10/30/15

"Happy Birthday Nancy!"

Love,
Darlene
(& Bob)

Cooking with Love!

Cooking with Love has no reason to doubt that all recipes, ingredients, instructions and directions will work wonderfully. However, the ingredients, instructions, and directions have not been tested in professional kitchens but rather in the kitchens of our homes and hearts. As always when you cook, the cook shouldn't hesitate to question procedures and directions before proceeding. Please note that all oven are not created equal. Test your oven for accurate temperature and hot spots and adjust recipes for baking time if necessary. The recipes in this book have been collected from various family, friends, neighbors, and other sources. Neither "Cooking with Love", nor any contributor, compiler, publisher, printer, distributor, or seller is responsible for errors or omissions.

Printed in Canada
TEACH Services, Inc.
254 Donovan Road
Brushton, New York 12916
Phone: 518 358-3494
FAX: 518 358-3028
www.teachservices.com

Cooking with Love!

Our family's journey into our epicurean history…

The Avella-Feiner Family and Friends Cookbook

A Collection of Recipes
Compiled by
Elise Avella Feiner

Featuring

Chefs with Heart…
Whisking Up a Better World!™

Visit us on the web at:
www.cookingwithlove.com

E-mail us at:
elise@cookingwithlove.com

Forward...

"The dinner table is the center for the teaching and practicing not just of table manners but of conversation, consideration, tolerance, family feeling and just about all other accomplishments of polite society except the minuet." – Judith Martin
"Miss Manners' Guide for the Turn-of-the-Millennium"

We hope as you read this cookbook, you will feel as though you are on an epicurean tour through time. We would love to have you come away with feelings of love, family and traditions. This marvelous book started out as a joke inspired by my nephew, Philly, who wanted me to make a video of myself making "gravy" (our tomato sauce) so he could learn to cook our family favorites, has turned into this marvelous book. I knew that if no one took the time to preserve our family recipes and our friends' recipes we would lose them in future generations. The precursor to this book was a booklet I gave out one Thanksgiving with pictures of our family from previous holidays, including recipes of that days' feast. I personalized each one and used it as a place card. My family was so engrossed with the handouts that they forgot to eat. I knew then, that a cookbook sharing these traditions was necessary. Today with our families spread so far apart, we need something that keeps us together. This is so much more than just a cookbook, a true labor of love, and filled with so many wonderful memories that each and every recipe has brought back...a holiday party, a special birthday, a walk on the beach...

Twenty-seven years ago, who ever would have thought that an Italian girl from Brooklyn (that would be me) would marry a N.J.B (nice Jewish boy) from Philadelphia (that would be my husband Marc) whom she met in Cebu City in the Philippines? We brought together two different yet very similar backgrounds. My friend Barbara always said, "You never know if you are going to find meatballs or matzoh balls or both cooking on the stove." Would my grandmother, Clementina Massimiano from Paduli, Italy, married to my grandfather Giuseppe Mainella from Benevento, Italy, my paternal grandmother Elizabeth Barone from Casa Marciano, Italy, married to my grandfather Felice Avella from Tufino, Italy, my new family's grandparents, Nellie Billet from Poland married to Judah Reinisch from Austria, and Freda Feldman married to Morris Feiner both from Russia have ever foreseen the way their families would grow and flourish?

As our siblings and relatives married, they brought other ethnic backgrounds into our family tree; Thirza Castro Avella of Puerto Rican descent, Theresa Boohaker Feiner of Lebanese descent, Edith Jacques Mainella, of French-Irish descent, and the list goes on and on. My husband Marc, an obstetrician, opened his practice in a small upstate New York town of Utica. Here, we found our "new family," our incredible friends of Cuban, Polish, English, Irish, and Spanish descent, all of them ready to share their heritage and recipes with us. Enjoy the heritage we share with you and create the memories of your own heritage someday soon.

I would be remiss to say that every recipe with my name on it is an original; (although so many are); they are recipes I have collected through the years and tweaked to my taste. Since there were so many contributors to this book it was difficult to determine the origins of some of these recipes and violation of any copyright is unintentional. It is my philosophy that recipes are meant to be shared and passed on: what better way to keep our traditions and heritage alive. Even though this book is copyrighted, it would give me no greater pleasure than to have you share and pass on these recipes. It is very hard to call any recipe your own, as everyone makes little changes to suit their taste. People of similar ethnic backgrounds cook very much the same way; in fact in some cases you may see two or three recipes for the same thing so that each branch of the family can have their own version. Finally, after reading, typing, retyping, correcting (and I know I still have missed a few things...please let us know if you find any mistakes), my "baby" was ready to be published.

I grew up in a family where I was always taught to be grateful for what you have and in return, give something back. For each cookbook sold we will send a donation to charity. If you purchase your book on our website, via the mail, or in retail locations, **select your preferred charity and write it on the enclosed postcard or letter and mail it to us, and a donation will then be made to your specified charity.** If you buy the book in other locations and **it is missing the postcard or letter**, it means that **the donation is going directly to where you purchased the book** (for example if you purchased it at the ARC Angel Gift Shop, a representative charities specific web site, or at a specific charity function or from a group using it as a fundraiser, **again**, the donation will go **directly to that group or organization** and the book may have a sticker to that effect.) **For a list of the participating charities in our "Chef's with Heart!" circle, see pages 565 – 566 in the back of the book.** If you order through our website, you may be asked to select your charity when you place the order.

We are Chefs with Heart...Whisking up a Better World!

If you are doing a fundraiser and don't have the time to compile your own recipes, contact us to find out how you can use this book for your organization. Visit us at **www.cookingwithlove.com** or e-mail us at **elise@cookingwithlove.com**

If you would like to be an independent contractor for us and sell our cookbook, visit us at **www.cookingwithlove.com** or e-mail us at **elise@cookingwithlove.com**

Dedication

This cookbook is dedicated with love to the following people:

With the utmost thanks to my mother, Katherine Avella, who always encouraged my abilities in the kitchen, and for giving me my first cookbook at age 8; Betty Crocker's Cooking for Boys and Girls.. Her incredible patience, guidance and love gave me the foundation that I stand on today. Through her ability to teach the recipes of our Italian Heritage, she taught all of us what a home filled with love and family is all about. I wish she had gotten to see the finished product, but she loved the rough draft. She is greatly loved and profoundly missed. She made all this possible!

My wonderful husband, Marc, you are my world. He has always been there, not only for me, but for both of our families as well; our sharing of holiday traditions would never have been possible without his generosity and love. Our children, Jeffrey, Steven ("my very own Emeril"), David, and Lauren (a special thanks to Lauren for all her computer expertise with Word), who asked me to put this book together so they would have their heritage and traditions preserved. Lauren was invaluable in putting this book into the proper format, and helping with the proofreading. No two parents could be more blessed than we are to have the four of you. You continue to fill us with love, joy and pride!

My grandmother, Clementina Mainella, for setting the example for the women in our family to follow. She was a phenomenal cook. She believed that education was the way to the future. She passed on her love of cooking, her love of family, and her recipes to my mother, and my Aunts: Fifi, Edith, and Jean. My Aunt Fifi, for teaching me the art of pasta making, being my roommate for all those years, for always being there for me and so much more…My Aunt Edith, who taught me that you can learn the cooking of other ethnic groups with ease as she did, and my Uncle Frank, who always shared their home with our family, allowing us to enjoy our summers in Bayville and our winters in Brooklyn and Florida sharing in his success. My Aunt Jean who taught me to cook with color, and my Uncle Pat for teaching me to always look before you leap!

My mother-in-law, Betty Feiner, for sharing her recipes, her wisdom, and her incredibly wonderful son Marc. My father- in-law, Jerry Feiner, who is greatly missed (you would have been so proud of your grandchildren), my Feiner brothers, Ivan and Kevin, and my wonderful sisters-in-law Tre and Barbara (my sounding board and best friend), Aunt Shirley and Uncle Harvey, Aunt Adele and Uncle Alvin, Uncle Gene (whose generosity, knowledge of family history and photos help to make this book so special), and Uncle Pinky, great cooks, and great families to be a part of. A special thanks to Marc's Nanny Nellie, for sharing with me, her recipes of my "new" family's Jewish foods and traditions. She was a vibrant woman and great cook. A special thanks to Dot Shavers, for sharing her "Feiner" fried chicken and all those wonderful stories of the Feiner boys growing up.

My brothers, Phil and Joe (thanks for always being there), who ate all my early mistakes, or buried them well. My sister-in-law Thirza, for sharing her Puerto Rican heritage and recipes, especially her turkey marinade…you are greatly missed.

My Aunts' Jenny, Mary, Julia, Frances, Mae, and Flo, the memories of Sunday morning visits were filled with the aromas of food and love, and my cousin Ann D'Amico for carrying on their recipes and sharing them with me. "Aunt Dottie" and "Uncle" Jimmy DeClementi, an incredible cook, for all his great recipes. My Aunt Lizzie, Uncle Ernie, cousins Maryann, Michele, Toni, Tom, Nick and Pam, Warren, Frank, Maureen, John G, and so many other cousins for teaching me that love, family and food are where it's at.

My wonderful family of friends, Ro Di Pierdomenico ("My Favorite Oldest Sister-In-Law"), Jeane Cassata (my "other mother") my "sister" Fran and Norm Zierler, and my other "sister and brother" Camille and Rene Sanabria, Carl Cassata, Rae and Steve Rosenfeld, Barbara and Stuart Schwartz, Debby, Shelley and Kayla Lipson, Maria and Tim Trainor, Johann and Bernie Gigliotti, Eileen and Anthony Furino, Carmen and Jorge Ferreiro, Cathy and Dick Sleeper, Helen and Dan Popeo (Dan is responsible for some of my favorite quotes found in the book), Cyndi and Billy Koury, Tony and Eleanor Picente who got me through some hard times way back when, Joppy Basile, Joanna and Frank Basile, Brenda and Charlie Antzelevitch, George and Zayda Koerner, Brenda and Robert Johnson (a special thanks to Brenda for supplying the handwritten recipes from her grandmother's collection) Nancy Barfield, Suzanne Bakiewicz, Janet Saporito, Candi Mitchell, Carol and Angelo Facci, Rose Pacifico (so much love was learned in your kitchen), Joanne Pacifico Del Guidice, Kenny and Debbie Schwartz , Basia, Zach and Jonah, Barbara, George and Ariana Cacoulidis, Rich and Julie Venezio, Brit, Jen and Nick, and Jeanne and Barry Donalty (their profound loss touched our souls), and my dearest and oldest friends, Sue Marquino, Pat Werner, Pat McGreevey, Andrea Kudrick, David Di John, Tina Terenzi, and Kathy Sullivan, and others, too numerous to mention, for sharing their traditions, recipes, and encouragement with me. I hope you enjoy seeing your family's recipes preserved here.

To Oscar Lirio, M.D. and Paula for giving me, and so many others, a second chance at life, no words can thank you enough…

My "children" by osmosis: Mindy and Joshua Rosenfeld, David and Aviva Zierler, Jeremy and Sam Zierler, Jonathan, and Zachary Zierler, Andrew Sanabria, Mike Alsheimer, Rich Kiersnowski, Adam Morton, Andrew Massoud, my "Japanese daughter," Sachi Ide (who has brought another culture to our family), Felicia and Kristin Furino, Kassie, Jonathan, Kyle, and Tessa Trainor, Kristin and B.J. Gigliotti, Brittany Butler, Sandra, Sherylynn, and Renee Koerner. My nieces and nephews, Michael, Sherry and Daniella Avella, Phil Avella, Sharon Vega Avella, Doug and Melissa Avella, Jennifer, Danielle, Karen, Abby, and Jody Feiner, Nicole and John-Michael Latini, who have become my biggest fans, for always sharing my table, and always asking for more. I hope the memories of preparing for the holidays together will always remain in your hearts. This book is for your husbands and wives so they can feed you in the style to which you have become accustomed. May you always keep our traditions and fill your children's lives with the love of family, and the love of tradition.

To the wonderful physicians at Medical Arts OB/GYN; they are the reason we came to the Utica area in the first place...Harold and Sue Baum, Bob and Sheila Smith, Mark and Ewa Godecki, you gave us a wonderful life here. Our new associates, Jim and Ronni Tichenor, and Scott and Elena Beattie, the incredible office staff who have also become "family." May all of you and your wonderful families, always be blessed with health and happiness!

Very special thanks to my niece, Nicole Latini, who beautifully illustrated all the divider pages for this book. She did an incredible job! She is truly a gifted and talented artist; I know her talents will take her far! Thanks to James R. Tichenor, M.D. for his computer assistance. Thanks to Rob Jenkins for all his invaluable help with the artwork, layout and design, to Christa Dunn for teaching me what was needed to develop a successful website, Don Whiting for the web design, and to Tim Trainor for allowing me to use all the resources available at Trainor Associates, for constructing our website **www.cookingwithlove.com**, and for just being such a dear and special friend. To Arlene and Steve Teuchert at The Gallery for their infinite patience and for taking the time to solve the software mysteries that held up our initial setup of the book. Vito Marrone of Marrone Photography in Utica, New York, for allowing me to reprint so many of these incredible pictures...he took all the good ones! Vito is the best of the best...To Timothy Hullquist at TEACH Services, Inc., Rachel Scofield at Athena Publishing, Robert O'Malley at Trendex Industries, and Jim Meyers, Meyers Bookbinding, I am forever indebted to you for your kindness, patience, and wisdom; each of you taught me something new about the publishing industry and each in your own way, brought this book into print . Quinn Peeper, M.D., a colleague of my husband Marc who came up with the idea for the cover, and finally to Mike Williams at Best Buy in New Hartford, who salvaged the cookbook when my hard drive crashed and it was all gone....this book is here because of you!

To so many of our neighbors in the restaurant community in the Utica – New Hartford area, Symeon Tsoupelis, Symeon, Jr. and Shelley Tsoupelis of Symeon's Restaurant, George Frattasio and Judy Gorea of Georgio's Restaurant, Jeff, Theresa, Jeff, Jr. and Caprice Daniels of Café Daniele, Dean and Jason Nole of Café Ca Nole, Chuck Sadallah of Daylight Donuts and Coffee, and our other area restaurants who helped out. Thanks for all your support and your recipes that added the finishing touches to this book. We are so fortunate to live in such a caring and giving community.

To Carol Zuchowski (and her husband Tom) who kept my house running while I was running...

And finally, my dear father, Samuel Avella, for being a loving, kind and generous man, a wonderful husband, father, and grandfather. When I was growing up, we kept an imaginary shaker labeled "Bottle of Love" to shake over our food. He taught me that it doesn't matter how good the food looks, it only tastes good when it's cooked with love. We miss you so much... your "shaker of love" is always in my heart.

I have decided to share this book with everyone who might want it because my son Jeff, who was a medical student at the SUNY at Buffalo School of Medicine when I started this project, was the President of the Operation Smile Chapter there. They were raising funds to enable children who cannot afford surgery for facial abnormalities to receive free care from plastic surgeons who travel the world and volunteer their time and expertise. I suggested we do a cookbook and immediately thought of our family cookbook which I had already started. So, our idea to use this as a fund raising project in conjunction with the cookbook was born. Jeffrey is now in his plastic surgery residency at Johns Hopkins. Jeffrey, your grandfathers would be so proud of what you have accomplished!

We decided to turn this book into a fundraiser not only for Operation Smile, but for many other worthy causes named at the end of this book. In every family, there is a cause that is near and dear to them; we decided to leave the selection up to you. If you don't have a charity near and dear to your heart, we ask that you consider four charities near and dear to our hearts, **Operation Smile**, **CURE** (Citizens United for Research in Epilepsy), **The Lower Eastside Girls Club,** and **St. Jude's Children's Research Hospital** when choosing a charity to donate to.

To paraphrase a very common idea, everything I learned about life, I learned around our family's kitchen table...I hope that your family will share the lessons you learned around your table with us! Please send your thoughts to elise@cookingwithlove.com; we'd love to hear from you!

I think that this story, written by my son Jeff, when he was a student at The University of Pennsylvania will give you a good look at our family and our traditions…

"A Family Thanksgiving"

She arrives at 12:00 noon, along with my Uncle Phil and his family, bearing gifts and food of special significance. A great commotion ensues as jackets are taken, and greetings exchanged. All attentions shift from the goings-on in the kitchen to the new arrivals. The steaming pots await the return of my mother's watchful eye, as she turns her attention to the scene at the door. I am the first to meet her as she comes in, and I stoop down to greet her tiny frame with a kiss on the cheek. This is how it is done. She is my grandmother, the hub around which the family clings, like spokes attached at the core of tradition and family. Here in the home of my parents, holidays are unique in their own special way. The manner in which they are celebrated has followed the legacy of countless years, steeped in "Old Country" values, and blended with family customs accumulated over the years. Each generation adds its own special flair to a growing pool of customs. From generation to generation, our traditions have been passed along this way, evolving at each step. Holidays are sacred to us, not only for the religious meanings anymore, but also for the presence and participation of family in our lives.

My heritage is an interesting one. My mother comes from an Italian, Roman Catholic family. My father's family is a mix of Jewish European heritage. I have been fortunate enough to have all the best values from each culture instilled in me. Above all, family is the most important value to us. It is the single principle that has guided us from a history of discrimination and poverty in Europe, to a new future here in America. Before I go further, I feel that I must portray my definition of the word "family." To many, family is simply a group of individuals related through marriage and genetics. For us, family encompasses a much broader spectrum. It goes so far as to include close friends of our parents and relatives whom we respect as much as we respect our own flesh and blood. We even go as far as to bestow upon them the title of "Aunt" or "Uncle", as a symbol of this respect. This point must be made clear, in order to understand my description of the holidays, or their meanings are lost. It is this concept of family that represents the nucleus of our culture, around which everything revolves. This is entirely reflected in the way in which we celebrate our holidays.

Thanksgiving is one such holiday my family has been proud to adopt and celebrate. It is an American holiday, bearing no religious or cultural significance other than a sense of American pride. It is a family holiday. The way we celebrate Thanksgiving most closely resembles Thanksgiving at my grandmother's house on Schenck Avenue in Brooklyn. Our family jokingly referred to it as the "Mission House", because my grandmother would invite every relative, friend, and friend's friend. Everyone was welcome. This tradition was probably a folk survival from my great grandmother's tiny village in Paduli, Italy. The town was so small and poor; that people had to rely on each other, and the village became a close knit family unit much like a very large family. I am unable to comment on the food served except to say that it was traditional Italian food. I am only aware of the food that has survived in our traditions to this day.

These early Thanksgiving celebrations were important events. After all, eating is an intimate social interaction. These holidays served to bring everyone together, to strengthen the bonds. One is reminded of the story of a sick, old man on his deathbed. He convenes his family and asked the eldest son, a strong boy, to bring him a fasces, a bundle of sticks. His son looks puzzled, but he does as he is told. The man asks everyone present to try to break the bundle of strong twigs, but no one is strong enough to snap the entire bunch. The old man takes the bundles, unties the cord, and proceeds to snap each twig individually. "Remember my children", he says to his family, "our family is like this bound bundle of twigs, when tied together, they are so strong nothing can break them apart, but sever the cord that binds them and anyone can break them apart."

The quote's a rather simple anecdote, but the concept behind it is very powerful. So powerful in fact, that the Roman Army used the fasces with an ax in the middle as a symbol of their power. Now, my family has no army, but we have all been there for each other. We have weak links, and we have strong links like all families, but the fact that we stick together keeps us strong. Our holidays have merely become a way of reinforcing this idea.

The Thanksgiving celebrations at my house are a culmination of our values and traditions. Early in November, we begin planning. It's a lot more difficult to get the family together now that we've moved far apart. Our most memorable Thanksgivings have included well over forty friends and relatives. Each year, the preparations usually begin days in advance. The women still do most of the cooking, but everybody gets in on the action. My grandmother usually comes over a day or two in advance to help my mother prepare the food. Her specialty is rolling the tiny meatballs for the soup; we call "Soup a la Sandella". My other grandmother, Mom Mom, often helps, but my Dad says she makes golf balls, not tiny meatballs. Each year, my mother draws up a menu. We always have turkey, but there is more to the food than the American aspect. We include antipasto. Usually, we bring out platters of cold cuts, salads, shrimp and olives.

My brother, Steven, makes spinach dip encased in a hollowed out round of rye bread. He makes it the same way every year. Breadsticks are also found at every Thanksgiving, but they are never store bought. Every year, my mother says she too tired to make them, but my Uncles Joe and Phil insist that it's not Thanksgiving without them. Every year, tradition wins out over a weary Mom, and instead, we all help to hand roll, seed, and bake them. We always have a bowl of chestnuts for my grandfather who passed away a decade ago. We have baby corn for my other grandfather, Poppy, who has also passed away. Nobody really eats them anymore, but they have become part of our tradition. The main part of the meal consists of the turkey, but there is always a pasta dish, in this case it's baked macaroni (for the American holiday), created by my Irish-French Aunt Edith. There is usually some sort of Jewish dish, usually a potato pie or kugel, invented by my "Aunt Barbara" one of those family friends, who is like an aunt. This represents a new tradition, adapted for both sides of the family. The pasta dish when we go with Italian fare is usually lasagna. The sauce or "gravy" as true Italians call it is prepared differently in every family. My mother prepares it as her mother, and grandmother did, using five essential elements: salt, pepper, tomatoes, basil and garlic. The sauce would simmer all day engulfing the entire house in its aroma. The meatballs frying on the stove have little chance of making it into the gravy, as my brother David begins the tradition of tasting them, and sneaking them out to us one by one. The trays of candies and cookies, and special pies; mincemeat for my Uncle Frank, apple pie made for my father by my "Aunt" Rae, (another friend) and a pecan pie for my Aunt Theresa (of Lebanese descent) who was born in Alabama. These foods have remained basically the same for generations, with slight modifications here and there. My mother spends the entire week preparing for the feast.

When Thanksgiving arrives, our house is thrown into chaos. Last minute preparations are hastily assembled; the house is clean and spotlessly prepared. Many of the dishes and serving implements we use have a long history in our family, having been passed on for generations. Many of the items we use on the table have been in the family since my great grandmother's time, while others have recently become part of our tradition. The table itself is usually placed in the family room because of the large amount of space it requires. The night before, we usually disassemble the couch and move everything out of the family room. Most years we rent a bunch of tables and place them together to make a rectangle so that everybody sits facing each other. My mother has a tablecloth that is over thirty feet long to cover the tables. We use this cloth only once a year for the Thanksgiving table. My sister, Lauren, sets the table with some of my mother's "good plates" and napkin holders shaped like turkeys (made by my cousins.) These napkin holders have also become part of our tradition. The tablecloth is covered with miniature chocolate turkeys, metallic confetti in the shape of turkeys, dishes, and a floral arrangement.

Each person has a place card with his name on it. Many of these place cards have been reused since we moved to this house in Upstate New York. The job of the place cards usually falls to my brother David, because he is the lefty in our house. He makes sure that the lefties, one in each family, are in good position. Finally, the table is ready, and the guests begin to arrive.

The guests from out-of- town usually arrive a few days before so that they can spend some time with us. Our local family and friends arrive around 12 or so on Thanksgiving Day. They come with cakes, desserts, and even entrees. It is in this way, each guest adds something to the whole experience. When my grandmother, Nanny, arrives, it feels like we are "officially" under way. Though she only lives fifteen minutes away with my Aunt Fifi, their arrival is a major event. She doesn't drive, so it's an immediate family member or close friend who goes to pick her up. Most of the time, it's her son Philip and his family. My other grandmother, who lives in Florida, has usually arrived a few days before. When they all arrive, everything begins. The adults sit in the kitchen while they talk and begin to eat from the myriad of platters scattered around the kitchen. The kids nosh on all the snacks, and hang around the kitchen. When we were little, we usually had snowball fights, or built forts. These days, I usually spend more time with the adults or my older cousins. The adults lead the conversations, but we're allowed to participate. It wasn't always this way. When my father was a kid, the children weren't allowed to be around when the adults were talking. In my mother's case, the adults would switch and began speaking Italian. These days, the social structure is different. It's more laid back. There are more gray areas now. In fact, one of our favorite parts of the day is when my cousins Maryann and Michele come from Staten Island, and we get to catch up on all the "family dirt." We still respect our elders, but the social "rules" are not the same. The dinner itself reveals some of these changes in contemporary adult-child interactions.

My mother decides when to start the dinner. Every year, we make a list of things we are thankful for, and I think my mother keeps these individual lists somewhere safe. They are sacred to us. The year that my mother was pregnant with my sister, and my Aunt Barbara was pregnant with my cousin Abby, my Mom mailed everyone a card and asked each invited guest to write something they were thankful for. She placed all the cards on our front door, and that's how she and my Aunt announced that they were pregnant. They were thankful for "new arrivals." These lists are always made before we sit down to eat. At the table, my father makes a toast. Other relatives say something, or sometimes even some of us children follow them.

This is a relatively new development, as the children were not always allowed to participate to the extent that they do today. The rest of the dinner is typically socializing. We all get up to eat at the same time. A new tradition is that now, dinner is almost always buffet style. This evolved because the kids were too small to pass the platters of food. When dinner is over, the adults and some of the children spend time in the kitchen where we might talk about recent events, people and anything else that might happen to come up. Guests leave any time during the evening, but close family usually stay late into the night. The cleanup is rarely left for the next day. This is when my Aunts Fifi, Rae, and Barbara, and Barbara spring into action. We all follow an unwritten social code. Everybody knows his role. Somehow, everything always winds up going smoothly, and the house is put back in order.

Holiday celebrations in my family have always been governed by tradition. My parents are simply following the examples of their parents. My grandpa Sam used to say, "It doesn't matter what you prepare as long as it's cooked with one ingredient..."Love". My mother keeps an empty bottle labeled <u>"Love"</u> in the kitchen and would tease my grandfather by sprinkling it over all the food. I have always tried to follow the examples and traditions set by my parents. The traditions we observe have been taking place in the homes of our ancestors, it is this link that preserves memories, and defines our culture. My generation will carry these traditions on in our own way, just like our parents' generation has. We pass on our values with the hopes of creating a responsible new generation to take our place when we have gone.

Reprinted with permission of Jeffrey M. Feiner, M.D.

Our Contributing Chefs with Heart...
Whisking up a Better World!

Antzelevitch, Brenda
Archibald, Marcia
Arcieri, Joan
Arcuri, Nick
Avella, Katherine
Avella, Philip
Avella, Thirza
Avramidis, Athena
Bakiewicz, Suzanne
Bamberger, Sheila
Barfield, Nancy
Basile, Sr. Frank
Basile, Joanna
Basile, Joppy
Blaker, Nancy
Blackburn, Louise
Borten, Pearl
Brophy, Jane Oster
Brown, John
Burlingame, Mimi
Burlingame, Sarah
Butler, Brittany
Calogero, Mark
Caplan, Samantha
Cardinale, Patty
Carlucci, Jean
Casazza, Virginia
Cassata, Jeane
Catapano, Neva
Christiano, Fanny
Christiano, Mary
Circelli, Cindy
Collins, Shirley
Cocalis, Taylor
Cotrupe, Sandra
Cully, Kitty
D'Amico, Ann
D'Amico, Nina

D'Andrea, Frances
Daniels, Jeffery, Jr.
Daniels, Jeffery, Sr.
Dardano, Tina
deCaronea, Marina
DeClementi, Vincent
DeSimone, Flo
DeSimone, Tom
DiCarlo, Billy
DiPierdomenico, Maria
DiPierdomenico, Rose-
marie
Dunn, Mona
Facci, Carol
Feiner, Abby
Feiner, Barbara
Feiner, Betty
Feiner, David
Feiner, Elise
Feiner, Freda
Feiner, M.D., Jeffrey
Feiner, Jody
Feiner, Lauren
Feiner, M.D., Marc,
Feiner, Steven
Feiner, Theresa
Ferreiro, Carmen
Finnegan, Maureen
Flomenhoft, Shirley
Forgeron, Barbara
Frank, Lisa
Frattasio, George
Fsadni, Joanne
Furino, Eileen
Furino, Theresa
Gaffney, Mary
Gigliotti, Johann
Gilsenan, Mona

Glorius, Jean
Godecki, M.D., Mark
Golden, Marie
Gorea, Judy
Grimaldi, Sr., Anthony
Grimaldi, Sr., John
Grimaldi, Millie
Gruman, Ann
Grundel, Edith
Halpin, Liz
Hamar, Eva
Hamlin, Irina
Herr, Nancy
Hull, Valerie
Jendzo, Phyllis
Johnson, Brenda
Juliano, M.D., Julie Ann
Jungkind, DeAnn
Kahler, Kathy
Kaplan, Sylvia
Karam, Mary Ann
Karam, Segean
Kent, Caroline Wilson
Koerner, George
Koerner, Zayda
Koury, Cyndi
Koury, Mary Frances
Koury, Sadie
Koury, Shemony
Kunkel, Joyce
Lanier, Hilda
LaRosa, Cathy
Latini, Nicole-Lynn
Latini, Phyllis
Lewandrezwski, Johanna
Limongelli, Carmela
Longo, Diane
Mahlon, Patricia

Maida, Elizabeth
Maida, Ernest
Maida, Michele
Mainella, Clementina
Mainella, Edith
Mainella, Jr. Joseph
Mainella, Josephine
Mainella, Jr., Frank S.
Mainella, M.D., Frank S.
Mainella, Pasquale
Mainella, Warren
Massimiano, Lucy
Massoud, Judy
Mehta, Kavita
Mercurio, Antoinette
Merrill, Joanna
Miller, Michael
Mitchell, Candie
Mollico, Thomas
Mollico, Toni
Montelegro, Barbara
Montero, Deb
Monticciolo, Fran
Nanna, Lisa
Napoli, Rockie
Nole, Dean
Nole, Jason
Orilio, Don
Ostrow, Hannah
Pacifico, Rose
Philipson, Aviva
Picano, Lynn
Plescia, Nellie
Popeo, Helen
Potter, Carol Koury
Reinisch, Nellie
Rosen, Debby
Rosenfeld, Rae
Ryen, Linda
Sack, Lee
Sadallah, Chuck
Sanabria, Camille
Sanito, Angelina
Sanito, Sr. Nicholas

Saporito, Janet
Saracino, Elizabeth
Scattaglia, Toni
Schabert, Kathy
Schwartz, Barbara
Schwartz, Nettie
Schwartz, Ruth
Schwendemann, Giannina
Selinsky, Karen
Shavers, Dot
Sleeper, Catherine
Smith, David
Smith, Gina Mastrovito
Smith, Sheila
Socolof, Vicki
Spirakis, Peggy
Sternick, Sam
Sulzman, Eleanor
Tarantino, Jenny
Tehan, JoAnn
Terenzi, Edith
Terenzi, Christina
Tichenor, Veronica
Trainor, Katherine
Trainor, Maria
Trainor, Tessa
Trociuk, Iryna
Tsoupelis, Ann
Tsoupelis, Jr., Symeon
Tsoupelis, Sr., Symeon
White, Hal
Zierler, Aviva
Zierler, Estelle
Zierler, Frances
Zuchowski, Carol

TABLE OF CONTENTS

The Feiner's 2004: Steven, David, Elise, Marc, Lauren and Jeffrey

My Parents: Samuel and Katherine Avella
My father was a barber and my mother taught elementary school in Brooklyn. My father had several barbershops in Brooklyn and Queens. Among his customers were Phil Silvers, Danny Kaye, and Steve Lawrence long before they were famous!

Marc's Parents: Jerry and Betty Feiner
Marc's parents were in the jewelry business and were located on Jewelers' Row on Sansom Street in Philadelphia

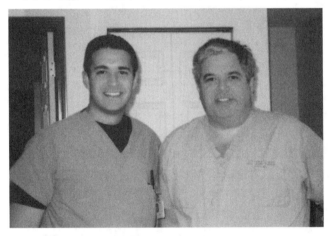

Two of my four favorite guys:
Jeffrey M. Feiner, M.D., and Marc A. Feiner, M.D.
Like father like son...Jeff is blessed to have inherited his father's surgical abilities. Let's hope he also has his caring ways. Marc's patients adore him!

Appetizers and Beverages...

The Marc A. Feiner Family
L-R: Elise Avella Feiner, Marc, Lauren, Jeffrey, David, and Steven Feiner

"Each day of our lives, we make deposits in the memory banks of our children."
-Charles Swindoli "The Strong Family"

My Recipe Terminology:

Double boiler- is a pot that is made to fit inside another pot; water or liquid goes into the bottom pot and the top pot sits inside the groove of the bottom pot. It's used to melt chocolate, make sauces, etc. It's great if you have one, but if you don't, a larger pot with a smaller one that will fit inside works well too. The two pots must fit together fairly tight to work (you can't have too much space). Don't put too much water in the bottom pot when you use them. **Be careful of the steam,** because the seal will not be as tight with a real double boiler.

Melt in the microwave – if you are melting chocolate or cheese for a recipe, start out in thirty second increments, so you don't burn the product. Remember, cheese and chocolate will continue to melt after cooking, so stir a little if you see solid pieces left before you microwave again, it's probably already done!

Egg Pan- an egg pan is a pan that my mother kept just to cook eggs in. She felt if you put meat in it, the eggs would stick and the pan would lose its effectiveness. Hers were all cast iron pans, but you can use non-sticks pans for this purpose as well. We also keep them in a plastic bag; wash them by hand so they don't get mixed up with the other pans. You will so happy of you decide to do this; you will make perfect sunnyside up eggs, crepes, and manicotti and blintzes.

Brown meat – if a recipe is not specific, just heat a few tablespoons of oil in a skillet, frying pan or Dutch oven (depending on the size of what you are browning) and just sear the meat to give it color. It shouldn't cook through because you will probably continue to cook it somewhere else (crock-pot, oven, grill). The purpose is to sear the meat to keep the juices in!

Peel and crush – My favorite expression when it comes to garlic…I know that some cooks tell you never to crush garlic, but rather slice it thin. I've been using a garlic press for years and it works beautifully. Just be careful if browning crushed garlic, it can burn quickly. If it does, discard it and start again because your food will be bitter!

Grated Cheese – You will see in a lot of the recipes I just state grated cheese; anything you like is fine although I usually use Pecorino-Romano, Locatelli- Romano, or Parmesan Cheese. I know that the chefs on the Food Network would argue with me, but I really can't tell the difference in the finished product. But please, use freshly grated, or grate it yourself, **nothing in the cans or bottles please!**

Candy Thermometer – A necessity if you are making candy. I once sent my (much younger at the time) daughter Lauren into the store to buy me a candy thermometer after mine broke; she came out and told me they didn't have any. I thought that was strange and went in to see for myself…she was looking in the candy aisle!

Confectionary Sugar, Confectioners' Sugar, Powdered Sugar – all one and the same things!

Dice – Since we don't have prep chefs like the TV chefs do, the pieces don't all have to be of perfect size and shape; just cut in small squares…

Chop – most of us, me included, have not quite mastered the art of chopping like a chef, try a rocking motion on the blade, but don't sweat the small stuff, just make the pieces smaller than when you started!

Symeon's Spices – Symeon's is a local Greek Restaurant that sells their incredibly delicious spice mix. They use it in their salad dressing, marinades and recipes. Once you try it, you'll become addicted to it, and find a million uses for it…in marinades, on French fries, on vegetables, etc. You can substitute our Passion Spice Mix for Symeon's Spices if you can't find them. See our website:

www.cookingwithlove.com

AVIVA'S EGGPLANT APPETIZER
Aviva Philipson

3 large eggplants
6 cloves of garlic, crushed

⅛ teaspoon black pepper
⅛ teaspoon salt

Do not peel the eggplants. Pierce the skin with a fork several times. Bake in a 400° oven for about 25 minutes until soft. While eggplant is baking, do all the remaining prep work for the recipe; see below. When the eggplants are done, let them cool until you can handle them. Peel and cut down the middle. Remove the bulk of the seeds, but don't go too crazy trying to remove them all or you'll have no eggplant left. Place the eggplant, garlic, salt and pepper in a food processor, and pulse **until fine, but not mush**.

While eggplant is cooking do the following:

3 medium onions, peeled and diced in the food processor, set aside
1 large green pepper, remove seeds and dice in food processor, set aside
3 cloves of garlic (peel, crush, and set aside)
1 (3 ounce) jar of capers, (optional) drained; you can use half the jar so it will be less salty
1 small jar of pimentos, drained

1 (13 ounce) jar of green olives, drain, and chop in food processor, not too fine, set aside
1 (7 ounce) jar of Kalamata olives, or container of olives, remove pits, and chop on processor, not to fine, set aside
4 (8 ounce) cans of Hunts® Tomato Sauce (open the cans and have ready)
4-5 tablespoons of olive oil
⅛ teaspoon of black pepper
⅛ teaspoon of garlic salt

Heat the olive oil in a very large frying pan. Add the onions, peppers, and crushed garlic. Sauté until soft; add the chopped eggplant, capers, pimentos, and both types of olives. Cook for about 10 minutes. Add the tomato sauce and cook for another 10 minutes. Add the garlic salt and pepper. Be very careful with the salt, as the olives are very salty. When cool, refrigerate in containers. Taste the next day before adding any additional salt. Serve with Aviva's flatbread crackers, (recipe below) or any crackers of your choice. Serves 12

Aviva Philipson, was a customer of mine at "By Invitation Only", made this recipe. She would always bring this to the store when she made it. We became good friends, and I asked her for the recipe. She invited me over and taught me how to do it. This is also great on sandwiches or on Italian toast like a Bruschetta with mozzarella. The pita flatbread crackers are the best. This is basically a caponata.

AVIVA'S FLATBREAD CRACKERS
Aviva Philipson

1-2 packages of paper thin Pita Bread
Olive oil

Seasonings of your choice (seasoned salt, garlic salt, oregano, basil, parsley, poppy and sesame seeds, and parmesan cheese)

Preheat oven to 400°. Place or open the round flat bread on a round cookie or pizza sheet. Using a pastry brush, brush each round with olive oil. Sprinkle with seasoned salt, garlic salt, oregano, basil, parsley, poppy, sesame seeds, and parmesan cheese. You can add or eliminate whatever you prefer. I usually use it all. Place the pita bread into the hot oven (you can place directly on rack if you want) for about 5-6 minutes until lightly browned. Remove and let cool. Do the next round the same way, and continue until they are all done. Do them **ONE** at a time. When cool break into pieces; serve with eggplant.

They can also be done in a sweet version to serve with a sweet dip or fruit, or as a snack. Preheat oven to 400°. Melt a stick of butter. Do these one at a time as well. Lightly brush the top of each pita with the melted butter. Sprinkle with cinnamon and sugar, and mini chocolate chips if desired. Bake on a pizza pan or round pan for 5-6 minutes until just brown. Let cool. Break into smaller cracker size pieces. See our website www.cookingwithlove.com for a source for paper thin pita bread.

The seeded ones are great with the eggplant dip, or eaten by themselves. The sweet ones are a great snack with a cup of hot chocolate or coffee. They store very well in zip lock bags.

ALMOND CHEESE SPREAD
Elise Feiner

1 (8 ounce) package Philadelphia® Cream Cheese, softened
2 cups shredded Swiss cheese or mozzarella
⅓ cup mayonnaise
2 tablespoons scallions, chopped

⅛ teaspoon nutmeg
⅛ teaspoon black pepper
½ cup sliced almonds (you can use the flavored Sunkist® Almonds), divided

Preheat oven to 350°. Mix the cream cheese, shredded cheese, mayonnaise, scallions, nutmeg and pepper. Add ⅓ cup almonds to the mix. Mix well. Place in an ovenproof dish and bake for about 15 minutes. Stir once during the cooking. Sprinkle with remaining almonds before serving.

BABA GANNOUJH
Elise Feiner

1 large eggplant
2 large cloves garlic, peeled
1 teaspoon salt

¼ to ⅓ cup tahini
⅛ cup lemon juice
Olive oil for drizzling

Slice eggplant in half lengthwise and put upside down on a greased foil lined pan or a disposable cookie sheet sprayed with PAM®. Put under the broiler until the outside skin is charred black and the pulp inside is soft; watching carefully. (15 to 30 minutes). Scrape out eggplant and put in bowl to cool, preferably in refrigerator for several hours. Pour off extra liquid before using, or Baba Gannoujh will be too watery. In a food processor or with a mortar and pestle, mince garlic, and scrape down sides or the bowl. Add eggplant, salt, and ¼ cup tahini. Pulse the food processor to mix. Slowly add lemon juice. Taste; adjust salt and lemon or tahini. Place on a flat plate and with the back of a spoon make a circular depression. Drizzle olive oil in the depression to serve. Serve with pita bread.

AVIVA'S BABA GANNOUJH
Aviva Philipson

1 eggplant
½ cup tahini
¼ onion, peeled and grated
2 cloves of garlic, peeled and crushed

2 tablespoon lemon juice
2 tablespoons water
Salt and pepper to taste
Olive oil for drizzling

Pierce the eggplant with a fork several times. Place the eggplant on a sheet on aluminum foil in a 400° oven and bake until soft and charred on the outside. When cool, remove the skin. Place the eggplant in a Cuisinart®. Add tahini, lemon juice, garlic, onion, salt and pepper. Add the water a little at a time until the tahini is a white color. Pulse until the eggplant is fine but not mushy and all ingredients are blended. Drizzle with a little olive oil. Serve with pita bread.

This is a delicious Middle Eastern appetizer and very popular in Upstate New York.

PEPPERONI DIP
Elise Feiner

1 (8 ounces) container sour cream
2 (8 ounces) packages Philadelphia® Cream Cheese, softened
¼ teaspoon garlic salt

6 ounces pepperoni, chopped
1 small can Durkee® Onions, divided

Preheat oven to 350°. Mix everything together using half the can of onions. Place into a small casserole dish. Bake for 15 minutes. Top with remaining onions and bake another 10 to 15 minutes. Serve with crackers. The new Ritz® Sticks would be great with this.

Aviva and Herb Philipson
Herb owned several Army and Navy stores in our community and was a beloved showman. Aviva is a fabulous cook. Herb is great missed by all!

CORNED BEEF DIP
Iryna Trociuk

2 cups sour cream
2 tablespoons parsley (fresh or dried)
2 tablespoons dill weed (fresh if possible)

2 tablespoons onion, finely chopped or grated
2 (3 ounce) packages corn beef, shredded
2 cups Hellmann's® mayonnaise

Mix all the ingredients together and serve in a hollowed out loaf of rye bread. Cube an extra loaf of bread for dipping. You can make this a day ahead of time.

CHIPPED BEEF DIP
Elise Feiner

5 (6 ounce) packages dried chipped beef, finely chopped
2 (8 ounce) packages Philadelphia® Cream Cheese
1 tablespoon minced onions
1½ cups sour cream

½ teaspoon garlic salt
1½ teaspoons Worcestershire sauce
¼ teaspoon black pepper
1 large loaf rye or pumpernickel bread

Preheat oven to 450°. In a large bowl, combine all ingredients except the bread. Place in an ovenproof dish. Bake for 10 minutes. Cut off the top of the bread, remove the inside to form a bowl, and cut the removed bread into small cubes. Set cubes aside. Put the spread back into the bread and bake at 450° for another 10 minutes or until bubbly. Serve with crackers, breadsticks, and bread cubes.

ELISE'S ARTICHOKE DIP
Elise Feiner

1 can of plain artichokes hearts, drained and finely chopped
1½ cups of shredded mozzarella

1 cup grating cheese (I use Pecorino Romano, but Parmesan is fine)
1 cup of mayonnaise

Preheat the oven to 350°. Spray Pyrex®, corning ware®, or other oven proof 8 x 8-inch dish with PAM® (I have also used a disposable aluminum cake pan.) Mix all ingredients together in a mixing bowl. Bake until golden brown, about 20 to 25 minutes. This can be done ahead and refrigerated until time to bake. Just bake it right before serving. Serves 6

Variations: Add one cup of sour cream and a box of Knorr® Vegetable soup mix to the above; or 1 cup of sour cream, a package of Lipton® Recipe Secrets Golden Onion Soup mix and top with buttered bread crumbs.

We always make this at the holidays. It's a fast and easy dip, and can be assembled ahead of time and then baked.. If you are bringing it to a party, use a disposable aluminum cake 8 x 8- inch pan, and bake just before you go.

My nieces (L-R) Jennifer and Danielle Feiner

CRAB DIP IN A CROCK
Katherine Avella

1 (8 ounce) package Philadelphia ® Cream Cheese, softened
¼ cup Parmesan cheese
4 medium green onions, thinly sliced (¼ cup)
¼ cup mayonnaise
2 teaspoons sugar
1 teaspoon ground mustard

1 clove of garlic, finely chopped
1 can (6 ounces) crabmeat, drained, cartilage removed and flaked
⅓ cup sliced almonds, toasted
Assorted crackers or raw vegetables

Spray the inside of a 1 to 2½-quart slow cooker with cooking spray. Mix all ingredients except crabmeat, almonds, and crackers, in a small bowl until blended. Stir in crabmeat. Spoon into a slow cooker. Cover and cook on low heat setting 1 hour to 1 hour 15 minutes or until cheese is melted. Sprinkle with almonds. Serve warm with crackers. Dip will hold up to 3 hours.

MACADAMIA CRAB SUPREME
Elise Feiner

2 (8 ounce) packages Philadelphia® Cream Cheese, softened
1 pound back fin crabmeat
1 cup white wine

1 cup mayonnaise
Salt and pepper, to taste
2 cups macadamia nuts, chopped

Preheat oven to 325°. Combine all the ingredients and place in an ungreased casserole dish. Bake for about 25 minutes or until brown and bubbly. Serve with crackers.

CRAB DIP
Elise Feiner

1 cup fresh crabmeat
1 cup mayonnaise
1 cup cheddar cheese, grated

½ cup scallions, minced
Freshly ground black pepper

Mix the crabmeat, mayonnaise, and grated cheese in the top of double boiler. Cook over medium heat until melted through. Stir in scallions and black pepper. Spoon the dip on to toasted baguettes or crackers. Serve hot. You can also mix everything together and microwave for 3-4 minutes (add an extra minute or two if necessary.)

Our English-Italian Cousins come to visit…
L-R: Dino Grassi, Stephen Gaan, Steven Feiner, David Feiner, Maddelena Stevens-Grassi, Elise and Marc Feiner, Angela Stevens (standing) Katherine Avella and Fifi Mainella. This is the beauty of family, even the distances between oceans can't keep us apart.

HOT CHEESE DIP
Elise Feiner

1 package Velveeta®, large
1 package Mexican Velveeta®, small
3 tablespoons oil
1 box frozen chopped spinach, defrosted

1 large red pepper, diced
1 large green pepper, diced
1 large red onion, peeled and diced
2 loaves uncut bread, (rye or pumpernickel)

In a large skillet, heat the oil. Add the onions and peppers until just beyond crisp. Squeeze any excess liquid from the spinach. Add the spinach and cook until heated through. Melt the Velveeta in a large microwave safe bowl, one minute at a time until melted. Add the vegetables to the cheese. Remove the top from one of the loaves of bread and hollow out the middle to use as a bowl. Add cheese to the bread. Cut the other loaf into cubes to dip in the cheese mix. This is also good with crackers or breadsticks. You might want to keep the bread on a hot plate so the cheese stays warm.

CARAMELIZED ONION DIP
Elise Feiner

2 large Vidalia or sweet onions
3 tablespoon of extra-virgin olive oil
½ teaspoon oregano
Salt and pepper to taste
1 tin of anchovy fillets, drained well and chopped

¾ cup Kalamata or black olives, pitted (I mix both)
2 (5 ounce) containers of Boursin Garlic and Herb Cheese spread
1 scallion finely chopped for the top
Tortilla or Pita Chips

Preheat the oven to 500° Mix the onions, olive oil, oregano, salt and pepper to taste. Add in the anchovies and place mixture in a small pan and place in the oven for 20 minutes, stir mix once during the cooking time. Remove from the oven and let cool a little. Place mixture in a food processor. Add the Boursin cheese, and olives and pulse until smooth. Place in a serving bowl and top with scallions. Serve with tortilla scoops, bagel or pita chips.

My husband Marc likes anything with anchovies; this is a dip that is right up his alley!

Vincent and Carol DeClementi then… When I was quite young, Vinny was one of my first crushes.

L-R: Carol and Vincent DeClementi and Marc Feiner today… Vinny however, has been married to Carol for many, many, years, and Marc and I have been together for 28 years. Our friendship has lasted through all those years.

AVOCADO CASSEROLE DIP
Elise Feiner

2 large avocados
¼ cup crumbled Stilton or Danish Blue Cheese
¼ cup walnut halves or pistachio nuts

½ pound proscuitto, thinly sliced
1 tablespoon Lea and Perrins™ Worcestershire sauce
Salt and pepper

Preheat oven to 375°. Cut the avocado in half and scoop out the flesh, leaving the skin intact, and roughly dice the avocado. Place avocado in an ovenproof casserole or Pyrex® dish and add the crumbled blue cheese, walnuts or pistachios, proscuitto, Worcestershire sauce and season with salt and pepper; mix well. You can bake and serve in the dish or spoon the mixture into the avocado shells and bake for 5 minutes; place under the broiler for 2 minutes right before serving. Serve with crackers, pita bread or toasted baguettes

CRAB DIP FURINO
Eileen Furino

1 pound of Muenster cheese or American cheese, cut into cubes
¼ cup milk
2 tablespoons butter

6 ounces crab meat, chopped
¼ cup dry sherry
2 teaspoons pimentos, chopped
1 clove of garlic, peeled and crushed

Cook the cheese, milk, and butter in a microwave on medium for 5-8 minutes. Stir every 2 minutes. Stir in the crab, pimentos, sherry, and garlic. Microwave on medium setting for another 2 to 3 minutes. Serve with French bread.

This is a great appetizer, fast and easy to make. Aunt Eileen made it for us one New Years Eve...it was delicious! When we all moved to the Utica, area we all left our families behind. Our friends became our families. We spent so many wonderful holidays and vacations with the Furinos. Our children will always have those wonderful memories.

"MOCK" HORNED DORSET DIP
Elise Feiner

1 (12 ounce) bag of frozen chopped onions (thawed and drained) I use Ore-Ida® or 1 cup of fresh chopped onions

1 cup of mayonnaise
1 cup cheddar cheese

Mix everything together and bake in a small baking dish that has been sprayed with PAM®. I usually double this recipe because it's so good. Bake at 375° for about 30 to 45 minutes or until golden brown. Serves 6. Serve with crackers, Wheat Thins®, Triscuits®, Pepperidge Farm® Butterfly's work well with this. We have this as an appetizer at every holiday. It's great to bring when you have to bring something to a party, just make it in an aluminum square baking dish.

There is a restaurant called the Horned Dorset in Leonardsville, New York, where they always serve this as an appetizer; this is my version. If you are ever traveling through Upstate NY on Route 8 be sure to stop in Leonardsville. Be careful not to go through the town too fast or you'll miss the restaurant. The restaurant is in the middle of nowhere, but wait until you go inside; it's beautiful...Be sure to go upstairs and check out the library! Reservations are recommended (315 855-7898). If you didn't know any better you'd think you were dining in Manhattan. I don't know where I got the recipe from, but everyone in Upstate New York makes it. It takes five minutes to put together and tastes great.

HOT GARLIC ARTICHOKE DIP
Elise Feiner

1 (14 ounce) can artichoke hearts, drained and chopped
1 cup mayonnaise
1 (8 ounce) container sour cream

1 cup shredded Swiss or mozzarella cheese (about 4 ounces)
1 envelope Lipton® Recipe Secrets Garlic Mushroom Soup Mix

Preheat oven to 350°. In a 1-quart casserole (sprayed with PAM®), combine all ingredients. Bake uncovered 30 minutes or until heated through.

VARIATION: For a Cold Garlic Artichoke Dip, omit Swiss cheese. If desired, stir in ¼ cup grated Parmesan cheese. Do not bake.

PEPPERONI PIZZA DIP
Diane Longo

1 (8 ounce) package Philadelphia® Cream Cheese, softened
½ cup sour cream
1 teaspoon dried oregano
⅛ teaspoon garlic salt
⅛ teaspoon crushed red pepper (optional)

½ cup pizza sauce (I usually make my own)
1 cup chopped pepperoni
¼ cup sliced green onions
Small amount of green pepper diced
1 cup shredded mozzarella

In a small mixing bowl, mix the cream cheese, sour cream, oregano, garlic salt, and red pepper. Spread evenly in a 9 or 10-inch quiche pan or Pyrex dish®. Spread the pizza sauce over the top. Sprinkle chopped pepperoni, green onions, and green peppers. Bake at 350° for 10 minutes. Top with mozzarella and bake 10 minutes more until the cheese is melted. Serve with crackers or sweet peppers strips, broccoli or cauliflower.

Diane Longo, our neighbor and good friend from Thistle Court gave me this recipe. I've used it several times. It is delicious and easy to make. See recipe index for Avella Pizza Sauce.

L-R: Cyndi Koury, Diane and Bob Longo, wonderful neighbors and friends. Cyndi was one of the first people I met when we moved upstate. Our children grew up together. Bob works for Remington and he and Diane were our neighbors on Thistle Court. My children were always popping up in their kitchens looking for treats. My children never knew which of these houses to call home. Diane is a great cook and baker as is Cyndi.

SHRIMP SPREAD
Rockie Napoli

1 (8 ounce) package of Philadelphia® Cream Cheese, softened
½ cup mayonnaise

2½ cups cheddar cheese, shredded
1 can tiny shrimp, drained
2-3 tablespoons onion, peeled and finely chopped

Mix everything together. Microwave one minute at a time until bubbly. Serve with crackers.

HOT SPINACH AND MOZZARELLA DIP
Elise Feiner

1 package chopped spinach (thawed and drained)
1 cup Hellmann's® Mayonnaise
1 cup Parmesan cheese

2 cups mozzarella
Paprika to taste

Mix all of the ingredients in the bowl, except for the paprika. After mixing, transfer it to a shallow baking dish. Sprinkle the top with a little paprika. Bake at 350° for 30 minutes or until bubbly. Serve with tortilla chips, pumpernickel bread etc. Enjoy!!!!!

SPINACH JACK ARTICHOKE DIP
Elise Feiner

2 cans artichoke hearts, plain, diced
1 large onion, finely chopped
4 cloves garlic, peeled and crushed
3 tablespoons oil

2 packages frozen chopped spinach
1 (4 ounce) package cream cheese; softened
1 bag shredded Monterey Jack cheese
½ cup Parmesan cheese

In a large skillet, heat the oil and sauté the onions, artichoke hearts and garlic until soft. Add the cream cheese and sour cream. Add the Parmesan cheese and set on low heat. Microwave the spinach until defrosted, drain and add to the mix. Place in an ovenproof dish that has been sprayed with PAM®; add the Monterey Jack cheese on the top and place in a 350° oven until the cheese is melted. You can also add mushrooms if you like. Serve with tortilla chips, pita chips, fried bowtie pasta. Serve with salsa, chopped tomatoes and sour cream on the side. I am going to try substituting creamed spinach for a different twist.

SNOW BALL DIP (CLAM DIP)
Katherine Avella

1 large round loaf of French, Italian, Pumpernickel or Rye Bread (whichever you prefer)
2 (8 ounce) packages Philadelphia® Cream Cheese, softened
3 (6½ ounces) cans chopped clams, drained (reserve ¼ cup of the liquid)
2 tablespoons grated onion

2 tablespoons beer
2 teaspoons Worcestershire Sauce
2 teaspoons lemon juice
1 teaspoon hot-pepper sauce, or to taste
½ teaspoon salt
Parsley springs for garnish
Raw vegetables for dipping

With a sharp knife, cup the top from the bread; set aside. Hollow out the loaf, leaving a 1½ to 2-inch thick shell. Cut removed bread in cubes. Set both aside. Keep the cubes in a zip lock bag.

In a large bowl, beat the cream cheese until smooth; stir in the clams, the reserved clam liquid, onions, beer, Worcestershire sauce, lemon juice, pepper sauce and salt until well blended. On a baking sheet make a cross with two sheets of foil, each long enough to cover the bread. Center the bread shell on foil. Pour clam mixture into shell; cover with bread top. Wrap the loaf with foil. Bake in a preheated 250° oven for three hours to blend, and the clam mixture to get piping hot. Remove the top. Serve loaf on a large platter surrounded by the bread and raw vegetables for dipping. Toast the bread cubes in the oven for the last five minutes baking time.

SPINACH ARTICHOKE DIP
Elise Feiner

1 (14 ounce) can artichoke hearts, drained and chopped
1 (10 ounce) package frozen chopped spinach, thawed and drained

1 cup mayonnaise
1 cup grated Parmesan cheese
2½ cups shredded Monterey Jack cheese

Preheat oven to 350°. Lightly grease a 1-quart baking dish. In a medium bowl, mix together artichoke hearts, spinach, mayonnaise, Parmesan cheese and 2 cups Monterey Jack cheese. Put mix in the prepared baking dish, and sprinkle with remaining ½ cup of Monterey Jack cheese. Bake in the center of the preheated oven until the cheese is melted, about 15 minutes. Enjoy!

CHICKEN WING DIP
Brenda Johnson

2 (8 ounce) packages Philadelphia® Cream Cheese
1 cup blue cheese salad dressing
6 ounces Frank's Red Hot Sauce

2 cups cooked chicken, diced
1 cup celery, diced
8 ounces Monterey Jack Cheese (shredded)

Melt the cream cheese (one at a time) over medium heat; stir in the blue cheese dressing and the Red Hot Sauce. Remove from the heat and stir in the chicken and celery. Spray a 13x9-inch pan with PAM. Pour mix into the pan. Sprinkle with Monterey Jack cheese and bake at 350° for 25 minutes. Serve with Tortilla chips or Scoops, or Pita crackers.

Brenda says that her sister-in-law is the queen of appetizers and dips and she gave her this recipe. She says it's fabulous!

SPINACH AND CHEESE DIP
Elise Feiner

1 cup Spinach Dip Mix (recipe follows); Freeze any extra
1 cup shredded cheddar cheese
1 cup shredded mozzarella cheese
1 cup sour cream

1 cup real bacon bits
1 cup red onion, diced fine
1 (16 ounce) jar of salsa picante or mild salsa

Preheat oven to 350°. Put the spinach dip in an oven-proof dish sprayed with PAM®, top with cheddar cheese and mozzarella cheese. Heat in the oven for about 10 minutes; stir thoroughly and place back in the oven for 5 more minutes. Remove from the oven and set in the center of a large ovenproof serving platter. Spoon some of sour cream onto the center of the dip, diced onions on one side and the bacon bits on the other. Serve with salsa on the side with tortilla chips, pita chips, potato chips, or your favorite crackers.

1½ tablespoons unsalted butter
3 tablespoons all purpose flour
2 cups half and half

½ cup Parmesan cheese
1½ teaspoons kosher salt
1 (16 ounce) package frozen chopped spinach

Defrost the spinach in a colander in the sink. When defrosted, place spinach in a clean dish towel and squeeze until dry. Set aside. Melt butter in a large frying pan. Slowly whisk in flour and cook briefly to form a roux (a mixture or flour and butter that is browned.) Add the half and half and cook until it thickens. Turn off the heat and mix in the cheese, and salt. Set aside to cool. Add the spinach to the cooled cream sauce and mix thoroughly. Freeze any leftover dip.

WHITE PIZZA DIP
Elise Feiner

1 envelope Lipton® Savory Herb and Garlic Soup Mix
1 (8 ounce) container sour cream
1 (8 ounce) cup ricotta cheese

1 cup shredded mozzarella cheese (about 4 ounces)
¼ cup chopped pepperoni (about 1 ounce)

Preheat oven to 350°. In a 1-quart casserole, combine soup mix, sour cream, ricotta cheese, ¾ cup mozzarella and pepperoni. Sprinkle with remaining ¼ cup mozzarella cheese. Bake uncovered 30 minutes or until heated through. Serve with bread or crackers

FETA SPREAD
Elise Feiner

1 puff pastry sheet
½ teaspoon oregano

1 (8 ounce) package Feta cheese
1 egg, beaten

Spread the puff pastry sheet out. Sprinkle the oregano over the feta cheese. Press the oregano into the cheese. Place the cheese in the middle of the puff pastry sheet. Wrap the puff pastry around the cheese. Place seam side down on a lightly greased cookie sheet. Brush with the egg. Bake 350° for 20 minutes or until golden brown. Serve with bread, fruit, and crackers.

PEPPERONI PUFFS
Elise Feiner

1 package puff pastry
Pepperoni slices

1 small mozzarella cheese cut in small cubes

Roll out the puff pastry and cut into 3x 3-inch squares. Place a few slices of pepperoni and a cube of mozzarella in the middle of each square. Fold up the square and twist on the top so they don't open during baking. Bake at 400° for about 10 minutes or until golden brown. Another variation is to add a tiny bit of pizza sauce and a little grated cheese to each square.

TACO STICKS
Elise Feiner

3 (7 ounce) cans potato sticks
2 (6 ounce) cans French Fried onions or cheddar onions or one of each
1 (12 ounce) can salted peanuts

⅓ cup butter, melted
1 envelope taco seasoning mix

In a large bowl, mix the potato sticks, onions and peanuts. In a separate bowl, combine the butter and taco seasonings; mix well. Pour the butter over the potato stick mixture and toss lightly to coat. Place on three ungreased 15x10-inch disposable cookie sheets. Bake uncovered in a preheated 250° oven for about 30 minutes. Store the sticks in airtight containers. You can also add some pretzel sticks if desired, but you may have to increase the butter a little.

REUBEN DIP
Elise Feiner

½ pound corned beef, chopped but not too fine
1 cup shredded Swiss cheese

1 cup Thousand Island dressing (1 small bottle)
½ (16)small bottle of sauerkraut or small can squeeze well

Mix everything together, and place in a baking dish or Pyrex® dish that has been sprayed with PAM®. Bake 350° until the cheese is melted. Serve with small rye squares. This can be mixed ahead and then baked when ready to serve.

I've made this as an appetizer at the holidays. It's fast, easy and delicious.

JOJO'S BRUSCHETTA
Joseph A. Mainella, Jr.

For every cup of extra virgin olive oil add:

1 teaspoon Polaner® chopped basil
1 teaspoon Polaner® chopped garlic in olive oil
½ teaspoon of McCormick® Italian Seasoning
1-2 teaspoons Regina® Balsamic Vinegar
1 loaf of Italian Bread cut on an angle into thin slices (let sit out overnight)

1-2 tomatoes cut into small cubes
Black Forest Ham cut into small pieces, or shrimp, or sausage (cooked)
Grated Cheese
Provolone Cheese cut into pieces

Mix together the olive oil, basil, garlic, McCormick Italian Seasoning, and vinegar. Brush the bread with the oil mixture. Add tomatoes to remaining oil mixture. Place grated cheese over the oil mixture on top of the bread. Top the grated cheese with ham, shrimp or sausage. Add some of the tomato mix on top of the meat. Add another layer of grated cheese. Top with provolone cheese. Bake 400° on a cookie sheet for about 10 to 13 minutes until cheese is melted and bubbly.

This is cousin JoJo's recipe. He made these when I was in Florida. They make a wonderful appetizer and the ham kicks it up.

Clockwise from bottom left:
Steven Feiner, Philip Avella, Jr., Jeffrey Feiner,
Michael Avella and David Feiner
1985

BRUSCHETTA
Elise Feiner

1 Loaf French or Italian Bread Sliced on the diagonal into thin slices

Oil Mixture for the top of French bread:

½-¾ cup olive oil
6-8 cloves of garlic (peeled and crushed)
Dash of garlic salt

Black pepper to taste
3 tablespoons grating cheese

Mix everything together in a bowl.

Tomato Mixture:

5-6 medium vine ripened tomatoes (or any tomato) diced
into very small cubes.
6-8 leaves of fresh basil, finely chopped
1 tablespoon dried oregano
Garlic salt and pepper to taste
2-3 tablespoons olive oil (more depending on your taste)

4-5 cloves of fresh garlic cut in half so they can be easily
removed
Mozzarella cut into small cubes (fresh in water, not
packaged if possible)

Make the tomato mixture early in the day. Remove the garlic, before serving. Line the slices of bread on a cookie sheet. Just before serving, brush or spoon a little of the oil mixture onto the slices of French bread. Place under the broiler for a few minutes to lightly toast. Watch **CAREFULLY** or they will burn. Remove from heat, and place tomato mixture on top. Top the Bruschetta with the cubed mozzarella when you are ready to serve it. Serves 6.

A delicious, quick appetizer to make. It's one of Steven and David's favorites.

JUDY'S KIELBASA
Judy Massoud

2 pounds Kielbasa (Hillshire Farms®)
½ cup ketchup
½ cup brown sugar (dark)
½ cup Progresso® red wine garlic vinegar

1 teaspoon ginger
1 tablespoon soy sauce
Pot with boiling water

Bring water to a boil. Put the kielbasa (keep whole) in the water and bring back to a boil. Boil for 10 minutes. Slice kielbasa in ½-inch slices. Put in a baking pan. In a pot, mix the ketchup, sugar, vinegar, ginger, and soy sauce. Heat through **but don't boil it**. Pour over the kielbasa. Let kielbasa marinade 24 hours. Do not remove marinade. Put baking pan in oven at 350° until heated thoroughly, approximately 25 minutes. Serves about 10 as an appetizer.

Judy made this for a buffet table at Mike Alsheimer's graduation party and it was a big hit. She was kind enough to share the recipe with me.

MARINATED SALAMI
Pearl Borten

1 (1 pound) Hebrew National® Beef Salami
⅔ cup apricot jelly

⅓ cup barbeque sauce

Mix the jelly and sauce together. Peel and score the salami. Spoon the jelly mixture over the salami. Place in a foil pan. Bake at 325° for 1 hour. Baste when half done. Let it get crispy on top. Put salami on a cutting board with cocktail rye bread. Serve with a bowl of mustard and a sharp knife for cutting.

This is a quick and easy appetizer from Mom Mom's friend Pearl.

MAPLE KIELBASA
Carol Zuchowski

1 smoked or regular kielbasa   Maple syrup

Place the kielbasa into a pot of water and bring to a boil. Let boil 30 minutes. Remove. Let cool and slice on an angle into ½-inch pieces. Place on a cookie sheet and brush with maple syrup. Bake at 350° for about 10 minutes, turn, brush the other side with syrup; bake another 10 minutes or until golden.

Carol got the recipe from her sister Darlene's father-in-law Joe Serbaniewicz. We made it Easter Sunday and it was great!

Carol Zuchowski with granddaughter
Chloe Dobbins

Chloe and Bailey Dobbins

MUSHROOM NACHOS
Josephine Mainella

24 large mushrooms; clean with a damp towel or zucchini slices (cut 1-inch thick) can be substituted for mushroom caps
4-6 tablespoons butter, melted
2 ounces pepperoni or chorizo sausage sliced thinly (about 24 pieces)
1-2 jalapeno peppers, finely chopped

1½ cups shredded Monterey Jack or sharp cheddar cheese (6 ounces)
1 small red bell pepper, roasted, or 2 pimentos, cut into 24 pieces
¼ cup minced green onion

Line a baking sheet with foil. Remove stems from mushrooms. Brush entire surface of caps with melted butter. Arrange caps rounded side down on sheet. Preheat broiler. Set 1 piece of sausage in each cap. Sprinkle with jalapenos, then cheese. Top with red peppers or pimentos. Broil 6 inches from the heat until cheese is melted. Transfer to heated platter. Sprinkle with minced green onions and serve. Serves 6.

Elise Feiner and Josephine Mainella
(Aunt Fifi)

Aunt Fifi never married and always
lived with us. She was my
"roommate" for years…After my
mother's death she came to live with
me again…she was always like
another mother to me!

MOZZARELLA STICKS
Elise Feiner

1 large mozzarella cut into thirds lengthwise, and then into sticks
Flour (about ½ cup)
2 eggs beaten, add more if necessary

2 tablespoons Parmesan cheese and extra to sprinkle on top
Flavored Italian Breadcrumbs

Beat the eggs and parmesan cheese together. Place the flour and breadcrumbs onto two separate paper plates. Dip the mozzarella sticks into the flour, then into the egg mixture, and then into the bread crumbs. Arrange on a sheet of waxed paper on a cookie sheet and place in the refrigerator for about ½ hour to 1 hour. Deep-fry the sticks in a deep fryer or large frying pan with enough oil to cover the sticks. They should be well browned but don't over fry or they will start to leak. Drain on paper towels. Sprinkle with Parmesan cheese and serve with marinara sauce (see index for Avella Marinara Sauce).Serves 4.

These are a favorite in the Feiner house and with kids and adults everywhere

PEPPER PISSALADIERE
Ann D'Amico

Olive oil
1 pound ripe tomatoes, peeled and chopped
½ teaspoon dried oregano
½ teaspoon sugar
Salt and freshly ground pepper
4 tablespoons butter

3 large onions, peeled and thinly sliced
2 large green peppers
1 (9-inch) pastry crust, prebaked for about
6 minutes at 350°
2 tablespoon grated cheese

Heat about two tablespoons of olive oil in a large sauté pan. Add the chopped tomatoes, sprinkle with the oregano and sugar, and season to taste with salt and pepper. Cook over low heat for 15 minutes, or until excess moisture has evaporated. Stir tomatoes with a wooden spoon. Cool; in another pan, sauté the onions in butter until soft; cool. Cut the peppers into long strips about ½- inch wide. Place on a cookie sheet and place under the broiler; broil for a few minutes until lightly browned. Sprinkle the bottom of the pie crust with the parmesan cheese. Cover with the onions; add tomatoes, dot with the pepper chunks. Brush the top of the tart and pepper chunks with olive oil. Bake 350° for 30 minutes.

ONION SQUARES
Elise Feiner

1 egg, well beaten
2 cups Bisquick® baking mix
¾ cup milk
2 tablespoons poppy seeds
3 tablespoons butter
2 cups chopped sweet onions

3 scallions, thinly sliced
1 egg
¾ cup sour cream
½ teaspoon salt
¼ teaspoon black pepper
Paprika

Blend the well beaten egg, poppy seeds and milk with the Bisquick. Turn onto a greased 9x 9-inch pan. Fry the onions and scallions in the butter until tender and lightly browned. Spread over the dough. Beat the other egg with the sour cream and season with salt and pepper. Bake at 400° for 25 minutes. Cut into squares. Sprinkle with paprika and serve very hot. Serves 12 to 15 as an appetizer. It's also good as a side dish with a steak.

L-R: Marc, Lauren and Jeffrey Feiner

SWEET KIELBASA APPETIZERS
Marie Golden

3 rings of Kielbasa   1 cup ketchup
2 cans of jelled cranberry sauce

Cut the kielbasa into ½-inch pieces. Mix the cranberry sauce with the ketchup in a medium bowl and blend well. Place the kielbasa and the sauce into a crock-pot. Cook on low heat until warm.

My hairdresser Marie said these sound horrible but are so easy to make and are delicious with a barbeque sauce coating. Her brother-in-law loves these.

Marie Golden, my favorite
hairdresser and friend
She earns her keep; it takes a
lot of work to keep my hair
"gray free"

PHYLLO CHEESE APPETIZERS
Elise Feiner

1 pound package of Phyllo dough   ¼ teaspoon salt
¾-1 pound unsweetened butter, melted, add more as   ⅛ teaspoon black pepper
needed   ¾ cup grated cheese
1 (16 ounce) container Ricotta cheese   1½ cups mozzarella shredded
2-3 eggs   1 cup Monterey Jack, or Muenster cheese, shredded

Mix everything together except the phyllo dough and butter. The mixture should be creamy but not too loose. If too thick, add another egg. The mix should be able to hold its shape. Take a piece of phyllo dough, butter with a pastry brush, put another piece on top, butter the second piece, and put a third strip on top, butter the third strip. Workings quickly, cut the phyllo dough into 2 to 3-inch strips (I usually cut each large sheet into 5 strips) and keep covered with a damp towel while you work on each triangle. Place about a 1 to 2 teaspoons of filling in one corner. Start to fold into a triangle and continue folding like a flag. Brush with butter to hold down the phyllo sheets. (You can also roll these in to an egg roll shape by placing some filling at the bottom of the sheets, start to roll and then fold the sides in, and continue rolling.) Seal seams with butter. Brush with butter or beaten egg yolk and sprinkle with sesame seeds. Place on a greased cookie sheet. They can be frozen at this point, or baked at 400° for about 15 to 20 minutes or until golden brown. They made a few extra minutes if you bake them frozen. Makes about 70, serves about 12.

There was a restaurant in Utica called the Polonaise that used to make these. When they closed, I had to learn how to make this myself because this is one of Lauren's favorite appetizers. They are great to eat, but a pain to make. You must work very quickly when working with phyllo dough. This goes so must faster with two people making them, but you can easily do it by yourself.

"The real measure of your wealth is how much you'd be worth if you lost all your money."
-Unknown

SAUSAGE CHEDDAR BALLS
Elise Feiner

1 pound bulk Italian sausage	3 cups Bisquick®
4 cups shredded cheddar cheese	½ teaspoon cayenne pepper
½ cup milk	1 package Lipton® Onion Soup mix
2 eggs, beaten	Paprika

Preheat an oven to 375°. Grease cookie sheets. Brown the sausage in a frying pan with a little oil in it. Set aside and cool. Combine the sausage, cheddar cheese, milk and eggs. Blend well. Add the Bisquick, cayenne pepper, and soup mix; mix well. Roll into 1-inch balls (use a small cookie scoop). Place on prepared sheets, sprinkle with paprika. Bake 10 to 15 minutes or until golden brown.

POTATO PUFFS IN PHYLLO
Elise Feiner

Leftover mashed potatoes	¼ cup vegetable oil
1 stick butter, melted	Salt and pepper, to taste
1 large onion, chopped	1 package Phyllo dough
2 cloves garlic, peeled and crushed	Melted butter, (start with 1 stick)
2 eggs, beaten	1 egg plus one tablespoon of water for an egg wash
1 cup cheddar cheese, grated	Sesame seeds (about ¾ cup)
1 cup grated mozzarella cheese	

Preheat oven to 375°. In a large frying pan, heat the oil and sauté the onions, garlic, and a little salt and pepper to taste. Add to the leftover mashed potatoes. Add the eggs and cheeses. Layer about three sheets of phyllo dough that have all been brushed with melted butter. Cut the phyllo dough into strips about 3 to 4-inches wide. Place about a tablespoon of the mixture in one corner and begin folding like a flag to turn into a triangular shape. Spray a cookie sheet with PAM™, and place the triangles on it. Brush the top with an egg wash; sprinkle with sesame seeds. They may be frozen at this point on a cookie sheet and when frozen, transfer to a zip lock bag. If you aren't freezing, bake for about 25 minutes or until golden brown, or bake frozen, and add a little extra cooking time. Serves 8.

I invented these after having a lot of leftover potatoes. These are great to make and freeze for last minute company or a party, just pop them in the oven. They taste like potato knishes.

SHRIMP WRAPPED WITH BACON
Nick Arcuri

Fresh jumbo shrimp, peeled, deveined and boiled	Barbeque sauce, Hickory Farm® Garlic if available
Bacon slices, partially cooked	

Boil the shrimp in lightly salted water until pink about 3 minutes; drain and set aside. Fry the bacon in a frying pan until cooked **about halfway and set aside.** Wrap the partially cooked bacon around the shrimp. Place on skewers. Brush with barbeque sauce. Place under the broiler. Broil until bacon is done. Turn over, brush with barbeque sauce. Broil until the other side is done. You can also use scallops if you want.

Nick Arcuri made these one Christmas Eve at his house and generously gave me the recipe.

The Feiner and Marquino Kids…

Front L-R: David, Steven and Lauren Feiner, Jennifer Marquino. Back L-R: Jeffrey and Elise Feiner, Susan Marquino holding Kristen. Sue and I have been friends since Junior High School!

ROASTED VEGETABLES AND FONTINA PUFF PASTRY
Athena Avramidis

1 package of Pepperidge Farm® Puff Pastry
1 small eggplant, sliced lengthwise
1 zucchini, sliced lengthwise
1 red pepper, roasted, seeded and sliced

1 box sliced mushrooms
2-3 cloves of garlic, peeled and crushed
4 ounces Fontina Cheese

Cut one sheet of puff pastry in half. Roll out to make two 4 x10-inch sheets. Roast some sliced eggplant, some zucchini sliced lengthwise and one red pepper (you can season them and you can use olive oil.) In a small saucepan, sauté some mushrooms and garlic. Slice some Fontina cheese, about 4 ounces. Preheat oven to 375°. Line a baking sheet with parchment paper. Set the pastry sheets on the paper. Arrange the sliced cheese on top, leaving one inch border. Arrange eggplant, the mushrooms and the zucchini. Slice the red pepper thin juliennes. Arrange them on top in a crisscross fashion. Fold the sides of the puff pastry (about 1-inch). Bake the tarts for 40 minutes or until golden and puffed. Cut the tarts crosswise. Serve warm or room temperature.

Athena Avramidis gave me this recipe at one of our birthday lunches. It's easy and delicious.

SALMON CHEESECAKE APPETIZER
Elise Feiner

3 tablespoons dry unflavored breadcrumbs
5 tablespoons grated cheese (Parmesan or Pecorino Romano)
½ cup onion, peeled and chopped
½ cup chopped green pepper
3 tablespoons butter
3 (8 ounce) packages Philadelphia® Cream Cheese, at room temperature

1 (3 ounce) package Philadelphia® Cream Cheese, at room temperature
½ cup heavy cream
¼ teaspoon black pepper
4 eggs
6 ounces smoked Salmon (lox) diced
½ cup shredded Swiss cheese
½ cup shredded Monterey Jack cheese

Grease the sides and bottom of a 9-inch spring form pan. Combine the breadcrumbs and 2 tablespoons of the grated cheese; sprinkle into the pan, coating the bottom and the sides. Refrigerate until ready to use. In a medium skillet, sauté the onions and the peppers in the butter until tender. Set aside. In a mixing bowl, beat the cream cheese until fluffy. Beat in the heavy cream, pepper and remaining grating cheese. Add the eggs and beat on low speed until combined. Fold in the onion/pepper mix, salmon, Swiss and Monterey Jack cheeses. Wrap two thicknesses of heavy-duty aluminum foil around the spring form pan. Pour salmon mixture into the pan. Place in a larger baking pan filled with hot water about 1½-inch deep. Bake at 325° for 30 to 40 minutes, or until the center is almost set. Cook on a wire rack for 1 hour. Refrigerate overnight. Cut cheesecake into wedges and serve with your favorite crackers. Serves 12 to 14. This is great for a Sunday Brunch or a luncheon.

L-R: Sisters Marie Caccavale, Jean "Dolly" Caccavale, Phyllis Caccavale Foster
and cousin Elizabeth Silvestri Saracino

PHYLLO SPINACH TRIANGLES
Elise Feiner

3 tablespoons olive oil
1 onion, chopped
½ cup chopped green onions, white and green parts
3 garlic cloves, minced
2 pounds fresh baby spinach, trimmed, washed and roughly chopped
½ lemon, juiced
2 eggs, lightly beaten

12 ounces crumbled Feta cheese
½ teaspoon freshly grated nutmeg
¼ cup finely chopped oregano
¼ cup finely chopped chives
½ cup grated Parmesan
½ pound unsalted butter, melted
1 pound Phyllo pastry sheets
Sesame Seeds

Heat olive oil in a large skillet and place over medium heat. Sauté onions and garlic for 3 minutes until soft. Add the spinach, season with salt and pepper, and continue to sauté until the spinach is limp, about 2 minutes. Add lemon juice, remove from heat and place in a colander, and squeeze out excess liquid by hand. Set aside to cool. The filling needs to be cool and dry to prevent the phyllo from becoming soggy. In a medium bowl, beat the eggs with feta cheese, nutmeg, chives, oregano, and grated cheese. Season, then fold in the cooled spinach mixture until well blended.

Preheat oven to 350°, brush 2 baking sheets with some melted butter. Unroll the Phyllo dough and lay a sheet flat on a work surface. Take care to keep the Phyllo covered with a damp, not wet, towel as you work to prevent drying out and becoming brittle. Brush the sheet with melted butter, and then sprinkle evenly with some oregano and chives. Repeat with 2 more sheets of Phyllo, stacking on top of each other. With a sharp knife or pizza cutter, cut the sheets lengthwise into thirds or fourths to form 2½-inch strips. Eventually, you will repeat this with all the sheets of dough as you finish each set of triangles. Place a heaping teaspoon of filling near 1 corner of the layered Phyllo strip. Fold the end at an angle over the filling to form a triangle. Continue to fold the triangle along the strip until you reach the end, like folding up a flag or roll egg roll style; place in the middle of the sheet, start to roll, and then, turn both ends in and continue to roll. Brush the top with butter and dust with Sesame Seeds, place on prepared baking sheet, and cover while preparing the remaining pastries. Repeat until all the filling and Phyllo strips are used up. You can freeze them at this point. Bake for 20 to 30 minutes until the triangles are crisp and golden. Serve hot, warm or cold. Makes about 40 triangles.

These are my niece Abby's favorite appetizers. She always calls me a few days before Thanksgiving to make sure that I am making these for her. She always takes the leftovers back with her! These are easy to make ahead and freeze. Don't bake them before freezing.

JOHN'S COCONUT SHRIMP
John Grimaldi, Sr., Executive Chef

2 pounds of frozen, cooked, deveined, shrimp with the tails left on (15-20 count, no bigger)
1 can of Sprite ®
12 eggs
Flour for breading
1-2 bags of Angel Flake Coconut

Oil for frying
1 (16 ounce) can of Coco Casa Coconut Cream
1 quart of heavy cream
Grand Marnier
Cantaloupe and Honeydew slices

Defrost the shrimp. Beat the Sprite and eggs together. Dip the shrimp into the egg mix then into the flour, back into the eggs and then into the coconut. Deep Fry. Slice the melons in small pieces and place one piece of shrimp on a piece of melon. Make a Sauce by mixing the Coco Lopez with the heavy cream. Add Grand Marnier to taste. Drizzle over the shrimp. Another variation of the sauce is to mix the coconut cream(about ½ can with about (8 ounces)sour cream, add chopped pineapple (drained) and some finely chopped red peppers to taste.

L-R: Kevin, Barbara and Abby Feiner
Kevin is Marc's baby brother and following in family tradition, Barb and Kevin are now on Jeweler's Row in Philadelphia at Feiner's, Ltd. They have the most beautiful pearls and Kevin can create anything, he has hands of gold!

SAUSAGE AND CHEESE STARS
Elise Feiner

Round Wonton Wrappers (I have used square, if you can't find round but you may need to cut them down a little))
1 pound pork sausage (sweet or hot)

1 (8 ounce) package shredded Cheddar cheese
1 (8 ounce) package shredded Monterey Jack Cheese
1 (regular size) bottle of Hidden Valley® Ranch Dressing

Grease mini muffin tins with PAM®. Place one wonton into each cup (if you use large wonton or egg roll wrappers cut into quarters), they will extend over the tops. Bake at 350° for 5 minutes. Cool. Crumble and fry the sausage in a frying pan which has been sprayed with PAM® or has had a bit of oil added to it. Drain and pat dry. Mix with remaining ingredients. (These may be made ahead and held up to this point. Fill the cups and bake again at 350° for 5 to 10 minutes.

L-R: Lisa Philipson, Beth Burke, Michele Schulman, Andi Dinerstein

L-R: Gary Philipson, Robert Schulman, D.D.S., Murray Burke, and Rick Dinerstein

STUFFED MUSHROOMS WITH PECANS
Elise Feiner

18 large fresh whole mushrooms
8 slices bacon, fried and crumbled (save the drippings)
½ teaspoon McCormick® Seasoned Salt
¾ loaf white bread made into crumbs
½ (14 ounce) can College Inn® Chicken Broth
1 large onion, peeled and diced
3 ounces blue cheese, crumbled

Salt and pepper to taste
4 tablespoons butter
¼ cup chopped green bell pepper
2 teaspoons parsley
1 cup grated cheese
1 small can chopped pecans

Clean the mushrooms. Remove the stems and chop them finely. In a large frying pan, add 3 tablespoons of the bacon drippings and 4 tablespoons butter and heat. Sauté the onions, peppers, and pieces of mushroom stems. Turn into a large mixing bowl and add remaining ingredients. Stuff the mushroom caps. Place in a large baking pan. Add about ¼-inch of water to the pan. Cover with foil and bake at 325° for 15 minutes. Remove foil; bake another 15 minutes or until golden brown.

Family Friends...
Michele and Bob Schulman, D.D.S.

L-R: Flo, Bob and Michele Schulman. Flo is a casino person just like me...lucky too!

20

STUFFED MUSHROOMS ITALIANO
Katherine Avella

6 large button mushrooms
2 links sweet Italian sausage (meat taken out of casing)
¾ cup seasoned Italian bread crumbs
¾ cup grated Pecorino Romano cheese
¼ cup grated Parmesan
1 tablespoon garlic powder

½ teaspoons freshly ground black pepper
1 tablespoon dried parsley
¼ cup extra-virgin olive oil
Olive oil for the top
¼ cup shredded mozzarella

Preheat oven to 375°. Wash and pat dry mushrooms. Take off stems and chop into small pieces. Place mushroom caps in baking dish. In a small skillet, lightly brown the sausage in a little oil (don't cook completely). Place teaspoon of sausage in bottom of mushroom. Press meat down into mushroom. In a small bowl, combine mushroom pieces, breadcrumbs, Pecorino Romano, Parmesan, garlic powder, pepper, and parsley. Add olive oil until mixture is moist. If too dry add, more oil. Fill each mushroom cap generously with stuffing mixture and place in baking pan. Drizzle a little olive oil over each one. Pour little water in bottom of pan. Cover with foil. Bake for 30 minutes. Remove foil, sprinkle mozzarella on each mushroom and bake uncovered for another 10 minutes. Serves 6.

CHEESY MUSHROOMS
Elise Feiner

12-16 large mushroom caps
12-16 cubes sharp cheddar cheese

4 tablespoons butter cut into 16 cubes
Salt and pepper to taste

Place mushroom caps on a cookie sheet, bottoms up. Place a cube of butter and a cube of cheese in each mushroom cavity. Sprinkle a little salt and pepper to taste. Bake at 325° for 15 to 20 minutes.

Cousins Betty and Joe Arcara
My Cousin Betty and I have always given this family a run for their money and now her daughter Bettina is following in our footsteps.

STUFFED MUSHROOMS
Iryna Trociuk

1 pound whole fresh mushrooms
½ cup fine breadcrumbs
½ cup finely shredded Swiss cheese
4 tablespoons grated onion and juice
½ teaspoon salt

½ teaspoon pepper
2 tablespoons or more milk or cream
Grated Parmesan cheese
Butter

Remove stems; chop stems and save. Wipe mushroom caps with oil. In a bowl, mix chopped mushrooms with fine breadcrumbs, add the Swiss cheese and toss. Add onion and juice, salt and pepper; toss. Add milk so mixture is moist and holds together. Stuff caps; sprinkle with breadcrumbs and Parmesan cheese and dot with butter. Place on cookie sheet in 375° for 25 minutes. It depends on size of mushrooms whether you need more or less cooking time.

Iryna is a fabulous cook. My son David says no one makes chili like Mrs. Trociuk. Iryna says that these mushrooms make the best appetizers.

TIROPITA (CHEESE FILLED TRIANGLES)
Peggy Spirakis

1 pound sharp Feta cheese	1 pound Phyllo dough
1 (8 ounce) tangy cottage cheese	1½ pounds butter (start with 2 sticks at a time, and add
3 extra large or 4 large eggs	more as needed)

Mash the feta cheese in a bowl to get out all the lumps. Add cottage cheese and eggs and mix thoroughly. Unroll the phyllo dough and cut in thirds across the width. Melt the butter completely. Take a ⅓ of a sheet and brush with butter lightly using a pastry brush. Fold the sheet lengthwise and lightly brush the top with butter, down the length. Put about 1 teaspoon of cheese in the corner close to you on the left hand side. Fold over in a triangle and then fold it like a flag. Place seam side down on ungreased cookie sheet. Brush tops with melted butter. Bake at 350° for 10 to 15 minutes, or until the tops are golden brown. Remember to keep the phyllo dough covered with a damp cloth while you are working with it or it will dry out.

This recipe came from a friend who used to teach with Uncle Joe. She gave me several Greek recipes that are wonderful.

ELISE'S SWEDISH MEATBALLS
Elise Feiner

2 cups fresh breadcrumbs	Salt and pepper
½ cup milk	3 cups beef broth
1 pound ground beef	2 cups heavy cream
1 pound ground pork	3 tablespoons Gravy Master®
3 eggs	¼ cup Kahlua®
Salt	1 teaspoon nutmeg
Pepper	1 teaspoon allspice
1 cup yellow onion, chopped, plus 6 cups yellow onions, sliced	¼ teaspoon cloves
	¼ teaspoon cinnamon
1 cup salted butter, divided	3-4 tablespoons cornstarch
½ cup sugar	¼ cup cold water

In large mixing bowl, soak bread crumbs in milk for 5 minutes. Add meat, eggs, salt, pepper, and chopped onions. Mix well and roll into 1 to 1½-inch meatballs. Sauté meatballs in ¼ cup butter approximately 20 minutes. In a separate frying pan, sauté sliced onions with ¼ cup butter, sugar, and pepper until caramelized, about 10 to 15 minutes. Remove mixture from both pans and place on separate plates. Deglaze both sauté pans with the remaining ½ cup butter and beef broth, scraping up the browned bits. Cook over high heat for 1 minute. Add everything from both pans into one large pot and add cream, onions, gravy master, Kahlua and spices and bring to a simmer. Mix cornstarch and water. Whisk the cornstarch into the mixture to thicken. Add meatballs and simmer approximately 20 to 30 minutes. Serves 12.

I got this recipe from a neighbor in Baltimore, when Marc was a Resident at Franklin Square hospital.

L-R: Mary Ellen Shaw, a close family friend and Carol and Tom Zuchowski. Carol is our housekeeper and she and her husband Tom are like part of the family. Without her, I could have never gotten this book finished, she ran the house and helped with Aunt Fifi so I could be free to work on the book. She has been with us for years.

SWEDISH MEATBALLS
Edith Mainella

1 loaf Italian bread (cut in cubes)
2 pints heavy cream
2 pounds ground beef
1 pound ground pork
½ pound ground veal
2 eggs
3-4 cloves garlic, peeled and crushed
½ teaspoon nutmeg
Sprinkle of parsley (about a teaspoon)
2 teaspoons salt

½ teaspoon thyme
2 chopped onions
Lots of grated cheese
⅛ teaspoon black pepper
Oil to Fry
1 teaspoon instant coffee
4 cans beef broth
Leftover heavy cream from the bread
A few teaspoons Wondra® flour to thicken the sauce.

Soak the bread in cream. Squeeze out the bread and save the cream. Add the bread to the ground meats. Then add the eggs. Add the garlic, nutmeg, parsley, salt, thyme, onions, grating cheese, pepper. Shape into small meatballs, 1-inch in diameter. Heat the oil and fry the meatballs; remove from pan onto paper towels. Reserve some of the drippings to make the sauce. Take some of the dripping from the frying pan and mix with the Wondra flour. Slowly add the beef broth, cream and coffee. Add the meatballs to the sauce and simmer for one hour. Add more flour if necessary. Sauce should not be too thick. Serves 8.

These were very popular in the seventies. They are making a comeback again. You can keep these warm in a crock-pot.

PEPPERONI CRISPS
Steven Feiner

¼ pound thinly sliced pepperoni (large rounds) don't use the small size pepperoni from sticks; use the one the size of salami

Preheat oven to 325°. Line cookie sheets with parchment paper. Place the pepperoni slices on the cookie sheets in a single layer and bake until the edges start to curl and they are getting crisp. Remove to a rack to cool, they will continue to crisp as they cool. Serve as you would any cracker i.e. with cheese, dips, etc. You can do these with Salami too.

Steven found this in Gourmet Magazine but it was done with Genoa Salami. My boys love these!

VEGGIE PIZZA
Cathy Kahler

2 packages crescent rolls (she uses 1½)
1 (8 ounce) package Philadelphia® Cream Cheese
1 cup mayonnaise
1 package ranch salad dressing (dry)
Assorted vegetables:
2 carrots, finely chopped

½ cup red bell pepper, chopped
½ cup chopped green bell pepper
½ cup fresh chopped broccoli
½ cup chopped green onions
Shredded cheddar cheese, sharp or mild

Line a jelly roll pan with roll pieces. Bake at 375° for about 10 minutes or until brown. Let cool. Combine the cream cheese, dressing, and mayonnaise. Spread on the cool crust. Sprinkle with the veggies cut up in small pieces. Then top with shredded cheese. Serves 8.

Cathy made this for a neighborhood party when we lived in South Woods and it was wonderful.

"I cannot believe that the purpose of life is to be happy. I think the purpose of life is to be useful, to be responsible, to be compassionate. It is, above all to matter, to count, to stand for something, to have made some difference that you lived at all."
-Leo Rosten

CHICKEN NUGGETS
Elise Feiner

1 cup flour
1 cup seasoned breadcrumbs
1 teaspoon baking powder

2 packages boneless, skinless chicken breasts cut into 1-inch cubes

Mix the flour, breadcrumbs, and baking powder together. Dip the cubes in the flour mix, coating completely. Deep fry or fry in a frying pan in about 1½ to 2-inches of oil. Serve with chicken dipping sauce. (See recipe index)

Lynn Picano and John Picano, M.D.
John is a radiologist and Lynn one of our school nurses (that alone should earn her a place in heaven.) We are lucky to count them among our good friends

PIZZA MEATBALLS
Elise Feiner

1½ pounds ground beef
1 teaspoon onion powder
2 eggs
1 cup panko (Japanese) breadcrumbs or plain breadcrumbs
4 cloves of garlic, peeled and crushed

1 teaspoon Worcestershire sauce
Salt and pepper, to taste
2-3 teaspoons McCormick® Italian seasoning
8 ounces mozzarella cheese cut into ¼ inch cubes

Sauce:
2-3 tablespoons vegetable oil
2 or 3 (15-ounce) cans Del Monte® tomato sauce
1 (15-ounce) can crushed tomatoes
3-4 cloves garlic, peeled and crushed

3 teaspoons dried basil
2 teaspoon dried oregano
1 chopped medium onion

Preheat oven to 350°. Line a flat baking sheet with parchment paper or waxed paper. In a large bowl add ground beef, onion powder, eggs, panko crumbs, garlic, Worcestershire, salt, pepper, and Italian seasoning. Mix thoroughly. Shape into 1-inch balls. Take a cube of the mozzarella and push it into the middle of the meatball. Roll the meatball into a ball again. Place on lined baking sheet. Do this until all of the meatballs have been formed. Bake in the oven until browned, about 15 to 20 minutes or you can fry them. Make sure the cubes of cheese are well surrounded and not too big or they will leak out of the meat. In a medium saucepan, place a few tablespoons of vegetable oil. Heat the onions until soft and golden. Add the garlic, and then quickly add the tomatoes so the garlic doesn't burn. Add remaining seasonings. Cook for 20 to 25 minutes on low simmer. Add the sauce to a crock-pot, on medium heat) Keep hot while the meatballs cook. Add the meatballs once they are done cooking. Serve with toothpicks. Serves 6.

My cousin Ann D'Amico said that my grandmother used to make her meatballs similar to these.

L-R: Bernie and Connie Gigliotti and Cindy Gigliotti Circelli
The Gigliotti's deserve a medal, they run our local driving school and have taught all our children to drive…and lived to tell the tale!

COCKTAIL MEATBALLS
Toni Mollico

3 pounds chop meat
3 cans tomato soup
1 cup sugar

2 tablespoons lemon juice
Garlic powder

Add as much garlic powder as you like to chopped meat. Mix well. Roll into very small meatballs. In a large pot, add soup, sugar, and lemon juice. Just make little meatballs and put in pot on stove, you can cover them or leave them uncovered; and let them simmer. Do not stir; gently shake pot to stir meatballs. Simmer 3 hours, shake, and do not stir with a spoon.

Cousin Toni says that these are the best appetizers and she always has requests to make them.

Elise Feiner (hidden on Left), Toni and Tom Mollico
on their wedding day.

L-R: Angelo Facci, Tom and Toni Mollico, and Carol Facci

SPINACH-MUSHROOM PINWHEELS
Elise Feiner

PASTRY:
1 (8 ounce) package cream cheese, softened
⅔ cup butter, softened
2 cups all-purpose flour
1 tablespoon all-purpose flour

1 teaspoon baking powder
½ teaspoon salt
¼ teaspoon baking soda

FILLING:
1 (10 ounce) package frozen chopped spinach, defrosted
2 tablespoons butter
2½ cups chopped mushrooms
1 cup chopped onion
½ teaspoon dried oregano

½ teaspoon salt
½ teaspoon lemon juice
⅛ teaspoon garlic powder
½ cup grated Parmesan cheese

In a large bowl, beat together cream cheese and ⅔ cup butter. Mix in 2 cups flour, a teaspoon baking powder, ½ teaspoon salt, and ¼ teaspoon baking soda; beat well. Divide dough into two balls; wrap in plastic wrap. Chill 30 to 60 minutes or until pastry is easy to handle. Preheat oven to 400°. Heat spinach in large frying pan over medium-low heat; drain. Squeeze out excess liquid; set aside. In a large frying pan, melt the 2 tablespoons butter. Stir in mushrooms and onion. Cook and stir over medium heat for 3 minutes or until onion is tender. Mix in spinach, remaining 1 tablespoon flour, oregano, salt, lemon juice and garlic powder. Cook and stir until mixture thickens. Stir in Parmesan cheese. Set aside to cool. On floured surface, roll a pastry ball into a 12x7-inch rectangle. Spread with half the spinach mixture to within ½-inch of edges. Starting with a short side, roll up dough and filling, jelly-roll style. Moisten edges with water; pinch to seal. Repeat with remaining pastry. Cover; chill 1 hour. Slice logs into ½-inch thick slices. Place on ungreased baking sheets. Bake 20 minutes or until golden. Remove to wire racks; cool. Serves 10.

Our English Cousins

Anthony, and Angela Stevens, Katherine Avella,
Lisa Stevens Gaan with Helen Gaan. Although Anthony
and Angela are gone, we still see Lisa and her family
when we are in London. Her son Stephen spent the
summer with us.

ITALIAN WONTONS
Elise Feiner

6 ounces bulk sweet Italian sausage	4 ounces Mozzarella cheese, shredded
2 tablespoons parsley	Cooking oil for deep frying
¼ cup finely chopped onion	2 tablespoons grated Parmesan cheese
40 wonton wrappers	Marinara sauce (optional)

In a large skillet cook the sausage and onion over medium heat until sausage is brown and onion is tender, stirring to break meat into small pieces. Drain well. Cool completely. Stir in mozzarella cheese, parmesan cheese, and parsley. Place one rounded teaspoon of filling in center of wonton wrapper. Moisten the edges of the wrapper with water. Starting with one corner, fold the wrapper over the filling forming a triangle. Press to seal well. Bring the two other pointed ends of the wonton wrapper up over the stuffed center. Moisten and press together. Cover and chill if not frying right away. Fry wontons, a few at a time, in deep hot oil 1 to 2 minutes. Serve with marinara sauce (See index for Avella's Marinara Sauce) on the side for dipping if desired.

SWEET AND SOUR MEATBALLS
Ann D'Amico

Meatball mixture (your own or see index)	Chili Sauce
Grape Jelly	

Make your regular meatball mix but **eliminate the garlic**. Shape into 1-inch meatballs, and fry. Make a sauce that consists of equal amounts of chili sauce and grape jelly. Heat both until melted. Toss with the meatballs. You can keep these warm in a crock-pot if you'd like.

My cousin Ann missed her calling. She should have been Martha Stewart. Ann, who is a fabulous cook, gave me this recipe. She said it sounds terrible but taste wonderful. She makes it for parties all the time.

The D'Amico's: Ann and Philip

My cousin Ann is something else, she was one of the first preemies to survive a very low birth weight in the days when babies that weighed 1 pound 12 ounces didn't survive. She was the first baby in the United States to use an incubator…She was on display in the incubator at the 1939 World's Fair in Flushing, New York! Phil is the best…super kind, super patient, and one of the best things that ever happened to this family.

HAM BREAD
Elise Feiner

2 packages of pizza dough (I use store bought for this)
2 (2-3 cup) bags of shredded Mozzarella
8 slices of ham cut about ¼-inch thick (I usually use Boars Head® baby ham, but any boiled ham from the deli is fine)

Grated cheese
1 egg and 1 tablespoon of water beaten together to form an egg wash (set aside)

Cut the ham into very tiny cubes. Stretch the pizza dough on a lightly oiled surface (I use a cookie sheet) until it is about the size of a 13-inch rectangle. Divide the ham in half, and spread the ham and 1 bag of the mozzarella over the dough leaving about a 2-inch border. You can sprinkle with a little grating cheese if you want to. Roll the dough up like a jelly roll to form a loaf; seal the edges by pinching them together. Place the dough back on the cookie sheet, seam side down. Repeat with the second loaf. Brush the top with the egg wash. Bake in a 350° oven for 25 to 30 minutes, or until golden brown. The loaf should sound hollow when tapped lightly with your knuckles. Cool on a wire rack. Slice to serve. Serves about 4 people per loaf.

These are very easy to make and great when you are having a crowd; just slice and serve. You can make them in advance and just reheat them when needed.

COCKTAIL REUBENS
Elise Feiner

3 ounces corned beef
1 cup sauerkraut, drained well
½ cup shredded Swiss cheese

½ cup Thousand Island salad dressing
1 loaf cocktail rye or pumpernickel bread, sliced

Preheat oven to 375°. Chop the corn beef. Placed corned beef, sauerkraut, cheese and dressing in a bowl. Stir to combine. Arrange slices of bread on a cookie sheet. Top each slice of bread with corned beef mixture. Bake for 10 to 12 minutes until the cheese is melted. Serve warm. Makes 20 slices.

Our Italian Cousins…
Guido and Giovanna Politano, Maria Campestre, Katherine Avella and Margarita Campestre on a visit to Rome…

"If nothing is going well, call your grandmother."
-Italian Proverb

BROCCOLI OR SPINACH BREAD
Elise Feiner

2 packages of prepared pizza dough (I buy it at the grocery store)
4 boxes of frozen chopped spinach or chopped broccoli, defrosted and drained
1 cup grated cheese (Parmesan or Locatelli Romano)
4 cloves of garlic, peeled and crushed
1 egg and 1 tablespoon of water beaten together to form an egg wash (set aside)

1 large onion, peeled and diced
4 tablespoons butter
Salt and pepper to taste
Dash of mint if using the spinach
2 bags (2-3 cup size) shredded Mozzarella Cheese

In a large frying pan, sauté the onions and garlic in the butter until lightly browned and starting to caramelize. Add the broccoli or spinach, grating cheese, salt and pepper and mint if using the spinach; cook for about 10 minutes. Place in a strainer and drain any liquid. Let cool a little. Stretch the pizza dough on a lightly oiled surface (I use a cookie sheet) until it is about the size of a 13-inch rectangle. Divide the vegetable mix in half, and spread the vegetables and 1 bag of the mozzarella over the dough leaving about a 2-inch border. You can sprinkle with a little more grating cheese if you want to. Roll the dough up like a jelly roll to form a loaf; seal the edges by pinching them together. Place the dough back on the cookie sheet, seam side down. Repeat with the second loaf. Brush the top with the egg wash. Bake in a 350° oven for 25 to 30 minutes until golden brown. The loaf should sound hollow when tapped lightly with your knuckles. Cool on a wire rack. Makes 2 loaves.

These are great as an appetizer for a crowd. They are fast and easy to make. You can make them ahead and freeze them. Just reheat when needed.

L-R: Lauren, Elise, David, and Marc Feiner

BAKED BRIE
Ronni Tichenor

1 brie round or wedge
1 jar red pepper jelly (not the hot one)

Crackers
Fruit

Put the red pepper jelly on a wedge of brie or a whole wheel if it's small, and then microwave it for about 30 seconds on high, or just until you see the brie start to melt. Serve it with fruit (apples, grapes, pears) and crackers. Be careful not to buy the spicy red pepper jelly.

Ronni Tichenor made this for an appetizer one night when we were there for dinner. It was excellent and simple to do. Ronni is an incredible cook and makes the best desserts!

"Watch your thoughts; they become your words. Watch your words; they become your actions. Watch your actions; they become your habits. Watch your habits; they become your character. Watch your character for it will become your destiny."
-Frank Outlaw

GRANDMA'S HORS D'OEUVRES
Joanne Fsadni

½ pound Jarlsberg cheese (cut and sliced into small pieces)
1 pound Boar's Head® boiled ham (cut ¼-inch thick and sliced into small pieces)
¼ pound Genoa salami (cut ¼-inch thick and sliced into small pieces or cubes)
1 pound Mozzarella cheese (grated)
1 pound low fat cottage cheese
2 pounds Ricotta cheese

4 extra large eggs (for filling)
6 cups flour
1 pound cream cheese
1 pound sweet butter
2 teaspoons baking powder
2 teaspoons salt
½ cup low fat milk
3-4 extra large eggs (for dough)

Mix together in large bowl, the Jarlsberg cheese, ham, salami, and mozzarella. Set aside. Then mix together in another bowl, the cottage cheese, ricotta, and eggs. Then, add the cheese mixture to the salami/ham mixture. Place filling into refrigerator while mixing dough. Make the dough. Mix together well the flour, cream cheese and sweet butter. Then add the baking powder, and salt. Gradually add the low-fat milk, and 3-4 extra large eggs. Knead dough well. Place in refrigerator in large bowl with plastic wrap. After both dough and filling have been slightly chilled, grease large cookie sheet with high sides.

Place ¼ of dough on a floured pastry board. Roll out to desired thickness, approximately ⅛-inch. Place dough on greased cookie sheet or ungreased non-stick pan. Spread half of filling on dough to within 1 to 1½-inches from edge of pan. Brush edges of dough with a little beaten egg to help it stick to top crust. Roll out another ¼ of the dough on floured pastry board and place on top of filling and bottom crust. Press top crust onto bottom crust with a fork and trim excess dough back to cookie tray. Poke several holes in top with fork and brush with beaten egg. Repeat with remaining dough and filling for a second tray. Bake in a 350° preheated oven for about 45 minutes or until top is light golden brown. Trays can be cut into 2 sections, wrapped tightly in foil and plastic wrap and frozen. Defrost and cut into bite size pieces. Heat on a cookie tray for 10 minutes; serve.

My cousin Joanne says, "Here's one from my Grandmother. She called it her Hors d'Oeuvres recipe" and always had half tray sections of it wrapped, frozen ready to go wherever she went. It's always a hit. Joanne's grandmother was my Aunt Julia, my father's oldest sister.

L-R: Jean "Dolly" Caccavale, Mae Avella and Julia Silvestri

The Avella Family:
(L-R Back Row) Flo Avella, Sam Avella, Frances Avella Moreira, Ralph Tarantino, Julia Avella Silvestri, Manuel Moreira
Front Row: (L-R) Mary Avella Caccavale, Jenny Avella Tarantino, Katherine Avella, and Mae Avella. Although, I always say I learned to cook from my mother, my father's six sister's were great cooks and my Aunt Julia a wonderful baker, so I was doubly blessed from both sides.

DOLMATHES - STUFFED GRAPE LEAVES
Peggy Spirakis

1 pound of chopped meat
1 large onion, peeled and finely chopped and cooked in a
small amount of butter and olive oil until golden brown
4 springs of dill, chopped
8 sprigs flat parsley; chopped
Salt and pepper to taste
¼ cup (plus a shake) of Carolina® Rice
½ teaspoon grated cheese
1 tablespoon olive oil

⅓ can Delmonte® or Hunts® tomato sauce
a dash of sugar
2-2½ teaspoons of dried mushrooms
A pinch of oregano
The juice of 1½ lemons
1 jar of Grape leaves (remove brine and wash)
2 packets of chicken bouillon

Place the grape leaves in boiling water and simmer 10 to 15 minutes if the leaves have tough veins. When selecting, try to use medium size tender leaves first. The very large leaves can be used to line the pot. Combine everything together but the grape leaves, lemon juice, and the bouillon. Take a grape leaf, vein side up. Cut off any remaining stems. Place the meat mixture above the stem area. The amount will depend on the size of the leaf. Figure a rounded teaspoon for a medium size leaf. The leaf will look triangular in shape. Place the filling at the lower end just above where the two rounded ends are. Then fold those two sections up. Then fold in from the right and left sides. Roll the leaf up to close it. Line a large pot with some of the large grape leaves. Throw a few springs of dill and parsley on the bottom. Place the rolled stuffed leaves in the pot seam side down (to prevent unrolling during cooking). Make a circular design in the pot. Place row upon row. When all the meat mixture is used up and all the leaves are in the pot, squeeze 1½-lemons over the top. You should have at least 4 rows of leaves. Cover the top with some flat grape leaves. Place an upside down dish smaller than the pot on top to act as a weight. Mix bouillon with some water and add to the pot. Water level should be half way up the pot. Bring to a boil over medium heat. Lower to a simmer-boil. Check after 45 minutes. Taste a few stuffed leaves from the center and side of pot. Rice should be well cooked and leaves tender. If the rice isn't cooking, it is because there isn't enough water in the pot. Add more water. When finished, drain off the liquid.

HANKY PANKYS
Frank S. Mainella, Jr.

1 pound fresh, ground Italian sweet pork sausage
1 pound chopped meat
2-3 tablespoons vegetable oil
1 medium onion, diced fine
½ teaspoon garlic powder
Salt and black pepper to taste
Dried parsley to taste

1-2 cups grating cheese
1 pound of Velveeta®, shredded
2 eggs, beaten
1 cup corn flake crumbs
1 (16 ounce) package each of cocktail rye and pumpernickel
breads

Brown the sausage and chopped meat with the onions in the oil that has been preheated. Drain any liquid from the meat. Add the Velveeta, salt, pepper, and parsley. Add the grating cheese, and corn flake crumbs. Let cool slightly and add the 2 eggs. Heap by the tablespoonfuls onto the bread. You can freeze them at this point. When ready to serve bake at 350° (about 35 to 40 minutes) until thoroughly heated and browned. You can do these in advance and freeze on cookie sheets; when frozen, put in plastic bags to store.

Frankie was the first to respond to the call for family recipes for the book and he sent in Aunt Edith's favorite appetizer. She made these all the time. They are fast, can be done in advance, frozen and make great appetizers for a party or holiday.

APRICOT BAKED BRIE
Ann D'Amico

1 egg
1 tablespoon water
1 whole baby brie, chilled

¼ cup apricot preserves
1 sheet frozen puff pastry sheet
Leaf shaped cookie cutter

Preheat the oven to 375°. Mix the egg and water together. Thaw the puff pastry and unfold and roll on a lightly floured board to approximately a 14-inch square. Brush brie with apricot preserves. Place on rolled pastry. Cut leaves out from remaining pastry. Set aside. Brush pastry edges around the brie with egg mixture. Fold remaining pastry over the brie and trim the edges. Place on a cookie sheet seam side down. Brush top with egg mixture and place leaves around the top. Brush again with egg mixture. Bake 25 minutes or until pastry is puffed and golden. Cool 15 to 20 minutes before serving.

Ann says that she doesn't bother with making the leaves, she just pulls the pastry up and twists it.

FOCACCIA
Elise Feiner

1 envelope dry yeast
1 tablespoon sugar
1 cup warm water
3½ cups flour
2 tablespoons kosher salt
Freshly ground black pepper
1 (15 ounce) container Ricotta cheese
2 eggs
3 ounces Genoa Salami, cut in thin strips

2 ounces pepperoni slices cut in thin strips
1 bag (2-3 cup) shredded mozzarella cheese
½ cup grated cheese (Locatelli-Romano)
1 small can black olives, sliced and drained (optional)
1 tablespoon garlic, peeled and crushed
½ tablespoon dried parsley
Salt and pepper, to taste
2 teaspoons olive oil

Preheat oven to 350°. Make crust: In a large mixing bowl, or Cuisinart® with a dough hook, mix the yeast, sugar and warm water for a few minutes to dissolve the yeast. Mix the flour and salt together, and add to the yeast mix. Starting on a low speed, mix until dough starts to form, then increase your speed until the dough is formed. Place in a bowl with a little olive oil on the bottom. Turn the dough over. Cover with a towel and place in a warm spot and let rise until double in bulk. Punch the dough down. Use a large cookie sheet or a disposable aluminum cookie sheet, spray with PAM®, and spread dough to cover the bottom of the pan. Sprinkle with the kosher salt and black pepper. Cover the dough and let rise again. In the meantime, combine the ricotta, 1 cup of mozzarella, eggs, salami, pepperoni, grated cheese, garlic, parsley and olives. Add salt and pepper to taste. Take your fingertips and make indentations all over the crust. Spread the filling over the crust. Sprinkle with remaining mozzarella. Bake 35 minutes until golden brown. Slice into squares.

This is a great appetizer. You can add anything you want, mushrooms, peppers, etc. We've been making this for years! It's sort of a fast version of our Easter meat pie.

L-R: Bernie and Johann Gigliotti, Charlene Koury
Bernie, Johann, and Charlene and her husband Jay are great friends and so special to us.
Bernie and Johann are the friends we call at 9:00 pm when everyone else has eaten, to
go out to dinner. We're the only 4 people who will just pick up and go on the spur of the
moment, and have a great time together laughing and joking.

APPLE/PEAR AND BRIE PUFFS
Elise Feiner

2 apples, peeled and cubed (small) or 2 pears, peeled and cubes
4 tablespoons butter

4 tablespoons brown sugar
1 puff pastry sheet
1 brie triangle, chilled

Preheat oven to 375°. In a medium frying pan, melt the butter and brown sugar. Add the apples, stirring frequently. Cook until apples are soft but not mushy and well coated with caramel mix. Set aside. Thaw puffy pastry sheet flat. Cut puff pastry sheet into approximately ½-inch squares and place them into mini muffin tins, pressing them into the shape of the muffin hole. Place a 1-inch slice of brie in the center of each puff pastry and then top it with approximately 1 tablespoon of apple mix. Bake 10 minutes or until puff pastry corners are toasted light brown. Let cool 5 minutes before serving. Makes about 20 puffs.

I had these at a party in Philadelphia and tried to recreate them at home.

CHEESE NUGGETS
Elise Feiner

1 cup grated sharp cheddar cheese
¼ cup soft butter
¾ cup Wondra® flour
¼ teaspoon Worcestershire sauce
¼ teaspoon salt

¼ teaspoon of paprika or
1 jar (6 ounces) stuffed green olives (can be stuffed with pimentos, almonds, etc.
Cooking with Love's Passion Spice Mix

In a small bowl, using a fork, blend the cheese, butter and Worcestershire sauce. Stir in the flour, salt, paprika or Cooking with Love's Passion Spice Mix and mix well. With your hands, knead slightly to form a dough. Preheat oven to 400°. Drain the olives very well; dry on paper towels. Using about 1 teaspoon of the dough, mold it around each olive, making a ball, covering the olive completely. Arrange the olives on a cookie sheet sprayed with PAM®. (At this point, you can freeze them by placing them on a tray in the freezer for 30 minutes. Remove to a zip lock bag to store and refreeze). To serve, preheat oven to 400°. Remove frozen olive balls to a cookie sheet. If frozen, bake for 15 to 25 minutes otherwise bake 15 minutes until golden. Cool on wire racks or serve immediately. Serve at once. Makes 16. Cooking with Love's Passion Spice Mix is available on our website **www.cookingwithlove.com**

BACON AND CHESTNUT BITES
Janet Saporito

1 pound sliced bacon
1 small can of sliced water chestnuts

1 cup Duck Sauce (in the Chinese food section of your grocery store)

Cut bacon in thirds. Wrap 2 slices of water chestnut into ⅓ slice of bacon. Secure with a toothpick and place ½-inch apart on a jelly roll pan. Bake at 425° approximately 20 minutes or until bacon is crisp. Serve with duck sauce for dunking.

BARBEQUE CHICKEN WINGS
Elise Feiner

5 pound bag of frozen chicken wings
4 tablespoons butter, melted
3 cups ketchup
1 cup sugar
1 cup brown sugar
1 cup white vinegar

1 cup maple syrup
3 tablespoons Lea and Perrins® Worcestershire sauce
1 teaspoon chili powder
Dash of red hot sauce, if desired
Garlic salt and black pepper to taste
1 (18 ounce) bottle of barbeque sauce (use ¾ of the bottle)

Preheat oven to 350°. Melt 4 tablespoons of butter in a pan. Place the chicken wings in a single layer on the bottom of the pan. Make the sauce by mixing all the remaining ingredients together; then spoon half of the sauce on the wings. Cook for 60 minutes, turning every 15 minutes; adding the rest of the sauce after 30 minutes.   Increase the temperature to 425° and cook for another 45 minutes or until meat comes away from the bone. If the sauce starts to cook too quickly, lower the heat a little or cover with foil. You can drain some of the liquid at the end to make the wings crisper.

L-R: Eileen Burt Furino, John Burt, Anthony Furino, D.D.S.
Eileen is from Philadelphia and Anthony from Long Island, they have been close friends of ours for years. Anthony is responsible for all the great smiles in this book. John and Dorothy (Eileen's parents) relocated here from Philadelphia. Dorothy was a gourmet cook!

BUFFALO CHICKEN WINGS
Elise Feiner

2 quarts canola or vegetable oil
3½ pounds chicken wings (remove tips, cut in half)
1½ sticks unsalted butter
1 bottle (5 ounce) Frank's® Red Hot Sauce

½ teaspoon Tabasco sauce
½ teaspoons cayenne pepper
Garlic salt to taste
Celery salt to taste

Heat 4-inches of oil in a deep fryer or medium pan over high heat until a deep fryer thermometer registers 400°. Line a baking sheet with paper towels; set aside. Add half of the wing pieces to hot oil, and fry until dark golden brown, 15 to 25 minutes. Remove to paper towels. While wings are cooking, melt butter in a small saucepan over medium heat. Add hot sauce, Tabasco sauce, garlic and celery salt, and cayenne pepper. Cook stirring occasionally, until heated thoroughly. Lower the heat, and keep warm until ready to use. Toss fried wings with sauce mix in a large plastic container with a cover. Serve with blue cheese and celery sticks. This makes mild wings. Increase hot sauce, Tabasco and cayenne to your taste.

Everybody who lives in Upstate N.Y. has their own version of Buffalo wings.

PARMESAN PUFFS
Janet Saporito

1 cup aged grated parmesan cheese
1 cup mayonnaise

Dash Lea and Perrins® Worcestershire sauce
1 long loaf of French bread

Mix cheese, mayonnaise and Worcestershire sauce. Slice bread on the diagonal into slices ½-inch thick. Spread at least 2 tablespoons of mixture on each slice of bread. Place each slice on a baking sheet. Bake at 425° for about 10 minutes or until tops start to brown. Recipe is easy enough to make quickly for more or less bread.

SHRIMP TOAST
Janet Saporito

½ pound shrimp, cleaned
2 green onions cut in ½-inch lengths
1 egg
1 tablespoon dry sherry
1 tablespoon cornstarch
½ teaspoon salt

⅛ teaspoon pepper
¼ cup minced water chestnuts
1½ teaspoons minced ginger
6 slices day old bread, crust removed
2 cups oil

Separate shrimp, onions, egg, sherry, cornstarch, salt and pepper in a blender. Cover and whirl until smooth paste is formed. Remove to a bowl and stir in chestnuts and ginger. Spread 2 tablespoon shrimp mixture on each slice of bread. Freeze 15 minutes, or until bread can be sliced easily. Cut diagonally in quarters. In medium skillet, heat oil; add a few pieces, shrimp side down. Fry over medium heat about 1½ minutes or until golden, turn and fry a few more seconds or until bread is browned. Drain on paper towel.

Janet and Ben Saporito and first grandchild Christina Molinari

Rebel and Janet…
Janet breeds and
shows Shar-Pei's

VODKA PIZZA PIECES
Elise Feiner

¾ cup red onions	1 cup heavy cream
1 cup chopped fresh mushrooms	1½ cup Pizza Sauce (see index) or use store bought
4 slices of proscuitto, chopped	1 pound of Pizza Dough or store bought Pizza crust
4 ounces Vodka	Ricotta cheese (optional)
4 tablespoons butter	Grated cheese

Melt the butter in a pan. Add the red onions, mushrooms and proscuitto. Cook for about 4 minutes. Add the vodka and cook until the vodka is reduced by half. Add the Pizza Sauce, and the heavy cream. Cook another 4-5 minutes. Let cool for about 8 to 10 minutes. Preheat oven to 500°degrees. If you are shaping the dough yourself, spray a Cookie sheet with PAM and stretch out the dough. If using a store bought crust, place in onto a cookie sheet sprayed with PAM. Spread the vodka sauce over the pizza dough. You can place some ricotta on top if you want to. Sprinkle with grating cheese. Bake about 15-20 minutes until the crust in golden brown. Cut into small squares to serve.

OLIVES AND ORANGES AND ALMONDS...OH MY!
Elise Feiner

2 pounds Spanish olives (Manzanilla olives of your choice) with pits in	10-12 cloves or garlic, peeled and left whole
2 oranges, unpeeled, sliced into ⅛ circles; removed the pits	2 sprigs or rosemary
1 cup whole almonds or pecans (or mix them)	2 mini limes (optional) cut in small circles
¼ cup white wine vinegar	Garlic salt to taste
⅛ cup sherry	Black Pepper to taste
2 bay leaves	¼ teaspoon Spices

Preheat the oven to 300° Mix the olives with all the remaining ingredients in a large mixing bowl (don't add too much garlic salt as the olives are already salty). Transfer the mix into a baking pan and cover with foil, and bake for 2 hours. Drain out and oil and set aside to use as a dipping sauce. Serve warm or at room temperature.

This recipe is based on a recipe by Tyler Florence. I added my own twist with the lime and whole garlic cloves, and some of the spices. The garlic cloves roast and become sweet, and the orange slices become like candy. This is a great appetizer.

L-R: Sharon and Philip Avella, Jr. (my nephew and Godchild) announcing the good news that they are expecting their first child

SESAME CHICKEN NUGGETS
Elise Feiner

2 eggs, slightly beaten
1 cup flour
1½ teaspoon salt
4 tablespoons sesame seeds

1 cup milk
2 packages boneless, skinless chicken breast, cut in
1-inch cubes or strips

Mix all ingredients together. Dip the chicken into the batter. Let drain; then deep fry or fry in a frying pan in about 1½ to 2-inches of oil. Serve with chicken dipping sauce. (See recipe index).

When I was working at Doctor's Hospital in Staten Island, we made these for all the hospital parties!

L-R: Lauren Feiner, "my Japanese daughter" Sachi Ide, David, Jeffrey and Steven Feiner celebrating Thanksgiving…Sachi, Lauren and David were all classmates at Exeter. We have stayed close to her, and she is now a part of our family.

The Torch being passed…
L-R: Aunt Fifi Mainella supervising Melissa Avella making "gravy" and Steven Feiner and Melissa Avella making Lasagna…Abby Feiner making breadsticks…we can now die happy; the next generation will eat!

BARBECUED KIELBASA
Maria Trainor

2-3 whole links of cooked Kielbasa

Jack Daniels® Old No. 7 Mustard

Cut the kielbasa into ½ to 1-inch pieces on the bias or on a slant (like cutting French bread for Bruschetta), so they won't fall through the grill. Place on a hot barbeque grill. Cook until well browned, crisp, and heated through. To serve dip into Jack Daniels Mustard.

Maria made this for an appetizer at the lake for Fourth of July...fabulous! If you live in the Utica area in upstate New York, we use Hapanowicz's Wedding Kielbasa for this. Their homemade kielbasa is the best. Their number is (315) 736-8288 and address is 19 Clinton Street, New York Mills, N. Y. Their web address is www.hapkielbasa.com

Tim and Maria Trainor
Tim helped make this book a reality, and Maria is my partner in cooking...couldn't ask for better, loving friends!

The Trainor Kids L–R: Kyle, Tessa, Kate and Jonathan
These kids are the kids you always wished could be yours!

HUMMUS PIZZA
Chuck Sadallah

1 package of fresh pizza dough or homemade pizza dough
½-1 cup Hummus (see index) or use store bought
2-3 onions, peeled and sliced
4-6 tablespoons olive oil divided
1 tablespoon sugar
¼ cup balsamic vinegar

Kalamata olives
Kasseri cheese or parmesan cheese, or cheese of your choice
Flavored Olive oil (3 tablespoons olive oil, fresh rosemary, basil, salt and pepper)

In a large frying pan, heat the about 3 tablespoons of olive oil, a few springs of fresh rosemary, and fresh basil, a little salt and pepper for a few minutes. Remove and set aside. In the same pan, add the two-three tablespoons of olive oil and add the onions. When the onions start to sweat, add 1 tablespoon sugar, and the balsamic vinegar. Cook mixture over low heat about 40 minutes, until well caramelized. Set aside and let cool slightly. Mix the hummus into the onions; add 1½ tablespoons flavored oil. Divide the pizza dough in two, and roll out thinly. Shape the dough onto a pizza pan or if you have it onto a pizza stone. Place the onion-hummus mix on the top. Add Kalamata olives and cheese or your choice. Drizzle with remaining oil. Bake in a 500° oven for about 8 minutes until crisp and nicely browned.

I was talking to Chuck in Barnes and Noble one day and he told me about this appetizer he invented...it sounded delicious. He has owned several restaurants in this area and is a great chef. Stop in and see Chuck at his new place, Daylight Donut and Coffee at 22 Genesee Street, New Hartford, New York whenever you're in the area.

The Schwartz Kids...
L-R: Debbie Schwartz Lipson, Deborah Karden-Schwartz and Kenny Schwartz

ROASTED RED PEPPER SPREAD
Elise Feiner

3-4 roasted red peppers
1 clove of garlic, peeled and crushed
¼ cup almonds, very finely chopped

Salt and pepper to taste
Mayonnaise

Pulse the red peppers in a food processor. Stir in the garlic, salt and pepper and almonds and a few tablespoons of mayonnaise. Spread on the top of bread, or use as a base for bruschetta.

We had this at a restaurant in Baltimore at Harbor Place, and I tried to duplicate it. They served it as a spread on their French bread.

Lindsay Greene, soon to be Dr. Lindsay Greene.
Lindsey is a Medical Student in Buffalo

Her proud parents, Ted and Kathy Greene,
our neighbors and friends…

MARIA'S QUESADILLAS
Maria Trainor

3-4 tablespoons olive oil
2-3 tablespoons balsamic vinegar
Salt and pepper to taste
4-5 Portobello mushrooms (washed and trimmed)

4 10-inch tortilla
1 bag Sargeanto® Shredded Mexican Cheese mix
3 scallions, sliced thinly

Carefully clean the Portobello mushrooms and remove some of the middle. Heat a barbeque grill. Place the mushrooms on the grill and drizzle olive oil and balsamic vinegar over the mushrooms. Add salt and pepper to taste. Turn and grill until they are done about 10-12 minutes. Slice the mushrooms in ½-inch pieces. Place a little olive oil in a large frying pan and place the tortilla into the heated oil. Place some cheese, a few mushroom slices and the scallions and then sprinkle a little more cheese over one half of the tortilla. Fold the tortilla in half, and grill until the cheese is melted and the tortilla is nicely toasted. Cut into three pieces to serve.

L-R: Tessa, Maria and Tim Trainor

Lauren Feiner and Jonathan Trainor

Connie DiMare
Maria's Mother and an incredible cook!

VEGGIE QUESIDILLAS
Elise Feiner

3-4 tablespoons olive oil
2-3 tablespoons balsamic vinegar
Salt and pepper to taste
Eggplant, zucchini, peppers and other veggies of your
choice

4 10-inch tortillas
1 bag Sargeanto® Shredded Mozzarella Cheese mix
3 scallions, sliced thinly

Place the vegetables on the grill on low heat and drizzle olive oil and balsamic vinegar over the vegetables. Add salt and pepper to taste. Turn and grill until they are done about 6-8 minutes. Place a little olive oil in a large frying pan and place the tortilla into the heated oil. Place some cheese, a few vegetables and the scallions and then sprinkle a little more cheese over one half of the tortilla. Fold the tortilla in half, and grill until the cheese is melted and the tortilla is nicely toasted. Cut into three pieces to serve.

Top L-R: Marc, Elise, Barbara and Kevin Feiner
Seated L-R: Betty Feiner, Louise and David Altman, Theresa and Ivan Feiner

L-R: Betty and Marc Feiner

L-R: Marc and Elise Feiner

BAKED MUSHROOM CROUSTADES
Maureen Finnegan

PART I:

24 slices of white bread 3 tablespoons softened butter	24 2-inch wide small muffin or tartlette pans

Coat each muffin tin with softened butter. Using a fluted cookie cutter, cut out a 3-inch circle from each slice of bread and carefully press into the muffin tin until it forms a delicate cup. Preheat the oven to 400° and bake croustades until they are lightly browned along the edges.

PART II: The filling and preparing the ingredients

4 tablespoons butter 4 tablespoons shallots, finely chopped ½ pound mushrooms, minced 1 cup heavy cream Salt and white pepper to taste	1 teaspoon parsley, very finely chopped The juice of a ¼ of a lemon 2 teaspoons grated parmesan cheese Butter

Melt the four tablespoons in a sauté pan. When the butter becomes frothy, add the shallots and cook over moderate heat until they soften, but do not brown. Stir in the mushrooms and cook until all the moisture has evaporated, approximately fifteen minutes. If the mixture is still too loose, add one tablespoon of flour and thoroughly combine so that the flour is not visible. Add 1 cup of heavy cream, stirring continuously until it comes to a boil. Lower and cook for 1-2 additional minutes. Remove pan from heat and stir in the salt and pepper, parsley, and lemon juice. Fill the prepared croustades with mushroom mixture, mounding the tin slightly. Sprinkle each with parmesan cheese. Dot with butter. Put on a cookie sheet and bake for three minutes. Briefly place under broiler until brown and bubbly.

This recipe came from my cousin Maureen who has says these are great appetizer or hors d'oeuvres. Maureen owned a restaurant in Manhattan called Factor's Find Café in the eighties and this was on her menu. This was one of our favorite restaurants. It was written up in Fine Dining Magazine who said "Factor's Find Café is a most unusual establishment in a most unlikely location and, it has a split personality, one for day and one for night..." See the next page for pictures of Maureen who never seems to grow old. I always tease her that my fondest memory of her will be of a New Years Eve in the seventies when she was dressed in tight gold lamé pants and looking like a Dresden doll. She never changes, never gains a pound, and is always so put together.

L-R: Elmer and Shirley Snyder, Dave and Louise Altman, Phil and Ann D'Amico, Maureen and Norman Finnegan,
Mary Ann and Michele Maida, Lauren Feiner, and Toni and Tom Mollico

Maureen Finnegan
Maureen is an antiques experts, restaurateur,
and a former English teacher.

L-R: Maureen Finnegan, Katherine Avella, Jean Mainella,
Josephine Mainella, Flo Avella at Sherry Avella's
baby shower

Top: Hannah Weiner Bottom: Sarah Weiner

The Weiner's Clockwise from Bottom Left: Hal, Nicole,
Hannah, Sarah, Rebecca, and Zach

TZATZIKI DIP
Elise Feiner

1 medium cucumber, peeled, sliced in half, seeded and finely chopped
1 cup plain yogurt
1 tablespoon olive oil

1 teaspoon lemon juice or white wine vinegar
½ teaspoon salt
1 clove garlic, peeled and minced
1 teaspoon Cooking with Love's Passion Spice Mix

In a medium bowl combine all the ingredients and chill for at least 1 hour to allow the flavors to blend. Serve as a dip with pita bread.

They make a great Tzatziki Dip at Symeon's Restaurant here in town. However, this is not too bad.

PEGGY'S TZATZIKI DIP
Peggy Spirakis

2 cups plain yogurt
2 large cucumbers, peeled, seeded and coarsely grated
1 tablespoon garlic, peeled and minced

1 tablespoon white vinegar
2 tablespoons olive oil
Salt and pepper to taste

Put yogurt in a cheesecloth lined sieve over a bowl. Drain several hours or overnight in the refrigerator. Peel, seed and grate cucumbers. Drain well. Add garlic, vinegar, oil, salt and pepper to cucumbers and mix well. Add yogurt; mix well. Serve with pita bread.

RED PEPPER SPREAD
Katherine Avella

1 cup roasted red peppers, rinsed and drained
1 (8 ounce) package cream cheese, softened
1 (1 ounce) packet Hidden Valley® Original Ranch Salad Dressing and Recipe Mix

Baguette slices and sliced ripe olives

Blot dry red peppers. In a food processor fit with a metal blade, combine peppers, cream cheese and salad dressing mix; process until smooth. Spread on baguette slices and garnish with olives, if desired.

We Italians love roasted peppers and use them for just about everything but dessert...hmmm roasted pepper ice cream???

TEX-MEX DIP
Sarah Burlingame

1 can refried beans
2 medium avocados, mashed
1 tablespoon lemon juice
2 cups light sour cream
1 packet taco seasoning mix

1 can green chilies (¼ cup) chopped
1 large can black olives, sliced
2 medium tomatoes, diced
2 cups shredded Cheddar cheese (part skim-milk)

In a 9x13-inch baking dish, layer refried beans. Mix the avocado, ¾ cup sour cream, and lemon juice in a bowl. Spread over the beans. Mix remaining sour cream with taco seasoning and spread over avocado layer. Layer chilies, olives, and tomatoes. Sprinkle cheese over the top. Serve cold with tortilla chips.

David's friend Sarah loves to cook. She has great low fat recipes, this is one of them!

"The children despise their parents until the age of 40, when they suddenly become just like them...thus preserving the system
-**Quentin Crewe**

SPINACH DIP STEVEN
Elise Feiner

2 (10 ounce) boxes of frozen chopped spinach, thawed and squeezed very dry
1 (16 ounces) container sour cream
1 cup Hellmann's® Mayonnaise

1 package Knorr® Vegetable soup mix
4 scallions chopped finely
1 large round loaf of pumpernickel or rye bread to serve and a smaller one to cut up and cube

In a medium bowl, stir spinach, sour cream, mayonnaise, soup mix, and scallions until well blended. Cover and chill overnight. Cut a hole out in the middle of the rye or pumpernickel bread. Remove the bread from the lid and cut in cubes. Remove most of the bread from the middle of the bread and cut into cubes. Cut up remaining bread and cube. Fill in the middle of the bread with dip. Serve on a large tray and surround with bread cubes. Cover well until ready to serve or the bread will dry up. Serves 6.

This originally came from the Knorr's soup box, but I changed it. I eliminated the water chestnuts and doubled the spinach so it wouldn't be as watery. This is usually Steven's job at the holidays. This is one of those recipes I always want to take it off the menu, but they never let me do it.

SHRIMP DIP
Edith Mainella

1 (8 ounce) package of Philadelphia® cream cheese
½ cup mayonnaise
3 tablespoons ketchup
2 teaspoons lemon juice

2 teaspoons Lea and Perrins® Worcestershire sauce
2 tablespoons grated onion
Baby shrimp (use as many as you like) or dice large shrimp

Mix everything together except the shrimp. When smooth, fold in the shrimp. Serve with crackers.

I found this recipe in Aunt Edith's recipe files. It was one of her favorite appetizers.

SALSA
Elise Feiner

1 cucumber, peeled, seeded and diced in small pieces
1 large ripe red bell pepper
½ pound ripe plum tomatoes, quartered, seeded, cut into ⅓-inch cubes
1 tablespoon minced shallots
¼ cup minced fresh basil
3 scallions, very thinly chopped in circles
¼ teaspoon cayenne pepper

2 tablespoons minced fresh coriander or cilantro (optional) or substitute parsley
1 teaspoon minced fresh thyme
4 tablespoons extra virgin olive oil
1 tablespoon fresh lime juice
½ teaspoon salt
¼ teaspoon freshly ground black pepper

Roast pepper directly over an open flame or under a broiler until the skin in charred, turn frequently with tongs. Transfer to a brown paper bag, close the bag and set aside for 10 minutes. Peel, core, and seed the pepper. Cut the pepper into ¼-inch cubes; place in a medium bowl. Add tomatoes, cucumbers, shallots, basil scallions, coriander, thyme, cayenne pepper. In a small bowl, whisk together the olive oil, lime juice, salt and black pepper. Pour dressing over the vegetables and combine by stirring. Serve at room temperature or chilled.

I make this in the summer. David and Steven love this. I omit the cilantro because I hate the flavor, but the original recipe called for it. I had also added 1 clove of garlic, crushed but found it too strong, but you could add it if you like. This is great with tortilla chips.

"The way to cure homesickness is to go home"
-Edna Ferber

PESTO SPREAD
Elise Feiner

1 (8 ounce) package Philadelphia® Cream Cheese
⅓ cup pesto sauce
2 tablespoons grated cheese

1 tablespoon pitted black olives, chopped
1 tablespoon pimientos, chopped

Beat the cream cheese, pesto sauce, and grated cheese in a small bowl. Gently stir in olives and pimentos. Refrigerate at least one hour or until ready to serve. Serve with crackers.

PESTO DIP
Helen Popeo

2 cups loosely packed fresh basil
⅓ cup of pine nuts
2 medium cloves of garlic

½ cup Parmesan cheese
½ cup of extra virgin olive oil

Put basil, pine nuts, garlic and parmesan cheese in a food processor. Process to a rough paste; with machine running, slowly pour the olive oil through the feed tube. If sauce seems dry (it should be a thick paste), add a little more olive oil. Serve with baguette points.

Helen made this wonderful dip for Uncle Jorge Ferreiro's birthday party. It was wonderful. Helen and Dan are two of the nicest people you could ever meet.

LAYERED PESTO DIP
Elise Feiner

1 (8 ounce) package Philadelphia® Cream Cheese
¼ cup grated cheese
⅓ cup pesto sauce

½ cup roasted red peppers, chopped
1 cup shredded Mozzarella cheese
¼ cup pepperoni, finely chopped, optional

Preheat the oven to 350°. Mix the cream cheese and grated cheese together. Add the pepperoni if desired. Place in the bottom of a 9-inch pie plate. Then layer the pesto sauce on the top. Sprinkle with the roasted peppers and mozzarella. Bake 15 minutes or until heated. Serve with crackers, vegetables, or toasted sliced Italian Bread.

JOYCE'S CREAMY GUACAMOLE DIP
Joyce Kunkel

3 medium avocados, peeled
1 tablespoon lemon juice
1 (8 ounce) package Philadelphia® Cream Cheese, softened
¼ cup finely chopped onion (1 small)
½ teaspoon salt
¼ teaspoon garlic salt
2 teaspoons olive oil

1 tomato, finely diced
¼ teaspoon hot pepper sauce (optional)
1 (10 ½ ounce) can bean dip
Shredded lettuce, chopped tomatoes, ripe black olives (sliced)
10 ounces Kraft® Natural Mild cheddar cheese, shredded

Mash avocados with lemon juice. Dice the single tomato and set aside. Combine avocado mixture, cream cheese, chopped onions, salt, garlic salt and olive oil together. Blend well. I like to put it in a food processor to make it smooth. Fold in the diced tomatoes. Chill before serving if desired. Evenly spread bean dip into a platter. Top with remaining ingredients. Serve with avocado mix and corn chips. Garnish with chopped tomatoes and ripe black olives.

Joyce was Aunt Edith's neighbor in Sarasota. She and her husband were wonderful to my Aunt Edith and Uncle Frank when they moved to Sarasota.   This is a great appetizer.

GUACAMOLE WITH BACON
Elise Feiner

4 medium size avocados, mashed
2 tablespoons lime juice
1 teaspoon grated onion
2 teaspoons olive oil

1 tomato, finely diced
8 drops Tabasco (optional)
½ teaspoon salt
4 slices of bacon, fried and crumbled

Mash the avocados and add the rest of the ingredients. Mix well. Serve with tortilla chips, Doritos or Fritos. Serves 6.

L-R: Cousins Carl, Sophia and Joanne Fsadni. Joanne and her partner Barbara are the creative force behind Fidgit™ and Perri Meno-Pudge™ two characters you will be hearing more of in the near future!

SUNFLOWER CHEESE BALL
Elise Feiner

1 (8 ounce) package cream cheese, softened
1 teaspoon Dijon mustard
½ teaspoon garlic salt
2 tablespoons white wine

1 cup pitted black olives, chopped
½ pound cheddar cheese, shredded
2 tablespoons minced parsley (optional)
½ cup sunflower seeds, shelled

Beat the cream cheese with the mustard, garlic, and wine until smooth. Beat in the olives, cheddar cheese, and parsley. Form into a ball wrap in waxed paper. Chill; then roll in sunflower seeds. Serve with crackers.

L-R: Kevin and Philip (Pinky) Feiner

GUACAMOLE DIP
Elise Feiner

1 small onion, peeled and grated	2 tablespoons lemon juice
1 tomato	2 tablespoons mayonnaise
6 peeled avocados	1 teaspoon salad oil
2½ teaspoons salt	4 drops Tabasco (optional)

On a chopping board, finely chop the onion and tomato. Chop the avocados, or mash if you prefer, add the salt, lemon juice, Tabasco, mayonnaise, salad oil and. Mix all ingredients together. Serves 8.

CAESAR SALAD DIP
Elise Feiner

1 (8 ounce) package Philadelphia® Cream Cheese	1 cup romaine lettuce, chopped
1 cup grated cheese	½ cup croutons
½ cup Kraft® Classic Caesar Salad Dressing	Anchovy fillets, optional

Beat the cream cheese with the grated cheese and salad dressing. Place in a round serving bowl. Garnish with the shredded lettuce leaves and croutons. Top with anchovy fillets if desired. Serve with crackers.

Aunt Flo celebrating her 90th Birthday with, all her nieces and nephews

Front L-R: Nina Frank, Flo Avella, Elise Avella Feiner,
Middle L-R: John Anselmo, Ann Silvestri, Betty Saracino, Phyllis Foster, Betty Arcara,
Ann D'Amico, Joe Arcara
Back L-R: Dolly and Marie Caccavale, Marc Feiner, Phil D'Amico, and Joseph Avella (missing Philip Avella)

"Only Eve can claim she was the original cook."
-Laraine Dell

GUACAMOLE AVRAMIDIS
Athena Avramidis

2 ripe avocados cut unto small pieces
1 tomato (seeded and chopped)
⅓ red onion (finely chopped)
Cilantro (finely chopped)

Dash salt
Juice of ½ lime
Dash of Tabasco sauce

Cut the avocado in half and twist to remove the pit, scoop out the meat and cut into small pieces. Mix with remaining ingredients and serve with tortilla chips.

Athena's recipe is a little more on the chunky side. It's excellent. You can use parsley if you don't like the taste of cilantro.

BLT DIP
Elise Feiner

1 (16 ounce) container sour cream
½ teaspoon onion powder
1 package Oscar Meyer® center cut bacon

½ cup shredded American cheese
1 tomato, chopped and divided
1 cup lettuce, shredded

Mix the sour cream and onion powder. Place in a round serving dish. Fry the bacon until crisp. Crumble the bacon. Sprinkle the bacon over the sour cream. Top with the cheese, ¾ chopped tomato, lettuce, and remaining tomato. Refrigerate. Serve with crackers, pretzels, or vegetables.

L-R: Cathy Sleeper, Carmen Ferreiro, Nancy Blaker, Roseanne Hart,
Elise Feiner, Athena Avramidis, Carol Mandour, Iryna Trociuk

EASY GUACAMOLE
Elise Feiner

3 avocados, peeled, pitted and diced
1 tablespoon sour cream
2 (3 ounce) packages cream cheese, softened
2 tablespoons salsa

1 pinch salt
1 dash ground black pepper
1 dash garlic salt
1 dash onion powder

In a small bowl, mix together the avocados, sour cream, cream cheese and salsa. Blend to desired consistency. In another small bowl mix the salt, pepper, garlic salt and onion powder. Stir into the avocado mixture. Cover and chill in the refrigerator a half hour before serving.

CHICKEN CURRY DIP
Catherine Sleeper

4 boneless skinless chicken breasts
4 tablespoons vegetable oil
2 bunches of seedless grapes, cut into tiny pieces
1 cup raisins
4 scallions, finely chopped

4 tablespoons curry powder
Black pepper to taste
½ cup walnuts, chopped (optional)
6-8 tablespoons mayonnaise, more if needed

Heat the vegetable oil in a frying pan. Cook the chicken breasts until done. Let cool, and then cut into **very tiny, tiny** cubes. Add the cut up grapes, raisins, scallions, curry powder, black pepper, walnuts, and mayonnaise. Serve with crackers. This is very spicy; you may want to cut back a little on the curry powder.

Cathy's recipe is a favorite here in town, especially in the Ferreiro house!

Catherine and Richard Sleeper, M.D.

Cathy is a New York City girl like me and Dick is from Long Island. He is a plastic surgeon here in town. We'll leave the things he is responsible for in this town to the imagination!

BEAU MONDE CHEESE DIP
Ann D'Amico

1 cup sour cream
1 cup mayonnaise
1 (3 ounce) package cream cheese with chives and onions
1 (4 ounce) package Blue cheese, crumbled
2 teaspoons Beau Monde (in spice aisle)

2 teaspoons dried parsley
2 teaspoons onion flakes
2 teaspoons dried dill
2 teaspoons dried tarragon
1-2 loaves of Pumpernickel or rye bread

Place all the ingredients except the bread in the Cuisinart® and blend until smooth. Take a large round or oblong loaf of rye or pumpernickel bread and cut around to make a hollow bowl. Cut up the bread you remove into cubes to dip into the cheese dip. Serve in a hollowed out rye or pumpernickel bread. You may want to buy an extra loaf to cut up more cubes. Serves 10 as part of an appetizer assortment.

My cousin Ann D'Amico made this dip years ago, long before the serving of dips in a loaf of bread was popular. This is delicious and so easy to make.

L-R: Cousins
Phil and Ann D'Amico and
Joan Calabrese in the
background toasting
Aunt Flo Avella at her
90th Birthday!

PARMESAN CRACKERS
Elise Feiner

16 ounces of Parmesan cheese (left in a wedge)

Grate the cheese using the medium holes of a cheese grater. Place a piece of parchment paper on cookie sheets. Drop the cheese on to the paper in round circles (or use a round mold to get the shape). Press down the bottom of a glass or your fingers to flatten them. Preheat the oven to 350°. Bake about 10 to 12 minutes until golden and crisp. Very carefully remove the crackers while they are warm with a spatula. Makes about 48 crackers.

I like to use these with the onion dip or mix them on a platter with the pepperoni crisps (see index). My mother has made these for years, and I had forgotten about them until I had spilled some cheese on a cookie sheet when I was baking breadsticks and it baked into a cracker. If you already have cheese that is grated finely, it will work too, but it doesn't work as well.

L-R: Philip Avella, Gisele Ruiz, Sharon Avella, Josephine Mainella, Douglas Avella, Melissa Avella, Elise Avella Feiner, Joseph Avella, Marc Feiner, Michael Avella holding Daniella Avella, Sherry Avella, and Vincent DeClementi

RYE BOAT
Brenda Johnson

1 small unsliced rye bread	2 teaspoons dill weed
1 pint sour cream	1 small onion grated
1⅓ cups mayonnaise	1 small jar chipped beef, chopped

Rinse the chipped beef as per package directions; chop the beef. Mix all the remaining ingredients (except the bread) with the beef in a bowl and refrigerate.

When you are ready to serve the beef, cut out the middle of the bread to form a bowl. Carefully remove the inside of the bread, and cut the piece you removed into cubes. Place the dip in the middle of the bread and place the cubes around the outside of the bread to serve.

"If you have only one smile in you, give it to the people you love. Don't be surly at home, then go out in the street and start grinning 'Good morning' at total strangers."
-Maya Angelou

EASY VEGETABLE DIP
Elise Feiner

¼ cup toasted almonds
3 cloves garlic
3 heaping tablespoons parsley

4 tablespoons flavored breadcrumbs
2 cups mayonnaise

Put first four ingredients in the food processor and chop fine. Blend in mayonnaise. Serve with crisp, raw vegetables.

L-R: Joe Avella, Steve and Rae Rosenfeld, Michele and Mary Ann Maida, Elise and Marc Feiner, Barbara and Kevin Feiner celebrating Thanksgiving…

L-R: Fifi Mainella, Frank Mainella, Katherine Avella, Jean and Edith Mainella

ONION DIP
Elise Feiner

2 large yellow onions
1 medium purple onion
4 tablespoons butter
¼ cup Wesson® oil
⅛-¼ teaspoon cayenne pepper
½ teaspoon kosher salt

½ teaspoon garlic salt
1 teaspoon Symeon Spices
¼ teaspoon black pepper
4 ounces Philadelphia® Cream Cheese (softened)
1 (8 ounce) container sour cream
½ cup Hellmann® mayonnaise

Peel the onions and then cut them in half and then slice them thinly. In a large frying pan, heat the butter and oil. Add the onions, cayenne pepper, kosher salt, garlic salt, Symeon Spices, black pepper. Sauté the onions for about 12 minutes. Reduce the heat and continue to caramelize the onions until they are brown. Set aside and let the onions cool. In a Kitchenaid® or other mixer, blend the cream cheese, sour cream and the mayonnaise until they are well blended and smooth. If you like the dip on the smooth side, add the onions and blend again. If you like the dip on the chunky side chop the onions into smaller pieces, and then fold into the mix. Reseason if necessary.

This is based on the recipe in the Barefoot Contessa but I changed some of the seasonings and added the purple onion. It's easy to make and can be used with chips, vegetables or crackers. After making this, you'll never want store bought onion dip again!

Daniella Faith Avella

Parents:
Michael and Sherry Avella

Grandparents:
Philip and Phyllis Avella

Great Grandparents:
Samuel and Katherine Avella

L-R: Andy and Suzanne Bakiewicz, Nancy Barfield, Stuart and Barbara Schwartz – very close and very dear friends.

L-R: Abby and Jody Feiner

L-R: Barbara, Abby, Kevin, and Jody Feiner

L-R: Karen, Ivan and Danielle Feiner
Ivan is Marc's older brother and is also an attorney in Philadelphia

L-R: Jeff Feiner, Uncle Joe Avella ...
a rare occurrence an MD and Lawyer together and smiling!

SPINACH PINWHEELS
Elise Feiner

2 (10 ounce) packages frozen chopped spinach; thawed, drained, and squeezed dry
1 (8 ounce) package cream cheese softened
½ cup mayonnaise
½ cup sour cream
10 slices bacon, fried and crumbled

1 envelope Hidden Valley® Ranch Party Dip Mix
4 green onions, chopped
½ cup chopped pecans (optional)
½ cup blue cheese, crumbled (optional)
1 package 8 to 10-inch flour tortillas, flavored is fine

In a medium mixing bowl, combine the cream cheese with sour cream and mayonnaise. Add the Hidden Valley mix and blend well. Add the bacon and green onions and mix again. Stir in the spinach and mix well. Fold in the pecans and blue cheese if desired. Place the tortilla on a piece of plastic wrap. Spread the mix on the tortillas to about ½-inch from the edge and use the plastic wrap to roll up tightly. Wrap the tortilla in plastic wrap and chill overnight. Cut into ½-inch slices to serve. You can also substitute shrimp for the bacon.

CUCUMBER SANDWICH APPETIZERS
Carmen Ferreiro

1 (8 ounce) package cream cheese, softened
1 small cucumber, peeled, grated, and squeezed dry
1 teaspoon grated onion

1 loaf Pepperidge Farm® White Bread; remove the crusts
A drop green food coloring

Mix the cream cheese, cucumber, onion, and green food coloring. Color should be a light green. Spread on the bread, and top with another piece of bread. Cut into triangles. Wet paper towels, squeeze well, and put on the bottom of a tray. Place the sandwiches on the tray, stacked up. Cover with a damp towel and refrigerate. You can also add an envelope of Good Seasonings® Italian Dressing mix if you want to.

These are great appetizer, tasty, colorful and very quick to make.

CREAM CHEESE HOLIDAY WREATH
Elise Feiner

2 (8 ounce) packages of Philadelphia® cream cheese, softened
¼ cup mayonnaise

⅓ cup Parmesan or Locatelli Romano Cheese
12 crisply cooked bacon slices, crumbled
¼ cup scallions, finely chopped

Combine the cream cheese and mayonnaise, mixing until well blended. Add the remaining ingredients; mix well. Chill. Place a small drinking glass in the middle of a serving platter. Drop the mixture by tablespoonfuls to form a ring around the glass. Smooth with a spatula. Remove the glass. Garnish the wreath with a little sprinkle of dried or fresh parsley and make a pimento or red pepper (roasted) bow by shaping from a long strip of pepper or pimento. Serve with crackers

This was a recipe from Philadelphia® Cream Cheese that I found in a magazine years ago. I changed it a little. I've made it several times. It's delicious and can be done ahead of time. It looks very pretty on a holiday buffet table.

Left Side

Gene and Glenn Feiner holding Noah Gabriel Feiner, our newest addition...

Right Side:

L-R: Donna, Noah, and Glenn Feiner

CHICKEN BREAST APPETIZERS
Mark Calogero

1 box of prepared chicken cordon bleu, or make your own (see recipe index)

Bake according to the package directions and allow to cool. Slice into ¼ -½-inch slices and arrange on a platter. Serve cold with the following mix:

1 (8 ounce) container sour cream
½ package of Good Season® Italian Dressing

2 ounces of Blue cheese, crumbled

Combine the sour cream, dressing and blue cheese until well blended. Refrigerate. Slice the cold cordon bleu breasts into thin slices and arrange on a serving platter leaving room in the center for a bowl with the dipping sauce. Add dipping sauce to the bowl, and serve. This recipe may be done in advance. You can also use 1(16 ounce) container of sour cream with 1 package of Ranch dressing and ¼ cup of blue cheese.

This is my husband Marc's favorite appetizer. He always orders it at Georgios Restaurant. I asked Mark Calogero how it was made and he told me to use packaged cordon blue. He also told me how to make the sauce. You can of course use homemade chicken cordon bleu.

OYSTER CRACKER APPETIZERS
Mary Christiano

2 bags Oyster Crackers
½ cups Wesson® Oil
1 tablespoon dill weed
½ teaspoon garlic salt

1 teaspoon celery salt (optional)
1 package Hidden Valley® Salad Dressing Mix
¼ cup grated cheese (Parmesan or Locatelli)

In a large plastic container, mix the oil, dill, garlic salt, salad dressing, and grated cheese. Quickly pour in the crackers and mix well. Place the cover on. Shake a few times. Keep in the container. You make these a few days in advance. They keep well. You can also bake them at 250° for 15-20 minutes if you prefer them crisper.

Phyllis' Aunt Mary made these for a party. It's a fast, easy appetizer to make and place in small bowls around the room when you are having a party. They are great to put out at a bar. You can also add some salted peanuts to the mix if you want. You can also substitute Ritz ® Cheddar Cheese Bits for the Oyster Crackers.

FREEZER CHEESE BALLS
Edith "Bubbe" Grundel

½ pound sharp Cheddar cheese
1 (8 ounce) package cream cheese or Neufchatel
¼ pound blue cheese
¼ cup butter or margarine

1 clove garlic, minced or mashed
⅔ cup coarsely chopped walnuts or pecans
Assorted crackers or wafers

Allow cheeses and butter to soften outside the refrigerator for several hours. Shred or cut the Cheddar into small pieces and put into the large bowl of an electric mixer. Add cream cheese, blue cheese, and butter; beat until blended. Add garlic and beat until creamy. Cover and chill cheese mixture for about 3 hours or until firm enough to shape into balls. Divide in half and shape into balls. Divide in half and shape each into a smooth ball; wrap in clear plastic film, then wrap in a plastic bag. Refrigerate or freeze until needed. Allow frozen cheese balls to stand at room temperature 3 or 4 hours before serving. Sprinkle nuts on a piece of waxed paper and roll each ball in about ⅓ cup of the nuts, pressing in lightly. Serve with crackers or wafers. Make 2 balls, each about 3 inches in diameter.

This recipe comes from Judy Oster's mother. She always makes these as gifts as the holidays.

"God couldn't be everywhere; so he created mothers."
-Old Jewish Proverb

CAPANATA
Elise Feiner

2 medium eggplants, skin left on, cut into ½-inch cubes
1-2 large onions, peeled, chopped coarsely
1 whole stalk of celery hearts or celery, cut into ¼-inch slices
1 clove garlic, peeled and crushed
1 (10 ounce) jar manzanilla or green olives with pimento, cut into ½'s or ⅓'s
1 pound fresh plum tomatoes cut in small cubes
4 tablespoons garlic flavored red wine vinegar
1 (3½ ounce) jar capers, drained

4 tablespoons sugar
Salt and pepper to taste (about ½ teaspoon salt, about ⅛ teaspoon pepper)
1 (10 ounce bottle) extra virgin olive oil
1 small can tomato paste
1 (14 ounce) can Hunt's® petite diced tomatoes
Pinch of oregano
Pignoli (optional)

Peel and cube the eggplant. Heat about 4 tablespoons of the olive oil in a large frying pan and brown the eggplant in batches until brown, about 5 minutes. Add a little more oil if needed. Remove from the pan. Add another 2 tablespoons of olive oil and heat and add the celery, onions and garlic, sauté about another 10 minutes, adding more oil if needed. Add the eggplant back to the celery mix. Sauté the mix about another 5 minutes. Add the plum tomatoes, tomato paste, and diced tomatoes. Cook about another 8-10 minutes. In a small pan, heat the sugar and vinegar to a boil and set aside. Add the capers and olives to the eggplant mix and sauté another 5-10 minutes. Add the vinegar mix to the eggplant, and any remaining olive oil. Stir well. Cook about another 5 minutes. Remove from the heat. Add the Pignoli if desired. Let cool. Serve chilled or at room temperature. You may freeze in smaller containers and let come to room temperature when ready to serve.

This is a delicious appetizer to serve at any type of function. My brother Joe likes to make it when he is at his home in Puerto Rico. He, my son Steven, and my cousins Warren, Frank and John are always calling me for one recipe or another...I am starting to feel like Food 911 myself! Hopefully, this book will help them all out.

L-R: Aunt Fifi Mainella
and
Thirza Avella

PINWHEELS
Elise Feiner

2 (8 ounce) packages cream cheese, softened
1 (1 ounce) packet Hidden Valley® The Original Ranch Salad Dressing & Seasoning Mix
2 green onions, minced

4 (12-inch) flour tortillas
1 (4 ounce) jar diced pimientos, rinsed and drained
1 (2¼ ounce) can sliced ripe olives, rinsed and drained
6 slices of crispy bacon, crumbled

Mix cream cheese, seasoning and salad dressing mix and onions until blended. Spread on tortillas. Blot dry pimientos and olives on paper towels. Sprinkle equal amounts of pimiento, bacon and olives over cream cheese mixture. Roll tortillas tightly in Saran Wrap®. Chill at least 2 hours. Cut rolls into 1-inch pieces. Discard ends. Serve with spirals facing up. Makes 3 dozen appetizers.

MOCK CHOPPED LIVER WITH GREEN BEANS
Elise Feiner

1 cup dried lentils; cooked until soft, drain
2 cups chicken broth
1 pound Green beans, boiled or steamed until cooked, but not mushy
¼ cup peanuts (or more)

½ cup chopped walnuts
2 cups diced onions
2 garlic cloves (or more)
¼ cup unsweetened peanut butter
Salt and pepper to taste

Sauté the onions and garlic in about 4 tablespoon oil until brown and soft. Remove. Cook the lentils in chicken broth until done about 30 minutes, drain if necessary. Steam the green beans in a pot with about 4 tablespoons of lightly salted water. Then, blend it all together in the food processor with remaining ingredients until smooth.

The Feiner Girls with their grandmother…
L-R: Lauren, Danielle, Betty, Jennifer and Abby

HERRING SALAD
Pearl Borten

1 (16 ounce) jar of Herring Tidbits in wine; drain well
1 red onion, sliced in thin rings
2 carrots, coarsely grated
3 tablespoons sugar

5 squirts of lemon juice
½ cup mayonnaise
½ cup sour cream

Mix everything together except herring. Mix well. Add herring and chill.

HUMMUS
Rae Rosenfeld

1 can (15½ -17 ounces) garbanzo beans, don't drain
3-4 cloves garlic, peeled and crushed
1 teaspoon salt

¼ cup lemon juice, plus a little more
¾ cup Tahini paste
Paprika

Blend the garbanzo beans, garlic, salt, and lemon juice in a food processor or blender until pureed. Add the tahini and blend again. Sprinkle with paprika before serving. Serve with pita bread. You can also place chopped cucumbers, chopped tomatoes, crumbled feta cheese and chopped olives on the top of the hummus for a more festive look. Serves 6.

I think Rae got it from Beth Arcuri one of the teachers at Hughes School I made a few adjustments because the original recipe called for ¾ cup lemon juice, half the liquid from the beans and a cup of Tahini. I found it a little strong but you could use the original if you want to.

The Rosenfelds: L-R: Steve, Rae, Josh and Mindy
I met Rae and Steve through Mindy and my son Jeff…
they have been best friends since kindergarten and so
have we!

CHOPPED LIVER
Elise Feiner

2 pounds calves liver or chicken livers
8 eggs, hard boiled (set 2 aside for the end)
3 medium onions, peeled and cut into slices
2 teaspoons mayonnaise
1 teaspoon sugar

1 medium onion (peeled and finely diced (set aside)
Chicken fat or Naya fat, or the fat from a chicken breast and back, rendered down
Salt and pepper to taste

Separate and place the calves liver on a disposable aluminum cookie sheet and broil on both sides until cooked and brown. Make sure liver is cooked **but not dry**. Cut in the middle to test. Remove any hard brown areas from liver. Keep all the remaining liquid in pan. Set aside. In a frying pan, add the skin from the chicken and render it down to use to fry the onions. You may need to add a little Wesson oil if you don't have enough chicken fat. Cook onions until soft and slightly brown, add sugar, and salt and pepper to taste. Set aside. Peel the hard boiled eggs. Place the liver, onions (with the oil that remains in the pan) and 6 hard boiled eggs through a food grinder twice. Use a Kitchenaid® if you have it. You can also use a food processor but be careful not to over process it. After you have put it through the grinder, add the liquid from the liver, mix in the one remaining raw finely diced onion, and the 2 remaining hard boiled eggs (chop or mash the eggs first) add salt and pepper to taste; mix well. Refrigerate. Serve with crackers. Serves 6.

After asking several people how to make chopped liver, I took their suggestions and modified them and came up with this recipe. I always used chicken livers but everyone said use beef. I can remember making this for Marc when I was pregnant and wanting to gag. It was truly a labor of love to prepare it. This liver was so good that Estelle Zierler risked a gout attack to eat it, and David Zierler, then, a confirmed vegetarian, finished the container. Not bad for a nice Italian girl from Brooklyn.

The Zierler-Cassata-Sanabria Clan: Back Row (L-R): Jonathan, Sidney, Norm Zierler, Carl, Jeane Cassata, David Zierler, Camille and Rene Sanabria.
Front L – R: Jeremy, Fran, and Zachary Zierler, and Andrew Sanabria
This is my other family in New Hartford New York, they are much more than friends to all of us!

ANTIPASTO
Elise Feiner

1-2 bags of iceberg salad mix
1 jar marinated artichoke hearts
1 (12 ounce) can solid white tuna
Green and black olives
8-10 pieces of Genoa Salami cut in strips
A handful of pepperoni cut in thirds

4-5 thick slices provolone cheese, cubed
A few slices of smoked mozzarella, cubed
3-4 hard boiled eggs cut in slices
Roasted peppers (see recipe)
Pepperoncini
Anchovies (optional)

Lay the salad mix out on a large platter or bowl. Layer all the remaining items on top of the lettuce, ending with circles of hard boiled eggs. Serve with the dressing of your choice (I like Good Seasons Italian). You can add anything else you want, (tomatoes, cucumbers, etc.) but this is a basic antipasto.

MOCK CHOPPED LIVER
Elise Feiner

1 cup dried lentils
2 cups chicken, vegetable or beef broth
1 large sweet onion, chopped
1 tablespoon vegetable oil
1 cup walnuts, lightly toasted

¼ teaspoon salt
½ teaspoon pepper
Garnishes: chopped green onions, walnut halves, baby leaf lettuce

Bring lentils and chicken broth to a boil in a large saucepan over medium heat; cover, reduce heat, and simmer, stirring occasionally, 30 minutes or until lentils are tender. Drain lentils, if necessary. Sauté chopped onion in hot oil in a large skillet over medium-high heat until onion is tender. Process one-third of lentils, one-third of onion, and one-third of walnuts in a food processor, in 3 batches, until mixture is smooth, stopping to scrape down sides. Stir together lentil mixture, salt, and pepper. Line a 3-cup mold with plastic wrap. Spoon into a mold. Cover and chill 8 hours. Unmold onto a serving plate. Garnish, if desired

Aviva Zierler's grandmother, Mom Mom (Jean Greenspan) told me that she substitutes a can of LeSueur Early (Baby) Peas for the lentils; drain and rinse them before using.

Daniella Faith Avella

The Loiacano Family

L-R: Cindy, Adrienne, Michael and Jon

Cindy was our children's teacher and became a good friend to all of us. They are now awaiting the birth of their first grandchild.

FRUIT KABOBS WITH PROSCUITTO
Mimi Burlingame

Cantaloupe Melon, peeled and cubed
Proscuitto, thinly sliced
Fresh mozzarella, tiny little balls in water

Olive oil (about ½ cup)
1 medium shallot, peeled
Fresh basil

Place proscuitto, mozzarella and cantaloupe on bamboo skewers alternating melon, proscuitto, mozzarella ball, proscuitto and melon. Chop shallots, basil and olive oil in food processor; process until smooth and set aside. Right before serving, drizzle over the kabobs.

Sarah's mother Mimi made these at a barbeque at their house...delicious!

David Graduates from SUNY Buffalo...
L-R: Jeff, Lauren, Marc, David, Elise and Steven celebrate!

GRAPE "NUTS"
Elise Feiner

4 ounces of Philadelphia® Cream Cheese (at room temperature)	3 tablespoons of Sherry
	1 bunch of seedless grapes
8 ounces of blue cheese or Boursin Cheese	1 cup of pistachios or walnuts finely ground

Mix the blue cheese or Boursin cheese with the cream cheese in a bowl until well blended. Add in the sherry and blend again. Take a piece of the cheese mixture and place a grape in the middle of it. Cover the grape with the cheese and roll around in your hands until it is covered. Roll the grapes in the nuts. Chill.

Uncle Phil and the girls…
Clockwise from the left: Nicole Latini, Lauren Feiner, Melissa Avella, and Abby Feiner

DEVILED EGGS
Elise Feiner

12 eggs	¾ teaspoon salt
¼ cup mayonnaise	⅛ teaspoon pepper
1 tablespoons white vinegar	⅛ teaspoon paprika
1 teaspoon dry mustard	¼ cup sharp Cheddar cheese, grated
1½ teaspoons Lea and Perrins® Worcestershire sauce	A little extra paprika to sprinkle on the top

Hard boil the eggs. Peel and let eggs cool completely. Cut the eggs in half lengthwise. Remove the yolks (being careful not to damage the whites), and place in a medium bowl. Mash the yolks with a fork until fine. Add remaining ingredients (you may need more mayonnaise if the eggs are large or you prefer it a little looser. Place the yolk mix back into the egg whites. I use a pastry tube with a star tip. It makes it easier to fill and looks a lot prettier. Sprinkle with paprika. Place a toothpick in each half and cover with Saran Wrap®. The toothpicks will prevent the Saran Wrap™ from sticking. Refrigerate until ready to serve. Serves 12

Follow the recipe for perfect hard boiled eggs (see index) so you don't have greenish tinged yolks. These are great for parties. Fast and easy to make and you can do them ahead of time. To make the eggs flat, carefully cut a very small piece from the bottom so they won't roll in the tray.

"One cannot think well, love well, sleep well, if one has not dined well."
-Virginia Woolf

ANTIPASTOS KEBABS
Elise Feiner

Marinated black and green olives
Hard salami, sliced 1-inch thick, cubed
Cubed Monterey Jack, Colby cheese, and Provolone cheese

Cheese tortellini, cooked according to package directions
Small bottle of Italian Salad dressing

Marinade all ingredients in bottled Italian dressing of your choice for a day or so. Place on bamboo skewers a few hours before serving.

"The Godfather" Joe Avella with his girls, daughter Melissa (L) and Goddaughter, Lauren Feiner (R) We call my brother DeNiro, because with darker hair, he could be Robert DeNiro's twin right down to the mole on his face!

TACO ROLL-UPS
Maria Trainor

1 package Mission® Flour Tortillas (Large Diameter)
1 (8 ounce) package Philadelphia® Cream Cheese
3-4 (or more as needed) scallions, very thinly chopped

1-2 cans chopped black olives, drained well
1 jar of Salsa
1 bag Shredded Taco Cheese (4 cheese mix)

Place the flour tortilla on a piece of Saran Wrap®. Spread a thin layer of the cream cheese on the tortilla. Sprinkle the scallions, and then sprinkle the chopped black olives. Dab a little salsa on the top (not too much or it will become soggy) and use a spoon to pat down the mix. Sprinkle with the Taco Cheese mix. Roll very tightly using the Saran Wrap® to keep tight. Repeat with remaining tortillas. Refrigerate for a few hours. Cut off the ends, and then cut each tortilla roll into 10 pieces. Makes about 100 appetizers.

Maria made these at camp as an appetizer and everyone loved them. They are fast and easy and can be done in advance. You can use a lower fat cream cheese if you'd like.

Tim and Katherine "Kassie" Trainor

Back Row L-R: Tim Trainor, David Feiner, Jonathan Trainor Front Row L-R: Abby Feiner, Lauren Feiner, Mackenzie Raehm, Sarah Burlingame, Andy Giambroni enjoying a day on the lake in Old Forge, New York!

UNCLE PAT'S FIGS
Pat Mainella

6-8 figs
Smoked mozzarella, or smoked Gouda (or any cheese of
your choice) cut in cubes

Proscuitto about ¼ of a pound

Remove the top stem of the fig and cut the figs in quarters but **DO NOT** cut all the way through. Place a cube of cheese in each fig. Wrap the fig with proscuitto.

My Uncle Pat's fig trees were his pride and joy. The ones in the back yard on Arlington Avenue grew the biggest figs you ever saw. I can remember picking and eating them right off the trees. I remember the loving care that my Uncle Pat gave those trees as he wrapped them with black tarp to protect them every winter. What I wouldn't give to have a shoot of one of those trees so I could have a tree of my own now.

L-R: Clementina Mainella (my grandmother), Katherine Avella (my mother) Aunt Fifi, Uncle Frank, Uncle Pat Mainella

When I was about to get married, my Uncle Pat had already passed away. Aunt Jean handed me a cigar box. I opened it and it was loaded with silver dollars. It was money Uncle Pat put away for my wedding dress. I insisted on paying for the dress with those coins (of course in the late seventies, silver prices were through the roof) What a fool I was, but I bet Mr. Kleinfeld of Kleinfeld Bridals was a Happy Camper!

My mother Katherine Avella and her brother Pat Mainella

SALAMI PESTO BRUSCHETTA
Elise Feiner

½ cup pesto (see recipe index)
4 10-inch tortilla wrappers (you can use flavored ones) or
French Bread sliced on the diagonal into ½-inch slices;
toasted lightly

¼ pound Genoa Salami or Pepperoni slices (small slices)
¼ cup red or yellow bell peppers, chopped
¼ cup sliced black olives
¾ cup shredded mozzarella

Spread a little pesto evenly over the tortilla rounds or the baguette slices. Place the salami or pepperoni over the pesto. Toss the peppers, olives, mozzarella, and grated cheese over the salami. If you are using the tortilla, place on a piece of Saran Wrap™ and roll tightly; chill. Slice into 8-10 pieces before serving. If using the French bread, serve immediately.

Roll-ups are great appetizers for a party; you can do them in advance, and fill them with virtually anything. Try making one with a layer of pesto and mixed Italian cold cuts, toss in a few roasted peppers...delicious!

Back Row L-R: Lenore Mami, Marsha Cassata, Claire Akselrad, Fran Cassata Zierler, Samantha Caplan Zierler, Elise Feiner, Lauren Feiner, Aviva Akselrad Zierler

Front: Camille Cassata Sanabria, Jeane Cassata taken at Sam's Bridal Shower...

John and Dorothy Burt – Dorothy was a
fabulous gourmet cook and passed her skills to
her daughter Eileen Furino

Ted and Marge DaBruzzo
My Uncle Teddy was a fabulous musician and used to have
a dance band for years!

Katie and Mike Cominsky
Katie (McDonough) is as Irish as they come and Mike is
Jewish, what a great match, producing two fabulous kids,
Manny and Marshall

Barbara and Stuart Schwartz
Barb is the first person I met when I moved here. She is a
Brooklyn girl like me and they are among our dearest
friends.

Bocce Boys L-R: Jeffrey Feiner, Marc Feiner,
Joe DiPierdomenico, Philip DiPierdomenico

Bettina and Luis Liza

ICED TEA PUNCH
Cathy LaRosa

12 tea bags
4 teaspoon dried rosemary leaves
2 quarts of boiling water
2 cups sugar

2 quarts lemon-lime soda, chilled
1 cup fresh lemon juice, strained
Fresh lemon slices
Ice Ring

Place the tea bags and rosemary in a large saucepan. Add boiling water and steep 5 minutes. Remove tea bags. Stir in sugar until dissolved. Strain and cool. Chill until ready to serve. In a large bowl, add the tea, soda, lemon juice; stir gently. Garnish with lemon slices. Add an ice ring. To make an ice ring, fill a tube mold with water (first spray with PAM®. When almost solid, add some lemon slices, orange slices, maraschino cherries; refreeze. When solid, add more water to cover and freeze until firm. Unmold and float in punch.

Cathy, our neighbor on Thistle Court, made this punch for a luncheon that she had. It is a great punch and wonderful in the summer.

ELISE'S CHOCOLATE KISSED HOT COCOA MIX
Elise Feiner

1 (14 quart) box nonfat dry milk, sifted
1 (1 pound) jar Coffee-mate® creamer, sifted
1 (2 pound) Ghirardelli® Chocolate and Cocoa Mix or 2-
pound box Nestlé's® Quik

1 (2 pound) bag confectioner's sugar sifted
1 (15 ounce) jar chocolate malted (Ovaltine®) milk mix
3 (12 ounce) bags Nestlé's® Mini Chocolate Chips
(optional)

Sift all ingredients and combine all together in a **VERY** large bowl. Mix well. Store in airtight containers (like jars or Tupperware.) I also give this with bags of mini marshmallows and the following instructions. If making into gift bags (see below) omit mini chips and add them later.

Instructions: **To make, mix ⅓ cup of the dry mix with ⅔ cup boiling water. Stir and top with mini marshmallows, if desired**.

This is my kid's favorite hot cocoa mix. It makes a ton and I always end up sending it off to the dorms at school with them. These make great stocking stuffers. Buy cone shape bags and measure out ⅔ cups of mix. Place mix in bags; top with a tablespoon of mini chips and 20-30 mini marshmallows; tie with a pretty bow and tag with directions! Each bag makes 2 cups.

BRANDY ALEXANDER
Josephine Mainella

¾ cup brandy
½ cup Crème de Cacao®

1 pint vanilla ice cream

Mix together until smooth or put in blender. Serve immediately. Serves 4.

Left Side L-R: Marc and Jerry Feiner Right Side: L-R: Ivan holding Jennifer, Jerry holding Steven, Marc holding Jeffrey and Danielle, and Kevin Feiner in the rear. When the kids were young my father-in-law had shirts made that said "I'm a Feiner Kid," and his shirt said "I'm the Feiner".

61

MIDORI PUNCH
Elise Feiner

Orange juice
Vodka
Midori®

1 large honeydew, seeds removed, scooped out with a
melon scooper

In a large punch bowl, mix four parts orange juice, one part vodka, two parts Midori. Blend well and chill. You can also scoop little honeydew melon balls into the punch bowl. For you new cooks, using the same type of measurement utensil, keep the proportions the same (cup, pint, gallon). For example, if you were using a cup, it would be 4 cups OJ, 1 cup vodka, 2 cups Midori.

This makes a great summer punch. This was a recipe from the Midori Company.

Jeff's Graduation from The State University of New York School at Buffalo School of Medicine and
Biomedical Sciences – Marc gave Jeff his hood at the graduation ceremony, what an incredible moment!
L-R: Steven, Marc, Jeffrey, Elise, David and Lauren Feiner

CHOCOLATE CAKE SHOOTER
Samantha Caplan

½ ounce Frangelico® Hazelnut
½ ounce Vanilla Vodka or Absolut® Citron

1 sugar coated lemon wedge

Add vodka and Frangelico to a shaker with ice. Shake. Garnish with a sugar coated lemon. Shoot the drink. Bite into the lemon slice. You can also substitute Grand Marnier.

Sam says this tastes just like a piece of chocolate cake!

Lauren Feiner and Samantha Caplan Zierler

CHOCOLATE MARTINI
Jeffrey Feiner, M.D.

½ ounce Godiva® Liqueur
½ ounce Crème de Cacao
1 ounce Gray Goose® or Absolut® Vodka
2 ounces sugar syrup

Ice cubes
4 Hershey's® Kisses (unwrapped)
1 large Hershey® Bar, grated

In a shaker, mix the Godiva, Crème de Cacao, vodka, and ice. In a martini glass, dip the rim in the sugar syrup and them into grated chocolate. Place a Hershey Kiss at the bottom of the glass. Strain the chocolate martini into the prepared glass. Top with a few more grated chocolate pieces.

This recipe is included for two of my favorite people: Anthony Furino and Frank Basile...drink up!

PINK SQUIRREL
David Feiner

4 ounces crème de cacao
4 ounces crème de noyaux

4 ounces heavy cream

Shake well with crushed ice. Strain into a chilled cocktail or martini glass. Serves 4.

PEPPERMINT PATTIE
Elise Feiner

1 cup of hot chocolate (see index for Elise's Chocolate
Kissed hot cocoa mix) or prepared mix
1½ ounces Peppermint Schnapps

½ ounce Crème de Cacao®
Candy Cane or Peppermint Stick

Mix hot chocolate according to directions. Mix the cocoa with the Schnapps, and Crème de Cocoa in a large mug. Add in a candy cane to swirl around. Sit in front of a fireplace and enjoy! Makes 1 cup.

COSMOPOLITAN
Jeffrey Feiner, M.D.

1½ ounce Vodka
1 splash Rose's lime juice

½ ounce Cointreau
1 splash cranberry juice

Shake the vodka, lime juice, Cointreau, and cranberry juice in a glass half filled with ice. Strain into a glass. Serve in a cocktail or martini glass. Garnish with lime.

Between the University of Pennsylvania graduation and the start of Medical School, my son Jeff took a bartending course and worked in Davio's Restaurant in Center City, Philadelphia, to earn little cash.

L-R: Maddelena Stevens-Grassi,
Angela Grassi, Katherine Avella,
Lauren Feiner, Dino Grassi,
Josephine Mainella, and
Steven Gaan
David Feiner kneeling in the front
on a trip to Niagara Falls

MANHATTAN
Katherine Avella

8 ounces of rye whiskey
2 ounces of vermouth

Dash of Angostura® bitters (optional)
Maraschino Cherries

Blend in a pitcher with crushed ice. Strain into a martini glass. Garnish with a cherry.

My mother always used to make this on Sunday when her Barone cousins visited.

L-R: Tina Massimiano, with cousins Michele and Mary Ann Maida. My cousins Michele and Mary Ann have always been there for me. We are following in our mother's footsteps. My mother and my Aunt Lizzie were the closest of cousins, more like sisters. They could carry on a whole conversation and never say a word. We are just like them!

SANGRIA
Elise Feiner

4 bottles dry red wine
1 cup brandy
½ cup sugar
2 oranges, sliced with peel on, remove seeds
2 lemons, sliced with peel on, remove seeds

2 apples, sliced with skin on, remove seeds
2 peaches, sliced with skin on, remove pit
1 honeydew melon, cubed
2 cinnamon sticks

Mix all ingredients in a large punch bowl. Let flavors blend for several hours or make the day before. Serve the sangria on ice.

We've been making this since the early seventies. It's great for a barbeque on a hot summer day.

WHITE WINE SANGRIA
Elise Feiner

2 (750 ml) bottles White Wine, California Zinfandel
2 bananas, sliced 2-inches thick
1 orange, rind reserved, cut in circles
6 peaches, sliced in 6 pieces each, pitted
1 red Delicious apple, remove core, chopped medium dice
6 plums, sliced in 6 pieces each, pitted

2 lemons, save rind, juiced
1 cup red grapes
2 cups ice
Sugar
8 ounces 7-Up®, optional

Place all fruit in a glass pitcher. Add 2 cups ice, lemon juice, orange and lemon rind, all the white wine and allow to sit in the refrigerator until just before serving. At the last minute, add sugar, to taste and soda, if desired. This is a little lighter than your regular Sangria. Great in the summer! Makes 5 to 6 servings.

L-R: Mom Mom Betty Feiner, David Feiner, and Josephine Mainella at David's graduation from SUNY Buffalo...
Aunt Fifi calls David "my boy" and David calls her "Jezebel..."

STOLI DOLI'S
Maria Trainor

1 bottle of Stoli™ Vodka   2-3 fresh pineapples cut into large cube

Place the pineapple pieces into a large container and pour the vodka over them. Cover, and let it sit on the counter for up to a week. When ready to use place in a martini shaker with lots of ice. Shake to chill and then strain into a martini glass. Serve with a few pieces or pineapple in it for an extra punch.

Maria made these for Jonathan's graduation party. They were a great hit. Lauren had them at the Picano's graduation party and wanted Maria to include the recipe here for future reference!

MOJITOS
Katherine Trainor

1 bottle of Bacardi™ Light Rum   Several sprigs of fresh mint leaves
1 (2 liter) bottle of Club Soda   Fresh lime
1 cup of simple sugar

Mix all the ingredients together except the mint and limes, and let chill well. Make a mash of the mint and the limes. Stir into the mojitos. Fill a large punchbowl or jumbo lemonade jar with a spigot and serve over crushed ice.

L-R The future "Dr" Matt Cully and Lauren Feiner chillin' at the Trainor's Camp after a long day of sun and fun!

THE BEE'S KNEE'S LEMONADE
Elise Feiner

2 cups sugar   2 vanilla beans
¾ cup honey   2¾ cups freshly squeezed lemon juice (about 27 lemons)
2½ cups water, more if needed

Using a juicer or if you have a juice attachment to a KitchenAid ™, juice the lemons and set aside. In a large pot, mix the sugar, honey, and 2½ cups of water over a medium heat. With a sharp knife, score the vanilla beans lengthwise, and using the dull side or back of a knife, scrape the seeds from the vanilla pod into the saucepan. Add the pods as well. Let the mixture come to a boil and cook for about 4 to 5 minutes, or until the sugar is dissolved. The mixture will start to thicken. Remove from the heat source and let cool. Place the lemon juice in a large jar or container. Stain the sugar mixture directly into the pitcher, removing pods. Add enough water to make one gallon of liquid. Stir well. Taste and adjust sweetness before serving. Chill well.

My niece Sherry's father is a "vanilla expert." He worked in a flavor developing plant in New Jersey and traveled to Madagascar to consult with vanilla bean growers. He gave me enough vanilla beans to last forever. I use them to flavor sugar, lemonade, and even iced tea!

David's
Graduation
from The State
University of New
York at Buffalo

L-R: Jeffrey,
Marc and Elise
Feiner

L-R: Ivan, Jeffrey and Theresa Feiner…Jeff's Godparents

The new Mr. and Mrs. Brett Smith
Brett is in a partner is a youth sports marketing company
called Fuse, and is now doing ad specialties as well.
Check out his website www.fusemarketing.com

"The New Docs": Antoinette Valenti, M.D.,
Jeffrey Feiner, M.D., and Lindsey Gutierrez, M.D.

L-R: Drs. Marc and Jeffrey Feiner
Medical School Graduation
Second to his birth, his father giving him his hood at graduation
was one of the most beautiful, and moving days of my life

L-R: Sherry, Aunt Fifi holding Daniella, and Michael Avella
My father and mother would have adored their first great-grandchild.

The "Fidgit Girls," Joanne Fsadni and Barbara Kimmel

Breakfast, Brunch and Eggs...

The Philip J. Avella Family
Standing L-R: Philip Jr., John-Michael Latini, Nicole Latini, Michael Avella
Sitting L-R: Phyllis and Philip J. Avella, Sr.

"In a big family, the first child is like the first pancake. If it's not perfect, that's okay, there are a lot more coming along."

– Antonin Scalia, Associate Justice US Supreme Court

Equivalents:

¼ cup of egg substitutes = 1 egg
1 stick of butter or margarine = ½ cup
¼ pound of cheddar cheese = 1 cup grated
1 teaspoon of dried herbs = 1 tablespoon of fresh herbs
1 large onion = 1 cup chopped
6 ounces of chocolate chips =1 cup
1 medium lemon yields 2-3 tablespoons of juice
1 medium lemon yields 1 tablespoon of grated zest
1 medium orange yields 6-8 tablespoons of juice
1 medium orange yields 2 tablespoon of grated zest
1 cup of heavy cream = 2 cups whipped
14 graham cracker squares = 1 cup crumbs
1 cup whole almonds = 8 ounces
1 cup whole walnuts = 6 ounces
2 tablespoons = 1 fluid ounce
4 tablespoons = ¼ cup
5⅓ tablespoons = ⅓ cup
1 cup = 8 fluid ounces
⅛ teaspoon garlic powder = 1 small clove
1 cup raw rice = 3 cups cooked
2¼ cups firmly packed brown sugar = 1 pound
2 cups granulated sugar = 1 pound
3½ cups of confectioners sugar = 1 pound
1 teaspoon of baking powder = ¼ teaspoon baking soda & ½ teaspoon of cream of tartar

1 ounce chocolate square = 3-4 tablespoons cocoa plus 1 tablespoon of butter
10 mini marshmallows = 1 large marshmallows
4 cups of flour = one pound
8 ounces of cooked noodles = 7 cups
8 ounces of uncooked noodles = 2-3 cups cooked
1 pound package of pasta cooked = 12 cups
4 ounces of pasta, uncooked = 2¼ cups cooked
3 medium bananas = 1 cup mashed
3 cups cornflakes – 1 cup crushed
1 tablespoon of cornstarch = 2 tablespoons flour
1 cup of breadcrumbs = 2 ounces
1 pound of nuts in the shell = ½ pound shelled
1 cup of egg whites = 8-10 whites
1 cup of egg yolks = 12-14 yolks
16 marshmallows = ¼ pound
3 teaspoons = 1 tablespoon
2 tablespoons = ⅛ cup
4 tablespoons = ¼ cup
8 tablespoons = ½ cup
12 tablespoons = ¾ cup
16 tablespoons = 1 cup
2 cups = 1 pint
2 pints = 1 quart
4 cups = 1 quart
4 quarts = 1 gallon
8 ounces = 1 cup
4 ounces = ½ cup

PERFECT HARD BOILED EGGS
Elise Feiner

6 eggs
Pinch of salt

Cold water
Ice bath (bowl of water filled with ice cubes)

You can half this or double it depending on the number of eggs you need. Over boiling gives eggs a rubbery feel, and a green tinged color to the yolks. To make a perfect egg, place eggs in a deep saucepan in a single layer (**Note**: if you increase the numbers of eggs make sure your pan is big enough so that the eggs always remain in a single layer). Pour in enough cold water to cover eggs by 2-inches. Add a pinch of salt. Set the saucepan over heat and then bring the water to the boil. Immediately remove the saucepan from the heat and place a cover on top of the pot. Let the eggs sit for 10 minutes, and then **IMMEDIATELY** place the eggs in a bowl of ice water for 4 minutes or run cold water over them to cool them. Then, refrigerate or peel depending on why you are using the eggs. Use them to make egg salad, serve in salads or just eat as is. If you are going to dye them for Easter eggs, your eggs are now ready for dipping and dyeing. Remember, if you're going to eat the eggs, don't leave them out of the refrigerator for more than two hours. Serves 3-6 depending on how you are using them.

THE BEST SCRAMBLED EGGS
Elise Feiner

12 eggs
¾ cup heavy cream
½ teaspoon salt
Pinch of black pepper

3 tablespoons fresh herbs or your choice (chives, tarragon, basil, and parsley) or 1 tablespoon dried herbs
6 tablespoons butter

Mix the eggs, salt, pepper (you can add more salt and pepper to your own taste), cream and herbs together with a whisk to scramble them. Heat the butter in a large non stick skillet but don't let the butter get brown. Add the eggs to the butter. Cook the eggs on a low to medium heat, stirring gently with a spatula. Do not over cook, in fact if you are putting the eggs in a chafing dish; undercook them a little as they will continue to cook in the chafing dish. Serves 6 to 8. You can double this recipe or halve it easily.

This is great to serve at a breakfast buffet. Be careful when you put eggs in a chafing dish if there is direct heat underneath them because the eggs may get a greenish tinge from heat (something like what happens when you over cook a hard boiled egg and the yolk turns green. It doesn't affect the taste. I made these at Juliann's brunch in the Hampton's.

SCRAMBLED EGGS
Elise Feiner

6 eggs
Salt and pepper to taste
1-2 tablespoon milk or cream

2-3 tablespoons butter

In a small mixing bowl, add the eggs, salt and pepper, and milk; using a fork or a whisk, scramble well. In a Teflon pan (**I keep a pan that I only use for eggs**) melt the butter. Add the egg mix, and gently stir with a spatula or large spoon, turning frequently until all the eggs have solidified. Serve immediately. If you are adding mozzarella or onions, add them to the butter before you add the eggs.

This is our "everyday" scrambled egg recipe. I like to cut up small cubes of mozzarella and scramble it into my eggs for lunch or sauté some onions and add them in too!!

SUNNYSIDE UP EGGS
Elise Feiner

6 eggs
Salt and pepper to taste

2-3 tablespoons of butter

In a small non-stick pan, melt ⅓ of the butter over a low heat. Carefully break 2 eggs into the pan so you don't break the yolks. With a fork, carefully lift the whites a little bit at a time, peeling it back from covering the yolks, to allow the whites to solidify. Be careful when doing this around the yolks. Continue to move the whites, pushing them to the sides of the pan, until all the whites are cooked. Carefully remove to a serving dish. Repeat two more times with remaining eggs. Serves 3.

I hate my eggs over easy. Take a little extra time and care, and you will always get perfect Sunnyside up eggs, well cooked, no running white and perfect yolks.

HASH BROWNS A LA ABBY AND JODY
Elise Feiner

Leftover potatoes (baked or boiled) cut into 1-inch thick slices or 1 bag of Ore-Ida® Frozen Hash Browns (defrosted)
2-3 onions, peeled and diced or sliced
1 stick butter

Garlic salt
McCormick® Seasoned Salt
Black pepper to taste

In a large frying pan over medium heat, melt the butter and sauté the onions until they begin to brown. Season with garlic salt, and black pepper to taste. Add the potatoes. Season with a little McCormick Seasoned Salt. Fry until brown and very crisp.

My nieces Jody and Abby love these potatoes and I always make them when they come to visit.

More of the Feiner Girls: L-R: Jody, Lauren and Abby Feiner
Can't deny that those three are cousins…

BUTTERMILK PANCAKES
Ann D'Amico

2 eggs
2 cups buttermilk
¼ cup melted butter
1¾ cups flour
2 teaspoons sugar

2 teaspoons baking powder
1 teaspoon baking soda
1 teaspoon salt
Optional: Add ½ cup blueberries, chopped apple, or chopped peaches to batter.

Mix dry ingredients together. Add buttermilk, eggs, and butter. Mix to incorporate. **DON'T OVER MIX**. Fold in fruit if using. Lightly butter the griddle. It should be hot. I have an electric one and put it at 375°. Use an ice cream scoop mold, or ⅓ cup measure to pour batter. Turn when they bubble and are golden on the edge, about three minutes. Serve with warm maple syrup.

My cousin Ann always makes these for her house guests. You are truly blessed when you receive an invitation to stay with Ann and Phil…they're the best!

Ann and Phil D'Amico

L-R: Nina D'Amico, Flo Avella and Ann D'Amico

FRENCH TOAST
Elise Feiner

8 slices of Challah (egg bread) or White Bread
3 eggs
3 tablespoons sugar

2 teaspoons vanilla extract
2 tablespoons milk or heavy cream
Butter for the frying pan or griddle

Mix everything but the bread together. Dip the bread into the egg mixture. Heat a large frying pan or griddle pan. Melt enough butter to cover pan, being careful not to burn the butter. Fry in a buttered frying pan until brown on both sides adding more butter if needed. Top with syrup, butter, and/or confectioners' sugar.

My kids love French toast, especially if we have leftover Challah! Get creative...use English Muffins, croissants, different types of bread for your French Toast.

HASH BROWN CASSEROLE
Elise Feiner

12 eggs
1 (12 ounce) can evaporated milk
1 teaspoon salt
1 teaspoon garlic salt
½ teaspoon pepper
½ pint heavy cream
¼ teaspoon cayenne pepper
1 (30 ounce) package frozen shredded hash brown strips, defrosted

2 cups shredded cheddar cheese
1 cup Monterey Jack Cheese
½ stick butter
1 large onion, peeled and diced
1 medium green pepper, chopped
1 cup cubed, fully cooked ham
Paprika
1 (4 ounce) can button mushrooms
1 small can Durkee® Fried Onions

In a large bowl combine the eggs, milk, salt, garlic salt, pepper, heavy cream and cayenne pepper. In a small frying pan, melt the butter. Add the onions, peppers, and mushrooms and cook until soft. Add the potatoes, onions and pepper mix, cheeses, and ham. Pour into a greased 13 x 9-inch baking pan. Pour egg mixture over the top. Bake uncovered at 375° for 35 minutes. Top with fried onions and sprinkle paprika. You can also add some additional cheese on the top if you'd like. Bake an additional 15 minutes or until a knife inserted in the middle comes out clean. Serves 12.

Great for brunch! You can use leftover potatoes if you have them, but the frozen hash browns are better. I make this the day after we've had spiral ham for dinner.

OVERNIGHT FRENCH TOAST
Barbara Schwartz

1 stick of butter cut into small pats
8 eggs or egg beaters
3 cups milk
1 tablespoon vanilla

½ teaspoon salt
¼ teaspoon pepper
½ tablespoon sugar
Large loaf of Italian or French bread

Spray a large 8 x 14-inch glass pan with PAM® or butter well. Cut the bread into 1-inch thick slices. Place in the prepared dish very tightly, placing pats of butter on as many pieces as you can. In a blender, add the eggs, milk, vanilla, salt and pepper, and sugar. Beat for 1 minute. Pour over the bread mixture in the pan. Cover and refrigerate. When ready to serve put into a cold oven (do not preheat) set to 350°. Bake 1 hour. Let stand for 5 minutes. Serves 4 to 6 as a main course, 6 to 8 as part of a brunch.

Aunt Barbara serves this for brunch. It's great if you have company staying over, because you can do it a day in advance, and bake it in the morning.

"A friend is someone who knows the song in your heart and can sing it back to you when you have forgotten the words."
-Donna Roberts

HOLIDAY FRENCH TOAST
Elise Feiner

½ cup (1 stick) unsalted butter
1 cup packed brown sugar
2 tablespoons corn syrup
1 (8 to 9 inch) round loaf Challah (egg) bread, sliced in 6 (1-inch) thick slices, discard the crust

5 large eggs
1½ cups half and half or heavy cream
1 teaspoon vanilla
1 teaspoon Grand Marnier® or Kahlua®
¼ teaspoon salt

In a small pot, melt butter with brown sugar and corn syrup over moderate heat, stirring, until smooth and pour into a 13 x 9 x 2-inch baking dish. Trim crusts from bread slices. Arrange bread slices in one layer in baking dish, squeezing them slightly to fit. In a bowl whisk together eggs, half and half or cream, vanilla, Grand Marnier or Kahlua and salt until combined well and pour evenly over bread. Chill bread mixture, covered, at least 8 hours or up to 1 day. Preheat oven to 350° and bring bread to room temperature. Bake bread mixture, uncovered, in middle of oven until puffed and edges are pale golden, 35 to 40 minutes.

This is great if you need something a little upscale for a special brunch. The Grand Marnier or Kahlua really add to the flavor. Be careful if you have children at the brunch, you might want to make the Overnight French Toast for them. This French Toast is delicious, BUT WATCH IT CAREFULLY BECAUSE THE BOTTOM CAN BURN EASILY!

MATZOH BRIE
Elise Feiner

8 eggs
1 large onion peeled and diced (or you can use the frozen diced onion, about 5 tablespoonfuls)
6 tablespoons butter
8 sheets Egg and Onion Matzoh (You can use plain matzoh too)

Salt and pepper to taste (about ⅛ teaspoon pepper, and ¼ teaspoon salt)
2 tablespoon milk or heavy cream
Dash of garlic salt

Peel and dice the onion. In a mixing bowl, put eggs, salt, pepper, cream or milk, and beat until well scrambled. Break the matzoh into halves or quarters and run under hot water until fairly wet but not soaked. Squeeze the excess water out of the matzoh, making sure that most of the water has been removed. Crumble the matzoh into the egg mix and whisk again. If the mixture is too loose, add another board of matzoh which you have also soaked and squeezed. Place butter and onions in a Teflon frying pan (egg pan) Sauté the onions until golden brown, stirring frequently, add a dash of garlic salt.   Add the egg mixture to the onions after they have browned. Stir constantly over medium heat until the mixture is dry; the same as you would if you were making scrambled eggs). Serves 4 to 5. (I always use one board of matzoh to 1 egg.)

Mom Mom showed me how to make this originally, then I doctored it up so it tastes great. I remember the first year we were married and I made Matzoh Brie during Passover, and then served it with bacon. Your father almost died. What did I know; he ate bacon the rest of the year...I told him I gave up my religion for him, but drew the line at giving up pork! Italians and pork...as Emeril says," it's a pork fat thing!" This is a very easy recipe to double or triple.

ITALIAN QUICHE
Elise Feiner

1 pie crust, frozen
1 pound ricotta cheese
1 bag mozzarella cheese, shredded
4 eggs
½ teaspoon salt
⅛ teaspoon black pepper

¾ cup grated cheese
1 tablespoon parsley
1 slice (½-inch) thick boiled ham, cut in tiny cubes
8 slices pepperoni slice, cut finely
6 slices bacon, fried and crumbled

Mix all ingredients together; pour into pie crust. Bake 375° for 50 minutes to 1 hour. Make sure edges of crust are not too brown, if so, cover with foil.

MATZOH MEAL LATKES
Elise Feiner

4 eggs, divided
1½ teaspoons salt
1 teaspoon baking powder
1 cup matzoh meal

¼ cup water
Butter for frying
Granulated sugar

Beat the eggs yolks with the salt and baking powder. Add the matzoh meal and water. Blend well. The mixture will be thick. Allow to set for a few minutes. Beat the egg whites until stiff. Fold into the matzoh meal mixture; refrigerate for about an hour.. Heat the butter in a large frying pan. Drop the matzoh meal mix by tablespoonfuls in the butter and fry until golden brown on both sides. Sprinkle with granulated sugar. Serve with applesauce or sour cream.

This is one of Marc's very favorite foods. He loves these for breakfast! One of his favorite memories is of his Grandmother, Nanny Nellie, making him matzoh meal latkes.

Marc's Grandparents: Juda and Nellie Reinisch Marc's grandparents used to own Germantown Butter and Egg which later became Breakstone.

L-R: Nellie Reinisch, Jerry and Betty Feiner

SPANISH OMELET'S
Katherine Avella

Sauce:
2-3 tablespoons of oil
1 can plum tomatoes (break apart with your fingers)
A few leaves of fresh basil, cut into small pieces
½ green pepper, seeded and diced into very small pieces

½ onion, peeled and diced
1 stalk of celery with the leaves, washed and cubed, cut the leaves in small pieces
Salt and pepper to taste

In a medium saucepan, heat the oil. Add the onions and sauté until soft but not browned. Add the pepper and celery; cook until soft. Add the tomatoes, breaking them apart with your fingers, basil, salt and pepper to taste. Bring to a boil, and then let simmer for about 25 minutes.

Omelets:
12 -14 eggs
Salt and pepper to taste

2 tablespoons milk
¼ cup grating cheese

Beat the eggs with remaining ingredients. Make your individual omelets in an omelet pan or a frying pan by taking about ½ cup egg mixture and cooking until it solidifies. Place in plate, add some of the hot tomato mixture to the middle of the omelets and then fold in half (To clarify this, it's like making a thicker crepe. The omelets will be about ¼ -inch thick. Lay flat in dish, fill with tomato mix and fold over forming a half moon shape.) Serves 6.

Katherine Avella upon her graduation from Brooklyn College in 1936. It was rare for a woman to graduate from College in those days, but my mother was ahead of her time

POTATO AND EGG OMELET
Katherine Avella

5-6 potatoes peeled and cut into small cubes (about ½ -inch in size)	Salt and pepper to taste
1 large onion, peeled and diced	1 tablespoon parsley
12 eggs	1 cup grated cheese
	Enough oil to coat the bottom of a large, deep frying pan

In a large bowl, beat the eggs, salt, pepper, parsley and grated cheese. Heat the oil in the frying pan. Add the onions and potatoes and fry until they are fairly well browned and cooked. Lower the heat to medium, and add about three-quarters of the egg mixture to the frying pan, and use a fork (just more the fork around the potato/egg mix) to help the eggs solidify between the potatoes (this will take about 10-15 minutes) When the omelet starts to appear completely firm, cover the frying pan with a large round dish or plate holding the dish to the top of the pan tightly, and flip the pan so the omelet lands in the dish. The dish will be on the bottom, and the pan on the top. **Be very careful when doing this** as the omelet will be heavy and the pan very hot. Remove the pan from the dish, and return the pan to the stove. Then, add the remaining eggs back into the frying pan, and slide the omelet off the dish back into the pan on top of the egg mix, and continue cooking until it coagulates. Again, place the dish over the pan and flip as before to put the omelet into the dish. Serve in wedges. Serves 6.

Nanny has been making this omelet for years. It was always a staple on Friday nights when you weren't allowed to have meat on Friday. It is great as a light supper or lunch served with a side salad. You can cut the recipe in half for a smaller group. This is great leftover in sandwiches the next day!

L-R: Josephine Mainella, Frank S. Mainella, M.D., Katherine Avella
My mother and Aunt adored both of their brothers. My Uncle Frank was a surgeon on
President Street in Brooklyn affiliated with Adelphi and Community Hospitals. His partner
was Dr. Harry Berman, that Italian-Jewish combo again. My Aunt Edith even kept a set of
Kosher dishes in their house when he and his wife came to dinner.

SAUSAGE STRATA
Frances Zierler

One large loaf of Italian Bread cut into cubes	1 cup heavy cream
2 tubes of Jimmy Dean® Bulk sausage (regular)	½ cup grating cheese
6 eggs per tube of sausage plus 4 additional eggs	1½ bags grated cheddar cheese
2 cups milk	

Grease an 11 x 15-inch Pyrex® pan. Cover with the bread cubes. Brown the Jimmy Dean sausage in a large frying pan. Drain off any excess grease. Whip the remaining ingredients together, except for the cheddar cheese. Place the sausage over the bread cubes. Sprinkle the cheddar cheese over the sausage. Pour the eggs over the top and bake at 375° for about 1 hour to 1¼ hours.

Aunt Fran makes this for brunch, it's wonderful. It's great to make if you are having a large group for breakfast or brunch. This is great leftover.

BACON MONKEY BREAD
Elise Feiner

1 pound bacon
3 teaspoons vegetable oil
¾ cup green peppers, seeded and diced
¾ cup onions, peeled and chopped
3 (7½ ounce) cans refrigerated buttermilk biscuits

½ cup butter, melted
½ cup shredded cheddar cheese or favorite cheese of your choice

Preheat oven to 350° Fry the bacon until very crisp. Drain well. Crumble and set aside. Heat the oil in a frying pan; when hot add the peppers and the onions sauté until tender and golden brown. Cut the biscuits in quarters and place in a mixing bowl. Add the vegetables, bacon, butter and cheese. Toss until well coated. Place in a large tube or angel food pan which has been well greased or sprayed with PAM®. Place tube pan on a cookie sheet as it gives off a lot of grease. Bake at 350° for 30 minutes. Invert onto a large serving platter. Serve warm. Serves 8.

This is great for a Sunday Brunch or as an appetizer. I make it on Easter Sunday and serve it as an appetizer. My son Jeffrey thinks this is the best! If it breaks apart as you are taking it out of the pan, just push it back together on the serving plate...it's made to be pulled apart easily.

ZUCCHINI TORTE
Helen Popeo

5 eggs
½ cup grated cheese
¼ cup oil
3 cloves garlic, peeled and crushed

1 pound sausage meat, cooked
½ cup fresh parsley
4 cups zucchini, grated

Cook sausage meat first; drain grease. Then, in bowl add in ingredients except the zucchini. Lastly, add the grated zucchini. Grease a 10-inch pie dish and add the torte mixture. Bake for 45 minutes at 350°. You can sprinkle with paprika before baking (I don't). Enjoy!

NANNY JEANE'S FRIED BOLOGNA AND POTATOES
Jeane Cassata

6 eggs
Salt and pepper to taste
About a tablespoon of water, milk, or cream

5-6 slices of bologna
1 bag of potato chips
2 tablespoons vegetable oil (more if needed)

In a mixing bowl, scramble a few eggs, salt, pepper, and a drop of water. Set aside. In a hot frying pan with a little oil, fry pieces of bologna that have been cut into triangles. Wet the potato chips with a little hot water; squeeze out excess water. Add potato chips to the egg mixture. Add the egg mixture to the frying bologna and scramble.

Nanny Jeane gave me another great recipe. This is like a potato and egg omelet kicked up a notch and without the work of frying the potatoes. Delicious!

L-R: Rene Sanabria, Camille Sanabria, Fran Zierler, Carl Cassata, Nanny Jeane Cassata, Norm Zierler

MUSHROOM QUICHE
Elise Feiner

1 (8-inch) pie crust, frozen
3 tablespoons butter
3 tablespoons flour
1 cup light cream
1 pound fresh mushroom slices (you can mix different
types e.g. crimini, button, etc.)
2 tablespoons butter

1 clove garlic, peeled and crushed
3 shallots, minced
2 egg yolks
1 tablespoon light cream
Salt and pepper to taste
2 tablespoons white wine
½ cup Swiss cheese, grated

Preheat oven to 400°. Bake pie crust 7 minutes; remove and set aside. Lower the heat to 350°. In a small saucepan, melt the 3 tablespoons of butter with the 3 tablespoons of flour, quickly add the cream. Cook until thickened. Cool; set aside. In a large skillet, melt the 2 tablespoons of butter, sauté the mushrooms, shallots and garlic. Drain off any excess liquid. Add mushrooms to the cream sauce. Beat the egg yolks with the 1 tablespoon of light cream and add to the mushroom mix. Blend in salt, pepper and wine. Check for seasonings. Pour mixture into pie crust. Top with Swiss cheese. Bake 350° for about 20 to 30 minutes or until brown and firm.

PECAN AND PINEAPPLE FRENCH TOAST
Elise Feiner

3 tablespoons butter
4 eggs
½ cup orange juice
¾ cup heavy cream
1 (8 ounce) can crushed pineapple
¼ cup sugar

1 tablespoon orange zest
1 teaspoon vanilla
¼ teaspoon nutmeg
1 loaf French bread, cut in 1-inch slices
½ cup chopped pecans

Topping:

¼ cup butter, softened
½ cup firmly packed brown sugar

1 tablespoon light corn syrup
½ cup chopped pecans

Butter or grease a 9 x 13-inch baking pan and layer the bread in the pan. Mix all the remaining ingredients and pour over the bread. Mix everything together for the topping except the pecans. Spread topping mix over the bread; sprinkle with the pecans. Cover and refrigerate overnight. In the morning, preheat the oven to 350°; bake 40 to 45 minutes until golden brown.

PEPPERONI CREAM CHEESE
Elise Feiner

1 large container of whipped cream cheese

1-2 cups sliced pepperoni

Put the pepperoni into a food processor and process until very finely chopped. Fold into cream cheese until well blended. Serve with bagels.

I made this one Sunday morning just for fun. The kids love it, and ask for it at every Sunday Brunch to put on their bagels... talk about a Jewish-Italian household!

L-R: Karen, Jody, Abby, Danielle and Lauren Feiner, quite a group of beauties and brains in the same package.

CARMEN'S QUICHE
Carmen Ferreiro

2 cups cooked smoked ham
2 cups shredded cheddar cheese
⅔ cup chopped green onions (scallions)
1 (10 ounce) package frozen chopped broccoli, defrosted
and well drained

1½ cups milk
3 eggs
¾ cup Bisquick® baking mix
¼ teaspoon salt
¼ teaspoon pepper

Heat the oven to 400°. Grease a large Pyrex® pie plate. Lightly sauté the ham, onions, and broccoli. Add the cheese at the end. Pour into the pie plate. Mix all the other remaining ingredients in the blender. Pour this mixture over the mixture in the pan. Bake until golden brown 35 to 40 minutes. Cool 5 minutes and serve. Serves 8.

Carmen and Jorge Ferreiro, M.D.
They are originally from Cuba. Jorge is a gifted surgeon
and Carmen a gourmet cook...she makes the best flan!

The Ferreiro Kids L-R: Eric, Marc, Cristina,
and Alex

Jorge Ferreiro, M.D
Jorge is a wonderful surgeon...my mother paid him the
ultimate compliment...she said he was the same kind of
doctor as her brother Frank, hands of gold and a heart full of
compassion...

Carmen Ferreiro and her son Alex

CRAB QUICHE
Jean Carlucci

Crust:

½ cup butter, chilled
3 tablespoons vegetable oil
2 cups flour

5-6 tablespoons ice water
½ teaspoon salt

Place the butter, oil, flour and salt in a mixer with a paddle attachment. Mix on medium speed until the mix resembles cornmeal crumbs. Add the water and process just until it holds together; about 10 seconds. Chill in refrigerator about 1 hour. Roll dough into a circle about 9 to 10-inches, and ¼- inch thick. Place in a glass 9-inch pie plate.

Filling:

1 pound fresh crabmeat, not frozen
2 tablespoons fresh tarragon
2 tablespoons chopped fresh basil
2 tablespoons chopped fresh chives
1 cup grated Monterey Jack Cheese
1½ cups Gruyere cheese or Swiss cheese

2 cups heavy cream
4 eggs plus 1 yolk
Salt and pepper to taste
¼ teaspoon cayenne pepper
¼ teaspoon paprika

Sprinkle the bottom of the pie crust with ½ cup Monterey Jack cheese and ¾ cup gruyere cheese. Top with crabmeat. Place the chopped herbs over the top of the crab, top with remaining cheese. Beat the cream, eggs, salt and pepper, paprika, and cayenne pepper. Pour over the crab/cheese mixture. Crimp edges of the pie crust. Bake 350° 1 hour and 15 minutes. Serves 6. Let stand about 20 minutes before serving.

QUICHE LORRAINE
Ann D'Amico

1 (9-inch) frozen pie crust
8 slices bacon, fried and crumbled
6 slices Swiss cheese (thin, about 2-inches x 3-inches)
4 eggs, beaten
2 cups light or heavy cream (or one of each)
1 tablespoon flour

½ teaspoon powdered mustard
¼ teaspoon nutmeg
½ teaspoon salt
Freshly ground black pepper
Few grains of cayenne pepper

Preheat oven to 400°. Fry the bacon until crisp. Drain and crumble; sprinkle into the bottom of an unbaked pie shell. Arrange the cheese slices over the bacon. Combine the eggs, cream, flour, nutmeg, salt, pepper, mustard, and cayenne pepper in a bowl, and beat for 1 minute. Pour into the pie shell. Bake on the lowest rack for 15 minutes. Reduce heat to 325° and bake 30 minutes longer. Insert knife into the center; if clean, it is cooked. Serve cut into wedges.

For a different effect, take 6 ounces of very fine noodles and cook as directed in lightly salted water until almost tender; do not overcook, drain. Grease a quiche pan or pie plate well. Place the noodles in the pan to form a crust. Then continue with above directions. You can also add ½ cup of Parmesan cheese and 1 medium chopped onion sautéed in a little of the bacon fat to the above recipe for a different twist.

ZUCCHINI TART
Ann D'Amico

4 cups zucchini (peel if you don't like the skin), cubed
1 cup Bisquick® baking mix
6 eggs, beaten
½ cup grated cheese
2 tablespoons parsley, chopped

1 small mozzarella cheese, cubed
⅛ teaspoon pepper
½ teaspoon oregano
½ teaspoon salt
1 can mushrooms, sliced

Preheat oven to 350°. Mix everything together. Bake in a greased square or 9 x 13-inch pan. It is done when a knife inserted into the middle comes out clean.

BACON-CHEDDAR CHEESE SCONES
Elise Feiner

4 slices bacon, chopped
3 cups all-purpose flour
1 tablespoon baking powder
1 tablespoon sugar
1½ teaspoons salt
1 stick unsalted butter, cut into pieces

6 ounces sharp cheddar cheese, grated (about 1½ cups)
½ cup parmesan cheese
½ cup thinly sliced green onions
½ teaspoon freshly ground black pepper
1 cup heavy cream, plus 2 tablespoons

Preheat the oven to 400°. In a medium skillet, cook the bacon, stirring, until crisp, about 5 minutes. Remove with a slotted spoon and drain well on paper towels. Into a large bowl, sift together the flour, baking powder, sugar, and salt. Cut in the butter, cheddar cheese, and parmesan cheese, green onions, and pepper with a pastry blender or fork, and work just until it starts to form lumps and come together. Add the bacon. Add 1 cup of the cream and work just until it becomes a sticky dough, being careful not to overwork. Turn out onto a lightly floured surface and pat until it comes together. Form into 2 large circles, about 7-inches in diameter and ¾-inch thick and cut each into 8 wedges with a sharp knife. Transfer to baking sheet with a spatula, leaving ½-inch space between each wedge. Brush the tops of the wedges lightly with the remaining 2 tablespoons of cream and bake until golden brown, 22 to 23 minutes. Remove from the oven and let cool slightly on the baking sheet. Serve warm. Serves 8.

BLINTZES
Nellie Reinisch

Batter:
½ cup flour
½ teaspoon salt
2 well beaten eggs

⅔ cup milk
1 tablespoon butter, melted

Sift flour, add salt and sift again. Combine eggs, milk and butter, and add to flour mix and beat until smooth. Pour enough batter into a hot greased 6-inch frying pan to make each crepe. Spin the batter around to cover the pan. When it coagulates, turn it over and let cook until the other side coagulates. It should just take a minute or two. Don't let them brown. Place on dish towels to cool until you are ready to fill them. You can made them a day in advance and refrigerate them until ready to fill. Place about a tablespoon of blintz filling in the middle of each pancake. Fold in the sides and bottom to make a sealed rectangle. When ready to serve, fry in a frying pan with butter until lightly browned and heated through.

Cheese Filling:
½ pound cottage cheese
1 egg yolk beaten
2 teaspoons melted butter

1 tablespoon of sugar
¼ teaspoon cinnamon
2 teaspoons grated orange rind

Combine all ingredients together. Add salt to taste. Fill Blintzes and brown as directed in the recipe above. Serve with sour cream or strawberry jam or topping of your choice.

Potato Filling:
2 pounds of potatoes
3 onions peeled, and diced finely

4 tablespoons sweet butter
Salt and pepper to taste

Peel the potatoes and boil in lightly salted water. Drain well. Put the potatoes through a ricer or mash if you don't have a ricer. Sauté the onions in the butter until golden brown. Add salt and pepper to taste. Add the potatoes to the onions. Re-season the mix with salt and pepper. Fill the blintzes with the mix and fry as above.

This was another of Nanny Nellie's recipes. This makes a great lunch or light supper. Choose your filling choice. Blintzes freeze very well. Freeze them right after you fill them. They are handy to have in the freezer when you don't have time to make dinner.

"A mother understands what a child does not say"
-Old Jewish Proverb

HAM AND ASPARAGUS STRATA
Katherine Avella

1 pound fresh asparagus, trimmed and cut into 1-inch pieces
4 Thomas® English Muffins split them in half and toast
2 cups shredded Colby-Jack cheese, divided
½ pound provolone cheese sliced
1½-2 cups cooked ham, diced
½ cup chopped red and green peppers

8 eggs
2 cups Crowley® Half-and-Half
1 teaspoon salt
1 teaspoon ground mustard
½ teaspoon black pepper
½ cup grating cheese

In a large skillet, bring about 2 to 3-inches of lightly salted water to a boil. Place the asparagus in the boiling water and cook for about two to three minutes. Drain immediately and plunge the asparagus into an ice bath (fill a bowl with ice cubes and some water.) Drain and pat dry.

Place six of the toasted English muffins flat side down in a well greased 13 x 9 x 2-inch baking pan. Fill in any remaining spaces with the rest of the muffins. Place the slices of provolone cheese over the muffins. Sprinkle with the ham, red and green peppers, and asparagus pieces, and top with 1 cup of the shredded cheese. In a large bowl, mix the eggs, Half-and-Half, salt, mustard, pepper and grating cheese; pour over the ham mixture. Cover and refrigerate overnight. Preheat the oven to 375.° Take the pan out of the refrigerator about ½ hour before you bake it. Top with the remaining cup of shredded cheese. Bake, uncovered at 375° for 45 to 55 minutes or until a knife inserted into the middle comes out clean. Serves 6 to 8.

In the sixties, my brother Phil, cousin Ronny, Joe Mancuso and John Ferraro were in a singing group called the Jo-Vals…
The "Jo-Val's"… L-R: Cousins Philip Avella and Ronald DaBruzzo

ASPARAGUS OMELETE
Elise Feiner

12 large eggs, beaten
½ cup milk
¾ cup grating cheese
2 tablespoons butter
2 tablespoons extra-virgin olive oil
1 medium onion, peeled and diced

½ pound thin asparagus, blanched in boiling water, chilled and diced
¼ cup assorted fresh chopped herbs: thyme, chives, basil, etc
Salt and pepper to taste

In large bowl combine the eggs with the milk and grating cheese. Heat the butter and oil in a large sauté pan, until the butter is foamy. Add the onions and cook until the onions are translucent and golden, being careful not to burn them. Using a large wooden spatula, stir in the eggs and turn the heat down to very low. Using a spatula let the eggs cover he bottom of the pan. When the eggs begin to cook and take shape, stir in the diced asparagus and the herbs. Cook until the omelets solidify. Serves 6.

SPINACH QUICHE
Elise Feiner

1 prepared pie crust (frozen)
2 (10 ounce) boxes chopped frozen spinach, cooked as directed
1 medium onion, peeled and chopped
3 tablespoons butter
¾ cup parmesan cheese

1 pound ricotta cheese
1 cup light cream
3 eggs, slightly beaten
⅛ teaspoon black pepper
½ teaspoon salt
¼ teaspoon nutmeg

Preheat oven to 400°. Bake pie crust for 5 minutes and remove from oven; set aside. Lower the oven to 350°. Cook the spinach and drain well. In a medium frying pan, heat the butter; add onions and sauté until golden. Add the spinach, salt, pepper and nutmeg to the onion. In a large bowl, mix together the ricotta, parmesan cheese, eggs and cream. Add the spinach mix and mix well. Turn into pie crust. Bake at 350° for 50 minutes or until firm and set in the center.

BAKED SAUSAGE AND NUTELLA
Elise Feiner

½ pound Jones® Breakfast sausages
4 Panini, pita bread, or English Muffins

1 (13 ounce) jar Nutella® spread

Preheat oven to 450°. In a large sauté pan over medium-high heat, cook sausages until all sides are brown. Slice lengthwise. Slice bread lengthwise and spread bottoms with hazelnut chocolate spread. Place sausages on hazelnut chocolate spread. Top with remaining half of bread. Bake sandwich in oven until bread is lightly toasted.

I love Nutella and sausage, but I couldn't imagine this combo until I tried it when we were in Europe.

GRANDPA'S PANCAKES
Brenda Johnson

2 cups Aunt Jemima's Original Pancake Flour
2 eggs
½ cup milk

½ stick butter, melted
Chopped, peeled, or grated apple (optional)

Beat 2 eggs until frothy. Add milk and melted butter. Add in the flour; blend well. You can add the apples into the batter if you like. Cook on a hot, greased griddle or pan by pouring the batter into round circles. Cook one side then flip over, cook other side.

Brenda says some of her best memories are of her grandfather Mike Plescia making these pancakes for all his grandchildren on Sunday morning. He would stack them sky high, no one could ever finish them! She remembers him grating the apples into the batter. She says these are the best pancakes!

Mike Plescia...Brenda's Brother Mike looks like their grandfather

Mike and his car...Brenda say her grandmother Nellie sent him out with $50.00 one Christmas Eve to buy fish and he came back with this car instead!

Mike Plescia and his granddaughter Brenda Plescia Johnson

Irina and John Hamlin, D.D.S.

Joanna and Frank Basile
Close friends and neighbors, Frank and Joanna were integral in
setting up the ARC Gala, a tremendous fundraiser in our area.

L-R: Tim Trainor, Robin Butler, Maria Trainor, Marc Feiner, Bernie Gigliotti, Elise Feiner, Johann Gigliotti,
Charlene and Jay Koury, Eileen and Anthony Furino

L-R: Frances Barone, Josephine Mainella, Flo Avella, Daniella and Phyllis Avella

Bread, Rolls, Muffins and More...

The Ivan J. Feiner Family
L-R: Karen, Danielle, Jennifer, Ivan, Theresa

"Happiness is having a large, loving, caring, close-knit family in another city."

-George Burns

Fun Things:

Melt chocolate in the top of a double boiler and place in a parchment cone or icing bag. Write messages around the borders of your plates. How about "I Love You", surrounding a Valentine's Day Dessert...

I learned to do this when we had the balloon decorating business. Melt chocolate on the top of a double boiler. Blow up some 5" balloons. Prepare a cookie sheet with a sheet of parchment or waxed paper. Place about ½ - ¾ teaspoon of melted chocolate on the sheets to make a base for the balloons.   Dip the inflated balloon in the melted chocolate about three-quarters of the way up, and place on the bases on the cookie sheet. Refrigerate. When the chocolate hardens, pop the balloon carefully by pulling gently near the knot and inserting a pin; release the air very slowly. Refrigerate the chocolate until ready to use. Fill with fruit, pudding, cookies, tiramisu, mousse, etc. - use your imagination. If you don't have a balloon, use a small stress ball (so it will be malleable when you have to remove it) wrapped in saran wrap and sprayed with PAM™.

Use glasses at different heights filled with marbles as candle holders. For safety, melt some wax on the bottom first to help secure the candles, and **don't move them once they are lit**.

Fill a small vase with water for your flowers and place inside a large vase. Fill the larger vase with candy, fruit, seashells, rocks, bubblegum, marbles; let your imagination run wild. A wonderful way to hide the stems, and theme your table!

Use mini vases, teacups, sugar bowls, teapots filled with flowers and place at each table setting.

For the holidays, use an inexpensive ornament at each place setting, spray a pinecone or fruit with gold or silver and place beside each place setting **(don't** eat the sprayed fruit).

For a cocktail party, fill a small shot glass with cocktail sauce and hang a few stuffed shrimp on the outside.

Skewer different kinds of marinated olives and place the skewers in jumbo martini glass (available at most kitchen supply stores). You mix them with skewers or small cherry tomatoes, a basil leaf, and a mini ball of mozzarella, for more color (that's for you Aunt Jean!).

Wash a bunch of fresh grapes and thoroughly dry. Let sit on paper towels (changing frequently) until they are completely dry. Melt some semisweet chocolate in the top of a double boiler. Dip the dry grapes into the chocolate. Place on a piece of wax paper and refrigerate to harden. When hardened, place on top of a fruit platter...this is great at Thanksgiving.

BASIC WHITE BREAD OR ROLLS
Josephine Mainella

1 package yeast
2 cups lukewarm milk or (1 cup water and 1 cup milk)
2 tablespoons sugar

1 tablespoon salt
6 cups flour
4 tablespoons melted butter

Place the lukewarm liquid in a bowl. Add yeast, sugar, and salt. Stir until dissolved. Add flour 1 cup at a time. After adding 3 to 4 cups of flour, add melted butter. Add remaining flour; form into a ball. Cover; let rest 10 minutes. Knead on a floured board for 10 to 15 minutes. Place back into a lightly greased bowl and cover. Let rise until double in size 1½ to 2 hours in a warm spot. Punch down to deflate. Knead three minutes. Divide into desired proportions (2 loaves or 28-30 rolls). Place in either a loaf pan or if making rolls, place on a cookie sheet sprayed with Pam and lightly floured. Cover and let stand in a warm place until double in bulk. For a hard crust, brush the tops with melted butter before baking, for a soft crust, brush with milk before baking. Bake at 375° for 40 minutes for bread. Bake 425 ° for 15 to 20 minutes for rolls.

GARLIC BREAD
Elise Feiner

Olive oil
6 cloves or garlic, peeled and crushed
Salt and pepper (dash of each)

3 tablespoons grating cheese
Oregano, or basil, or any spice you like
1 large loaf of Italian or French bread

Split the loaf of bread in half. In a bowl, place the oil, garlic, salt, pepper, and grated cheese, and any spices you like. Brush over the bread and score the loaf in 3-inch pieces. Bake at 350° until golden brown.

My kids love garlic bread. This is one of my two favorite versions. I have a great spice mix that I use and just mix with olive oil.

L-R: Josh Rosenfeld, Lindsey Ulrich, Mindy Rosenfeld, and Jake Stookey

GARLIC BREAD WITH MOZZARELLA
Elise Feiner

1 large loaf of Italian or French bread
1 stick of butter, softened
3 tablespoons olive oil
6 cloves garlic, peeled and crushed

Salt and pepper to taste
3 tablespoons grated cheese
1 (2-3 cups) bag shredded mozzarella

Preheat oven to 450°. Cut the loaf in half. In a small bowl, place the oil, garlic, salt, pepper, and grated cheese. Add the butter and blend well with a fork. Spread on both sides of the bread. Score the bread into 3-inch sections but don't cut all the way through. Sprinkle with mozzarella. Bake until golden brown and mozzarella is melted. You can also wrap the loaf in foil and bake it at a lower temperature (350°), if you do this omit the mozzarella. Place the two halves back together and wrap in foil. Bake about 15 minutes. Unwrap the bread, sprinkle the mozzarella on the top and place back in the oven until the cheese melts.

GARLIC CHEESE BREAD
Elise Feiner

3 to 4 cloves garlic, peeled and crushed
1 cup butter, room temperature
1½ tablespoons dry basil
¼ teaspoon oregano
1½ teaspoons capers (tiny ones)

2 teaspoons pimentos
1 loaf Italian bread
½ pound sliced mozzarella, American cheese, or cheese of
your choice

Preheat oven to 350°. Place all ingredients in a food processor except the bread and cheese. Slice bread in ¾-inch slices, but don't cut it all the way through so it resembles a fan. Spread each side of the bread slices with butter spread. Place a piece of mozzarella or cheese of your choice between each slice. Brush top and side of bread with butter. Wrap the loaf in foil. Bake for 15 to 20 minutes, or until cheese is melted. Open foil, and brown under broiler if desired (**watch carefully** so it doesn't burn.)

L-R: Camille Sanabria, Elise
Feiner, Fran Zierler
my "sisters", not related by
blood but by heart!

SESAME SEED BRAIDED BREAD
Elise Feiner

1½ cups hot milk
¼ cup sugar
1 tablespoon salt
½ cup butter
2 packages yeast

½ cup warm water
2 eggs
6½ cups all purpose flour
Egg Wash: 1 egg mixed with 2 tablespoons water
Topping: 2 tablespoons melted butter; sesame seeds

Stir the sugar, salt, and butter into the hot milk. Cool to lukewarm. In a large mixing bowl, sprinkle the yeast over the warm water. Stir to dissolve. Add the milk mixture to the yeast. Add the two eggs and three cups of the flour; beat 2 minutes at high speed with the dough hook attachment of a mixer. Gradually add the remaining 3½ cups of flour; until dough is stiff. Turn onto a lightly flour board and knead for 10 minutes. Place dough in a lightly greased bowl. Turn the greased side to the top of the bowl. Cover with a towel. Let rise in a warm place until double in bulk. Place on a lightly floured board. Divide the dough in half. Cut each half into thirds roll each third into a 28-inch long strip. Braid the three strips together, pinch the ends. Place on a large greased cookie sheet forming a circle with an opening of 6-inches in the middle. Cover the bread with some of the egg wash. Braid the remaining three strips, form a smaller circle and place on top of the first circle. Brush with the melted butter. Cover with a towel and let rise until double in bulk, about 1 hour. Preheat oven to 375°. Place the cookie sheet on the middle rack of the oven. Brush the remaining egg wash on the bread. Sprinkle with sesame seeds. You can also use poppy seeds if you prefer. Bake for 45 minutes to 1 hour. If getting too brown, cover with foil.

The aroma of this bread baking just fills the house with love!

L–R: Cousins Lauren Feiner, Nicole Latini, Sharon Avella, Sherry Avella

ONION BREAD
Elise Feiner

1 package of yeast	2 teaspoons salt
1 cup lukewarm water	3 tablespoons melted butter
2 teaspoons sugar	½ cup coarsely chopped onions
Approximately 3¼ cups flour	2 teaspoons paprika

Sprinkle the yeast into the warm water and stir until dissolved. Add 1 teaspoon sugar and 2 cups of flour. Stir and then beat well. Add 1½ teaspoons of salt and the remaining teaspoon of sugar. Stir in another ½ cup flour (saving ½ cup for kneading). Pour ¼-cup flour on a board and knead until smooth and satiny. Add remaining flour as needed. Put into a greased bowl, turn and cover; let rise until double in bulk, about 1 hour. Punch down and divide. Place in 2 greased 9-inch round layer pans. Brush with butter and sprinkle with the onions. Push the onions down into the dough's surface so it looks indented. Let rise until double in bulk about 45 minutes. Sprinkle with the remaining ½ teaspoon of salt and paprika. Bake at 450° for about 20 to 25 minutes.

ONION SHORTCAKE
Louise Blackburn

1 large onion, thinly sliced	1 (1 pound) can creamed corn
¼ cup butter	1 cup sour cream
1 box Flako® Corn Muffin Mix	¼ teaspoon salt
1 egg, beaten	1 cup grated cheddar cheese
⅓ cup milk	

Preheat oven to 425°. In a medium frying pan sauté the onions in butter. Combine the muffin mix, egg, milk, and creamed corn. Pour muffin mixture into a greased 9 x 9-inch square pan. In a bowl, combine sour cream, salt, onions, and ½ of the cheese. Spread the sour cream mixture on top of the muffin mixture. Sprinkle the remaining cheese on the top. Bake for 30 minutes. Serve warm.

I got this in a recipe exchange from Louise. It's delicious and smells wonderful when baking! Great with a Mexican meal.

CHALLAH
Elise Feiner

4½ - 5½ cups flour	1 teaspoon cold water
2 tablespoons sugar	⅓ cups butter, melted
1 cup very warm water	¼ cup poppy or sesame seeds (for top), optional
1½ teaspoons salt	Few drops yellow food coloring
4 eggs at room temperature	
2 packages yeast	

In a large bowl, thoroughly mix 1¼ cups flour, sugar, salt, and undissolved yeast. Mix melted butter, and yellow food coloring into the warm water. Mix the water mixture with the flour mixture. Gradually add to the dry ingredients and beat 2 minutes at medium speed, scrapping the bowl occasionally. Add 3 eggs, the white of the remaining egg (reserve yolk), and another ½ cup flour. Beat at high speed 2 minutes, scrapping occasionally. Beat in enough additional flour to make soft dough. Turn onto a lightly floured board; knead until smooth and elastic about 8 to 10 minutes. Place in a greased bowl turning to grease the top. Cover and let rise until double in bulk; about 1 hour. Punch down; turn onto a lightly floured board. Divide the dough in half. Divide each half into three pieces and make one into a 12-inch braid and the other into a 10-inch braid. Place the 10-inch braid on top of the 12-inch braid. Place on a greased cookie sheet. Beat remaining egg yolk with a little water. Brush over the bread. Sprinkle with poppy seeds. Let rise again for one hour. Bake at 400° 20 to 25 minutes or until golden brown and bread sounds hollow when tapped on the bottom. Cool on a rack.

This is a wonderful Challah for the Jewish holidays or for Shabbat.. It smells wonderful when baking. The yellow food coloring gives it a great color.

L-R: Marc A. Feiner, M.D., Betty Feiner, and Elise Feiner

SESAME TWIST
Elise Feiner

1¼ cups milk
3 tablespoons honey
2 tablespoons butter
2 teaspoons salt
1 envelope dry yeast

¼ cup warm water
4 cups sifted flour
1 egg, slightly beaten
Sesame seeds

Scald the milk, honey, butter and salt in a medium saucepan. Cool to lukewarm. Sprinkle the yeast in warm water and then stir into cooled milk mixture. Beat in 2 cups of flour to form a smooth, soft dough. Gradually add the remaining 2 cups of flour to make stiff dough. Turn onto a floured board; knead until smooth. Turn into a greased large bowl, turn to cover completely. Let rise 1½ hours or until double in bulk. Punch down; knead a few times; divide in half. Divide each half in three equal pieces 14-inches long; make a braid. Place on a greased cookie sheet. Cut off one third of the second half of the dough and set aside. Divide the remaining dough in three equal parts and roll into 12-inch long roll. Make another braid; place on top of first braid. Take the reserved dough and divide in thirds. Roll into 10-inch strips. Make a third braid; place on top of second braid. Let rise again until double in bulk. Brush loaf with one egg beaten with a drop of water. Sprinkle with sesame seeds. Bake at 375° for about 45 minutes. You may need to cover with foil if getting too dark. Bread should hollow on the bottom when tapped if it is done.

I can't remember where I got this recipe but I have been making it for years. It makes a pretty presentation with the three braids on top of one another. I have done bread in the bread machines but nothing compares to doing it yourself from scratch. I find the breads from the bread machines too dense.

L-R Front Row: Lauren, Elise, and Marc Feiner
L-R Back Row: David, Steven, and Jeffrey Feiner

BACON CORNBREAD
Elise Feiner

1 cup flour
1 cup cornmeal
4 teaspoons baking powder
2 tablespoons sugar
1 teaspoon salt

1 egg
1 cup milk
2 tablespoons butter, melted
12 slices bacon

Preheat oven to 400°. Place flour, cornmeal, baking powder, sugar and salt in a bowl and toss to mix. Beat the egg with a fork; add to flour mix. Add the milk and melted butter. Stir until thoroughly moistened; but do not over mix it. Fry the bacon until almost cook; it should be soft, not crisp. Drain on paper towels. Lightly grease a 9-inch square baking dish and then place a piece of waxed paper on it. Arrange the slices of bacon on top of the waxed paper. Place the batter carefully over the bacon strips. Bake for 30 minutes or until well browned. Remove from the baking dish and let cool for a few minutes. The bacon will be on the top. Remove the waxed paper. Cut into squares. Serves 6.

This is also great at a breakfast buffet or as a side dish with chili!

SKILLET CORNBREAD
Elise Feiner

1 tablespoon butter
1 tablespoon oil
1 cup flour
1 cup cornmeal
2 tablespoons sugar
1 tablespoon baking powder
1 teaspoon freshly ground black pepper

½ teaspoon salt
1 cup milk
¼ cup butter, melted
2 eggs, slightly beaten
¼ cup bacon, fried and crumbled
¾ cup Shredded Cheddar cheese or Monterey Jack

Preheat the oven to 425°. Place one tablespoon of butter and oil in a large ovenproof or cast-iron skillet (10-inch in diameter). Place the skillet in the preheated oven for 5 minutes. In a medium mixing bowl stir together the flour, cornmeal, sugar, baking powder, ½ teaspoon of black pepper, and salt. Make a well in the center of the mix; set aside. In another bowl, blend together the milk, the ¼ cup of butter, and the eggs. Add egg mixture all at once to the dry mixture. Stir until just moistened. The batter will be slightly lumpy. Put the batter into the prepared pan and spread with a spoon. Sprinkle the remaining ½ teaspoon of black pepper. Add the bacon and cheese and blend. Bake 20 minutes or until a toothpick inserted near the center comes out clean. Serves 8.

CORNBREAD WITH ONIONS
Elise Feiner

2½ cups yellow cornmeal
½ cup white flour
½ cup whole wheat flour
2 tablespoons sugar
1 tablespoon salt
3 eggs
1½ cups buttermilk

½ cup corn oil (or canola oil)
1 (14-ounce) can cream style corn
⅓ cup chopped green onions
2 cups sharp Cheddar, grated
2 or 3 tablespoons sun dried tomatoes, chopped

Preheat oven to 425°. In a large bowl, combine the yellow cornmeal, white flour, whole wheat flour, sugar and salt, and mix together. In a separate bowl, beat eggs slightly, and blend into mixture. Blend in buttermilk and oil. When well blended, add the remaining ingredients 1 at a time (the batter will be lumpy). Grease 2 (9 x 11-inch) pans, or 3 (8 x 10-inch) pans. Pour batter into pans, shake pans and tap on counter to distribute evenly. Bake 30 to 45 minutes.

CORNBREAD
Elise Feiner

1½ cups self rising corn meal
2 eggs beaten
⅓ cup oil
1 cup cream style corn or 1 small can
1 cup sour cream

2 teaspoons baking powder
1 stick butter, melted
¼ cup sugar
1 (8 ounce) bag shredded cheddar cheese

Mix dry ingredients together; mix other ingredients together. Combine and mix well. Put in a well greased or sprayed 12 tin muffin pan. Bake 425° for 25 to 30 minutes.

If you are really pressed for time and need a fast cornbread or corn muffins use a small box of Jiffy® corn muffin mix and substitute ¾ of a cup of Helluva Good® French Onion Dip for the milk in the recipe…it's wonderful!

Gary and Lisa Philipson and their children Evan, Jeremy and Rachel…many of Gary's mother Aviva' recipes are in this book. Gary is following in his father's footsteps and now runs the Philipson's in our area.

CHEESE BREAD
Edith Mainella

½ cup grated cheese
2 teaspoons salt
2 tablespoons sugar
2 packages yeast

2 cups lukewarm water
2 tablespoons oregano
4½ cups flour (divided into 3 cups and 1½ cups)
Additional grating cheese for the top

Combine the cheese, salt, sugar, yeast, lukewarm water, and oregano with 3 cups of flour. Blend slowly with a spoon. Mix in remaining flour. Cover with waxed paper and a towel. Let rise 45 minutes. Punch down and place in a buttered casserole (round) pan. Sprinkle with grated cheese. (You may substitute onion salt, garlic salt, caraway seeds or Good Seasons® dressing for the cheese.) Bake 375° for 55 minutes. Serve warm with butter.

L-R: Frank S. Mainella, M.D., Teriann, Edith and Joseph Mainella, Jr.

PEPPERONI PIZZA BREAD
Elise Feiner

½ cup of warm water
2 tablespoons onions, chopped very fine
1 tablespoon heavy cream or half and half
1 tablespoon sugar
2 tablespoons butter, softened
¼ cup marinara sauce
1 teaspoon salt
⅛ teaspoon black pepper
½ teaspoon garlic salt

½ teaspoon dried oregano
2 cups bread flour
2 teaspoon active dry yeast
⅓ cup chopped pepperoni
¼ cup chopped mushrooms
½ cup mozzarella, shredded
4 tablespoons grating cheese

In a small bowl, dissolve the yeast in the warm water, add the sugar. Set aside. In a small frying pan, sauté the mushrooms and onions until golden and soft. In a mixing bowl mix the flour, salt, pepper, oregano, and bread flour. Add the yeast, heavy cream, and tomato sauce to the dry mixture and mix with a dough hook. Add the onion mix, pepperoni, grating cheese and mozzarella; blend well. Let rise and punch down. Divide and shape into two loaves; place into buttered loaf pans.   Let rise a second time. Bake 375° about 45 minutes or until golden brown. In a hurry, use store bought pizza dough!

In this house, anything with pepperoni is a go. This tastes just like pizza and is fast and easy to make.

L-R: Joseph, Melissa and Thirza Avella

SAUSAGE BREAD
Elise Feiner

2 packages of prepared pizza dough (I buy it at the grocery store)
2 pounds of Italian sweet sausage (you can use hot if you like); bulk or remove it from the casing
2 bags shredded mozzarella cheese

1 egg, beaten
½ cup grated cheese (Parmesan or Locatelli Romano)
2 cloves of garlic, peeled and crushed
2 medium onions, peeled and diced (optional)
1 red pepper (optional)
1 green pepper (optional)

1 egg and 1 tablespoon of water beaten together to form an egg wash (set aside)

In a large frying pan, fry the sausage with the garlic until it is well cooked; drain any liquid. If the sausage did not break apart while frying, use a knife and chop it into small pieces. Add the grating cheese to the sausage. Stretch the pizza dough on a lightly oiled surface (I use a cookie sheet) until it is about the size of a 13-inch rectangle. Divide the sausage mix in half, brush the dough with beaten egg, and spread the sausage and 1 bag of the mozzarella over the dough leaving about a 2-inch border. You can sprinkle with a little more grating cheese if you want to. Roll the dough up like a jelly roll to form a loaf; seal the edges by pinching them together. Place the dough back on the cookie sheet, seam side down. Repeat with the second loaf. Brush the top with the egg wash. Bake in a 350° oven for 25 to 30 minutes until golden brown. The loaf should sound hollow when tapped lightly with your knuckles. Cool on a wire rack. You can also sauté some onions and green peppers in a little butter and add to the bread before rolling it (Make sure you drain the peppers and onions well before rolling in the bread.) If you decide that you want to add peppers and onions take 2 medium onions, peel and dice them. Take one green and one red pepper, wash, remove seeds and cut into thin slices. Melt about 2-3 tablespoons of butter in a medium frying pan. Sauté the onions and peppers until soft and golden. Sprinkle with a little garlic salt and black pepper. Drain off any remaining liquid before using. You can do them ahead and then reheat them. Serves 12.

Papa David Feldman, Nanny Freda's Father, Marc's great-grandfather…

Ida and David Feldman
Marc's Great Grandparents

My son David is named in his honor…
my mother-in-law Betty always said
what a great man he was!

Fathers and Daughters…Lovely, never, ever change… Just the way you look tonight!

Dr. Marc Feiner and Lauren

Dr. Charles Antzelevitch and Lisa

L-R: Abby and Kevin Feiner, Karen and Ivan Feiner

Shelley and Kayla Lipson

Jennifer and Ivan Feiner

Jorge Ferreiro, M.D. and Cristina

BANANA BREAD FEINER
Elise Feiner

½ cup vegetable oil (Wesson®)
1 cup sugar
2 eggs, slightly beaten
3 ripe bananas, mashed with a fork
2 cups all purpose flour
1 teaspoon baking soda
½ teaspoon baking powder

½ teaspoon salt
3 tablespoons milk
½ teaspoon vanilla extract
1 (6 or 12 ounce) bag miniature chocolate chips, depending on your preference
½ cup chopped nuts (optional)

Beat oil and sugar together. Add eggs and mashed banana pulp and beat well. Sift together the four, baking soda, baking powder and salt. Add sifted dry ingredients, milk, and vanilla. Mix well and stir in chocolate chips, and nuts if desired. Pour into mini loaf pans or a large loaf pan which has been greased and floured. Bake at 350° for about 20 to 25 minutes for the mini loaves and 60 minutes for the large loaf. Cool well. Serves 6 normal people or one to two growing Feiner Boys! Use leftover slices for French Toast.

This is the Feiner kid's favorite banana bread. We have mailed it to schools all over the U.S. It also bakes up well in mini loaves or cupcake tins as well. Not only do the Feiner kids love it but it has become a favorite of the Rosenfeld and Ferreiro kids, too. A really easy recipe that keeps very well, if it lasts that long. It also freezes well wrapped in foil.

ANN'S PUMPKIN BREAD
Ann D'Amico

4 eggs
⅔ cup water
½ teaspoon baking powder
2 cups pumpkin
3 ⅓ cups flour
2 teaspoons baking soda
1½ teaspoons salt
⅔ cup butter, softened

2 ⅔ cups sugar
1 teaspoon cinnamon
½ teaspoon ground cloves
¼ teaspoon ginger
⅛ teaspoon nutmeg
1 cup raisins
⅔ cup walnuts, chopped

Cream butter and sugar. Add eggs, pumpkin and water. Mix all dry ingredients together and add to the mix. Add the raisins and walnuts. Butter and flour three loaf pans. Pour in pumpkin mixture. Bake at 350° until a wooden stick inserted into the center comes out clean (about 50 to 60 minutes). Makes 3 loaves.

PUMPKIN BREAD
Elise Feiner

3 eggs
1½ cups sugar
1½ cups pumpkin
1 cup plus 2 tablespoons oil
1½ teaspoons vanilla
2¼ cups flour
1½ teaspoons baking soda
1½ teaspoons baking powder

1½ teaspoons salt
1½ teaspoons cinnamon
¼ teaspoon pumpkin pie spice
¼ teaspoon ginger
¼ teaspoon nutmeg
¾ cup chopped pecans (optional)
6 (ounce) package chocolate chips (I like mini chips)

Beat eggs and sugar together. Add pumpkin, oil, and vanilla, mixing thoroughly. Sift dry ingredients; add to pumpkin mix and blend well. Add pecans and chocolate and stir to blend. Greased and flour 2 loaf pans. Bake in a 350° oven 50 to 60 minutes.. This freezes well.

If you are using fresh pumpkin you can prepare it in the microwave by cutting in quarters, remove the seeds, cover with Saran Wrap™ and microwave each quarter until soft. I got this recipe when we were living in Baltimore, Maryland.

"Everyone is kneaded out of the same dough but not baked in the same oven."
-Yiddish Proverb

PUMPKIN NUT BREAD
Fran Monticciolo

3½ cups all purpose flour
1 teaspoon cinnamon
2 teaspoons baking soda
1 teaspoon salt
½ teaspoon baking powder
½ teaspoon allspice
2 cups sugar
⅔ cup brown sugar

1 cup oil
4 eggs
⅓ cup water
2 cups (16 ounces) pumpkin
½ cup walnuts
¾ cup raisins

Preheat oven to 350°. Grease two 9 x 5-inch loaf pans or one 3 pound coffee can. Mix flour, cinnamon, baking soda, salt, baking powder and allspice. Set aside. In a large bowl, mix the sugars and oil. Add eggs, water and pumpkin, beat well. Gradually add the dry ingredients and stir until well blended. You can do all this with an electric mixer. Stir in the nuts and raisins. Pour batter into pans. Bake 55 to 60 minutes or until a cake tester inserted in to the center comes out clean; remove from the oven. Let sit 10 minutes. Cool on wire rack.

I spoke to Fran recently and she told me that she has retired from teaching. It seems like yesterday that she was starting out!

HAWAIIAN BANANA NUT BREAD
Elise Feiner

4½ cups flour
1½ teaspoons baking powder
1 teaspoon baking soda
2 teaspoons salt
3 sticks unsalted butter, softened
2 cups firmly packed light brown sugar
1 cup sugar
3 teaspoons vanilla

6 large eggs
2 tablespoons freshly grated lemon zest
2⅔ cups ripe bananas (about 6 large), mashed
6 tablespoons sour cream
1½ cups macadamia nuts, chopped
1 cup sweetened coconut flakes, toasted lightly and cooled
1 (12 ounce) package mini-chocolate chips

Heat the oven to 400°. Place the coconut on a cookie sheet and toast lightly about 10 minutes stirring frequently. Let cool. Lower the oven to 350°. Into a bowl sift together the flour, the baking powder, the baking soda, and the salt. In a large bowl with an electric mixer cream the butter with the sugars, beat in the vanilla, the eggs, one at a time, the lemon zest, the bananas, and the sour cream. Add the flour mixture, beat the batter until it is just combined, and stir in the macadamia nuts, chocolate chips and the coconut. Pour the batter into a buttered and floured loaf pans and bake the bread in the middle of a preheated 350° oven for 40 to 50 minutes, or until a tester comes out clean. Cool the bread on a rack. Freezes well.

CRANBERRY PUMPKIN BREAD
Elise Feiner

4 eggs
2 cups pumpkin puree
1 cup vegetable oil
4 cups sugar
4½ cups all-purpose flour

2 tablespoons pumpkin pie spice
2 teaspoons baking soda
1 teaspoon salt
4 cups cranberries, craisins, or chocolate covered cranberries or any combination of the three

Preheat oven to 350°. In bowl combine eggs, pumpkin puree and oil. Add dry ingredients and mix well. Add cranberries and mix well. Divide dough into 2 (8 x 4-inch) loaf pans. Bake for 50 minutes.

"Women rely on friends...that's where we gain sustenance and find safety. We can count on our women friends when we need a good laugh or a good cry."
-Cokie Roberts

LEMON BREAD
Ann D'Amico

1 cup sugar
6 tablespoons butter, softened
Rind of 1 lemon
2 eggs
1½ cups flour
½ teaspoon salt

1 teaspoon baking powder
½ cup milk
½ cup chopped nuts
¼ cup sugar, scant
Juice of one lemon

Preheat oven to 325°. Cream the butter and shortening together. Add lemon rind. Beat in the eggs. Sift flour, salt and baking powder together, and add to butter mix, alternating with the milk, beginning and ending with the flour. Stir in the nuts. Pour into a greased loaf pan and bake at 325° for 35 to 45 minutes. Dissolve ¼ cup sugar in lemon juice and pour over hot bread. Allow to cool in the pan. When cold, slice and serve with sweet butter.

My Cousin Ann says this is her favorite recipe.

OATMEAL BREAD
Ann Gruman

2 cups boiling water
1 cup rolled oats
⅓ cup butter
⅓ cup light molasses
4 teaspoons salt

2 packages yeast
¼ cup warm water
2 eggs
5½ cups sifted all purpose flour

Mix together the 2 cups of boiling water, rolled oats, butter, molasses and salt and cool to lukewarm. Add 2 packages of yeast to a little warm water. When light add to the above mix. Blend in eggs. Add flour. Mix until dough is well blended. Place dough in a well greased bowl and cover. Place in the refrigerator for at least 2 hours. Shape chilled dough in two loaves on a well floured board and place in greased 9 x 4 x 3-inch pans and cover. Let rise in warm place until double in bulk. Bake 1 hour at 375°.

This recipe was given to my Aunt Edith by her neighbor, Mrs. Gruman. They lived next door to each other on Arlington Avenue. I found the recipe in my Aunt Edith's recipe box. It was written in Mrs. Gruman's hand and was a reflection of the times. It was written on very formal stationary, from Mrs. Gruman to Mrs. Mainella. So different from our casual relationships with our friends and neighbors today!

ZUCCHINI BREAD
Gina Mastrovito-Smith

3 eggs
1 cup oil
2 cups sugar
2 cups zucchini, peeled and grated
2 teaspoons vanilla
1 teaspoon baking powder

1 teaspoon baking soda
3 cups flour
½ teaspoon salt
2 teaspoons cinnamon
Nuts and raisins (optional)

Beat eggs, add oil and sugar. Add vanilla and zucchini. Combine dry ingredients except nuts. Mix together. Place in a greased loaf pan. Sprinkle with chopped nuts (walnuts) and with a little cinnamon sugar. Bake 350° for 45 minutes or until a knife inserted into the middle is dry.

Maryann Mastrovito invited Trish Alsheimer, Judy Massoud and I out to lunch after Gina's wedding. Gina invited us to see her new house and have dessert. She made this bread and brownies for us. It was delicious. She didn't put the raisins or nuts in the bread, they're optional. She sprinkles chopped walnuts and cinnamon sugar on top.

ORANGE BREAD
Elise Feiner

2 packages of dry yeast	¾ cup milk
½ cup warm water	¼ cup butter
⅓ cup sugar	¾ cup orange juice
¼ cup grated orange rind	2-2½ cups flour
1 tablespoon salt	Additional flour if necessary
¼ teaspoon baking soda	

In a small bowl, mix the yeast in warm water. In a large mixing bowl combine the ½ cup sugar, grated orange rind, salt and baking soda. Heat the milk with the butter; cool to lukewarm. Add the milk mixture to the large mixing bowl. Add the orange juice and yeast mixture. Using a mixer at medium speed add 2-2½ cups of flour. Beat the soft dough until it looks elastic; about 3 to 4 minutes. Do not beat the dough too long. By hand, add enough flour to make a stiff dough, usually about 3 cups total. Knead on a floured board for about 6 minutes. The dough should not be sticky. Place in a greased bowl and cover with Saran Wrap®. Place in a warm place and let rise until double in bulk. Punch dough down. Divide in half. Let the dough set for 5 minutes. Shape into two loaves. Bake at 350° for about 35 minutes.

You can also use this dough to make Cinnamon Monkey Bread (see index)

STRAWBERRY BREAD
Elise Feiner

2 cups fresh strawberries, washed	1 teaspoon baking soda
2 large eggs	½ teaspoon baking powder
1 cup sugar	½ teaspoon ground cinnamon
½ cup vegetable oil	¼ teaspoon salt
1½ cups all-purpose flour	½ cup chopped macadamia nuts or pistachio nuts

Topping:	
1 quart fresh strawberries, washed and sliced	¼ teaspoon vanilla extract
⅓ cup granulated sugar	1 teaspoon grated orange peel
1 tablespoon Grand Marnier	

Preheat the oven to 350°. Grease a 9-inch round cake pan and set aside. Place the strawberries in a food processor, and puree on high speed. In a large bowl, beat together the eggs, sugar, and oil. Add the strawberries and whisk until well blended. In a separate bowl, sift together the flour, baking soda, baking powder, cinnamon, and salt. Add into the strawberry mixture, blending until moistened. Fold in the nuts, do not over mix. Pour into the prepared pan and bake until a tester inserted into the middle comes out clean, about 50 minutes. Remove from the oven and cool on a wire rack. Serves 8.

For topping: In a bowl, combine all the ingredients and stir. Cover and let soak in the refrigerator for 2 hours. Cut cake into 8 pieces. Top with strawberry topping and whipped cream (see index for whipped cream).

CINNAMON MONKEY BREAD
Elise Feiner

Melted butter	The dough from your favorite roll or bread recipe (See Orange Bread, above)
Cinnamon sugar	

Grease a large tube pan with butter. Pinch the dough off into little balls about 1-inch in diameter. Roll the balls in melted butter and cinnamon sugar (you can make your own by mixing cinnamon and sugar together or you can buy it pre-made.) Place the dough balls in a haphazard fashion until the pan is half full. Allow the dough to rise (about 30 minutes) and then bake at 375° about 45 minutes. To serve, invert on a serving plate and let your guests pull off a ball.

This was very popular in the 80's. We called it Monkey bread or Bubble Bread. It's great for company for breakfast. It is making a comeback today!

TONI'S STRAWBERRY BREAD
Toni Scattaglia

3 eggs, beaten
⅔ cup butter (unsalted), softened
2 cup sugar
2 teaspoon baking soda

3 cups of strawberries, washed, dried and chopped fine,
3⅓ cups of flour
2 teaspoon vanilla
1 (6 ounce) bag mini chocolate chips

Preheat oven to 350°. Cream the eggs, sugar and butter together. Add baking soda to the strawberries. Add the flour, alternating with the strawberry mix to the egg and butter mixture. Mix in the vanilla. Place in a greased loaf pan and bake for 50 to 55 minutes.

Our neighbor, Toni was a fabulous baker and cook. She would always send over her baked goods and cookies at the holidays. It is fast and easy to make and great to take care of an abundance of strawberries in the summer. The chocolate chips are my idea, and I increased the amount of strawberries slightly. It tastes like chocolate covered strawberries; and freezes well. Tragically, Toni died very young, but she will live on through her wonderful recipes. This is my favorite strawberry bread.

MONKEY BREAD
Sylvia Kaplan

4 cans Pillsbury® Hungry Jack Biscuits
¾ cup sugar
1 teaspoon cinnamon

½ cup chopped nuts
½ cup raisins

Cut biscuits into quarters and roll into balls. Mix the cinnamon and sugar together in a small bowl. Roll balls into the sugar cinnamon mix. Place in a well greased angel food or Bundt pan, placing nuts and raisins between the layers. Make topping (see below) and pour over biscuits. Bake 350° for 40 to 45 minutes. Pull apart to serve.

Topping:
1 cup of sugar (white or brown)
1½ teaspoons cinnamon

¾ cup butter
¼ cup evaporated milk

Place in a medium saucepan on the top of the stove. Bring to a boil. Pour over biscuits.

My sister-in-law Barbara's Aunt Sylvia gave me this recipe at Barbara's bridal shower. This is great if you're serving a brunch, or even for dessert. You can add more nuts and raisins if you would like.'

L-R: Jonah, Zachary and Basia Schwartz…Barbara and Stuart's grandchildren

More fathers and daughters...Thank heavens for little girls!

John Burt and Eileen Burt Furino

Bernie and Kristin Gigliotti

Katherine and Timothy Trainor

Anthony Furino and his girls...
Felicia and Kristin

HONEY ROLLS
Lucy Massimiano

1 cup milk	3¼ cups flour
½ cup oil	1 package dry yeast
2 tablespoons honey	2 eggs divided (reserve 1 egg white for topping)

Heat the milk, ½ cup oil, and 2 tablespoons of honey until warm about 120 to 130°. Set aside. Blend 1½ cups of the flour, yeast, eggs and warm liquid mix together. Beat 3 minutes by hand. Stir in the remaining 1¾ cups flour. Dough will be soft and sticky. Cover and let rise until double in bulk about 45 to 60 minutes. Generously grease round or square pans. Punch down the down and knead for 30 seconds. Drop by tablespoons side by side in pan. Make the topping. Drizzle half over the rolls. Cover; let rise again in a warm place until double in bulk 20 to 30 minutes. Drizzle the remaining topping over the rolls. Bake 25 to 30 minutes in a 350° oven or until golden.

Topping:

⅓ cup sugar	2 tablespoons butter
1 tablespoon honey	1 reserved egg white

Blend all ingredients together. Mix well.

Cousin Lucy is from the Philippines and is an excellent cook. They used to visit us quite often when we lived in Brooklyn, or we would visit them in Auburn, New York. There was never an empty spot at her table; she truly "Cooked with Love."

Our newest additions twins Missy and Nikki,
with parents Cathy and Steve Appel
Cathy and Steve waiting a long time for these
two beautiful gifts but they were well worth the
wait!

L-R: Missy and Nikki Appel

Their cousin Steffanie Freedoff...
David's daughter

ROLLS SANITO
Nicholas Sanito Sr.

1 pound of flour (about 4 cups)
¼ teaspoon salt
3 tablespoons sugar
1 large egg

2 ounces oil
1 package of dry yeast dissolved in about ¼-½ cup warm water
1 egg beaten with 1 tablespoon of water (egg wash)

In a deep bowl, put the flour; add the salt and sugar and mix well. Make a well and add the egg, yeast mixture, and oil. Mix well. Dough should be wet. Sprinkle flour on the top and let rise 1 hour. Take out and put on a board, punch down and let rise again in a greased pot. Turn over so all dough is greased. Take out and punch down again. Roll into long roll and cut into pieces 2 inches thick. Roll into a strip again and make into a knot. Let rise again. Mix another egg with a drop of water. Brush with egg wash. Bake 350 to 375° for about 35 minutes.

Uncle Nicky always used to make these delicious rolls. I don't know why, but for some reason I am the only one who seems to have a copy of this recipe so here it is for all to enjoy. We always had a great time with Uncle Nicky...I remember as a kid he always used to take us to Jones Beach...he loved to drive and was a chauffeur for awhile when he retired. We miss him!

Angie and Nick Sanito, Sr.
I have such wonderful memories of my Uncle Nick and trips to
Jones Beach.

Nick and Pam's daughter
Nicole Sanito Makrides
and Nick Makrides

Nick Sanito Jr (my cousin refers to himself as "Cousin Fat
One"...)he's the best and his great wife cousin Pam
Sanito

96

SOUR CREAM BISCUITS
Jo Anne Merrill

4 cups biscuit mix (I use Bisquick™)   6 ounces 7-Up®
1 cup sour cream

Preheat oven to 400°. Mix the sour cream into the biscuit mix, using a pastry blender or two table knives, until mixture is crumbly. Add 7-Up all at once, stir quickly with a large fork. Turn out onto lightly floured board and quickly knead 6 to 8 times. Don't over mix or biscuits will be tough. Pat into a square and cut into about 18 equal pieces using a knife dipped in flour. You can also use a 2 to 3-inch biscuit cutter. Bake biscuits for about 7 to 10 minutes. Another variation of this is to mix ¼ cup 7-Up, ¼ cup buttermilk, 2 cups Biscuit mix, and 2 tablespoons butter. Mix first three ingredients together, place on floured board, knead, Cut into 1-inch thick biscuits, brush top with butter and bake 450° for 15 to 20 minutes.

This recipe has been passed around for years and usually changed a little by each of us.

POTATO ROLLS
Elise Feiner

1 package yeast   Cooking oil
1 cup warm water (105° - 115°)   1½ cups warm cooked potatoes put through a ricer
2 eggs   ½ cup nonfat dry milk
⅓ cup sugar   4½-5 cups sifted all purpose flour
1 tablespoon salt

Sprinkle yeast into water. Let stand 10 minutes; then stir until dissolved. Into a large mixing bowl, put the eggs, sugar, salt and ⅓ cup oil, potatoes, milk, and the yeast mix. Beat at low speed until blended. Gradually add 2 cups flour and beat well. Add the remaining 2½ to 3 cups flour by hand. Mix until the dough pulls away from the side of the bowl. Let rise until it doubles in bulk. Roll out on a floured board until about 1½ inches thick. Cut with a floured 2¼-inch biscuit cutter. Roll edges lightly in oil and put into baking pan (13x9x2-inch). Let the rolls rise a second time. Bake in a preheated 400° oven for about 25 minutes. Makes about 20 rolls.

BUTTER BISCUITS
Elise Feiner

4 tablespoon sugar   ¼ cup warm water
6 tablespoons shortening   1 cup buttermilk
½ teaspoon salt   ½ teaspoon baking soda
2½ cups all purpose flour   Melted butter for the tops
1 package dry yeast

Sift the dry ingredients together. Dissolve the yeast in warm water. Add yeast, shortening and buttermilk to the dry ingredients. Mix well, turn onto a floured board. Knead 20 times. Roll out ¼ -inch thick, and cut into rounds or squares. Butter each biscuit and stack in twos (one on top of the other) Let rise 2 hours. Bake at 400° for 15 50 20 minutes. Makes about 2 dozen.

L-R: Glenn, Sharon, Gene, Florence, Larry, Betty and Jerry Feiner at Larry's Bar Mitzvah. Larry is now a physician (ENT) in Philadelphia.

And more fathers and daughters...Sugar and Spice and Everything nice!

Frank Mastrovito and Gina Mastrovito-Smith

Laura Jendzo Skonberg
and Richard Jendzo

Lauren and Marc Feiner

R-L: Lauren and Marc Feiner, Ariana and George Cacoulidis

Left: Steve Rosenfeld with daughter Mindy

BASIC MUFFIN BATTER
Elise Feiner

1½ cups flour	1 stick unsalted butter
⅓ cup sugar	1 cup sour cream
1½ teaspoons baking powder	1 large egg
¼ teaspoon baking soda	1 teaspoon vanilla extract
¼ teaspoon salt	

Preheat oven to 400°. In a bowl, sift together flour, sugar, baking powder, baking soda and salt. Melt the butter and in a medium bowl, mix butter with sour cream, egg, and vanilla. Stir the butter mix (if you are adding anything else, add it at this point) into the flour mix. Prepare 12 muffins tins by either well greasing them or by spraying them with PAM®. Divide the batter into the muffin tins, and bake for about 20 minutes or until golden brown. Depending on what you add, this may take a little longer. This is a basic muffin mix. Get creative and add your favorite things. For example, mini chocolate chips, chopped nuts, coconut, fresh fruit, dried fruit, poppy seeds, favor extracts, etc. These can be whatever you want them to be! Makes 12 muffins.

BLUEBERRY MUFFINS
Ann D'Amico

½ cup butter	½ teaspoon salt
1¼ cups plus 2 tablespoons sugar, divided	½ cup milk
2 eggs	2 cups fresh blueberries, divided
2 cups flour	2 tablespoons flour
2 teaspoons baking powder	

Toss 1½ cups of blueberries with the 2 tablespoons of flour and set aside.

Preheat the oven to 400°. Cream the butter; gradually add 1¼ cups of sugar. Beat at medium speed with an electric mixer. Add eggs, one at a time, beating well after each addition. Sift together flour, baking powder and salt. Add to creamed mixture, alternating with milk. Mash ½ cup of blueberries with a fork; stir into the batter. Fold in remaining flour coated blueberries. Divide batter into 18 well greased muffin tins. Sprinkle the tops of the muffins with remaining 2 tablespoons of sugar. Bake at 400° for 30 minutes. Cool in the pan 10 minutes before removing.

CHOCOLATE IN THE MIDDLE MUFFINS
Elise Feiner

8 ounces semisweet chocolate chips	3 tablespoons flour
1 stick unsalted butter	¼ teaspoon salt
1 teaspoon vanilla	4 eggs
½ cup sugar	

Preheat the oven to 375°. In the top of a double boiler, melt the chocolate and butter together. Add in the vanilla. In a large mixing bowl, mix the sugar, flour and salt. Add this to the chocolate mix and mix well with an electric mixer on low speed. Add the eggs one at a time. Beat until batter is creamy, and lighter in color; refrigerate. Butter a muffin tin well and sprinkle some cocoa in each tin. Shake the tin to coat the sides with the cocoa. Place mixture into muffin tins. Bake for about 11 minutes. The middle will be gooey.

Lauren loves these muffins as well as any kind of cake that has gooey chocolate in the middle...then it's off to the gym!

"A mother is a person who seeing there are only four pieces of pie for five people, promptly announces she never did care for pie."
-Tenneva Jordan

PEACH MUFFINS
Ann D'Amico

2 cups flour
1½ cups granulated sugar
1 tablespoon baking powder
½ teaspoon salt
¼ cup butter, melted

2 eggs, lightly beaten
1 cup milk
6 tablespoons butter
1 cup plus 2 tablespoons packed brown sugar
3 cups sliced peeled ripe peaches (cut in small pieces)

Preheat oven to 375°. In a mixing bowl, combine the flour, granulated sugar, baking powder and salt. Add the butter, eggs, and milk; mix until smooth. Set the batter aside. Grease 18 muffins tins well. Place one teaspoon of butter and 1 tablespoon of brown sugar in each muffin tin. Place in a 375° oven for 5 minutes. Remove from oven and lower oven to 325°. Arrange the peaches in the muffin tins. Fill each half full with batter. Bake at 325° for 25 minutes or until brown. Remove from pans immediately. They may fall apart a little when you take them out, not to worry...just place the peaches back on the top, when cool sprinkle with confectioners' sugar. It's like a pineapple upside down cake in a muffin tin!

Make these in the summer when the peaches are fresh and sweet...I can't even describe how good these taste...just watch them disappear!

LEMON MUFFINS
Ann D'Amico

2 cups all-purpose flour
½ cup plus 2 tablespoons sugar
1 tablespoon baking powder
1 teaspoon salt

1 stick butter
½ cup fresh lemon juice
2 eggs, beaten
Finely grated rind of 1 lemon

Preheat oven to 400°. Butter or spray muffin tins with PAM®. Combine flour, ½ cup sugar, baking powder and salt; blend well. Melt butter. Remove from heat and stir in lemon juice, eggs and lemon rind. Stir egg mix into dry ingredients and blend until well moistened. Spoon into muffin cups and sprinkle the top of the batter with the remaining 2 tablespoons of sugar. Bake 15 to 20 minutes or until slightly browned. Makes 12 muffins.

ORANGE MUFFINS
Elise Feiner

1½ cups plus 2 tablespoons all-purpose flour
½ cup sugar
2 teaspoons baking powder
½ teaspoon salt
1 egg, lightly beaten
1 stick plus 1 tablespoon (9 tablespoons) melted unsalted butter

1 cup milk
4 tablespoons orange juice concentrate, thawed
2½ teaspoons finely grated orange zest
½ cup chopped pecans
¼ cup firmly packed light brown sugar

Preheat the oven to 400°. Lightly grease 2 mini muffins tins or 1 regular muffin tin and set aside. In a large bowl, sift together 1½ cups of flour, the sugar, baking powder, and salt. In a bowl, beat the egg, 8 tablespoons of the butter, the milk, orange juice concentrate, and 2 teaspoons of the zest. Add the wet ingredients to the dry, combining just until moistened. Do not to over mix. Divide the batter among the prepared muffin tins, filling each halfway. To make the crumbs: in a small bowl, combine the remaining 2 tablespoons of flour, the chopped pecans, the brown sugar, and the remaining 1 tablespoon of melted butter and ½- teaspoon of grated zest. Mix well and sprinkle 1 teaspoon on top of the batter for each muffin. Bake until the muffins are golden brown and a tester inserted into the middle comes out clean, about 14 to 16 minutes or a little longer for regular size muffin tins. Remove from the oven and let sit for 5 minutes in the pans, and then cool on wire racks. Serve with orange butter (see index for 2 varieties of orange butter) on the side.

CHOCOLATE MACADAMIA NUT MUFFINS
Elise Feiner

2 cups flour
½ cup sugar
1 tablespoon baking powder
1 teaspoon salt
⅓ cup unsweetened butter, chilled
1 cup semisweet chocolate chips

1 cup macadamia nuts, chopped
1 egg, lightly beaten
1 cup milk
1 teaspoon vanilla extract
Miniature chocolate chips (optional for the tops)

Preheat the oven to 350°. In a food processor, mix the flour, sugar, baking powder and salt. Add the butter and process until the mixture looks like coarse meal. Stir in the chocolate chips and ¾ cup of the nuts. In another bowl, mix the egg, milk and vanilla. Add to the dry ingredients and mix until combined. Grease or line muffin tins with paper liners. Spoon into prepared muffin tins. Sprinkle with remaining chopped nuts (and mini chocolate chips if desired). Bake for 25 minutes

PEANUTTY BANANA MUFFINS
Elise Feiner

1½ cups flour
½ cup sugar
1 teaspoon baking powder
½ teaspoon baking soda
½ teaspoon salt

1 egg
½ cup butter, melted
1 teaspoon vanilla
1½ cups bananas, mashed (about 3 medium)
1 cup peanut butter chips

In a bowl, mix the flour, sugar, baking powder, baking soda, and salt together. Set aside. In a separate bowl, mix the egg, butter, vanilla and bananas. Stir in the dry ingredients that you have set aside. Fold in the peanut butter chips. Generously grease or line a 12 muffin tin pan. Bake at 375° for 18 to 22 minutes or until a cake tester inserted into the middle come out clean. Cool five minutes before removing from the pan.

This is a nice change from the banana bread. You can also substitute chocolate chips or combine both types of chips.

BASIL ZUCCHINI MUFFINS
Elise Feiner

2 eggs, beaten
¾ cup milk
⅔ cup oil
2 cups flour
¼ cup sugar

1 tablespoon baking powder
1 teaspoon salt
2 cups zucchini, shredded
3 tablespoons fresh basil, chopped
½ cup grated cheese, divided

In a large bowl, mix the eggs, milk and oil and ¼ cup of the grating cheese. In a separate bowl, mix the flour, sugar, baking powder and salt. Mix the dry ingredients into the egg mix; mix until flour is moistened. The batter will not be too smooth. Gently fold in the zucchini and the basil. Grease muffin tins or spray with PAM®. Fill the muffin tins about ¾ full. Sprinkle with the remaining ¼ cup grating cheese. Bake at 425° for 20 to 25 minutes. Remove from pans. Depending on the size of your pans, you may get 18 muffins out of the batter. Serve with a salad for lunch.

I like to do these in mini muffin tins and adjust the baking time accordingly. These are a great way to deal with an overabundant vegetable garden. The aroma is fabulous!

"True friends are the ones who never leave your heart, even if they leave your life for awhile."
–Author Unknown

CORN MUFFINS
Ann D'Amico

1½ cups yellow or white cornmeal
½ cup flour
1 tablespoon sugar (optional)
4 teaspoons baking powder

1 teaspoon salt
½ stick butter
¾ cup buttermilk
2 eggs

Preheat oven to 425°. Butter muffin tins or spray with PAM®. Combine dry ingredients and blend well. Melt butter; remove from heat. Stir in buttermilk and eggs. Stir butter mixture into dry ingredients and blend until well moistened. Spoon into a 12 cup muffin and bake 15 to 20 minutes until lightly browned. Let stand 5 minutes before removing from the tins. These can be done in mini muffin tins and served with chili or soup and salad. Adjust baking time.

Standing L-R: Elise Feiner, Elizabeth Maida, Philip D'Amico, Joseph Avella, Teddy Barone, Ann D'Amico
Sitting L-R: Ernest Maida, and Billy Foster
This picture was taken at a party given in honor of my mother getting her Master's Degree when she was 65 years old.

LIGHT LEMON MUFFINS
Ann D'Amico

2 cups flour
½ teaspoon baking powder
½ teaspoon baking soda
½ teaspoon salt
1 cup sugar
1 stick unsalted butter (softened)
1 tablespoon lemon zest
1 cup ricotta

1 egg
1 tablespoon lemon juice
½ teaspoon almond extract (you can use vanilla extract as well)
¼ cup thinly sliced almonds
granulated sugar or cinnamon sugar to sprinkle over the top

Preheat the oven to 350°. Spray a muffin tin or line with paper muffin liners that have been sprayed with PAM®. Mix the flour, baking powder, baking soda and salt together. In a large mixing bowl with a Kitchenaid or mixer beat the sugar with the softened butter and lemon zest until light and fluffy. Add in the ricotta cheese. Beat in the egg, lemon juice and extract. Place the batter into the muffin tins. Sprinkle with the sugar (or cinnamon sugar) and almonds. Bake 20-25 minutes until lightly brown. Do not over bake.

Ann says that these are delicious and very light!

*There are two kinds of people in the world, the givers and the takers,
I'm a giver and so are you...never be a taker!*
-Vincent "The General" DeClementi

CRUNCHY RASPBERRY MUFFINS
Elise Feiner

1½ cups whole wheat flour
¼ cup sugar
¼ dark brown sugar; firmly packed
2 teaspoons baking powder
¼ teaspoon salt
1 teaspoon cinnamon

1 egg; lightly beaten
½ cup butter, melted
½ cup milk
1¼ cups fresh raspberries
1 teaspoon lemon zest

Topping:

½ cup chopped pecans
½ cup light brown sugar, firmly packed
¼ cup whole wheat flour

1 teaspoon cinnamon
2 tablespoon butter

Sift the flour, sugar, brown sugar, baking powder, salt and cinnamon together. Make a well in the middle. Add the egg, butter, and milk into the middle. Mix with a wooden spoon until combined, but do not over mix. Add the raspberries and lemon zest gently; just mix to combine. Spray a muffin tin with PAM® . Fill ¾ of the way. Make the topping by mixing the ingredients together until crumbly. Top each muffin with some of the topping mixture. Bake at 350° for 20 to 25 minutes.

HAM AND CHEESE MUFFINS
Elise Feiner

1¾ cups flour
⅓ cup rye flour
2 teaspoons baking powder
¼ teaspoon salt
1 tablespoon light brown sugar
½ cup cooked ham, finely chopped
¾ cup shredded Swiss Cheese
1 egg; lightly beaten

1 cup milk
¼ cup vegetable oil
¾ teaspoon spicy mustard
½ teaspoon Worcestershire sauce
1 scallion finely chopped (optional)
¼ teaspoon cayenne pepper

Mix the flour, rye flour, baking powder, salt, and brown sugar together. Make a well in the middle and add the egg, oil, milk, mustard, Worcestershire sauce, and cayenne pepper. Fold in the ham, Swiss cheese and scallions. Spray a muffin tin with PAM®. Fill ⅔' of the way. Bake at 400° for 20 to 25 minutes. Makes 12.

These are great with a salad for a light lunch.

BACON CHEDDAR MUFFINS
Elise Feiner

1½ cups flour
½ cup shredded cheddar cheese
¼ teaspoon cayenne pepper
¼ cup sugar
2 teaspoons baking powder
2 tablespoons butter
½ medium onion finely diced

¼ red pepper finely diced
1 egg, beaten
¾ cup milk
⅓ cup oil
8 sliced of bacon, crisply fried and crumbled

In a small frying pan, sauté the onions and red peppers until soft. Set aside. Grease a muffin tin with PAM®. Mix the flour, cheese, sugar pepper, and baking powder together. Make a well in the middle. Mix the egg, milk and oil together in a small bowl. Add to the middle of the well. Stir until just mixed (it will be lumpy). Fold in the bacon and onion pepper mix. Spoon into muffin cups. Bake at 400° for 20-25 minutes.

Great with a bowl of soup for a light lunch.

And still more fathers and daughters…And they're Daddy's Little Girls…

Elise Avella Feiner and Samuel Avella

Kristin Furino and Anthony Furino

Vincent "The General" DeClementi and
Giannina DeClementi Schwendemann

Abe Akselrad and his girls…from L-R: Gila, Aviva and
Rebecca

Joseph and Melissa Avella… Then

Joseph and Melissa Avella…Now

PIZZA DOUGH - NANNY'S
Katherine Avella

14 cups all purpose flour	5 packages dry yeast (Fleischmann's® Rapid Rise)
8 teaspoons salt	4 eggs
2 tablespoon sugar	3-5 cups warm water
3 tablespoons olive oil	

This can be mixed together in a mixer with a dough hook, or a Cuisinart™. If not, mix the yeast with the flour. Make a large circle of flour on a wooden mixing board. Break the eggs in the middle. Add the salt, sugar, and olive oil. Slowly start to add the water. The dough should be soft but not too sticky. If doing it by machine, mix everything except the water. Add the water slowly so you don't add too much. The dough should be soft, not sticky. Place dough in a large pot with a little olive oil on the bottom, turn, and cover with a layer of Saran Wrap™ which has been lightly greased. Cover with a heavy towel or blanket; place in a warm dark place. Let rise until double in bulk about 1 hour. Punch dough down, cover and let rise again. Punch dough down again and let rise a third time. Punch down. Preheat oven to 450°. Separate dough into 3 to 4 pieces. Keep covered with a cloth as you work. Lightly grease a pizza pan with a little olive oil. Wipe off excess oil. Start to stretch the dough being careful not to tear it. When fully shaped, bake crust for a few (about 3 to 5) minutes until barely lightly brown to prevent soggy crust. You can omit this step if you want to, and increase the baking time. Remove from the oven. Top with pizza sauce, add mozzarella, grating cheese, and whatever other toppings you want (pepperoni, mushrooms, black olives etc.) Dot the top with another layer of sauce. Return to the oven and bake until hot and bubbly about 15 to 20 minutes. Lift the dough with a spatula, the crust should be crisp and brown on the bottom when done. Don't use too much sauce or your crust will be too soggy. This will make enough for 2 to 4 pizzas depending on your pan size.

This is the dough that Nanny used to make every Friday when I was a kid. It smells wonderful as it rises. It's a great pizza crust and easy to make. I saw a hint on the food channel that you should put the mozzarella on the bottom and then put the sauce; the crust won't get soggy. Any of these pizza dough recipes can be used to make pizza frite (fried dough.) Pull off pieces of dough and deep fry in ail. Either sprinkle with confectioners' sugar or dip in marinara sauce. You can also put a little cube of mozzarella in the middle before frying them if you are going to dunk them in marinara sauce.

Nanny Katherine Avella with her Grand-daughters (L) Melissa Avella and (R) Lauren Feiner

PIZZA DOUGH
Maria DiPierdomenico

	2 tablespoon honey
½ cup light red or white wine	2 teaspoon salt
1½ cups warm water	2 tablespoons plus 2 tablespoon olive oil
3 ounces brewer's yeast	6 cups flour

Place wine, water and yeast in a large bowl and stir until dissolved. Add the honey, salt and olive oil and mix well to combine. Add 2 cups of the flour and mix with a wooden spoon until it becomes a loose batter. Add 4 more cups of the flour and stir for 2 to 3 minutes, incorporating as much flour as you can with the wooden spoon. Bring the dough together by hand and turn out onto a floured board or marble surface. Knead for 6 to 8 minutes, until dough is smooth and firm. Place in a clean, lightly-oiled bowl and cover with a towel. Let rise in the warmest part of the kitchen for 45 minutes. Makes one large rectangle pizza. Shape into a very lightly greased rectangular cookie sheet. Top with sauce and cheese of your choice. Bake in a 500° for about 15 to 20 minutes.

PIZZA DOUGH DOMENICO
Rosemarie DiPierdomenico

4 packages yeast
4 cups warm water
2 tablespoons sugar

2 tablespoons salt
4 tablespoons olive oil
4 pounds flour (about 16 cups)

Dissolve yeast in 1½ cups of warm water and a pinch of the sugar. Add salt, sugar, olive oil, and remaining water and then add flour. Mix with a dough hook or knead until it forms a soft, sticky dough. Let rise 1-1½ hours or until double in bulk. Punch down. Knead on a board with additional flour if necessary. Let rise again. Grease a cookie sheet or round pizza pan with a little oil. Divide the dough in thirds. Lightly grease a pizza pan or cookie sheet. Press the dough into the pan. Top with tomato sauce, mozzarella and whatever toppings you desire. Bake at 450° until crust is well browned about 15 to 20 minutes.

To tell if rising is complete, lightly press 2 fingers ½-inch into the dough. If indentations remain, the dough is ready for shaping.

This is Rosemarie Di Pier's recipe. It makes great pizza dough. You can also fry this and coat with powdered sugar for a sweet taste or dip in tomato sauce for a salty snack.

PIZZA BREAD WITH MUSHROOMS, ONIONS AND OLIVES
Ann D'Amico

1 pound pizza dough (store bought is fine)
4 large onions, peeled and sliced
2 large boxes of stuffing mushrooms, sliced

1 stick of butter, divided in two
1 jar (small) pitted Kalamata olives sliced, or cured olives
(pitted and sliced)

In a large frying pan, melt the half stick of butter and sauté the onions until golden brown. Drain; and set aside. In the same pan, add the remaining half stick of butter and sauté the mushrooms until soft. Drain; set aside. Preheat the oven to 350°. Roll the pizza dough into a rectangle. Mix onions, mushrooms and olives together. Spread the mixture on top of the dough. Roll tightly like a jelly roll to shape like a baguette. Make dents in top to look like bread. Bake 350° until golden about 15 to 20 minutes.

POPOVERS
Elise Feiner

2 eggs
1 cup flour
1 cup milk

1 teaspoon salt
½ teaspoon black pepper
4 tablespoons prime rib meat drippings

Preheat oven to 450°. Put the popover pan in the oven or baking pan in preheated oven for 10 minutes. In large bowl, beat eggs until frothy with a mixer. Gradually beat in flour and milk. When batter is smooth, add salt and pepper. Remove the hot pans from the ovens. Divide the drippings evenly among the popover pans. Pour in the batter. Place pans in the middle of a 450° oven and bake 10 minutes. **Do not** open the oven during the baking! Reduce heat 375° and bake another 15 to 20 minutes. After baking insert a knife into each popover to allow the steam to escape. Makes 10. You can also add three tablespoons of fresh chopped herbs to the batter if you'd like (chives, basil, thyme, etc. Blend them in with the flour.)

My nieces L-R: Karen, Danielle and Jennifer Feiner way back when…

GIANT POPOVERS
Elise Feiner

6 tablespoons butter
6 eggs
2 cups milk

2 cups all purpose flour
1 teaspoon salt

In a small saucepan, melt the butter. Preheat the oven to 375°. Liberally grease eight (8) deep (7 ounce) custard cups or popover pans. Set custard cups in a jelly roll pan. In a large mixing bowl, on low speed, beat the eggs until frothy. Beat in the milk and the melted butter until well blended. Beat in the flour and salt. Fill each custard cup ¾ full with the batter. Bake 1 hour and then **quickly make a slit** in the top of each popover with a knife, to let out the steam. Bake another 10 minutes. Immediately remove the popovers from the cups and serve. Makes 8.

SPINACH AND ROASTED GARLIC PIZZA
Elise Feiner

1 package prepared pizza dough
1 bag shredded mozzarella cheese
2 heads roasted garlic
½ cup olive oil

1 (16 ounce) container ricotta cheese
1 (10 ounce) package frozen spinach, thawed and
squeezed dry
¾ cup grating cheese

Roasted Garlic:
Take 2 full heads of garlic and cut off the top quarter. Place cut side up on a small disposable aluminum baking dish. Drizzle with 1 tablespoon of olive oil and salt and pepper to taste. Turn the garlic over and roast cut side down or wrap each in aluminum foil (cut side up) in a 325° oven for about 1 hour or until the cloves are soft. Remove from the oven and let cool. Squeeze the garlic into a container and set it aside. Preheat oven to 475°. Spray a large cookie sheet with PAM® and blot excess spray. Spread the pizza dough over the pan to form the crust. Mix the roasted garlic you have prepared with the ½ cup olive oil. Spread the roasted garlic over the crust. Mix the grating cheese, ricotta cheese and about ⅔'s of the bag of mozzarella together. Drop all over the crust. Top with the spinach. Top with remaining mozzarella cheese. Bake for about 15 to 20 minutes until browned and bubbly. You can substitute chopped broccoli for the spinach.

CROISSANTS
Elise Feiner

¼ cup lukewarm water (100-110°)
2 tablespoons sugar
2 packages yeast
4 cups flour
1½ teaspoon salt

1 cup warm milk
1 cup butter
1 egg yolk
1 tablespoon water (level)

Measure the water into a small bowl. Add 1 tablespoon of sugar and the yeast. Stir to dissolve. Mix in ⅔ cup flour. Shape into a ball. Cut a slit in the shape of a cross on the top of the ball. Place in a bowl; cover with a towel. Let rise 15 minutes until double in bulk. Combine remaining sugar and flour, salt, and milk in a large bowl. Mix well. Turn onto a floured board. Top with the risen yeast mixture. Knead the dough and yeast mixture together until smooth and elastic. Place in a large greased bowl and turn over so all sides are covered with grease. Cover with a towel; let rise 1½ to 2 hours until doubled in bulk. Punch down. Let rise another 30 minutes until doubled in bulk again. While the dough rises, knead the butter with your hands until it is free of lumps and of easy spreading consistency but still cold. Chill if needed. Turn dough onto a floured board and roll to a rectangle 18 x 10-inches. Spread butter over ⅔ of the dough leaving a 2-inch border all around. Moisten the edges with cold water. Fold the unbuttered third up to the middle of the buttered third. Fold the buttered ⅓ down so the top edge is even with the bottom. Pinch the edge of the top to enclose the butter. Roll out gently to another 18 x 10-inch rectangle dusting any tears in the dough with flour to repair it. Fold the dough into ⅓'s as before. Roll into another 18 x 10-inch rectangle again. Fold into ⅓'s as before. Be sure edges are even. Sprinkle lightly with flour; chill 2 to 3 hours.

Butter a cookie sheet. Divide the dough into 3 pieces. Work one piece at a time; refrigerate the other pieces until ready to use them. On a floured surface, roll dough into a 13-inch circle. Cut into 6 to 8 wedges. Roll up into a crescent shape from the wide end. Bend a little to form croissant shape. Place 2-inches apart on cookie sheet. Cover with plastic wrap. Let rise 1 hour. Remove plastic wrap. Brush with egg yolk. Bake 375° 20 minutes. These may be frozen. Makes 18. Before rolling you can fill them with cream cheese, strawberry preserves, chocolate, etc. if you like.

These are so time consuming to make but once you make them you will never each a store bought croissant again. They are outstanding. You can also put a pan of water in the bottom of the oven to create steam to make them super flaky. All the folding is what makes the croissant flaky. Try these once, you won't be disappointed.

SCONES
Ann D'Amico

1½ cups flour	½ teaspoon cinnamon
4 teaspoons baking powder	½ cup craisins, currants, golden raisins, or nuts, or ½ cup
5 tablespoons butter, ice cold	blueberries or chopped apples
5 tablespoons sugar	1 egg yolk, lightly beaten, to glaze
⅔ cup buttermilk	1 tablespoon sugar, to sprinkle

Mix the flour and baking powder together in a bowl. Make a well in the center and add 5 tablespoons icy cold butter cut into small pieces, and sugar. Cut into flour mix until it looks like coarse crumbs. Don't over mix. Add ⅔ cup buttermilk, cinnamon and raisins, and mix with flour. Place on a floured board. Knead a few times not more than 30 seconds. Roll on a board or between wax paper or parchment paper until ⅜-inch thick. Cut out rounds or leave in a circle and score into 8 wedges, but don't cut through. Brush with beaten egg yolk. Sprinkle with sugar. Let stand 15 minutes. Bake 400° until golden 12 to 15 minutes. Cool and cut into wedges. Serve with clotted cream (whipped cream mixed with cream cheese and raspberry jam).

My cousin Ann gave me this recipe which she got from the Savoy Hotel in London. She said they are great for breakfast.

CROUTONS
Elise Feiner

1 large loaf of Italian or French bread (one day old bread	½ cup grating cheese
works best), cut into small cubes	⅛ teaspoon black pepper
1 stick of butter	Garlic salt to taste

Heat the butter in a large frying pan or medium-low heat. Add the cheese, black pepper, garlic salt, and then add in the cubed bread and stir frequently until they are well coated with the butter mixture. At this point you have two options. You can continue cooking them in the frying pan until they are crisp, or transfer them to a cookie sheet and bake in a 400° oven for about 10 minutes or until they are as crisp as you like them. You can also add a little dried oregano, basil or rosemary if you like but this is optional. It would depend on what you what using the croutons for. For example, for pea soup or stracciatella I would leave them plain, but it's up to your own taste.

I always make these with pea soup or stracciatella. My kids love them right out of the frying pan. Store in a plastic container.

PUFF PASTRY
Elise Feiner

¾ cup butter (12 tablespoons)	1 teaspoon salt
2 cups flour	6 tablespoons water

Soften 6 tablespoons of butter in a small mixing bowl. Add the flour and blend thoroughly into the butter. Add the salt and water and knead lightly to make dough. On a floured board, roll the dough into a rectangle about ¼-inch thick. Soften remaining butter slightly. Divide the dough in thirds in your mind. Spread the butter over ⅔ of the rectangle and leaving a 1-inch border unbuttered around the edges. Fold the unbuttered third of the dough over the center third; fold the remaining third on top.

Turn the dough 90° and roll into another rectangle about ⅓-inch thick. Fold into fourths like this; take the short ends of the rectangle in to meet the center; then fold one half over the other as if you were closing a book. Repeat this procedure again, turning 90° before you start. Cover and refrigerate about 1 hour. Roll out into a rectangle again and fold in fourths like before. Roll the rectangle out a final time to about ¼-inch thick. This is a great puff pastry for beef Wellington. Encase the beef in pastry and brush with egg. Bake as you would for any Wellington. See recipe index for Beef Wellington or Pork Wellington.

The reason for all the folding is to make the pastry flaky. If the dough becomes too soft when you are working it, place in the refrigerator for a few minutes. This is great to make if you have the time. It is so much better than store bought puff pastry.

L-R: Cousins David, Jody, and Steven Feiner

ELISE'S FAMOUS BREADSTICKS
Elise Feiner

1⅓ cups warm water
2 packages active dry yeast
3 teaspoons salt
2 tablespoon sugar (level)
½ cup vegetable oil (Wesson)
4 cups Gold Medal flour

2 egg yolks and 1 tablespoon water for an egg wash (add more as needed)
Natural (not hulled) Sesame Seeds (about 1-1½ pounds or about 3-3½ cups)

In a mixing bowl, dissolve yeast in warm water. Add sugar, salt, oil, and **half the flour**. Beat vigorously under smooth. Mix in the remaining flour. Knead in bowl or on a floured cloth covered board until smooth. If you do it in a Kitchen Aid mixer (use dough hook) or a Cuisinart (use dough blade), you don't even need to knead the dough; just follow the directions above except instead of beating vigorously, turn on mixer and mix the first addition of flour. Then, add the last two cups of flour and process until the dough forms a ball. It makes perfect dough almost every time. Once in a while depending on weather conditions the dough may be a little sticky when you remove it from the mixing bowl. If that happens add 1 to 2 tablespoons of flour more (add one at a time) and mix or process again. The dough should not be sticky but medium firm. Cover the dough and let the dough rise until double in bulk. Punch the dough down once. The dough will be very elastic and easy to stretch and roll.

Preheat the oven to 400°. Pinch off a small amount of dough and roll into a pencil shape. (I make them between 4 to 7 inches long and but don't make much wider than a pencil). Dip into an egg wash mixture, and then roll in sesame seeds. Continue until **ALL** the dough is **USED**. Place on a cookie sheet sprayed with PAM®, 1-inch apart. I use disposable aluminum cookie sheets. Bake 30 to 35 minutes or until golden brown. The amount of time you need to bake them will depend on how thick you roll them and how crisp you like them (This depends on how accurate your oven temperature is too.) Start checking after 20 minutes. After baking about 15 minutes rotate the cookie sheets top to bottom and front to back; bake for remaining 15 to 20 minutes. I find it best to do two cookie sheets at a time and rotate them midway. Makes about 6 dozen.

This is my favorite recipe. I can't even remember where I got it, I've had it so long. I always double and triple the recipe; in fact the recipe above is doubled from the original. I can't remember a single Thanksgiving and Christmas without them. It's one of the few recipes that will always bind us as a family because everybody gets in the act when we make these. Somebody cuts, somebody rolls, somebody dips, etc. In 2000, I was tired after my surgery and wasn't going to make them...mass mutiny!!! Everyone went nuts. Michael, Philly, Sherry, Sharon, Abby, Melissa and the four Feiner's protested. So at 1 o'clock in the morning we started to make the breadsticks, and finished at 3:30 am. Of course, all the helpers were starting to drop by the wayside, but we did have our breadsticks. I caution you, hide some so they make it to the holiday table!

FRISELLE
Carmela Limongelli

4 cups flour
6 eggs
4 teaspoons baking powder

2 tablespoons salt
2 tablespoons black pepper
3 heaping tablespoons lard (Crisco is fine)

Take the four cups of flour and make a flour well (leave the middle open like a doughnut hole.) Mix the rest of the ingredients in a bowl. Pour into the center of the well. Knead the flour with the wet ingredients until well blended and a dough is formed. Grease or spray cookie sheets with PAM®. Shape into a long loaf or 2 if needed. The loaf should be about 4-inches wide and about 3-inches high. Bake at 375° for about 15 minutes. Slice into pieces about 2-inches wide. Return to the oven, and bake another 10 to 15 minutes until golden brown.

My mother's cousin, Carmela, was a fabulous cook. She used to spend a lot of summers in Bayville at Uncle Frank's. When I was a teenager we used to share one of the bedrooms and we would talk into the middle of the night. She would tell me what it was like when she was growing up. She would teach me how to bake the Italian specialties of her family, and I would sit there in the middle of the night and write then down.

The bond that links your true family is not one of blood, but of respect and joy in each other's life. Rarely do members of one family grow up under the same roof."
-Richard David Bach

DANIELE'S GARLIC KNOTS
Jeffery Daniels, Jr.

1 pound pizza dough
Olive oil
5-6 cloves of garlic, peeled and crushed
Garlic salt, to taste

Salt and pepper, to taste
2-3 tablespoons freshly chopped parsley
½ teaspoon oregano
½-¾ cup parmesan cheese

Take the pizza dough and break off small pieces. Roll into a pencil shape and then shape into small knots. Bake at 375° until golden brown about 20 to 30 minutes. Mix all the other ingredients in a bowl. Add the knots to the bowl. Toss with mixture. Enjoy!

Jeff Daniels, Jr. from Daniele Restaurant gave me this recipe years ago. Easy to do and much quicker than garlic bread

TARALLE LIMONGELLI
Carmela Limongelli

2 pounds flour (about 8 cups)
1 package yeast dissolved in 2 beaten eggs
10 eggs
1 tablespoon plus 1 teaspoon salt
2 tablespoons whiskey

2 tablespoons oil
½ teaspoon black pepper, optional
4 tablespoons grated cheese (optional) if using decrease
salt to 1 tablespoon

Dough to be very soft. Make well with the flour. Beat eggs; add remaining ingredients to the middle of the well. Form into soft dough. Let dough rise at least 1 hour. Break off pieces of dough and shape into donut or circle shape (should have a hole in the middle).
   Place rings into a large pot of boiling lightly salted water. When they rings raise to the top of the pot, remove the taralle, and place on clean dish towels. With a sharp knife score around the side of each taralle about half way through.. Bake directly on oven rack for 15 minutes at 400°. Lower heat to 350° Turn. Bake for 10 more minutes..

This recipe is similar to my Grandmother's but Carmela added her own touch. I remember her baking these in Bayville and all the men sitting around with their coffee eating these. These are very hard and are made to be dunked. I have many wonderful memories of times spent with Carmela and her sons, Danny, Eugene, and Enzo. In fact, Enzo works on the grounds crew at Shea Stadium and in my groupie days, he always had tickets for us. In fact, when I was 18, He brought my favorite player, Wayne Garrett to dinner...I thought I would die!

"My Groupie" Days...
L-R: Wayne Garrett # 11 and Elise Feiner

Carmela's son, cousin Enzo Limongelli
at Shea Stadium

110

MY NANNY'S TARALLE (BOILED)
Clementina Mainella

13 eggs
2 pounds Wondra® Flour
2 jigger's anisette, brandy, or whiskey
2 teaspoon coarse pepper

2 tablespoon salt or 1 tablespoon salt and 4 tablespoon grated cheese
2 tablespoons olive oil

Dough to be very soft. Make well with the flour. Beat eggs well, and add remaining ingredients. Place in the middle of the well. Work into the flour to form soft dough. Knead the dough until well blended. When you press lightly with your fingers, it will spring back when kneaded enough. Let dough rest at least 20 minutes to 1 hour Shape into donut shape. Bring a large pot of water to a boil. Place the taralle into the pot of boiling water. When they rise to the top, remove, and place on clean dish towels. Score around the side of each taralle with knife, but don't cut through. Bake on grate or oven rack directly for 15 minutes at 400°, turn. Bake for an additional 10 minutes at 350 °.

This is my grandmother's recipe, passed from her mother. These are really hard in texture and are made to dunk in coffee.

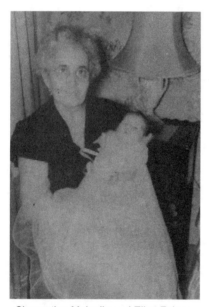

Clementina Mainella and Elise Feiner
Me with my grandmother…
She was so thrilled to finally have a
granddaughter after 4 grandsons

Freda Feldman Feiner and Marc Feiner
Marc with his grandmother…

ZEPPOLE WITH RICOTTA
Josephine Mainella

1 (16 ounce) container ricotta cheese
3 tablespoons sugar
3 eggs, lightly beaten
4 teaspoons baking powder

1 cup flour, sifted
¼ teaspoon salt
Oil for frying

In a deep bowl, mix ricotta, eggs, sugar, and baking powder. Let stand 1 hour. Sift the flour and salt together. Add to ricotta cheese mixture. Blend until smooth. Drop by tablespoonfuls into hot oil in a deep fryer or frying pan filled with a few inches of oil. Sprinkle with confectioner's sugar or granulated sugar.

Another variation used at Easter and St. Joseph's Day.

ZEPPOLE WITH RICOTTA - SFINGI SAN GUISEPPE
Frances D'Andrea

2 pounds ricotta cheese
3 cups flour
2 tablespoons baking powder
3 tablespoons sugar
1 tablespoon vanilla

6 large eggs, lightly beaten
½ cup milk
Oil to fry
Confectioners' sugar, to sprinkle on the top

In a large bowl, mix the ricotta, flour, baking powder, sugar, vanilla, and eggs. Add the milk; the batter should be on the thick side. Let stand for 30 minutes. Heat about 3 inches of oil in a frying pan or use a deep fryer set to 350°. Drop the batter by tablespoonfuls into the **HOT** oil, a few at a time. Turn until they are golden about 3 to 4 minutes. Drain on paper towels. Sprinkle with confectioner's sugar before serving.

There are so many recipes for zeppole, this is just another variation. It is Judge D'Andrea's wife Frances' recipe. She was a close family friend. It is a little sweeter than the other two. You tend to see these on March 19, St Joseph's Day. Of course in our family, as in most Italian families we have our share of Joseph's: my grandfather, my brother, Aunt Fifi (Josephine), cousins Joe Mainella, Joe Sanito, and Jo Jo Mainella, just to name a few. This recipe is in honor of all the Josephs.

Uncle Harry and Aunt Gert Feiner
Uncle Harry was one of the many
Feiner Brothers. He was an avid
stamp collector and would send our
children very old stamps every year
for the holidays. We miss them…

ZEPPOLE WITH YEAST
Josephine Mainella

3 packages dry yeast
4 cups lukewarm water
4 tablespoons oil

2 teaspoons salt
8 cups flour (about 2 pounds)
Confectioners' or granulated sugar for topping (optional)

Stir yeast into one cup of warm water. Let stand. In a pot, place flour, add yeast, remaining water. Add salt. Mix in oil until all flour is blended, about three minutes. Cover and let stand about 3 hours or until triple in size. Knead for about three minutes. Let rise again for about 1 hour. Dough should be soft. Place a little oil on a plate. Dip fingers in oil. Using a kitchen scissor dipped in oil cut off pieces of dough and pull from both ends to form 3-inch strips. Do not touch the middle of the strips. Deep fry the dough quickly until golden brown. Sprinkle with confectioners' or granulated sugar if desired. If you don't like it sweet you can dunk them into marinara sauce and grating cheese. You can also put a small cube of mozzarella in the middle before frying if not using the sugar.

This is the original fried dough of Italian street fairs and amusement parks.

"No matter what you've done for yourself or for humanity, if you can't look back on having given love and attention to your own family, what have you really accomplished?"
-Elbert Hubbard

HOT BUTTERED PRETZELS
Ann D'Amico

2½ cups all-purpose flour plus more for work surface
½ teaspoon salt
1 teaspoon sugar
2¼ teaspoons regular instant yeast

1 cup warm water (about)
Pretzel salt or kosher salt
3 tablespoons unsalted butter, melted
Vegetable cooking spray

Preheat the oven to 500°. Line baking sheets with parchment paper; set aside. In a medium bowl, whisk to combine flour, salt, sugar and yeast. Slowly add the water; the quantity will be determined by the humidity in the air. Transfer to a lightly floured work surface. Knead until soft and smooth about 5 minutes. Dust the dough with flour, and place in a plastic bag. Seal the bag, leaving room for the dough to expand. Let rest at room temperature for about 30 minutes. Spray work surface with cooking spray. Transfer rested dough to work surface. Divide dough into 8 equal pieces, about 2½ ounces each. Roll each piece into a long thin rope, 28 to 30 inches long. Twist each rope into a pretzel shape. Dip each pretzel in warm water. Place on prepared sheets. Sprinkle lightly with pretzel salt. Let rest, uncovered, for 10 minutes. Bake until golden brown, 8 to 9 minutes. Brush thoroughly with all the melted butter. Serve warm.

Ann sent this recipe which was adapted from "The King Arthur® Flour Baker's Companion: The All-Purpose Baking Cookbook" by King Arthur Flour. Check out their website and order their catalog and cookbook, its great! http://www.kingarthurflour.com

ITALIAN TARALLE WITH PEPPER AND NUTS
Josephine Mainella

Group 1:

3 cups white flour (Gold Medal)
1 cup whole wheat flour
2 tablespoons baking powder

¾-1 tablespoons salt
½ -¾ tablespoons coarsely ground pepper

Group 2:

¾ cup warm oil (6 ounces)

¾ cup warm white wine (6 ounces)

Group 3:

½-1 cup chopped nuts any kind or mixed them up

In a Cuisinart®, put ingredients from group 1 and pulse. Add ingredients from group 2 and mix until dough forms a soft ball. If needed, add a little more liquid (but don't ever exceed 2 cups total). Remove from Cuisinart and knead in ingredients from group 3. Let dough rise for about 1 hour in a covered bowl. Preheat oven to 350°. Divide dough into small pieces. Roll into thin long strips about 6 inches long, and then shape into rings and place on an ungreased cookie sheet for ½ to 1 hour. Then, bake at 350° for 10 to 15 minutes on the lower rack, move to upper rack and bake another 10 to 15 minutes, depending on the size of the rings. They should be a light to medium brown, depending on your preferences.

Of all the things Aunt Fifi bakes these are the most delicious. Actually, they are addicting. They are great with a cup of coffee or just to eat as a snack. You can add more pepper or nuts if desired. They stay very well in a tin can or waxed paper bags.

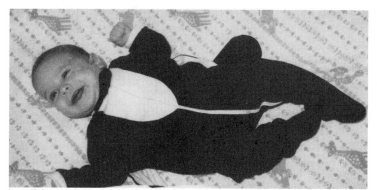

Aunt Fifi would always hold David and rock him for hours…calling him "my boy…"
Aunt Fifi's boy, David Feiner age 3 months – February, 1984

QUICK AND DELICIOUS PIZZA
Elise Feiner

Individual Pita Breads in the size of your choice (thicker ones)
Pizza Sauce (see Avella Pizza Sauce) the sauce does not have to be heated

Mozzarella (whole not shredded) sliced very thinly
Grating Cheese Pecorino Romano or Parmigiana

Take a few tablespoons of the sauce and spread over the bottom of the pita bread. Lightly sprinkle with grating cheese. Lay thin slices of mozzarella over the tomato sauce. Spoon a little sauce over the mozzarella, sprinkle generously with grating cheese. Bake at 400° about 8 to 10 minutes or until cheese is melted and bread is crisp.

MAKE SURE YOU BUT A PIECE OF ALUMINUM FOIL IN THE OVEN, ON THE SHELF BELOW THE PIZZA SO IT CATCHES ANY OVERFLOW OF MELTED CHEESE, OTHERWISE CLEANUP WILL BE A MESS.

Always keep some pizza sauce made and in the freezer so you can make these whenever you want. If you are careful, you can make these ahead and freeze them. Wrap them in aluminum foil and then place in a zip lock bag. After they freeze you can stack them. Take one out and pop it in the oven. You may have to bake them a few extra minutes if frozen.

ZEPPOLE TARANTINO
Jenny Tarantino

1 package active dry yeast
⅛ teaspoon salt
⅛ teaspoon sugar
1 cup warm water

1¼ cups flour, spooned into a cup
1½ cups corn oil or vegetable oil

Dissolve yeast, salt and sugar in water; stir in flour, blending well. Cover and let rise in a warm area 1½ hours or until double and double in bulk. Heat oil in a shallow pan (6-inch diameter and 1-inchdeep) to 375°; drop by level tablespoons four at a time, fry each side two minutes or until golden brown. Drain well on paper towels, sprinkle with confectioners' sugar while hot. Serve warm. Depending on the weather you may need to add up to 2 cups of flour. The dough will be very sticky. I also like a little more salt (1 teaspoon). You can also use these to dip into marinara sauce and grating cheese. Makes about 18.

My cousin Ann sent this recipe that I believe is my Aunt Jenny's recipe I can remember so many Sunday's spent at a huge table with my entire father's family at my Aunt Jenny and Uncle Ralph's house. I think I am the most like my Aunts Jennie and Julia, in looks and in likes (cooking and baking…I know I inherited these talents from them). My six aunts adored their brother Sam or Sem as they called him.

The Avella's (Clockwise from the top) Julia, Mary, Mae, Sam, Frances…
Missing Jenny and Flo (not born yet)

ZEPPOLE WITH BAKING POWDER
Antoinette Mercurio

3 cups flour
1 teaspoon salt
1 tablespoon oil

1 tablespoon baking powder
Water (lukewarm) about 1-1¼ cups
Confectioners' sugar, for topping

In a bowl, mix above ingredients to form soft elastic dough. Oil fingers and shape in pencil like shapes. Preheat a frying pan with about 1 to 2 inches of oil in it. Deep fry the pencil like pieces of dough. Sprinkle with confectioners' sugar if desired.

A Typical Thanksgiving Dinner this year
featuring a sing-a-long…
Standing: Philip Avella
Sitting from front to back: Edith Mainella,
Katherine Avella, Josephine Mainella, Barbara
and Kevin Feiner, Michael and Sam Avella

STRUFOLI
Antoinette Mercurio

3 cups flour
5 large eggs, place in a pan or warm water to heat up
1 teaspoon baking powder
1 tablespoon oil

2 tablespoons grating cheese
1 tablespoon salt
1 tablespoon coarse ground pepper

Mix above ingredients well. Knead. Let rest ½ hour or more in a covered dish in a warm place. Roll into long pencil like strips and cut into ½-inch pieces. Deep fry at 300°

This is Uncle Tony's sister Antoinette's recipe. What a fabulous cook she is. These are delicious to snack on. These are not your typical sweet dessert, like you would normally associate with the term strufoli; these are a savory type.

Top Row L-R: Anthony Grimaldi, Jr., Millie Grimaldi, Nick Sanito Sr., Angie Sanito, Ted DaBruzzo,
Anthony Grimaldi Sr.
Bottom Row L-R: Carol Grimaldi, Joan Arcieri, Ida Grimaldi, Antoinette Mercurio, Marge DaBruzzo

The Cacoulidis Family:
George and Barbara Cacoulidis and their daughter Ariana.
Barb and I connected the first time we met at a tradeshow
and have been friends ever since.

Bonnie and Bob Loomis…
Bob was the Principal of the kids school and remains a good
friend

L-R: Samantha Caplan (soon to be Zierler), Jeremy Zierler,
and Zachary Zierler

Mr. and Mrs. Jeremy B Zierler
How could these babies be of
marriageable age? I am aging fast!

Tony and Eleanor Picente
Eleanor is responsible for keeping my children sane and
preventing me from becoming insane!

L-R: Pat Yozzo, Lauren Feiner, Cindy Loiacano, and Vicki
Angell…our kids' teachers and good friends!

Casseroles and Crock Pots...

The Joseph C. Avella Family
Clockwise from the top: Douglas, Joseph, Thirza and Melissa

"The reason grandparents and grandchildren get along so well
is that they have a common enemy."
-Sam Levenson

My Favorite Things:

Paper Dishes or paper towels for flour or breadcrumbs when you have to bread something; use them and trash them...

A nine piece glass nesting bowl set – these are great to do all your prep work especially when doing things like stir frying or anywhere where you need to add ingredients quickly. Just place everything in its own bowl until you need it and dump it in when you're ready!

PAM® – the "wonder drug of the kitchen"...I spray PAM® on everything, cookie sheets, casserole pans, crock pots, spatulas, spoons, measuring cups (great if you're measuring sticky things like honey or peanut butter. Makes cleanup a breeze...use it! However, **don't use the garlic flavored on your cookie sheets**!

Disposable aluminum pans – I rarely ever use a real cookie sheet anymore when making cookies or breadsticks. I use the disposable and wash them in the dishwasher so they are good for a few uses. The ultimate in lazy cooking tips!

Cheap plastic containers – great for leftovers or for meals for college kids or older parents...cook a little extra and wrap the leftovers to share. Label with the name, date, and cooking directions...they will bless you for it! Your very own "meals on wheels"...

Buy a Cookie Baller - okay so a Dough Scoop – these are great when making cookies all one size, cocktail meatballs, etc.

Ore Ida® Frozen Onions – they are your friend...you may never cut an onion that you have to sauté again after using these. The only places they don't work are in salads or in something like sausage and peppers where you want bigger slices but other than that, they're wonderful!

Shredded Cheeses: What a great world we live in, you don't even have to grate your cheese anymore, it's already done for you!

A kitchen torch – great for crème brulee, baked Alaska, meringues, etc. Word of warning do not use near little kids, anything flammable, or with long hair – **a little common sense goes a long way here!**

Pan Scrapers – They cost about a dollar in Bed Bath and Beyond® and sure make clean-up easier!

Frozen appetizers, desserts, etc – great for unexpected company; either make your own or visit BJ's or Costco and keep a few boxes in the freezer if you have the space!

Large Pots – When you make soup or "gravy" (tomato sauce) make tons divide and freeze it...do the work once and when you're pressed for time, microwave to defrost, cook some pasta and dinner.

Peeled Whole Garlic – this is another great invention. Check the produce department of your grocery store for this product. I know BJ's carries it. I don't like the ones in oil, these are just whole unpeeled garlic cloves...what a time saver. Unless you really do large volumes try to buy a small container or buy a larger one and split it with a friend because they can get moldy (white) if you open them and don't use them frequently. In my house I could buy them in tubs, and it wouldn't be enough!

Store Bought Pizza Dough – great for unexpected company...keep some sauce in the freezer, a bag of shredded mozzarella in the refrigerator and instant dinner! Just because you're a great cook doesn't mean you can't take a shortcut now and then.

If you are having a crowd for breakfast, make your sausages and bacon ahead of time on cookie sheets in the oven, no grease all over, but watch carefully, they cook quickly. Just place the sausages on sheets, and separate the bacon slices and you can overlap them slightly and as they shrink, they'll separate. Keep warm in chafing dishes! This is much easier than frying in large quantities.

Plastic Garbage Bags – these make great mixing bowls if you to mix large quantities, like when you make Muddy Buddies. Easy clean-up too...just toss and go!

CHICKEN AND BROCCOLI CASSEROLE
Shirley Flomenhoft

2 (10 ounce) packages frozen broccoli
2 whole cooked chicken breasts
¼ cup butter
¼ cup flour
½ teaspoons salt
Dash black pepper

2 tablespoons dry white wine
½ teaspoons dry mustard
1 cup chicken broth
½ cup light cream (or milk)
1 cup shredded cheddar cheese
Grated Parmesan Cheese

Cook broccoli; drain and cut spears into smaller pieces. Remove skin and bone from chicken breasts; slice meat. Melt butter in a medium sauce, blend in flour, salt and pepper, mustard. Stir in chicken broth and cream. Cover and cook over medium heat, stirring constantly, until sauce thickens and bubbles, (about 1 minute) add cheese and stir until melted. Stir in wine. Remove from heat. Arrange broccoli spears in the bottom of greased 8 to 9-inch baking dish. Overlap slices of chicken on broccoli. Pour sauce over, sprinkle with Parmesan cheese. Bake in a 350° oven for 35 minutes or until heated and top starts to bubble. Serve with rice.

Aunt Shirley was very excited over the cook book project and contributed this and many other recipes.

The Flomenhoft-Weiner Family L-R: Nadia, Brad Weiner, Leslie Solitrin, Marc Solitrin, Shirley and Harvey Flomenhoft, Terri Freedman, Marc Freedman, Hal Weiner

CHICKEN AND DUMPLINGS
Katherine Avella

1 medium onion, peeled and chopped
3 stalks celery, thinly sliced
3 cloves garlic, peeled and crushed
6 tablespoons butter
½ cup flour
2 teaspoons sugar
1 teaspoon salt

1 teaspoon basil
½ teaspoon black pepper
4 cups College Inn® Chicken Broth
1 package frozen baby peas
1 whole store bought oven roasted chicken; cut into cubes
(about 5 cups)

Dumplings:
2 cups Bisquick®
2 teaspoons dried basil or herb of your choice

⅔ cup milk

In a deep saucepan or large frying pan, melt the butter and add the celery, onions, and garlic; sauté until the onions are starting to caramelize and get light brown. Add the flour, sugar, salt, basil, black pepper and broth(you may want to dilute the flour with some of the broth before adding it in to prevent lumps); bring to a boil. Cook, stirring frequently for 1 minute. Lower the heat, add the peas and cook another 5 minutes; stir constantly. The sauce should be thickening. Add the chicken. Pour into a large (at least 13 x 9 x 2-inch baking pan that has been sprayed with PAM®. In a separate bowl, mix the Bisquick with the basil. Stir in the milk. Drop by tablespoonfuls over the chicken mixture forming 12 dumplings. Preheat the oven to 350°; bake for 30 minutes. Cover the pan with aluminum foil (lightly) and bake an additional 12 minutes or until the dumplings are done. Serves 4-6.

This is one of Marc's favorite dinners and so easy to make with the ease of rotisserie chickens already pre-cooked. This can be ready in no time at all.

DRESSED-UP ZUCCHINI CASSEROLE
Elise Feiner

1 (12 ounce) package or can of chicken flavored
Stove Top® dressing mix
½ cup butter for Stovetop mix, melted
6 cups zucchini, peeled and sliced
¼ cup onion, peeled and chopped

½ stick butter
1 cup sour cream
1 cup cream of chicken soup
1 cup carrots, grated

Combine crumb and seasoning Stove Top packets with ½ cup melted butter or margarine. Layer half of the mixture in 9 x 13-inch pan. Sauté the zucchini and onions in half a stick of butter for about 5 minutes. Drain well. Spread over the Stovetop mixture. Combine sour cream and undiluted Cream of Chicken soup with 1 cup grated raw carrots. Pour over zucchini. Top with rest of Stovetop mixture. Bake 30 minutes at 350°. Serves 6.

This is a great side dish to serve with chicken or pork.

HAM AND POTATO CASSEROLE
Elise Feiner

1 clove garlic, peeled
2 tablespoons butter, softened
1 large onion, peeled and sliced
2 tablespoons olive oil
4 ounces Black Forest ham sliced ¼- inch thick, finely diced
4 ounces grated Swiss cheese

4 large eggs, lightly beaten
½ cup heavy cream or half and half
¼ cup grated cheese
1 pound Yukon Gold potatoes, peeled and grated
Salt and pepper, to taste
3 tablespoons butter, cut into tiny cubes

Preheat the oven to 375°. Cut the clove of garlic in half and rub it all over a 2 quart baking dish. Take the other half and crush it and add it to the 2 tablespoons of butter. Rub all over the dish. In a small frying pan, heat the olive oil and sauté the onions until golden brown. In a large mixing bowl, combine the ham, cooked onions, Swiss cheese, eggs, grated cheese and cream. Carefully squeeze the water out of the potatoes and add to the egg mixture; season with salt and pepper. Place the mixture in the prepared pan. Place butter cubes over the top and bake for 40 to 45 minutes or until lightly browned. Serves 4 to 6.

TACO PIE LAUREN
Elise Feiner

2 pounds ground beef
1 can (10 ¾ ounce) Campbell's® Condensed Tomato Soup
1 jar (16 ounces) thick and Chunky Salsa (I use Tostitos® Mild)
1 can (use the soup can to measure) milk

6 flour tortilla or 8 corn tortillas cut into tiny triangles
4 cups Sargento® Mexican Cheese Mix or any Mexican Cheese Mix, shredded

In a skillet over medium high heat, in a little oil or sprayed with PAM®, cook beef until browned, stirring to separate the meat. Pour off the fat. To cut the tortillas, cut the circles in half and then half again to make 4 quarters. Then cut each quarter into small triangles. In a large oval rectangle pan or Pyrex® pan, spray with PAM. Add the soup, salsa, milk, tortillas, and half the cheese, and the browned beef. Cover. Bake at 400° 30 minutes or until hot. Sprinkle with remaining cheese. Bake uncovered for about 10 to 15 more minutes until cheese melts and it's browned. Serves 4

This recipe was a Campbell® Soup recipe, but I changed it a little. It takes 10 minutes to make; a great fast one pan dinner. David, Lauren and Marc just love it.

"Nani" Jeane Cassata and her
"adopted" granddaughter
Lauren Feiner...
Jeane has only grandsons, so
Lauren has become her
official granddaughter!

MOZZARELLA AND EGGPLANT CASSEROLE
Elise Feiner

1 large eggplant, peeled and cut into ½- inch cubes
1 stick of butter
1 medium onion, cubed
2 cloves of garlic, crushed
1 pound of chopped meat
1 tablespoon fresh parsley

1 teaspoon Worcestershire sauce
2 teaspoons salt
⅛ teaspoon of black pepper
1(2-3 cups) bag shredded mozzarella
1 unbaked pie crust

In a large frying pan, sauté the eggplant in 6 tablespoons of the butter until soft. Cover and let cook for a little while. Remove the eggplant from the pan and drain with a slotted spoon. Sauté the onion and the garlic in the remaining 2 tablespoons of butter until the onions are soft, and starting to brown. Add the chopped meat and sauté until browned. Drain off any excess grease from the meat. Mix the meat with all the remaining ingredients except the mozzarella. Add the eggplant mix; blend well. Pour into the pie shell. Top with the mozzarella. Bake at 375° for about an hour. If getting too browned, cover with foil. Let cool a few minutes before serving.

SALMON CASSEROLE
Nancy Barfield

1 can of salmon
1 package of cooked spinach
1 can of cream of tomato soup

1 tablespoon of Worcestershire sauce
1 bag of golden egg noodles
1 small package of sharp cheddar cheese, grated

Mix the spinach, soup, salmon and Worcestershire sauce. Cook the bag of noodles according to package directions. Put the noodles in a baking dish, spread the salmon mixture over the noodles, then put the cheese on top. Depending on the size of your pan you could layer this more than once. Cook at 350° for about 35 to 40 minutes, until mixture is heated through and cheese has melted.

Nancy says this makes a great side dish.

TACO BAKE
Lauren Feiner

1 package Kraft® Deluxe Macaroni and Cheese Dinner
1 pound ground beef
1 (1¼ ounce size) package taco seasoning mix

¾ cup Breakstone® sour cream
1½ cups Kraft® Shredded Cheddar Cheese, divided
1 cup salsa

Prepare the dinner as directed on the package. Meanwhile, brown meat in a skillet; drain. Add taco seasoning-mix and ¾-cup water to meat. Simmer 5 minutes. Stir sour cream into prepared Dinner. Spoon half of the Dinner mixture into a 2 quart baking dish; top with layer of meat mixture, 1 cup of cheese and remaining Dinner mixture. Cover. Bake at 400° for 15 minutes. Top with salsa and remaining cheese. Bake uncovered, 5 more minutes. Serves 6.

This is a mix of two of Lauren's favorite things...mac and cheese and taco pie; a perfect marriage. This was generously reprinted with permission of the Kraft Foods. Visit their website kraftfoods.com for more recipe ideas.

A much younger Lauren Feiner at Halloween... maybe she was already getting ready for Las Vegas and her life in Casino Management??? Or maybe she's practicing to be a showgirl if all else fails...

LINGUINI - SAUSAGE CASSEROLE
Elise Feiner

1 box (1 pound) linguini
2 tablespoons butter
1 pound Italian Sausage, (sweet, or you can mix sweet and hot) bulk
1 tablespoon olive oil
1 medium onion, peeled and finely chopped (1 cup)
1 green pepper, seeded and finely chopped
3 teaspoons oregano
1 (3.5 ounce) can pitted black olives, chopped
½ cup parsley, finely chopped

½ teaspoon salt
½ teaspoon pepper
3 eggs, slightly beaten
1 (15 ounce) container ricotta
¼ cup grated Locatelli-Romano
3 tomatoes thinly sliced
1 package shredded mozzarella
1 cup shredded Swiss or Gruyere cheese
1 tablespoon grated Parmesan cheese
Cream sauce (optional)

Cook linguini in lightly salted water until almost but not completely done. Toss with butter in a large bowl; cover. Preheat oven to 375°. Lightly grease and flour a 10-inch spring form pan. Heat the oil in a large skillet; remove the sausage from casing if necessary and brown, stirring for about 10 minutes. Remove any excess fat. Add the onion, green pepper, and 1 teaspoon of oregano; sauté 5 minutes. Combine the sausage mixture, olives, parsley, salt and pepper with the linguini; toss gently to combine. Whisk together the eggs, ricotta, remaining oregano, and Locatelli Romano cheese in a medium bowl until light and fluffy. Stir in linguini mixture; toss gently to combine. Press half the linguini mixture into the prepared pan. Arrange half the tomatoes over the linguini. Sprinkle half of the mozzarella and Swiss cheese. Repeat the layers again. Sprinkle the tomatoes on the top with the parmesan cheese. Cover tightly with aluminum foil. (You can refrigerate for 2 days at this point if you'd like). Bake at 375° or 50 minutes of until set. Remove foil; bake an additional 5 minutes. Let stand 10 minutes. Slice into wedges. If you want to freeze this omit the tomatoes from the recipe. Defrost overnight in the refrigerator and then place the tomato slices on the top (you will use half the amount). Bake 375° for 1 hour and 45 minutes covered with foil. Remove foil; bake another 15 minutes. Serve with cream sauce if desired. Serves 6.

Cream Sauce:

¼ cup butter
¼ cup flour
¼ cup milk
1 cup heavy cream

Pinch of ground nutmeg
1 teaspoon salt
⅛ teaspoon white pepper
½ cup grated Locatelli Romano

Melt butter in a medium saucepan. Whisk in the flour. Gradually add the milk and cream stirring constantly. Cook over medium-high heat, stirring constantly until the sauce comes to a boil and is thick and smooth. Lower heat and let simmer, still stirring 2-3 minutes. Remove from pan. Stir in nutmeg, salt and pepper. Stir in grated cheese. Keep warm until ready to serve.

NINA'S RICE CASSEROLE
Nina D'Amico

Meatballs, cooked 1 per person or leftover meatloaf, crumbled
1-2 cups peas, depending on the number of meatballs used
2 cups rice, cooked and drained according to package directions

¼ cup Reggiano Parmigiano, grated
2 eggs, beaten
2 cups marinara sauce

In a bowl mix sauce, meat, rice and peas. Grease a 9 x 13-inch casserole dish. Spread in the meat mix evenly. Beat eggs and cheese together. Pour over the top. Bake at 350° for 30 minutes until set.

Nina is Ann's 91 year old mother-in-law. It's a great way to use up your leftovers.

Our Italian Cousin comes to visit...
L-R: Phil, Joe, Katherine, and Michael Avella, Maria Campestre, Josephine Mainella, Philip Avella, Jr., Marc Feiner

PINEAPPLE CASSEROLE
Ann D'Amico

1 large can crushed pineapple (drained)
¼ cup sugar
½ cup water with 1½ tablespoons of cornstarch dissolved in it
2 beaten eggs

Dash salt
1 small can of mandarin orange segments (drained)
Can of apricot halves, drained
A few pats of butter, cubed
Cinnamon

In a large bowl, mix everything but the mandarin orange segments, apricots, butter and cinnamon. Mix well. Add the oranges. Pour into a buttered 9 x 13-inch casserole. Place apricot halves on the top. Dot the top with butter, and sprinkle with cinnamon. Bake at 375° until well set. Serve by the spoonfuls. Make be served hot or cold.

The original called for ½ cup sugar, and not to drain the pineapple. I found it was too sweet, so I changed it. It is great with any kind of meat as a side dish.

Seated L-R: Nina D'Amico, Ralph Tarantino, Jenny Tarantino, and Julia Silvestri

Standing L-R: Katherine, Samuel and Flo Avella at Julia's 85th Birthday Party

TUNA PIE
Elise Feiner

4 tablespoons butter
1 small green or red pepper, chopped (⅓ cup)
1 small onion (about ¼ cup), peeled and chopped
¼ cup plus 2 tablespoons Original Bisquick® baking mix
¾ teaspoon salt
¼ teaspoon black pepper

3 cups milk
4 (6 ounce) cans tuna in oil drained
1 (14 ounce) package frozen chopped broccoli, thawed and drained
1 tablespoon lemon juice

For Biscuits:

2¼ cups Bisquick® Original baking mix
⅔ cup milk

1 (6 ounce) cup cheddar cheese, shredded

Heat oven to 425°. Grease the bottom and sides of a rectangle pan 13 x 9 x 2-inch with shortening. Melt butter in a 3 quart saucepan over medium heat. Cook bell pepper and onion in butter 3 to 5 minutes stirring occasionally, until softened. Stir in Bisquick, salt and pepper. Cook over medium heat, stirring constantly until smooth and bubbly, remove from heat. Gradually stir in milk. Heat to boiling, stirring constantly. Boil and stir 1 minute; remove from heat. Stir in tuna, broccoli, and lemon juice. Pour into pan; keep hot while making the biscuits. You can also do this in individual baking dishes or small disposable aluminum pans if you want to freeze it in individual portions. Make swirl biscuits. Place biscuits on top of the tuna mixture. Bake uncovered 20 to 25 minutes until mixture is bubbly and tops are golden brown. Serves 8.

Swirl Biscuits:

Stir Bisquick and milk until soft dough forms. Place dough on surfaced sprinkled with Bisquick; knead 10 times. Roll dough into a 15 x 9-inch rectangle. Sprinkle with cheese. Roll up tightly, beginning at 15-inch side. Pinch edge of dough into roll to seal. Cut into 12 slices, about ¼ -inch wide.

The original recipe came from a Betty Crocker® cookbook, but I changed it and added more tuna, and seasonings. I made this to freeze for Jeff, so he would have quick dinners. I divided it into smaller portions and froze it so he could bake it later.

MOUSSAKA
Peggy Spirakis

8 long narrow eggplants (or 5 to 6 medium sizes)
Extra olive oil, for greasing pan and brushing eggplant
2 cups chopped onion
¼ cup water
3 tablespoons olive oil
3 pounds very lean ground beef or ground lamb
½ teaspoon salt
Pepper, to taste (ground fresh)
¼ teaspoon nutmeg
½ teaspoon cinnamon
1 teaspoon sugar

2 tablespoons butter, plus 4 tablespoons, for topping
1 (15-ounce) can tomato sauce
¼ cup ketchup
½ pound Parmesan or Romano cheese, freshly grated
12 to 14 Royal® (or any brand) milk biscuits finely crushed or cracker meal
11 large eggs
1 cup milk
15 x 10-inch deep pan greased (with olive oil)
Jelly roll pan

Peel and slice eggplant into ¼-inch slices lengthwise. Sprinkle with salt. Place in a colander to drain (about 30 minutes). Rinse and let dry between paper towels. Preheat oven to 350°. Place eggplant onto well oiled jelly roll pans. Brush with olive oil. Bake 10 to 15 minutes until tender. Set aside. In a large skillet cook onions in ¼-cup water, 3 tablespoons olive oil and ¼ teaspoon salt until onions are clear. Remove and set aside. In the same skillet, brown meat. Add cooked onions, salt, pepper, nutmeg, cinnamon, sugar, tomato sauce, ketchup and 2 tablespoons of butter. Cook; stirring well. Reduce sauce until almost dry and set aside. In 15 x 10-inch greased pan sprinkle ½ of the cracker crumbs to cover the bottom (the rest will be used for the top). Place a layer of eggplant close together over cracker crumbs. Top with ⅓ of the grated cheese. Add ½ of the meat mixture. Spread evenly. Repeat once more and top with eggplant and cracker crumbs. Sprinkle the remaining Parmesan cheese. Beat 11 eggs and 1 cup of milk together well or substitute the béchamel sauce (see recipe for béchamel sauce below). Spoon entire mixture on top of moussaka, wetting all crumbs and cheese. Drizzle top with 4 tablespoons melted butter. Bake in 350° oven for 50 to 60 minutes until golden brown on top and knife inserted in center comes out clean. Cool and cut into diamonds or squares. Serve warm. This recipe freezes well. Thaw and cut into pieces and heat through. Serves about 15.

BÉCHAMEL SAUCE FOR MOUSSAKA
Peggy Spirakis

If you want more traditional moussaka use béchamel custard as follows:

4 tablespoons butter
4 tablespoons flour
2 cups milk
2 cups heavy cream
¼ teaspoon freshly grated nutmeg

¼ cup lemon juice
3 egg yolks
½ cup Parmesan cheese
Salt and Freshly ground black pepper

In a saucepan, melt the butter. Add the flour to make a roux. Cook the roux over medium heat for 3 or 4 minutes, or until it becomes a very pale tan color. Slowly add the milk, whisking constantly. Add the nutmeg and the lemon juice. Simmer, stirring constantly, over low heat for 15 minutes. The mixture should be fairly thick. In a separate bowl, whisk the eggs together. Take ½-cup of the hot milk mixture and whisk it into the beaten eggs. This will temper the eggs. Whisk the egg/milk mixture back into the milk mixture. Add the Parmesan cheese and stir. Over very low heat, cook this mixture for 3 more minutes. Be careful not to let the mixture simmer. Season well. **Remember, this substitutes for the 11 eggs and 1 cup of milk in Moussaka recipe above.**

Sam's Bridal Shower

L-R: Lenore Mami, Marsha Tolino, Fran Cassata Zierler, Jeane Tolino Cassata, Camille Cassata Sanabria and Samantha Caplan (soon to be Zierler)

BAKED RICE CASSEROLE
Katherine Avella

4 cups rice
1 stick of butter
2 tablespoons chopped or dried parsley
Salt and pepper to taste
3-4 eggs, beaten

1 quart of milk
1 cup grated cheese
3 tablespoons unflavored bread crumbs
3 tablespoons butter cut into small cubes for the top of the casserole

Preheat the oven to 375°. Using 2½ cups of water for each cup of rice, bring the water to a boil. Add rice slowly; cover and cook over a low flame. When the rice is cooked, put into a large mixing bowl. Quickly add the butter so it will melt. Add the milk, eggs and cheese. Add the salt and pepper to taste. Put into a greased baking pan. Sprinkle with breadcrumbs and dot with butter. Bake about 25 to 30 minutes or until golden brown. Allow to set before serving. Cut into squares or spoon to serve. Serves 8 to 10.

ORIENTAL CABBAGE CASSEROLE
Elise Feiner

1 medium head of cabbage, chopped
1 cup of celery, chopped
1 red bell pepper, seeded and chopped in small pieces
1 cup of onions chopped

3 scallions finely chopped
1 can Chinese vegetables
1 can water chestnuts, sliced
½ stick Butter

Cheese Sauce:

3 tablespoons butter
3 tablespoons flour
1½ cups heavy cream or 1 can cream of mushroom soup
½ pound sharp cheddar cheese, grated

Dash of Tabasco Sauce
1 teaspoon Accent
Chinese noodles

Boil the cabbage in a small amount of salted water for five minutes and drain. Sauté all the vegetables except the cabbage in the butter. Butter a baking dish and layer the cabbage, then vegetables, repeating until all the layers are used. Pour the cheese sauce over all and top with Chinese Noodles. Make the cheese sauce by melting the butter and add the flour stirring quickly so it doesn't get lumpy. Add the cream or the soup stirring quickly so you don't get lumps. Heat until it thickens. Add the Tabasco, and Accent. Stir in the cheese until it melts.

L-R: Joanne Keats, Toby Usenheimer, Susie Zeidner, Sheila Bamberger

NANCY'S SLOPPY JOES
Nancy Barfield

2 pounds ground beef (brown first in a frying pan; drain grease)
Fried Potatoes (great if you have some left over baked or boiled potatoes) I used oil to fry them in a pan

1 (10 ounce) box of spinach, cooked according to package directions, set aside
3 or 4 eggs scrambled with milk
1 can of stewed tomatoes with onions and peppers
grated cheddar cheese

Cook the ground beef and potatoes I put them in the same frying pan. Add in the cooked spinach Add in the eggs and mix well. Add in the can of stewed tomatoes; then after that is all cooked at the last minute add in the grated cheese and serve.

Nancy says, "I also put on grated parmesan cheese after I put it on the plate. It's good, makes a lot and very fast to make."

Nancy Barfield in a rare quiet moment…

My cousin Joan and Ron Calabrese's newest grandchild Nicholas Moore with his big sister Meghan Kangmeister

ZUCCHINI CASSEROLE FANTASTIQUE
Elise Feiner

6-7 zucchini, peeled and sliced
1 large onion, peeled and chopped
1 stick butter
1 cup carrots, grated
1 can cream of chicken soup
1 package Stovetop Stuffing® Chicken Flavored

1 cup sour cream
1 pound sweet Italian sausage, fried, crumbled, and drained well
½ cup parmesan cheese
1 large mozzarella cheese, or 1 package of Swiss cheese, cut in slices

In a large pan, sauté the onions in the butter. Add the zucchini and cook until softened; add the remaining ingredients except the mozzarella, or Swiss cheese. Top with the mozzarella or Swiss cheese. Pour into a baking pan that has been sprayed with PAM®. Bake at 350° for 45 minutes to 1 hour until heated thoroughly and cheese is melted. If the cheese is getting to brown, cover with foil for awhile. Serves 6.

You can't deny genetics...L-R: my son Jeffrey Feiner at his high school
graduation and my father Sam Avella both age 18...bookends!

"If your children spend most of their time in other people's houses, you're lucky; if they all congregate at your house, you're blessed."
- Mignon McLaughlin

And still more Fathers and Daughters…

Erica and Frank Basile

Sophia and Carl Fsadni

Marc and Lauren Feiner

L-R: Maryann Maida, Michele Maida, and Elise Feiner,
"The Third Daughter," and Ernest Maida

Robert Pavelock,
M.D.
and daughter
Natalie

Marc
Freedman
and
daughter
Nikki

JAMBALAYA
Elise Feiner

1 cup onion, peeled and chopped
1 cup green bell pepper, chopped
1 cup celery, chopped
3 cloves garlic, finely chopped
1 (28 ounce) can diced tomatoes, undrained
2 cups fully cooked smoked sausage, chopped
1 tablespoon parsley flakes

½ teaspoon salt
½ teaspoon dried thyme leaves
¼ teaspoon pepper
¼ red pepper sauce or Tabasco Sauce
¾ pound uncooked, peeled deveined medium shrimp, thawed if frozen
4 cups hot cooked rice

Mix all ingredients, except shrimp and rice in a 6 quart slow cooker or crock-pot. Cover and cook on low setting 7 to 8 hours until vegetables are tender. Stir in shrimp. Cover and cook on low heat setting for about 30 minutes or until shrimp are pink and firm. Serve with rice.

MUSHROOM STEW
Maria Trainor

3 pounds pork cubes
6-8 cloves of garlic, sliced thin
Olive oil, enough to cover the pan
1 green pepper, cut into small cubes
1 large onion, peeled and diced
2 bay leaves
Dash of crushed red pepper

2-3 large cans of Cora crushed tomatoes, plus half that amount of water
Salt and pepper to taste
1 can straw mushrooms
1 box of button mushrooms sliced
1 package of sliced portabella mushrooms (cut into smaller pieces)

Place the olive oil in a hot frying pan. Add the garlic. Brown the pork cubes then remove and set them aside. Add the peppers and onions to the frying pan and cook for a few minutes. At this point you can cook this in a crock-pot, or on top of the stove. In either case, add all the remaining ingredients to a crock-pot or large pot. Cook in the crock-pot on low for 6 hours, or cook on top of the stove on medium to low heat for about 2 to 3 hours.

Maria, Jonathan, Kristin Gigliotti and I went to see Lauren when she was a student at Phillips Exeter Academy. For three days, we exchanged recipes. This is delicious, and freezes very well. This is also great served in a bread bowl for a luncheon.

STOVETOP IN A CROCK-POT
Elise Feiner

2 packages of Stovetop® Savory Herb Stuffing
1 package of Jiffy® Cornbread Mix, prepared according to package. Let cool and cube it.
2 cups of chopped onion
2 cups of chopped celery

1 cup of butter
½ teaspoon sage
½ teaspoon thyme
About 4 cups of chicken broth
1 egg

In a medium frying pan, sauté the onions and celery in the butter until soft and light brown. Mix all the remaining ingredients together in crock-pot; place it on high for 15 minutes, then on low for at least 3 to 4 hours.

This is great way to save oven space on Thanksgiving. Put it up when you put your turkey in, and by dinnertime it's ready to go.

L-R: George and Sherylynn Koerner and
Marc Feiner at the top of Diablo Mountain
in San Francisco

CROCK POT DRESSING
Elise Feiner

8-inch pan cornbread prepared and cubed
1 bag Pepperidge Farm® Stuffing Mix
1 sleeve saltine crackers
5 eggs, beaten
1 medium onion
Garlic salt to taste
1 cup chopped celery

1-2 teaspoon sage or poultry seasoning
1 teaspoon each of parsley and oregano
½ teaspoon black pepper
2 cans cream of chicken soup
4-5 cups chicken broth
2 sticks butter
1 jar mushrooms, drained (optional)

Lightly grease crock pot. Crumble cornbread into a mixing bowl. Sauté the celery, onions and mushrooms in the butter. Beat the eggs and add the spices to the eggs. Add remaining ingredients into crock pot. Add egg mix and butter/vegetable mix. Dot the top with butter. Cook on high 2 hours or on low 3 to 4 hours. Serves 12.

L-R: Gene Feiner,
Freda Feiner,
Ida Feldman,
and Jerome Feiner
on the Boardwalk in
Atlantic City, NJ

SUPER BOWL XXI CHILI
Iryna Trociuk

2½ pounds ground sirloin
2 tablespoons vegetable oil
8 garlic cloves, peeled and chopped
2 medium onions (peeled and chopped)
2 green peppers (chopped finely)
1 (2 pounds 8 ounce) large can red kidney beans, drained
1 large (12 ounce) can tomato paste
2 (1 pound 13 ounce) canned plum tomatoes diced or use
Crushed tomatoes
1 (15 ounce) can Hunts® Tomato Sauce

6 Hershey® kisses
2 teaspoons Tabasco sauce
4 teaspoons (or more) Chili Powder
2 teaspoons salt
1 teaspoon pepper
1 teaspoon cinnamon
½ teaspoon red pepper flakes
½ teaspoon Lea and Perrins® Worcestershire sauce

If you are doing this is a crock-pot use a large frying pan to brown the meat, if you are doing it on top of the stove use a large pot or Dutch oven. Brown garlic and ground sirloin in the oil. Drain all the fat. Add the red kidney beans, onions, green pepper; mix. (If you are doing this in the crock-pot add to the crock-pot at this point). Add plum tomatoes, salt, pepper, chili powder, Tabasco sauce, cinnamon, red pepper flakes, Worcestershire sauce, tomato paste and tomato sauce. Stir. Simmer over low heat if doing this on the stove stirring occasionally until desired thickness (about 1 to 1½ hours), or if doing this in the crock-pot cook on low for about 5 to 6 hours or automatic for 4 to 5 hours. Add the Hershey kisses at the very end (the secret ingredient) and stir well. You can adjust any of the seasonings from the Tabasco sauce to the Worcestershire sauce to your own taste. When ready to serve, sprinkle with shredded Colby and Monterey Jack Cheese or a Mexican Cheese Mix (comes packaged this way.) Serve with Tortilla chips and enjoy, or for an interesting twist, place some Fritos at the bottom of your serving bowl, add chili, top with cheese...yummy! Serves 6.

David had gone over to the Trociuk's to watch the Super Bowl and came home raving about Iryna's Chili. Whenever she made it, she would always freeze some for David to have when he came home from Exeter on his vacations. David begged me to get the recipe from her. She was generous enough to share her recipe with us and it has become a favorite of David and Marcs. I made some minor modifications, added the tomato sauce and kisses. This freezes very well if it lasts that long. Iryna did hers on the stove, but I did it in the crock-pot and it was great.

PORK TENDERLOINS IN THE CROCK-POT
Elise Feiner

2 package boneless pork loin chops (6 to a package) or
2 pork tenderloins
3 eggs, beaten
½ teaspoon garlic salt
⅛ teaspoon black pepper
3 tablespoons grated Parmesan cheese
¾ cup flour
¼ cup vegetable oil
1 large Bermuda onion (red), peeled and sliced
1 large Vidalia onion, peeled and sliced
5 potatoes, peeled and cubed
¼ cup Kahlua

1 (13¾ ounce) can Chicken Broth
1 can cream of mushroom soup
1 can Red Dog® Beer (or any beer)
2 tablespoons honey
½ tablespoons garlic salt
3 tablespoons mustard
1 box sliced mushrooms
1 handful olives (mixed, any kind you like)
½ pint heavy cream
1 (16 ounce) container sour cream
1 small can French Fried Onions (Durkee®)
Blue cheese, crumbled

Beat the eggs with garlic salt, pepper, grated parmesan cheese. Roll the tenderloins in flour, then in the egg mixture, and then back in the flour. Heat the oil in a large frying pan. Add the tenderloins and brown then, but don't cook them. Remove from the oil and set aside. Add the onions to the pan and sauté until soft and slightly brown. Remove from the pan and place in the crock-pot. Add all the rest of the ingredients (except for the blue cheese and fried onions) to the crock-pot. Add the tenderloins. Cook on automatic for 6 hours. Serve with buttered noodles, or the Fran's Cabbage and Noodles (see recipe index). You can add a little flour at the end to thicken the sauce if desired. Add the flour to cold water first and then whisk it in quickly. Let cook about ten minutes after you add the flour. Slice to serve. After you slice it put some of the sauce on it, top with crumbled blue cheese and fried onions.

SPIRAL HAM IN A CROCKPOT
Carol Zuchowski

1 large Spiral Ham
1 cup of water

Aluminum Foil

Wrap the spiral ham in aluminum foil. Place in the crock-pot and add one cup of water. Cook on low 6-8 hours or on high 4-6 hours. Be careful of the liquid when you lift it out, have something nearby to let it drain into. Cut and serve. It's so moist; you'll never want to make it in the oven again!

PORK CHOPS IN GRAVY
Elise Feiner

2 pounds boneless pork chops (the thicker ones are best or pork tenderloins)
3 tablespoons oil
2 cans cream of mushroom soup or cream of celery or
1 can of each
Garlic salt and black pepper to taste

1 can cream of onion soup
1 can Coke® or Pepsi®
1 package dry onion soup mix
1 small can of mushrooms

In a large skillet or frying pan, heat the oil. Brown the pork chops lightly. Remove. Place all the ingredients except the mushrooms in the crock-pot, and cook on low all day (about 7 hours). Add mushrooms to pot about 30 minutes before serving. Serve over rice or noodles.

L-R: Maddelena, Angela
and Dino Grassi

PEPPER STEAK IN A CROCK-POT
Elise Feiner

2 pounds beef round steak
2 tablespoons oil
¼ cup soy sauce
1 cup chopped onions
2 cloves garlic, peeled and chopped
1 teaspoon sugar
½ teaspoon salt

¼ teaspoon pepper
 ¼ teaspoon ground ginger
1 (16 ounce) can whole plum tomatoes with liquid, broken up
2 large green peppers, cut in strips
1 tablespoon cornstarch
½ cup cold water

Cut the beef into 3 x 1-inch strips. Heat the oil in a skillet. Brown the strips. Transfer strips to a crock-pot. Add everything but the tomatoes, green peppers, cornstarch and water. Cook on low for 5 to 6 hours or until meat is tender. Add the tomatoes and green peppers; cook on low for an additional hour. Mix the cornstarch and water and make a paste. Stir into the liquid in the crock-pot and cook on high until thickened. Serve with rice.

You can also use 4 fresh tomatoes cut into 8 pieces each if you want to. I found this on the internet and it's great! I love crock-pot recipes because you can start them in the morning and never have to worry about your dinner. Crock-pot recipes are great for the working Mom or student.

CROCK-POT STUFFED PORK CHOPS
Elise Feiner

4 boneless pork center chops
⅓ cup celery, chopped fine
¼ cup carrots, chopped fine
½ cup onions, chopped fine
1 tablespoon olive oil
2 tablespoons butter
¼ cup chopped pecans
2 cups soft breadcrumbs

1 egg
½ teaspoon sage
½ teaspoon thyme
1 teaspoon parsley
Kosher salt
Freshly ground black pepper
4-6 medium potatoes, peeled and quartered
3 teaspoons butter, cut in small cubes

Cut each chop horizontally through the center, but not completely through to butterfly. Place between plastic wrap and gently pound with a meat mallet to thin the chops out. Season with salt and pepper to taste. You can also substitute thin pork cutlets if you can find them. Melt 2 tablespoons of butter with the olive oil in a skillet over medium heat. Sauté the celery, onions, and carrots until lightly browned and tender. Put the vegetable mix into a mixing bowl; add breadcrumbs, chopped pecans, sage, parsley, thyme, salt and pepper. Mix until moistened. Place some of the stuffing mix into each chop; or onto each thin pork chop (roll up) and secure with a toothpick. Place the potatoes in the crock-pot; dot with cubes of butter. Season with salt and pepper to taste. Place the pork rolls on top of the potatoes in the crock-pot. Sprinkle with any remaining stuffing mix. Cover and cook on low for 7 to 9 hours.

CROCK-POT PORK AND POTATOES
Elise Feiner

6 boneless pork chops
6 potatoes peeled and sliced ¼-inch thick
1 small can mushrooms
½ (12 ounce) bag frozen onions

Salt and pepper to taste
1 bag shredded cheddar cheese
1 can cream of mushroom soup
½ pint heavy cream (optional)

You can use more pork chops and potatoes depending on the number of servings you need. Peel and slice the potatoes into ¼-inch thick rounds, and layer them halfway up your crock-pot sprinkling the onions, cheese, and salt and pepper as you layer. Sprinkle salt and pepper on the pork chops. Place the pork chops over the potatoes; top with the soup (you may want to add an additional can of soup if you increase the other ingredients. Cook on medium heat for 6 to 8 hours. The juice from the pork mixes with the soup and makes scalloped potatoes. You can also add half pint of cream if desired.

PORK CHOPS IN THE CROCK-POT
Elise Feiner

6-8 pork chops (boneless)
¼ cup Wondra® Flour
½ teaspoon garlic salt
¼ teaspoon black pepper
Vegetable oil
2 cans cream of mushroom soup
1 (12 ounce) can of Pepsi®

1 can (13¾ ounce) College Inn® Chicken Broth
1 package Lipton® Onion Soup Mix
3 tablespoon mustard
1 container or box sliced mushrooms
1 pint heavy cream
3 cloves garlic, peeled and left whole
Salt and pepper to taste

Mix the Wondra flour, garlic salt and black pepper together. Dredge the pork chops in the flour mixture. (Save some of the remaining flour mixture in case you want to thicken the sauce at the end of cooking.) In a large frying pan, place enough vegetable oil to cover the bottom of the pan. Heat the oil; brown the chops. When nicely browned but not completely cooked, remove from pan and place in a crock-pot.

Add the chicken broth to the drippings in the pan and scrap the bottom of the pan. Pour the whole mix over the chops in the crock-pot. Add all the remaining ingredients except for the mushrooms, to the crock-pot. Stir well. Let the chops cook on low for 6 to 8 hours, or high 4 to 6 hours. Add the mushrooms and heavy cream during the last half hour of cooking. Serve over rice. If you would like the sauce to be a little thicker use a few tablespoons of the leftover flour mixture, and add it to cool water. Mix the flour and water until very thin. Add to crock-pot and allow to thicken a few minutes before serving. Throw out any of the remaining flour mixture. Serves 4 to 6.

BBQ PORK SANDWICHES
Elise Feiner

2-3 pork tenderloins, small thin ones
2 onions peeled and diced or 1 (12 ounce) bag of frozen diced onions
2 (13¾ ounce) cans College Inn® Chicken Broth

Garlic salt and pepper to taste
2 (16 ounce) bottles of your favorite barbeque sauce (I like Jack Daniels®)

Place the tenderloins, chicken broth, garlic salt and pepper in a crock pot and cook on high for about 4½ to 5½ hours. Remove the pork from the crock-pot and shred the pork by pulling it apart with 2 forks or by using your fingers. Remove the onions from the crock-pot with a slotted spoon and add it to the shredded pork. Remove all but about ¼ to ½ cup of the liquid from the crock-pot and discard the excess liquid. Add the pork to the remaining cup of liquid in the crock-pot. Add the barbeque sauce and cook another 1½ hours. Serve on buns. You can also serve this over nacho or tortilla chips. Place the nacho chips in a soup bowl. Pour some melted Cheese Whiz® over the chips, and top with the pork. It's great this way. Serves 6 to 8.

This is a great recipe and so easy to do. It takes about 5 minutes to throw it in the crock-pot, and then just let it cook. It's great on a cold winter night. It freezes well if you have any leftover. My son David and husband Marc love this! When we were in New Orleans, they served it with the Cheese Whiz and tortilla chips, mmmmm good.

BARBEQUE TURKEY BREAST
Elise Feiner

7-10 pound turkey breast
Salt and pepper
3 large onions, peeled and diced
3 cloves garlic, peeled and crushed
½ cup ketchup
1 cup cider vinegar

1 can beer
1 stick butter
1 tablespoons soy sauce
1 tablespoon Lea and Perrin® Worcestershire sauce
½ teaspoon black pepper

Season the breast with salt and pepper. Brown the turkey breast in a large pan in a tiny bit oil. Add turkey breast and remaining ingredients to a crock pot and let simmer 6 to 8 hours. Remove the breast, discard all the bones and skin and shred the turkey. Return to the sauce and let cook another half hour. Serve on hard rolls. Serves 6.

CHICKEN IN A CROCK-POT
Elise Feiner

6 large boneless skinless chicken breasts
½ cup dry white wine Vermouth
1 can cream of mushroom soup
1 (4 ounce) jar sliced mushrooms

1 cup sour cream
¼ cup flour
Paprika
Salt and pepper, to taste

Mix the flour together with the sour cream and set aside. Sprinkle the chicken breasts with salt, pepper, and paprika. Place in the crock-pot. Mix the soup, wine, and mushrooms together and then add in the flour mix. Pour over the chicken. Sprinkle a little more paprika over the chicken. Cover and cook on low for 6 to 8 hours. Serve over rice or noodles.

CHICKEN AND POTATOES IN A CROCK-POT
Elise Feiner

6 boneless skinless chicken breasts
3 tablespoons oil
5 potatoes, peeled and cubed
1 can cream of chicken soup

1 can cheddar cheese soup
½ teaspoon poultry seasoning
1 package Goya® Sazon seasonings
½ pint (8 ounces) heavy cream

In a large skillet, heat the oil and brown the chicken breasts lightly. Transfer the chicken to a crock-pot. Place the potatoes on top of the chicken. Mix the soups, seasonings, and heavy cream together. Pour over the chicken potato mix. Cover and cook on low about 6 to 8 hours.

CHICKEN STROGANOFF
Elise Feiner

6 boneless skinless chicken breasts
6 slices bacon
1 (8 ounce) container sour cream

1 can cream of mushroom soup
¼ cup flour
Freshly ground black pepper

Mix the sour cream, soup, flour and black pepper together. Wrap a piece of bacon around each chicken breast. Place the chicken in a crock-pot. Top with the sour cream mixture. Cover and cook on low about 8 hours. Serve over egg noodles.

L-R: Juda Reinisch, Ruth Kreger Lincoln, Betty Reinisch Feiner,
Freda Feldman Feiner, Ida Weinblatt Feldman, Nellie Billet Reinisch

BEEF STROGANOFF WITH WINE
Elise Feiner

3 pounds beef round steak
½ cup flour
2 teaspoons salt
⅛ teaspoon pepper
½ teaspoon dry mustard
2 medium onions, thinly sliced and separated into rings

2 (4 ounce) cans sliced mushrooms, drained or ½ pound mushrooms sliced
1 (10 ½ ounce) can condensed beef broth
¼ cup dry white wine
1½ cups sour cream
¼ cup flour

Trim the excess fat from the steak and cut into 3-inch strips about ½-inch wide. Mix the ½ cup flour, salt, pepper and dry mustard; toss with the steak strips and coat them thoroughly. Place the steak strips in the crock-pot; add in the onion rings and mushrooms. Add the beef broth, and wine and mix well. Cover and cook on low for 8 to 10 hours. Before serving, mix the sour cream with ¼ cup flour; stir into the crock-pot. Serve over noodles or rice. Serves 6.

BEEF STROGANOFF
Elise Feiner

2 pounds beef stew meat
1 cup chopped onions
¾ -1 cup flour
½ teaspoon garlic salt
Vegetable oil
1 can Cream of Golden Mushroom soup (*make sure it isn't regular Cream of Mushroom)
1 can Cream of Onion soup

1 (6 ounce) jar of mushrooms, drained (I use quartered fresh mushrooms)
¼ teaspoon pepper
1 (8 ounce) package cream cheese at room temperature, cubed
1 (8 ounce) container sour cream
Hot cooked noodles or rice (I use wide noodles)

Mix beef cubes, flour, garlic salt, and pepper together in a zip lock bag. Heat a few tablespoons of oil in the bottom of a large frying pan (enough to just cover the bottom of the pan.) Brown the cubes of meat for a few minutes; add and brown the onion. Place meat in the crock pot; add the soups. Add water to one of the cans of soup and use this water to scrape the drippings from the bottom of the frying pan and add to the crock pot. Cover and cook on low heat setting for 6 to 8 hours or until beef is very tender. After cooking for about 4 to 5 hours, add the mushrooms. About 30 to 45 minutes before serving, stir in cream cheese into beef mixture until melted. Stir in sour cream into beef mixture; cook until thoroughly heated. Serve over noodles or rice. Serves 8.

STUFFED STEAK ROLLS
Elise Feiner

2 pounds sandwich steaks, (not Steaks Umms) cut by butcher
1 (6 ounce) box Stove Top® Stuffing or other seasoned stuffing mix
4 slices bacon, diced
1 rib celery, diced
1 bunch green onions, diced

1 can cream of celery soup, undiluted
1 can cream of onion soup, undiluted
1 can cream of mushroom soup, undiluted
¼ - ½ cup water
1 medium onion, coarsely chopped
2 (14-16 ounce) cans stewed tomatoes

Pound each steak until thinned to about ¼-inch. Sauté bacon, celery, and green onions; drain off fat. Combine bacon and vegetable mix with the stuffing mix (including the seasoning packet that came with the mix, if any). Stir in the cream of celery soup and enough water to moisten. Place onions in the crock-pot. Spread stuffing mixture on each flattened steak; roll up and secure with a toothpick; place on top of onions. Spoon any extra stuffing around the rolls. Mix the cream of onion soup and cream of mushroom soup with the stewed tomatoes. Spoon the cream of onion soup-tomato mix over the rolls. Cover and cook 8 to 10 hours on low, or 4 to 6 hours on high. You can also use pork cutlets, veal or chicken cutlets thinly pounded. Serves 6.

This is one of my favorite meals. I've done it with pork, beef, and veal. It's easy, very delicious and great reheated.

"If you have never been hated by your child you have never been a parent."
- Bette Davis

CHILI
Elise Feiner

2 tablespoons olive oil	1 teaspoons cumin
2 pounds sirloin steak, cut into 1-inch cubes	1 teaspoon dried basil
½ pound ground beef	2 (13¾ ounce) cans beef broth
12 ounces chorizo sausage, casing removed, cut into	2 cans whole plum tomatoes, drained
½ cubes	1 cinnamon stick
1 large yellow onion, coarsely chopped	3 bay leaves
1 large (2 pounds 8 ounce) can red kidney beans, drained	Sour cream
¼ cup chili powder	Shredded cheddar cheese
1 tablespoon garlic salt	

Place oil in a large, heavy Dutch oven over medium heat. Brown the sirloin in batches. Remove to a bowl with a slotted spoon. Add ground beef, chorizo and onions to the pot and brown. Stir the meat to separate it. Put the sirloin back into the pot. Stir in remaining ingredients. Bring to a boil, reduce heat, and simmer for 2 hours. Stir occasionally, breaking up tomatoes. This can also be done in a crock-pot. After you've browned all the meats, add them to the crock-pot. Add remaining ingredients except sour cream and cheddar cheese. Cook on auto for 4 to 5 hours. Before serving, remove the cinnamon stick, and bay leaves. Top with sour cream and shredded cheddar cheese. Serves 6.

You can decrease the amount of chili powder if it's too overpowering for you.

Front seated L-R: Josephine Mainella, Nina Frank
Standing L-R: Flo Avella, Phyllis Foster, Katherine Avella, Betty Arcara, Elise Feiner,
Marie Caccavale, Jean "Dolly" Caccavale, Phyllis Avella

BEEF AND PORK BARBEQUE
Elise Feiner

1½ pounds small beef cubes	½ cup brown sugar
1½ pounds small pork cubes	¼ cup vinegar
2 cups chopped onions	1 teaspoon salt
¼ cup chopped green peppers	2 teaspoons Worcestershire sauce
1 (6 ounce) can tomato paste	1 teaspoon dry mustard

Combine all the ingredients in a crock-pot. Cover and cook on low for about 12 hours or on high for about 6 hours. Stir and serve. Serves 6

CROCKPOT IDEAS
Carol Zuchowski

My housekeeper Carol uses the crock-pot for much more than I thought possible… Rinse off a boneless or spiral ham. Wrap in aluminum foil. Add pineapple is desired. Add 1 cup of water and cook on low for about 7 hours. Make your regular meatloaf mix; shape in a loaf. Place a long piece of aluminum foil across the crock-pot and place meatloaf on it; cook in the crock-pot; you can add ½ cup of water. Cook on low 7 to 8 hours. Season a turkey breast, add 3 cups of water and cook on low 9 hours.

ZAYDA'S SHORT RIBS
Zayda Koerner

4 pounds of short ribs
2 tablespoons sweet paprika
1 tablespoon kosher salt or
1½ teaspoons regular salt
¼ cup dark brown sugar, firmly packed
2 tablespoons chili powder

6 cloves garlic, peeled and crushed
1 tablespoon ground cumin
2 teaspoons Coleman's dried mustard
¼ teaspoon cayenne pepper
1 bottle of Jack Daniel's Barbeque sauce or any Honey
Mustard Barbeque Sauce

Mix the paprika, salt, brown sugar, chili powder, garlic, cumin, mustard and cayenne pepper in a bowl. Rub the mix all over the ribs. Refrigerate the meat for a few hours, overnight is even better. Place the meat in a crock-pot on low for 7½ hours. Preheat the oven to 325°. Take a large baking sheet that has been sprayed with PAM® and place the ribs on the pan in a single layer. The ribs will have given off a lot of liquid in the crock-pot. Mix the liquid with the barbeque sauce in a saucepan and bring to a boil; reduce to a simmer and cook for about 10 minutes until mixture begins to thicken. Set aside about 1 cup to use as gravy and spread the rest over the ribs in the baking sheet; coat well. Bake for about 15 to 20 minutes until crisp.

You can also use baby back ribs, but short ribs are the best. Zayda made these for us when we visited them in California.

L-R: Marc and Elise Feiner, Zayda, Sherylynn, Renee, and George Koerner (missing Sandra). The Koerner's were our neighbors in South Woods and although they moved to California we still remain close. The girls have become real beauties!

SLOPPY JOES
Carol Facci

3 pounds ground beef
1 cup chopped onions
2 cloves garlic, peeled and minced
¼ teaspoon garlic powder
1½ cups ketchup
1 cup chopped green peppers
½ cup water

4 tablespoons brown sugar
4 tablespoons prepared mustard
4 tablespoons Lea and Perrins® Worcestershire sauce
4 tablespoons vinegar (wine or cider)
3 teaspoons chili powder
Hamburger buns

In a large skillet, brown the ground beef, onions, and garlic. Cook until the meat is brown and the onions are tender. Drain off the fat. In any size crock-pot; combine the ketchup, green peppers, water, brown sugar, mustard, vinegar, Worcestershire sauce, and chili powder. Stir in the meat mixture. Cover and let cook on low 6 to 8 hours or high 3 to 4 hours. Spoon onto hamburger buns. Serves 8 to 10.

Carol says this is a favorite of her family. Her sons love it when they come back from playing on the road with their band "Full Blown Chaos".

L-R: Angelo and Carol Facci, Toni Mollico and Tom Mollico My cousin Toni and I have always been inseparable.

BURGUNDY POT ROAST
Elise Feiner

5-7 pound bottom round or other meat for pot roast
1 cup flour (Gold Medal ®)
2 teaspoons garlic salt
2 tablespoons McCormicks® seasoned salt
½ teaspoon black pepper
¾ cup Wesson® Oil
5 potatoes, peeled and cubed (place in cold water until needed, dry off with a clean dish towel before adding to the oil)
3 stalks of celery cut 1-inch pieces
1 small bag of mini baby carrots, washed and left whole (dry off with a clean dish towel before adding to the oil)
1 large onion, peeled and chopped, or 1 (12 ounce) bag of frozen chopped onions

3 cloves of garlic, peeled and crushed
1 (13¾ ounce) can College Inn® Beef Broth
1 cup red wine (Holland House® is fine) or Livingston or Inglenook Burgundy
2 (8 ounce) cans Hunts® Tomato Sauce
2 bay leaves
1 package Knorr® Beef Stew Mix
1 (.7 ounces) envelope Good Season® Dry Italian Dressing
4-6 cups water
Salt and pepper to taste
1 can straw mushrooms (Optional)
1 (1.55 ounce) Hershey Bar

The best thing to do with this recipe is to **do all the prep work ahead of time,** cut all the vegetables, open all the cans, etc. as you will be working quickly once you start. Mix the Gold Medal flour, garlic salt, seasoned salt, and black pepper in a large zip lock bag. Place the beef in the zip lock bag and shake until well coated. (Save the leftover seasoned flour to thicken the stew later if needed). Heat the Wesson oil in a large frying pan, and then brown the roast until well browned but not fully cooked. Place in crock-pot. To the same frying pan (add a little more oil if needed) add the potatoes, onions, celery, carrots and garlic and sauté for a few minutes until soft and slightly browned. Add to the beef in the crock pot. Add the beef broth, red wine and tomato sauce to the frying pan. Bring to a slight boil and pour over the meat in the crock-pot. Add bay leaf, Knorr Beef Stew Mix, Italian Dressing, and water to the crock-pot (the amount of water will depend on how much room you have left in the crock-pot.) Add salt and pepper to taste. Add the mushrooms about a half hour before the roast is done. Cook on low for 6 to 8 hours, or high 4 to 6 hours. Add the chocolate bar and allow to melt into the sauce before serving.

Before serving, remove the bay leaf. You may want to use some of the extra flour to thicken the stew. Dissolve a few tablespoons of leftover flour in cool water until mixture is very thin, and then add to the crock-pot. Allow to thicken for a few minutes before serving. Discard any leftover flour. This can also be done in a large Dutch oven on top of the stove. If you would like to do this on top of the stove, use a large Dutch oven or casserole pot. Start by browning the beef roast and remove to a platter. Add vegetables as above, remove to a platter, add all ingredients to the Dutch oven or large stockpot; add the rest of ingredients. Bring to a boil, and then simmer for about 2½ to 3½ hours.

SHREDDED SHORT RIBS
Katherine Avella

3 – 3½ pounds of boneless beef short ribs
¼ - ½ teaspoon black pepper
2 onions, peeled and kept whole
1 tablespoon garlic salt
Water, about 1 – 1½ cups
2 cans (13 ounces) College Inn Chicken Broth
5-6 tablespoons vegetable oil

4-5 onions, peeled and thinly sliced
¼ teaspoon black pepper or more to taste
1-2 teaspoons garlic salt (to your taste)
½ -1 cup garlic flavored red wine vinegar or more to taste
½ - 1 cups of reserved broth from the Crock-Pot, strained (optional)

Spray a crock-pot with PAM™. Place the short ribs, ¼-½ teaspoon black pepper, 2 whole Onions, the 1 tablespoon of garlic salt into a crock-pot. Add the chicken broth and about 1 cup of water over the top of the ribs and onions to cover them well. Cook on low about 8 to 10 hours (I always do mine overnight), or on high 6 to 8 hours. Remove the beef from the crock-pot, discard the onions and save about two cups of the broth (strain it first before setting it aside). Using two forks shred the short ribs by pulling them in opposite directions, until all the meat it shredded. In a large frying pan, heat the 3-4 tablespoons of vegetable oil. Add the sliced onions and sauté over medium heat until golden brown and caramelized about 20 minutes. Season the onions with the remaining black pepper and garlic salt. Add the shredded beef, and continue to cook until well blended about 10 minutes. Add the vinegar about a cup or more to taste. Blend well; add remaining reserved water from the crock-pot about 1½ cups to moisten the beef. You don't want to make it too wet, just moistened. Heat through and re-season to taste. You can serve this as a main course, or we like it best in sandwiches with Fran's Delicious Red Peppers (see index).
I always keep some of this in the refrigerator, just to munch on, or for sandwiches. It doesn't look pretty, but it tastes great...kind of like a Sloppy Joe without the sauce!

136

ELISE'S POT ROAST
Elise Feiner

¼ cup vegetable oil (Wesson®)
¾ cup all-purpose flour
½ teaspoon garlic salt
⅛ teaspoon black pepper
3-4 pound pot roast (rump roast, bottom round, etc.)
3 medium onions, peeled and sliced
5 or 6 potatoes, peeled and cubed
2 bay leaves

1 teaspoon garlic salt
¼ teaspoon black pepper
2 cups veal, beef or chicken stock
2 (8 ounce) cans Hunts® tomato sauce
1 (12 ounce) can Red Dog® Beer or any beer is fine
1 package Good Season® Italian Dressing Mix (dry)
1-1½ cups water (optional)
4 tablespoons unsalted butter

Crock-pot instructions:

Peel and cube the potatoes and place in cold water until ready to use. Peel and slice the onions. Wash the carrots. If you are not using baby carrots, peel and cut a few carrots into small pieces. Add the stock, tomato sauce, beer, bay leaf, Good Seasons Dressing mix, 1 teaspoon of garlic salt and ¼ teaspoon pepper, (the second amounts listed) to the crock-pot now. Mix the flour with the ½ teaspoon of garlic salt and ⅛ teaspoon of black pepper (the first amounts listed in ingredient list). Dredge the pot roast completely in the flour mixture. Save the extra flour to thicken the sauce later. In a frying pan, heat the oil. Brown the pot roast on all sides until well browned but not cooked. Remove pot roast and add it to the crock-pot now. Add the onions, potatoes, and carrots to the oil and brown lightly, and then add to the crock-pot. Add a little of the liquid from the crock-pot to remove all the drippings from the pan and pour back into the crock-pot. If the roast is sticking out of the liquid too much or the fluid level is not about 2-inches from the top of the crock-pot you can add the water. When everything is in the crock-pot set on automatic and cook 6 to 8 hours. About 30 minutes before serving, cook your rice or put up water for noodles. About 15 minutes before serving take about 4 tablespoons of the unsalted butter and four tablespoons of the leftover flour mix (throw the rest away now) and knead together to make a paste. Slowly add it to the crock-pot whisking it in with each addition and let cook for another 10 to15 minutes to thicken the sauce. While this is cooking throw the noodles into the water, when they are cooked the sauce will be perfect. Drain the noodles. Put the pot roast and sauce on top of the noodles or slice the meat and top with the sauce. Serve the vegetables on the side. Serve with rice or egg noodles.

Stovetop Directions:

Peel and cube the potatoes and place in cold water until ready to use. Peel and slice the onions. Wash the carrots. If you are not using baby carrots, peel and cut a few carrots into small pieces. Mix the flour with the garlic salt and black pepper (the first amounts listed in ingredient list). Dredge the pot roast completely in the flour mixture. Save the extra flour to thicken the sauce later. In a large pot or Dutch oven, heat the oil. Brown the pot roast on all sides until well browned but not cooked. Remove pot roast; place it in a plate for now. Add the onions, potatoes, and carrots to the oil and brown lightly. Add the stock, tomato sauce, beer, bay leaf, Good Seasons Dressing mix, garlic salt and pepper (the second amounts on the ingredient list) to the pot. Put the roast back in the pot. Cover and bring to a boil, then lower to a simmer and let simmer for about 3 to 4 hours About 30 minutes before serving, cook your rice or put up water for noodles. About 15 minutes before serving take about 4 tablespoons of the unsalted butter and four tablespoons of the leftover flour mix (throw the rest away now) and knead to make a paste. Slowly add it to the crock-pot, whisking it in with each addition and let cook for another 10 to 15 minutes to thicken the sauce. While this is cooking throw the noodles into the water, when they are cooked the sauce will be perfect. Drain the noodles. Put the pot roast and sauce on top of the noodles or slice the meat and top with the sauce. Serve the vegetables on the side. Serve with rice or egg noodles.

This is great dinner in one pot. You can make it ahead and reheat it. It's great for leftovers too. It smells wonderful when cooking as well. Serve with a good with rye bread and some butter. The meat also makes good sandwiches the next day.

Cousins Nick and Pam Sanito
celebrating his birthday in Florida

More Fathers and Daughters...Grandfathers, Godfathers, Fathers – in Law, etc.

Father-in-Law Jerome Feiner with
Daughter-in-Law Barbara Sussman Feiner

Godfather Michael Barone, M.D. with
Goddaughter Elise Avella Feiner

Godfather Joseph Avella with Goddaughter Lauren Feiner

Granddaughter Basia Adi Schwartz
with Grandfather Stuart Schwartz

Norm Zierler with daughter-in-law Samantha Caplan Zierler

Michael Avella with daughter Daniella

Meats...

The Kevin Feiner Family
L-R: Kevin, Abby, Barbara and Jody

"Call it a clan, call it a network, call it a tribe, or call it a family. Whatever you call it, whoever you are, you need one."

– Jean Howard

Hints:

If you over salt food, put a peeled raw potato into the food and it will absorb the excess salt. Obviously, remove it before serving.

Cream whips better if the bowl and beaters are well chilled.

Egg whites that are to be whipped for a meringue should be at room temperature. Don't let the beaters touch anything greasy.

A stick of butter will soften if placed in a microwave for one minute on 20% power. (if you have a new or very powerful oven this may be too long, so check frequently.

If you need softened butter for a recipe and forgot to leave it out, grate it into the recipe.

When measuring honey or anything sticky, spray the measuring cup with PAM® first.

To determine if an egg is hard boiled spin it. If it spins it's hard boiled, but if it wobbles it's raw!

To see if an egg is fresh, put it into a pan of cool salted water. If it sinks it's fresh, if it floats, throw it away!

If you are flouring a large amount of food (for example fried chicken pieces) spread long sheets of aluminum foil on the counter and flour on the foil. Discard when done.

To slice meats thinly as for jerky or stir fry's, partially freeze it before cutting.

For extra crisp French fries, fry once and remove before they are completely done. Drain on paper towels and cool. Fry again right before serving at a higher temperature.

When frosting a cake, place a thin layer of frosting on the serving plate to secure the bottom layer of the cake; it acts like glue.

Grind up a vanilla bean and place it into some granulated sugar and you'll have vanilla sugar – great to top fruits!

When working with filo dough always keep it covered with a damp cloth. Instead of brushing it with melted butter, place the melted butter in a spray bottle and spray it on the dough. To save time instead of making triangle shapes, try rolling it like an egg roll. Fold the sheet in half, making a rectangle. Place filling near the bottom; fold about ½-inch in on either side, and roll. Spray with butter to seal. Place seam side down on your baking sheet.

To soften a box of hard brown sugar, open it, place it in the microwave along side a cup of hot water and microwave for about 1½-2 minutes per ½ pound.

To freeze muffins: Cool completely; then wrap in foil and place in an airtight plastic freezer bag. To reheat, unwrap and bake in a 350° oven or a toaster oven for 10 minutes (if you like them soft) or 15 minutes (if you like them crusty.)

To keep vegetables green when cooking, dip your finger in water and then baking soda. Put your finger into the water you will cook the vegetables in **(before you boil or steam it obviously,)** and your veggies will stay green!

TENDERLOIN FILET WITH GRAND MARNIER
Elise Feiner

4-6 pound tenderloin of beef
1¼ cups Grand Marnier
1¼ cups barbecue sauce
2 cloves garlic, peeled and crushed

2 teaspoons onions, finely chopped
Salt and pepper to taste
1 package shredded Monterey Jack cheese

Place the tenderloin in a disposable aluminum plan or large roasting pan. Split the tenderloin in the middle but do not go very deep. Pour the Grand Marnier over the tenderloin. Then pour the barbecue sauce over the tenderloin. Season the tenderloin with salt, pepper, onions and garlic. Marinate 4 to 6 hours or overnight. Heat the barbecue or preheat the oven to 500°. Place the tenderloin on the barbecue and cook for about 45 minutes depending on how you prefer your meat. When just about done, pour the package of Monterey Jack cheese over the meat and close the lid for a few minutes until the cheese melts. If doing it in the oven, cook at 500° for 15 minutes and then lower the temperature to 350° and let cook for another 45 minutes or until done to the way you prefer it. Pour the cheese over it and return to the oven for a few minutes to melt the cheese. You can use Kahlua in place of the Grand Marnier if you prefer.

STUFFED BEEF TENDERLOIN
Elise Feiner

4 tablespoons butter
2 scallions, finely chopped
1 can of sliced mushrooms
1 clove of garlic, peeled and crushed
4 sprigs of parsley finely chopped

1 whole filet of beef
3 tablespoons of blue cheese
Melted butter
Garlic salt

Sauté the scallions, garlic and mushrooms in the butter; add the parsley. Slit the tenderloin and add the vegetables. Spread the blue cheese over the stuffing. Tie the tenderloin with cooking twine. Brush the filet with melted butter, and sprinkle with garlic salt. Cook on a barbeque grill until desired doneness is achieved. This may also be done in the oven. Cook at 500° for 30 minutes. Decrease temperature to 350° and cook until desired doneness.

STEAK MADEIRA
Elise Feiner

1 good size London Broil
¾ cup red wine vinegar
½ cup ketchup
¼ cup vegetable oil
1 tablespoon salt
¾ teaspoon black pepper

¾ teaspoon dried mustard
¾ teaspoon celery salt
¼ teaspoon garlic salt
¼ teaspoon dried thyme leaves
¼ teaspoon ground cloves

Mix together and let marinade 4 to 6 hours or overnight. Remove the steak from the marinade and cook the steak on a grill or under a broiler until desired doneness is achieved.

Madeira Sauce:

¼ cup unsifted all purpose flour
1 can (10 ½ ounce) condensed beef broth, undiluted

½ cup Madeira wine
Salt and pepper to taste

In a small saucepan mix a little of the beef broth with the flour. Keep adding broth until there are no lumps. Heat until it starts to boil. Add the Madeira and let simmer for a few minutes. Add salt and pepper to taste. To serve slice the London Broil, and spoon the sauce on the slices or pass around in a gravy boat and let everyone add it to their own meat.

EASY BEEF GOULASH
Janet Saporito

1 pound ground beef
1 pound of spaghetti, broken into 2-inch lengths
1 large onion, peeled and chopped

Approximately 8 beef bouillon cubes
Approximately 8 cups of water

Brown the ground beef; drain. Add onions, stir and sauté for 2 minutes. Add 2-4 cups of water; add spaghetti. Add more water to cover pasta. Add bouillon cubes. Simmer, covered on medium heat, about 15 minutes, until pasta is tender. Stir occasionally. Add more water if too much evaporates. Add more bouillon to taste. Sauce thickens and is great for leftovers.

Janet said, "I learned to make this as a child at summer camp, cooking it on a camp fire. I've continued to make it for over 30 years at home on the stove top."

STEAK PIZZAIOLA NANNY
Katherine Avella

4 tablespoons vegetable oil
2 pounds of beef, cut into thick slices or cubed beef for stew
2 (1 pound 12 ounce) cans crushed tomatoes
1 (8 ounce can) Hunts® Tomato Sauce
¾ cup-1 cup flour
1 teaspoon garlic salt

⅛ teaspoon black pepper
6 cloves garlic, peeled and crushed
1 small onion, peeled and diced
1 teaspoon oregano
2 teaspoons basil
Salt and pepper to taste

Mix the flour, garlic salt and ⅛ teaspoon black pepper in a zip lock bag. Add the cubes or slices of beef; shake to coat well. In a medium to large frying pan, heat the oil. Add the cubes and brown lightly but do not thoroughly cook them; set them aside. Add the onion and garlic to the pan, and sauté until the onions are soft. Add the meat to a crock pot or large deep casserole pan. Add the garlic onion mixture to the meat. Add the tomatoes, and all remaining seasonings. If doing on top of the stove let simmer for about 2 hours; if doing in a crock-pot, set on high for 5 to 6 hours. Serve over rice or pasta. Serves 6.

This is a quick and easy dinner to prepare, especially if you do it in a crock-pot. Serve it with a salad and some crusty Italian Bread.

STRIP STEAKS
Elise Feiner

4 strip steaks
4 tablespoons olive oil
2 tablespoons oregano
2 tablespoons basil
2 tablespoons onion salt

2 tablespoons garlic salt
½ cup flour
4 tablespoons butter, melted
4 cloves garlic, peeled and crushed

Coat the steaks with olive oil. Season the steaks with salt and pepper to taste. Mix the flour, oregano, basil, onion and garlic salt. Dip the steaks in the flour mixture. To make the steaks, preheat the broiler. Place the steaks on a broiling pan. Broil the steaks for 5 minutes, then turn, and cook the second side for an additional 3 to 5 minutes. In a small, melt the butter; add the garlic and sauté for a few seconds. Spoon over the steaks before serving.

This gives steaks a great flavor. I tried to copy a steak from a restaurant in Philadelphia. You can also place some crushed garlic on it if you like a strong garlic taste. You can use any kind of steak (rib eye, T-bone etc.) here.

"A friend drops their plans when you're in trouble, shares joy in your accomplishments, feels sad when you're in pain. A friend encourages your dreams and offers advice, but when you don't follow it, they still respect and love you."
-Doris Wild Helmering

SAUERBRATEN
Elise Feiner

1 (4-5) pound top or bottom round of beef
Salt and freshly ground black pepper
4 tablespoons canola oil
4 cloves garlic, coarsely chopped
2 large onions, thinly sliced
2 bay leaves

4 tablespoons tomato paste
¼ cup ketchup
1 cup red-wine vinegar
2 cups red wine, such as burgundy
¼ cup sour cream

Season beef well with salt and pepper. Tie meat tightly every 2-inches with kitchen twine, and once from end to end, to help keep meat together. Heat 2 tablespoons of oil in a large, heavy casserole over medium heat. Brown meat evenly on all sides, including the ends. Transfer to a plate, and set aside. Reduce heat to medium low; add remaining 2 tablespoons oil, garlic, and onions. Cook, stirring often, until softened, 5 to 7 minutes. Add bay leaves, tomato paste, ketchup, red-wine vinegar, and red wine. Bring to a boil over medium-high heat. Return beef to pot, and add about 2 cups water. Cover with a tight-fitting lid. Reduce heat to simmer. Cook for 1 hour, turn beef, and continue to cook until tender, about another 1½ hours. Remove pot from heat. Let cool slightly, and transfer beef to a cutting board with a well. Remove twine, and let beef rest for 15 minutes. Skim any fat from the casserole. Taste the sauce, and season with salt and pepper to taste. Stir in sour cream. Slice meat against the grain into ¼-inch slices. Place meat back into a platter; spoon some sauce over it. Serve immediately with additional sauce. I like this over noodles.

PEPPER STEAK
Katherine Avella

2-3 packages beef strips cut for stir fry
½ teaspoon meat tenderizer
4 teaspoons sugar
2 tablespoons soy sauce
¼ teaspoon black pepper

2-3 tablespoons vegetable oil
2 teaspoons cornstarch
1 large onion, peeled and sliced
2 peppers, red and green, seeded and sliced in ¼ inch strips

Marinate the beef slices in meat tenderizer, sugar, soy sauce, black pepper for about 1 hour. In a large skillet, heat the oil. Sauté the onions and the peppers until lightly colored. Set aside. Add cornstarch into the meat, and mix well with your hands. Heat the oil in the pan again and sauté the meat until done. Add the sautéed vegetables. Heat through. Serve over rice. Serves 4.

PRIME RIB OF BEEF
Elise Feiner

1 (10 pound) standing rib roast or a boneless prime rib
3 garlic cloves, peeled and cut into slivers
5 cloves of garlic, peeled and crushed
Fresh rosemary and thyme, coarsely chopped
Olive oil

1 teaspoon sea salt
1 teaspoon cracked pepper
½ cup red wine
½ cup beef stock

Peel the garlic and cut it into narrow slivers. With the tip of a sharp knife, poke holes over the fatty part of the beef, and insert the garlic slivers. Mix the olive oil, thyme, rosemary, crushed garlic and salt and pepper to make a paste. Rub the roast with the paste so that the meat and fat are evenly covered. Put the roast rib side down in a roasting pan. Place the pan on the middle rack of a preheated 500° oven and roast for 30 minutes. Cooking at the higher temperature will seal in the juices. Lower the heat to 350° and continue to cook for 1½ to 2 hours depending on how you like your meat done. Use a meat thermometer inserted into the fleshy center of the roast where it will not hit a bone or fat. This will give you a true reading: 120-125° for rare; 125-130° for medium rare; 135° for medium; 140° for well done) Remember the center will be rarer than the end pieces.

Remove roast from the oven; transfer to a heated platter. Allow the meat to rest 15 to 20 minutes before carving. Meanwhile carefully pour off the fat from the pan. Reserve pan juices and brown bits that have scraped from the bottom of the pan. Pour this, the red wine and stock into a small sauce pan and simmer gently. You may want to thicken it with a little flour slurry (a few tablespoons of Wondra flour mixed with cold water); add salt and pepper to taste. Serve immediately.

MARIA'S FILET MIGNON
Maria Trainor

5-6 pound whole beef tenderloin (filet mignon)   **Salt (or garlic salt) and pepper to taste**

Season a whole filet mignon with salt and pepper or garlic salt. Place on the grill on high heat for 15 minutes. Reduce heat and cook until desired doneness. Slice thinly and serve in sandwiches.

Maria says this is great on the grill. She makes this at their camp in Old Forge in the summer.

ORANGE BEEF WITH CASHEWS
Jane Oster Brophy

1 pound beef cubes (I cut them into smaller pieces)   **2 teaspoons vinegar**
2 tablespoons brown sugar   **2 teaspoons ginger**
2 tablespoons garlic   **4 green onions**
2 tablespoons oil   **⅔ cup orange juice**
2 tablespoons cornstarch   **½ teaspoons red pepper**
4 cups broccoli flowerets   **½ cup salted cashews (I put in extra)**
2 teaspoons water

Combine beef, brown sugar, 2 tablespoons soy sauce, and garlic in a zip-lock bag. Shake to coat well. Place broccoli and water on a plate. Cover with Saran Wrap®. Microwave the broccoli for 2 minutes. Stir onions, soy sauce, orange juice, cornstarch, vinegar, ginger and red pepper in a bowl. Whisk to mix well. Heat oil in a large skillet. Add beef and marinade (contents of zip-lock bag). Stir-fry for 10 to 15 minutes or until beef is mostly cooked through. Add broccoli; heat. Add cashews; heat. Add onion-orange juice mixture. Cook 2 to 3 minutes or until thick. Serve with rice.

Judy Oster's daughter Jane is a great cook, in fact, she should be a professional chef. She is however, a Nurse Midwife!

Jane Oster Brophy and John Brophy

Their son Samuel Eitan Brophy

Their newest addition
Aaron Yehuda Brophy

LONDON BROIL
Elise Feiner

3 to 4 pound London broil   **1 tablespoon dried parsley**
1 medium onion, peeled and sliced   **1 tablespoon dried oregano**
½ cup vegetable oil   **1 tablespoon dried basil**
½ cup water   **2 tablespoons McCormick® Montreal Steak Seasoning**
½ cup red wine vinegar   **1½ teaspoons McCormick® Seasoned Salt**
1 tablespoon garlic salt   **4 tablespoons Kahlua**
1 tablespoon Cooking with Love's Heavenly Greek Spice
Mix

Mix all the ingredients together except for the London Broil. Take a sharp knife and make small slits all over both sides of the London broil. Place into the marinade. Turn occasionally, making a few more slits each time. Marinate at least 6 hours or overnight. Barbeque on a grill about 6 to 7 minutes on each side for medium (depending on the thickness), or broil in the oven.

This is a great and flavorful marinade. The steak is great leftover in sandwiches.

JOAN'S BEEF BRISKET
Edith Mainella

1 large beef brisket
Salt and pepper
3-4 tablespoons vegetable oil
1 cup cooking sherry
1 cup teriyaki sauce
4 cups water

2 medium onions, sliced
5-6 carrots, peeled and sliced in
2 to 3-inch pieces
5-6 potatoes, peeled and quartered
1 package Lipton Onion Soup Mix
Salt and pepper

Sprinkle the brisket with salt and pepper. In a large Dutch oven, heat the oil. Place the whole brisket into the pot and sear the brisket on both sides (about 5 to 10 minutes). Add onions, Remove meat and set aside; add the potatoes and carrots; brown the potatoes and carrots and sauté for about 15 minutes. Remove the vegetables. Place the meat back into the pot; add the onion soup mix, sherry, teriyaki sauce, and water. Bring to a boil and then lower to a simmer. Let simmer for about 3 to 4 hours on low. After the second hour, add the vegetables back and cook for the last hour or two until meat is done and vegetables are soft.

This recipe was given to me by Aunt Edith who got it from her friend Joan. It was first way I learned to make brisket. I used to make it this way all the time. I like this because it is done on the top of the stove instead of in the oven. The vegetables take on a great flavor when cooked in the liquid.

EDITH'S PEPPER STEAK
Edith Mainella

Leftover roast beef cut in 1½-inch cubes
2-3 onions, peeled and sliced
2 green or red peppers, seeded and cubed
Teriyaki sauce to taste
Red wine to taste

Ketchup to taste (lots)
A-1® Steak Sauce
2 cans sliced mushrooms
Salt and pepper to taste

Cube the leftover roast beef. In a large frying pan, heat a little oil, brown the cubes slightly and remove and set aside. In the same oil, sauté the onions and peppers until soft. In a bowl, mix the wine, ketchup, A-1 Steak Sauce, teriyaki sauce, to taste. Add the beef back to the onion mix. Pour sauce over meat mix. Add mushrooms in; heat thoroughly. Taste and reseason if necessary.

My Aunt Edith always used to make this whenever we had leftover roast beef. I always remember her making this when we were in Bayville for the summer. It's wonderful over rice.

MEATLOAF
Katherine Avella

2-2½ pounds of chopped meat
4 eggs
½-¾ cup grating cheese
⅛ teaspoon black pepper
¼ teaspoon salt

1 envelope of Lipton® Onion Soup Mix
½ - ¾ cup unflavored breadcrumbs
4 tablespoons ketchup
3 tablespoons mustard
¼ cup water

Mix everything but the meat together in a large bowl. When well blended, add the meat and mix thoroughly. Use your hands. Place in a large glass or aluminum pan (or a loaf pan) that has been sprayed with PAM®. Bake at 375° for 45 minutes to an hour until well browned. Serves 4 to 6.

This is Nanny's recipe. Everyone loves this except Steven, he hates meatloaf. It is a great dinner when served with mashed potatoes and gravy. You can make the mix the night before if you are working, just refrigerate it and bake the next night for dinner. This is very easy to double for a large amount. This makes great sandwiches when it's leftover! You can add more ketchup or mustard to taste. This can also be done in a crock-pot, just shape in a loaf and cook on high for about 7 to 8 hours. Add about ½ cup of beef stock to the pot when you start to cook it. Drain the juices and discard periodically so the meatloaf browns. For something different, you can layer strips of bacon across the bottom of the pan and bring them up the sides and criss-cross them on the top of the meatloaf before baking (this only works if you put the meat in a loaf pan.)

EYE OF THE TIGER
John Grimaldi, Sr. , Executive Chef

6-8 pound filet mignon, have butcher cut it so that it is flat like a jelly roll; basically cut in half but not all the way through, and each half in half, not all the way through, to make a long thin sheet
Fresh Italian Breadcrumbs from 1-2 loaves of bread, do in food processor, but not too fine
½ cup olive oil

3-4 cloves of garlic, peeled and crushed
Salt and pepper to taste
2-3 tablespoons finely chopped fresh parsley
¾ cup grated cheese; parmesan or Locatelli Romano
3 (12 ounce) lobster tails, removed from shell, NOT cooked
A few sprigs flat leaf Parsley
About ½ cup chopped walnuts

Mix the breadcrumbs with the olive oil and place on a cookie sheet. Toast in a frying pan until golden brown; let cool. When cool, crumble to make the consistency of cornflake crumbs. Add the garlic, parsley, salt and pepper, and grating cheese. Mix well. Lay the meat on a long sheet of waxed paper. Lay the uncooked lobster tails across the width of the meat tail to head, head to tail, tail to head. Sprinkle with crumb mixture reserving a little to sprinkle on the top of the meat. Roll like a jelly roll and tie with kitchen twine 1-inch apart across the entire roast. Sprinkle with remaining crumbs. Bake 350° 1 hour and 25 to 40 minutes. Slice into about 10 to 12 slices. Top with a piece of flat leaf parsley and a few chopped walnuts. Serve with burgundy sauce.

Burgundy Sauce:

2 cups of burgundy or port wine
6 cups beef stock
1 stick of butter

Salt and pepper to taste
3 blocks cheddar cheese, shredded or 4 bags of shredded cheddar

In a large saucepan, melt the butter and cheddar cheese until the cheese looks like the satin of a tuxedo. Gradually add the beef stock and the wine; add salt and pepper to taste. The sauce should look like cheese whiz with a burgundy color.

My cousin John is an Executive Chef. He said when this is sliced; it looks like the eye of the tiger. It's definitely a dish to do when you want to make an impression. John says the lobster will be a little softer than a boiled lobster and that's why you add the breadcrumbs to absorb most of the moisture. John is now at Italian Deli in Long Island called Seven Brothers Gourmet Food Market. It's located at 2914 Long Beach Road, Oceanside, New York 11572. The phone number is 516 678-5999. Be sure to stop in if you need catering, you can trust John!

BEEF MARSALA
Elise Feiner

2 (¾ pound) beef top round steaks, each cut into ¼-inch thick slices
1-2 eggs
3 tablespoons milk
½ cup Wondra® flour
1¼ cup bread crumbs
¼ cup grating cheese
1 teaspoon salt

⅛ teaspoon black pepper
¾ cup butter
1 clove of garlic, peeled and sliced
¾ cup water cold
2 teaspoons flour
½ cup Marsala
1 beef bouillon cube or package of bouillon

On a cutting board, pound the beef sliced until they are about ⅛-inch thick. Cut into 4 x 2-inch pieces. In a dish, beat the egg with the milk. Pour Wondra flour on waxed paper or paper plate. On waxed paper, combine breadcrumbs, grating cheese, salt and pepper. Dip meat in the flour, then egg mixture, and finally, crumb mixture. In a large frying pan, melt 2 tablespoons of the butter. Add the garlic and ⅓ of the meat, until meat is lightly browned. Remove to a platter and repeat with remaining meat, adding more butter as needed, don't exceed ½ cup butter. In a cup, mix the 2 teaspoons of flour and water. Remove the garlic from the pan. Add the remaining ¼ cup butter and melt. Add the flour/water mixture, Marsala, bouillon. Cook, stirring until thickened. Pour over the meat. Great with rice or noodles. Serves 6.

L-R: Kyle, Jonathan, and Tessa Trainor, David, Lauren and Steven Feiner, and Katherine Trainor enjoying the summer in Old Forge, New York

BRISKET IN A BAG
Elise Feiner

1 whole beef brisket	½ bag, mini carrots
Garlic salt and pepper	5-6 potatoes, peeled and quartered
3-4 garlic cloves, peeled and cut in half	2 cup water
3-4 tablespoons vegetable oil	4 tablespoons flour
2 small onions, peeled and left whole	Oven Brown in Bag

With a sharp knife, make holes in the brisket and insert the garlic pieces. Sprinkle the brisket with garlic salt and pepper. In a large frying pan, heat the oil. Sear the brisket on both sides for about 10 minutes. Place the flour into a large oven brown in bag, and shake. Place the brisket, and remaining ingredients in to bag. Bake in a 325° oven for about 4 to 5 hours.

Brisket is a staple in the Jewish home, when I was first married and cooking my first brisket, I couldn't understand why it wouldn't brown. It was in the oven forever. I called my mother to ask what I was doing wrong. She said, "What kind of a brisket did you buy?" What kind of briskets are there? I bought a corned beef brisket, not a beef brisket. What did I know??? I could have cooked that baby a million years and it would never have turned brown!

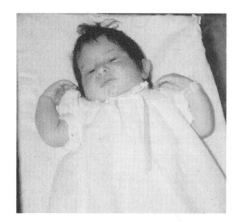

Lauren and Elise Feiner...my baby is all grown up!

"What do girls do who haven't any mothers to help them through their troubles?"
-Louisa May Alcott

BEEF STEW
Elise Feiner

3-4 pounds sirloin cut in 1-inch cubes
1 cup flour (Gold Medal®)
2 teaspoons garlic salt
2 tablespoons seasoned salt (McCormick®)
1 teaspoon black pepper
¾ cup Wesson® Oil
5 potatoes, peeled and cut into
2- inch cubes (place in cold water until needed, dry off with
a clean dish towel before adding to the oil)
3 stalks of celery cut 1-inch pieces
1 small bag of mini baby carrots, washed and left whole
(dry off with a clean dish towel before adding to the oil)

1 large onion, peeled and chopped, or ½ bag (10 ounces) of
frozen chopped onions
3 cloves of garlic, peeled and crushed
1 (13¾ ounce) can College Inn® Beef Broth
1 cup red wine (Holland House® is fine) or Livingston
Burgundy
1(13¾ ounce) can Hunts® Tomato Sauce
1 bay leaf
1 package Knorr® Beef Stew Mix
4-6 cups Water
Salt and pepper to taste

The best thing to do with this recipe is to do all the prep work ahead of time, cut all the vegetables, open all the cans, etc. as you will be working quickly once you start. Mix the flour, garlic salt, seasoned salt, and black pepper in a large zip lock bag. Place the beef cubes in the zip lock bag and shake until well coated. (Save the leftover seasoned flour to thicken the stew later if needed). Heat the oil in a large frying pan, and then fry the cubes in a few batches until well browned but not fully cooked. As each batch is done, remove and place in crock-pot. To the same frying pan (add a little more oil if needed) add the potatoes, onions, celery, carrots and garlic and sauté for a few minutes until soft and slightly browned. Add to the beef cubes in the crock pot. Add the beef broth, red wine and tomato sauce to the frying pan. Bring to a slight boil and pour over the meat in the crock-pot. Add bay leaf, Knorr Beef Stew Mix, and water to the crock-pot. Add salt and pepper to taste. Cook on low for 6 to 8 hours, or high 4 to 6 hours. This can also be done in a large Dutch oven on top of the stove. Before serving, remove the bay leaf. You may want to use some of the extra flour to thicken the stew. Dissolve a few tablespoons of leftover flour in cool water until mixture is very thin, and then add to the crock-pot. Allow to thicken for a few minutes before serving. Discard any leftover flour. If you would like to do this on top of the stove, use a large Dutch oven or casserole pot. Start by browning the cubes and remove to a platter. Add vegetables as above, remove to a platter, and add the remaining ingredients, adding the meat and vegetables. Bring to a boil, and then simmer for about 2½ to 3 hours. Serves 6.

BEEF WELLINGTON
Elise Feiner

4-5 pounds filet of beef
1 package puff pastry
4 tablespoons butter
½ pound fresh mushroom, chopped fine
2 cloves garlic, peeled and crushed

¼ medium onion, peeled and chopped
Salt and pepper to taste
2 tablespoons brandy
1 egg plus 1 tablespoon of water

In a skillet, melt the butter and add the garlic, onions, mushrooms, salt and pepper. Sauté for a few minutes until the vegetables are soft and almost cooked. Add the brandy and cook until most of the liquid had evaporated. Remove from heat and set aside. Make sure you remove any excess liquid at this point. Preheat oven to 500°. Trim any excess fat from the beef. Season the beef with salt and pepper. Cook for about 35 minutes. Do this early in the day and let cool to room temperature. Roll the puff pastry out. Spread the mushroom mix over the pastry about where the beef would be placed. Put the beef on top of the mushroom mix. Brush the edges of the pastry with the water and egg. Seal the pastry around the beef, overlapping the edges and moistening the edges to seal the seam. Use extra pastry to decorate the top of the dough. Place the beef on a lightly greased cookie sheet. (You can do this ahead of time and refrigerator. Remove to room temperature before baking). Brush the top of the pastry with beaten egg and water. Bake in a 450° oven for about 45 minutes to 1 hour. Let stand 10 minutes before carving.

This is a great special occasion's recipe. I made this when Uncle Ernie Maida retired from the New York Transit Authority at a dinner in his honor. If you feel really adventurous, make your own puff pastry. See the recipe in the index.

*"I think, at a child's birth, if a mother could ask a fairy godmother to endow it
with the most useful gift, that gift would be curiosity."*
-Eleanor Roosevelt

BEEF CUBES IN WINE
Shirley Flomenhoft

2 pounds beef cubes (remove fat)   1 cup sherry wine
1 can Campbell ® Golden Mushroom Soup

Place in a casserole and cook at 325° for 3 hours. Serve over rice.

This is another quick and easy recipe from Aunt Shirley.

BEEF BRISKET SCHWARTZ
Barbara Schwartz

1 large Beef Brisket (about 5-6 pounds), trimmed   1 package Lipton® Onion Soup Mix
1 (36 ounce) bottle Heinz® Ketchup   Black pepper
1 (1 liter) bottle Ginger Ale   Garlic salt
1 tablespoon soy sauce   Wondra® flour to thick sauce
2 cloves garlic, peeled and left whole

Sprinkle the brisket with a little garlic salt and black pepper. In a large pan brown the brisket on both sides for a few minutes. In a large roasting pan, mix the remaining ingredients (ketchup, ginger ale, onion soup mix, soy sauce, garlic. Remove the brisket from the pan, and add to the liquid mixture. Bake at 375° for about 1½ hours to 2 hours. Remove from pan and slice. Return to pan and cook for another 1½ hours to 2 hours. I have also just left it in and sliced it when it was finished. You can also do this is a crock-pot. Just put all the ingredients in the crock and remove the browned brisket to the crock-pot and let cook on automatic about 6 hours. If you like the sauce to be thicker, take a few tablespoons of flour mixed with cold water. Stir until it is smooth. Add to the hot liquid stirring as you add it. Let cook a few minutes before serving. Serves 6.

Barbara invited us for dinner one night and made this brisket. It was delicious and very different from the other brisket recipes. I love brisket any way, but the kids seemed to prefer this one. It has a little sweet taste to it. It's always good to have a few brisket recipes so life isn't boring. Barbara was the first person I met when I moved to New Hartford; she recognized another Brooklyn girl and took me under her wing. We've been friends... family, ever since!

L-R: Barbara Schwartz, Jeffrey Feiner, M.D., Stuart Schwartz...
as proud as his own parents!

"One loyal friend is worth ten thousand relatives"
-Euripides

BEEF BRISKET - REINISCH
Nellie Reinisch

1 large beef brisket
4 onions, peeled and sliced
McCormick® Season All Seasoned salt
6 cloves of garlic, peeled and cut in half
2-3 cloves of garlic, peeled and cut in ⅓'s
3 carrots, peeled and cut into 3-inch pieces
2 stalks celery, cut into 3-inch pieces

1 can mushrooms
5-6 potatoes, peeled and quartered
1 (8 ounce) can tomato sauce
Black pepper
Paprika
4-5 tablespoons vegetable oil

Preheat the oven to 350°. In a large skillet, heat the oil. Sprinkle the brisket with black pepper, seasoned salt and paprika. With a small knife make little holes in the fat side of the brisket and insert the garlic pieces that have been cut into thirds throughout the brisket.
Sear the brisket until brown about 10 minutes. Remove. In a large enamel roasting pan, place the onions; sprinkle with seasoned salt. Mix the garlic cloves that were halved in with the onions. Place the carrots and celery on top of the onions. Add the tomato sauce, seasoned salt, pepper, and paprika to taste. Place the brisket on top of the vegetables. Cover with foil and bake at for 2 hours. Parboil the potatoes and add them to the brisket after it cooks two hours. (I usually just peel and cube them and put them in raw at the beginning. Add the mushrooms. Cover again and let cook another 1 to 2 hours.

This is another version of Nanny's Nellie's brisket. She said that she put an inch of water in the pan, but Mom Mom said that the vegetables give off enough liquid and not to add the water. The aroma of this cooking is wonderful. I love this brisket!

BEEF BRISKET – REINISCH TOO...
Nellie Reinisch

8-10 pound brisket
Garlic cloves
1 quart beef stock (unsalted or low salt)
3 large onions, sliced
3 tablespoons vegetable oil
2 teaspoons salt
2 teaspoons McCormick® Season All Seasoned Salt

1 teaspoon freshly ground black pepper, to taste
1 teaspoon onion powder
1 teaspoon garlic powder
1 cup ketchup
1 cup chili sauce
1 cup brown sugar

Preheat oven to 500°. Make slits in the brisket and stuff brisket all with garlic. Place brisket in a baking dish bake until browned on top, turn brisket and return to oven until browned on both sides. Reduce oven to 350°. Add enough beef stock to casserole to come up 1-inch on sides, cover with foil and bake one hour. While brisket is cooking, heat a large skillet over medium high heat and sauté onions in vegetable oil, until caramelized and most liquid has evaporated, about 20 minutes. Set aside. Remove brisket from oven after one hour and add caramelized onions and all remaining ingredients, moving meat around to combine ingredients. Cover and continue to bake until very tender, another 2 to 3 hours. Remove brisket to a carving board and slice. Strain extra cooking liquids and pour over sliced brisket. Brisket may be returned to casserole dish and allowed to cool, then served the next day; (reheated in oven). Brisket is better if made a day in advance.

Nellie and Juda Reinisch
(Marc's Grandparents)
We were so happy that Marc's
grandfather was able to make it
to our wedding, he passed away
a few weeks later. You'd never
know how sick he was by how
dapper he looked.

GERMAN ROUMALADE
Janet Saporito

2 pounds of beef for Braciole
½ cup diced bacon, raw
½ cup diced dill pickles
½ cup diced onions
¼ cup mustard

4 beef bouillon cubes
Water
3 tablespoons flour
Salt and pepper to taste

Spread beef with mustard. Mix pickles, bacon and onions. Spread mixture on to beef about ½-inch from the edges. Starting with the narrowest end, begin rolling beef. Use toothpicks to secure edges and close ends.

Cooking:

May be done stove top or crock-pot. In a crock-pot: place meat rolls in pot. Cover with water. Add bouillon cubes. In the crock-pot, cook on low for 7 hours or high on 5 hours.

On the stove top: Place rolls in a pot, cover with water and add bouillon cubes. Simmer on low until tender about 2½ hours.

Remove beef rolls from pot. Carefully remove toothpicks. Use flour/water mixture to thicken gravy. Add salt and pepper to taste.

Janet says, "I never really went by measurements for this. Probably better if you made it first and adjusted as you go along. I'm not so sure how my measurements are."

PEPSI® POT ROAST
Elise Feiner

4 pound pot roast
Dash of salt and black pepper
1 package onion soup mix
1 can cream of mushroom soup

1 can (12 ounces) Pepsi®
1 large onion, peeled and diced
3 carrots, peeled and sliced in rounds
2 stalks celery, chopped

Season the pot roast lightly with salt and pepper. Brown the pot roast in a large skillet. Place the roast in a crock-pot or large Dutch oven. Add remaining ingredients. Cook for about 6 hours on high in the crock-pot or simmer 3 to 4 hours on low in a Dutch oven on top of the stove. Serve over noodles or rice.

EASY FILET MIGNON
Elise Feiner

4-5 pound beef tenderloin
3 tablespoons butter, softened

Garlic salt to taste
Black pepper to taste

Season the softened butter with the garlic salt and pepper and rub all over the filet. Preheat the oven to 500°. Place the filet in a roasting pan. Roast 25 minutes for rare, 35 minutes for medium. Remove from the oven and immediately cover with heavy duty aluminum foil. Let rest 25 to 30 minutes before slicing.

This is Steven's favorite meal. In the sixth grade his teacher, Vicki Angell, asked the kids what their favorite food was. Steven wrote that he loves "flaming yon." She was puzzled, then realized he meant filet mignon and laughed for hours!

"When you teach your son, you teach your son's son."
- The Talmud

PEPPER STEAK SAPORITO
Janet Saporito

For Marinade:

2 tablespoons soy sauce
2 teaspoon cornstarch
½ cup cold water

1¼ pounds flank steak

1 large bell pepper
1 large tomato
1 onion

¼ teaspoon meat tenderizer
¼ teaspoon baking soda
3 tablespoons oil

1 teaspoon salt
3 tablespoons oil

Sauce:

4 tablespoons stock or water
½ teaspoon salt
½ teaspoon sugar

1 teaspoon sesame oil
2 tablespoons oyster sauce (bottled)
1 tablespoon corn starch

Preparation:

Combine soy sauce, cornstarch, water, meat tenderizer, and baking soda together. Slice beef across the grain and place in marinade. Add 3 tablespoons of oil. Turn occasionally. If marinated less than 2 hours reduce water to 2 tablespoons. Rinse pepper and cut in think chunks; sprinkle with a little salt. Let sit 20 minutes. Cut tomato in chunks; cut onions to same size as peppers and set aside.

Prepare sauce mix by mixing all the ingredients together.

Put 3 tablespoons oil in skillet over high heat. Add onion stirring constantly until light brown. Add peppers. Cook another 2 minutes. Add tomatoes and 1 teaspoon salt. Remove from heat and set aside. Stir fry the flank steak. Stir in sauce mix. It will thicken gradually. Add pepper/tomato mix. Serve at once with rice.

L-R: Cousins Brad and Hal Weiner, Leslie Weiner Solitrin, Marc Feiner, Ivan Feiner, Terry Weiner Freedman, and Kevin Feiner

STEAK PIZZAIOLA
Frank S. Mainella, M.D.

¼ cup olive oil
12 cloves garlic, peeled and crushed
2-2½ pound London Broil, or flank steak (have butcher cut it into Scaloppini like slices)
Salt and pepper to taste

2 (28 ounce) cans crushed tomatoes
2 teaspoons oregano
2 teaspoons basil
6 tablespoons Worcestershire sauce

Heat half the oil in a large frying pan or a casserole over medium-high heat. In the meantime, sprinkle the steak with salt and pepper to taste. Add the garlic to oil and fry for about 15 seconds. Quickly add some of the steak to the oil and garlic mixture, add about 3 tablespoons of the Worcestershire to the steak, and brown it on both sides about 2 to 3 minutes. Remove the steak to a dish, and add the rest of the oil and heat it before adding the remaining steak and Worcestershire sauce. Remove the rest of the steak to the platter. Add the tomatoes, salt, pepper, oregano, basil, to the oil in the pan. Bring to a boil, and reduce to a simmer for about 25 to 30 minutes. Add the steak back into the sauce and continue simmering for about 1½ hours. The meat should be tender. You can serve this over rice or pasta. Serves 6.

Uncle Frank sent this recipe along. The Worcestershire sauce was one of Aunt Edith's secret ingredients. She also used to make something similar with leftover roast beef. She would cook it with lots of onions, cube the beef, add Worcestershire sauce, and ketchup and tomato sauce and seasonings.

Avella-Mainella Clan…

Back Row L-R: David Feiner, Phil, Phyllis, Melissa, and Flo Avella, Frank S. Mainella, MD, Marc Feiner, MD, Elise Feiner, Thirza and Joe Avella, Lauren Feiner

Front Row L-R: Jeffrey Feiner, Phil Avella, Jr., Steven Feiner, Katherine Avella, Josephine Mainella, Nicole Latini, Michael Avella, John-Michael Latini

"Life is not about the breaths you take but about the moments that take your breath away."
-Author Unknown

UNCLE TOM'S BARBEQUED SKIRT STEAK
Thomas Mollico

2 pounds of trimmed skirt steaks
1 package of McCormick® Montreal Steak Grill Mates Marinade Mix
½ cup McCormick® Montreal Steak Grilling Sauce

Mix the marinade mix packet according to package directions. Cut the skirt steaks into 3 to 4-inch pieces. Place the steaks in a large zip lock bag. Add the marinade mix and the ½ cup of the grilling sauce. Place the marinade mix and the steak into the refrigerator 1 hour or overnight. Grill on the barbeque.

Uncle Tom says that when he makes this for the Mollico's and the Facci's, he needs 10 pounds of skirt steaks. He said you can use any kind of grilling sauce that you like. This is also good done on the George Foreman® Grill. He serves it with grilled eggplant and any kind of potatoes you like. He says that they always beg him to make his famous skirt steak!

L-R: Tom Mollico, Toni Mollico, Mary Ann Maida, Brian Mollico, Steven Feiner and Michele Maida, some of my closest and most favorite cousins

L-R: Brian Mollico, Steven and David Feiner, John Grimaldi Jr. Jeffrey and Lauren Feiner, Christopher Grimaldi...all very much younger on a trip to Mystic, Connecticut.

ROASTED WHOLE FILET/ TENDERLOIN OF BEEF
Theresa Feiner

1 filet of beef (about 5 pounds), well trimmed and tied   4-5 cloves of garlic, crushed
2 tablespoons extra virgin olive oil

Have butcher trim and tie filet. Rub olive oil and garlic over entire surface. Preheat oven to 425°. Place filet in the roasting pan and roast until thermometer inserted in thickest part reads 120° for rare, 125 to 130° for medium rare, or 135 to 140° for medium. Cover roast loosely with foil and let stand for 15 minutes before slicing. Serve with sauce of choice or gravy from drippings.

My sister-in-law Theresa makes a mean filet of beef. My other sister-in-law Barbara wanted to make sure this was included in the book!

ESTELLE'S ROAST BEEF
Estelle Zierler

6-8 pound rump roast   3 large onions, peeled and thinly sliced
2 (8 ounce) cans Hunt's Tomato Sauce   Salt and pepper to taste
2 (8 ounce) cans of water

In a large baking dish (9 x 13-inch), place the onions, tomato sauce, water and salt and pepper to taste. Place the roast on the top of a baking rack and place over the onion-tomato mix. Bake at 350° until a meat thermometer registers medium. Slice and serve with the tomato and onion sauce served over it.

Fran said that her mother- in- law Estelle always made this roast and her family loved it, until Norm stopped eating beef and she never made it again...what a loss! We resurrected it here for all to enjoy once again. I miss my card playing partner and casino buddy. We all miss Estelle and her joie de vivre!

Estelle Zierler

Estelle and Sidney Zierler

Lest we forget to give Sidney credit where credit is due, he drove a cab in Manhattan for years and is an accomplished drummer and jazz musician!

Felicia Furino and B.J. Gigliotti

The Bakiewicz's
L-R: Andrzej, Matthew, Alexandra, and Suzanne

Kristin Gigliotti and Jonathan Trainor...
Hockey Buddies and Best buddies!

L-R: Kristin Furino and Kristin Gigliotti

The Feiner Boys L-R: Pinky (Philip), Gene
and Jerry with their baby picture

Marc and Elise Feiner

RACK OF LAMB
Elise Feiner

1½ - 2 tablespoons olive oil
2 garlic clove, minced
4 tablespoons thinly sliced scallion including the green part
1 teaspoon dried rosemary, crumbled
1½ cups fresh Italian bread crumbs

1 (1¼ pound) trimmed single rack of lamb (7 or 8 ribs) or 2 small ones
Salt and pepper, to taste
¼ cup mayonnaise
¼ cup mustard

In a small skillet heat the oil over moderate heat until it is hot but not smoking, add the garlic and cook it, stirring, for 30 seconds. Add the scallion and the rosemary and cook the mixture, stirring, for 10 seconds. Stir in the bread crumbs and salt and pepper, to taste, and remove the skillet from the heat. Mix the mayonnaise and mustard in a small bowl, set aside. Heat an ovenproof skillet over moderately high heat until it is hot; brown the lamb, seasoned with salt and pepper, turning it for 5 minutes or until the sides and the ends are browned evenly. Pour off any fat from the skillet, arrange the lamb, fat and meat side up, and coat both sides of the rack with mayonnaise/mustard mixture. Then press the crumb mixture evenly on the fat and meat side of the lamb. Spray a roasting pan with PAM®. Place rack on pan. Bake the lamb in the middle of a preheated 375° oven for 35 to 50 minutes, or until a meat thermometer registers desired doneness. Let it stand, uncovered, for 10 minutes. Serve 1 to 2.

This is one of my favorite dinners to make. The crust of mustard and mayonnaise mixed together is great. I save all my stale Italian bread and make it into crumbs, freeze them until you need them!

LEG OF LAMB
Katherine Avella

5 tablespoons olive oil
6 cloves garlic, peeled and crushed

Black pepper
2 tablespoons rosemary

Mix the oil, garlic, pepper and rosemary together. Rub all over both sides of the leg of lamb. Place on a rack in a roasting pan. Bake in a 350° preheated oven until desired doneness. Test with a meat thermometer to check for desired doneness.

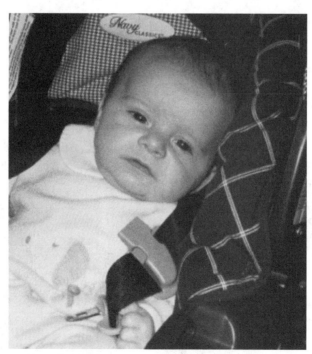

Noah's arrival into our family was truly a miracle. Glenn and Donna had been praying for a baby for years and just when they were about to say that's it, Noah Gabriel Feiner arrived with more coincidences attached to his arrival then there is room on the page to list. While Glenn and Donna are blessed to have him, Noah is one lucky baby to come into a family filled with so much love to give him. Blessings go both ways!

Noah Gabriel Feiner...our new source of love and joy!

"A baby is God's opinion life should go on"
–Carl Sandburg

The Gigliotti's: L-R: Bernie, Kristin and Johann

Michele Circelli and Concetta Gigliotti

L-R: Steven Feiner and Michael Alsheimer

Christina Malecki and Steven Feiner

L-R: Jeffrey Feiner, Michael Avella and Daniella Faith Avella

Nancy Neilson, M.D. and Jeffrey Feiner "her golden boy" on match day...State University of New York meets Johns Hopkins!

SAUSAGE AND PEPPERS
Elise Feiner

2-3 packages sweet Italian sausage (about 1½ to 2 ½ pounds)
4-5 large onions, peeled and sliced
¼ teaspoon black pepper
1 teaspoon garlic salt
Vegetable oil

6 green, yellow and red peppers (you can just use green if you want, I like color) washed, seeded, sliced or cubed
1-2 packages all beef hot dogs, sliced ¼ to ½-inch thick
Italian bread or rolls
Aluminum cookie sheets

Preheat oven to 400°. Cut up your onions, peppers and hot dogs; do this ahead of time and put them in separate zip lock bags in the refrigerator. Spray a large disposable aluminum cookie sheet with PAM® (remember if you are using an aluminum pan, put something solid underneath so it won't buckle when you take it out of the oven.) Cut the sausage links or long pieces of sausage into 1½ - 2-inch pieces with a scissor. Bake for about 30 minutes or until well browned. Cut a piece to make sure it is cooked. You shouldn't see any pink inside. When you are ready to prepare the dish, (I do this while the sausages are cooking) place a thin layer of vegetable oil in a *very large frying pan*. Start to sauté the onions, season with garlic salt and pepper (the above amounts are just a guide, season to taste), when the onions are starting to brown (about 5 to 6 minutes), add the peppers. Cook until the peppers are starting to get soft (about another 5 minutes) Stir the pepper and onion mix often but not constantly so the onions don't burn; add the hotdogs. Cook until the hot dogs are just starting to brown. Add the cooked sausage and mix well. If your frying pan is not big enough, mix everything in a large disposable baking pan. You can keep this warm on the grill if you are having a barbeque. To do this on a barbeque, start the sausages first in a large metal pan, and then do the peppers and onions the same way as above. It is easier to do it in the oven. Serve this with long Italian rolls or even better yet, crisp loaves of Italian bread cut into heroes. Serves 6.

This has been an Avella family favorite forever. I can remember my father, and then Uncle Phil doing this on the grill when I was a kid. The whole yard would have this incredible aroma the smell of summer! I used to do it the same way. One day, Aunt Toni was visiting, and she asked me what I was making. She said, "I make the sausage in the oven, it's so much easier"...she sure was right. It is much easier to do it in the kitchen and just take it out to the grill in the summer or serve it right to the table in the winter. In our house, they say they love the sausage and peppers, but in truth, they love the hot dogs and peppers. They fight over the pieces of hot dogs so we now add more hot dogs then before. Everyone yells at Lauren to stop eating all the hotdogs out of the pan, then they turn around do the same thing. My boys love to eat a nice hero (hoagie, sub) sandwich filled with this.

ROOT BEER HAM
Edith Mainella

12 to 15 pound spiral cut ham
2 liters A/W® root beer
1½ cups dark brown sugar

4 tablespoons hot spicy mustard
2 tablespoons dry mustard
1 pound green seedless grapes

Preheat oven to 220°. Rinse the ham thoroughly and pat dry. Place ham in roasting pan with a lid. Pour 1 liter of root beer over ham. Add half the grapes and ½ cup of brown sugar. Bake covered, for 6 hours, basting often. When done, remove ham from juices and discard juices. Return ham to roaster. In saucepan, combine remaining brown sugar and 2 cups of root beer. Bring to a boil and reduce until thickened enough to coat ham. Remove from heat and stir in both kinds of mustard. Brush sauce over top of ham and return to 300° oven uncovered to let brown. Add more sauce as needed. Add remaining grapes during final 15 to 20 minutes of cooking. Be careful not to burn top of ham. Serve remaining sauce separately.

Aunt Edith sent this recipe from Florida. She loved to make ham, both fresh ham and spiral ham. We always had ham on New Year's Day in our family, and tradition continues to this day.

Frank and Edith Mainella enjoying their
retirement in Sarasota, Florida.
My Aunt Edith and Uncle Frank were a special
breed and they don't make them like this any
more. They opened their hearts, homes, and
pockets to all their relatives and friends.

PORK TENDERLOIN WITH VEGETABLES
Elise Feiner

3 packages of boneless pork tenderloins (about 4 to a package)
3-4 tablespoons of butter
4 onions, peeled and sliced
2 red peppers, peeled, seeds removed and sliced
1 box of sliced mushrooms

¼ teaspoon black pepper
½ teaspoon garlic salt
2-3 tablespoons Wondra® flour
¾ cup white wine
½ cup chicken broth
Enough vegetable oil to cover the bottom of a frying pan

Heat a large frying pan. Add the oil and then lightly brown the boneless pork tenderloins on both sides. Remove from the pan and set aside. Add a little more oil if necessary. Add the butter to the oil in the frying pan and then add the onions. When they are starting to get golden brown, add the peppers, and mushrooms. Sprinkle with the pepper and garlic salt. You may adjust the seasonings to your taste. Sprinkle the vegetables with Wondra flour and mix well. Add the wine and chicken broth and allow to cook for about another 10 minutes. Place the pork tenderloins in a large baking pan that has been sprayed with PAM®. Top with the vegetable mix. Cover with foil. Bake 350° about 45 minutes. Serves 6 to 8.

PORK CHOPS IN MUSTARD
Elise Feiner

8 boneless pork loin chops
2 cans Family Size Campbell® Chicken and Rice Soup (or 4 small ones)
1 small jar of Gulden's® Mustard
Salt and Pepper

1 large plus one medium onion, peeled and sliced
1 can Campbell's® Golden Cream of Onion Soup (undiluted)

Trim any fat off the chops, and set aside. Season the pork chops with salt and pepper. Spread both sides of the chops with very generously with mustard. Place the trimmed fat from the pork chops in a large deep frying pan or casserole pot. If there is not enough fat on the chops use a little oil (Wesson®) just enough to coat the bottom of the pan. Render down the fat and sauté the onions for a few minutes. Add the pork chops and brown well. Remove the chops and place on a dish. Add the two large cans of soup and 1 large can of water or the 4 small cans of soup and two small cans of water (half of what you would normally use), and onion soup. Cook for a few minutes, and then put the pork chops back in the pan. Bring to a boil and then lower to a simmer. Cover the pan and let cook about 45 minutes to an hour. Check after 45 minutes and if sauce is not thickening a little, cook for about another 15 to 20 minutes with the cover off. You can also do this in a crock-pot. Prepare as above except after you brown everything put it in the crock-pot on low for about 5 to 6 hours.

I got this recipe from a neighbor of mine on Lewiston Street in Staten Island. Her name was Gloria and she would always make these. These reheat really well and I think they taste better leftover. You can serve them with mashed potatoes, and use the rice mix as gravy. The mustard really gives this a great taste.

PORK MADEIRA
Elise Feiner

2 tablespoons butter
2 tablespoons corn oil
1½ pounds pork tenderloin, cut and trimmed into ½-inch slices
1 medium onion, chopped
1 large red pepper, cored, seeded and cut into strips
1 tablespoon paprika
1 tablespoon flour

1¼ cups chicken stock
5 tablespoons Madeira wine
2½ cups sliced mushrooms
1 teaspoon tomato paste
⅔ cup heavy cream
Salt and pepper to taste

Melt the butter and oil together in a large skillet. When the butter begins to foam, add the pork slices, in batches if necessary and cook over high heat about 4 minutes, until just beginning to brown. Remove the pork with a slotted spoon and drain on paper towels. Add the onion and peppers to the butter and cook for about 2 minutes, stirring occasionally. Add the paprika and flour and cook, stirring for 1 minute. Remove the pan from the heat and blend in the stock. Return the pan to the heat and add the Madeira, mushrooms, and tomato paste. Simmer 2 to 3 minutes. Add the pork back into the pan and season with salt and pepper to taste. Cover and simmer very gently until the pork is tender and cooked through, about 20 minutes. Stir in the cream and adjust for seasonings. Heat through gently on low heat. Serve hot with rice or noodles.

PORK CHOPS WITH BALSAMIC VINEGAR
Elise Feiner

3 tablespoon all purpose flour
1 teaspoon fresh rosemary, chopped
½ teaspoon salt
½ teaspoon black pepper
6 (½-inch thick) boneless pork chops
4 tablespoon butter

4 tablespoon olive oil
3 garlic cloves, peeled and crushed
1 (13¾ or 14.5 ounce can) College Inn® Chicken Broth
⅓ cup Balsamic Vinegar

Combine the flour, rosemary, salt and pepper. Dredge the pork chops in the flour mix. Melt the butter and oil in a large frying pan over medium heat. Add the garlic and sauté 1 minute. Add the pork chops and cook about 4 to 5 minutes on each side. Remove the chops. Add the chicken broth and vinegar, stirring to incorporate the drippings on the bottom of the pan. Cook about 7 minutes until the liquid is reduced by half. Add the pork chops and cook an additional 5 minutes or until done.

This is based on a dish made at the Chesterfield Restaurant in Utica, New York.

PORK AND PRETZELS
Elise Feiner

6 boneless pork chops, trimmed ¼-inch thickness
¼ cup mayonnaise
½ cup sour cream
½ teaspoon garlic salt
½ teaspoon Worcestershire sauce
⅛ teaspoon celery salt

Dash of black pepper
Dash of paprika
2 cloves of garlic, peeled and crushed
2 cup crushed pretzels
4-6 tablespoons butter
¼ teaspoon dried sage

Pound pork chops to ¼-inch thickness. Mix the mayonnaise, sour cream, garlic salt, Worcestershire sauce, celery salt, black pepper, paprika, and garlic together. Place the pork chops in the marinade for about 2 to 3 hours. When ready to cook, dredge the pork chops in the pretzels. Melt the butter in a large frying pan. Add the pork chops; sprinkle with sage. Cook 4 to 5 minutes on each side or until done.

PORK LOIN
Elise Feiner

1 large loin of pork, butter flied
2 large onions, peeled and sliced
3 cloves of garlic, peeled and cut in half
4-5 cloves of garlic, peeled and crushed
¼ cup olive oil

⅛ cup Balsamic vinegar
2 teaspoons garlic salt
⅛ teaspoon black pepper
Gravy Master® for color

Mix all the ingredients together except the pork loin, the garlic cloves which were cut in half and Gravy Master. Place the pork loin in a large roasting pan after you spray it with PAM®. With a knife make slits in the pork loin and insert the garlic halves. Take the garlic and onion mix and rub all over the port loin and insert some of the marinade into the middle of the loin. Let the pork marinade in the mix for a few hours. Pour out about half of the remaining marinade and add about half cup of water to the baking pan. Bake at 350° until a meat thermometer registers the correct doneness for pork. Use the remaining drippings to make nice brown gravy. To make brown gravy, take a few tablespoons of Wondra® flour and dissolve in about 1½ cups cold water. (Try to remove as much of the grease from the drippings as possible if you are health oriented...if you are flavor oriented, leave some of the grease). Add to the drippings in the pan. Pour that mix into a medium sauce pan. Season with black pepper and garlic salt to taste. Add Gravy Master® for color and flavor. Stir constantly and bring to a boil. Lower the heat and let it simmer for a few minutes. The gravy will only thicken after it comes to a boil. If too thick add more water, if too thin add a little more flour (mix with a little cold water first.)

Uncle Gene Feiner and Rose Parrotta
Rose owns the Happy Rooster Restaurant in
Philadelphia. It's located at 118 South 16th
Street. Call for a reservation 215 563-1481 if
you're in the neighborhood.

NANNY'S KIELBASA
Katherine Avella

1½ pounds kielbasa, sliced
1-inch thick, on a slant
2 tablespoons oil
1 pound of sauerkraut

Garlic powder
Black pepper
2 large onions, peeled and sliced

Put oil in a large frying pan and heat. Add sliced kielbasa and brown. Remove to a platter. To the oil, add sliced onions and cook until golden. Add the sauerkraut with liquid. Add garlic powder and black pepper to taste. Stir together. Add browned kielbasa. Mix; cover and stew for about 10 minutes. Let stand about 5 minutes before serving.

AUNT THIRZA'S LOIN OF PORK
Thirza Avella

5-6 pound pork loin, butterflied
5-6 cloves of garlic, peeled and cut in half
1-2 medium onions, peeled and cut in slices
1 packet of Sazon Goya® seasoning mix (con culantro y achiote)
Wesson® oil about 1-½ cups
Garlic flavored wine vinegar (about ½ cup)
Garlic salt (about 1-2 tablespoons)
Onion powder or salt (about 2 teaspoons)
Oregano (about 4 tablespoons)
Parsley (about 4 tablespoons)

Basil (about 4 tablespoons)
Black pepper to taste (about ¾ teaspoon)
Paprika (about ½ tablespoon)
McCormick® Season All Seasoned Salt (about 2 teaspoons)
Cooking with Love's Passion Spice Mix (about 1 teaspoon) (this is a spice from a local restaurant and can be ordered from our web site)
Water (enough to made it a little looser) about ¼ cup
1-2 carrots, peeled and sliced thinly
8-10 green olives cut in half

Place the sliced carrots, green olives, and some of the sliced onions in a separate bowl; set aside. Mix remaining ingredients together, except for the pork onions, garlic cloves, and water. Mix well. Add the onion slices to the marinade. If the marinade is too pasty add a little water to thin it. Add a little marinade mix to the carrot mix, cover and refrigerate. Marinade the pork in this marinade overnight. When ready to bake the pork make a few holes with a knife and stick the garlic halves into the holes. Stuff the carrot, onion, and olive mixture into the middle of the pork loin; tie with more kitchen twine if necessary. Spray a roasting pan and rack with PAM®. Place the pork loin on the rack. Keep as much of the onion and about 1 cup of the liquid from the marinade and discard the rest. Put the remaining cup of marinade and onions over the loin, in the pan. Roast the loin at 350°, basting frequently until a meat thermometer registers correct temperature; about 1 to 1½ hours. Check with thermometer so it doesn't overcook or it will be dry. Remove the pork when the temperature reaches 10° below the temperature listed for pork. Let sit 15 minutes before slicing to keep the juices in and the temperature to rise 10°. Slice and serve with brown gravy. Take a few tablespoons of Wondra flour and mix with 1 cup of cold water until it is thin and very runny. Add to the drippings from the pan, adding a little more water if needed; heat until boiling. Lower to a simmer and cook a few minutes until thick. Add garlic salt and pepper to taste; add Gravy Master for color.

L-R: Jeffrey, Lauren, Steven, Elise and Marc Feiner missing David

PORK ROAST
Thirza Avella

1 (5 to 7 pound) pork loin
1 whole head garlic, cloves separated and peeled
1 tablespoon McCormick® Season All Seasoned Salt
1 teaspoon garlic salt
3 tablespoons vegetable oil

Gravy:

6 tablespoons oil or butter
4 tablespoons flour
1 medium onion, peeled and finely chopped
½ medium green bell pepper, seeded and finely chopped
1 stalk celery, finely chopped
2 cloves garlic, peeled and crushed
½ bunch green onions, green and white parts chopped separately

1 large onion, chopped
2 stalks celery, chopped
½ medium green bell pepper, seeded and chopped
2 tablespoons teriyaki sauce
1 teaspoon Worcestershire sauce

2 cups beef stock
½ cup heavy cream
1 pound sliced mushrooms
2 tablespoons teriyaki sauce
Salt
Freshly ground black pepper

Preheat the oven to 450°. Pierce the roast all over with the tip of a paring knife and stuff one clove of garlic into each hole. Sprinkle on all sides with seasoned salt and garlic powder and rub into the meat. Heat the oil in a Dutch oven over medium-high heat and brown the roast evenly on all sides, about 10 to 15 minutes. Add the chopped onion, celery, bell pepper, and enough water to come 1-inch up the sides of the pan. Add the teriyaki sauce, Worcestershire sauce, and stir to combine and loosen any browned bits on the bottom of the pan. Cover and bake for 45 minutes. Reduce the oven temperature to 350° and add a more water as necessary to come 1-inch up the side of the pan. Continue to cook until very tender, about 3½ hour's total cooking time.

Melt 4 tablespoons of the butter in a medium saucepan. Whisk in the flour and cook, stirring constantly, over medium heat, until milk chocolate-colored roux is formed, about 15 minutes. Add the onion, bell pepper, celery, garlic, and the white part of the green onions, and cook until the vegetables are soft but not browned, about 5 minutes. Whisk in the beef stock and heavy cream and cook until thickened, 10 to 15 minutes. While the sauce is simmering, melt the remaining 2 tablespoons of butter in a medium skillet over medium-high heat. Add the mushrooms and cook, stirring, until tender and golden brown around the edges, about 5 minutes. Add the mushrooms and teriyaki sauce to the gravy and simmer about 3 minutes. Remove the roast from the pan. Strain juices from meat through a fine mesh strainer into the gravy and simmer until heated and thickened, about 5 minutes. Season with salt and pepper, to taste, and serve with pork.

My sister-in-law Thirza was a whiz with pork and a great cook!

FRESH HAM
Edith Mainella

Large fresh ham
6-8 slices of bacon

1 orange, cut into thin slices

Place the ham in a roasting pan that has been sprayed with PAM®. Preheat an oven 350° oven. Cover the ham with bacon strips and orange slices. Bake about ½ hour per pound. Cover with aluminum foil if the bacon is getting too brown.

Aunt Edith always made a fresh ham at the holidays, and we always fought over who would get the crispy skin.

HAM AND COLA
Elise Feiner

5 pounds precooked ham (I like the spiral ham)
½ cup brown sugar
1 teaspoon dry mustard

1 teaspoon prepared horseradish
1 can Coca Cola®

Mix the brown sugar, mustard, and horseradish together. Add enough cola (about ¼ cup) to make a paste. Save the rest of the cola. Rub the paste all over the ham and place in a crock-pot. Add the remaining cola. Cover and cook on high 1 hour. Turn and reduce heat to low and cook 6 to 7 hours.

INCREDIBLE PULLED PORK
Elise Feiner

1 cup roasted garlic mix (see below)   **1 (6-7 pound) boneless pork shoulder or butt roast**

Make the roasted garlic mix for the rub. To learn how to roast the garlic see the **recipe index for Roasted Garlic Dipping Oil**. It will take about **10 full bulbs of garlic** to make one cup of garlic paste for the mix. Preheat the oven to 275°. Trim any extra fat from the pork roast. Rub the garlic mix all over the pork roast and into any openings. Place the roast fat side up in a pan and place in the oven for 6-8 hours and no more than 10 hours. Place on a board and allow to sit for about 10 to 15 minutes before serving. Pull the pork apart with a fork or tongs so it's in chunks. I like to serve this with couscous.

Ingredients for the roasted garlic mix:

1 cup roasted garlic cloves   **2½ tablespoons dried rosemary**
2½ tablespoons salt   **The zest of one lemon**
1 tablespoon dry mustard powder   **1 teaspoon black pepper**
1 tablespoon paprika   **1 tablespoon of Herbs de Provence**
1 tablespoon thyme

Squeeze the cloves of garlic after they have been roasted. Place all the ingredients in a food processor, and make into a paste. Spread over roast as directed above.

My kids love barbequed pork in the crock-pot, this is a little different twist on the pulled pork.

SWEET AND SOUR PORK
Elise Feiner

1 pound pork tenderloin or stir fry pork strips   **4 slices pineapple**
1 green bell pepper, cubed   **½ cup cornstarch**
1 red bell pepper, cubed   **5-6 cups of oil**

Marinade:
½ teaspoon salt   **1 tablespoon cold water**
½ tablespoon soy sauce   **1 egg yolk**
1 tablespoon cornstarch

Sweet and Sour Sauce:
3 tablespoons rice wine vinegar   **3 teaspoons cornstarch**
4 tablespoon sugar   **1 teaspoon garlic salt**
4 tablespoons ketchup   **1 teaspoon sesame oil**
5 tablespoons cold water

With a meat tenderizing hammer, pound the pork until it is thin; cut into one-inch squares or strips. Mix the marinade ingredients together in a bowl. Place the pork in the marinade for at least an hour. Cut the pineapple into the same size squares; set aside. Mix the ingredients for the sweet and sour sauce and set aside. Heat the oil. Coat the pork pieces in the cornstarch while the oil is heating. When the oil is hot, fry the pork cubes for about 3 minutes; remove fro the oil. Reheat the oil when ready to serve and refry the pork cubes until crispy; set aside. Remove all but about 3 tablespoons of the oil from the pan and fry the peppers and pineapple, stirring constantly. Add the sweet and sour sauce mix, stirring constantly. Continue to stir fry until the sauce has thickened. Turn off the heat. Add the pork back in and mix well again. Serve with white rice.

EASY PORK CHOPS
Elise Feiner

12 boneless pork loins   **3-4 tablespoons butter**
Cooking with Love's Passion Spice Mix   **4-6 cloves of garlic, peeled and crushed**

Liberally sprinkle both sides of the pork chops with the Cooking with Love's Passion Spice Mix. Heat a large grill pan or frying pan that has been sprayed with PAM™. Add the butter and melt the butter with the garlic for about 1 minute. Add the chops and brown on both sides until thoroughly cooked and browned about 8 minutes.

PORK WELLINGTON
Elise Feiner

1½ teaspoons unsalted butter
1 pork tenderloin (about 1½ pounds)
2 teaspoons McCormick® Season All Seasoned Salt
4 tablespoons vegetable oil

1 sheet Puff pastry
1 egg
4 tablespoons mustard
3 cups mushroom pate (see below)

Preheat the oven to 400°. Use a disposable aluminum cookie sheet and grease the center with the butter. Season the tenderloin with the seasoned salt on all sides. In a large skillet, heat the oil. Sear the tenderloin in the oil, turning frequently until brown and internal temperature reaches 110° (check with a meat thermometer) about 18 to 20 minutes. Remove from the pan and let cool for about 15 minutes. On a lightly floured board, roll the puff pastry to a large rectangle about 12 x 16-inches. Rub the tenderloin with the mustard. Place the mushroom mix in the middle of the rectangle. Place the tenderloin on top of the mushroom mix. Beat the egg with a little water. Brush the edges of the pastry with the egg mix. Wrap the pastry around the tenderloin cut off any excess pastry (you can use this to make cutouts to decorate the Wellington. Place the pork seam side down on the prepared cookie sheet. You may want to place this sheet on a regular cookie sheet for safety. Brush the pastry with the remaining egg/water mix. Bake for 15 to 20 minutes; turn. Bake until the temperature reaches 150 to 160°. Remove from the oven. Let sit about 5 minutes before serving.

I love Beef Wellington but this is another version which is very easy to do. It's great if you're on a budget and need a less expensive cut of meat, but you still want an elegant meal. If you are serving more than 3 to 4 people you can use a boneless loin of pork as well, just adjust cooking time.

L-R: My Grandfather Felice Avella and Great Grandfather
Emmanuele Avella...check out those handlebar moustaches!

MUSHROOM PATE
Elise Feiner

4 tablespoons unsalted butter
½ cup shallots, peeled and minced
3 cloves garlic, peeled and crushed
1½ pounds mushrooms, cleaned and finely chopped
¼ teaspoon salt
⅛ teaspoon pepper

¼ cup white wine
1½ teaspoons soy sauce
1½ teaspoons balsamic vinegar
1½ teaspoons Worcestershire sauce
½ teaspoon basil
3 tablespoons grated cheese

In a large frying pan, melt the butter. Add the shallots and garlic, and stir for about 3 minutes. Add the mushrooms, salt, pepper and cook until the mushrooms start to brown and caramelize. This should take about 20 minutes. Add the wine, soy sauce, vinegar, and Worcestershire sauce; cook stirring to scrap the pieces from the bottom of the pan. Let the liquid evaporate. Stir in the basil and grated cheese. Remove from heat. Let cool until needed. Make sure all liquid is gone. This is used for making a pork or beef Wellington if you don't like the liver pate. You can also serve it with crackers if you want.

I am not a fan of liver so I always use mushrooms when I make a Wellington. I got a recipe similar to this in the seventies and changed it a little through the years. If you are a fan of liver, you could easily cook and chop some liver and add it to the mix.

CROQUETTAS DE JAMON (HAM CROQUETTES)
Thirza Avella

3 pounds cooked ham, cut into a large dice
1 white onion, diced
2 red peppers, diced
2 cloves garlic, sliced
2 tablespoons tomato paste
¼ bunch parsley, chopped
½ teaspoon fresh grated nutmeg

½ cup heavy cream
½ cup flour, plus ½ cup
Salt and freshly ground black pepper
2 large eggs lightly beaten
2 cups Panko crumbs or plain breadcrumbs
Vegetable oil for frying

Place about 4 tablespoons of oil in a large frying pan. Add the ham, onions, peppers, and garlic and sauté for a few minutes. Add tomato paste and caramelize. Add parsley, nutmeg, and heavy cream. Sprinkle with ½ cup of the flour. Season with salt and pepper to taste; cool. Pulse the ham mixture in a food processor until finely ground. Shape into logs or round croquettes. Place the remaining flour in a dish; dip the croquettes in the flour. Place the 2 beaten eggs in a bowl. Dip the floured croquettes in the egg. Place the Panko crumbs in a dish. Dip the croquettes from the egg into the crumbs. Heat a frying pan filled 1-inch of oil to 375°. Fry the croquettes until golden brown. Serves 6.

This is a very typical Latin recipe. When my friend Nancy Barfield and I went to Spain, we lived on these for lunch and dinner. This is a great way to use up leftover ham. Try them with the mustard sauce in the recipe index.

BARBEQUED SPARERIBS
Elise Feiner

2-3 racks of pork or beef baby back ribs
2 onions, peeled and left whole

Boiling water
Marinade or barbeque sauce of your choice

In the days before the spareribs came precooked, we started from scratch. Take the racks of baby back ribs, (amount will depend on the number of guests you are having). Place a large onion or two in a large (18 quart) pot with the spareribs. Bring to a boil and then reduce to a simmer for about 35 to 45 minutes. Remove from the water. Marinade in your favorite barbeque sauce or marinade overnight. I like to use a mix of ketchup, duck sauce, garlic salt, and apricot Saucy Susan sauce. Barbeque the ribs on the grill on medium heat. Watch **carefully** because any sauce with high sugar content will burn easily. These ribs are basically cooked at this point so they don't need to be on the grill very long.

L-R: Cousins Michele Maida, Jeffrey "Dr. Carter" (as the girls call him) Feiner and Mary Ann Maida

CROWN ROAST OF SPARERIBS
Thirza Avella

2 racks of spareribs (about 4-5 pounds)
¼ teaspoon garlic salt
⅛ teaspoon black pepper
¾ cup butter
½ cup chopped onions
½ cup green pepper, seeded and chopped

1 (8 ounce) can creamed corn
½ cup heavy cream
½ teaspoon dried rosemary
1 (8 ounce) package cornbread stuffing mix
¾ cup Dinosaur® or Sweet Baby Ray's® Barbeque sauce or your own choice

Preheat the oven to 350°. Ask the butcher to trim the racks so that they are the same height all the way across. Save the trimmings. Wipe the ribs with a damp paper towel. Shape the racks into a standing crown by standing them up on their narrow edge with the meaty side of the ribs facing the outside of the circle. Fasten with bamboo skewers or wooden picks. Sprinkle with garlic salt and pepper inside and out. Line a small roasting pan with aluminum foil. Place the meat crown into the pan; tuck the leftover trimmings pieces (so they can flavor the stuffing) inside the crown; against the ribs. Add about 2 cups of water to the pan. Roast covered for 1½ hours. Meanwhile, place the butter in a skillet and heat it. Sautee the onions and green peppers until tender about 5 minutes. Remove from heat. Add the corn bread stuffing and stir until moistened. Set it aside. At the end of the 1¼ hours, remove the crown from the oven. Pour off the pan drippings, save about ½ cup. Stir the reserved drippings into the corn bread stuffing. Brush the whole crown inside and out with barbeque sauce. Place the stuffing inside the crown. Cover the center of the roast and the ends of the crown with aluminum foil. Roast an additional 45 minutes so that the ribs are browned and nicely glazed. When you take the crown out of the pan, lift the aluminum foil liner so the stuffing doesn't fall out. Carefully place the crown on a platter, remove any foil from the top, and fold under any visible foil in at the bottom.

The much younger Avella's
Clockwise from the Left: Thirza, Joseph, Douglas and Melissa
Turn back a few pages and see if Joe doesn't look like my grandfather and great grandfather…same pose and everything!

BALSAMIC PORK LOIN
Elise Feiner

4 cups red wine
3 cloves garlic, peeled and chopped
1 cup balsamic vinegar
1 teaspoon fresh rosemary, chopped
Boneless pork loin (3-4 pounds)
Garlic salt to taste

Black pepper
3 cloves garlic, peeled and crushed
2 teaspoons fresh rosemary, chopped
¼ cup brown sugar
¾ cup balsamic vinegar
2 tablespoons extra virgin olive oil

Place the 4 cups of wine and 3 cloves of garlic in a heavy saucepan. Reduce the volume to about ¼ cup over high heat. Add the vinegar and continue to reduce the sauce to about ⅓ cup. Add the teaspoon of rosemary and cook for about 5 minutes or until the sauce is fairly thick. Remove from the heat and strain. Set aside. Preheat oven to 325°. Combine the 3 cloves of crushed garlic, 2 teaspoons rosemary, brown sugar and the ¾-cup olive oil in a large saucepan. Bring to a boil over high heat; reduce to low heat and cook about 5 minutes making sure the sugar has dissolved. In a large enough pan to fit the pork, heat the olive oil until very hot, but not burned. Add the pork loin sprinkled with garlic salt and black pepper. Brown on both sides. Place pork in a roasting pan and brush with the brown sugar mix. Bake for about 15 minutes and brush with the brown sugar mix again. Continue to bake until the pork is done, basting with the brown sugar (check for doneness with a meat thermometer.) Drizzle the balsamic sauce that you made earlier over the meat. Serves 6.

Betty and Jimmy Saracino

Phyllis and Richard Jendzo

Dorothy and Vincent DeClementi

Rosemarie and her son Philip Di Pierdomenico

Jeffrey and his Mom Elise Feiner

Fran and Norm Zierler

VEAL AND PEPPERS
Katherine Avella

2 pounds veal cubes	2-3 green peppers, seeded, and cut into strips
½ - ¾ cup flour	1 box fresh mushrooms, sliced
1 teaspoon garlic salt	4 packets chicken bouillon
⅛ teaspoon black pepper	2 cups hot water
4-6 tablespoons oil	½ - ¾ cup white wine
2 medium to large onions, peeled and sliced	Salt and pepper to taste

Mix the flour with the garlic salt and black pepper. Flour the veal cubes. In a Dutch oven or deep sauté pan, heat the oil. (Add more oil if necessary as you brown the rest.) Brown the cubes of veal until nicely golden. Remove to a platter. Add the onions to the oil, and sauté until starting to soften, add the peppers, cook until soft and the onions are golden about 10-15 minutes. Add the chicken bouillon dissolved in the hot water; add wine, and the veal cubes. Heat to boiling and then lower to a simmer for about 15 minutes. Add the mushrooms and salt and pepper to taste. Continue to simmer about another 15 minutes. Serve over rice, mashed potatoes or noodles. If you prefer a red sauce, decrease the bouillon to two packets, and the water to 1 cup. Add one can of crushed tomatoes at the same time you add the bouillon. You may need to simmer it for an extra 10 to 15 minutes. I would also add about 1 teaspoon of dried basil with the tomatoes. Serves 4.

VEAL BIRDS
Katherine Avella

2 pounds veal scaloppini sliced on the thicker side (cut in 2 to 3 pieces, not too small)	Salt and pepper, to taste
2 large onions, (peeled and sliced)	½ - 1 cup white wine
2 cups chicken or beef broth (if using bouillon packets use 2 packets to 1 cup of water)	2-3 tablespoons oil

Brown veal in a little oil with the onions. When the veal stops foaming, add the broth, salt and pepper, and the white wine. Simmer 25 to 30 minutes. Serve over white rice or mashed potatoes.

VEAL CUTLETS GALLIANO®
Elise Feiner

1-1½ pounds veal cutlets	1 teaspoon pepper
1 large onion, thinly sliced	½ cup white wine
2 cloves garlic, minced	3 ounces Galliano®
1 cup flour	1 tablespoon parmesan cheese, grated
½ cup oil	2 beef bouillon cubes
2 tablespoons butter	4 ounces mushrooms, sliced
1 tablespoon tarragon	Juice of half a lemon
1 tablespoon salt	

Sauté onion in butter and oil until tender and slightly browned. Combine flour, tarragon, salt and pepper in a plastic bag and coat the veal cutlets. Remove onion from the skillet with a slotted spoon, draining butter and oil mixture back into the pan. Add garlic to reserve butter and oil and lightly brown. When brown, add veal cutlets and cook until brown. Return onions to skillet. Add white wine, water and Galliano. Bring to a boil, and then reduce to a simmer. Add beef bouillon cubes and mushrooms and simmer for 10 minutes. Sprinkle Parmesan cheese and squeeze lemon over the cutlets. Cover and heat five minutes, then serve.

This came from a newspaper article when we lived in Staten Island. It's excellent.

"All people are made from the same dough, they are just cooked in different ovens"
-Old Jewish Proverb

VEAL FORESTIER
Elise Feiner

1 pound veal cutlets for scaloppini cut about ¼-inch thick
¼ cup Wondra® flour
4 tablespoons butter
½ pound fresh mushrooms, sliced

½ cup dry vermouth
2 tablespoons water
¾ teaspoon salt
Dash pepper

On a cutting board with a meat mallet, pound the cutlets to ⅛-inch thick, and cut into 3 x 2-inch pieces. (Better yet, have the butcher do it for you.) On waxed paper, coat the cutlets lightly with the flour. In 10-inch skillet over medium-high heat, in hot butter, cook the meat a few pieces at a time, until lightly browned on both sides, removing pieces as they brown, and adding more butter if necessary. Add mushrooms, vermouth, salt and pepper to skillet; heat to boiling; cover and simmer until the mushrooms are tender, about 5 minutes. Return the meat to the skillet; heat through. Place on a serving plate.

VEAL ROAST
Elise Feiner

3 pounds boneless veal roast
Salt and pepper
½ cup butter
½ cup onion, peeled and diced

½ cup white wine
1 tablespoon all-purpose potato
1 cup fresh mushrooms, sliced
1 tablespoon rosemary, crumbled

Season the meat with salt and pepper to taste. In a large skillet, sear the meat on both sides in the butter until golden brown. Remove from the skillet. Add the onion to the frying pan and brown them. Add the wine and the flour; stir well. Add the mushrooms and rosemary. Put the meat on a rack in a roasting pan. (Spray the pan and the rack with PAM® first.) Pour the contents of the skillet over the top of the meat. Roast in a preheated 350° oven for 1¾ hours or until a meat thermometer reads the correct temperature for veal. Serve with mashed potatoes or rice if desired. Serves 6 to 8.

OSSO BUCO
Virginia Casazza

4 veal shanks cut three inches thick (about 3½ to 4 pounds)
½ cup of all purpose flour
Salt and pepper
6 tablespoons extra-virgin olive oil
3 tablespoons unsalted butter
1 medium carrot, diced
1 large Spanish onion, peeled and diced
1 celery stalk, chopped into ¼-inch slices

2 tablespoons chopped fresh thyme leaves
4 cloves of garlic, peeled and crushed
2 bay leaves
2 cups marinara sauce (see index)
2 cups chicken or veal stock
2 cups dry white wine
Gremolata

Preheat the oven to 375°. Mix the salt and pepper into the flour. Dredge the shanks with salt and pepper. In a heavy 8-quart casserole, heat the olive oil and butter together until very hot. Place the shanks in the pan and brown all over, turning to get every surface, 12 to 15 minutes. Remove the shanks and set aside. Reduce the heat to medium, add the carrot, onion, garlic, celery and thyme leaves and cook, stirring regularly, until golden brown and slightly softened, 8 to 10 minutes. Add the tomato sauce, bay leaves, chicken stock and wine and bring to a boil. Place shanks back into pan, making sure they are submerged at least halfway. If shanks are not covered halfway, add more stock. Cover the pan with tight-fitting lid of aluminum foil. Place in oven for 2 to 2½ hours and cook until meat is nearly falling off the bone. Serves 4

Remove the casserole from the oven and let stand 10 minutes. Before serving, sprinkle with the Gremolata.

Gremolata:
¼ cup finely chopped Italian parsley
¼ cup pine nuts, toasted under the broiler until dark brown
Zest of 1 lemon

Zest of one orange
2 cloves of garlic, peeled and crushed

Mix the parsley, pine nuts and lemon and orange zest, and garlic together in a small bowl. Set aside until ready to serve.

This was one of Cousin Virginia's favorite dishes. She served it with a delicious risotto (see index).

VEAL CUTLETS
Katherine Avella

1½ pounds veal for scaloppini (cutlets)
Plain bread crumbs
Wondra® flour
6-8 eggs, beaten
½ teaspoon salt

⅛ teaspoon black pepper
2 tablespoons dried parsley
1-1½ cups grated cheese (Locatelli Romano or Parmesan cheese)
Wesson® oil or other vegetable oil for frying

Cut the veal pieces into small size cutlets about 3 x 2-inch or leave them large if you like them that way. Get two large paper plates or pieces of waxed paper or aluminum foil, and fill one with plain breadcrumbs, and one with flour. Beat the eggs, salt, pepper, parsley, and grated cheese together in a large mixing bowl. Dip the cutlets in the flour, then the egg mixture, then the breadcrumb mixture. (You may freeze them at this point by placing them on a sheet of waxed paper in a single layer on a disposable cookie sheet; after they freeze you can put them in a zip lock bag and fry later.) Place them on a platter as you bread them with wax paper between each layer. If you have any of the egg mixture left over, add remaining breadcrumbs to it and mix until firm, adding more breadcrumbs if necessary. Shape into round patties and fry these as well. They are delicious too. Place about ¼ - ½-inch of oil in a frying pan and heat. Test the oil to see if it is hot by throwing a little of the breadcrumb mix into the oil; if it bubbles, it's hot enough to begin frying. Fry the cutlets until golden brown on both sides. This will take a few minutes (about 4 to 6 minutes for veal.) Place on a platter lined with paper towels as they finish cooking. Layer paper towels between each layer of cutlets. Remove the paper towels before serving.

This is one of the Feiner kid's favorite meals. If you are using chicken cutlets you may want to pound them between two sheets of waxed paper to thin them out a little. However, today you can find thin chicken cutlets in most stores. When you buy the veal cutlets be careful if you ask for cutlets, in some places this means it will have a bone. You may need to ask for scaloppini. Chicken cutlets are made exactly the same way, substituting chicken for veal. The chicken will be a little bit thicker (you will use boneless chicken breast); you can flatten with a meat mallet if you want them very thin by placing them between two sheets of waxed paper and pounding to the desired thinness. You can also ask the butcher to do this for you. This recipe was my grandmothers, handed down to my mother, and then to me. These are delicious just fried with a salad and side dish.

VEAL PARMIGIANA
Katherine Avella

Prepared Veal cutlets (see recipe previous page)
2-3 bags grated mozzarella cheese, or whole mozzarella thinly sliced
½-¾ cup grating cheese for the top

Recipe for Avella Marinara Sauce (see index)
1 pound Pasta (I like spaghetti with this)

To make the cutlets Parmigiana, make the marinara sauce recipe and the veal cutlets as per the directions. In a shallow baking dish, cover the bottom with marinara sauce. Place a single layer of prepared cutlets on top of the sauce. Top with another sparse layer of marinara sauce. Top with mozzarella and grated cheese and more marinara sauce. Bake at 350° for about 20 to 25 minutes or until cheese melts; cover with foil if getting too brown, or place pan under the broiler until the mozzarella melts, about 7 minutes (**watch carefully**.) If making Parmigiana, serve with spaghetti or angel hair pasta. Cook pasta according to package directions and fix with marinara sauce and grating cheese. Serves 6

Good looking kids if I do say so myself

L-R: Lauren, Jeffrey, David and Steven Feiner – all that orthodontic work paid off – thanks Uncle Anthony Furino!

Camille Sanabria says no one does braces like Anthony and asks every kid she sees with beautiful teeth if he's their orthodontist!

ATHENA'S VEAL ROLLS
Athena Avramidis

8 veal cutlets	Few tablespoons flour
½ pound bacon cut into small pieces	5 - 6 tablespoons butter
¼ teaspoons lemon rind	2 large onions, peeled and cut in pieces
½ cup breadcrumbs	3 tablespoons tomato paste
1 teaspoon basil	1-2 carrots, peeled and cut in pieces
Salt and pepper to taste	½ cup butter
1 egg, beaten	2½ cups beef stock

Mix together the bacon, lemon rind, breadcrumbs, basil, and egg. Sprinkle some fresh pepper. Salt and pepper the veal cutlets (pound them thinner if needed). Put some of the filling in the middle of each cutlet and roll them up. Tie with thread. Roll them in a little flour. In a large sauté pan, melt the butter. Sauté the rolls until brown on all sides. Remove to a Pyrex® baking pan. In the same sauté pan with the drippings, brown the onions and carrots. Add the tomato paste and the stock. Simmer for about 1 to 2 minutes. Cover the rolls with the sauce and bake at 350° for 1½ hours.

Athena made this for a holiday party at her house. They were a great hit. They are great to make if you're having a large group, just triple the recipe; great with mashed potatoes.

Lee Avramidis, M.D., and Athena Avramidis
Lee and Athena are our Greek friends. He is our pediatrician and she
is a fabulous cook and tennis player

STUFFED BREAST OF VEAL
Elise Feiner

1 large onion, diced and sautéed	½ tablespoon paprika
4-6 tablespoons butter	1 (5 to 6 pound) breast of veal, with a deep pocket cut into it
⅛ teaspoon pepper	1 loaf egg bread (Challah)
½ teaspoon garlic salt	4 eggs beaten
1 package onion soup mix	½ cup grated cheese
¼ cup melted butter	1 teaspoon sugar

Preheat oven to 375°. Sauté the diced onion in the 4-6 tablespoons of butter. Sprinkle with garlic salt and pepper. Mix onion soup mix with melted butter and paprika. Then, rub mix into the inside and outside of the veal breast. Break the egg bread into pieces and put into a colander and run hot water over bread to moisten. Drain well. In large bowl, put drained bread, sautéed onion mix, eggs, grated cheese and sugar. Mix very well. **Season with additional garlic salt and pepper to taste.** Stuff the bread mixture into veal breast. Tie the veal roast together with kitchen twine to prevent the stuffing from coming out as it cooks and expands. Cover with foil Place into oven for 2½ hours. Remove foil and cook another 45 minute to 1 hour. Serves 6 to 8.

I made this for dinner one night and it was outstanding. Buy a big veal breast with bones in place and have the butcher cut a very deep pocket in it. You may need to tie or sew the opening shut. I served it with the potato pie, roasted peppers, and escarole, a meal to die for.

VEAL MARSALA
Elise Feiner

8 tablespoons unsalted butter
1 pound of thin veal cutlets for scaloppini
¾ cup flour (more if needed) to coat the cutlets
2 shallots, peeled and finely chopped

6 ounces of Marsala wine
6-8 fresh mushrooms sliced
Salt and Pepper to taste

Melt the butter in a large frying pan over medium heat. Lightly dredge the veal cutlets in the flour and shake off any excess flour (I use Wondra® flour). Fry the veal cutlet on one side until golden brown. Turn over and add salt and pepper to taste and add the shallots. Lightly brown on remaining side about 4 minutes.

Increase the heat to high and add the Marsala and heat to a boil to evaporate the alcohol. Add the mushrooms and cook for a few more minutes. Place the veal on a serving dish and spoon the sauce over it.

This is one of my favorite ways to make veal although it doesn't come close to the best Veal Marsala which is made at Café Del Buono in New Hartford, New York. Eric makes the best! Stop in for dinner if you are in upstate New York. Their address is Commercial Drive, New Hartford, New York (across from the Sangertown Mall) and phone is 315 736-3023. He also makes an amazing Caesar Salad!

VEAL ROLLS
Katherine Avella

2 cloves of garlic, peeled and chopped
6 tablespoons extra virgin olive oil divided
½ - ¾ cup unflavored bread crumbs
3 tablespoons fresh parsley, finely chopped
salt and pepper to taste
6 veal cutlets (thin for scaloppini)

6 ounces Fontina cheese, thinly sliced
2-3 plum tomatoes, thinly sliced in circles and then cut in half
⅓ cup white wine

Mix the garlic with half of the olive oil and set aside. Preheat the oven to 350°. In another bowl, mix about ½ cup of the breadcrumbs with the parsley. Add this mix to the olive oil and garlic mix. Add a little salt and pepper to taste. Season the veal by sprinkling a little salt and pepper on the cutlets. Lay the cutlet flat and place a piece of the Fontina Cheese and 1 to 2 slices of the tomato halves at one end of the cutlet. Sprinkle a little of the breadcrumb mixture on the top of the tomatoes Roll the cutlet from the stuffed end into a roll and secure it with toothpicks use about 4 per roll. Spray a baking dish with PAM. Place the rolled veal into the baking dish and top with the remaining breadcrumbs, remaining olive oil and the wine. Bake 20 to 25 minutes. Let cool a little and then slice each cutlet into 4 to 5 pieces (rounds) using the toothpicks as a guide so each round is held together with a toothpick.

This is great for a light supper or a brunch with a salad but I really like it as an appetizer for a holiday or special dinner party. It looks very festive on the plate with the tomato showing through. You can garnish the top with parsley if you like. It will serve 2-3 as a main course.

After 4 sons, my friend Fran Zierler is finally getting some females to even out her household. Fran with daughters-in-law Aviva on the left and Samantha on the right!

David and Aviva Zierler

Samantha Caplan (soon to be Zierler) singing
with the band...you go girl!

L-R: Ronnie and Michael Tichenor

"Nanny" Jeane Cassata I am so blessed to have had Jeane come into my
life especially since my Mother is gone...she is always there for me.

L-R: Andrew Lowitz,
Steven Feiner, Kevin
Abbass, Paul Mancuso,
Ann Custadaro, David
Marks, Meredith
Schabert, David Feiner,
Lauren Feiner, and
Jeffrey Feiner

Poultry...

The Norman B. Zierler Family
L-R: David, Zachary, Fran, Jonathan, Norm, Jeremy

"Food is the most primitive form of comfort."
-Sheila Graham

More Hints:

Flies or bees bothering you? Spray them with hairspray and they'll take a dive.

Sealed envelope: Put in the freezer for a few hours, then slide a knife under the flap. The envelope can then be resealed. (hmmm...)

Use empty toilet paper roll to store appliance cords. It keeps them neat and you can write on the roll what appliance it belongs to.

For icy door steps in freezing temperatures: get warm water and put Dawn dishwashing liquid in it. Pour it all over the steps. They won't refreeze. (Wish I had known this for the last 40 years!)

Crayon marks on walls? This worked wonderfully! A damp rag, dipped in baking soda. Comes off with little effort (elbow grease that is!).

Permanent marker on appliances/counter tops (like store receipt BLUE!) rubbing alcohol on paper towel.

Opening brand new jars can be a feat in itself. Well, I have found a way to make it the easiest thing to do. Instead of banging a jar of jam, pickles, etc., with a knife until it loosens up, I simply reach into the drawer and pull out the handy nutcracker. It adjusts to the size of the jar and I simply give it a good twist and off pops the lid! You can also use disposable rubber gloves to open jars...increases your grip!

Blood stains on clothes? Not to worry! Just pour a little peroxide on a cloth and proceed to wipe off every drop of blood. Works every time! You learn this quickly working in a hospital...nail polish (acetone) remover works for sticky things like labels, and stickers.

Use vertical strokes when washing windows outside and horizontal for inside windows. This way you can tell which side has the streaks. Straight vinegar will get outside windows really clean. Don't wash windows on a sunny day. They will dry too quickly and will probably streak.

Spray a bit of perfume on the light bulb in any room to create a lovely light scent in each room when the light is turned on. Place fabric softener sheets in dresser drawers and your clothes will smell freshly washed for weeks to come. You can also do this with towels and linen.

Candles last a lot longer if placed in the freezer for at least 3 hours prior to burning.

Author Unknown (I received this in an e-mail forward – with many thanks to the original author)

BARBARA'S FABULOUS ROASTED CHICKEN
Barbara Schwartz

Chicken pieces of your choice,
(I prefer boneless breasts)

Cooking with Love's Passion Spice Mix
Vegetable oil

Wash of the chicken pieces and do not let dry. Coat them very liberally with Cooking with Love's Passion Spice Mix. Place a little vegetable oil in a baking dish. Place chicken in the dish. Bake at 350° for one hour covered with aluminum foil, placed **ACROSS** the top and **not tucked it**. Lower the oven to 250°; remove foil and cook for another 45 minutes.

This makes a delicious and moist chicken. Barbara makes this for company and on the Jewish holidays!

The Schwartz-Lipson Clan...

Back Row L-R: Kenneth Schwartz, Stuart Schwartz, Barbara Schwartz, Shelley Lipson

Front Row L-R: Debbie Karden Schwartz holding Zachary Schwartz, Basia Schwartz, Debbie Schwartz Lipson holding Kayla Lipson (missing Jonah Schwartz)

BARBEQUE CHICKEN PIZZA
Lauren Feiner

4 tablespoons vegetable oil
1 package pizza dough
1 green pepper (optional) seeded and sliced
2 packages boneless chicken cut in strips for stir fry
Salt and pepper to taste

1 small red onion, peeled and sliced thinly
½ - ¾ cup Jack Daniels® Barbeque Sauce
1 package shredded mozzarella cheese (2 or 3 cups)
Black olives, pitted and sliced, optional
2 Roma tomatoes, diced in tiny cubes

Preheat oven to 500°. In a large skillet, heat the vegetable oil. Add the strips of chicken, season with a little salt and pepper. Cook until the brown and almost cooked. Remove chicken and set aside. Add the peppers and onions to the oil and sauté until soft. Lightly spray a cookie sheet with PAM®. Shape the pizza dough in the prepared pan. Brush the top of the crust with the barbeque sauce. Mix the chicken, peppers and onions in the remaining barbeque sauce. Place the chicken mixture on top of the pizza shell. Top with mozzarella. Sprinkle the diced tomatoes. Bake for about 20 minutes or until brown and crisp.

Ever since Lauren went to Phillips Exeter Academy, this has become one of her favorite foods. I couldn't imagine barbequed chicken pizza but it's really delicious. This is the version we created at home.

L-R: Jeffrey, David and Steven Feiner holding Lauren Feiner

They may fight with their sister but don't let anyone else harm a hair on her head...those boys adore her!

CHEESEY CHICKEN ROLLATINI
Elise Feiner

12 chicken cutlets
¾ cup seasoned bread crumbs
¼ pound Swiss cheese
¼ pound cooked ham
½ pound mozzarella
Fresh parsley, to taste
3 eggs, beaten
1 clove garlic, finely diced

1 small onion, finely diced
Salt and pepper, to taste
1 small can mushrooms, stems and pieces
1 (13¾ ounce) can chicken broth
1 tablespoon brown mustard
Grated cheese
Melted butter as needed

Trim chicken cutlets of any excess fat and pound each cutlet with a mallet. In a bowl, dice or shred Swiss cheese, ¼-pound mozzarella, ham, onion, garlic and parsley; mix well. Add bread crumbs, salt, pepper, grated cheese and melted butter; Mix thoroughly. On each chicken cutlet, place a scoop of the mixture and flatten with a fork. Secure each cutlet with a toothpick. Roll each cutlet in beaten egg and then seasoned bread crumbs. Fry rollatini in oil in a skillet until lightly browned. Place rollatini in a large baking dish. Add half the chicken broth; cover the pan with aluminum foil and bake at 325° for 35 to 45 minutes. Remove from oven and leave uncovered for about 10 minutes. Top each chicken cutlet with drained mushrooms and remaining shredded mozzarella. Mix remaining broth with brown mustard and pour over chicken. Bake uncovered for an additional 10 to 20 minutes. Serve over white rice.

I got this recipe when we were living in Staten Island in the early eighties. It's a good main dish for company too!

CHICKEN ALMANDINE
Shirley Flomenhoft

Chicken breasts boned (amount depending on the number of people; figure 1 piece for women, 2 pieces for men)
Flavored Italian Breadcrumbs

Melted butter or margarine (enough to coat chicken breasts)
Slivered almonds

Dip chicken breasts in butter or margarine. Then dip in breadcrumbs. Bake in a 325° oven for about 40 minutes or until brown. In the meantime, place a small of butter in a frying pan; add the slivered almonds. Keep turning the almonds until brown, watching carefully as they can burn quickly. Place almonds in a separate dish. Before serving, place almonds in a microwave for a few seconds to reheat. Place on top of the chicken breasts.

CHICKEN ACHARI
Caroline Wilson-Kent and Mona Gilsenan

2 pounds boneless chicken breasts and thighs
1½ cups yogurt, drained
1½ teaspoons mustard seeds
1 teaspoon Fenugreek seeds
5 whole red chilies
1 teaspoon Nigella (Kalonj) seeds
1 teaspoon fennel seeds

3 inches grated fresh ginger
4 cloves garlic, peeled and pressed
1½ teaspoons salt
3 green chilies, sliced and deseeded
2 tablespoons coriander leaves
½ cup oil

Remove the skins and cut the chicken into small pieces. Blend the yogurt with the salt, black pepper, ginger and garlic. Marinate the chicken for two hours in this mixture. Heat the oil in a heavy bottomed pan and add all the spices until they start to pop. Add the chicken gradually, removing as much of the marinade as you can (set the excess marinade to the side. Brown the chicken for 15 minutes in the spice mixture. Add the yogurt marinade and reduce the heat. Cover the pan and let the chicken cook for another 30 minutes. Uncover the chicken and reduce the gravy until thick. Garnish with green chilies and coriander leaves. Serves 6.

This recipe came from my wonderful clients at the Oberoi Hotels and Resorts. Through the years, they have come to be more to me then clients, they are my friends. They have contributed this wonderful Indian recipe that can be served at both a main course and an appetizer. If you have difficulties finding these spices e-mail us at elise@cookingwithlove.com .

CHICKEN CASSEROLE
Sam Sternick

5 chicken breasts, stewed
1 pint sour cream
1 can cream of mushroom soup
1 (4 ounce) can mushrooms, undrained
¼ cup sherry (optional)

1 cup or more of chicken broth
⅓ cup melted butter
1 package of stuffing

Remove the meat from the bones. Place in a greased casserole. Mix sour cream, soup, mushrooms, broth and sherry. Pour over the chicken. Sprinkle with stuffing. Drizzle with butter. Cover with foil. Bake at 350° for 45 minutes. Uncover for the last few minutes. Serves 6.

Sam Sternick sent this recipe when we were collecting our Birthday Club recipes. To all my supportive friends in the birthday club...yes, there finally is a cookbook! The Birthday Club is a group of my friends who have been meeting once a month for the past twelve years to celebrate birthdays, good times, and support each other in the bad times...we are so lucky to have each other!

CHICKEN BREASTS SUPERB
Elise Feiner

2-3 packages of boneless chicken cutlets
1 (16 ounce) container sour cream
¼ cup lemon juice
4 teaspoons Worcestershire sauce
1½ teaspoons celery salt
2 teaspoons paprika

6 cloves of garlic, peeled and crushed
2 teaspoon salt
½ teaspoon pepper
3 cups plain breadcrumbs
½ cup butter
¼ cup oil

In a large bowl, combine the sour cream, lemon juice, Worcestershire sauce, paprika, celery salt, garlic, salt and pepper. Add the chicken cutlets to the sour cream mixture and stir to coat each piece well. Cover the bowl and refrigerate several hours or overnight. Preheat oven to 375°. Spray a large cookie sheet with PAM®. Roll the chicken breasts in the breadcrumbs, coating them well. Melt the butter and oil together in a small saucepan. Spoon half the mixture over the breasts. Bake for 45 minutes uncovered. Spoon the remainder of the butter oil mix over the chicken. Bake another 10 to 15 minutes or until chicken is tender and nicely browned. Serves 4 to 6.

This is one of my favorite chicken recipes. The sour cream coating keeps the breasts very moist. My cousin, Joan Arcieri used to love these chicken breasts when she ate dinner at our house. I make these at least once a week. Lauren loves these. These are wonderful leftover.

CHICKEN MARSALA
Lisa Nanna

4 chicken breasts sliced thin
2 eggs
Salt and pepper to taste
1½ cups unflavored breadcrumbs

⅓ cup parmesan cheese
¼ cup butter
2 tablespoons olive oil
1 cup dry Marsala or port wine

Beat eggs with salt and pepper. Combine breadcrumbs and cheese. Dip the chicken in the egg mixture and then into the breadcrumbs. Let stand 15 minutes. Melt butter with oil in a large frying pan. When butter foams, add the chicken. Cook over medium heat until golden brown on both sides. Add wine, cover; simmer 15 to 20 minutes or until tender. Serves 2 to 4 depending on their appetites.

This recipe was contributed by Lisa Nanna, a friend from Trainor Associates. She said it is a family favorite in her house. Lisa has since moved out of the area to much warmer climates (lucky her) but her recipe will remain a favorite with all the friends she left back in New Hartford.

"Success depends on your ability to make and keep friends".
-Sophie Tucker

CHICKEN BREASTS SUPREME
Elise Feiner

4 tablespoons of oil (or enough to coat the bottom of a 10-inch frying pan)
2 packages boneless chicken breasts
6 cloves of garlic, peeled and left whole
½ (12 ounce) bag frozen chopped onions
1 can Campbell's® Cream of Chicken Soup or Cream of Chicken and Mushroom
1 can Campbell's® Cheddar Cheese Soup

1 can (13¾ ounces) College Inn® Chicken Broth
½ pint heavy cream
¼ teaspoon black pepper
1 teaspoons garlic salt
2 teaspoons paprika
Dash of nutmeg
4-6 tablespoons mustard

Place oil in the bottom of a large frying pan. Add garlic, left whole, chopped onions, and chicken breasts. Brown lightly. Just before they're done add about 4 tablespoons of mustard, and brown for a few more minutes. In the meantime, add the 3 soups, heavy cream, garlic salt, pepper, paprika, nutmeg and 2 tablespoon mustard to a crock-pot. When chicken is brown, add the entire contents of the frying pan to the crock-pot mix. Turn on high for about 5 hours. Serve over white rice or noodles.

CHICKEN CATALINA
Elise Feiner

1-2 packages of boneless, skinless chicken breasts or chicken cutlets

1 bottle of Catalina Dressing
Flavored Italian Breadcrumbs

Pour the dressing into a large bowl. Add the chicken and mix well. Refrigerate for a few hours. Dip into flavored breadcrumbs. Spray a large baking pan or cookie sheet with PAM®. Place the breaded cutlets on the pan or pans. Bake 350° for about 50 minutes until golden brown.

Old Family Friends…The Oppenheim Family
L-R: Evan, Ethan, Felice, David, Elana, and Eliza (in front)

"A mirror reflects a man's face, but what he is really like is shown by the kind of friends he chooses."
-Proverbs

176

CHICKEN CACCIATORE
Elise Feiner

¾ - 1 cup Wesson Oil
3 pounds boneless chicken breasts (cut in large cubes)
1 cup Wondra® flour
¾ tablespoon garlic salt
1 teaspoon black pepper
¼ cup olive oil
5 cloves garlic, peeled and crushed
3 (1 lb 12 ounces) cans crushed tomatoes

2 (8 ounce) cans Hunts® Tomato Sauce
1 (13¾ or 14.5 ounce) can College Inn® Chicken Broth
(with garlic if you can find it)
1 cup Red wine or Vermouth (Holland House® is fine)
1 (2.25 ounce) can black olives sliced, pitted and drained
3 tablespoon salt (approximately)
1 teaspoon black pepper
3 tablespoons dried basil

Place the Wesson oil in a large heated frying pan. Mix the flour, garlic salt and pepper together. Lightly coat the chicken with the flour mixture and brown in the Wesson oil. The pieces should be golden brown but not completely cooked. Add the olive oil to a crock-pot and place the garlic in the oil. When the first batch of chicken is just about done, turn the crock-pot on. **Do not leave on too long with the oil** before adding the chicken to the crock-pot. Add the chicken and remaining ingredients to the crock-pot. Add the rest of the chicken as it's browned. Add the leftover oil from the frying pan to the crock-pot. Use your judgment if there is too much oil. Cook on low 5 to 6 hours or on high 4 to 5 hours. Serve over spaghetti, angel hair, or capellini; topped with sauce and grating cheese. Serves 6.

This was adapted from Nanny's recipe which is done on top of the stove. You can easily do this on top of the stove in a Dutch oven. Her recipe used plum tomatoes which are put through a blender (You can use these too, or mix with crushed tomatoes if you like. You can also use any kind of chicken pieces, we just like boneless). Either way, it's delicious!

My Paternal Grandparents
Elizabeth and Felice
Avella...
put a moustache on my
brother Joe and voila...
my grandfather!

CHICKEN CARBONARA
Valerie Hull

2 packages parmesan & butter flavored rice (I've used Rice a Roni® and Uncle Bens...chicken flavor is good)
10 ounces bacon
1 pound chicken breasts (I cube it, cooks faster)
1 teaspoon garlic minced (can use powder if need be)

1 cup heavy cream
1 cup frozen peas, thawed and drained
3 green onions or (cooking onions will work as well)
2 ounces of parmesan cheese shaved. (I've only used sharp cheese but you can use whatever you like)

Cook rice to package directions and set aside (I found for two of us that one package of rice is plenty, also you can eat chicken with noodles or plain). Cook bacon until crisp, drain all but two tablespoons of drippings. Sauté cubed chicken until browned and cooked well. (The frozen bagged chicken works well, it's tender) Add garlic and cream, simmer until sauce thickens. Add peas, cook until heated through and stir in enough cheese to thicken. Serve over rice, garnish with onion, top with cheese.

Valerie says, "I use regular onions which I cook with the chicken and garlic. I keep leftover chicken and rice separate so that the rice doesn't soak up all the sauce from the chicken. It is so delicious that I usually eat 3 chunks of the chicken cold the next day for breakfast. I bought some light cream to try instead of heavy cream later in the week and I will let you know if it is a good alternative. I even tried buttermilk as it has fewer calories than heavy cream but the cheese would not mix with it. And I'm going to try it without the bacon to see how it is and to save myself some sodium. Also I thought diced tomatoes would be good as a garnish. Anyone who likes onions and garlic will like this recipe and use as much onion and garlic and you like." Valerie is one of the girls from my weight loss group.

CHICKEN CHEESY-ONION CASSEROLE
Elise Feiner

1 package (6 ounces) Stovetop® stuffing mix
3 cooked boneless chicken breasts, cubed
1 can (10¾ ounce) cream of chicken soup undiluted
1 (8 ounce) container sour cream
2 tablespoons (Lipton®) dry onion soup

1 (4 ounce) can mushrooms, pieces and stems, drained
½ (8 ounce) can water chestnuts, drained
1 (2 cups) bag shredded White Cheddar cheese
1 (2.8 ounce) can Durkee's® Fried Onions
2 tablespoons Parmesan or Locatelli Romano Cheese

Prepare stuffing according to package directions and set aside. Grease a two quart casserole or baking pan. Place the chicken in the prepared pan. Mix the soup, sour cream, dry soup mix, 1½ cups of the cheddar cheese, and half the can of onions. Spread over the chicken. Sprinkle with mushroom and water chestnuts. Sprinkle with ¼ cup cheddar cheese. Spread the stuffing mix over the top. Sprinkle the Parmesan cheese on top of the stuffing. Bake 350° for 25 minutes, sprinkle remaining cheese and fried onions over the top and bake another 10 minutes. Serves 6

I found a recipe similar to this in a magazine and then changed it. As my friend Fran says, everything tastes better with cheddar, so I added that, onions, etc. It's delicious.

CHICKEN FRANCAISE
Elise Feiner

1 pound boned and skinned chicken breasts
4 tablespoons pecorino cheese
8 tablespoons fresh parsley, chopped
2 eggs, well beaten
Flour for breading

½ cup olive oil
½ cup white wine
2 cups chicken stock or broth
6 thin slices lemons, seeds removed
4 tablespoons butter

Mix the cheese, eggs, and parsley together. Flour the chicken breasts; dip in the egg mixture and then back in the flour. Sauté the chicken breasts in the olive oil and remove. Add the wine to the oil and reduce. Add the stock and lemon slices. Boil for 5 minutes. Remove the lemon slices. Turn on low. Add the butter. Add the chicken back in and coat with sauce. Add a little flour to thicken if desired. This is a great dinner recipe and I'm not a lemon lover. Serves 4.

CHICKEN CORDON BLEU
Elise Feiner

4 double chicken breasts (about 7 ounces each), skinless and boneless
Kosher salt and freshly ground black pepper
8 thin slices ham
16 thin slices Gruyere or Swiss cheese

2 teaspoons fresh thyme leaves
¼ cup flour
1 cup Panko or plain breadcrumbs
1 teaspoon olive oil
2 eggs
2 teaspoons water

Preheat oven to 350°. Lay the chicken between 2 pieces of plastic wrap. Using the flat side of a meat mallet, gently pound the chicken to ¼-inch thickness. Lay 2 slices of cheese on each breast, followed by 2 slices of ham, and 2 more of cheese; leaving a ½-inch border on all sides to help seal the roll. Tuck in the sides of the breast and roll up tight like a jellyroll. Season the flour with salt and pepper; spread out on waxed paper or in a flat dish. Mix the breadcrumbs with thyme, kosher salt, pepper, and oil. Beat together the eggs and water. Lightly dust the chicken with flour, and then dip in the egg mixture. Gently coat the chicken in the bread crumbs. Place the chicken rolls in a baking pan and bake for 20 minutes until browned and cooked through. Serve whole hot, or chill and cut into pinwheels to serve with dipping sauce before serving. Serves 8.

Felicia Furino
and
Jeffrey Feiner
Anthony, Eileen ,
Marc and I always
joke that we want
them to get married,
in fact, we having
been trying to marry
them off for years!

178

MOM MOM'S CHICKEN BREASTS
Betty Feiner

2 package of boneless, skinless, chicken breasts
½ package onion soup mix

1 bottle Wish Bone® Thousand Island Salad Dressing
2 heaping tablespoons of Apricot Preserves

Mix together well. Marinade the chicken breasts in the mix. Bake at 350° about 35 to 45 minutes or until golden brown and thoroughly cooked.

Camp Green Lane Visiting Day…
L-R: Lauren, Jeffrey, Elise, Steven, Marc and David Feiner

CHICKEN CHRISTINA
Elise Feiner

6 (8-ounce) boneless chicken breasts
12 ounces butter, melted

1 package of Knorrs® Béarnaise sauce, prepared according to package directions;

Filling:
12 ounces cream cheese (at room temperature)
12 teaspoon chopped garlic
Salt and freshly ground black pepper

½ cup chopped fresh basil leaves
½ cup chopped fresh oregano leaves

Breading:
Flour, for dusting
4-5 eggs

6 tablespoon milk
Japanese bread crumbs (Panko), for breading

Preheat the oven to 350°. Mix together the filling ingredients and set aside. Lightly and evenly pound chicken breast to ½-inch thickness. Lay the breast flat (shiny side down), and place filling on ½ of the breast. Fold the chicken in half and tuck in corners. Hold together with a toothpick. Beat together the egg and milk to make an egg wash. Dip the chicken in flour and shake off excess flour. Dip chicken in egg mix, shaking off excess. Coat the chicken in Japanese bread crumbs. Place on a baking pan and lightly drizzle with butter. Bake until golden brown and the internal temperature of the chicken reaches 170° (check with a meat thermometer). Serve with béarnaise sauce.

Andrew Sanabria and Lauren Feiner then…

…and now

179

CHICKEN REUBEN
Katherine Avella

2 packages boneless chicken breasts (thin, but not too thin)
1 (16 ounce) bottle of Thousand Island dressing
½ pound of Swiss cheese sliced

½ - ¾ (16 ounce) bottle of sauerkraut; squeezed dry
Salt and pepper to taste

Spray a baking dish with PAM®. Place the chicken breasts in a single layer in the baking pan. Sprinkle with salt and pepper to taste. Place the sauerkraut on top of the chicken breasts. Place the Swiss cheese slices on top of the sauerkraut. Pour the dressing on top of the cheese. Cover with aluminum foil. Bake 375° for about 45 minutes to 1 hour. Remove the foil for the last 15 minutes and raise the heat to 400° to let the top brown a little. Serves 4 to 6.

This is my mother's recipe. It takes about 5 minutes to put together when you need to do something fast. This is a great dish to make for a luncheon too, but for a fast dinner, you can't beat it!.

"Nanny" Katherine Avella with her Grandson's:
L-R: Steven and David Feiner, Philip Jr., Douglas, and Michael Avella (missing Jeff)

GREEK STEWED CHICKEN
Peggy Spirakis

3 tablespoons olive oil
2-3 pounds of chicken pieces of your choice (I prefer breasts and legs)
2 teaspoon ground cinnamon
Kosher salt
Ground black pepper

2 onions, peeled and coarsely chopped
5 cloves garlic, peeled and crushed
3 cloves of garlic, peeled and left whole
½ cup white wine
2 cups water
1 (6 ounce) can tomato paste

Heat oil in a large skillet on high heat. Sprinkle chicken with cinnamon, salt, and pepper, brown on all sides, and set aside. Turn the heat to medium-high, add the onions and minced garlic, and cook for 3 minutes, stirring continuously. Add the wine and deglaze the pan; reduce until almost dry. Add water, tomato paste, and whole garlic cloves. Add chicken, cover, and simmer for 1 hour or until chicken is cooked through. Add water as needed. Serve this over white rice or with orzo pasta.

This is a traditional Greek chicken dish given to my by Uncle Joe's friend Peggy.

CHICKEN FAJITA PIZZA
Elise Feiner

1 pound of pizza dough (Store bought is fine)
2 tablespoons vegetable oil
1 pound of boneless chicken breasts, cut into strips
½ of a medium red pepper cut into strips
½ of a medium green pepper cut into strips
1 large onion, peeled and cut into thin slices

Garlic salt and pepper to taste
1 (8 ounce) bag shredded mozzarella
1 (8 ounce) bag of shredded Mexican cheese mix
½ (16 ounce) jar of salsa (I use Tostitos® Mild Salsa)
1 (8 ounce) container sour cream

Preheat oven to 450°. Lightly grease a medium size cookie sheet pan. Stretch the pizza dough into the pan. In a large skillet, heat the oil. Add the onions and peppers and cut until soft and golden. Remove and set aside. Add the chicken to the skillet (add a little more oil if necessary) and cook for about 5 minutes until chicken is no longer pink. Add the peppers and onions back to the skillet. Remove from the heat. Stir in the salsa and sour cream. Place the mozzarella over the bottom of the pizza crust. Place the chicken mixture on to of the mozzarella. (If there is too much liquid in the pepper/chicken mix drain the excess liquid off.) Place the Mexican cheese mix on the top. Bake 12 to 15 minutes until the crust is brown and cheese is melted and bubbly.

This is a great dinner for teenagers. It's fast and easy to make. It's one of my son David's favorites. It's a great change from regular pizza and teenagers love fajitas anyway you make them.

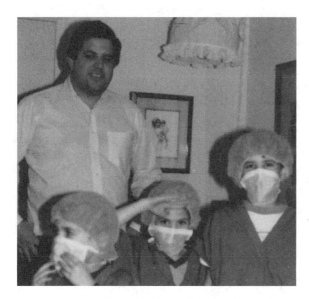 

Proud Dad, Marc Feiner, M.D. with his Junior "Docs" from L: David, Steven
and Jeffrey and Nurse Lauren Feiner…1988

LEMON ROASTED CHICKEN
Elise Feiner

1 large whole roasting chicken
1 large lemon
8 slices proscuitto
1 to 2 cloves garlic, peeled and finely chopped

½ cup fresh thyme leaves picked and finely chopped
Salt and freshly ground black pepper
4 ounces softened butter

Preheat the oven and an appropriately sized roasting tray to 425° Wash the chicken well and pat dry with kitchen paper. Using your fingers, separate the breast skin from the breast meat. Move your fingers gently down the breast, being careful not to rip the skin. Zest the lemon, keeping the peeled lemon to one side. Chop proscuitto and add to the bowl with the lemon skin, garlic and thyme. Season, with salt and pepper and then mix it all into the butter. Push this into the space you have made between the meat and the skin; rub and massage any that's left over in and around the bird. Make tiny cuts in the thighs. Cut the lemon in half and push it into the cavity. Then put chicken in the hot roasting tray and roast in the preheated oven for 40 minutes or until done when tested with a meat thermometer. Serves 4.

CHICKEN EN CROUTE WITH MADEIRA SAUCE
Elise Feiner

3 whole large chicken breasts, with skin and bones, cut in half
¾ pound mushrooms
2 medium onions
2 tablespoons butter
½ cup breadcrumbs
¾ teaspoon salt
¼ teaspoon black pepper
¼ teaspoon oregano
4 tablespoons vegetable oil
2 stalks of celery cut into 2-inch pieces
2 medium carrots cut into 2-inch pieces

¼ cup flour
1 (10 ounce) can beef broth
¾ cup Madeira
1 bay leaf
¾ cup water
Parsley sprigs
2 egg yolks
1 teaspoon of water
Broccoli Filling
Pastry Crust (if you are in a hurry, you can use prepared puff pastry -2 boxes)

Remove the chicken breasts from the bones to form boneless breasts. Reserve the bones. Cut the breasts in half. Refrigerate the breasts and the bones. Reserve 6 mushrooms for the sauce. Mince the remaining mushrooms. Peel and mince one of the onions. In a 10-inch skillet over medium heat, in the butter, cook the mushrooms and onions until tender and liquid is evaporated, about 5 minutes. Stir in breadcrumbs, salt, pepper, and oregano. Set aside. Prepare broccoli filling according to the directions below. Make the pastry one to two days in advance. With a meat mallet pound the breasts until they are ¼-inch thickness. Spoon about 2 tablespoons of the broccoli filling into the center of each breast leaving a ½-inch border all around. From the narrow end, roll jelly roll style. Mix the egg yolks with 1 teaspoon of water. Prepare the pastry crust according to the directions below. Roll the pastry and cut out rectangles 8 x 7-inches each. Spread 2 tablespoons of the mushroom mixture over the pastry rectangles, leaving 2-inches all around as a border. Top with a chicken roll. Brush egg wash around the border. Wrap the pastry around the chicken roll to resemble a package. Spray baking sheet with PAM®. Do all rolls the same. If you have extra pastry, cut pieces to look like a ribbon and bow and place on each bundle. Brush with remaining egg wash. Place on the baking sheet seam side down and refrigerate. You can do this the day before.

Bake at 375° for 45 minutes to 1 hour or until the pastry is golden brown. In the meantime start the Madeira sauce while chicken is baking. With a sharp knife, slice the remaining mushrooms. In a 3-quart saucepan over medium heat in 2 tablespoons vegetable oil, cook mushrooms until tender about 5 minutes. remove with a slotted spoon; set aside. Add 2 more tablespoons of oil to the same pot and add the chicken bones, celery and carrots, and the remaining onion, peeled and left whole. Cook until well browned about 20 minutes. Add the flour and cook flour until slightly browned, stirring frequently. Gradually stir in the beef broth, Madeira, bay leaf, ¾ cup water. Heat to boiling; reduce heat to low; simmered uncovered 15 minutes. With a slotted spoon, remove the bones, vegetables, and bay leaf, and discard. Return the cooked mushrooms to the sauce and heat through. Serve sauce on the side to spoon over the chicken bundles.

Broccoli Filling:
5 ounces frozen chopped broccoli, drained well
1 egg white
¼ cup mayonnaise

1 tablespoon minced onion
½ teaspoon salt
⅛ teaspoon black pepper

Thaw half of a 10 ounce package of frozen chopped broccoli. Drain well. In a small bowl with a wire whisk, beat the egg white until frothy. Beat in mayonnaise, onion, salt and pepper.

Pastry Crust:
12 tablespoon butter
2 cups flour

1 teaspoon of salt
6 teaspoons water

Soften 6 tablespoons of butter in a mixing bowl. Add flour and blend thoroughly. Add water and salt and knead lightly to form dough. Form into a ball, wrap in saran and refrigerate one hour. On a floured board, roll out into a rectangle about 18 x 12-inches, and ¼-inch thick. Slightly soften the remaining butter. Spread the butter over ⅔ thirds of the rectangle, leaving a one inch border around the edges. Fold unbuttered third over the center ⅓. Fold remaining ⅓ on top. Turn 90° and roll into another rectangle ⅓ of an inch thick. Fold in fourths as follows: First fold the short ends of the rectangle in to meet in the center (Imagine a line in the center of the rectangle, fold the lower half up to meet that line, then fold the upper half down to meet that line.) Then fold one half over the other. Turn 90° and repeat the same way. This is what gives you the layered pastry. Cover and refrigerate 1 hour. (The pastry can be made 48 hours in advance). Before using fold the same way again. Divide the dough in half; roll out to be able to cut each half into three rectangles as described in the recipe.

This is very time consuming, but if you have company that you need to impress, this dish will do it. Today, you can just buy the puff pastry and save some steps.

182

CHICKEN PAPRIKASH HAMAR
Eva Hamar

3 pounds chicken pieces, boneless breasts
1 medium onion, diced
½ cup butter
5 tablespoons paprika, heaping

4 tablespoons flour, heaping
2 pints sour cream
Salt and pepper to taste

Sauté the chicken is a large pot, with the onion, butter and salt and pepper until light brown for at least 30 minutes, keep covered; stirring occasionally. Add paprika (the more the better), sprinkle the flour over meat, and stir. Add sour cream. Simmer slowly for about 30 minutes longer. We like to serve this over white rice with a side dish of frozen green peas cooked with mushrooms. Serves 6.

Eva Hamar was our housekeeper for years. She emigrated here from Hungary. Among her many talents, she is a fabulous seamstress. She worked on movie wardrobes when she lived Hungary. She now lives in California with her family, Michael, Adam and Nickolett.

CHICKEN PAPRIKASH A LA LEE
Lee Sack

1 medium onion, peeled and diced
1 tablespoon oil
1 teaspoon salt
1 (6 ounce) can tomato paste

1 tablespoons Sweet Hungarian Paprika
1 cut-up chicken (this can be made with 1 to 1½ chickens)
¼ to ½ cup sour cream
½ teaspoon salt

Dice the onion and sauté in a large frying pan with the oil till the onion is translucent (not golden). Add the tomato paste, the paprika and the 1 teaspoon salt. Mix well together and coat the chicken pieces with the tomato onion mixture. This will coat up to 1-1½ chickens. (You can use chicken pieces of your choice, but have at least 1 good size breast.) Sprinkle with the additional ½ teaspoon of salt. Cover tightly and cook for at least 45 minutes, on a very low heat without peeking. (Trust the chicken.) Cook longer, if necessary. Remove the chicken from the pan to a platter and keep warm. Add the sour cream, in small amounts to the gravy, mixing well each time you add liquid. Return gravy to pan; warm slightly; adjust seasoning to taste. Serve chicken over rotelle or bowtie noodles, pour gravy over both

Lee is a good friend of Aunt Barbara's from Aruba. She made this for dinner when they were together in Canada. It was so good; they were licking their fingers! Try it with Lee's Cucumber Salad (see index).

CHICKEN PAPRIKASH
Elise Feiner

4 (12-ounce) chicken breasts
Salt and freshly ground black pepper
3 tablespoons sweet paprika
2 tablespoons flour
¼ cup oil
4 cups onions, thinly sliced
4 cloves garlic, peeled and crushed
2 tablespoons tomato paste
2 cups tomatoes, diced very small
2 tablespoons fresh marjoram leaves, minced

1 teaspoon fresh thyme leaves, minced
1 bay leaf
2 tablespoons balsamic vinegar
1 cup dry white wine
2 cups chicken stock
¼ cup heavy cream
1 small jar roasted peppers, cut into 1 inch strips
2 tablespoons parsley, chopped
1 cup sour cream

Cut each chicken breast into 3 pieces. Season the chicken with salt, pepper and 1 tablespoon of paprika. Lightly coat the chicken with flour. In a large sauté pan, heat oil. Sear chicken pieces until brown on all sides. Remove the chicken from the pan set aside. Add onions to the pan and sauté for 5 minutes until golden brown. Add the garlic. Cook for one more minute. Add the tomato paste, tomatoes, and remaining 2 tablespoons of paprika. Stir until well blended. Add the marjoram, thyme and bay leaf. Add the vinegar and wine and stir well to remove all the pieces stuck to the bottom of the pot. Add chicken stock. Season with salt and pepper to taste. Bring to a boil. Add the reserved chicken pieces and cover but leave a little of the cover off the pot. Simmer for 20 minutes. Add cream and sour cream and continue to simmer another 10 minutes or until the chicken is tender. Pour sauce and 1 roasted pepper in a blender; puree. Taste and adjust seasoning. Pour sauce over chicken. Reheat if necessary.

CHICKEN POT PIE
Elise Feiner

For Filling:
3 cups cooked chicken, cubed
5 potatoes, peeled, cubed, and boiled until soft but not thoroughly cooked

1 jar mushrooms (small)
½ bag frozen mixed vegetables or (around 10 ounce) box (peas, carrots, corn, beans) or whatever you like

For Sauce:
1 stick of butter divided in half
½ cup chopped onion (finely)
10 tablespoons of Wondra® flour
1 cup milk
1 cup cream
1 (13¾ or 14 .5 ounce) can College Inn® Chicken Broth

2 tablespoons white wine
¼ teaspoon dried thyme
¼ chopped fresh flat parsley
¼ teaspoon nutmeg
½ teaspoon black pepper
3 teaspoon garlic salt

For Crust:
You can used prepared pie crust or make a Bisquick® crust
2¼ cups Bisquick®

⅔ cup milk

Preheat oven to 400°. In a large saucepan, melt half the butter and sauté the onion until soft and translucent. Add the remaining butter and the flour and stir rapidly to prevent lumps. Quickly, add the milk, cream, chicken broth, and wine, stirring continuously to prevent lumps. Bring to a boil stirring constantly, lower to a simmer and then add the thyme, parsley, nutmeg, pepper, and garlic salt. Simmer for a few minutes to thicken and then remove from the heat. Add the mushrooms, vegetables, potatoes, and cooked chicken. Place the mixture in a casserole pan or individual soufflé dishes.

Make crust: Mix the Bisquick and the milk together with a fork until moist. Lightly flour a board with Bisquick and knead ten times. Roll out into a crust and place on the top of the casserole or individual soufflé dishes; crimp the edges, make a few slits. Brush with an egg yolk that has been mixed with a teaspoon of water. Bake 30 to 45 minutes or until golden brown. Serves 6.

I put this together when I had some leftover chicken so that I could make some different meals for Jeffrey while he was in Medical School.

CHICKEN VERONIQUE
Nancy Barfield

1 cup of cooked peas
2 cups of cooked chicken, cubed
1 can of cream chicken soup
1 can water chestnuts
½ cup of green grapes cut in half

1½ cups of instant Minute® rice
1 can of chicken stock (use enough to equal the water in the directions on the box)
1 teaspoon of Chinese Five Spices
1 can of Durkee's® French fried onion rings

Combine peas, chicken, and cream of chicken soup, water chestnuts, and Chinese 5 spice powder in a bowl. This can all be done one day ahead and refrigerate. Cook the rice with chicken stock instead of water. In a 9-inch square baking pan, put the rice around the edges of the pan leaving the middle empty. Take the grapes and fold it into the chicken mixture. Then, pour that mixture in the center of the pan; cover it with Durkee's French fried onion rings. Bake at 350° for about 45 minutes, or until mixture is heated through and onion rings are brown.

My friend Nancy Barfield is a busy event planner, but she likes to cook in her spare time. This is one of her favorite dinners to make when she has company.

L-R: David Feiner and Marc Feiner, M.D. at David's White Coat Ceremony at SUNY at Buffalo School of Medicine... Class of 2009

EASY CHICKEN BREASTS
Elise Feiner

6 boneless chicken breasts
½ stick butter
½ teaspoon garlic salt
Salt and pepper to taste

1 box or ½ pound sliced fresh mushrooms
1 small can of Durkee's® fried onion rings
1 cup shredded Monterey Jack Cheese

In a large pot, (use an ovenproof pot with a lid) melt the butter, garlic salt, salt and pepper together. Add the chicken turning until the chicken is well coated with the butter mixture. Cover the pot and place in a 350° oven for 1 hour. Remove the pot and add the mushrooms and continue to bake for about 15 minutes. Remove from the oven and add the cheese and onion rings. Bake uncovered until the cheese melts. If you don't have an ovenproof pot, start the chicken in a large frying pan, then transfer to a baking pan and cover it with foil.

CHICKEN/ TURKEY POT PIE WITH A TWIST
Elise Feiner

4½ cups frozen shredded hash brown potatoes, thawed
6 tablespoons butter

1½ teaspoons salt
¼ teaspoons pepper

Filling:

½ cup chopped onions
¼ butter
¼ cup flour
1 package chicken bouillon
1 teaspoon Worcestershire sauce
½ teaspoon dried basil

2 cups milk
3 cups cooked chicken or turkey, cubed
1 cup frozen peas, thawed
2 potatoes, peeled cubed and boiled
1 carrot, peeled and cut into small circles, boiled

Combine the hash brown potatoes, butter, salt and pepper. Press into individual greased ramekins or custard cups (10 ounce) size. If you want to make this family style, press into a greased casserole dish. Bring the potatoes up a little higher than the rim if possible.
Set them aside. Sauté the onions in butter in a medium saucepan. Add the flour, bouillon, Worcestershire sauce, and basil. In a medium pot, cook the cubed potatoes and carrots until tender but not mushy. Drain; set aside. Add the milk; bring to a boil; cook, stirring frequently until thickened about 3 to 4 minutes. Add the chicken, peas, potatoes and carrots. Spoon into the ramekins. Bake 375° for 35 to 40 minutes or until golden brown. Serves 6.

This is great for leftover chicken or Thanksgiving turkey; I love the potato crust!

My other "sons", my sons, and my daughter at Steven's Graduation from Trinity-Pawling
L-R: Adam Morton, Joshua Rosenfeld, Steven Feiner, Michael Alsheimer, Rich Kiersnowski, Andrew Massoud, David, Jeffrey and Lauren Feiner. Trinity Pawling is a phenomenal prep school. They also have a great "language retraining program" for kids with learning disabilities. Carol and Ted Kneeland have a great program set up if your child has difficulties in language processing. Consider their scholarship fund in making your donation choice.

DOT'S FEINER FRIED CHICKEN
Dot Shavers

Boneless chicken breasts, or breast pieces with ribs, or whatever pieces you prefer
McCormick® Season All Seasoned Salt

Gold Medal® Flour
Vegetable oil for frying

You can use whatever chicken parts you prefer, but cut into small pieces. I usually cut the boneless chicken into 3-4 pieces, and the whole breasts into about 4-5 pieces. Lay out sheets of aluminum foil on a table or counter, and place the chicken pieces in a single layer. Sprinkle the pieces of chicken very liberally with the Seasoned Salt on **both sides**; you should barely be able to see the color of the chicken. (Only use McCormick Seasoned Salt and Gold Medal flour in this recipe, as it really affects the taste of the chicken) Let the seasoned chicken sit at least 45 minutes to an hour. Pour a large quantity of Gold Medal Flour in the middle of the chicken and dredge easy piece in the flour until thoroughly coated, or place flour in a large bowl, throw in several pieces and mix with your hands. In a heavy frying pan with a lid (cast iron is great for this) place about ¾-1-inch of oil. Heat the oil, and test by dropping a bit of flour mixture into it. When it starts to bubble, it's hot enough to begin frying. Place chicken in a single layer **and keep the pot covered while frying.** Turn until golden brown on both sides but do not overcook. Use tongs to turn the chicken. Drain on a platter covered with paper towels. Layer paper towels between the layers of fried chicken. Serve with mashed potatoes. If you like legs or wings or whatever use them. They like boneless here so that's what I use. I always make some breasts with ribs for us. Don't do this in a deep fryer because it really needs the heavy pan with a cover. If you like the pieces large, it is not necessary to cut them. I started to cut them when the kids were small and that's how they prefer them but you can leave the pieces whole.

This recipe comes from Dot, Marc's parent's housekeeper and cook. She made this for Shabbat dinner every Friday in Elkins Park. It is THE best Fried Chicken. She taught me that the frying pan must be covered when it is frying. She also said that Magnalite frying pans (cast iron) are the best for this purpose and in fact she only used her pan for chicken. The outside of the pan is black from being so well seasoned. Wash the pan in warm soapy water or put in the dishwasher but DON'T EVER scrub with Brillo so the pan stays seasoned. This is great leftover as well. In our house, the kids like the boneless pieces but Marc and I love the pieces with the bones because the bones get so crispy that you can practically eat them. I always make both. You can always count on Steven's friends to show up on fried chicken night, so this is for all of you as well, my other " sons": Josh, Andrew Massoud, Mike, Rich and Adam, and for Uncle Steve Rosenfeld who always gets the leftovers sent to him. My "other sons" are pictured on the previous page.

CHICKEN FLORENTINE
Elise Feiner

12 boneless chicken breasts
¼ teaspoon salt
1 teaspoon garlic salt
¼ teaspoon paprika
3 tablespoons butter
¼ cup butter, melted

1 (10 ounce) package spinach
1½ cups white wine
1 tablespoon lemon juice
1½ cup flavored breadcrumbs
¾ cup sour cream

Cook spinach according to package directions; squeeze out liquid and set aside. Place the breasts in a shallow greased baking dish. Sprinkle with salt, garlic salt and paprika; dot with the 3 tablespoons of butter. Bake at 400° for 30 minutes. In a medium saucepan, combine the melted butter, spinach, wine, lemon juice and bread crumbs; bring to a simmer. Remove from the heat and blend in the sour cream. Remove the chicken from the pan and place a mound of stuffing, topped with a breast, back into the pan, continue with the other breasts. Bake for an additional 15 to 20 minutes. Serves 6 to 8.

GARLIC CHICKEN
Elise Feiner

3½ pounds chicken, cut into bite size pieces
Salt and pepper to taste
4 tablespoons flour
4 tablespoons olive oil
½ pound mushrooms, rinsed and drained well
18 large cloves garlic, UNPEELED
½ cup finely chopped onion

½ cup dry white wine
2 cups fresh tomatoes, peeled and seeded
½ cup chicken broth
4 springs Parsley
1 bay leaf
½ teaspoon thyme

Sprinkle chicken pieces with salt and pepper, dredge in flour and pat well to make the flour adhere. Heat the olive oil in a heavy skillet. When hot add the chicken pieces and cook uncovered, turning occasionally to brown well on all sides, about 10 minutes. Add mushrooms, unpeeled garlic, and onions and cook, stirring for another three minutes on high heat. Add wine, parsley, bay leaf and thyme and stir to dissolve brown particles on the bottom of the skillet. Bring to a simmer and add salt and pepper if needed. Cover tightly and cook 20 minutes. With a slotted spoon, remove the garlic cloves and squeeze out the flesh. Add pureed garlic to the skillet and bring to a simmer. Cook and stir two minutes. Remove bay leaf and sprinkle basil or parsley. Serve with white rice.

This recipe came from Lisa (I don't know her last name) in the beauty parlor I use to go to. She also had it published in the Observer Dispatch, our local newspaper. I have seen several versions of this recipe through the years.

BEER CAN CHICKEN
Mark Godecki, M.D.

3½-4 pound chicken
1 can of your favorite beer or soda
McCormick® seasoned salt

Black Pepper
½ lemon or small potato

Clean and wash the chicken well. Dry with a paper towel. Liberally season the chicken with seasoned salt, pepper, or seasoning of your choice. Place the lemon or potato in the neck of the chicken to seal in the flavors. **Empty out half the contents of the beer or soda can**. Place the chicken over the beer can which is sitting in a baking sheet or use the beer can rack they sell in the stores. Place the chicken over the barbeque and set the heat on **low-medium** on the right side and place the chicken on the left side of the grill. Cover it and let cook 1 to 2 hours, checking occasionally. You can do this in the oven as well. Preheat oven to 350°. Place the chicken (which is in a baking pan to which you have added ¼ cup of water) on the bottom rack of the oven so it stands up. Roast for about 1 to 2 hours. Check temperature with a meat thermometer.

Let the chicken stand about 10 minutes. **Be extremely careful when removing the chicken from the can or you can get badly burned. Use tongs if you have them.** Try to have someone to help you so they can hold the base while you remove the chicken.

Mark Godecki, my husband's partner was the first person I knew who cooked the chicken this way when we visited him at his camp on Lake Piseco for dinner.

Mark Godecki, M.D. and Ewa Godecki, D.D.S.
Mark is my husband Marc's partner and a great OB/GYN. They are originally from
Poland. Ewa's mother Helena makes the best Pierogi's… Move over Big Martha!

PULLED CHICKEN IN A THAI COCONUT MILK RED CURRY BROTH WITH JASMINE RICE
David Smith

This is a great dish to serve at a dinner party. Although there is considerable prep time, it can all be done well in advance, allowing you to be out of the kitchen and enjoying the company. When it comes time for dinner, 15 minutes, and you're ready to eat. This recipe works well with just about any protein, Prawns, Beef, or tofu are easily substituted in this recipe. The first thing you will want to do is roast the chicken, so it can cool and the meat can be pulled of off it. I prefer to work with Organic or free range chicken, the quality and taste of the meat is well worth the price difference. All you need to do is season the chicken with salt and pepper, and put it in a 400 degree oven for about an hour, till it is done. Once the chicken is done, you can let it cool for 20 minuets, and then refrigerate till it is cool enough to pull the meat from.

1 Roasted Chicken (store bought will work too)

The next step is the curry broth. For this you will need the following ingredients.

1 medium yellow onion
3 inches of ginger root
3 stocks lemon grass (finely chop inner white part of the stalk)
2 carrots
4 stalks of celery
2 cups low sodium chicken stock
2 cans of coconut milk

1 can of crushed tomatoes (unseasoned)
3 limes
1 tablespoon honey
¼ cup rice vinegar
¼ cup soy sauce
3 tablespoon red curry paste
1 teaspoon fish sauce

In a sauce pan, over medium heat, add a few tablespoons of oil, combine diced onion, ginger, lemongrass, carrots and celery. Sautee for a few minuets till they soften. To this add curry paste, chicken stock, coconut milk, zest and juice of limes, honey, soy, rice vinegar and fish sauce. Bring to a boil, and then simmer for 1 hour, or until reduced by ⅓. You will want to taste and adjust seasoning to taste. If you prefer a mild curry, start with 1 tablespoon curry paste, and adjust the heat to you taste. After 1 hour strain the broth through a fine strainer, and reserve.

The final step: Plating

As with all recipes, you should feel free to adjust them to your taste and liking. Also keep in mind what is fresh and available. If you don't care for asparagus, use broccoli or something else you like. Keep in mind what is in season, and what is available to you.

2 cups jasmine rice...cooked according to directions
2 Julienne shallots or 1 small yellow onion
1 head diced asparagus
10 medium shitake mushrooms; julienned
2 ears corn kernels

Any combination of fresh chopped Basil, cilantro and mint
1 Lime
1 Mango
¼ cup ground peanuts

Start over medium/high heat by quickly sautéing shallots in olive oil, about 2 minutes, then add asparagus, mushrooms and corn. Next top with Curry broth, add in pulled chicken and cook for about 8 minuets till vegetables are done. Serve in large cowls over jasmine rice. Garnish with a few pinches of fresh mixed herbs, squeeze of lime juice, Ground peanuts, and diced fresh mango. Please use this recipe as a guide line, and adjust any ingredient to meet your likes and needs. Most importantly have fun, food should be fun! Enjoy. Cooking and smiling, David Smith

David is the Executive Chef at The Cottonwood Restaurant and Bar in Truckee, California. I've know David since he was 16 years old. When we first came to New Hartford to interview for a position at Medical Arts, David had just gotten his drivers license. He and his younger brother Brett offered (or were volunteered) to baby-sit for Jeffrey, who was 4 at the time. He's grown into a wonderful young man, and fabulous chef. Stop in to see him: It's off Brockway Road (Old Hwy 267); P.O. Box 3487 - Truckee, CA 96160 PH (530) 587-5711; FAX (530) 587-3955
Email: info@cottonwoodrestaurant.com

L-R: David Smith, Jennifer
Smith Boylan holding Jamie
Boylan, Brett Smith

CHICKEN DIVAN
Shirley Flomenhoft

6 chicken breasts split
2 cans cream of mushroom soup
½ pint (8 ounces) or ¾ pint sour cream
¾ cup cooking sherry

3 packages frozen broccoli spears
Bread Crumbs
1 large (2-3 cups) bag Grated cheddar cheese

Cook chicken and remove chicken from the breasts. Cook broccoli spears according to package directions). Place a row of chicken and then a row of broccoli spears in a shallow greased 13 x 9-inch Pyrex® pan that has been sprayed with PAM®, alternating chicken with broccoli. Mix mushroom soup, sour cream and wine together. Pour over chicken and broccoli mix. Bake at 375° about 30 minutes (until bubbly.) Remove from oven and put grated cheddar and bread crumbs on top. Place under the broiler and **WATCH** carefully until cheese is melted. Serves 6 to 8.

GRILLED CITRUS CHICKEN
Irina Hamlin

Juice and grated zest of half a lemon
Juice and grated zest of half a lime
3 tablespoons olive oil
2 cloves garlic, peeled and minced
1 tablespoon dry white wine

1 teaspoon salt
½ teaspoon freshly ground pepper
⅛ teaspoon cayenne pepper
6 boneless skinless chicken breast halves

Combine the lemon juice, lemon zest, lime juice, lime zest, olive oil, garlic, white wine, salt and black pepper, and cayenne in a large bowl; mix well. Rinse chicken, pat dry. Add to marinade. Marinate, covered, in the refrigerator for 1 to 10 hours; drain. Grill over hot coals for 10 minutes or until chicken is cooked through, turning once. Serves 6.

Irina submitted this recipe to our birthday club group and it's finally made it into print!

Brian and Rachel Hamlin

CHICKEN ITALIAN COUNTRY STYLE
Elise Feiner

4 tablespoons extra-virgin olive oil
Coarse salt and pepper
2 pounds boneless skinless chicken breast, cut into chunks
2 tablespoons butter
2 shallots, chopped
3 small carrots, peeled and thinly sliced
10 crimini mushrooms, finely chopped

4 sprigs fresh tarragon leaves removed and chopped to about 2 tablespoon
¼ cup parsley leaves, chopped
1 cup dry red wine
1 (32-ounce) can chunky-style crushed tomatoes or diced tomatoes in puree

In a large skillet over medium high heat, warm the olive oil. Season the chicken with salt and pepper, brown it in the oil for 2 or 3 minutes on each side, and remove to a plate. Return pan to stove and reduce heat to medium. Add butter to the pan and sauté the shallots, carrots, and mushrooms. Sauté for 3 to 5 minutes until mushrooms darken and carrot bits are fork tender. Add tarragon and parsley and stir. Add wine and reduce liquid for 1 or 2 minutes. Add tomatoes to the sauce and stir to combine. Add chicken back to the pan and simmer chicken in sauce for 6 minutes or until chicken is cooked through and juices run clear. Serve this over rice or pasta. Serves 4.

LEMON CHICKEN BORTEN
Pearl Borten

2 packages boneless skinless chicken breast cutlets
Plain breadcrumbs
6 tablespoons vegetable oil for frying (more if needed)
4-5 cloves of garlic, peeled and sliced

Juice of 5 lemons
3-4 tablespoons of honey (5-6 if you like it sweeter)
1 bottle white cooking wine

Dip the chicken cutlets in bread crumbs and fry lightly in oil. Remove the cutlets from the pan. In the same pan, add the garlic, lemon juice, honey and white wine. Let it boil for 2 to 3 minutes. Place the chicken breasts in a large plastic container. Pour the lemon/wine mixture over the chicken breasts. Let marinate overnight. Preheat oven to 350°. Spray a large baking pan with PAM®. Place the chicken breasts on it in a single layer. Bake for 20 minutes covered, and uncovered for another 20 minutes. Serves 6.

JARLSBERG CHICKEN
Cyndi Koury

Butter (to grease the baking dish)
6 tablespoons butter
2 tablespoons oil
6 chicken breasts halves, skinned and boned
¾ pound large white mushrooms, washed, patted dry, and stemmed
1 large bunch broccoli, stemmed, peeled, trimmed, cut into spears and cooked al dente or artichoke hearts

Lemon pepper
2 tablespoons flour
½ cup chicken stock
1 scallion, sliced thinly
½ cup dry white wine
1½ cups shredded Jarlsberg or Swiss cheese
Salt and freshly ground white pepper
Shredded Jarlsberg cheese

Lightly butter a baking dish. Melt 2 tablespoons of the butter with oil in a heavy skillet over low heat. Add chicken and cook until juices run clear when pricked with a fork, 3 to 5 minutes each side. Don't overcook. Remove chicken to a platter. Set aside. Melt 2 more tablespoons of butter in skillet. Add mushrooms, and cook over medium-high heat until tender; 3 to 5 minutes. Arrange broccoli (or artichoke hearts) in a single layer in a baking pan. Place the chicken over the broccoli and season with lemon pepper. Preheat oven to 350°. Melt 2 remaining tablespoons of butter over low heat. Whisk in flour and cook stirring constantly about 3 minutes. Pour in chicken stock and wine whisking until thoroughly blended. Continue cooking until sauce thickens and coats a spoon. Add ¼ cup scallions and 1½ cup cheese and stir until melted. Taste and season with salt and pepper. Pour sauce over the chicken. Arrange mushrooms on the top and sprinkle the additional cheese. Bake 35 minutes. Top with additional shredded Jarlsberg cheese. Turn oven to broil and broil 3 to 5 minutes until cheese is bubbly and golden, watching carefully.

Cyndi Koury made this for my birthday one year. It was so delicious. It's a great dish to make for company because a lot of it can be prepared ahead.

L-R: Billy, Catherine and Cyndi Koury at Catherine's Graduation...Cyndi is a gourmet cook and baker!

JEFF'S FAVORITE BARBEQUE CHICKEN
Betty Feiner

3-4 packages Boneless chicken breasts cut in half (thin)
½ (40 ounce) bottle of Dai Day® Duck Sauce
½ - ¾ (9.4 ounces) bottle Saucy Susan Apricot Sauce
4 tablespoons Gulden's® Spicy Mustard

1 tablespoon garlic salt
1 package Lipton® onion soup mix (optional)
1 onion peeled and cut into long slices

Open the packages of chicken and rinse under cold water, remove any fat. Cut in half; don't make pieces too small (not as small as for fried chicken.) Mix the rest of the ingredients together; add the garlic salt ½ tablespoon at a time. If it looks like too much don't add the rest of it. The amount of garlic salt depends on how much chicken you use. You can adjust the mustard and garlic salt to your taste. Add chicken and let marinade for a few hours, or make the night before and refrigerate. If you are making this on the grill, let the marinade drip off before putting on the grill and do not leave unattended. **Because of the high sugar content in the duck sauce it can burn easily so watch them carefully.** Grill for about 8 to 10 minutes. Check to make sure they are done, but because they are not that thick they don't need to cook very long. You can also do them on the George Foreman grill. You can add a package of Lipton's onion soup mix to the marinade if you want to. Serves 6.

I think this recipe came from a friend of Mom Mom's originally and I jazzed it up a bit. It has become a summertime favorite in our house, but with the advent of the Foreman grill it can be done year round.

STIR FRY CHICKEN AND PEANUTS JEFFREY
Carmen Ferreiro

3 packages boneless, skinless chicken breasts or cutlets
1 cup cornstarch, more if necessary
1 tablespoon ground ginger
9 tablespoons Soy Sauce
3 tablespoons cooking Sherry (Holland House® is fine for this)
3 tablespoons sugar

1 tablespoon rice wine vinegar Vegetable oil for frying
2- 3 bunches scallions, washed and trimmed; cut in 1-inch pieces
2-3 green and red peppers, washed; cut in 1-inch cubes
5 cloves garlic; peeled and crushed
1 cup dry roasted peanuts

The secret to this recipe is to do all the prep work ahead of time. Crush the garlic and place it a little dish. Cut up the scallions and peppers and put in little bowls. Measure out the peanuts and set aside. Mix the sherry, soy sauce, sugar, rice wine vinegar, in a measuring cup and set aside. Remove the chicken from the package and remove any remaining fat. Cut into small cubes (about three pieces from each breast) Mix the cornstarch with the ginger. Dredge the chicken in the cornstarch mix. Save a few tablespoons of the cornstarch mix to use later if you need to thicken the sauce. Discard the rest of the cornstarch mixture. Place about ½ to 1-inch of oil in a frying pan and heat. When hot, add the chicken and fry until crispy on both sides. Remove to a platter which has been lined with paper towels. Remove most of the remaining oil, leaving just a thin layer on the bottom of the pan. Quickly add the green peppers and stir fry for a few minutes. Then add the scallions and garlic to the peppers cooking until the peppers are soft but not mushy. Add the chicken back to the vegetables. Add the soy sauce mix and stir well. If you want to thicken the sauce take about 2 tablespoons of the leftover cornstarch and add about ¼-½ cup of cold water to it. Mix until the cornstarch is dissolved and not lumpy. Add to chicken mixture. Cook for a few minutes until thick and all the chicken is coated. Add the peanuts and stir until all coated. Serve with rice. Serves 6.

Aunt Carmen says this is one of Uncle Jorge's favorite recipes. I made it one day and the kids loved it, except for Steven who prefers his chicken fried. This is Jeffrey's favorite chicken dish.

Jeff Feiner being roasted by his Dad at his graduation party...being given a Second Place Ribbon; the only time in his life he ever saw one!

Marc says Jeff is the kid that ruins the curve☺

NETTIE'S CHICKEN
Nettie Schwartz

Chicken pieces of your choice	**Cornflake crumbs**
1 bottle of low fat Italian Dressing	

Marinade chicken breasts or whatever parts of the chicken you prefer in a bottle of low fat Italian dressing. Place cornflake crumbs in a large bowl. Coat the chicken pieces with the cornflake crumbs. Spray a large baking pan or cookie sheet with PAM®. Bake in a 375° oven for about 35 to 55 minutes depending on the type of chicken pieces you have chosen. Check while baking and if the crumbs are getting too brown, cover with foil for awhile. Remove foil about 10 minutes before they are done to allow for a final browning.

Nettie Schwartz is a friend and the kids' Hebrew School Teacher.

JOHN'S STUFFED CHICKEN BREASTS
John Grimaldi , Sr.

⅓ **cup club soda**	½ **pound Italian proscuitto or boiled ham**
1 teaspoon lemon juice	**1 large mozzarella cut into small rectangles**
Salt and pepper to taste	**Fresh parsley, chopped**
Grated cheese	**Flavored breadcrumbs**
Parsley	**2 cups shredded mozzarella (for the top)**
2-3 packages of thin, boneless, skinless chicken cutlets	
(you can use the breasts but they will have to be pounded)	

Mix together the club soda, lemon juice, salt, pepper, grated cheese and parsley. Dip the chicken breasts into the club soda mixture. Then roll into flavored breadcrumbs. Refrigerate for about 2 hours. Place a chicken cutlet on a flat surface. Place ½ slice of proscuitto, a piece of mozzarella, fresh parsley, and breadcrumbs in the center of the cutlet. Roll up to form a log shape. Place into a large roasting pan and bake 350° for 45 minutes, turn every 15 minutes. Refrigerate, and slice each breast into ½-inch slices. Each roll will make about 6 slices. Place the slices of chicken breast into another baking pan. Preheat oven to 300° degrees. Add wine sauce (see below) to the chicken. Bake just to heat about 15 minutes in a 300° oven. Add the mushrooms, shredded mozzarella and slices of lemon placed over the top, and bake another 15 minutes.

Wine Sauce: for every 4 chicken breasts

1 cup of white wine or Marsala (add at the last 15 minutes)	**1-2 cloves garlic, peeled and crushed**
Parsley	**1 box sliced mushrooms**
⅓ **cup oil**	**1 lemon cut in thin slices**

Mix all the ingredients together except for the mushrooms, and lemon slices. Heat in a small saucepan; bring to a boil. Let simmer 5 minutes. If too loose thicken with a little cornstarch.

My cousin John is an executive chef in Staten Island and a fabulous cook. He always makes these for our parties. Serve the breasts whole or sliced in rounds for a buffet. We are always exchanging recipes.

John Grimaldi and Elise Feiner a very long time ago...check out the hat! My mother took me out in public like that...(That's Aunt Millie Grimaldi, John's mother in the background on the right.)

QUICK CHICKEN DINNER
Nancy Barfield

1 package of boneless chicken breast, sliced thin
A little black pepper
1 package of onion soup mix

1 can whole cranberry sauce
1 bottle Catalina salad dressing

Place the chicken breasts in a pan that has been sprayed with PAM®, and sprinkle with pepper. Mix together in another bowl, the onion soup mix, cranberry sauce and salad dressing; then pour over the chicken. Bake at 350° for 40 minutes

Nancy's cousin gave this to her. It's fast, easy and delicious. Serve with Stove Top Stuffing®.

CHICKEN CUTLETS
Katherine Avella

3 pounds of boneless thin chicken cutlets
Plain bread crumbs
Wondra® flour
6-8 eggs, beaten
½ teaspoon salt

⅛ teaspoon black pepper
2 tablespoons dried parsley
1-1½ cups grated cheese (Locatelli Romano or Parmesan cheese)
Wesson® oil or other vegetable oil for frying

Cut the chicken pieces into small size cutlets about 3 x 4-inch or leave them large if you like them that way. Get two large paper plates or pieces of waxed paper or aluminum foil, and fill one with plain breadcrumbs, and one with flour. Beat the eggs, salt, pepper, parsley, and grated cheese together in a large mixing bowl. Dip the cutlets in the flour, then the egg mixture, then the breadcrumb mixture. (You may freeze them at this point by placing them on a sheet of waxed paper in a single layer on a disposable cookie sheet; after they freeze you can put them in a zip lock bag and fry later.) Place them on a platter as you bread them with wax paper between each layer. If you have any of the egg mixture left over, add remaining breadcrumbs to it and mix until firm, adding more breadcrumbs if necessary. Shape into round patties and fry these as well. They are delicious too.   Place about ¼-½-inch of oil in a frying pan and heat. Test the oil to see if it is hot by throwing a little of the breadcrumb mix into the oil; if it bubbles, it's hot enough to begin frying. Fry the cutlets until golden brown on both sides. This will take a few minutes (about 7 to 10 minutes depending on the thickness.) Place on a platter lined with paper towels as they finish cooking. Layer paper towels between each layer of cutlets. Remove the paper towels before serving.

CHICKEN CUTLETS PARMIGIANA
Katherine Avella

Chicken cutlets (see recipe above)
2-3 bags mozzarella cheese
½-¾ cup grating cheese for the top

Recipe of Avella Marinara Sauce (see index)
1 pound of spaghetti

To make the cutlets Parmigiana, make the marinara sauce recipe and chicken cutlets as per the directions. In a shallow baking dish, cover the bottom with marinara sauce. Place a single layer of prepared cutlets on top of the sauce. Top with another sparse layer of marinara sauce. Top with shredded mozzarella and grated cheese and more marinara sauce.   Bake at 350 ° for about 25 to 30 minutes or until cheese melts; cover with foil if getting too brown , or place pan under the broiler until the mozzarella melts, about 7 minutes **(watch carefully.**) Serve with spaghetti or angel hair pasta. Cook the pasta according to package directions and fix with marinara sauce and grating cheese. Serves 6.

My grandmother's sister Orsola Massimiano Barone We always called her "Toots– a-layla" Because as kids we could never say Zia Orsola. She is Aunt Lizzie and Aunt Frances', Uncle Teddy and Uncle Mike's mother"

TURKEY
Elise Feiner

We do our turkeys one of three ways:

Marinate the turkey in Aunt Thirza's special marinade mix. The makes the most phenomenal turkey. We always have this for Thanksgiving. See index under marinades.

Just sprinkle the top of the skin with garlic salt and bake it at 350° until temperature (when checked with a meat thermometer) reaches the appropriate temperature for poultry.

Take a stick of butter, and soften it. Add (to taste) garlic salt, grating cheese, pepper, a little basil, oregano, paprika, the juice of half of a lemon (save the lemons for when you are ready to roast the bird) and parsley. Make into a paste. Divide in half. Sprinkle the turkey with a little paprika. Take half of the butter mixture and forced it under the skin. Use your fingers to push in all around under the skin. Rub the rest of the butter mix all over the turkey skin. Cut a lemon in half, remove seeds and put it into the turkey cavity. Bake. If the turkey starts to get brown cover with foil.

NICOLE'S CHICKEN CUTLETS IN LEMON SAUCE
Nicole Lynn Latini

2- 3 packages boneless chicken cutlets, if using breasts, pound to flatten them
½-1 stick of butter

Flour
3-4 eggs mixed with salt and pepper to taste

Lemon Sauce:

1 stick of butter
2-3 tablespoon flour
Juice of one lemon, and some of the pulp

1 tablespoon chopped parsley
1 chicken bouillon dissolved in hot water (optional)

Dip the chicken cutlets into flour, then into the egg mixture, and then back in the flour. Layer them on waxed paper until ready to sauté. Heat a large sauté or frying pan. Melt a ½ stick of butter, and start to sauté the chicken breasts until lightly brown. Add more butter as needed. Set the sauté pan aside. Place the sautéed chicken breasts into a baking dish sprayed with PAM® or lightly buttered, and bake for about 30 minutes in a 350° oven.

Turn the heat under the sauté pan to medium. Add one stick of butter to the sauté pan, scrapping the browned drippings on the bottom. Add the flour and blend well. Add the juice of one lemon and some of the pulp, add chopped parsley. If too thick add a little chicken bouillon dissolved in hot water. Cook until slightly thickened. Add to the chicken at serving.

When my niece Nicole was working in the Uptown Grill Restaurant, she became quite the chef. She made this recipe for a dinner she served to Nanny.

FETA STUFFED CHICKEN BREASTS
Elise Feiner

3 ounces of feta cheese, crumbled
1 teaspoon oregano
4 boneless chicken breasts (about 6 ounces each)
Kosher salt and pepper

3 tablespoons olive oil
½ cup chicken broth or stock
Juice of ½ lemon
3 tablespoons unsalted butter

Mix the feta cheese and oregano together. Make a pocket in each chicken breast by inserting a paring knife in the thicker side of the breast. **Don't go all the way through**. Stuff the cheese mix into the pocket. Season the breasts with salt and pepper on both sides. Heat the oil in a frying pan over medium-high heat. Add the breasts and cook until well browned on each side about 7 minutes per side. Cover the pan and cook until the chicken reaches 160° when checked with a meat thermometer. Cook another 5-8 minutes. Set the chicken aside. Add the chicken stock to the frying pan and cook, deglazing the pan as you do with a wooden spoon. Add the lemon juice and butter; reduce heat to low and swirl the pan until the butter melts and sauce is slightly thickened. Spoon the sauce over the chicken to serve. (If the sauce doesn't thicken to your liking, take about 2 teaspoons of Wondra flour mixed in a little cold water and add it to the pan).

SESAME PECAN CHICKEN
Elise Feiner

2 large cloves garlic, peeled and crushed
Salt and pepper to taste
1-2 packages boneless, skinless chicken cutlets
1 cup buttermilk
¼-½ cup pecans
¼ cup walnuts
½ cup sesame seeds

¼ cup flour
1 teaspoon paprika
1 tablespoon butter
1 tablespoon corn oil
½ cup heavy cream
1 tablespoon Dijon mustard

Combine garlic, 1 teaspoon salt and the buttermilk. Marinate the chicken in the mixture at least two hours. Place the pecans, walnuts, sesame seeds, flour and paprika in the food processors and blend but not too fine. Wipe most of the marinade off the chicken. Dip chicken into the flour and nut mixture, pat lightly and refrigerate for several hours. (Place on wax paper).

Melt the butter and oil in skillet until almost smoking. Turn the heat down and sauté the chicken until golden brown about 4 to 5 minutes on each side. Drain on paper towels. Remove most of the excess at from the skillet. To the skillet add the cream, mustard, freshly ground black pepper and if desired, more salt. Whisk occasionally until mixture thickens. Pour sauce over the chicken. If extra sauce is desired double the cream and mustard. This recipe originally called for 2 large chicken breasts boned and split but I use chicken cutlets. Depending on how many you feed and their appetites, you might buy one or two packages of chicken cutlets. Serve 4.

Antoinette is Jeff's friend from Medical School. They are now doing their residencies at Johns Hopkins...Antoinette in Psychiatry, Jeff in Plastic Surgery

The Valenti Family:
L-R: John, Angelina, Amy, Antoinette Valenti, M.D., and John at the Medical School Graduation dinner.

CHICKEN RIGGIES PLESCIA-JOHNSON
Brenda Johnson

3 teaspoons minced garlic
Olive oil
2 (28 ounce) cans crushed tomatoes
1 (28 ounce) can whole peeled tomatoes
8 medium boneless chicken breasts, cubed
1½ bottles of hot or mild cherry peppers (cut up in quarters with seeds)
Dash of red wine (optional)

Salt and pepper to taste
1-2 teaspoon basil
½ teaspoon oregano
½ pint heavy cream
1 red and 1 green bell pepper (quartered)
1½ pounds Rigatoni macaroni
Grated cheese (Optional)

Heat the oil in a large frying pan. Add garlic and cook for one minute until golden, add the chicken pieces and cook until browned. Add the cherry peppers and the cherry pepper juice. Add red wine to taste. Add the bell peppers. Break up the 1 can whole peeled tomatoes, and add to the pan. Add the 2 cans of crushed tomatoes. Add salt and pepper to taste. Add in basil and oregano. Bring to a boil and then **simmer** for about an hour. Cook the rigatoni according to package directions. Just before serving, add the heavy cream to the sauce. Mix the sauce with the rigatoni and serve. You can top with grated cheese if you'd like.

Don't let the name Johnson fool you, Brenda's maiden name is Plescia and she is an old fashioned Italian cook! These are delicious!

STIR FRIED CHICKEN AND BROCCOLI
Elise Feiner

3-4 packages stir fry boneless chicken strips or cut boneless breasts into cubes
5-6 tablespoons of oil
2 cloves garlic, peeled and thinly sliced

1-2 packages fresh broccoli flowerets
1-2 carrots sliced thin on an angle
1 can straw mushrooms
6 scallions cut in 1-inch pieces

Marinade for the chicken:
1 teaspoon cornstarch
½ teaspoon salt
1 teaspoon sugar
1 teaspoon soy sauce
1 clove of garlic, peeled and crushed

⅛ teaspoon black pepper
1 teaspoon hoisin sauce
1 teaspoon sesame oil
½ teaspoon rice wine vinegar

Liquid for Broccoli Mix:
9 tablespoons soy sauce
3 tablespoons sugar
3 tablespoons cooking sherry

1 tablespoon rice wine vinegar
2 packages chicken bouillon dissolved in ½ cup hot water

Mix the broccoli mix ingredients together and set aside.

For the Frying Pan:

3-4 tablespoons oil

6 cloves of garlic, crushed

Mix the cornstarch, salt, sugar, soy sauce, garlic , pepper, hoisin sauce, sesame oil, and vinegar together. Add the chicken strips and refrigerate for a few hours. In a large frying pan or wok, heat 5 to 6 tablespoons of oil, and the 2 thinly sliced garlic cloves. Add the marinated chicken strips and quickly stir fry until just about done. Remove to a platter. Add the carrots and scallions to the oil and quickly stir fry them. Remove and place with the chicken. Add another 3 to 4 tablespoons of oil, and the 6 cloves of crushed garlic to the pan. Quickly stir fry the broccoli. When it is turning bright green and starting to soften, add the liquid broccoli mix. Cook for a few more minutes. Add the chicken, vegetables, and the can of straw mushrooms back to the pan and heat thoroughly. If you want a little thicker sauce take about 2 tablespoons of cornstarch and dissolve in about 5 ounces of water. Stir until well blended and smooth. Add to pan, whisking it in quickly. Allow to cook a few minutes to thicken. Serve over rice. Serves 6.

CHICKEN BREASTS WITH MANGO SALSA
Elise Feiner

8 skinless, boneless chicken breasts
4 teaspoons fresh oregano, chopped
2 teaspoon fresh thyme, chopped
2 teaspoon fresh basil, chopped
2 teaspoon kosher salt
1½ teaspoons sugar
¼ teaspoon allspice
¼ teaspoon cayenne pepper

2 large mangos cut into ½-inch cubes
2 small bananas cut into ½-inch pieces
1 medium red pepper, washed, seeded and cut into very tiny cubes
4 scallions, thinly sliced
½ cup fresh lime juice
4 tablespoons honey

Mix the oregano, thyme, basil, salt, sugar, allspice and cayenne pepper in a large bowl. Rub the mixture all over the chicken and refrigerate for about 30 minutes. In another bowl, mix the mango, banana, red pepper, scallions, lime juice and honey together.
Cover and set aside in the refrigerator to chill. A quick way to cube the mango is to slice down the mango from the top to the bottom around the large pit. This will give you two halves, if you slice it leaving about a ¾-inch center piece where the pit is. Then score each half vertically into a few rows, and then score it horizontally to create small cubes. Push the skin up from the outside and the cubes should pop up. You can them release them with a gentle tap of the sharp knife or by carefully running a small paring knife under the cubes.
Heat a large grill pan sprayed with PAM® if you have one, or you can do this on the grill, or use a George Foreman® grill. Cook the chicken on both sides until thoroughly cooked about 6-8 minutes on each side, depending on the thickness of the chicken breasts. You can them top the chicken with the salsa mixture or serve it on the side. This serves 8, but you can easily cut it in half.

When we lived in the Philippines we ate, and learned a lot of uses for mangos, including how to cut them easily. I had two housekeepers, Lita and Annie in the house my friends and I rented, who were great cooks. They often made this for dinner.

CHICKEN IN A CLAY POT (BIHAR)
Kavita Mehta

3 pound roasting chicken
½ teaspoon crushed garlic
½ teaspoon finely grated fresh ginger
1 tablespoon grated onion
¼ teaspoon ground cardamom
¼ teaspoon ground turmeric
¼ teaspoon ground mace

Salt to taste
¼ teaspoon saffron strands
I tablespoon boiling water
3 tablespoons ghee or butter
⅓ cup strong chicken stock 1 bay leaf

Stuffing:

1 tablespoon, ghee of oil
1 large onion, finely chopped
1 teaspoon finely chopped garlic
3 teaspoons ground coriander
I teaspoon ground cumin
250 g (8 ounces) minced lamb
½ teaspoon dried fenugreek leaves, optional

1 bay leaf
1½ teaspoons salt
½ teaspoon ground black pepper
¼ teaspoon each ground cardamom, cinnamon and cloves
1 cup long grain rice
2 cups hot water

Remove skin of chicken. You will find (if you have not done this before) that a skinned chicken is indeed a pathetic sight, but the reason for this procedure is that the flavors are not lost on the skin, but penetrate the flesh instead. However, without the protective skin which contains most of the fat, the breast meat is inclined to be dry, so remember to put the chicken breast downwards when cooking so that the breast is immersed in stock and remains moist. Make small slashes in the flesh of the breast, thighs and drumsticks. Combine garlic, ginger, onion, cardamom, turmeric, mace and salt. Dissolve saffron in boiling water and add. Rub the mixture well into the chicken, cover and marinate overnight in refrigerator or for at least 2 hours at room temperature. Fill the chicken with cooked and cooled stuffing, truss the bird and place in clay casserole breast downwards. Melt the ghee or butter and pour over the chicken. Pour stock into the casserole and add the bay leaf. Bake in a moderately slow oven 325° for 2 hours or a slow oven 300° for 4 hours if this is more convenient. Take the dish to table and uncover it there, slipping a knife between not and lid to break the seal. Serve with a pilau such as mattar pilau or with plain boiled rice.

Stuffing:

Heat ghee or oil and fry onion and garlic until soft and starting to turn golden. Add ground coriander and cumin and fry 1 minute, then add lamb and fry, stirring, until lamb is browned. Add all remaining ingredients except rice and water. Cover and cook on low heat for 15 minutes, stirring occasionally. Add rice and hot water; bring to the boil, stirring. Then turn heat very low, cover tightly and cook for 20 to 25 minutes or until liquid is absorbed by rice. Cool slightly before using.

I met Kavita Mehta, when we were working together on a job for one of my corporate clients, The Oberoi Hotels and Resorts. She supplied me with all of the Indian Spices used for our event. She has a wonderful website... check out: indianfoodsco.com

Bernie's Angels!
Top Row L-R: Bernie Gigliotti, Katherine Trainor
3rd Row: L-R Lauren Feiner, Kristin Gigliotti, Shannon Babula, Alana Nicoletta, Cecilia Tripp
Middle Row: Regina DeMauro, Marita Tolfa, Mary George, Emily Balzano, Lori Kasuda, Katie Mc Coy
Front L-R: Caitlin Dwyer, Kacie Cunningham

ZUCCHINI STUFFED CHICKEN
Carmen Ferreiro

2½ pounds chicken parts (I use boneless chicken breasts)
½ cup Progresso® Italian style breadcrumbs
1 small zucchini, grated
1 egg
4 tablespoons parmesan cheese

1egg, beaten with 1 teaspoon water
1½ cups Progresso® Italian Style Breadcrumbs
3 tablespoons oil
3 tablespoons butter

Loosen the skin on each chicken piece to form a pocket. I create a pocket on the boneless breasts with a knife. Mix the ½ cup breadcrumbs, zucchini, egg, and parmesan cheese. Spoon into the pockets. Hold together with toothpicks if necessary. Dip filled chicken into the egg and water mixture to coat; then into breadcrumbs. In a frying pan, heat the oil and butter. Add chicken and brown on each side. Transfer to a baking pan and bake 15 to 20 minutes at 375°. Serves 6.

Aunt Carmen said that this dish is a favorite in her house. Between her and Uncle Jorge, I'm not sure who the better cook is.

L-R: Jorge Ferreiro, M.D.
and Carmen Ferreiro

TONI'S BAKED CHICKEN
Toni Mollico

Boneless skinless chicken cutlets
1 onion, peeled and sliced

Vegetable oil
Flavored breadcrumbs

Dip the breasts in oil, and then dip into the breadcrumbs. Fold in half. Add a little oil and the sliced onions to a baking pan that has been sprayed with PAM®. Add the chicken cutlets to the pan. Cover the chicken with aluminum foil and bake 34 to 40 minutes in a 350° oven.

Aunt Toni made these for us for dinner when we were all newlyweds. She gave me the recipe because it was great for a quick dinner. Add a potato and a salad and you're done.

Toni and Tom Mollico on their
wedding day

TURKEY OR CHICKEN CROQUETTES
Katherine Avella

4 tablespoons butter
1 tablespoon onion, finely chopped
4 tablespoons flour
1 cup milk or chicken broth
Salt and pepper, to taste
2 cups finely chopped cooked chicken or turkey

2-3 eggs
Salt and pepper (for the eggs) to taste
1 tablespoon milk
2 tablespoons grated cheese
Plain Breadcrumbs

Heat the butter, add the onion and cook until soft and slightly browned; add the flour. Stir over low heat for about a minute. Add the milk or broth, salt and pepper and cook until thick and smooth. Add the chicken or turkey. Reseason. Chill thoroughly. Shape into croquettes (can make logs, circles, or pyramid shaped). Make a mix of a 2-3 eggs, salt and pepper, 1 tablespoon milk, a little grating cheese. Dip the croquettes into the egg, and then dip into plain breadcrumbs, and fry until golden brown. While the croquettes are frying, make a white sauce (see index.) Serves 4.

My mother always made these when we had leftover chicken or turkey. Hers were the best!

Katherine and Samuel Avella (my parents)

Nanny (Katherine Avella) and grandson Michael Avella
at his wedding

L-R: My nephews Philip Avella, Jr. and Michael
Avella at my wedding

L-R: Joe DiPierdomenico, Marc Feiner, Philip DiPierdomenico, Philip Avella, and Joseph Avella

R-L: Sandra Nolan, Robert Smith, M.D., Marie George, and Carol Feduccia at Bob's Retirement Dinner

L-R: Lauren Feiner, Lauren Sleeper, Brittany Venezio, Cristina Ferreiro and Abby Feiner

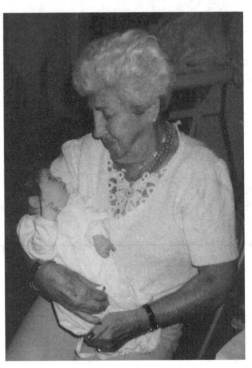

Nanny Nellie Reinisch with great granddaughter Lauren Feiner May 1985

L-R: Jeffrey Feiner, Brittany Venezio, Rich Venezio, Marc Feiner, Jennifer Venezio, Julie Venezio sightseeing in New York City

Seafood...

The Stephen Rosenfeld Family
Clockwise from the top: Joshua, Rae, Mindy and Steve

"I've been on a diet for two weeks and all I've lost is two weeks."

-Totie Fields

And Even More Hints:

To clean artificial flowers, pour some salt into a paper bag and add the flowers. Shake vigorously as the salt will absorb all the dust and dirt and leave your artificial flowers looking like new! Works like a charm!

To easily remove burnt on food from your skillet, simply add a drop or two of dish soap and enough water to cover bottom of pan, and bring to a boil on stovetop.

Spray your Tupperware with nonstick cooking spray before pouring in tomato based sauces and there won't be any stains.

When a cake recipe calls for flouring the baking pan, use a bit of the dry cake mix instead and there won't be any white mess on the outside of the cake. I like Baker's Joy ® myself…

Wrap celery in aluminum foil when putting in the refrigerator and it will keep for weeks.

When boiling corn on the cob, add a pinch of sugar and milk to help bring out the corn's natural sweetness.

Cure for headaches: Take a lime, cut it in half and rub it on your forehead. The throbbing will go away.

Don't throw out all that leftover wine or broth: Freeze into ice cubes for future use in casseroles and sauces.

To get rid of itch from mosquito bites, try applying soap on the area and you will experience instant relief.

Ants, ants, ants everywhere ... Well, they are said to never cross a chalk line. So get your chalk out and draw a line on the floor or wherever ants tend to march. See for yourself.

Use air-freshener to clean mirrors. It does a good job and better still, leaves a lovely smell to the shine.

When you get a splinter, reach for the scotch tape before resorting to tweezers or a needle. Simply put the scotch tape over the splinter, then pull it off. Scotch tape removes most splinters painlessly and easily.

-Author Unknown (I received this in an e-mail forward – with many thanks to the original author)

STUFFED SHRIMP
Phyllis Latini

1-2 pounds of raw shrimp, cleaned and deveined
1 row of Ritz Crackers, crushed
1 can of crab meat, drained
1 can of clams, minced or chopped, drained
1 clove of garlic, peeled and crushed

1 small onion, peeled and minced
1 tablespoon lemon juice
2 tablespoons of parsley flakes
Black pepper to taste
1 stick of butter

For the top of the shrimp:
½ - ¾ stick of butter
¼ cup white wine

2 teaspoons lemon juice
Paprika

Slit the belly of each shrimp. In a small frying pan, melt the stick of butter. Add the onions and garlic and sauté until golden. In a bowl, mix the crushed crackers, crab meat, clams, Parsley flakes, lemon juice, and black pepper. Add this mix to the sautéed onions and garlic, and mix well. Stuff each shrimp by putting the mixture into the belly of the shrimp. Pack a 9 x 12-inch glass baking dish with the shrimp. Make a small mixture of butter, lemon juice and white wine (cooking wine is good). Spoon over each shrimp. Garnish with paprika for color. Bake at 375° for about 30 minutes or until they look done and turn pink.

My niece Nicole sent this recipe from her grandmother's (Shamma) kitchen. Phyllis is a fabulous cook. Nic says these are great as a main course or hors'oeuvres.

REVIVING FROZEN SHRIMP
Joppy Basile

Bring a pot of water to a rapid boil. Throw frozen shrimp in and cook for **ONE** minute. Immediately drain. Place on a rack and cover with ice and allow to cool about 5 minutes. Squeeze a bit of lemon over them.

Maria Trainor told me that Joppy, does her shrimp this way; they taste so fresh you'd never know they were frozen.

MANELE'S BAR-B-QUE SHRIMP
Edith Mainella

3 pound shrimp, unpeeled
Olive oil
Freshly ground black pepper, lots of it
Salt
Lemon juice

Tabasco
Lea & Perrins® Worcestershire Sauce
2½ sticks butter
10 cloves of garlic, peeled and crushed

Place the whole shrimp, keeping the shells on, in a single layer on an oven proof dish. Drizzle olive oil over the top of the shrimp. Pepper the shrimp until they are black; when you think you have enough pepper, add more. Add lots of salt, lemon juice, Tabasco sauce, and Worcestershire sauce. Remember you are seasoning through the shells. Melt 2 sticks of butter; add the garlic and sauté for 3-4 minutes. Pour over the shrimp. Cut up the remaining ½ stick in small cubes and put the butter on top of the shrimp and you can either broil until the shrimp are cooked; 10 to 15 minutes or bake at 450° for 5 minutes, turn; pepper them again, and bake for a few more minutes. Be sure to taste and see if they are done. Serve with newspapers on the table and lots of napkins. Use French or Italian bread to sop up the oil and butter. Serve with cold beer and a salad. To eat, suck the shells first, peel the shrimp, dip back in the sauce. Serves 6.

When my cousin Warren was in law school, we made several trips to New Orleans. These were served at Pat Manele's Restaurant. My Aunt Edith loved these and used to make them in Bayville and East Hills all the time. Every time I make this recipe, I think of her.

Warren Mainella, U.S.M.C.
I was in high school when Warren was in Viet Nam. I wrote him a letter, and lit a candle every day until he arrived home safely. Then, I just prayed to say thanks!

Frank S. Mainella Jr. holding Melissa Avella

SHRIMP CEVICHE WITH MANGO AND JICAMA SALAD
David Smith

The key to making this dish is preparing the shrimp 24 hours before you need them. If you do not have 24 hours you can cheat and quickly blanch the shrimp in salted boiling water for about 2 minutes. If you go this route, be careful not to overcook the shrimp. Assuming you have 24 hours, follow these steps:

Take approximately 1½ pounds of any type of shrimp. The larger the shrimp the longer it will take to cook. I recommend using a 16/20 prawn. This means that there are 16 to 20 prawns in a pound. You need to remove the shells, leaving the tail on. Prawns also need to be de-veined. In a bowl, juice 3 lemons and 3 limes. Combine this with one tablespoon of granulated sugar, a pinch of salt and pepper, and one small diced red onion. Next, add your shrimp into this mixture, and toss so that the shrimp are coated in the juice. If there is not enough juice to cover the prawns, add the juice of another lemon and lime. Cover this mixture and refrigerate for 24 hours. This is plenty of time to cook the shrimp, but when finished taste one to make sure they are properly seasoned.

To present the ceviche salad, peel and julienne one ripe mango and one medium Jicama. Add ½ a bunch of chopped cilantro, three tablespoons olive oil, and one tablespoon rice wine vinegar, one teaspoon ground cumin, and a pinch of salt and pepper. Toss and let rest until ready to serve. Fresh tomatoes or any hot or sweet chili work great in this salad also. To plate this dish place a bed of fresh spring greens on a plate. Top this with a small handful of Jicama salad, and then the prawns. Drizzle some of the ceviche juices over the whole dish so that the citrus flavors mingle with all three layers of the salad. You can garnish this dish with a few of the leaves of the cilantro, or a diced green onion. Serves 4.

David is the executive chef of the Cottonwood Restaurant and Bar in Truckee, California. David says, "With the advent of summer, my thoughts turn from the heavy, filling dishes of winter to lighter fare. Dishes like beef stroganoff, or braised lamb, popular on a cold night in February, go unnoticed on a hot July evening. Summer dishes tend to be lighter, and also will take advantage of the plethora of fresh ingredients that become available. One of my favorite summer dishes is ceviche. This dish can be prepared as an entree or appetizer, and will be the hit of any summer barbecue. Classic ceviche uses lime or lemon juice to cook shrimp, resulting in a light fruity dish. I've also developed a recipe for an Asian halibut ceviche, which relies on this same cooking process, but introduces Asian flavors to this South American dish. Here you can find recipes for both these dishes, or you can use these recipes as guide lines for other forms of ceviche, taking advantage of the fresh bounty that land and sea has to offer. "

EASY STUFFED SHRIMP
Elise Feiner

24 shrimp with tail unpeeled but the remainder of the shrimp peeled, deveined, and butterflied
1 pound lump crabmeat
1 stick butter
½ pound mild cheddar cheese, grated
1 can cream of mushroom soup

4 ounces of heavy cream
6-8 slices of Italian bread made into breadcrumbs
Garlic salt
Salt and white pepper
Paprika or Symeon spices
2-3 tablespoon butter, melted

Lightly sauté the crabmeat in the butter; add the cheese, mushroom soup, cream, and fresh breadcrumbs. Season with salt, pepper, and garlic salt. Increase breadcrumbs if too loose. Stuff the shrimp with the mixture. Sprinkle with paprika or Symeon spices. Bake at 350° about 13 minutes. I have a great shortcut here. Instead of stuffing the shrimp individually you can either separate the shrimp into individual casseroles or place them in a large casserole in the following way. Place the shrimp with the tails up around the perimeter of a buttered casserole dish. Spread the crabmeat stuffing over the shrimps so the tails are still visible. Drizzle with a little butter and bake the same way.

This is an easy way to make stuffed shrimp. I got the idea to top the shrimp from a restaurant in New Hampshire called Master MacGraiths. They do a great stuffed shrimp.

"Christmas gift suggestions: To your enemy, forgiveness. To an opponent, tolerance. To a friend, your heart. To a customer, service. To all, charity. To every child, a good example. To yourself, respect."
-- Oren Arnold

LOBSTER FRA DIABLO
Katherine Avella

2-3 whole lobsters
3 (2 pounds 3 ounce) cans plum tomatoes put into the
blender to puree
1 (2 pounds 3 ounce) can crushed tomatoes
5-6 cloves of garlic, peeled and crushed

Salt and pepper
1 tablespoon basil
3-4 tablespoons vegetable oil
Crushed red pepper (optional)

In a large stock pot, (about 18-quarts or more) heat the oil; add the garlic. Add the tomatoes, salt, pepper, and basil. Bring to a boil, and reduce to a simmer for about 25 minutes. Bring back to a boil and add the lobsters; reduce heat to medium; let cook for about 15 minutes. Cook the spaghetti according to package. Use the sauce to fix the spaghetti. Serve lobsters in a platter. Serves 3 to 4.

Fra Diablo means "of the devil in Italian." You can add as much crushed red pepper as you want to make it "red hot."

BROILED LOBSTER
Maria Trainor

Lobster Tails (frozen)
Melted Butter to brush on

Paprika
Melted Butter to Serve

Defrost the lobster tails in the refrigerator. Crack the center of the **TOP** of the shell from beginning of the tail. Gently pull the lobster out of the shell and place either on top of the shell of remove from the shell completely. Brush the uncooked lobster with melted butter and sprinkle with paprika. Bake in a shallow pan or cookie sheet at 350° for about 20 minutes or until firm and white. Place under the broiler for a few minutes. Serve with melted butter

Maria gave me this recipe and it is easy and delicious. This is how we do the tails for Christmas Eve dinner.

CLAMS OREGANATA
Katherine Avella

Cherrystone clams
2 loaves Italian bread, made into fresh breadcrumbs in the
blender (not too fine)
2 teaspoons oregano
Salt and pepper to taste

2 teaspoons parsley
5 cloves garlic, peeled and crushed
1 cup grated cheese
Olive oil

Soak the clams in cold water to which you have added 1-3 tablespoons of cornmeal. Open the clams and pour out most of the juice. If any sand remains remove the remaining clams from shells, wash and return clams to the shells. Line clam shells with the clams back in them up on a baking sheet. Mix all the remaining ingredients together to form a breadcrumb mix. Use enough olive oil to dampen the crumbs. Spoon breadcrumb mixture generously on the top of the clams. Drizzle a little olive oil over the crumbs. Bake at 350° until crumbs are golden. Serve with lemon wedges.

My Uncle Pat loved to go clamming on the beach in Bayville, Long Island. All of the kids would tag along with him, and we would bring back bushels of clams. I can still see him shucking them in the backyard. My mother always make these for appetizers.

LOBSTERS
Elise Feiner

Fresh live lobsters one per person

Butter, melted

Fill a large pot with enough water to cover the lobsters. Lightly salt the water. Bring the pot of water to a boil. Add the lobsters and bring the water back to a boil. Set your timer for 16 to 20 minutes depending on the size of the lobster. When the bell goes off, the lobsters are done. Drain well before serving. Serve with melted butter, lemon wedges, a plastic bib, lobster or nut crackers.

LOBSTER ROLLS
Elise Feiner

1 to 2 pounds cooked lobster meat
Salt and pepper to taste
1 to 2 stalks of celery, finely diced

1 medium to large onions, peeled and finely chopped
Mayonnaise
Hot dog buns

Mix everything together but the buns to taste. Butter the buns and broiler until golden. Fill with lobster mix.

STEVE'S CLAMS ON THE BARBIE
Steven Feiner

1-2 bags small (Littleneck) clams
Aluminum foil, heavy duty

2 sticks butter, melted
6 cloves garlic, peeled and crushed

Place a double layer thickness of aluminum foil on your barbeque grill (You can use disposable pans too.) Preheat the grill. Rinse the clams in cold water. Place on the grill and cover. Cook until the clams are opened. Remove to disposable aluminum pans. Serve with melted butter to which the garlic has been added.

Steven had these at a friend's house and now always makes them at home on the barbeque!

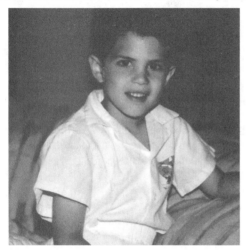

Steven "Butch" Feiner...then

Steven "Butch" Feiner ...now ...my wild colt
heading off to Thomas Cooley Law School in Lansing, Michigan
Steve is a great cook, at least someone takes after their mother...

L-R: David Feiner, Adam Morton, Steven Feiner

SHRIMP MARINARA
Maria Trainor

Large bag of frozen cooked shrimp, peeled, deveined and
tails removed; thawed

Marinara sauce well heated (your own or see index)
Linguine or spaghetti

Place the thawed shrimp in a pot of boiling water for **one minute;** place in an ice bath. Dry. Heat enough marinara sauce for the amount of pasta you are making. Add shrimp to sauce to **heat for a few minutes**. Cook pasta; top with shrimp sauce, and grated cheese if desired. This is best served over spaghetti.

I must confess that I don't make much fish at home except around the Christmas holidays. However, as my children have gotten older, they have become lovers of seafood and shellfish and so we have started to make much more shellfish at home. They love to come home from school for a lobster dinner, complete with corn on the cob, cornbread, and a shrimp cocktail for starters. This dish is one of Lauren's favorites.

"The wildest colts make the best horses."

-Plutarch

MUSSELS MARINARA WITH SPAGHETTI
Rosemarie DiPierdomenico

4 bags Mussels
1 large bunch flat leaf parsley (pull off stems), washed, and chopped
12 cloves garlic, peeled and crushed
2 bottles Inglenook Chablis

Black pepper to taste
¾ cup olive oil
1-2 cups water
3 pounds spaghetti
Marinara sauce (see next page for sauce)

Soak the mussels in cold salted water. Roll with your hands and let sit for a few minutes. Wash and debeard the mussels. Change the water a few times to remove all sand. If any of the mussels are opened before you cook them, or remain closed after they are cooked, discard them. In a very large pot (about 16 to 20 quart pot or a large stockpot) place the crushed garlic, parsley, black pepper, olive oil, and one bottle of the wine. Add the mussels. Add about 1 to 2 cups of water. Cover the pot and bring to a boil (about 5 to 7 minutes) Cook for about another 10 to 12 minutes or until the mussels are open and tender. Make the marinara sauce in advance. (Recipe on next page). Have your water boiling for the spaghetti before you put the mussels in. Cook the spaghetti, so that it is ready before the mussels are ready to come out (just by a minute or two). Use the sauce to fix the spaghetti, and save enough to refill the gravy boat 2 or 3 times. Put in a separate pot if necessary. After the spaghetti is fixed, and the mussels are done, remove about ¾ of the liquid from the mussel pot and add the remaining marinara sauce to the mussels. Mix well in a large bowl, and serve with spaghetti. Serves 12.

This has become a Christmas Eve staple. My "favorite eldest sister-in-law" and most wonderful cook Ro taught me how to make theses. We had gone to Hampton Bays for a barbeque a few years ago, and she made the mussels. I was flabbergasted at my children going crazy over these mussels. They begged me to make them, and now, they are learning how to make them themselves. Jeff made them himself for the millennium Christmas Eve. The aroma when these are cooking is fabulous. Stuart Schwartz, a confirmed "non mussel eating" man has even become a believer.

JoJo "Julius" Di Pierdomenico "My Oldest Brother"
Joe was absolutely the most handsome man I ever saw in a New York State Trooper's Uniform…a great man and greatly missed…

His Grandson Joey Sapio

Jerry and Juliann (DiPierdomenico) Sapio

L-R: John, Tyler and Andrea DiPierdomenico

FEINER'S FAVORITE MARINARA SAUCE FOR MUSSELS
Rosemarie DiPierdomenico

2 (1 pound 12 ounce) cans Chunky Crushed tomatoes
(Furmano's®)
2 (2 pounds 3 ounce) cans Italian plum tomatoes
4 cans regular crushed tomatoes
1 large onion, peeled and chopped
6-8 cloves of garlic, peeled and crushed

Salt and pepper to taste
3 tablespoons dried basil
2 cups (about ½ bottle) of Inglenook® Chablis or any white
wine
Olive oil (about ¼ cup)

Open all the cans of tomatoes and place the 2 cans of plum tomatoes in the blender (one at a time) and turn quickly on and off just to liquefy. In a very large pot, cover the bottom with olive oil. Heat, and then add the garlic and onions. You may need to add a little more olive oil at this point. Sauté for a few minutes until lightly browned. Add the pureed plum tomatoes and the rest of the crushed tomatoes, salt, pepper, basil, and the wine. (I usually add about half of the bottle). Cook about 45 minutes to an hour. I usually make this a few days in advance. Set aside enough sauce to fix the 3 pounds of spaghetti. Use to fix the spaghetti as per the directions in the mussel recipe. Set aside extra sauce for the gravy boat. Add the mussels to remaining sauce as directed in the mussels marinara recipe, **being sure to drain about ½ to ¾ of the liquid** from mussels or the sauce will be too watery (you do want to retain a little of the liquid for the garlic and wine flavor). Serves 12.

This is the accompanying sauce to the Mussels Marinara. It is Ro Di Pier's recipe, and is wonderful. You can also use this as an everyday marinara sauce if you'd like, but I keep it special by only using it with the mussels on Christmas Eve. Have lots of bread ready for dipping in the sauce.

GARLIC BUTTER SHRIMP
Frank J. Basile, Sr.

1 pound frozen or fresh shrimp, peeled and deveined,
medium to large shrimp
½ cup butter
1 clove of garlic, minced

1 tablespoon snipped fresh parsley
Dash red pepper
3 tablespoons white wine
Shredded lettuce (optional)

Thaw shrimp if frozen. For sauce, melt butter in a saucepan. Stir in garlic, parsley and red pepper flakes. Cook for one minute. Stir in wine. Heat through. Set aside. Thread shrimp onto 4 long or 8 short skewers. Grill on the greased rack of an uncovered grill directly over medium coals for 6 to 10 minutes or until shrimp are opaque on the inside, turning over halfway through grilling time, brushing frequently with the sauce. Serve on a bed of shredded lettuce. Use extra sauce for dipping if you want. **Hint:** Make extra sauce to dip instead of using the contaminated sauce from the raw shrimp.

Maria Trainor gave me this recipe. She said that Frank Basile made these as an appetizer when they had dinner there, and that they were delicious.

The Basile's Clockwise from Top: Joanna, Frank, Jr., Jeffrey, Erica, and Frank Basile, Sr.

CLAMS CASINO
Rockie Napoli

3 cans minced clams, (juice of one can only)
2 sticks melted butter
Parsley and garlic powder to taste

Flavored breadcrumbs
Paprika

Mix the clams, butter, parsley and garlic powder together.   Add flavored breadcrumbs until you get a nice consistency (about ½ a can). Spread in a baking dish. Sprinkle with paprika. Bake 350° for 30 minutes.

OPEN FACED BROILED CRAB SANDWICHES
Iryna Trociuk

1 (8 ounce) package of crab delight (Louis Kemp®)
3 green onions, chopped
1 cup grated cheddar cheese
⅓ cup mayonnaise

¼ teaspoon Tabasco or cayenne pepper
1 large tomato, cut into 8 slices
4 sourdough English Muffins, split

Preheat the broiler. Flake crab in a bowl. Add green, onions, cheese, mayonnaise and Tabasco. Lay muffins split side up on a baking sheet, and broil until golden, 2 to 3 minutes. Remove muffins from oven and lay a tomato slice on each half. Top with about ½ cup crab mixture. Return to oven and broil until bubble and brown, 3 to 5 minutes.

Iryna said that these make a great brunch dish!

Michael Trociuk, M.D.
and
Iryna Trociuk

STEAMERS
Jeffrey Feiner

4-6 pounds steamer or littleneck clams
3 cups dry white wine (I use Inglenook® Chablis)
1 onion, diced
8-10 cloves garlic; crushed
12 black peppercorns

1 (13 ¾ or 14.5 ounce) can College Inn ® Chicken Broth
Good handful of fresh parsley, chopped
4-5 fresh basil leaves, finely chopped
3 cups water

Place clams in cold water to which you have added 1-3 tablespoons of cornmeal. Let the clams sit about ½ hour. Rinse well in cold water. **Discard** any clams with **broken shells or** those that are **open before** cooking or **closed after** cooking. Wrap the clams by dozen - dozen and a half in cheesecloth before putting them in the pot (cut pieces of cheesecloth in large rectangles, place the clams in the middle and tie with kitchen twine). This makes it easier to serve later on. Place the wine, onions, garlic, peppercorns, parsley, basil, and water in a large steamer or pot. Add the clams. Bring to a boil, keep covered. Stir or mix by shaking the pot for about 6 to 8 minutes or until clams are opened. Serve with melted butter. Serves 8.

Jeffrey loves steamers and they are so easy to make! Adding the cornmeal, allows the clams to open to eat it, and release the sand from the inside of their shells.

L-R: Sherry, Michael and Daniella Avella

Mindy Rosenfeld and Jake Stookey

Marc, David, and Elise Feiner at David's Graduation From the
State University of New York –with honors

L-R: Abby, Lauren, and Jeffrey Feiner

Daniella Faith Avella
Looks just like a doll with her Daddy's Face!

The Johnson's L-R: Alexander, Gabrielle, Brenda holding
Garrett, and Robert

SALMON STEAKS WITH TARRAGON CRÈME SAUCE
Nancy Blaker

4 salmon fillets
¼ cup melted butter or margarine
1 teaspoon salt, divided
¾ teaspoon pepper, divide
¼ cup minced onion

½ teaspoon dried tarragon (to taste)
2 tablespoons flour
1 cup milk
1 teaspoon lime juice

Preheat the broiler. Lightly grease the broiler pan. Place salmon in the pan, lightly baste with butter or margarine, salt and pepper. Broil 5 inches from the heat for about 15 minutes. In a small saucepan over medium heat, cook onion and tarragon in remaining butter, until the onion is transparent. Add flour stirring constantly for 1 minute. Gradually add the milk and lime juice stirring until thick. Add salt and pepper. Pour sauce over the salmon. Serves 4.

Nancy is a wonderful friend, great cook and fellow needle pointer and knitter. She and I love to share recipes. This is a favorite of hers.

SOLE TOPPED WITH SUMMER SALAD
Nancy Blaker

¼ cup flour
¼ teaspoon salt
⅓ teaspoon black pepper
⅛ teaspoon garlic powder
Paprika to taste
4 sole fillets
1 tablespoon margarine or butter

2 tablespoons salad oil
1 medium cucumber (peeled, seeded, cubed)
1 large tomato (peeled, seeded, and cubed)
¾ teaspoon basil
2-3 tablespoons low calorie Italian Dressing

Combine flour, salt, pepper, garlic powder and paprika. Coat fillets with flour mixture. Heat the margarine or butter with 1 tablespoon of oil. Cook the fillets over medium heat for 2 minutes per side. Remove fillets. Cover to keep warm. Wipe out skillet and add 1 tablespoon oil. Add cucumber, tomato, and basil to the skillet. Cook constantly until warm but crisp. Stir in salad dressing. Spoon over the fish and serve.

Nancy's husband Mark is a cardiologist, so therefore, we depend on her to add some healthy recipes to this otherwise cardiologist's nightmare of recipes, laden with cream, butter and cheese.

Mark Blaker, M.D. and Nancy Blaker

FRENCH FRIED CALAMARI RINGS
Josephine Mainella

1 pound fresh or frozen squid
1 egg, beaten

⅓ cup milk
1 cup bread crumbs

Wash squid. Slice into ¼-inch rings. Drain on paper toweling. Combine egg and milk. Dip squid rings into the egg mixture, then coat with crumbs. Place in a single layer in a fry basket. Fry in a deep fat fryer (350°) for 20 to 30 seconds or until lightly browned. Make 6 appetizer servings or 3 entrée servings. Serve with cocktail sauce.

FRIED CALAMARI
Tom DeSimone

1 large bag of frozen calamari rings, thawed and drained
Flour
Salt and Pepper

Garlic salt
Parmesan cheese
Parsley

Season the flour with salt and pepper. Place the drained, thawed, calamari rings in the flour mixture. Place in a strainer to shake off excess flour. Deep fry but don't over fry or they will be tough. Season with parmesan cheese, garlic salt and parsley when done. Do not overcook the rings. Serve with cocktail sauce or a little marinara sauce. For a different twist, mix equal amounts of flour and graham cracker crumbs.

Tom and Flo owned a catering hall called Alfredo's Ristorante in New Hartford for years. All of our Bar and Bat Mitzvah's were held there. Tommy is a fabulous chef. Tommy could rival any New York City catering hall. Mike and Philly even worked there for awhile. His calamari is the best!

SQUID WITH PEAS
Josephine Mainella

4 tablespoons olive oil
2-3 cloves garlic, peeled and chopped
Crushed red pepper flakes to taste
3 pounds squid (cut into rings)

1 cup dry white wine
Salt
Parsley to taste
1 pound fresh peas (frozen or canned)

In frying pan at medium heat add the olive oil, garlic, and crushed red pepper. Add cut up squid and let cook until pale pink. Add 1 cup dry wine, parsley, and 1 teaspoon salt. Add the peas. Cook between 20 to 25 minutes.

SEAFOOD IN A BOWL
Thirza Avella

2 (1½ pound) whole lobsters or individual lobster tails
1 pound live Littleneck clams
¼ cup white wine
¼ cup water
1 pound sea scallops

½ cup cognac
1 shallot, finely shopped
2 cups chilled butter, diced
Salt and pepper, to taste
6 small individual bread bowls

In a steamer, steam lobster and clams, approximately 10 to 15 minutes. Remove the lobster and clams. Reserve the juices. Crack and separate the claws and tails from the lobster discard the shells. In a shallow sauté pan, add the wine, water, and scallops. Cook on medium heat until the scallops are done. Reserve the juices. Combine the reserved seafood juices, combined; they should equal 1½ cups liquid. If there's not enough liquid, add some water. In a large heavy pan, add the reserved juices, cognac, and shallots, reduce by half. Remove from heat add 2 cubes of butter. Whisk until melted and return to medium heat continue to whisk while adding the remaining butter. The sauce should thicken to the pouring consistency of cream. Add the salt and pepper, to taste. Serves 6.

Cut the top off each loaf of bread and hollow it out. Leave an inch thick crust on the sides and bottom. Fill the bread hollow with the seafood and top with the cognac sauce. Serve immediately.

WARREN'S BARBEQUE TROUT OR STRIP BASS
Warren Mainella

1 whole trout or strip bass, scaled and gutted
Fresh diced tomatoes
Oregano to taste
½ can (small) black olives
1 stalk celery, chopped fine
½ fennel stalk, chopped

Basil to taste
McCormick's Italian seasoning to taste
Salt and pepper to taste
Olive oil to drizzle
1 teaspoon lemon juice
½ stick butter cut in ¼-inch cubes

Scale and gut the fish, but leave the whole fish intact. Fill the cavity with fresh diced tomatoes, oregano, black olives, chopped celery, chopped fennel, basil, McCormick's Italian Seasonings, salt, pepper, olive oil, and lemon juice. Use a little of all of the preceding, using your judgment for the amounts; it will depend on the size of the fish. Cut up about ½ stick of butter in small cubes and insert into the fish. Wrap the whole fish in aluminum foil loosely. Put on a low flame on the barbeque. Turn after 15 minutes. Cook for another 15 minutes. Open the foil and check for doneness. When it's soft to the touch, it's done.

This is Cousin Warren's barbequed fish recipe. He said it is the most delicious fish you have ever tasted. It was one of Uncle Frank's favorite. Who would have thought that Warren, who always wanted me to make him a sandwich, would become such a great cook!

Cousins Elise Feiner and Warren Mainella

Warren Mainella holding Jeffrey Feiner riding on Command

Warren with Chico and Booger at his new home in Savannah, Tennessee

Warren riding Booger and dragging Chico along on his ranch!

GEFILTE FISH LOAF
Brenda Antzelevitch

1 jar of gefilte fish (6 piece size)
1 large can carrot slices, drained
½ cup mayonnaise
¾ cup matzoh meal

1 tablespoon sugar
½ cup of the jellied liquid from the gefilte fish

Place into a large bowl and mash everything together with a fork. Spray a loaf pan with PAM®. Place mashed ingredients into a loaf pan. Bake 350° for 1 hour. Slice and serve. This can also be served cold. Serves 6.

Brenda got this recipe from a friend. She said it is fast, easy and delicious. The carrots give it a jewel like quality and it looked beautiful when you serve it. It takes away the fish taste when made this way.

The Antzelevitch Family L-R: Brenda, Charlie, Lisa and Danny

Brenda and Dr. Charles Antzelevitch

Dr. Charles Antzelevitch and Lauren Feiner.

Charlie is the Director of the Masonic Medical Research Lab in Utica, New York and a world renowned speaker in the field of cardiology.   Three of my kids did summer research fellowships there. We in New Hartford are so blessed to have a man of Charlie's caliber and integrity living among us.

GEFILTE FISH
Nellie Reinisch

10-12 pounds carp, white or pike fish, reserve the skin and bones
2 pounds of onions, peeled and sliced
1-2 sticks butter or margarine
6-8 eggs
About 4 ounces of cold water
3 tablespoons cracker meal
About 3 tablespoons salt
¼ teaspoons black pepper

2 full quarts of cold water
3-4 carrots, sliced
3 large raw onions
1 strip of celery
Remaining ½ of cooked onions
Salt and pepper to taste
1 tablespoon sugar
¼ cup cold water

Remove the bones and skin from the fish and save. Sauté onions in margarine or butter to a light golden look. Do not make brown. After the onions cool, add half of the onions to the fish meat. Then add the eggs, about 4 ounces of cold water, cracker meal, salt and pepper. Chop all of this together until texture of the fish is silky looking. Taste to adjust seasonings. Do all this while chopping. Shape into oval patties. Prepare the pot to cook the fish as follows: Put the fish bones on the bottom and sides of the pot. Add 2 full quarts of cold water. Add the carrots, raw onions, celery, remaining cooked onions, salt and pepper to taste. Place the oval patties, slowly around the pot. Cover fish with fish skin so pot of fish doesn't get dry. Bring to a boil and cook on medium to low heat. While this is cooking add 1 tablespoon of sugar. In about 1½ hours add ¼ glass of cold water over the fish. Cook fish for 3½ hours on low to medium heat. Taste while cooking for seasonings.

This is Nanny Nellie's recipe written in her own hand. It was given to me by Aunt Shirley to include in the book. She was a fabulous cook and every one of her recipes has been wonderful so far.

"Nellie's Girls" L-R: Adele Freedoff, Shirley Flomenhoft, and Betty Feiner
Beautiful inside and out!

HADDOCK OREGANATA
Tom DeSimone

8 pieces haddock fillets
Olive oil
1 loaf Italian bread crumbs or dried crumbs
½ cup grated cheese
1 tablespoon fresh parsley

3 cloves garlic, peeled and crushed
Salt and pepper to taste
1 teaspoon lemon juice
Additional lemon juice to top fish
½ stick butter cut in ½-inch cubes

Mix all the ingredients together except the haddock, additional lemon juice and butter cubes together. Place the haddock in a pan sprayed with PAM®. Top each piece with the bread crumb mix. Sprinkle with a little lemon juice. Top with butter cubes. Bake in a 375° oven 15 to 20 minutes.

This is one of the specialties at Alfredo's Catering Hall. Tommy DeSimone was gracious enough to share it with me.

FRIED FLOUNDER
Katherine Avella

Whole flounder, scaled, cleaned and head removed
½ cup flour

Salt and pepper to taste
Oil for frying

Dip in flour seasoned with salt and pepper. Fry until golden brown and fish is completely cooked.

FLOUNDER FILLETS IN TOMATO
Katherine Avella

2-3 tablespoons olive oil
1 small onion, peeled and dices
1 (2 pound 3 ounce) can plum tomatoes (crush with your fingers)

Salt and pepper to taste
1-1½ pounds flounder fillets
Grating cheese

Place the oil in a large skillet and heat. Add the onions and sauté until lightly golden. Add the tomatoes, salt and pepper; bring to a boil. Reduce heat and simmer about 20 minutes. Add the flounder fillets; simmer until the flounder is cooked and tender about 15 minutes. Sprinkle with grating cheese.

We Italians do everything in sauce!

FISH 'N CHIPS
Elise Feiner

Vegetable oil, for frying
1½ to 2 pounds fresh haddock
Salt and pepper
½ cup flour
2 large eggs

2 tablespoons cold water
2 cups plain bread crumbs or panko crumbs
½ teaspoon dried mustard powder
¼ teaspoon cayenne pepper

Pour about 2-inches of vegetable oil into a large frying pan. Heat oil over medium high heat. Cut haddock into 4 servings, 6 to 8 ounce portions and season with salt and pepper. Place a couple of scoops of flour in a paper dish. Combine egg and water in second bowl.
    Season plain bread crumbs with mustard and cayenne pepper in the third paper dish. Coat fish in flour, then egg, and then bread crumbs. Gently set coated fish into hot oil and fry 5 minutes on each side until medium golden brown in color. When the fish is evenly golden all over, remove and drain on brown paper bags if you have them or otherwise, paper towels will do.

Chips:

2½ pounds fingerling potatoes, quartered lengthwise
1 tablespoon vegetable oil
2 tablespoons melted butter

McCormick® Season All seasoned salt
Apple Cider Vinegar

Preheat oven to 550°. In a large bowl, toss potato wedges with oil and melted butter. Spread potatoes in a single layer on a cookie sheet. Roast potatoes 20 minutes, turning once, until deeply golden all over. Season with seasoned salt, and sprinkle with apple cider vinegar. Drain on paper towels. Serves 4

Since my gastric bypass surgery I have become a fish eater. This is delicious. I love Panko crumbs (Japanese Breadcrumbs), they make a really crisp crust. To make the chips, use the small finger potatoes or waxy potatoes as they are sometimes called. They have a firmer texture. We became fans of vinegar on our fries when we lived in Baltimore, and you can't live in upstate New York with becoming a fan of a Friday Fish Fry!

L-R: Glenn Feiner,
Sharon Feiner Fischer,
and
Larry Feiner, M.D.

L-R:
Glenn and
Steven Feiner
I think my son
Steven and his
cousin Glen
look alike

FISH FILLETS
Elise Feiner

Fish filet of your choice, such as flounder, haddock
4 tablespoons butter, melted
Salt and pepper to taste

Garlic powder
A few saltine crackers, crumbled

Melt the butter, add salt and pepper to taste, and garlic powder. Place the filets on a pan. Brush with the butter mixture. Top with saltines. Drizzle remaining butter over the saltines. Broil for about 5 to 6 minutes being careful not to burn the crumbs. Fish will flake easily when cooked.

FISH FILLETS WITH CAPER MAYONNAISE
Katherine Avella

1 teaspoon vegetable oil
Salt to taste if desired
Freshly ground pepper to taste

1 pound boneless fish fillets with the skin left on
2 tablespoons mayonnaise
2 tablespoons drained capers

Preheat the broiler to high. Brush the surface of the filets with a little oil, salt and pepper. Brush a large baking dish with a little oil, salt and pepper. Place the fish skin side down in the pan. Blend the mayonnaise and capers together. Brush the mixtures uniformly on the top of the fillets. Place the fillets about 4-inches from the source of the heat; broil. If the fillets are about ½-inch thick they should broil properly in about 3 to 4 minutes. Fish flakes when done.

BEER BATTER FISH FRY
Elise Feiner

6 pieces of haddock filets
12 ounces of beer or enough to cover the fish
1 egg, beaten
¼ cup evaporated milk

1½ cups Bisquick® baking mix, sifted
1 teaspoon salt
¾ cup beer

Place the fish in a container with the beer; refrigerate 24 hours. When ready to fry, make a batter of the egg, milk, sifted Bisquick® and salt. Add ¾ cup fresh beer to the batter. Dip the fish in the batter and fry to a golden brown. You can also use frozen or other fish of your choice. You can also cut these in small pieces and use as an appetizer. Serves 6 as a main course.

Friday nights are fish fry nights in Upstate New York; you can't live here if you don't like fish!

FLOUNDER FILLETS (CUTLET STYLE)
Katherine Avella

⅛ teaspoon black pepper
2 tablespoon dried parsley
1-1½ cup grated cheese (Locatelli Romano or Parmesan cheese)
Wesson® oil or other vegetable oil for frying

1½-2 pounds flounder fillets
Bread crumbs, plain
Wondra® Flour
6-8 eggs
½ teaspoon salt

Get two large paper plates or pieces of waxed paper or aluminum foil, and fill one with plain breadcrumbs, and one with Wondra Flour. Beat the remaining ingredients together in a mixing bowl. Dip the fillets in the flour, then the egg mixture, then the breadcrumb mixture. Place them on a platter as you bread them with wax paper between each single layer. If you have any of the egg mixture left over, add remaining breadcrumbs to it and mix until firm, adding more breadcrumbs if necessary. Shape into round patties and fry these as well. They are delicious too. Place about ¼ to ½-inch of oil in a frying pan and heat. Test to see if it is hot by throwing a little of the breadcrumb mix into the oil, if it bubbles, it's hot enough to begin frying. Fry the fillets until golden brown on both sides. Place on a platter lined with paper towels as they finish cooking. Layer paper towels between each layer of cutlets as they finish frying.

FRESH CALAMARI IN BEER BATTER
Josephine Mainella

3 pounds cleaned squid with tentacles
1 cup flour (all purpose or whole wheat)
2 eggs
1 (12 ounce) can light or dark beer
1 teaspoon onion powder
½ teaspoon garlic powder

⅛ teaspoon cayenne pepper or more to taste
½ teaspoon salt
Oil for deep-frying
Seasoned salt
Lemon wedges
Cocktail sauce

Cut squid into 1-inch rings. Combine flour, eggs, beer, onion powder, garlic powder, cayenne pepper and salt. Dip small handfuls of squid rings and tentacles in flour mix. Heat the oil. Deep fry squid 1½ minutes, separating the pieces with tongs so they don't clump. Drain and repeat with remaining squid. Garnish with lemon wedges and cocktail sauce for dipping. Serves 6.

ASIAN HALIBUT CEVICHE
David Smith

Unlike the shrimp in the Shrimp Ceviche with Mango and Jicama Salad (see index), it is mandatory to prepare the fish 24 hours before it is needed, because the fish will not hold up to being blanched, and it will loose a lot of flavor. For this recipe, you will need one pound of fresh halibut. Alaskan halibut is available throughout the spring and summer, but a fresh California halibut, or one from the Northwest will work also. You will need to take the halibut and dice it small ¼ inches). The easiest way to do this is to cut strips off your filet and then line them up together to dice. You should avoid putting any pieces of halibut that have excessive amounts of sinew or cartilage, as this will not cook up as tender as the other fish.

In a medium bowl, combine the juice of four oranges, four lemons, ¼ cup soy sauce, ¼ cup rice wine vinegar, two tablespoons of peeled chopped fresh ginger, and a splash of Tabasco (or a few chili flakes). Toss this mixture with the fish, cover and refrigerate for 24 hours. You will know when the fish is done because it will become soft, not chewy, and the flesh of the fish will appear cooked all the way through. After 24 hours it is important to taste and season the fish. I find that usually the mixture needs a bit more soy sauce to increase the salt content, and I like to finish it with ¼ cup of honey to sweeten. Everyone's taste for salt and sweet are different, so it is important to taste dishes and season them according to what you like. This ceviche is very versatile, and can be served or presented many ways. A few suggestions are to serve it with crispy fried wonton skins, as an appetizer. You can also toss the mixture with fresh greens and serve it as a salad. This will also work as a cold noodle salad, tossed with almost any type of noodle. Of course, to make things simple, you can always just eat it as is!

David's Dad, Bob, was my husband Marc's partner at Medical Arts, OB/GYN. David says, "I hope that you enjoy these recipes and they will inspire you to try them. Do not fear the ceviche concept. If you are using a good, fresh product, it is very safe. If in doubt, why not come in to the restaurant and let us serve you some of our own!

The Robert Smith Family
L-R: Terrence Boylan holding Jamie , Jennifer Smith Boylan, Robert Smith, M.D., Sheila, David and Brett Smith

FISH IN A POUCH
Elise Feiner

Any fish fillet or small whole fish of your choice
For each piece of fish you'll need:
2 teaspoons extra virgin olive oil
Sea salt to taste
Black pepper to taste
1 teaspoon freshly chopped parsley

1 sprig fresh oregano
3-4 pitted black olives
2 slices of lemon
½ clove garlic, peeled and slivered
2 teaspoons fresh lemon juice

This can be done in the oven or on the grill. Preheat the oven to 400°, or preheat your grill. Take each piece of fish and place it in a piece or foil or parchment paper (large enough to be able to fold it over and make a packet) and top with above ingredients. Place the foil or parchment packages on a baking pan and place in the oven or on the grill. Bake for about 20 minutes, or until the fish begins to flake. Use parchment in the oven, foil in the oven or on the grill. The parchment will burn on the grill.

Jerome and Betty Feiner on their wedding
day May 30, 1946

More cousins… Paul and Pnina Feiner's Family
Back Row L-R: Ken and Justin
Front Row L-R: Elliot, Judy, Pnina, Benjamin, Paul
Seated: Sharon

CHILEAN SEA BASS
Elise Feiner

4-5 tablespoons unsalted butter
5 pounds of onions, mix several different kinds, Vidalia,
Spanish, Bermuda, and Maui, peeled and thinly sliced
14 plum tomatoes, peeled, seeded and chopped
5 shallots, peeled and cut in half
5 cloves of garlic, peeled and cut in quarters

4 fresh basil leaves, chopped
2 tablespoons extra virgin olive oil
1 teaspoon salt
½ teaspoon ground white pepper
12 Chilean Sea Bass Fillets (about 3 pounds)

In a large heavy pan, heat the butter until melted and add the onions. Cook, stirring frequently over very low heat, until they caramelize and are rich golden brown color. This will take about 1½ hours. When done put the onions in a food processor. Add the tomatoes, shallots, garlic, and basil and process until smooth. In the same pan that you browned the onions, add the olive oil. Add the onion mix and cook over low heat about 30 minutes. Preheat the oven to 425°. Put the pieces of sea bass into a roasting pan that has been sprayed with PAM®. Sprinkle them with salt and pepper to taste. Put the onion mix on the top and bake for about 10 to 15 minutes. Serve by placing 2 pieces of fish topped with some sauce for each person. Serves 6.

Debbie and Anthony Pedicini, Jr.

Tyler and Cassandra Domenico

Samantha Mia Smith daughter of Kris and
Gina Mastrovito-Smith

Jamie Marissa and Philip Di Pierdomenico, Jr.

L-R: Sharon Feiner Fischer and
Barbara Feiner
Sharon is an event planner in Atlanta,
Georgia, and Barbara is a gem in
more ways than one…

Soups and Salads...

The Stuart Schwartz Family
Top Row L-R: Debbie Schwartz Lipson, Barbara and Kenneth Schwartz
Middle Row L-R: Sheldon Lipson, Stuart Schwartz, Debbie Karden Schwartz
Front Row L-R: Kayla Lipson, Basia and Zachary Schwartz...missing Jonah

"Children in a family are like flowers in a bouquet; there's always one determined to face in an opposite direction from the way the arranger desires."
-Unknown

– Uses for Alka Seltzer:

Clean a Toilet: Drop in two Alka Seltzer tablets, wait twenty minutes, brush and flush. The citric acid and effervescent action clean vitreous China.

Clean a Vase: To remove a stain from the bottom of a glass vase or cruet, fill with water and drop in two Alka Seltzer tablets.

Polish Jewelry: Drop two Alka Seltzer tablets into a glass of water and immerse the jewelry for two minutes.

Clean a Thermos Bottle: Fill the bottle with water, drop in four Alka Seltzer tablets, and let soak for an hour (or longer, if necessary).

Unclog a Drain: Clear the sink drain by dropping three Alka Seltzer tablets down the drain followed by a cup of Heinz White Vinegar. Wait a few minutes, and then run the hot water.

Uses for Bounce:

It will chase ants away when you lay a sheet near them.

It takes the odor out of books and photo albums that don't get opened very often.

Repels mosquitoes -Tie a sheet of Bounce through a belt loop when outdoors during mosquito season.

Eliminates static electricity from your television screen. Since Bounce is designed to help eliminate static cling, wipe your television screen with a used sheet of Bounce to keep dust from resettling.

Dissolve soap scum from shower doors. Clean with a sheet of Bounce.

Freshen the air in your home. Place an individual sheet of Bounce in a drawer or hang in the closet.

Prevent thread from tangling. Run a threaded needle through sheet of Bounce before beginning to sew.

Place a sheet of Bounce in your empty luggage before storing.

Freshen the air in your car. Place a sheet of Bounce under the front seat.

Clean baked-on foods from a cooking pan. Put a sheet in a pan, fill with water, let sit overnight, and sponge clean. The anti-static agent apparently weakens the bond between the foods.

Eliminate odors in wastebaskets. Place a sheet of Bounce at the bottom of the wastebasket.

Collect cat hair. Rubbing the area with a sheet of Bounce will magnetically attract all the loose hairs.

Eliminate static electricity from Venetian blinds. Wipe the blinds with a sheet of Bounce to prevent dust from resettling.

Wipe up sawdust from drilling or sand papering. A used sheet of Bounce will collect sawdust like a tack cloth.

Eliminate odors in dirty laundry. Place an individual sheet of Bounce at the bottom of a laundry bag or hamper.

Deodorize shoes or sneakers. Place a sheet of Bounce in your shoes or sneakers overnight.

Golfers put a Bounce sheet in their back pocket to keep the bees away

-Author Unknown (I received this in an e-mail forward – with many thanks to the original author)

BEEF OR VEAL STOCK
Elise Feiner

8 pounds beef or veal bones cut into 2-3 inch pieces
1 (6 ounces) can tomato paste
2 cups chopped onions
1 cup chopped celery
1 cup chopped carrots
2 cups red wine
Salt

20 peppercorns
7 cloves garlic, peeled and left whole
5 bay leaves
1 teaspoon thyme
2 gallons water

Make a bouquet garni by placing the peppercorns, garlic, bay leaves, and thyme in a cheesecloth and tie with kitchen twine. Set aside. Preheat the oven to 400°. Place your bones in a large roasting pan and cook for 1 hour. Remove from the oven and brush the bones with the tomato paste. Put the chopped vegetables over the bones. Put back in the oven for another 30 minutes. Remove from the oven and place the roasting pan on your cook top. Add the wine and scrap all the drippings from the bottom of the pan. Place the contents of the pan into a large stockpot. Make sure you have scraped the whole bottom of the roasting pan well. Add a little water if need be. Add the 2 gallons of water to the pot. Add the prepared bouquet garni to the pot. Add salt to taste. Bring to a boil and reduce to a simmer and let cook at least 4 hours. Remove from the heat. Remove any excess fat. Discard the bouquet garni. Discard the bones. Strain the stock. Freeze in either ice cube trays or small plastic container (I use 2 cup size) and use in any recipe that calls for stock.

This is time consuming but adds such a difference in flavor as compared to commercial stock. I always keep stock in the freezer.

SPINACH SOUP
Elise Feiner

Chicken Soup (College Inn® or Homemade) See recipe index for Elise's Best Chicken Soup
3 boxes frozen chopped spinach

Egg omelets (see Egg Omelets for Soup a la Sandella)
Little meatballs (see index Meatballs for Beef Soup)

Heat the chicken soup thoroughly. Add the spinach, egg omelets, and meatballs. Cook until the spinach is defrosted and soup is hot. If you don't have time to make omelet's, take 6 eggs, salt, pepper, about 1 teaspoon of dried parsley and ½ cup grated cheese and whisk together. Pour the egg mix into the soup stirring constantly while adding the egg to make egg ribbons.

BEEF SOUP
Elise Feiner

1 large onion, peeled and left whole
5 stalks celery, washed and left whole
1 (16 ounce) bag baby carrots washed
2-3 packages short ribs
1 package beef shanks or beef bones
1 (16 ounce) can Hunts Tomato Sauce

2 tablespoons salt
¼ teaspoon black pepper
1 pound chopped meat (chuck or ground round) for meatballs (see Recipe for Meatballs for Beef Soup next page)

Take the one pound of chopped meat and follow the recipe for meatballs for Beef Soup. Fill a 16 quart pot with the remaining ingredients and bring to a boil. Then, lower to a simmer and let cook for about 3 to 4 hours. Remove the short ribs and shank from the soup and let cool. When cool, shred the meat and return some of it to the soup. I usually keep some of the meat aside and then put it in a frying pan. (See below) skim the soup periodically. When soup is finished remove the onion, and the carrots. Let the carrots cool a little and then put them in a blender with about 1 cup of the soup to liquefy them. Add the carrots back into the soup. Taste for seasonings. Serve by cooking some small pasta (alphabets, shells, acini de pepi, bows, etc.) and adding it to the soup. When you cook the pasta and drain it, put it back into the pot you cooked the pasta in, and then add the soup to that pot. This way, you will have a lot of leftover soup remaining in the original pot to freeze. You can change the type of pasta or cook rice the next time. The cooked pasta doesn't always freeze well, the plain soup freezes beautifully. Serves 12.

My mother would shred some of the short ribs and take a frying pan with a few tablespoonfuls of oil. Cut up onions and fry until golden brown. Add the shredded short ribs to the onion. Season with salt and pepper and add a few teaspoonfuls of wine vinegar to it. It almost tastes like a sauerbraten. For specific recipe see the crock-pot section of this book for Shredded Short Ribs. Serve it with a salad after the soup has been eaten. If you don't want to do this, just add all the shredded short ribs to the soup.

This was Grandpa Sam's favorite soup. He could make a meal of it. It really is a complete meal in itself because of the vegetables, beef, and meatballs. When Jeff, Steve, David, and Lauren were little, they would eat this by the bowlful, loaded with grating cheese. It was so nourishing. As with all the soups we make homemade, my kids would be satisfied with the soup and want to skip the meal.

MEATBALLS FOR BEEF SOUP
Katherine Avella

1 pound of chopped meat (ground round or chopped chuck will do)
2 eggs
Pinch salt (about ⅛-¼ teaspoon) because the cheese is salty
Ground black pepper (about ⅛ teaspoon)

Grating cheese (Parmesan or Locatelli Romano) about ¾-1 cup
Parsley (dried) about ½ tablespoon
Plain breadcrumbs (don't use seasoned) about ¼ of a cup
Water about ⅛-¼ of a cup

Mix everything together but the meat. When well mixed, add the meat and mix well. Shape into balls about ¼-inch in diameter. These meatballs are **very tiny.** Take a tiny bit of meat with the tip of your fingers and shape into tiny balls. Put up a large pot of water with about 1 tablespoon of salt added to it. Bring to a boil, and throw in the meatballs. Boil for about 5 to 6 minutes until cooked. Use a large slotted spoon to add the meatballs to beef soup. Do not add the remaining water or pieces of meat in the water that might be floating around. If you need more broth, then strain some of the water that you cooked the meatballs in and then add it to the beef soup

This beef soup was grandpa's favorite meal in the middle of winter. I can remember how it always smelled so wonderful and hearty. It filled our kitchen with love. This is a little time consuming because the meatballs are so tiny, but well worth the effort.

SIMPLE SQUASH SOUP
Carmen Ferreiro

3 acorn squash
1 bunch of scallions
2 carrots
1 tablespoon of fresh ginger

Olive oil
Low fat chicken broth
Salt and pepper to taste
Curry powder to taste (optional)

Cut squash in half; remove seeds and place in microwave and cook until tender (about 15 minutes). Cool and scoop out the inside. In large saucepan, sauté scallions and ginger in olive oil. Add the carrots in chunks and the squash. Pour enough broth to cover the squash and carrots. Season and let it simmer until the carrots are tender. Put through the blender or use an immersion blender to make it smooth. Taste for flavor and serve. You can serve with a dollop of sour cream, chopped peanuts and chopped scallions. This soup freezes very well.

L-R: Leslie Weiner Freedman, Brad Weiner, Aunt Betty Feiner, Hal Weiner, Leslie Weiner Solitrin

CHICKEN SOUP - ELISE'S BEST
Elise Feiner

1 Purdue® Oven Stuffer Roaster
2 large onions, peeled and left whole
2 bags mini baby carrots or one bag of regular carrots,
washed, peeled and cut in thirds
5 stalks celery, washed; cut off loose top leaves and cut in
half

2-3 bay leaves
Salt and pepper to taste
Cold water

Open the package of chicken and remove all the gizzards and other goodies from both ends of the chicken. Wash under cold running water. Fill a very large stockpot (16-24 quart) ¾ of the way full with cold water. Add the chicken, onions, carrots, celery, bay leaves, salt and pepper to taste. Bring soup to a boil and them lower to a simmer. Simmer for about 3 to 4 hours. Remove onions and celery and discard. **MAKE SURE YOU REMOVE BAY LEAVES** and discard them. Remove the chicken to a large platter and let it cool. Remove all the skin and all the bones and discard. Shred the chicken, and set it aside. Let the soup cool. Remove all the carrots from the soup and place in a small bowl. Strain the remainder of the chicken broth through a large strainer into another pot or container. Wash the stockpot out. Return the strained soup back to the pot. After you remove the chicken and all the vegetable, you will see that the fluid level has dropped considerably. The broth that is left is very concentrated at this point. You can now add about 3 to 4 cups of water back into the pot, but add this one cup at a time being careful not to dilute the soup too much. You will probably have to reseason the soup with salt and pepper at this point. Take the carrots that you set aside, and take about 1 cup of the broth and place it into a blender, and liquefy it. Add this mix back to the soup. It will give your soup a beautiful golden color. You can also do this by leaving the carrots right in the pot using an immersion blender if you have one. If you are using the soup for Matzoh Ball Soup, **add the shredded chicken back into the broth.** If you want to use it for a soup for dinner with a pasta or rice, **add the chicken back in.** If you are using it for soup a la Sandella (see index), **add very little chicken** back to the soup, and make chicken salad with the rest. If you are making it with pasta for a first course or light supper or lunch, boil the pasta of your choice in salted water, but usually very small pasta is used (orzo, stars, alphabets, small shells, rings, etc.) Drain well and then add pasta to the soup. Serves 12 to 16.

This is the best chicken soup base there is. It's fast and simple to make, you can do it in advance and freeze it. You can make it with matzoh balls (see below), rice, pasta, or as the base for soup a la Sandella. It is Jewish Penicillin with an Italian Flair. We use bay leaves while Mom Mom and our other Jewish relatives use dill in their soup. My kids can live on this soup, loaded with grating cheese when it has pasta in it, or simmering with Matzoh balls (I could never make enough to satisfy David) I made this soup in winter as a first course but because it was loaded with vegetables, pasta and chicken it was often the only thing my kids would eat.

MATZOH BALLS
Elise Feiner

12 tablespoons vegetable oil (¾ cup) (Wesson)
12 large eggs, slightly beaten
3 cups matzoh meal (Manischewitz)

6 teaspoons salt
6 tablespoons chicken soup stock
6 tablespoons club soda

Blend the vegetable oil and eggs together in a large plastic lidded bowl. Mix matzoh meal and salt together. Add matzoh meal and salt mixture to egg and oil mixture; blend well. Add the soup stock and club soda (if soup is not made yet, you can use all club soda) and mix until well blended. The mix should be a little on the fluffy side. Cover the bowl and refrigerate a few hours or overnight (is best.) Bring **2 large** pots (16-24 quarts if you have one, but at least 8-quart) of salted water to a boil. Shape the matzoh meal mix into balls, the size of meatballs (about 2-inches in diameter). They will grow **MUCH** larger as they cook. Reduce the flame so that the water is slightly boiling and not at a full rolling boil. Place half the matzo balls in one pot and the other half in the other pot. Cover the pots and cook for 45 to 55 minutes. **The secret to good matzoh balls is the club soda that makes them light and not cooking them all in one pot if you are making a large quantity.** If they are too close together they will stay hard in the middle instead of being fluffy. You can add some of the liquid from the matzoh balls to the soup if you like or need to have more liquid; this is up to you. If you decide to use some of the liquid, strain it as you pour it into the soup so you don't get loose matzoh ball crumbs in your soup. Remove from the pots with a slotted spoon or flat strainer and add to the chicken soup (See recipe for Chicken Soup - Elise's Best.) Makes about 36 matzoh balls. This will serve about 16 normal people (3 each) or 10 people including the 3 Feiner boys.

Although these are David's favorite, the rest of the Feiner kids do quite well with these too. This recipe makes a ton of matzoh balls but the Feiner boys can eat about 6 or more each. They fight over the matzoh balls and have contests as who can eat the most. I try to make enough to have leftovers as well, since Aunt Phyllis and Uncle Phil love this too. When figuring how many to make, normal people can eat about 3 for a starter course. You can easily divide this recipe and make less, but if you are married to a Feiner boy think twice. The leftover soup freezes well.

221

ELISE'S MUSHROOM-BEEF BARLEY SOUP
Elise Feiner

3 tablespoons vegetable oil
3 pounds beef cubes
4 potatoes, peeled and cut into small cubes
4 stalks celery, cut into thin slices
3 to 4 (2.25 ounces) bags mini baby carrots, cut carrots in half
½ (12 ounce) bag chopped frozen onion
1 box (8 ounces) fresh, sliced mushrooms
2 cloves of garlic, peeled and crushed

2 bays leaves
¼ teaspoon black pepper
2 teaspoons garlic salt
1 teaspoon dried basil
2 (15 ounce) cans Hunts® Tomato Sauce
1 (13¾ or 14 ounce) can College Inn® Beef Broth
1 cup barley
2-3 quarts water

Place the oil into a large heated saucepan. Add the beef cubes, and brown then lightly. Remove the cubes, leaving remaining liquid in the pan, and place cubes in either a large crock-pot or a large Dutch oven or stockpot. Add the potatoes, onions, carrots, celery, garlic and mushrooms to the saucepan and brown lightly. Add the vegetables to the beef. Add the bay leaves, garlic salt, pepper, dried basil, beef broth, tomato sauce, and water to the pot you selected. Add the barley. If you are doing it in a crock-pot, cook on high for 6 hours, and then on low for 2 hours. If you are doing it on top of the stove in any of the other type pots, bring to a boil, and then cook on a low simmer for about 2-2½ hours. Check to see if the barley is cooked and allow additional time if necessary. You may need to add a little more liquid (water or beef broth is fine) if the soup is too thick. Serves 6.

This is a great soup for a cold winter's day. It's very quick to put together and freezes well.

My "All-Stars" David and Lauren Feiner at Phillips Exeter vs. Andover Varsity Baseball Game

ITALIAN SEMOLINA SOUP
Frances Zierler and Camille Sanabria

2 (1 pound) bags Semolina
12 large eggs
1 pound freshly grated Parmesan cheese

Chopped fresh parsley
1 large (16 quart at least) homemade chicken soup or stock (see index)

Bring chicken broth to boil. In another bowl, gradually whisk farina; eggs, cheese, parsley, in medium bowl. Form into large balls. Refrigerate at **least 2 days** in advance. Using a large hole cheese grater, grate the balls into the **boiling soup**. Allow to cook for at least 15 minutes. Season soup with salt and pepper. Ladle soup into bowls. Sprinkle with 2 tablespoons cheese and parsley. Makes 12 servings.

Fran said that this is a soup that her grandmother always used to make. They always have this at Thanksgiving.

(Left) Fran Zierler dancing with her son David at his wedding... and son Jeremy at his wedding (right)

222

LEE'S GAZPACHO
Lee Sack

2 cucumbers, no seeds
2 green peppers
1 cup onions, peeled and chopped
1 (24 ounce) large can Italian whole plum tomatoes

¾ cup wine vinegar
¼ cup olive oil
4 cloves garlic, peeled and minced
1 (48 ounce) can tomato juice

Mix the cucumbers, green peppers, onions and the plum tomatoes in a food processor, one vegetable at a time. Put the vegetables into a large bowl. Mix in the wine vinegar, olive oil, garlic, and tomato juice. Mix together and chill before serving.

Aunt Barbara Schwartz gave me this recipe that she got from her friend Lee.

ELISE'S BEST PEA SOUP
Elise Feiner

4-5 tablespoons vegetable oil
3 bags dried green peas
1 bag (32 ounces) baby carrots
4 large Idaho potatoes, peeled, cut in small cubes or 16 red tiny new potatoes, peeled and quartered
1 pint heavy cream
2 bay leaves
3 smoked ham hocks or bone from a spiral ham

Salt and pepper to taste
¼ pound boiled ham cut in ¼-inch thick slices (I like Boar's Head® Baby Ham) cut in small cubes, or leftover spiral ham
1 bag frozen chopped onions
2 cloves garlic, peeled and crushed
½ teaspoon sugar
⅛ teaspoon thyme
1(13 ¾ or 14 ounce) can chicken broth

Place the oil in a 16 quart stockpot and sauté the onions until soft and translucent; add potatoes and cook for about 5 to 8 minutes. Fill the pot with water and add all the remaining ingredients except for the heavy cream, and cubed ham. Keep flame on medium until it starts to boil. Then lower to a simmer and stir frequently. Simmer for about 3 hours. Remove the bay leaves and the ham hocks. Let the **soup cool slightly** and place into a blender in **small batches** (don not fill blender all the way or the heat will make it expand) and puree until smooth or use an immersion blender to puree it in the pot. Remove any ham from the hocks and add back to the pureed soup. Add the cubed ham pieces and the heavy cream to the soup. If you prefer the soup thicker, you can add a little flour that has been mixed with cold water, but **remember the soup gets thicker as it stands**. To make fresh croutons, take a loaf of Italian bread and cut it into cubes. In a very large frying pan, melt a stick of butter. Add garlic salt, and black pepper, and grating cheese. Toss in the cubes and stir frequently until golden brown. Serves 12.

My Aunt Edith always made pea soup on New Years Day and that has stayed our family's tradition. This is Steven's favorite soup. Serve it with a lot of grating cheese and fresh croutons.

Elise Avella Feiner High School Graduation Picture...
Editor-in-Chief of the Yearbook...I should have quit then!

ESCAROLE AND BEANS
Josephine Mainella

2 heads of escarole, washed
4-5 tablespoons olive oil
2 cans of Cannellini beans, don't drain
2 cans of water (use bean can)
1 large onion, peeled and diced

4-5 cloves of garlic, peeled and crushed
Salt and pepper to taste
1 - 2 cups chicken broth
Grating cheese

Wash the heads of escarole very well. Cut in small pieces about 3 inches long. Place a large pot of lightly salted water up to boil. When boiling, add the escarole and cook for about 15 minutes until soft. Drain; set aside. In a large saucepan, heat the olive oil. Add the diced onions and cook until soft and translucent about 7 to 10 minutes. Add the garlic and cook another minute. Add the beans, water, chicken broth, salt and pepper to taste. Cook for about 15 minutes. Add the escarole, cook an additional 15 minutes. Top with grating cheese.

This can be served as a side dish but it is usually served as a soup. This is another Italian peasant dish which was typical of the Neapolitan cooking our families all did. This was passed down from grandmother to daughter to granddaughter.

MUSHROOM SOUP WITH BARLEY AND WILD RICE
Sheila Smith

2 tablespoons butter or olive oil
¾ cup diced onions
¾ cup sliced leeks, white part wash well
¾ cup peeled and sliced carrots
¾ cup peeled and sliced parsnips
1 teaspoon minced garlic
1 pound cleaned and sliced mushrooms (portabella and/or baby bells are best)
2 teaspoons finely chopped fresh sage leaves
1 scallion, thinly sliced for garnish

1½ teaspoon kosher salt (omit if using salty broth)
¼ cup dry Madeira
¼ teaspoon freshly ground pepper
⅓ cup wild rice
¼ cup pearl barley
5 cup vegetable stock or water (I used ½ packet of the broth of Manischewitz® Matzoh ball soup mix)

I use the food processor to prepare the onions, carrots, parsnips, and mushrooms. Melt the butter over medium heat in a 3 quart saucepan. Sauté the onion, leeks, carrots, parsnips, and garlic until soft, about 5 minutes. Add the mushrooms, sage, salt, and pepper. Cook until the mushrooms have softened. Add the Madeira and reduce by half over high heat. Stir in the rice, barley, and vegetable stock. Bring to a boil, reduce the heat and simmer, covered for 50 minutes. Garnish with scallions.

My friend Sheila is another one of the Medical Arts wives. She is a very talented artist and sculptor, and has had many art shows showcasing her work. This recipe is from the Union Square Cafe in New York City. Sounds delicious!

Sheila Smith

CREAMY CRAB BISQUE
Katherine Avella

2 shallots, peeled and chopped
5 scallions cut in small pieces
4 tablespoons unsalted butter
¼ cup flour
3 cups milk
½ cup half and half

1 cup heavy cream
¼ teaspoon white pepper
½ teaspoon ground mace
1 teaspoon paprika
Hot pepper sauce
1 pound lump crabmeat salt and black pepper

Sauté shallots and scallions in butter over medium heat until softened; about 2 to 3 minutes. Blend in flour; cook 4 minutes. Slowly stir in milk, half and half and cream. Cook just until warm stir occasionally. Stir in white pepper, mace, paprika and Tabasco. Gently stir in crabmeat. **Heat, do not let boil**, and serve hot.

CRAB BISQUE
Elise Feiner

1 pound fresh lump crabmeat
1 (10¾ ounce) can cream of celery soup, undiluted
1 (10¾ ounce) can cream of mushroom soup, undiluted
1 (10¾ ounce) can tomato soup, undiluted
1 quart milk
½ cup dry sherry

2 tablespoons sugar
2 teaspoons freshly ground pepper
1 teaspoon salt
1 tablespoon Worcestershire sauce
5 drops hot sauce

Drain crabmeat, and remove any bits of shell. Set aside. Stir together celery soup and next 9 ingredients. Cook over medium heat, **stirring constantly**, until mixture is thoroughly heated. Stir in crabmeat. **Do not cook on high heat or it will burn**. Serve in a bread bowl. Serves 8.

CREAM OF BROCCOLI SOUP
Suzanne Bakiewicz

2 cups water
1½ pounds broccoli flowerets
1 medium onion, peeled and diced
1 large stalk celery, diced
3 tablespoons oil
½ stick butter
2½ cups chicken broth

Salt and pepper to taste
2 tablespoons cornstarch dissolved in about 5 ounces of cold water
1 pint heavy cream
½-1 quart milk
Dash of nutmeg
Garlic powder, cumin and dry mustard to taste

In a quart saucepan, boil the water, add the broccoli and celery. Boil for about 10 minutes. Let cool a little. Put the broccoli celery mix in the blender. Heat a medium saucepan, add the oil and butter. Sauté the diced onion on low heat until golden brown for about 10 minutes. Add to the broccoli mix and blend again until smooth. In a large pot, add the chicken broth to the broccoli mix. Add the heavy cream and the milk a little at a time or you might make it will be too thin. Add the spices; stir constantly. In separate bowl mix: Mix the cornstarch and water until smooth, and blend into soup. **Heat thoroughly but do not boil**. Simmer until you have to have some! Serves 6.

Suzanne's quote "(By the seat of my pants, I contributed this recipe!) I told you I wasn't much of a cook but somehow this turns out great!" Suzanne promises to learn to cook if I finally finish this book!

"In prosperity our friends know us; in adversity we know our friends"
-John Churton Collins

NEW ENGLAND CLAM CHOWDER
Elise Feiner

2 dozen large chowder clams or 3 (10 ½ ounce) cans of
 minced clams
½ pound lean salt pork, diced
1 cup chopped onion
3 cups diced, peeled raw potatoes
1 teaspoon salt

¼ teaspoon white pepper
2 cups light cream
2 cups milk
2 tablespoons butter
Paprika

Steam open the clams. Strain and reserve the liquid; coarsely grind or chop the clams. If canned clams are used, strain and save the liquid. Measure the clam liquid, fresh or drained. If there is less than 4 cups, add water to make it 4 cups. Fry pork fat in a skillet until golden. Remove pork and set aside. Drain off all but ¼-cup fat. Add onions and sauté for 5 minutes. Add potato, salt, pepper and clam liquid. Simmer until the potatoes are tender. Add the clams, cream, milk and butter. **Reheat carefully making sure it doesn't come to a boil.** Top with the crisp pork and sprinkle with a little paprika. Makes about 3 quarts.

STRACCIATELLE SOUP
Elise Feiner

Chicken soup
4 eggs
8 tablespoons grating cheese (Parmesan or Locatelli
Romano)

Salt and pepper to taste
1½ tablespoons semolina or flour

You can use canned chicken broth such as College Inn® or Homemade Chicken Soup (see recipe for Chicken Soup - Elise's Best.) If you are using the homemade chicken soup, remove all the vegetables, bay leaf, and chicken. Use the chicken for something else like chicken salad. Strain the broth well through a cheesecloth lined strainer. Set aside until ready to use or refrigerate until ready to use.

Beat the eggs well. Add the cheese, flour, and salt and pepper. **Return the chicken soup to boiling**. Then quickly add the beaten egg mixture to the boiling soup, stirring rapidly so the soup basically scrambles in the broth. This should take about 4 minutes. Serve in individual bowls with extra grating cheese if desired. Serves 4.

Variations: 2 variations (add either to soup before adding egg mixture)

Add 2 packages of chopped frozen spinach, cook separately in a small pot of boiling water for about 3 to 4 minutes, and drain well. Add to broth before adding egg mixture.

Pasta: Add small pasta that has been cooked according to package directions to the soup before adding egg mixture.

This is a favorite of Marc and Lauren, and easy to make especially if you have leftover chicken soup.

"Daddy's Little Girl": Lauren and Marc Feiner
then   and now…

CARROT SOUP
Elise Feiner

4 tablespoons butter
1½ cups sliced carrots
1 large onion, peeled and sliced
½ clove garlic, peeled and crushed
2 tablespoons rice
1 tablespoon dried parsley or 3-4 springs fresh
Zest of half of an orange

4 cups chicken stock
¼ teaspoon sugar
Salt and pepper to taste
Juice of half of an orange
¼ cup heavy cream
2 egg yolks

Melt butter. Add the vegetables, garlic and rice; mix well over low heat, about 5 minutes without browning. Add the parsley, orange zest, stock, sugar, and seasonings; bring to a boil. Lower heat and simmer 30 to 40 minutes, until the vegetables are tender. Put into a blender or puree until smooth. Return to pot and reheat. Add the orange juice. Mix egg yolks and cream well. Add a few spoons of the hot soup to the egg mixture to temper it. Stir the egg mixture back into the soup stirring slowly. **Reheat the soup without boiling**. Serves 4.

BLACK BEAN SOUP (FRIJOLES NEGRO'S)
Carmen Ferreiro

2 large cans Goya® black beans
2-3 tablespoons olive oil
1 medium onion, peeled and finely chopped
½ green pepper, finely chopped
1 bay leaf

4 cloves minced garlic or garlic powder
1 tablespoon red wine vinegar
½ teaspoon sugar
Ground cumin to taste
Salt and pepper to taste

Sauté the onions, peppers and fresh garlic in the olive oil in saucepan. (You can either chop everything very fine or put in the food processor). Pour in the black beans and add the rest of the ingredients (if you are using garlic powder, put it in at this time). Simmer for 30 to 45 minutes. Remove the bay leaf. Serve over white rice. If you prefer "soupier" beans, you can add some water. You can also add a few strips of bacon for flavor as you are cooking the onions and the peppers.

Carmen laughs and says, "this, of course, is not an 'authentic' black bean soup recipe. Who has time to soak beans overnight????? But, this is so quick and easy so that even the kids that are away from home can make it!"

CHICKEN TORTILLA SOUP
Elise Feiner

1 pound chicken breasts, cubed
3 tablespoons oil
1 can Campbell's® Fiesta Nacho Cheese Soup
1 can cream of chicken soup
Salsa to taste

1 soup can filled with milk
1 (small) jar salsa; mild
Tortilla chips, Crushed
Shredded cheddar cheese

In a frying pan, heat the oil. Brown the chicken cubes and set aside. In the top of a double boiler add the chicken and all the remaining ingredients except the tortilla chips and cheddar cheese. Bring to a boil over low heat; stirring constantly. You can also do this in a pot but don't leave unattended and stir constantly or it will burn. Serve topped with the crushed chips, cheddar cheese and salsa. You can also cut fresh tortillas in strips and bake until crisp.

This is our version of David's favorite soup from the Ground Round.

"Only the pure in heart can make a good soup."
-Ludwig Van Beethoven

CABBAGE SOUP
Nellie Reinisch

3 pounds beef soup meat or 1 pound short ribs or mix the two (trim fat from meat and bones)
Soup bones (beef)
3 quarts of water
1 large onion, peeled and left whole
1 tablespoon salt
1 (3 pound) head of cabbage shredded
1 small can of sliced red beets

1 small can of tomato sauce
1 can of Campbell's® Tomato soup
Salt and pepper to taste
¼ teaspoon sour salt
The juice of half of a lemon
1 tablespoon sugar or more
2 grated apples

In a large pot filled with three quarts of water, place the meat, and soup bones. Add the onion and salt and cook slowly for 1½ hours. Cut the cabbage into shreds. Soak cabbage in cold water and drain. Pour boiling water over the cabbage and drain. Put cabbage in the soup. Add the beets, tomato sauce and tomato soup. Cook another 45 minutes. Season with salt and pepper, sour salt, lemon juice, and sugar. Cook for another 90 minutes. Add the grated apples.

This is Nanny Nellie's famous cabbage soup recipe. She gave it to me years ago when she and Poppy Joe were still living in Miami.

MY MOTHER'S MUSHROOM BARLEY SOUP
Liz Halpin

1½ pounds flanken (beef short ribs)
½ cup barley
4 quarts water
1 cup sliced fresh mushrooms or 1 small can
2 carrots, sliced thinly
2 stalks celery, sliced thinly

1 potato, peeled and diced
1 medium onion, peeled and diced
1 bouquet garni (1 sprig of parsley, dill, bay leaf tied together in cheesecloth)
Salt and pepper to taste
1 can beef broth or beef stock

In a 6 quart pot, bring water to a boil with the flanken and bouquet garni. Simmer one hour. Then, add the vegetables and barley. Add the broth and simmer 30 more minutes. Remove the ribs. Trim the meat from the bone, dice it and add to the soup. Salt and pepper to taste. Taste vegetables to see if they are cooked, if not simmer a little longer. You can serve this is a bread bowl.

This recipe came from Aunt Rae Rosenfeld's neighbor, Liz Halpin.

VICHYSSOISE
Elise Feiner

4 leeks (only use the white parts)
1 medium onion, peeled
3 tablespoon sweet butter
5 medium potatoes, peeled
4 cups chicken broth

1 tablespoon salt
2 cups milk
2 cups medium or light cream
1 cup heavy cream

Finely chop the white part of the leeks and the onions and brown lightly in the butter. Add the potatoes, finely sliced. Add the chicken broth and salt. Boil gently for 35 to 40 minutes. Either crush in a strainer, put into a blender, or use an immersion blender to puree. Return to the heat and add the milk and medium or light cream. Season to taste and bring to a boil. Cool and then place into a fine strainer, and force through. When the soup is cold, add the heavy cream. Chill well before serving. Garnish with chopped chives if desired.

"Anybody who believes the way to a man's heart is through his stomach flunked geography."
-Robert Byrne

BAKED ONION SOUP
Elise Feiner

4 very large onions peeled and sliced (you can mix regular onions and Vandalia onions if you like)
½ stick of butter
2½ tablespoons olive oil
2 tablespoons sugar
2 tablespoons flour
3¼ cups hot water or homemade beef stock
½ cup dry white wine or sherry
Bouquet Garni (6 sprigs of parsley, 4 springs of thyme, 1 bay leaf, 1 garlic clove peeled and mashed, tie together in a cheesecloth)

Salt and pepper to taste
3 egg yolks
½ cup Madeira wine
½ pint heavy cream
Parmesan Cheese
8 slices of day old French bread
8-6 slices of Gruyere Cheese depending on the size of the slice and a little extra grated gruyere to add to the soup (You can also use Swiss Cheese if you prefer)
Onion Soup Crocks

In a skillet, sauté the onions in the butter, olive oil, and sugar slowly so that they caramelize and become brown. Stir frequently so they don't burn. Add the flour and cook the mixture another 3 minutes over low heat. Remove the pan from the heat and stir in the water or beef stock, white wine and the bouquet garni. Bring the liquid back to a boil, stirring, frequently. Reduce the heat and simmer the mixture covered for 1 hour stirring occasionally. Discard the bouquet garni and add salt and pepper to taste. In a dish, whisk together the egg yolks, Madeira, and heavy cream. Whisk about 3 tablespoons of the hot soup into the dish to temper it, and then add the mixture into the pot of soup. Toast the French bread slices in the oven (you can brush with a little olive oil and season it with spices of your choice if you'd like) until they are golden brown. Place the soup in the crocks; add a little grated gruyere cheese, parmesan cheese and the toasted bread to the soup. Top with the slices of Gruyere cheese. Place the crocks in a deep baking dish. Add water to the baking dish so that the water comes up half way around the sides of the bowl Bake at 450° until the cheese is melted about 10 to 15 minutes. Be very careful when handling the crocks as they will be very hot. Serves 6.

This is one of the best onion soup recipes I've ever had. I have changed it through the years and this is the end result. It is very rich and creamy and perfect for an onion soup connoisseur (of which I am one.) Its a little time consuming but well worth it.

HAL'S ONION SOUP
Hal White

6 tablespoons butter
8 onions peeled and sliced
1½ quarts boiling water
7 beef bouillon cubes
Salt and pepper to taste

1 cup dry white wine
6 thick slices of French bread toasted
½ cup grated Parmesan cheese
1 cup grated Swiss cheese

Melt the butter in a 2-quart saucepan. Cook the onions until transparent, stirring occasionally. Dissolve the bouillon cubes in the boiling water, and add salt and pepper to taste. Add to the onions; cook uncovered over low heat about 10 minutes. Add wine, stir, cook 10 more minutes.

Pour soup into deep earthenware casserole. Place toast on top and sprinkle with grating cheese and sprinkle Swiss cheese on the top. Bake in a preheated 425° oven about 20 minutes.

This recipe came from Aunt Barbara Schwartz. It was given to her by her friend Hal White who was quite a gourmet cook. He has since passed away, but Aunt Barbara is still close to his wife Shirley and his family.

"There are only two people who can tell you the truth about yourself; an enemy who has lost his temper and a friend who loves you dearly."
-Antisthenes

CRAB BISQUE BALTIMORE
Elise Feiner

6 tablespoons butter
1 cup finely diced onion
½ cup finely diced celery
½ cup minced leeks
¼ cup flour
1 cup fish stock or seafood stock
4 cups half-and-half

¼ cup dry sherry, plus sherry to pass at the table
½ teaspoon salt
¼ teaspoon white pepper
¼ teaspoon ground mace
Dash of Tabasco sauce
1 pound back fin crab meat, picked over for shells
Lightly whipped cream and paprika, for garnish

Melt butter in a soup pot, then sauté onion, celery and leeks until tender. Whisk in flour and cook several minutes, stirring. (Don't brown.) Take off the heat, whisk in the stock, half-and-half, sherry, salt, pepper, mace and Tabasco. Return to heat and bring to a boil, **stirring often**. Simmer 15 minutes. Stir in crab meat and continue to simmer another 5 minutes. Ladle into soup bowls. Garnish each serving with a dollop of whipped cream and a dash of paprika. Pass dry sherry at the table and add to taste. You may like to cook the soup in the top of a double boiler to avoid scorching and then transfer the soup to a crock-pot after it's made to keep it warm until serving time.

I got this recipe when Marc and I lived in Baltimore. We lived on crabs...broiled, steamed, in soups...

Lauren and Steven Feiner – they were so identical as babies that I once sent my
mother-in-law a picture of Lauren and she asked why Steven was wearing
earrings!
Lauren is now considering the possibility of law school, she is interested in casino
law...as long as the two of them don't do malpractice, we'll allow them to stay in
the family...

"In the final analysis, it is not what you do for your children but what you have taught them to do for themselves that will make then successful human beings."
-Ann Landers

MARIA'S TOMATO SALAD
Maria Trainor

1 loaf of round or very long and wide crusty bread or individual bread bowls
½ stick of butter, melted
Garlic salt
Roma tomatoes (remove middle and cut into smaller pieces) or regular tomatoes cut into slices
Fresh or wet mozzarella, cut into cubes

Red onions cut thinly
Lots of diced garlic
Fresh Basil
Dash of dried oregano
Salt and pepper to taste
Olive Oil
Balsamic vinegar

Make the tomato salad by mixing tomatoes, mozzarella, and remaining ingredients except bead, butter and garlic salt.. Remove the top and scoop out most of the bread from the middle. Brush the inside with melted butter and sprinkle with garlic salt. Preheat oven to 375°. About ten minutes before serving, place the bread in the oven for about 5 to 8 minutes to heat. Mix everything together but the mozzarella. About a half hour before serving, remove the garlic and add the mozzarella. Let the flavors blend for another half an hour. Fill the middle of the bread with the tomato salad. Replace the top and cut into sections. You can also do this in individual bread bowls. Serves 6.

ELISE'S TWO WAY TOMATO SALAD
Elise Feiner

6 tomatoes cut in thin slices or cubes
3 cloves garlic, peeled and cut in thirds
Salt and pepper to taste
Lots of fresh basil, finely chopped
1-2 teaspoons oregano

1 medium red onion sliced or cut in circles
Olive oil
Dash red wine vinegar (optional)
Mozzarella cheese cut in round slices, or cut into cubes
Whole Wheat Biscotti (about 4-6)

For the first way, take the tomatoes and **cube** them. Add the **sliced** red onions, garlic pieces, salt, pepper, oregano and basil and mix. Add the olive oil and dash of red wine vinegar. You can add cubed mozzarella to this salad. Otherwise, just serve over whole wheat biscotti (available at Italian specialty stores). Take the biscotti and dampen them with ice water, a little olive oil, and red wine vinegar. Allow to get soft but not mushy. Remove the garlic pieces, spoon the tomato salad over the biscotti. **The second way** is to **slice** the tomatoes in round ¼-inch slices, and arrange on a serving platter alternating with the slices of mozzarella (overlap slightly). Add red onions, **cut in thin circles** over the tomato/mozzarella platter. Place the pieces of garlic on top. Add lots of fresh basil. Sprinkle with oregano and salt and pepper to taste. Drizzle with olive oil. I don't use vinegar on the salad if I am arranging it on a platter. Toss on a few ice cubes and refrigerate until serving time. Remove garlic before serving.

SPINACH SALAD WITH MUSHROOMS
Elise Feiner

1 pound fresh spinach washed and patted dry
6 slices bacon, fried and crumbled (save about 2 tablespoons of the drippings)
3 eggs, hard-boiled
2 scallions thinly sliced
½ cup sugar
¼ cup red wine vinegar
½ cup olive oil

1 tablespoon parsley
1 tablespoon chives
1 teaspoon Worcestershire sauce
1 teaspoon prepared mustard
Freshly ground black pepper
½ shallot, finely chopped
2 teaspoons garlic salt

Starting from the sugar, mix all the remaining ingredients together to make the dressing (add the bacon drippings too). Mix and shake well. Place remaining ingredients in salad bowl; add dressing. Toss and serve. Note: This dressing is sweet (you may want to decrease the sugar to your taste).

"Sometimes it's just not worth the effort or the pain, no matter how much someone used to mean to you."

-Author Unknown

SPINACH SALAD
Elise Feiner

1 bag fresh spinach, washed and patted dry
6 slices crisp bacon, crumbled
4 fresh mushrooms, sliced
3 hard boiled eggs, sliced
½ small red onion, thinly sliced
½ cup olive oil

¼ cup balsamic vinegar
½ teaspoon garlic salt
⅛ teaspoon black pepper
2 tablespoons mustard
Dash of lemon juice

Mix the olive oil, vinegar, garlic salt, pepper, mustard and lemon juice together with a whisk until well blended. Place in an airtight container and shake well. Separate the spinach onto 4 plates. Divide the eggs, mushrooms, red onion and crumbled bacon evenly on the spinach. Add the dressing and toss. Serves 4.

RED KIDNEY BEAN SALAD
Josephine Mainella

1 large can of red kidney beans, drained (about 2 cups)
¼ cup wine vinegar
3 tablespoons olive oil
¼ teaspoons oregano

¼ teaspoon salt
⅛ teaspoon black pepper
¼ cup diced celery
2 tablespoons chopped onion

Combine beans with everything except the celery and chopped onion. Mix well. Then add in the celery and onions. Chill in refrigerator. Serve in lettuce cups. Serves 4.

RASPBERRY SALAD
Mary Frances Koury

Make a dressing with raspberry vinegar, olive oil, salt and pepper and a little fresh parsley. Pour over romaine lettuce, and add a can of mandarin orange segment (drained).

Cindy Koury got this recipe from her cousin Mary Frances, and made it for lunch once. It was delicious and she has shared the recipe with me.

PIECES OF EIGHT SALAD
Elise Feiner

½ cup sour cream
½ tablespoon mustard
1 tablespoon cider vinegar
2½ tablespoons honey
½ cup mayonnaise
3 tablespoons ketchup
1 egg yolk
1 teaspoon salt
⅛ teaspoon tarragon
2 leaves basil, finely chopped
⅛ teaspoon oregano
¼ teaspoon parsley

⅛ teaspoon dill
Pinch of chives
1 teaspoon lemon juice
¼ teaspoon onion salt
¼ teaspoon garlic salt
Pinch of nutmeg
⅛ teaspoon thyme
Combination of iceberg, romaine, endive and Bibb lettuce
1 box mushroom slices
1 can baby shrimp, drained well
Tomatoes cut in tiny cubes
3 hardboiled eggs, sliced

Add all the ingredients up to the lettuce in a food processor and process until smooth. Mix the lettuce varieties together. Mix in the mushrooms, tomatoes, and baby shrimp. Add the dressing. Decorate with hard boiled egg slices. Serves 6.

We had a salad like this in Kentucky. I tried to replicate the recipe. It's delicious!

ORIENTAL SALAD
Candie Mitchell

1 bag of cabbage coleslaw
3-4 scallions sliced
1 or more cups of frozen peas (not cooked)
1 package oriental (Ramen) soup; break noodles and add to salad (do not cook)
½ can of mixed nuts
¼ cup of sunflower seeds

2 tablespoons of sugar
½ cup of oil
Seasoning from soup
1 teaspoon salt
¼ teaspoon pepper
¼ cup of vinegar (I use apple cider vinegar)

Mix cabbage coleslaw, scallions, peas, and ramen noodles together. Add nuts. Make dressing; mix the 2 tablespoons of sugar, oil, seasonings from the soup mix, salt, pepper and vinegar. Toss the slaw mix with dressing. Serve immediately.

My friend Candie made this salad for Brittany Venezio's Graduation. It is very similar to the Bok Coy salad recipe; this is great for people who are not Bok Choy Fans. Sadly, Candie passed away recently. I will miss a good friend and a great cook!

NANNY'S TOSSED SALAD
Katherine Avella

1 head of lettuce, torn into pieces
2-3 cloves of garlic, peeled and cut in half
2-3 thin slices of red onion
Salt and pepper to taste

¼-½ teaspoon oregano
Red wine vinegar with garlic
Vegetable or olive oil
Crumbled blue cheese (optional)

Rub your salad bowl with the cut ends of the cloves of garlic and place them in the bowl (**count the number of cloves for easy removal**). Add the torn lettuce, and onion. Add pepper to taste and the oregano. Right before serving (or it gets soggy) add salt to taste. **Remove garlic cloves**. Add vinegar and oil to taste, and toss well. Add blue cheese if desired. Serves 6.

Marc loves this salad. It is so basic, but you can add anything you want to it, tomatoes, cucumbers, etc. Add some blue cheese if you like, but he loves it served with anchovies. This salad is great with veal or chicken cutlets.

CUCUMBER SALAD ROSENFELD
Rae Rosenfeld

2 cucumbers, peeled and sliced
1 large onion, peeled and sliced in thin rings
3 tablespoons white vinegar

2 tablespoons sugar
¾ cup mayonnaise

Peel and slice the cucumbers and put them in a mixing or serving bowl. Peel and very thinly slice the onions in circles and place on top of the cucumbers. Mix the sugar, mayonnaise and white vinegar together; add to the cucumber mix. Mix well and refrigerate. Prepare a day in advance where possible to allow flavors to blend. You can adjust any of the ingredients to taste. Serves 6.

This recipe was given to our family by Aunt Rae Rosenfeld. She said it is one of Uncle Steve's favorites. It is great for a "break the fast" at Yom Kippur, a barbeque, or just as a side dish.

L-R: Rae, Mindy and Steve Rosenfeld Steve is also from Brooklyn and Rae from Long Island. They are among our closest friends, more like family… Notice a pattern with the Brooklyn, Long Island roots developing???

Rae is one of the most talent crafters I have ever known, you name it, and she can do it. Blessed are those who have had the good fortune to be one of "Mr. Rosenfeld's" students.

NANNY NELLIE'S COLE SLAW
Nellie Reinisch

2 bags of packaged coleslaw mix
2 stalks celery cut in thin slices (optional)
12 tablespoons Hellmann's or Best Food Mayonnaise
4 tablespoons sugar

4 tablespoons water
4 tablespoons white vinegar
Salt to taste (about ½-1 teaspoon)

Mix all the ingredients together except the coleslaw and the salt, and set aside. Then add the first bag of coleslaw to a large plastic container. Lightly salt the coleslaw with half of the salt. Add about half of the mayonnaise mixture. Mix well. Add the second bag of coleslaw and the rest of the salt. Mix again. Add the rest of the mayonnaise mix. Mix well again. The mixture may appear to be a little dry but as the salt releases the moisture from the cabbage, the liquid will increase. Refrigerate, and stir every few hours (2 to 3 times). Stir before serving. Serve about 6 to 8.

If you want to increase or decrease the recipe, keep the proportions in the same ratio: 3 tablespoons of mayo: 1 tablespoon of water: 1 tablespoon of sugar: 1 tablespoon of white vinegar

This great recipe was handed down from Marc's Grandmother Nanny Nellie. Nan had the best recipes, very accurate and was always willing to share them. She and Poppy Joe used to own Germantown Butter and Egg before it was sold to Breakstone. She was a wonderful cook and her recipes were always so delicious. I first tasted this coleslaw at her apartment in Miami. I never cared for coleslaw until tasting hers. This is great by itself, or on sandwiches (corned beef, coleslaw and Russian dressing, or roast beef). Nanny's girls (Mom Mom, Aunt Shirley and Aunt Adele) love to tell how Nanny never taught them how to cook, so they could marry rich husbands and have a cook. I loved inheriting all Nanny's recipes.

FIFI'S GREEN BEAN SALAD
Josephine Mainella

½ pound fresh green beans
3 tablespoons olive oil
3 tablespoons wine vinegar

2 cloves of garlic, peeled and thinly sliced
¼ teaspoon salt
⅛ teaspoon black pepper.

Wash and snap the ends off the green beans. Prepare and cook green beans in lightly salted boiling water for about 4 minutes. Place in an ice bath; cool and drain. Mix olive oil, wine vinegar, sliced garlic, salt, and black pepper. Add to beans. Chill and serve

LETTUCE WEDGES WITH BLUE CHEESE DRESSING
Elise Feiner

1 cup mayonnaise
1 cup sour cream
6 ounces blue cheese, crumbled
¼ teaspoon salt
¼ teaspoon dried mustard
1 tablespoon Worcestershire sauce

2 tablespoons heavy cream
1 teaspoon lemon juice
12 slices of bacon, cooked and crumbled
½ cup Locatelli-Romano or other grating cheese
¼ cup chopped chives, fresh
1 large head of lettuce (iceberg) cut into 6 equal parts

Make the blue cheese dressing. Mix all the ingredients together **EXCEPT** the bacon, grating cheese, chives and lettuce wedges. Mix the bacon, grating cheese and chives together. Top each wedge of lettuce with blue cheese dressing and sprinkle with the chive mixture. Serves 6.

A restaurant in Baltimore that served this in place of a salad. This is my version.

Left Side

L-R: Barbara, Abby and
Lauren Feiner

Right Side
Toni Mollico and Lauren
Feiner

MARC'S CAESAR SALAD
Marc Feiner, M.D.

1 clove garlic, crushed	1 egg at room temperature
½ cup oil	Juice of half of a lemon
¾ teaspoon salt	1 clove garlic, peeled and halved
¼ teaspoon freshly ground black pepper	2 large head of romaine lettuce, washed and chilled
¼ teaspoon dried mustard	Croutons
1½ teaspoon Worcestershire sauce	¼ cup blue cheese, crumbled, optional
6 anchovy fillets, drained and chopped	2 tablespoons parmesan cheese

Several hours ahead, mix the one clove of crushed garlic, oil, salt, pepper, mustard, Worcestershire sauce, and anchovy fillets in a blender or food processor. Place in a covered container and refrigerate. Bring three inches of water in a small saucepan to boiling. Turn off the heat. Carefully lower the egg into the water and **let stand one minute, and then lift out**. Drain; set aside to cool. Make your own croutons (see recipe index) or use store bought. Just before serving, rub the inside of the salad bowl with the cut ends of the garlic clove and discard the two pieces of garlic. Cut out the coarse ribs from the romaine lettuce and tear into bite size pieces; place in the prepared bowl. Shake dressing well and pour over the romaine leaves. Sprinkle with parmesan cheese and toss until well coated. Break the egg over the center of the salad; pour lemon juice directly over the egg. Toss well again. Sprinkle croutons over the salad; toss well again. Serve at once. Serves 6. You can also add chicken to steak to this recipe. This is the best Caesar salad I've had!

This is Marc's (and the entire Feiner boy's) ultimate favorite salad! I put everything in the blender because Marc loves anchovies and I hate them. You can't taste the anchovies this way. I find preparation goes much faster if you have everything lined up in little bowls ahead of time. You can also place whole anchovy fillets on the top of the salad for anchovy lovers!

The Feiner Boys:
Back Row L-R: David, Steven and Jeffrey
Front Row L-R: Ivan, Kevin and Marc Feiner

LAYERED ANTIPASTO SALAD
Elise Feiner

½ to 1 head iceberg lettuce or romaine lettuce shredded	1 can or jar artichoke hearts, plain or marinated, sliced into pieces
5 Roma tomatoes cut in tiny cubes	1 large red onion, peeled and diced
5-6 fresh basil leaves	Roasted peppers (see index)
1 pound fresh mozzarella (little balls in water are best), sliced into rounds or in half	1-2 small cans black olives, pitted and sliced
¼ pound Genoa salami cut into strips	¼ pound pepperoni slices
1-2 (12 ounce) cans Bumblebee Solid White Tuna drained and broken up into pieces with a fork	4 slices provolone cheese
6 hard boiled eggs sliced into rounds	¼-inch thick, cut into small cubes
	Breadsticks (see Elise's Famous Breadsticks)

Layer the ingredients in order in a large glass (see through) salad or trifle bowl. When you make the breadsticks make some into small nugget-like sizes, and just before serving the salad top with the mini breadsticks or use croutons if you don't have breadsticks. Serve with creamy vinaigrette dressing. (See recipe index) or salad dressing of your choice. Serves 8.

CHICKEN CAESAR SALAD
Elise Feiner

1 loaf Italian bread, cut on an angle
3 tablespoons olive oil, plus ½ cup
1 garlic clove, minced, plus 3 cloves peeled
½ teaspoon dried oregano
Salt and pepper
3 anchovy fillets
2 teaspoons Dijon mustard

Juice of half of a lemon
2 tablespoons red wine vinegar
1 teaspoon Worcestershire sauce
2 romaine lettuce hearts, cut in 2-inch pieces
1 hard boiled egg
1 cup shredded Pecorino Romano
1 pound cooked grilled chicken, sliced in strips (optional)

Preheat the oven to 400°. Cut the Italian bread into angled slices. In a small pan over medium heat, add the oil, minced garlic, and oregano. Cook for 2 minutes. Dredge the bread in the oil mixture. Season with salt and pepper to taste. Spread the bread cubes in a single layer on a baking pan and bake for 10 minutes. The croutons should be crisp but don't overcook them. In a food processor, combine remaining garlic, anchovy, mustard, lemon, vinegar, Worcestershire, salt and pepper. Process the mixture for 30 seconds to make a paste. Add the olive oil and process again until combined. Place the romaine in a large salad bowl. Grate the hard boiled egg into the bowl. Add the dressing to the salad and toss to coat. Add the cheese, croutons, parsley and chicken, toss well. Season to taste with salt and pepper. Serves 4.

POTATO AND BEAN SALAD
Josephine Mainella

2 pounds white potatoes
2 pounds green beans, fresh
2 cloves garlic, crushed
3 scallions, sliced
Oregano to taste

Salt and pepper
½ cup olive oil
⅓ cup wine vinegar

Boil potatoes with skins on (cooking water should be 2 inches above the potatoes) for 45 minutes. Drain and cool. Wash string beans and snap ends. Boil in lightly salted water until tender; drain and cool. In a large serving bowl, peel and slice or cube potatoes, add string beans, garlic, scallions, oregano, salt and pepper to taste. Add oil and vinegar, toss to serve.

CARMEN'S SPINACH SALAD
Carmen Ferreiro

2 bags fresh baby spinach, washed and dried
1 small red onion, peeled and thinly sliced
12 slices bacon, fried and crumbled
Roasted red peppers cut in strips
Chopped walnuts
¼ cup raisins
6 fresh mushrooms, sliced

Feta cheese, optional
Croutons
Seedless red grapes, halved lengthwise
Salt and pepper to taste
Olive oil to taste
Balsamic vinegar to taste

In a large bowl, mix all the ingredients together. You can also top this with leftover chicken if you have any.

Carmen said that she had a salad like this at The Ground Round and tried to recreate it at home. This is her version. She said that this is Cristina's favorite salad.

"The ornament of a house is the friends who frequent it."

-Ralph Waldo Emerson

CAFE CANOLE APPLE-WALNUT SALAD
Dean and Jason Nole

2-3 shallots, peeled and very finely chopped
1½-2 cups extra virgin olive oil
¼ cup cider vinegar
Salt and pepper, to taste
½ teaspoon garlic salt
1-2 apples, peeled, sliced thinly and put into water with a
little lemon juice until ready to use

1-2 cups shelled walnuts toasted for a few minutes
⅛ teaspoon black pepper
1-2 cups blue cheese, crumbled
2 bags or heads Boston Bibb lettuce, washed
Lemon juice for the apples

Peel and slice the apples thinly and place in a bowl of cold water to which you have added a little lemon juice. Take a piece of aluminum foil and shape into a mini tray, and place the walnuts on it and put in a 350° oven to about five minutes to toast lightly. Break into small pieces by hand or with a little hammer, not fine though. Crumble blue cheese and set aside in a bowl. In a food processor, process the shallots until fine. While the processor is still running add the olive oil, and cider vinegar. The above amounts are just approximations, adjust to your taste. Add salt (very little because you are also adding garlic salt), pepper, and garlic salt to taste. Process the mixture for a few minutes. The mixture will look opaque. You can do this in advance and refrigerate. Bring to room temperature and shake before serving. Place the lettuce, a few slices of apples, walnuts and blue cheese on salad plates. **Just drizzle the dressing over the top. You don't pour this on and mix like a regular salad; it's just a little touch.** I use a plastic bottle type dispenser to drizzle the dressing.

This is great to for a buffet and then everyone can add what they want. The dressing is a light vinaigrette. Dean Nole was gracious enough to share the recipe but not the proportions but this is close. Everyone who tries this salad loves it. Enjoy.

L-R: Dean Nole, Lauren Feiner, and Jason Nole in the kitchen at Café
CaNole...hmmm Lauren in the kitchen????

Who would have ever thought that Lauren would be at Cornell's School of Hotel
Administration and working as a prep chef?

MOCK POTATO SALAD
Debby Rosen

1 large head cauliflower cut in small pieces
2 cups diced celery
1 cup red onion, diced
1-2 cups mayonnaise to taste
¼ cup cider vinegar

2 teaspoons salt
2 teaspoons sugar substitute
½ teaspoon freshly cracked black pepper
4 hard boiled eggs, peeled and chopped

Place cauliflower with about a tablespoon of water in a microwave safe casserole; cover. Cook on high 5 to 7 minutes and let stand covered another 3 to 5 minutes, until tender, but not mushy. Drain; combine with celery and onion. Mix the mayonnaise, vinegar, salt, pepper, sugar substitute. Pour over the cauliflower. Add the eggs, stir gently. Chill and serve. Serves 12.

Debby Rosen gave me this recipe and said it's delicious and great for people on low carb diets.

BOK CHOY SALAD
Nancy Blaker

Enough olive oil to coat the bottom of a frying pan
2 packages of Ramen Noodles, Chicken Flavored, broken up (in the soup aisle, orange package)
2 seasoning packets that come with the noodles

1 cup slivered almonds
2 tablespoons sesame seeds
2 tablespoons sesame oil

Mix all the ingredients together except for the olive oil and sesame oil. Heat a frying pan with the olive and sesame oils. Add the other ingredients. Lightly brown the mixture in the olive oil and sesame oil mix. Cool. Place is a zip lock or plastic container.

Salad Greens:

2 bunches of Bok Choy
1 bunch of scallions

1 bag of shredded carrots

Cut up the two bunches of Bok Choy into small pieces (the size of celery pieces, using some of the greens leaves too. Cut up one bunch of scallions (dice), add a small bag shredded carrots and refrigerate in a zip lock bag.

Dressing:

3 ounces of cider vinegar
9 ounces of olive oil

½ cup sugar
3 tablespoons soy sauce or teriyaki sauce

Mix the cider vinegar, olive oil, sugar and soy sauce together; shake well.

Do everything one day ahead and then mix all three sections together when ready to serve.

Aunt Carmen Ferreiro said that Nancy Blaker made this for a party at the Sleepers and everyone loved it. She made it at home and her kids really liked it. Maria Trainor thought that Andi Dinerstein made it originally, but wherever it came from, it's great! Carmen said that she used sesame oil for the sesame seeds, and used ¼ cup sugar and less olive oil in the dressing but this is the original recipe.

POTATO VINAIGRETTE SALAD
Katherine Avella

6 tablespoons oil
3 tablespoon vinegar
1 clove of garlic, peeled and crushed

¼ teaspoon salt
⅛ teaspoon pepper

Mix everything together to make the dressing. Shake well and refrigerate.

2 medium unpeeled potatoes, boiled in lightly salted water until cooked about 45 minutes

1 stalk of celery (about ½ cup), diced

Peel and dice the potatoes. Add the celery. Chill in the refrigerator.

Toss together:

½ cup pared diced and seeded cucumber
½ cup pitted and diced black olives

2 tablespoons minced onions

Put the potatoes, cucumbers, celery, olives, and onions together in a large bowl. With a fork carefully but thoroughly blend in about ¾-cup of the dressing mixture above (shake before adding). Cover the salad and chill about 1 hour before serving.

NANNY NELLIE'S POTATO SALAD
Nellie Reinisch

2 pounds new potatoes (red)
1 hard boiled egg
½ teaspoon dried mustard
Salt and pepper to taste

Drop of water
1 teaspoon white vinegar
Mayonnaise to taste

Boil the potatoes in lightly salted water until cooked (easily pierced with a fork). Mash the hard boiled egg with a fork. Add the mustard to the egg and mash again. Cut the potatoes, (leaving the skin on) into small cubes. Add the egg mix to the potatoes. Add salt and pepper, drop of water, vinegar and mayonnaise to the potatoes. Mix well. Serves 6.

This is another of Nanny Nellie's salad recipes. She was the best cook!

NANNY'S POTATO SALAD
Katherine Avella

10 pounds of potatoes
1 quart of mayonnaise
1 cup white vinegar
1 cup water
4 teaspoons sugar

1 teaspoon salt
1 medium onion, peeled and very finely chopped
1-2 small carrots, peeled and cut into very small pieces
2 gherkins cut into very small pieces
¼ cup chopped green peppers (optional)

Wash the potatoes, and leave their skins on. Place in a pot of salted water; bring to a boil, lower the heat and let cook for about 45 minutes or until the potatoes are cooked. (You can check the potatoes by inserting a fork, if it's soft and easily pierced, they are done). Let them cool. Peel and cube. Mix the mayonnaise, vinegar, water, sugar, salt together. When well mixed, add the onions, carrots, gherkins and peppers. Mix again. Add the potatoes. Mix well again. Refrigerate until ready to serve. This recipe can be cut in half for smaller quantity. Serves 15.

Nanny always made this potato salad for all our large parties and gatherings. It is a very traditional potato salad recipe.

LUCY'S POTATO SALAD
Lucy Massimiano

4 pounds potatoes boiled in salted water (2 teaspoons salt)
1 tablespoon salt
1 tablespoon sugar
½ teaspoon white pepper
⅓ cup salad oil

⅓ cup white vinegar
⅓ cup water
½ cup sour cream
½ cup mayonnaise
1 medium onion, chopped finely

Boil the potatoes in their skins for about 40 minutes. Let cool. Peel and cube the potatoes. In a large bowl, mix remaining ingredients. Add potatoes. Refrigerate for about 12 hours.

This recipe came from Cousin Lucy Massimiano. She is a native of the Philippines and excellent cook. She makes all the traditional Filipino dishes as well as American and Italian cuisine. She always had a family barbeque in Auburn in the summer, with tables laden with all these wonderful international dishes.

"The family, we are a strange little band of characters trudging though life sharing diseases and toothpaste, coveting one another's desserts, hiding shampoo, locking each other out of our rooms; inflicting pain and kissing to heal it in the same instant, loving laughing, defending and trying to figure out the common thread that bound all of us together."
-Erma Bombeck

POTATO SALAD - ELISE'S BEST
Elise Feiner

1 (8 ounce) package of Oscar Mayer Bacon, regular or thick cut (fried and cut in small pieces) save a little for garnish
3 pounds of very small red or new potatoes
3 teaspoons salt
6 hard boiled eggs, peeled and sliced (I do this on an egg slicer, first one way, then turn and do again)
1 extra hard boiled egg to garnish, sliced on egg cutter
1 bunch scallions, sliced thinly (save a little for garnish)

¼ teaspoon black pepper
1 teaspoon garlic salt
1½ cups mayonnaise
⅛ cup white vinegar
¼ cup hot water
3 tablespoons sugar
2 tablespoons Dijon mustard

In a medium skillet, fry bacon until crisp. Drain on paper towels. **Save** about ½ cup of bacon drippings. If doing the bacon in the microwave, save the paper towels, and when cool, twist and save the drippings. Scrub the potatoes. Do not peel them. Place in a large pot and cover with water. Add 2 teaspoons of salt, and bring to a boil. Lower the heat and then let them boil gently until tender, when they are easily pierced with a fork. This takes about 25 to 35 minutes. Drain. Let cool until you can handle them easily. Cut into ½-inch cubes. Place the potatoes in a large bowl. Add the scallions, eggs, 1 teaspoon of salt, black pepper, garlic salt, bacon and the mayonnaise. Toss gently, until combined.

In a small saucepan, heat the reserved bacon drippings, vinegar, hot water, sugar and Dijon mustard. Bring to a boil whisking constantly and boil for 2 minutes. Pour over the potato salad and gently blend. Garnish with reserved scallion, bacon and egg slices. Serve warm, room temperature or cold. Refrigerate leftover salad, and bring to room temperature before serving. Serves 6 to 8.

This is one of the best potatoes salad there is. I found it in a cookbook years ago and changed it to my taste. This is the result. It will be a little loose when first made, but thickens as it sets. I prefer it the next day, but it tastes great when just made. David and Marc love this one. This is the potato salad I always make at home when I have the time to prepare it. If I need a quick potato salad, I use Aunt Millie's.

L-R: David, Elise, Marc and Steven Feiner

TORTELLINI SALAD
Carol Koury Potter

Vinaigrette Dressing:

2 tablespoons Dijon mustard
⅓ cup red wine vinegar
¾ cup olive oil

2 cloves garlic, peeled and crushed
Salt and pepper (freshly ground) to taste
Dash lemon

Salad:
1 pound tortellini, cheese-filled or meat filled, cooked and cooled
½ cup fresh parsley, chopped fine
2 tomatoes, seeded and chopped in small cubes
1 cup broccoli flowerets, cooked, blanched, and cooled

⅓ cup red onion, finely chopped
1 cup black olives, chopped
1 red bell pepper, finely chopped
Finely grated Parmesan cheese

Whisk dressing ingredients together and set aside. Mix cooked tortellini with vinaigrette. Add remaining ingredients and toss. Cover and refrigerate; serve at room temperature.

This recipe is from a close family friend, Carol Potter. She is Billy Koury's sister. Cyndi had made this and I loved it. Carol sent the recipe to me, saying this is served at all the Koury family functions.

ORZO WITH TUNA MACARONI SALAD
Elise Feiner

1 pound orzo (or pasta of your choice); cooked as directed
1 large onion, peeled and chopped finely
2 stalks celery, cut in tiny cubes
1 (12 ounce) can Tuna Fish (solid white)
1 small can baby shrimp (optional)

Salt and pepper to taste
1 can black olive slices
2 scallions, finely chopped
1 box frozen peas, defrosted
1 cup mayonnaise (you may adjust according to your taste)

Mix all the ingredients except the orzo and mayonnaise together. Cook the orzo according to the directions in lightly salted water. Drain the orzo well, and run under cool water. Drain well again. Add the orzo to the other ingredients. Add mayonnaise to your taste. Chill. Serves 8.

NANNY'S MACARONI SALAD
Katherine Avella

2 pounds elbow macaroni
1 quart of mayonnaise
1 cup milk
⅔ cup heavy cream
⅓ cup white vinegar

4 teaspoons sugar
1 teaspoon salt
1 onion, peeled and finely chopped
2 gherkins, finely chopped
1 carrot, peeled and finely chopped

Boil the elbows in salted water according to the package directions. Drain well; Run cool water over the pasta, drain well again. Mix the remaining ingredients together while the pasta is cooking. When pasta is cool, add to mayonnaise mixture. Mix well. Refrigerate. Serves 10 to 15 as a side dish.

Summer barbeques always included a large bowl of Nanny's macaroni salad.

AUNT MILLIE'S POTATO SALAD
Millie Grimaldi

6 potatoes
2 hard boiled eggs
1 medium to large onion, peeled and chopped

2-3 stalks celery, cut into small pieces
Salt and pepper to taste
¾ cup mayonnaise or more to taste

Boil the potatoes in salted water in their skins for about 40 minutes. Let cool. Peel and cube the potatoes. If you like the mayonnaise mixture on the smooth side, follow the directions for the food processor; if you like it chunky, follow the directions to mix in a bowl. In a food processor add remaining ingredients. Pour over the potatoes and blend. May be served immediately or refrigerated. If you like, you can put everything in a bowl except the potatoes and mix well for a few minutes. Then pour over the potatoes and mix well again. This will make a more textured potato salad. Serves 6.

We once went to my Aunt Millie's for lunch, and she made this potato salad while we were sitting there. She served it warm, and it was excellent.

CALIFORNIA CHICKEN SALAD
Elise Feiner

Baby Salad Greens
Strawberries cut in slices
Cantaloupe, cubes
Apples, peeled and cut in small slices

Raisins
Pistachio Nuts
Crumbled Blue Cheese
Cooked Chicken Breast (one per person)

Place the greens in individual bowls or plates. Add the fruit along the edges. Sprinkle the raisins, blue cheese and pistachio nuts on top; add chicken slices. Make a dressing of sweet and sour sauce or duck sauce, balsamic vinegar, salt and pepper, a little oregano and basil, and lightly drizzle over the salad.

This is similar to a salad at Teddy's in Rome, N.Y. Carlos told us how to make it. Stop in to eat at Teddy's 851 Black River Boulevard North, Rome, New York. (315) 336-7839

241

PASTA SALAD WITH PIZZAZZ
Elise Feiner

3 slices pepperoni about ¼-inch thick (cut into cubes)
3 slices Genoa salami about ¼-inch thick, (cut into cubes)
4 slices provolone (mild) about ¼-inch thick (cut this into strips or cubes)
1 (2.25 ounces) can Black olives, pitted and sliced, drained
1 stick of butter
4-5 cloves of garlic peeled and crushed.
1 head or bag of broccoli floweret's, separated into small floweret's
1 medium zucchini, peeled and cut in rounds
1 can, jar, or box of mushrooms

1 bunch of scallions, cut into small 1 inch pieces
Salt and pepper to taste (I use garlic salt)
1 pound of rotelle or tricolor rotelle
¼ - ½ cup olive oil
⅛ - ¼ wine vinegar or balsamic vinegar
1 package of Good Season® Italian Dressing
1-2 teaspoon oregano
1-2 teaspoon basil
Lots of grating cheese (about 1-1½ cups)

Mix the salami, pepperoni, provolone, and black olives together and set aside. In a large frying pan, melt the butter and add the garlic. Sauté for about 1 minute; add the broccoli, zucchini, mushrooms, and scallions and sauté until the vegetables are soft to medium. Add salt and pepper to taste. Cook one pound of rotelle or tricolor rotelle pasta in boiling salted water according to directions. Drain and set aside. Make a mixture of the olive oil, balsamic vinegar, Good Seasons, oregano and basil. Mix well. Set aside. In a large bowl, add the pepperoni mix, cooked pasta, sautéed vegetables, dressing mix. Add the grating cheese and toss well. Serve at room temperature or chilled. Serves 8.

Our Wedding...
Back Row L-R: Kevin, Ivan, Elise, and Marc Feiner, Mary Ann Coyle Socik, and Tom Mollico
Middle Row L-R: Warren Mainella, Michele Maida, Toni Mollico, Frank Mainella, Jr.
Front Row L-R: Barbara Freedoff Forgeron, Theresa Feiner

SUMMER SALAD
Linda Ryen

1 package of spring salad mix
1 package of walnuts
1 can canned pears in lite syrup
1 package Feta Cheese

½ package Muenster cheese, cubed
1 package fresh raspberries
1 bottle Raspberry Vinaigrette Dressing (Maple Farms®)

Layer in the above order in a salad bowl. Put dressing on and serve.

Linda said this is a wonderful salad to serve. She uses low fat feta cheese and fat free dressing.

Linda and Jerry Ryen

Linda was a talent event planner in New Hartford, owning Jessie and Company. Jerry works for Utica National Insurance. Their daughter Jessica is a very talented columnist at the Observer Dispatch, our local newspaper.

PASTA SALAD WITH ASPARAGUS
Elise Feiner

1 large shallot, finely chopped
⅔ cup extra-virgin olive oil, eyeball it
1 pound asparagus, thin spears
2 heads of endive, cored and thinly sliced
½ small red bell pepper, chopped in tiny cubes
1 pound farfalle (bow tie) pasta cooked and cooled
½ cup frozen green peas
⅛ cup finely chopped parsley

6 tablespoons red or white wine vinegar
Salt and freshly ground black pepper
4 tablespoons grated cheese, divided
3 slices provolone ½-inch thick, cut into small cubes
1 small can black olives, sliced
1 handful pepperoni, thinly sliced or a few slices of salami
about ¼-inch thick (cubed) (or both)

Heat the shallot and oil in microwave safe covered dish for 45 seconds to one minute or in a small pan on the stovetop over medium low heat for 5 minutes. Allow oil to cool back to room temperature. Cut the bottoms of the asparagus off. Par boil the asparagus tops in 1-inch simmering lightly salted water covered for 3 to 4 minutes. Immediately place in a bowl with ice cubes to stop the cooking; when cool, drain. Cut asparagus into 1-inch pieces on an angle and add to a bowl. Combine sliced, cooked asparagus with shredded endive, red bell pepper, cooked pasta, green peas and chopped parsley. The peas will defrost as you toss salad. Pour vinegar into a small bowl and whisk in cooled shallot oil. Add 3 tablespoons of grating cheese to the oil/vinegar mix. Add the black olives, provolone cheese, and pepperoni or salami to the pasta. Pour dressing over salad and toss. Season salad with salt and pepper, to your taste and toss again. Top with one tablespoon grating cheese. Serves 10.

This is probably my favorite pasta salad. I find that sometimes the endive discolors a little in the salad, you could easily omit it.

The Emery's
Lisa, John and Mackenzie

Lisa is a teacher and
realtor, John Manages one
of our local Wal-Mart's, and
Mackenzie is a genius!

BROCCOLI - CAVATELLI SALAD
Betty Arcuri

1 pound of frozen Cavatelli with ricotta or cheese tortellini
1-2 cloves of garlic, peeled and crushed
⅔ cup olive oil
1 bunch of broccoli floweret's
1 cup roasted peppers (cut into small pieces)

1 teaspoon of salt
¼ teaspoon black pepper
2 tablespoons parsley
2 tablespoons basil (optional)
¼ cup grated parmesan cheese

Cook Cavatelli as per package directions and drain well. While cavatellis are cooking, heat oil in a frying pan; add crushed garlic and broccoli and sauté for 10 minutes. Add the above to the cooked Cavatelli along with the remaining ingredients. Stir until well blended and place in a serving bowl. Maria said that Joanna Basile recommends doubling or tripling this recipe for a larger crowd. Serves 4.

Maria Trainor got this recipe from Joanna Basile. It is Joanna's' Aunt Betty's recipe. She is a fabulous cook, and this salad is delicious. You can serve it hot as a main dish, or cold as a salad. Joanna says this is great for a picnic since it won't spoil in the sun.

The Basile Kids
L-R: Jeffrey, Erica,
and Frank, Jr.

243

MEDITERRANEAN ORZO SALAD
Elise Feiner

1 cup orzo pasta uncooked (6 ounces)
3 tablespoons red onions, chopped, finely
1 cup tomatoes, red ripe (about 2 small), chopped in small cubes
½ cup celery, chopped
2 tablespoons basil, fresh, chopped
2 tablespoons Kalamata olives, pitted, chopped, finely

2 tablespoons capers
1 teaspoon Dijon mustard, grained
¼ teaspoon sugar
1 tablespoon balsamic vinegar
2 tablespoons garlic oil
Salt and pepper to taste
3½ ounces feta cheese, crumbled

Bring a large quantity of lightly salted water to a boil and cook the orzo until just tender. Drain and allow to cool. Mix the pasta with the onions, tomato, celery, basil, olives, and capers. In a small bowl, whisk together the mustard, sugar and vinegar. Gradually beat in the oil until it emulsifies. Pour this vinaigrette over the pasta mixture and season with salt and pepper. Chill the salad. When it's cold, crumble feta cheese on the top before serving. Serves 4.

L-R: Lauren, Jennifer and Steven Feiner

A Day at the Races…
L-R: Ivan, Lauren, Steven, Jennifer and Marc Feiner at Saratoga

TUNA WITH CAPERS
Barbara Forgeron

Several Roma tomatoes, peeled and chopped
Coarse salt
1 pound pasta; cooked as directed
1 pound tuna in water, flaked
1-2 teaspoons lemon juice

6 tablespoons capers, well drained
4 tablespoons olive oil
Mint leaves, optional
Cayenne pepper, to taste

Sprinkle tomatoes with salt and let sit 30 minutes. Rinse off the salt. Meanwhile, place tuna in large bowl, add chopped mint and capers. Sprinkle with lemon juice. Add oil and season with salt and cayenne pepper. Toss. Add pasta and toss. Barbara likes shell shaped pasta. Serves 6.

This recipe comes from Cousin Barbara who lives in Palm Springs. She say's "We tend to eat lightly out here in the desert in the summer. Here is one of my family's favorite summer salads."

The much younger
Forgeron Kids:
L-R: Jeffrey, Alison, and
Benny

LEE'S CUCUMBER SALAD
Lee Sack

4 cucumbers
Salt
1 tablespoon onion, diced

¼ cup vinegar
½ cup water
1 rounded tablespoon sugar

Peel and slice 4 cucumbers as thinly as you can. Place in a bowl. Salt very liberally, and toss the cucumbers after each salting. Let sit a couple of hours.

After a goodly amount of liquid has come from the cucumbers, squeeze a small handful at a time as hard as you can and remove to another bowl. Don't bother rinsing. Dice about 1 tablespoon of onion, into very small pieces. Spread over squeezed cucumbers. Make a mixture of ¼-cup vinegar, in a ½-cup of water. Add about 1 rounded tablespoon of sugar. Taste, it shouldn't be too sweet or too tart. Pour vinegar/sugar/water over cucumbers and let sit in refrigerator, covered, for at least 2 hours. Serves 4.

Aunt Barbara said her friend Lee made this as a side dish with the Chicken Paprikash; it was delicious!

ELISE'S WHITEFISH SALAD
Elise Feiner

1 large smoked whitefish
Salt and pepper to taste
1 (8 ounce) package cream cheese softened

1 medium onion, peeled and finely chopped in food processor
2 stalks celery (washed), chopped finely in food processor
1 cup mayonnaise

Chop celery and onions in a food processor. Cut off the head of the fish and open the fish. Remove all the meat paying very **CAREFUL attention to remove all the bones**. Some are very small. Roll the pieces of fish between your fingers to break them up and remove the bones. Mash the softened cream cheese and mayonnaise together. Mix together the celery, onions, salt (**go very lightly on the salt,**) and pepper. In a large bowl, mix fish with mayonnaise mix, and celery mix. You may need more mayo depending on your taste, or the size of the fish. Serves about 6.

I think Mom Mom told me how to make this but I'm not sure. The cream cheese keeps the salad very white in color as opposed to the store bought which tends to be a little gray. You can do this a day ahead. It's great for Sunday Brunch or "Break the Fast" for Yom Kippur. B.J.'s sells smoked whitefish. If you've never tried it, it's a great change from tuna fish. The smoky taste is delicious! This salad is very smooth and usually eaten on a bagel with or without lox (smoked salmon.)

ELISE'S TUNA FISH
Elise Feiner

2 (12 ounce) cans Bumblebee® or Star-Kist® chunk White Tuna
1 medium-large onion, peeled and chopped
2-3 stalks celery, washed, chopped into a fine dice

1 carrot, peeled and grated
½ teaspoon sugar
Mayonnaise to taste

Open and drain the cans of tuna well. Place tuna in a food processor and pulse until the texture you prefer. I like it fine. If you like it on the chunky side, use a fork to break it apart. Remove to a bowl. Take the onion and celery and process it until it is fine. Add to the tuna in the bowl. Shred one carrot in the food processor using the fine shredding disc or grate the carrot; add to the tuna. Add the sugar; add mayonnaise to taste. Chill or serve at room temperature. Serves 6 to 8.

I have been making this tuna for as long as I can remember. When I was in high school living with my Aunt Jean and Uncle Pat for a few weeks, there was a German deli in Woodhaven, N.Y., that made the best tuna fish. One day Aunt Jean asked the man what made it so good and he said that the secret was the carrots and just a drop of sugar to take away the fishy taste. This tuna has become a legend in its own time. It's really is delicious. People always ask for the recipe.

"Friendship is like a bank account; you can't continue to draw on it without making deposits."
- Author Unknown

ELISE'S EGG SALAD
Elise Feiner

12 eggs, hard-boiled (see recipe for Perfect Hard Boiled eggs)
3-4 slices American cheese, yellow, cut in very tiny cubes

Salt and pepper to taste
Mayonnaise

With an egg slicer, cut the hard boiled eggs vertically, and then horizontally so the pieces in the egg salad remain chunky. Add salt and pepper to taste. Add enough mayonnaise to make it to the consistency you prefer. Fold in the pieces of American cheese. Serve warm or chilled

In our house, they like the egg salad on the chunky side and served warm on a bagel. Tuna fish and egg salad are a staple dinner in the summer in our house, and one of Marc's favorite meals.

L-R: Marc, Elise and Jeffrey Feiner

CHICKEN, TURKEY OR HAM SALAD
Elise Feiner

Leftover chicken, turkey, or ham (or boil the meat in lightly salted water if you want to make it for this purpose (see chicken soup recipe)
1 large onion, peeled and finely chopped

2-3 stalks of celery, washed and finely chopped
Salt and pepper to taste
Mayonnaise

The above amounts are just a guide, depending the amount of leftover meat. Take the chicken that is left over when making chicken soup, or place a chicken or boneless chicken breasts in a pot of lightly salted water and boil for about 30 minutes until cooked. When cooled, remove chicken from the bones, or use the boneless chicken. Place in a food processor and pulse until it is the consistency you like; or you can also dice it into tiny cubes by hand. I prefer it on the fine side, but that's a matter of taste. Place in a mixing bowl. Chop the onion and celery in a food processor until fine, and add to the mixing bowl. Add salt and pepper to taste. Begin adding mayonnaise about ½-cup at a time until it is the consistency you prefer. To make turkey salad, take the leftover turkey, and process it to the consistency you want, and make it the same way as the chicken salad. You can use leftover baked chicken, ham, or pork as well. If you are using leftover ham and have made the mustard sauce in the index to go with it, add the leftover sauce in with the mayonnaise. The amount of seasonings will vary with the amount of leftover meat.

This is a great way to use leftover chicken, ham or turkey. It's great in sandwiches, or on crackers. If you are making this to serve at a luncheon, just cook the chicken or turkey any way you feel comfortable, by boiling, baking, grilling, etc., it doesn't matter, you just need the cooked chicken or turkey.

"Having a place to go is a home. Having someone to love is a family. Having both is a blessing."
-Donna Hedges

TORTELLINI AND BROCCOLI SALAD
Elise Feiner

1 pound cheese tortellini, cooked as directed
1 box frozen broccoli flowerets, defrosted
1 jar mushroom pieces, drained
4 tablespoons butter, melted

¼ - ½ cup olive oil
Salt and pepper to taste
1 cup grated cheese
5 cloves garlic crushed

Cook the tortellini according to the directions. Drain and let cool. In a medium frying pan, heat the butter and add the garlic; sauté for about 1 minute. Add the broccoli and mushrooms, and heat through, stirring frequently. Add salt and pepper to taste. Add the grating cheese. Toss with the tortellini, add the olive oil. This may be served at room temperature or chilled. Serves 8.

CHICKEN AND RED ROASTED PEPPER SALAD
Carmen Ferreiro

Leftover cooked chicken, cut up as for chicken salad
Fresh roasted red peppers cut up
1 clove garlic (more if you are making a lot of chicken), peeled and crushed

Salt and pepper to taste
Olive oil to taste
Balsamic vinegar to taste
Fresh cilantro chopped

Mix everything together in a large bowl. You can substitute parsley for the cilantro if you don't like the cilantro. Serve with wedges of pita or slices of fresh bread

Carmen said she made this salad up one day, as a change from the traditional chicken salad.

BLT CHICKEN SALAD
Elise Feiner

¼ cup mayonnaise
¼ cup barbeque sauce
1 tablespoon lemon juice
½ teaspoon pepper
¼ teaspoon salt
2 cups cooked chicken breasts, chopped
2 medium tomatoes, chopped (use Roma if possible)
1 stalk of celery thinly sliced

5 cups iceberg, romaine, and Bibb lettuce
12 bacon strips, cooked
¼ medium red onion sliced in very thin circles (optional)
2 hard boiled eggs, chopped (optional)
Croutons (optional)
Seasoned slivered almonds (optional) (Sunkist Almond Accents)

In a small bowl, combine mayonnaise, barbeque sauce, lemon juice, pepper and salt. Cover and refrigerate 1 hour. In the meantime, chop celery, chicken, onions, bacon, tomatoes etc. Just before serving combine chicken, celery and tomatoes. Serve on the salad greens. Sprinkle with eggs, bacon, onions, croutons, and almonds. Top with dressing. You can also toss with the dressing after adding the chicken with the celery and tomatoes, but I like to add it at the end. Serves 4.

This makes a great summer dinner too! The combination of barbeque sauce and mayonnaise sounds awful, but is awfully good.

STRAWBERRY SALAD
Aviva Zierler

2 parts Balsamic Vinegar
1 part olive oil
Dash of honey to taste
1-2 bags of mixed salad greens

1-2 cups walnut halves
Maple syrup (enough to coat the walnuts)
Sliced fresh strawberries
Oil for frying

Coat the walnut halves in the maple syrup. Fry the walnuts for a few minutes until crisp. Refrigerate to harden. When ready to serve, place the greens in a large salad bowl. Mix the balsamic vinegar, oil and honey together until well blended. Toss with the salad greens. Top with the walnuts and sliced strawberries.

We had this salad at Aviva's bridal shower. It was made by her mother's friend Ann. She quickly told us how to do it so we could make it ourselves. It was excellent, and great for a buffet luncheon. For the novice cooks, 2 parts to one part means if you use 2 cups of vinegar, use 1 cup of oil, or 1 cup of vinegar, use ½ cup of oil.

L-R: Samantha Caplan Zierler, Aviva Akselrad Zierler,
and Fran Zierler (her daughters- in-law)

L-R: Jeane Cassata, Samantha Caplan, Aviva Akselrad,
Fran Zierler, and Camille Sanabria

L-R: Cousins Phyllis Jendzo, Laura Jendzo Skonberg
and Kim Jendzo

L-R: Betty, Marc and Ivan Feiner

And more Cousins…
The Fentons
L-R: JR, Francine, Brooks, and Raegan

And yet still more cousins…
L-R: Angela, Julieann, Laura, John, and Maria Juliano

Pasta and Rice...

The Anthony J. Furino Family
L-R: Felicia, Anthony, Eileen and Kristin

"The trouble with Italian food is that five or six days later you're hungry again."
-George Miller

Great Websites for Cooks:

http://www.cookingwithlove.com

http://www.kraftfoods.com

http://www.cookierecipe.com

http://www.foodtv.com

http://www.copykat.com

http://www.topsecretrecipes.com

http://www.epicurious.com

http://www.nabiscorecipes.com

http://www.breadworksinc.com

http://www.americanspice.com

http://www.culinary.com

http://www.appetizerrecipe.com

http://www.fantes.com

http://www.mastercook.com

http://www.bakeoff.com

http://www.recipecenter.com

http://www.gourmet.com

http://www.bonappetit.com

http://www.allrecipes.com

http://www.emerils.com

http://www.kingarthurflour.com

http://bakerscatalog.com

http://www.parmigianoreggiano.net

http://www.pennmac.com

http://www.surlatable.com

http://www.mozzco.com

http://www.goldnkrackle.com

http://www.freshpasta.com

http://www.florentynaspasta.com

http://www.anticaitalia.com

http://www.traversos.com

http://www.todarobros.com

http://www.pastacheese.com

http://www.chefscatalog.com

_____

_____

_____

_____

_____

BAKED ZITI
Elise Feiner

2 pounds of ziti
2 pounds of ricotta cheese
2 (8 ounce) bags of shredded mozzarella cheese
1-2 cups of Pecorino Romano or Parmigiana

Tomato Sauce (See recipe under Avella-Mainella Family's
Famous Gravy or Avella's Marinara Sauce)
1 large mozzarella, whole, cut in thin slices
Extra grated cheese for the top

Heat the tomato sauce. In a large bowl, mix the ricotta cheese, grating cheese, and shredded mozzarella. Cook the ziti but leave a little on the hard side because they will soften when they are baked. Drain well. Add tomato sauce to the ziti, stir in the cheese mixture until well blended. Place into a large casserole pan or large aluminum tray or if doing meals ahead into individual loaf pans for quick dinners. Top with additional tomato sauce, grated cheese and slices of mozzarella. Cover with aluminum foil so the mozzarella doesn't burn. Remove the foil for the last 15 to 20 minutes of baking. This freezes very well for a party. Freeze unbaked and then bring to room temperature before baking. Bake at 375° for about 1 hour until heated all the way through and slightly browned on top. If using small pans adjust the time accordingly. Serves 8 to 10.

This is fast and easy to make especially if you have gravy (tomato sauce) in the freezer. It's great for a buffet table, a barbecue, or great to keep one in the freezer for unexpected company. You can also use Marinara sauce for this. We don't use meat in our baked ziti. For a change of pace, make them with the vodka sauce instead of plain tomato sauce!

VODKA RIGGIES
Elise Feiner

6 scallions, chopped
5 slices proscuitto, chopped
4 tablespoons unsalted butter
2 ounces Vodka
1 cup milk or cream

1-2 cups tomato sauce
1 teaspoon black pepper
¾ cup parmesan cheese, grated
1 pound rigatoni

Sauté scallions in melted butter until soft, but not brown. Add proscuitto and sauté for one minute. **Stand back and carefully add vodka and ignite** until alcohol burns off. Add tomato sauce, milk or cream, and pepper. Heat for about 5 minutes. Add grated cheese and heat another two minute. Serve over cooked rigatoni. Serves 4.

This sauce is easy enough to make while the rigatoni are cooking.

PENNE A LA VODKA
Ann D'Amico

1 pound penne cooked
2 cups of your own tomato sauce (more if you like it redder in color)
1 cup heavy cream

½ cup Pecorino Romano cheese
¼ cup vodka
Fresh basil to taste

Pour sauce into a pot. Add cream and stir. Add cheese. Stir well. Chop basil into a chiffonade, add, along with vodka. Heat; stirring till bubbly. Add pasta; mix well.

Ann says this is easy to make. This is DELICIOUS and great for a quick dinner.

The Juliano Family
L-R: Laura, Maria, Julie Ann, John
and Angela

PENNE ALLA VODKA WITH PROSCUITTO
Elise Feiner

3 tablespoon unsalted butter
2 cloves garlic, finely chopped
3 ounces proscuitto, cut into strips or cubes
1 pound penne cooked according to directions
2 cups of your own sauce (more if you like it darker in
color) or 1 can (35 ounces) peeled Italian tomatoes, drained
and coarsely chopped

1 cup heavy cream
¾ cup Pecorino Romano
¼ cup vodka
Salt to taste
Fresh basil

In a very large skillet, melt the butter. Add garlic and cook for about 2 minutes, until light brown over low to medium heat. Stir in proscuitto and cook for another minute or two. Pour tomatoes into the skillet, and simmer for about 10 minutes. Add cream and stir for about 1 minute. Add the vodka, cook another 3 minutes. Season with salt. Add cheese. Stir well. Chop basil into a chiffonade. Heat, stirring until bubbly. Cook the penne in 6 quarts salted water until they are al dente. Drain, reserving some of the pasta water. Add pasta. Mix well. Add a little of the reserve pasta water if the sauce is too thick. Serves 6.

L-R: Marc and Elise Feiner, Rich and Julie Venezio, David and Lauren Feiner
In Front: Michelle Raehm…Michelle is from Utica but now lives and performs in Hilton Head with her band Target

ZITI WITH SPINACH
Elise Feiner

1 box frozen spinach (10 ounces) thawed
5 tablespoons olive oil
6 cloves garlic, sliced
½ cup white wine
1 cup chicken broth
1½ cups heavy cream

⅛ teaspoon black pepper
4 ounces proscuitto thinly sliced
½ cup blue cheese or gorgonzola, crumbled
1 pound ziti or pasta of your choice
½ cup locatelli-romano grated cheese
Pignoli (optional) toasted

Drain the excess liquid from the spinach and set aside. Put up a large pot of salted water to boil to cook the pasta. Heat 3 tablespoons of the oil in a medium frying pan. Quickly sauté the sliced garlic for about 1 minute, taking care not to burn it. Add the spinach and cook for another 1 to 2 minutes. Add the wine and cook for about another 2 minutes. Add the chicken broth, cream and black pepper. Bring to a boil, and then lower to a simmer and cook for about 13 minutes. Cool slightly and put in a blender and blend until smooth. In a large frying pan, heat the remaining olive oil and cut the proscuitto into thin stripes. Sauté in the oil until crisp. Drain on paper towels, reserving a little for the topping. Add the spinach mix to this pan. Add the blue cheese and stir until melted about 2 minutes. Cook the pasta according to your taste. Drain and toss with the spinach mix. Add grated cheese and top with fried proscuitto. Serves 6.

One of my favorites since I was a kid. I love spinach and blue cheese, what a great combo. I also add toasted pine nuts once in a while. I like this over fettuccine noodles for a great side dish too.

CHICKEN RIGGIES
Elise Feiner

2 pounds rigatoni
1½ sticks butter
2½ pounds boneless chicken breasts cut in cubes
1 large onion, peeled and diced
5 cloves garlic, peeled and crushed
½ cup flour

1 can (13¾ or 14½ ounce) College Inn® Chicken Broth
½ teaspoon each of dried basil and dried oregano
6 cherry peppers, cut into pieces (optional)
2 bell peppers, red or green, cut in cubes
2½ cups marinara sauce
1½ cup grated Parmesan or Locatelli cheese

Dredge the chicken cubes in flour and coat well. In a large sauté pan, melt the butter, brown the chicken cubes lightly, remove and set aside. In the same pan, sauté the onions until soft and translucent about 7 minutes. Add the garlic and cook another few minutes.
   Add the remaining ingredients including the chicken and simmer for about 45 to 60 minutes. Cook the rigatoni according to package directions. Pour the chicken mixture over the rigatoni and toss well. Top with additional grating cheese if desired. Serves 6.

You can't live in Upstate New York and not learn how to cook some version of chicken riggies. It's a staple here. This is one of David's favorite meals.

David and Elise Feiner at the Bellagio in Las Vegas

CANNELLONI CAPRICCIO
Elise Feiner

Shells: This is basically a crepe batter
4 eggs
1 cup water

1 cup sifted flour
Pinch of salt

Beat eggs, add flour, water and salt, and beat again. This mixture should be very loose; looser than a pancake batter. Grease a small frying pan (if you have cast iron pan they work well for the crepes, or a non stick pan is good too), about 4 to 5-inches in diameter.
   Pour about 3 tablespoons of the batter (I use a small gravy ladle for uniformity) in the pan and rotate pan to cover the bottom. There should be just enough batter to cover the bottom but not break apart. You want the crepes thin. Don't worry if the first few are not perfect, I always end up discarding the first one or two until you get the hang of it. Heat the crepe until it coagulates and then turn the crepe over. Let the other side coagulate and remove from the heat, placing on clean dish towels until they cool. They can be stacked when cooled and wrapped in wax paper or saran wrap until you are ready to fill them. Refrigerate until ready to fill. You can make the crepes a day in advance.

Sauce:
4 tablespoon butter
1 heaping tablespoon flour
1½ cups milk
½ teaspoon salt

1 egg yolk, beaten
2 tablespoons grated cheese
Dash white pepper
Dash of nutmeg

Melt butter in a small pan and add flour. Stir into a smooth paste; add milk. Stir continually and cook over low flame for 10 minutes. Sauce should have the consistency of thick cream. Add salt, pepper, and nutmeg. Remove from the stove, and stir in the grated cheese and egg yolk rapidly.

CONTINUED ON NEXT PAGE

CANNELLONI CAPRICCIO CONTINUED

Filling:

2½ cups cooked chicken, shredded or finely chopped or ground
¼ pound fresh mushrooms, chopped finely
Salt and pepper to taste

4 tablespoons butter
1 egg
½ cup well drained, cooked spinach
½ cup Parmesan cheese

Cook the spinach according to the package directions drain and set aside. You can boil chicken breasts in water if you don't have any cooked chicken leftover, or just buy a cooked chicken at the grocery store. Sauté the mushrooms in the butter in a medium frying pan. Add salt and pepper to taste. Mix the finely ground chicken with the spinach, mushrooms, egg, and cheese. Fill the shells by placing a heaping tablespoon or two into the center of each shell. Fold the ends in to make a long tube. Line a large shallow baking pan with a layer of sauce. Place the shells seam side down. Cover with remaining sauce and sprinkle with grating cheese. Bake 350° for 30 to 35 minutes or until set. Serves 8.

FRAN'S PASTA WITH ZUCCHINI
Frances Zierler

¼ cup oil
3-4 onions, peeled and cut in thin slices
2-3 large zucchini, peeled and cubed
2-3 large cans stewed tomatoes
1 (14½ ounce) can diced tomatoes

½ teaspoon dried basil
2 bags shredded white cheddar cheese
Salt and pepper to taste (I use a little garlic salt instead)
Grated cheese if desired (Locatelli Romano or parmesan)
1½ to 2 pounds pasta of your choice (I like bowties)

In a very large frying pan, heat the oil and sauté the onions until lightly browned and caramelizing. Add a little salt and pepper to taste. Add the stewed tomatoes and basil and cook for about 20 minutes. Add the cubed zucchini, cover, and cook until soft about another 60 to 90 minutes or so. Check for seasonings and add more salt and pepper if desired. In the meantime, boil a pot of salted water to cook the pasta. Cook pasta to your taste. Drain the pasta. Pour the tomato/zucchini mixture over the pasta. Add the cheddar cheese and mix well. Serves 6.

My friend Fran is a great cook. They are basically vegetarian in her house so she has to come up with a wide variety of creative meals. They love pasta and she can cook it a hundred ways. This is one of my favorites. It's even better leftover or cold for breakfast if you're a true Pastaholic!

CREAMY BROCCOLI LASAGNA
Katherine Avella

9 uncooked lasagna noodles
¼ cup chopped onions
¼ cup butter
¼ cup all purpose flour
2 teaspoons chicken bouillon granules
¾ teaspoon garlic salt
¼ teaspoon pepper

¼ teaspoon dried thyme
2½ cups milk
6 cups broccoli flowerets
1½ cups ricotta
2 (4 ½ ounce) jars sliced mushrooms
2 (6 ounce) packages Swiss cheese slices or mozzarella cheese slices

Cook noodles according to package directions (add a little oil to the water to prevent sticking).. Meanwhile, in large skillet sauté onions in butter, until tender. Add the flour, bouillon, garlic salt, pepper and thyme. Stir until smooth. Gradually add the milk. Bring to a boil. Cook and stir 2 minutes until thickened. Add broccoli cook for another 3 to 5 minutes. Stir in ricotta and mushrooms. Drain the noodles. In a greased 13 x 9 x 2-inch baking dish, line 3 noodles ⅓ sauce and ⅓ Swiss or mozzarella cheese. Repeat twice. Bake uncovered 350° minutes 35 to 40 minutes or until bubbly and broccoli is tender. Let rest 10 to 15 minutes before cutting.

"Friends are the family we choose for ourselves."
-Edna Buchanan

RAVIOLI
Katherine Avella and Josephine Mainella

Dough:

3 cups all-purpose flour

1 teaspoon salt

4 eggs

2 tablespoons olive oil

1 yolk, for egg wash

In an electric mixer fitted with a dough hook, combine flour and salt. Add eggs, 1 at a time and continue to mix. Drizzle in oil and continue to incorporate all the flour until it forms a ball. Sprinkle some flour on work surface, knead the dough until elastic and smooth. Wrap the dough in plastic wrap and let it rest for about 30 minutes in the refrigerator.

Cut the ball of dough in half, cover and reserve the dough you are not immediately using to prevent it from drying out. Dust the counter and dough with flour. Form the dough into a rectangle and roll it through the pasta machine, 2 or 3 times, at its widest (#1) setting or whichever is the widest on your machine. Turn down to the next number setting and crank the dough through again, 2 or 3 times. Continue until the machine is at its narrowest setting. The dough should be paper-thin, about ⅛-inch thick. Dust the counter and dough with flour; lay out the long sheet of pasta. Brush the top surface of dough with egg wash. Drop 1 tablespoon of cooled filling about 2-inches apart on **HALF the sheet of pasta**. Fold the unfilled half over the filling. Remove any out air pockets around each ravioli and form a seal. Use a pasta cutter or a crimper to cut each ravioli into a square or round shape. Use the tines of a fork to seal and crimp the edges of each ravioli. Check to make sure the ravioli are sealed before cooking. If making ravioli in advance, dust with cornmeal to prevent them from sticking. Yield 24; serves 4.

Filling:

1 pound ricotta

2 eggs

1 teaspoon parsley

Salt and pepper to taste

Dash of nutmeg

1 grated mozzarella (small)

1 cup grating cheese

Mix all ingredients together. Refrigerate to help solidify before filling the ravioli. Cook the ravioli in plenty of boiling salted water for 8 to 10 minutes. Ravioli will float to the top when cooked. Do not use a colander to drain, rather, lift the ravioli from water with a large strainer or slotted spoon or they will break. Serve with your favorite tomato sauce or see index.

This is my favorite type of pasta. We always had ravioli for the holidays or special occasions. I can remember Nanny and Aunt Fifi making them when I was a little girl and living in Brooklyn.

FARFALLE WITH SHRIMP AND PEAS
Billy Di Carlo and Marina deCaronea

¼ cup olive oil

2 tablespoons butter

2 scallions, chopped

10 shrimp per person, peeled and deveined

1½ cups frozen peas, defrosted

1 pound bowtie pasta (cooked according to package directions)

1 cup white wine

Salt and pepper to taste

A few strands of Spanish Saffron

Chopped fresh fennel for garnish

Cook the pasta according to package directions while you are doing the shrimp. Heat the oil and butter in a large frying pan. Sauté the scallions lightly; add the peas. Stir in the wine, cook until the wine is reduced. Add the shrimp and salt and pepper to taste. Cook until the shrimp is pink. Add the cooked pasta. Mix together. Sprinkle with fennel. Serves 4.

Mom Mom sent this recipe that was given to her from her friend in Florida, Billy Di Carlo. He heard about the cookbook and wanted to make a contribution. He said, "You are ready for a great eating experience."

MANICOTTI
Elise Feiner

Filling:

3 pounds of ricotta
6-8 eggs
1 large mozzarella grated, or two bags of shredded mozzarella
1-2 cups grated cheese (Parmesan or Locatelli Romano)

3-4 tablespoon parsley
Salt and pepper to taste
Extra grating cheese and extra mozzarella for the top if desired

Manicotti Shells:

4 eggs
1 cup water

1 cup sifted flour or Wondra® flour
Pinch of salt

Tomato Sauce:

You can use marinara sauce but, a meat sauce makes a much tastier manicotti. See index for Avella-Mainella Gravy and Avella Marinara sauce.

In a large bowl, mix all the ingredients for the filling together. The mixture should be of a firm consistency, but not too hard. You can add more eggs if necessary. It should maintain its shape when you scoop it out. Make the shells. Beat eggs, add flour, water and salt, and beat again. This mixture should be very loose; looser than a pancake batter. Grease a small frying pan about 4 to 5-inches in diameter (if you have cast iron they work well for the crepes or a non stick pan is good too.) Pour about 3 tablespoons of the batter (I use a small gravy ladle for uniformity) in the pan and rotate pan to cover the bottom. There should be just enough batter to cover the bottom but not break apart. You want the crepes thin. Don't worry if the first few are not perfect, I always end up discarding the first one or two until you get the hang of it. Heat the crepe until it coagulates, and then turn the crepe over. Let the other side coagulate and remove from the heat, placing on clean dishtowels until they cool. They can be stacked when cooled and wrapped in wax paper or saran wrap until you are ready to fill them. Refrigerate until ready to fill. You can make the crepes a day in advance. You can double this recipe if you have extra filling and freeze manicotti, unbaked.

Fill the shells by placing a heaping tablespoon or two into the center of each shell. Fold one end into the middle and then the other end into the middle to make a long tube. Line a large shallow baking pan with a thin layer of tomato sauce (you can you a meat sauce or marinara sauce; see recipe index for directions) Place the filled manicotti shells, seam side down into the tomato sauce. Cover the tops of the shells with additional sauce, sprinkle on some grated cheese and mozzarella if you'd like. Bake in a 400° degree oven for 45 minutes to an hour or until the manicotti are firm (check often, if getting too brown cover with aluminum foil). Serve with a salad and the meat from the gravy. Serves 12.

These crepes are delicious and give the manicotti a more delicate flavor than store bought manicotti tubes. They are really easy to make once you get the hang of it. In my mother's house, there were always cast iron pans that were just used for egg products. My mother said nothing would stick if they were only used for eggs. You knew better than to ever put meat in one of those pans. They were always kept wrapped in a plastic bag to keep them separated. Try to keep a small pan separate so that when you make the crepes or scrambled eggs you won't have a problem with sticking. This is my mother's recipe.

CAVATELLI
Katherine Avella and Josephine Mainella

2-3 eggs depending on the size
¼ cup oil
1 teaspoon salt
1½ pounds of ricotta

3 cups semolina flour
3 cups flour
You can add a little warm water if needed to make the dough soft.

Put the flour, semolina, and salt in the Kitchen Aid with the dough hook attachment. Add the oil, eggs and ricotta. Make a dough, but not too dry, a little softer than the Tagliatelle dough. Knead the dough on a lightly floured board for a few minutes. Cut in half and cut each half into 4 to 5 pieces. Cover the dough with Saran Wrap®. Put the dough through the Atlas Pasta machine on the widest setting (# 1) two times. Then put it through the fettuccine attachment, (broad cutter). They will be in long rods. Then cut in ½-inch pieces, shape, with fingers, by rolling the dough quickly with one finger so it curls over. Sprinkle with flour so they don't stick together. Freeze in plastic bags. Yield: 3 pounds.

These Cavatelli sure beat the store bought. They are so light and delicious. I remember as a kid, Aunt Fifi and my Mother making these for Christmas. I always love to stick my fingers in them to help shape them. These are the best!

PASTA A LA CARBONARA
Elise Feiner

1 pound of pasta of your choice (spaghetti, linguini, ziti)
½ pound pancetta, chopped, or substitute bacon or proscuitto
½ cup extra virgin olive oil
4-5 cloves of garlic, peeled and crushed
½ teaspoon crushed red pepper (optional)

½ cup dry white wine or chicken stock
2 large egg yolks
½ cup grated cheese (plus some for top)
1 teaspoon fresh parsley, finely chopped
Freshly ground black pepper and salt to taste

Bring a large pot of salted water to a boil and cook the pasta according to package directions, saving ¼-cup of the pasta water. While the pasta is cooking, heat a large pan over medium heat. Sauté the pancetta or bacon/ham in a little bit of the olive oil until it is brown and crisp about 3 to 5 minutes. Add the remaining olive oil, garlic, and red pepper; sauté for about 2 minutes. Add the wine or chicken stock (I use half of each) and reduce by half, about 2 minutes. Set aside. Beat the egg yolks and cheese together with a whisk. While whisking, add the ¼-cup of hot pasta water and whisk vigorously to temper your eggs. Add the parsley, and pepper; set sauce aside. Drain the pasta. Add the pasta to the broth/wine sauce. Add in the pancetta, then egg mixture. Toss. Remove from heat. Add salt to taste. Top with grating cheese. Serves 4.

This Northern Italian dish is one of Uncle Phil's favorites.

Katherine Avella and Philip Avella - circa 1945-46
This was one of my mother's favorite pictures and she gave
it to my father one Father's Day as part of his gift.

SPAGHETTI AGLIO E OLIO
Katherine Avella

1 pound spaghettini or spaghetti
6-8 cloves garlic, peeled and left whole, but cracked lightly with a knife
¼ cup extra-virgin olive oil

2 tablespoons Italian parsley
Pinch red pepper flakes
1 teaspoon salt

Bring a 6-quart pasta pot of salted water to boil over high heat. Add the spaghetti and cook according to package directions. Try to time it so that the garlic sauce is done when the pasta is done. Before you drain the pasta, save about 1 to 2 cups of the pasta water to moisten the pasta at the end if necessary.

Heat a 10-inch frying pan over medium heat and add the olive oil. Add the garlic and cook until golden brown, don't let the garlic get too brown, about 2 minutes. When the garlic is light brown, remove the pan from the heat, and add the parsley and red pepper flakes.
Drain the pasta and add it to the sauté pan. Mix the pasta and sauce well; season with salt and pepper, and serve immediately. Toss with grated cheese if desired. Serves 4.

My mother would often make this fast and easy spaghetti dish. It's delicious!

LASAGNA
Elise Feiner

1 pound of Lasagna noodles
2 pounds of chopped meat
2-3 tablespoons of oil
3 pounds of ricotta
6-8 eggs
1 large mozzarella grated or two bags of grated mozzarella
1-2 cups grated cheese (Parmesan or Locatelli Romano)

3-4 tablespoon parsley
Salt and pepper to taste
Extra Grating cheese for the top and the layers
Extra mozzarella for the top if desired
Tomato Sauce: You can use marinara sauce but, a meat sauce is much tastier See index for Avella-Mainella Famous Gravy or Avella Marinara sauce

Cook the noodles in boiling salted water and add a little oil so they won't stick. Cook according to package directions. I usually undercook them by a few minutes because they will continue to cook in the oven. Drain the noodles and run cold water over them; line the noodles up on kitchen towels or wax paper so they won't stick to each other until you are ready to use them. Set aside while you make the filling. In a medium frying pan, coat the bottom with the oil and brown the chopped meat until it is cooked. Break the meat apart with a fork while it is cooking so you don't have any lumps. The meat should change colors but not actually be too browned. Drain off any excess liquid and set the meat aside. In a large bowl, mix all the remaining ingredients well. Add the meat to the cheese mixture and well again. The mixture should be of a firm consistency, but not too hard. You can add more eggs if necessary. It should be easy to spread when you scoop it out. Line a large, deep baking pan with a layer of tomato sauce (you can use a meat sauce or marinara sauce; see recipe index for directions) Place a single layer of the lasagna noodles down into the tomato sauce. Spread a layer of the cheese mixture on top of the lasagna. Top with some tomato sauce and grated cheese, and another layer of tomato sauce. Add another layer of lasagna, and then cheese mixture, grating cheese, tomato sauce, continuing until you end with a layer of the noodles on the top. Finish with the last layer with tomato sauce and sprinkle on some grated cheese and mozzarella if you'd like (if you put mozzarella on the top, cover with foil and leave foil on for about 1 hour; remove foil for the last 15 minutes to allow top to brown.) Bake in a 375° oven for about 1 hour and 15 minutes or until the lasagna is firm. Let stand about 15 to 20 minutes before serving. Serve with a salad and the meat from the gravy. This will make 2 trays 13 x 9 x 4-inches. Bake one and freeze one. Let thaw overnight in the refrigerator before baking. Each tray serves 6 to 8.

This was always a favorite in my house growing up. Aunt Edith always made it for Christmas. We don't use sausage in our lasagna, but if your family prefers it you can mix some sausage into the chopped meat and brown it together.

LINGUINI AGLIO E OLIO
Katherine Avella

2 cups light olive oil
6 cloves garlic, peeled and crushed or 1½ tablespoon minced jar garlic
3 (2 ounce) cans flat anchovy fillets, drained and chopped

2 cups coarsely chopped pecans or hazelnuts
1 pound of linguini
Grated cheese for serving

Heat olive oil in a large skillet or saucepan over medium-low heat. Add garlic and anchovies and cook 15 minutes, being careful not to burn. Add nuts and cook 10 minutes longer. Meanwhile prepare linguini according to package directions. Drain well (but reserve a little water) and place in a large serving bowl. Pour on sauce, add water if too dry, and toss until well coated. Serve immediately with Parmesan. Serves 4.

If you're like me, you could eliminate the anchovies!

JEANE'S PESTO AND CREAM CHEESE PASTA
Jeane Cassata

1 pound pasta or your choice, cooked as directed
1 (8 ounce) package cream cheese, softened
3 tablespoons milk

2 cups pesto sauce (see recipe index or use store bought)
¾ cup grated cheese

Cook a pound of pasta (something like ziti or spaghetti.) Take a stick of cream cheese mixed with the milk, and soften in the microwave. Add the cream cheese to the drained pasta and mix well. Add the pesto sauce and mix again. Add grating cheese, and enjoy. Serves 4.

Nanny Jeane has great recipes, fast and delicious. This is one of them. It puts a new twist on the pesto by making it a little creamier.

FRAN'S GRANDMOTHER'S PASTA
Jeane Cassata

1 pound of pasta cooked according to package directions
2 sticks unsalted butter, softened

1 (8 ounce) package cream cheese, softened
1½-2 cups grated cheese

Cook pasta according to package directions. Drain; reserve some of the water. Mix equal parts of softened butter and softened cream cheese and toss with hot pasta. If too dry add a little of the pasta water. Mix well. Add a generous amount of grating cheese.

Jeanne and Fran said that this is how her mother and grandmother made "macaroni with butter." No doubt it must be delicious.

L-R: Nani Jeane Cassata, Fran Cassata Zierler, Camille Cassata Sanabria and Carl Cassata

FETTUCCINE ALFREDO A LA LAUREN
Elise Feiner

1 pint heavy cream
1½ sticks unsalted butter, softened
1½-2 cups freshly grated Parmigiano-Reggiano

Freshly cracked black pepper
1 pound of fettuccini, tortellini, hats, or pasta of your choice

Heat heavy cream over low-medium heat in a deep sauté pan. Add butter and whisk gently to melt. Stir in cheese and blend to incorporate. Season with freshly cracked black pepper. The sauce should start to thicken. If it is too loose, add more grating cheese, however, the sauce should not be too thick either…use your judgment here. In a large stockpot, cook pasta (fettuccini) in plenty of boiling salted water according to the directions. Quickly drain the pasta and add it to the sauté pan, gently toss the noodles to coat in the Alfredo. Transfer pasta to a warm serving bowl. Top with more grated cheese. Serve immediately. You can use this with tortellini or any other pasta. Serves 6 as a side dish; four as a main course.

I used to make my Alfredo sauce according to Aunt Edith's recipe, but one day I tried something different, and this was the result. This is closer to the Alfredo sauces made in the restaurants. It is a little thicker than Aunt Edith's. In her recipe, you don't cook the ingredients; just add the hot pasta to the ingredients. Both are delicious, and I make them both regularly, as my kids are big fans of Alfredo sauce.

FETTUCCINE ALFREDO EDITH
Edith Mainella

1 bag wide egg noodles (12 ounces) or 1 pound box of
fettuccine
6 egg yolks
1 stick butter at room temperture

2 half pints heavy cream
1½-2 cups grating cheese
Freshly ground black pepper to taste

Make your sauce mixture while the water for pasta is coming to a boil. In a large bowl, beat the egg yolks with a fork or whisk. Cut the butter into small or pieces, or you may melt it first and then add it. Add the cream, grating cheese, black pepper. Mix well. Cook the pasta in salted water according to package directions. Drain. Toss with the cream mixture. Let sit a few minutes. Stir again before serving. You can use this with tortellini or any other pasta. Serves 6 as a side dish, four as a main course.

I first learned to love this dish at my Aunt Edith's house. It was the first place I ever had it, and long before it was in vogue. It's so easy to make. I started to make it at home and the kids love it. Actually, it's Dante's (Jeff's dog) favorite meal.

257

TORTELLINI ALFREDO
Elise Feiner

1 pint heavy cream
1½ stick unsalted butter, softened
1½-2 cups freshly grated Locatelli-Romano

Freshly ground black pepper
1 pound tortellini, cheese-filled, cooked as directed

Heat heavy cream over low-medium heat in a deep sauté pan. Add butter and whisk gently to melt. Sprinkle in cheese and stir to incorporate. Season with freshly ground black pepper. In a large stockpot, cook pasta (tortellini) in plenty of boiling salted water according to the directions. Quickly drain the pasta and add it to the sauté pan, gently toss the noodles to coat in the Alfredo. Serve immediately. Serves 4 as a main course and 6 as a side dish. Read comments on previous page in above recipe Fettuccine Alfredo a la Lauren for guide to sauce thickness.

FETTUCCINE WITH BLUE CHEESE SAUCE
Elise Feiner

4 eggs
4 cups ricotta
6 ounces blue cheese, crumbled
¼ cup all purpose flour
1 tablespoon minced fresh parsley

2 teaspoons thyme
¼ teaspoon salt
⅛ teaspoon cayenne pepper
1 pound fettuccine, cooked and drained
Paprika

In a large mixing bowl, beat the first 8 ingredients 2 minutes until blended. Fold in fettuccine. Transfer to a baking dish sprayed with PAM®. Sprinkle with paprika. Bake uncovered at 325° 40 to 45 minutes. Let stand 10 minutes before serving. Cut in squares. Serves 4 to 6.

Our Wedding...
Marc and Elise Feiner, Katherine and Samuel Avella
June 4, 1978

When Marc first met my parents we were on a school break from medical school. He wanted to elope and get married before he returned to school. My father almost had a heart attack...his only daughter get married without a big wedding??? No way... I guess you can tell who prevailed. Like my mother said, "Where am I going to find shoes in three days?"

NANNY'S SPAGHETTI AND BROCCOLI
Katherine Avella

2 (16 ounce) packages frozen Green Giant® select broccoli pieces,
1 pound spaghetti, broken into 2-inch pieces
Salt (about 3 tablespoon added to the water)

¼ teaspoon black pepper
8-10 cloves garlic, peeled and crushed
1½ - 2½ cups grated cheese or to taste
½ cup olive oil

Bring an 8 quart pot of lightly salted (about 3 tablespoons) water to a boil. Toss in the spaghetti, garlic, olive oil, salt and pepper, broccoli. Bring back to a boil and let boil for about 5 minutes. Cover the pot. Turn off the heat and let the spaghetti absorb most of the water, until the spaghetti is cooked (about an hour and a half); stirring occasionally. Add in the grated cheese; blend well. You can add more water if you prefer it more "soupy." Top with additional grated cheese if desired. Serves 6.

This is the way Nanny makes it. I love it. It's much more like a soup than a pasta dish but on a warm winter's night it can't be beat. It tastes even better reheated the next day. I have tried this with small pasta like shells, but because the pasta actually cooks and absorbs the water you need substantial pasta like spaghetti or linguini so it doesn't get mushy.

PASTA WITH FRESH TOMATOES AND CHICKEN
Elise Feiner

5 tablespoons olive oil
8 cloves garlic, crushed, divided
1 teaspoon finely chopped dried oregano, divided
2 teaspoons finely chopped dried basil, divided
6-8 fresh basil leaves if available, chopped
30 to 36 fresh Roma tomatoes, quartered and then cut in thirds or fourths
Salt and pepper to taste
2 pounds chicken breasts on the thin side, seasoned with salt and pepper

2 (14½ ounces) cans College Inn® Chicken Broth
2 (2.25 ounce) cans sliced black pitted olives, one drained, and one with juice
1½-2 pounds of pasta, I use "hats or orchiette"
4 teaspoons garlic salt
Freshly ground black pepper
1-2 (5 ounce) cans Hunt's® Tomato Paste
2 (15 ounce cans) Hunt's® Tomato Sauce
1 (14 ounce can) Hunt's® Diced Tomatoes
Grating cheese

If you divide this recipe in half, divide all ingredients except for the oil. You will need the full amount in both cases. If you are picky and don't like the little pieces of tomato skins in the sauce, you can blanch the tomatoes before cutting them. Heat a large pot of boiling water. Add the whole tomatoes and let stay in the water 2 to 3 minutes. Remove to a bowl of ice water. Gently peel the skins off the tomatoes, and then quarter them. After you quarter them, cut them in thirds or quarters.

Pour 3 tablespoons olive oil in a skillet on medium heat and sauté half of the crushed garlic in the oil along with 1 teaspoon basil and ½-teaspoon oregano. Add the tomatoes, a cup at a time, to the skillet. Once all the tomatoes are in the pan, allow them to reduce by a fourth. Add 4 teaspoons garlic salt and black pepper to taste. In a separate bowl mix the chicken breasts with the remaining oregano, basil and crushed garlic. Stir well to coat. In a separate pan, cook the chicken with remaining 2 tablespoon of oil. Cook until chicken is brown; remove to a dish and when cool, cut into cubes (size depending on your preference – they like them small in my house.) Deglaze the pan with a little of the chicken broth, saving any liquid that may be in the pan and set aside. **NOTE:** I find it much faster to brown the whole piece of chicken and then cut it into cubes but you can cube it first ad then brown it if you want to.

Once the tomato mixture has reduced, add the chicken cubes, remaining chicken broth and liquid from the pan, tomato paste, diced tomatoes, and juice from the olives to the pan and allow it to continue to cook for approximately 30 minutes. Add the cans of tomato sauce and fresh basil and cook another 30 minutes. Add the chopped olives to the sauce. Cook the pasta (rotelle, shells, gemelli, etc, something that holds the sauce) in boiling salted water. Drain well. Add the sauce and top with grating cheese. 8 servings

This is one of Lauren's favorite dishes; she and Sachi always request this when they're home from school!

PASTA A LA MARCO POLO
Katherine Avella

½ - s¾ cup olive oil
4-5 cloves of garlic, peeled and crushed
Salt and pepper to taste
1 pound of spaghetti, cooked according to package directions
1⅓ cups chopped walnuts

1 cup chopped black olives
⅔ cup chopped parsley
½ cup chopped pimentos
2 teaspoons chopped basil
Grating cheese if desired

Bring a pot of salted water to a boil to cook the spaghetti. **Chop everything ahead of time and set aside.** While the spaghetti is cooking and almost done, heat the oil in a small frying pan. Add the garlic and sauté for a few minutes; add salt and pepper. Remove from the heat. Drain the spaghetti, but save some of the pasta water to add to the spaghetti if they are too dry, or just remove the spaghetti with tongs keeping them a little damp. Add the oil garlic mixture. Add remaining ingredients to the spaghetti. Toss well. Top with grated cheese if desired.

This is a take off on a Julia Child recipe I think. Nanny made it with her own twist.

"Keeping scores of old scores and scars, getting even and one upping always makes you less than you are."

-Malcolm Stevenson Forbes

JIMMY'S MACARONI AND BROCCOLI
Vincent DeClementi

1 head broccoli flowerets
½ - ¾ cup olive oil
4 cloves garlic, peeled and sliced thinly or crushed
Salt and pepper

Grating cheese
1 pound pasta (ziti, shells, bowties)
Water to boil pasta (salted)

Wash broccoli and cut up into small flowerets. Let dry. Bring salted water to a boil. Throw in the pasta of your choice. While the pasta is cooking, heat the oil in a large frying pan. Add the garlic, and as soon as it starts to sizzle, throw in the broccoli. Add a little salt and pepper to taste. Cook for about 5 to 7 minutes until the broccoli is soft but not mushy. When pasta is cooked, strain but leave a little water. Toss with the broccoli, and add grating cheese to taste. Add extra pasta water if too dry. Serve immediately. Serves 4 to 6.

Uncle Jimmy makes his macaroni and broccoli this way. I really like it, but also like the way Nanny makes it, which is a little soupier (the way Grandpa always liked it). This is a nice change and much quicker to do.

L-R: Dorothy and Jimmy DeClementi, Lauren and Jeffrey Feiner
Jimmy is one of those you call truly great men, and you know what's
behind all great men, in this case Dottie.

Eddie Schwendemann holding Lauren Feiner
What a kind and gentle man...so greatly missed!

FRAN'S MACARONI WITH BROCCOLI
Frances Zierler

1 pound of your favorite macaroni (ziti, hats, shells etc)
2 bags fresh broccoli floweret's, cut in smaller pieces
½ - ¾ cup olive oil
4-5 cloves garlic, crushed

Salt and pepper to taste
1 bag shredded white cheddar cheese
Grating Cheese

Put up a large pot of salted water to cook the macaroni. Throw in the macaroni and the broccoli at the same time if you like the broccoli soft. If you prefer the broccoli a little less soft, throw the broccoli in with the pasta when it is at the halfway point in its cooking time. In the meanwhile, heat the olive oil in a small pan, add the garlic and let it sauté on low so the garlic doesn't burn but the oil gets the garlic flavor. Add salt and pepper to taste. Just cook for a few minutes. Drain the pasta and broccoli mix, but don't drain it too well. Reserve a little of the water as you drain it into a separate pot in case you need to add more liquid to the pasta if it is too dry for your taste. Add the pasta/broccoli mix to the heated garlic and oil. Quickly stir in cheddar and grating cheeses.

This is Aunt Fran's version. The cheddar cheese adds a great touch to the dish!

LINGUINI WITH ANCHOVIES
Josephine Mainella

½ - ¾ cup vegetable oil
Anchovy fillets 2-3 small cans depending on your taste
2 tablespoons capers
¼ cup fresh parsley, chopped fine
4 cloves garlic, peeled and crushed

Red pepper flakes, optional
Freshly ground black pepper to taste
Approximately 2 cups water
1 pound pasta of your choice (linguini is my choice)

Heat a large pot of lightly salted water. Cook pasta according to directions. Drain, saving some of the water if you want to add more to the sauce. While pasta is cooking, make the sauce. In a medium saucepan, heat the oil; add in the garlic, capers, and anchovies and cook for about 5 minutes. The anchovies will dissolve. Add in the parsley, black pepper, and red pepper flakes if desired. Add about 2 cups of tap water to the oil mixture. Let simmer about 15 minutes. Toss with the cooked pasta. Add more water from the pasta water if too dry.

This is Aunt Fife's recipe. For almost her whole life, my mother did all the cooking in the house, and Aunt Fifi did the baking and made the pasta. In her old age, she's 897 now; she's became the chief cook and bottle washer, taking care of my mother until my mother's death at 89. Aunt Fifi now lives with us!

PASTINA
Katherine Avella

½ pound pastina
½ stick butter at room temperature

¼ cup grating cheese
½ pound ricotta (optional)

Cook the pastina according to package direction. Drain but don't drain too well, let some water remain in another pot in case the pastina is too dry. Mix the pastina with the butter and grated cheese, until the butter melts and it's well blended. If too dry just add a little of the hot pasta water. Variations: add the ricotta to the above mix; another variation is to boil the pastina in 4 cups of chicken broth. Add the butter and cheese and serve immediately. This is more of a soup dish.

This dish reminds me of Friday nights in the days when you couldn't have meat on Friday. Since I hated fish, I lived on this! It also reminds me of being a little child and staying home from school when I was sick; my mother would make this to make me feel better. It's a perfect dish for little children. You can easily cut the recipe in half because a LITTLE pastina makes a LOT of pasta.

ORZO WITH MUSHROOMS
Barbara Schwartz

1 cup orzo
1 stick butter
½ pound fresh mushrooms sliced

1 small onion, peeled and diced
½ teaspoon salt
⅛ teaspoon black pepper

Prepare orzo according to package directions by boiling in a pot of salted water. While orzo is cooking, melt the butter in a medium frying pan. Sauté the onions until they are golden but not yet brown. Add the mushrooms, salt and pepper. Cook until tender about 10 minutes. Drain the orzo. Toss the cooked orzo with the mushroom mixture. Sprinkle with grating cheese if desired.

COUSCOUS
Elise Feiner

1 tablespoon canola or vegetable oil
3 tablespoons butter
1 can (13¾ or 14 ½ ounce) College Inn Chicken Broth
1 to 1½ cups heavy cream
½ cup chopped scallions

1 (10 ounce) box Near East® Couscous (plain)
1 can (4 ounces) mushroom slices or
2-3 Roma tomatoes cut in tiny cubes
Salt and freshly ground black pepper
¼ cup grated cheese or more to taste

In a medium saucepan, combine the oil, butter, cream, chicken broth, and scallions, and bring to a boil. Reduce to a simmer. Stir in the mushrooms or tomatoes and couscous and cover the pan. Remove the pan from the heat and let stand for 5 minutes. When the couscous has absorbed all the liquid, fluff it with a fork, and add the salt, pepper, and grated cheese. Serve warm. 4 to 6 servings

LINGUINI WITH PESTO AND VEGETABLES
Elise Feiner

6 medium red potatoes, unpeeled and cubed or red baby
new potatoes (about 12, quartered)
1 pound of linguine or pasta of your choice (I like bows)
2 cups frozen baby peas
6 tablespoons olive oil
2 cups pesto sauce (see recipe index for Maria Trainor's
Pesto Sauce) or store bought

½ cup grating cheese
1 small onion, peeled and diced
1 small can of mushroom slices
4 tablespoons Pignoli nuts
Grating cheese for the top

Cook the peas according to the package directions. In a large skillet, heat the olive oil. Add the onions and sauté until golden. Add the cooked peas and mushrooms and cook until well heated. Remove from heat. Bring the potatoes to a boil in lightly salted water, and cook for about 13 to 15 minutes until done. At the same time, have a pot of salted water boiling to cook the linguine, trying to time them to be done at the same time as the potatoes. Drain the potatoes and the linguine. Place in a large bowl or serving platter. Add the pesto sauce. Add the peas and mushrooms mixture. Top with a little more grating cheese, and the pine nuts. Mix well. You can also add grilled chicken to this mix if you like.

I found the basic recipe for this in a magazine and added the onions, mushroom and chicken, but I use Maria Trainor's pesto recipe, it's the best!

L-R: Johann Gigliotti, Charlene Koury, Felicia and Eileen Furino, Elise Feiner, Maria and Katherine "Kate" Trainor, Cindy Circelli...wonderful friends! There is nothing better in this world than your mother and your girlfriends!!!

ORIENTAL SPAGHETTI
Cyndi Koury

1 pound of spaghetti
1 whole chicken breast
1 chicken bouillon cube
¾ cup boiling water
3 teaspoons corn starch
7 tablespoons soy sauce

1 teaspoon ginger
1½ teaspoons oil
3 teaspoons garlic powder
Chopped broccoli flowerets
Chopped carrots, chopped mushrooms
1 can water chestnuts

While cooking 1 pound of spaghetti or spaghettini according to package directions, do the following:

In a small bowl, combine 1 whole chicken breast, boned and skinned and cut into ½-inch cubes, 2 tablespoons soy sauce, 1 teaspoon ginger, 1 teaspoon garlic powder. Let stand for 30 minutes. Dissolve 1 chicken bouillon cube in ¾-cup boiling water and add 3 teaspoons cornstarch, and 5 tablespoons soy sauce. Heat 1½ tablespoons of oil in a large skillet. Add 2 teaspoon garlic powder, brown, and then add chopped broccoli (floweret's), chopped carrots, 1 can water chestnuts. Stir fry for 3 to 4 minutes over high heat until tender. Remove with a slotted spoon and set aside. Add the chicken to the skillet; stir fry for 2 minutes until cooked. Add the chicken bouillon to the chicken, boil stirring until it thickens. Add broccoli mix and add chopped mushrooms and stir until heated through. Add this mixture to cooked spaghetti while still hot. Toss and serve.

Cyndi Koury gave me this recipe. I haven't tried it yet but she says it's delicious.

TAGLIATELLE MAINELLA
Clementina Mainella, Josephine Mainella, and Katherine Avella

1½ - 1¾ cups white flour
1 cup semolina flour
½ teaspoon salt

1 cup eggs (measure as many as you need to fill a measuring cup)
1½ tablespoons oil

Have lots of brown grocery bags ready as you will lay the dough on these as you process it.

In the Kitchen Aid with the dough hook, add the dry ingredients and mix for a minute or two. Slowly add the eggs and the oil. Process until a smooth dough forms. If it is too wet slowly add another ¼ of a cup of Semolina flour. Add more flour if needed but do not make too dry.

Knead for a few minutes on a lightly floured board. Cut dough in half and each half into four to 5 pieces. Cover with Saran Wrap® and let dough sit for about 30 minutes. Start to process the dough in the Atlas pasta machine on the **# 1 SETTING**. Do each piece three times. Place on brown bags in a single layer. Starting with the first batch you did, turn the machine to **#2**, and do each piece three times again. You can cut the pieces if they get too long. Then move the machine to **#4** AND process each piece three times. Then move to **#5** and process TWO times. Change to the Tagliatelle cutter and cut all the pieces. You can also cut them manually with a pastry wheel cutter. Let dry on the brown bags. Each pound of fresh pasta equals two pounds of store bought pasta.

This recipe has been handed down from generation to generation. This is my grandmother's recipe and her original recipe calls for a half an egg shell full of oil. Nanny and Aunt Fifi have modernized and standardized the recipe through the years. I can remember as a kid, making them when you still had to turn the machine by hand. Now the machines have electric motors. I remember shuttling the pasta back and forth to be processed and the fun of cutting them with the pasta wheel. Today it is much easier to make and tastes just as delicious; once you taste the homemade pasta you'll never want store bought again! Now, my daughter Lauren helps me...

"Generation to Generation"...
L-R: Elise Feiner, Katherine Avella, Lauren Feiner, Josephine Mainella

*"When I stopped seeing my mother with the eyes of a child,
I saw the woman who helped me give birth to myself."*

-Nancy Friday

PASTA IN A POT
Nancy Barfield

1½ pounds of macaroni; any kind that is on sale, elbow, bows, shells, (or you can mix any leftover pasta)
2 large jars of sauce; I like to get one Marinara and one with meat

1 large container of sour cream
1 large package of mozzarella cheese, shredded
1 large package of provolone cheese

When making the sauce I like to add ground beef, onions, mushrooms, etc. Get a large round pot (make sure it's ovenproof; something you would cook macaroni or soup in). Make or heat your sauce. Cook the pasta in lightly salted water according to package directions. Butter the sides and bottom of your pan. Put in some pasta, then some sauce so that it cover the pasta, spread some sour cream, then mozzarella cheese, provolone cheese and repeat until you fill up the whole pot. Bake at 375° for about 45 minutes, or until mixture is heated through and the cheese on the top is golden brown.

My good friend Nancy Barfield gave me this recipe. It's great if you're having a crowd and you're on a limited budget. It's also a wonderful way to get rid of all those little leftover bags of uncooked pasta that we all have in our closets.

LINGUINI IN RED CLAM SAUCE
Katherine Avella and Josephine Mainella

1 pound of linguini or spaghetti
2 cans of whole baby clams or chopped clams depending on your preference.
2-3 tablespoons of oil
Salt and pepper to taste
6-9 Anchovy fillets (optional)
3 tablespoon fresh parsley

Half a medium onion, peeled and finely chopped
6-8 cloves of garlic, peeled and crushed
1 large can crushed tomatoes
1 (2 pounds 5 ounce) can whole peeled tomatoes (crush with your fingers)
3 tablespoons basil
Crushed red pepper (optional)

Heat a pot of boiling, salted water for the linguini when you make the sauce. Start the sauce when you heat the water for the linguini because this takes a little longer than the white clam sauce because the tomato has to cook. In a medium saucepan, heat the oil. Add the onions and sauté until soft but not brown. Add the garlic. Add the juice from the cans of clams (set the clams aside for now), anchovies, salt and pepper, parsley. Let the sauce cook over medium heat for about 10 minutes. Add the tomatoes and basil. Let simmer for about 30 minutes, and then keep on low. Put the **CLAMS** in **JUST** before the spaghetti are finished cooking or they will get rubbery (just heat them in the hot sauce for a few minutes. **IMPORTANT**: Do not strain the spaghetti well, use tongs to take the spaghetti out of the pot because you want the spaghetti moist as there is not a large amount of sauce here. If you absolutely must strain the spaghetti, put the colander over a pot so that you reserve some water. This way if the sauce is too dry you can add some of this water to the linguini. Serves 4.

If you prefer a stronger taste of clams, you can also buy bottle clam juice and add a little more of this to the sauce. You can also use fresh clams and steam them to serve on the side of the plate, just spoon some of the liquid over them after they are steamed. When you steam them, throw in a lot of peeled garlic, fresh parsley, and olive oil to the water you are using to steam them in to give them flavor. Another variation of linguini in clam sauce...just depends on your preference.

L-R: Flo Avella, Josephine Mainella, and Katherine Avella

LINGUINI WITH WHITE CLAM SAUCE
Katherine Avella and Josephine Mainella

1 pound of linguini or spaghetti if you prefer
2 cans of whole baby clams or chopped clams depending on your preference.
½ - ¾ cup of oil
1 tablespoon capers
Salt and pepper to taste

6-9 Anchovy fillets (optional)
3 tablespoon fresh parsley
Half of a medium onion, peeled and finely chopped
6-8 cloves of garlic, peeled and crushed
Water
1 cup dry white wine such as a Pinot Grigio (optional)

Heat a pot of boiling, salted water for the linguini when you start to make the sauce. Throw in the linguini while the sauce is cooking. In a medium saucepan, heat the oil. Add the onions and sauté until soft but not brown. Add the garlic. Add the juice from the cans of clams (set the clams aside for now), anchovies, capers, salt and pepper, and parsley, and wine if desired. Let cook over medium heat for about 10 minutes. Add about 1 cup of water to the oil mixture. Keep on low. Put the **CLAMS** in **JUST** before the spaghetti are finished cooking or they will get rubbery (just heat them in the hot oil for a few minutes. **IMPORTANT**: Do not strain the spaghetti well, use tongs to take the spaghetti out of the pot because you want the spaghetti moist as there is not a large amount of sauce here. If you absolutely must strain the spaghetti, put the colander over a pot so that you reserve some water. This way if the sauce is too dry you can add some of this water to the linguini. Serves 4.

If you prefer a stronger taste of clams, you can also buy bottle clam juice and add a little more of this to the sauce. You can also use fresh clams and steam them to serve on the side of the plate, just spoon some of the liquid over them after they are steamed. When you steam them, throw in a lot of peeled garlic, fresh parsley, and olive oil to the water you are using to steam them in to give them flavor.

This is a meal that my boys and Marc love. I'm not a clam eater but they smell delicious! Serve with crispy garlic bread and a salad and you have a meal.

"My boys"
L-R: Jeffrey, Steven, Elise and David Feiner

PASTA WITH ANCHOVIES
Jean Glorius

⅓ cup oil from 2 ounce can of flat anchovies and vegetable oil
⅓ cup Italian cured olives, pitted and cut in half
Freshly ground black pepper to taste
1 pound pasta of your choice (spaghetti, linguine, capellini)
3 cloves garlic, peeled and left whole

6-8 anchovy fillets or more to taste
1½ cup canned plum tomatoes, drained
¼ cup fresh parsley, chopped fine

Heat a large pot of lightly salted water to cook the pasta. When you drain the pasta retain a little of the cooking water in case the pasta is too dry. Cook according to the pasta directions. While they are cooking, make the sauce. Heat the oil in a saucepan, add the whole garlic cloves, cook for a few minutes and then discard the cloves. Add the anchovies and simmer on low until they dissolve. Add the tomatoes and olives and simmer an additional 5 to 8 minutes. Add the black pepper and parsley. Cover and simmer for 20 minutes. Toss sauce over cooked pasta. Add additional water if too dry. Serves 4.

PASTA FAGIOLI
Patricia Muhlon

1 small can Progresso® Cannellini Beans
2 tablespoons olive oil
2 stalks celery; diced
1 medium onion; diced
2 cloves garlic, peeled and sliced
3 fresh plum tomatoes; diced

Fresh basil cut in a chiffonade
Salt and pepper to taste
Dash crushed red pepper (optional)
8 ounces cooked Ditalini pasta (cooked according to package directions)

Sauté celery and onions until soft (not brown). Throw in garlic and basil. Toss in freshly diced tomatoes. Add entire can of beans, including liquid. Add salt, pepper and crushed red pepper to taste. Cook for 20 to 30 minutes, add cooked pasta. Cook pasta; save a little of the cooking water when draining the pasta. If too dry add a little of the cooking water. Recipe can be doubled, tripled, etc. Serves 2.

Cousin Nick Sanito sent this recipe from his sister-in-law. He says it's the best! Her comments are "Serve with freshly grated parmesan cheese and crusty Italian bread. Delicioussssssssssss!"

L-R: Marc Feiner and Nicky Sanito, Jr. fishing in Orlando, Florida

PASTA DOUGH
Elise Feiner

2⅓ cup all purpose flour (for better pasta, use 1⅓ cup all purpose flour and 1 cup semolina flour))
2 large eggs

1 tablespoons olive oil
½ teaspoon salt
⅓ cup water or heavy cream

This dough is designed for manual pasta machines. Mix 2 cups of flour and salt in a bowl, reserve ⅓ cup for later. Make a well in the center. Mix eggs, olive oil, and water and pour into well. Stir flour into egg mixture until dough forms into a ball. Turn out onto floured surface and knead for about 10 minutes, adding extra flour if too moist. Knead until dough is smooth and elastic. Cover with towel and rest for 30 minutes. Cut into 4 portions, keep pieces covered until used. Get out your machine and set dial on widest setting (#1 on the Atlas® machine). Flatten dough ball and run through rollers several times until smooth (you may add a bit of flour here too). Move rollers to next setting and roll again once. Continue to roll until pasta is the proper thickness (#5 or 6 on the Atlas). You may cut sheet in half if it's too long. Continue with other pieces and then put the finished sheet aside to dry for about 3 minutes. Attach desired pasta cutters and run the sheets through. You can use right away or spread out the pasta to dry overnight and then freeze extra. To cook, drop into large pot of boiling water with a bit of salt and oil. Cook until al dente, which should only take about 2 minutes for fresh. A tip - be sure the dough is fairly dry; otherwise it won't cut into separate strands. You can substitute heavy cream for the ⅓ cup water for richer pasta. This is great for fettuccini Alfredo.

PASTA AND CAULIFLOWER
Elise Feiner

4 cups of marinara sauce (see index)
1 large head of cauliflower (cut into flowerets, not too small)
Salt and pepper to taste

½ to 1 cup grated cheese
1 pound of the pasta of your choice (I like the small shells best, or Ditalini but it's up to you)

Place a pot of lightly salted water up to boil the pasta in. Cut the cauliflower into flowerets, but don't make them too small or they become invisible in the sauce. Place the cauliflower in another pot of lightly salted water and bring to a boil. Reduce the heat; simmer for about 10 minutes or until the cauliflower is tender. In the meantime, heat the marinara sauce. When the cauliflower has been cooking about 8 minutes, cook your pasta.   Drain the cauliflower well, and add to the marinara sauce. Season with salt and pepper. Drain the pasta, and coat with the cauliflower and tomato sauce. Add the grating cheese. Enjoy!

If you have extra sauce leftover, take two cans of string beans, peel 2 potatoes, cube and boil in lightly salted water, drain. Add to the string beans, and leftover sauce and you have another side dish. You can serve it hot of cold.

This dish reminds me of my best friend in elementary school, Pat Tromba's grandmother. She would always make this for dinner on Friday nights. I can remember her standing in her kitchen stirring this big pot with the pasta and cauliflower. I had never eaten it before, but loved it the first time I tasted it.

Friends since elementary school...Then...
L-R: Angela Sarcia, Meryl Redner, Linda Gebhart, Elise Avella, Pat Cooke,
Caroline Vecchione, Allyson Knowles, and Susan Alexander

Now...
Back Row L-R: Elise Avella Feiner, Susan Alexander Marquino, Patricia Tromba Werner
Front L-R: Angela Sarcia Murphy, Linda Gebhart Smart, David Di John, M.D. still together after all these years!
David and I have been friends the longest...since kindergarten!

PASTA E PISELLI (PASTA AND PEAS)
Katherine Avella

3 tablespoons olive oil
3 cloves of garlic, peeled and crushed
1 large onion, peeled and finely diced
2 (15 ounce) cans peas, I like the LeSueur Early (Baby)
Peas, don't drain
2 bags (2.25 ounce) baby carrots cut into thin rounds
1 (8 ounce) box fresh mushrooms or a can of mushrooms,
drained (optional)

4-5 (13¾ or 14 ounce) cans chicken broth, divided
½ teaspoon dried oregano
½ teaspoon dried basil
1½ cups grating cheese (or more to taste)
Salt and pepper to taste
1 pound of pasta (I suggest small shells or small bows,
tubetti, or ditalini)
Fresh chopped basil (optional)

In a medium saucepan over moderate heat, heat the olive oil. Add the onions, carrots and mushrooms, and cook until softened and starting to get a golden color. Add the garlic and cook a few more minutes. Add the cans of peas, (don't drain), 3 cans of the chicken broth, oregano, basil, salt and pepper; bring to a boil. Reduce the heat and lower to a simmer for about 20 minutes. In the meantime, cook the pasta in lightly salted water according to the package directions. Drain well (but reserve some of the pasta water in case mix is too dry). In a large serving bowl, add the pasta to the pea sauce. I usually add the fourth and fifth cans of broth only if necessary because this pasta tends to absorb liquid quickly. Add the grating cheese. Add a little water if too dry. Pass around fresh basil if you have any and additional grating cheese. If you don't have chicken broth handy you can just use additional water. Serves 6.

My mother made pasta with everything; potatoes, peas, beans, lentils, clams etc. This is one that as I kid I never cared for, but as an adult, I love it.

The Avella's 1954
Clockwise from the right:
Samuel holding Elise, Joseph, Philip and Katie
Alabama Avenue

MACARONI AND CHEESE ITALIA
Elise Feiner

1 pound of elbow or rotelle macaroni
8 tablespoons butter
8 tablespoons Wondra® flour
4 cups milk
2 cups heavy cream
1 large mozzarella cut in small cubes
1 cup Parmesan cheese

1 cup sharp cheddar cheese grated
½ small onion, peeled and grated
2 tablespoons Worcestershire sauce
2 teaspoons salt
Freshly grated black pepper
½ cup plain breadcrumbs mixed with ¼ cup parmesan
cheese for the topping

Prepare the macaroni according to the package directions but cook a few minutes less than suggested. Rinse and drain. In a large sauce pan, melt the butter. Stir in the flour and a little bit of the milk so it doesn't get lumpy. Continue adding the milk to keep it smooth. Add remaining milk and cream. Add the onion, Worcestershire sauce, salt and pepper. Stir in the parmesan cheese and the cheddar cheese. In a large, well greased casserole, pour in the sauce; add the cooked macaroni. Stir in the mozzarella cheese. Sprinkle with the breadcrumb mix. Bake at 350° for about 45 minutes. Serves 8.

PASTA AND LENTILS
Katherine Avella

1 large onion, peeled and chopped in small pieces
3 stalks of celery, diced in small pieces, use stems and leaves
4-5 tablespoons olive oil
4 cloves of garlic, peeled and crushed
1 (2 pound 3 ounce) can of plum tomatoes, (break up with your fingers if you like it chunky or put in blender if you like it smooth)
1 (15 ounce) can of Hunt's® Tomato sauce

6 fresh basil leaves, washed and cut fine
2 teaspoons dried basil
1 teaspoon dried oregano
1 teaspoon salt
¼ teaspoon black pepper
2 cans of Progresso® Lentil Soup or 1 bag of dried lentils cooked according to package directions
1 pound spaghetti, broken into 1 inch pieces
Parmesan Cheese

In a large saucepan, heat the olive oil. Add the onions, celery, and garlic and cook over medium heat for about 7 minutes to soften. Add the tomatoes, tomato sauce, salt, pepper, fresh and dried basil, oregano and salt and pepper. Let simmer on low heat for about 30 to 35 minutes. Add the 2 cans of lentils with their liquid and let cook together for another 15 minutes. Set aside. Boil a large pot of salted water and cook the spaghetti according to package directions. Drain the pasta over a pot retaining the boiling liquid. (You may need to add some of this water to the tomato mixture if too dry). Add the pasta to the tomato mix. Add the pasta water if necessary. Let stand 5 minutes. Top with grated parmesan cheese. You can also do this with dried lentils; cook according to package directions; reserve the liquid you use to cook the beans. Serves 4 to 6.

This is another great dish, especially on a cold winter's night. A good loaf of bread and a salad, a good bottle of wine and you're set!

L-R: Philip Avella Jr. Grandpa, Sam Avella, Michael Avella,
Nanny, Katherine Avella, Philip Avella Sr. in Staten Island, N.Y.

SPICY TORTELLINI
Marie Golden

1 jar Alfredo sauce or homemade (see index for tortellini Alfredo)

1 jar salsa (medium) or your choice
1 pound tortellini, cheese-filled; cooked as directed

In a medium saucepan, heat the alfredo sauce on low-medium heat. Add the salsa, and heat through. Cook tortellini according to package directions. Top with the sauce mix. Serves 4 to 6.

This is a quick and easy recipe from my friend and hairdresser Marie. She said it's great if you have unexpected company.

FRESH TOMATO AND MOZZARELLA PASTA
Maria Trainor

A few tablespoons of olive oil
5-7 cloves of garlic, peeled and crushed
4-5 pounds of plum tomatoes
Salt and pepper to taste
About 20 leaves of fresh basil cut in a chiffonade

3-4 balls of fresh mozzarella (in water), cut in tiny cubes
About 1 cup of grated cheese or more to your taste
1 pound of pasta (something with substance and grooves like a penne rigati)

Cut the tomatoes in half lengthwise. Then, lay the flat side down, cut in half again and then thirds. In a large deep frying pan, heat the oil and add the garlic. As soon as it starts to sizzle, add the tomatoes. Cook over high heat for about 5 minutes and then lower and let cook for about 40 minutes. Add salt and pepper to taste. In the meantime, have a pot of salted water ready to boil for the pasta. When the tomatoes have cooked about 25 minutes throw in the pasta and cook to your liking. Drain well. Return to the pot for a few minutes to dry up any excess water. Add to the tomatoes in the frying pan. Add in the basil and fresh mozzarella cubes. Mix well. Add grated cheese to your taste and top with a good amount of grated cheese. Serve immediately.

Maria is the most incredible cook, everything she makes is fabulous! Tim always says that she and I never know when to stop cooking and enjoy ourselves...but, that's how we do enjoy ourselves!

L-R: Tim and Maria Trainor, Cindy and Dave Circelli

SPAGHETTI PIE
Elise Feiner

1 teaspoon salt
½ pound dried spaghetti
2 teaspoons olive oil, plus 1 tablespoon
1 cup Marinara sauce (see recipe index, Avella's Marinara Sauce)
½ cup chopped green bell pepper
2 teaspoons minced garlic
1 teaspoon Italian seasoning

1½ cups cubed mozzarella (4 ounces)
½ cup chopped black olives, optional
4 ounces button mushrooms, wiped clean and thinly sliced
4 large eggs
½ cup milk
¾ cup sliced pepperoni
½ cup grated Parmesan

Bring a large pot of water to a boil over high heat. Add salt and spaghetti and stir to combine. Return to a boil, reduce heat to a low boil and cook until al dente, about 10 minutes. Drain spaghetti. Return to the pot and toss with 2 teaspoons olive oil and set aside. Preheat the oven to 375°. Lightly grease a 2-quart casserole dish with the remaining olive oil and set aside.

In a large mixing bowl combine the spaghetti, marinara sauce, bell pepper, garlic, Italian seasoning, and mozzarella and toss to mix well. Add chopped black olives and mushrooms, and mix to combine. In a separate bowl, whisk the eggs and milk. Transfer the spaghetti mixture to the prepared dish and pour the egg mixture over the top. Arrange the sliced pepperoni in an even layer over the top, and sprinkle with Parmesan. Bake until bubbly and golden brown on top, 20 to 25 minutes. Remove from the oven and let sit for 5 minutes before serving. Serves 6.

PASTA A LA PUTTANESCA
Elise Feiner

¼ cup extra-virgin olive oil
1 cup finely chopped onion
1 teaspoon minced shallots
6-8 cloves garlic, peeled and crushed
½ teaspoon dried oregano
½ teaspoon dried basil
2 tablespoons Anchovy fillets, minced
2 tablespoons drained capers
1 cup pitted Kalamata or Gaeta olives; halved

2 (28-ounce) cans Roma plum tomatoes, broken into
pieces, with juice
2 tablespoons tomato paste
2 (14 ounce) cans Hunt's® diced tomatoes
½ cup dry white wine
¼ cup fresh clam juice (optional)
2 cups plum tomato, medium diced
1 pound of pasta of your choice, linguine, spaghetti, penne
Salt and pepper to taste

In a large sauté pan heat the olive oil over medium high heat. Add the onion and shallots and sauté until soft and lightly caramelized, about 6 minutes. Add the garlic and cook an additional 2 minutes. Add the oregano, basil, and anchovy fillets. Sweat about 30 seconds, until anchovies begin to break down. Add capers and olives and sauté 1 minute. Deglaze the pan with white wine, add clam juice, let reduce by ⅓. Add the plum tomatoes and tomato paste and mix well. Add salt and pepper to taste **(don't forget the olives, anchovies and capers are very salty so be careful with the salt.** Cook pasta according to package directions; drain. Add cooked pasta to puttanesca sauce and toss well.

In Naples, it is said that the "ladies of the night" invented this sauce to lure their customers in. It was said that no one could resist the smell of this sauce when it was cooking

L-R: David, Jeffrey, Elise, Marc, Lauren and Steven Feiner

PASTA SFUZZI
Elise Feiner

4 tablespoons vegetable oil
2 eggplants, peeled and cubed
3 large onions, peeled and thinly sliced
12 cloves of garlic, peeled and put through the garlic press
Black pepper and salt or garlic salt to taste
Fresh basil, chopped
2 cups grated cheese
½ cup toasted breadcrumbs (optional)

Tomato sauce (marinara or regular meat sauce is fine - see
recipe index for Avella's Marinara Sauce or Avella-Mainella
Famous Gravy)
2 pound ziti pasta
2 large mozzarella or 5-6 small little fresh mozzarellas, cut
in very tiny cubes

Have tomato sauce made and heated in a separate pan. In a large frying pan, heat the oil. Add the onions and start to brown them. When golden, add the garlic, and when it starts to sizzle add the cubed eggplant, salt and pepper to taste. As the eggplant softens, it will start to absorb the oil and get a little dry. Add a few ladles of the tomato sauce to prevent it from burning. Cover and let simmer on a low flame until soft, but not mushy. Add breadcrumbs if desired.   Bring a pot of salted water to a boil. Cook the ziti. Drain well. Add the **HOT** eggplant mix, and as much tomato sauce as you prefer. Add the mozzarella, grating cheese and basil. Serve immediately. Serves 6.

I ate this at Sfuzzi's restaurant in Manhattan. I made this recipe up and it's very close. This is delicious and makes a great luncheon dish or a light supper when served with a salad and some nice crusty Italian bread. You can easily cut this in half. You can easily bake the eggplant as well. Place the cubes on a cookie sheet in a single layer with 3 tablespoons olive oil and toss. Bake at 400° for about 25 minutes, stir occasionally. You can also add ricotta to this dish if you'd like.

PASTA PATTATE (PASTA WITH POTATOES)
Katherine Avella

1 large onion, peeled and chopped in small pieces
3 stalks of celery, diced in small pieces, use stems and leaves
4-5 tablespoons olive oil
4 cloves of garlic, peeled and crushed
2 (2 pound 3 ounce) can of plum tomatoes, (break up with your fingers if you like it chunky or put in blender if you like it smooth)
1 (15 ounce) can of Hunt's® Tomato sauce

6 fresh basil leaves, washed and cut fine
2 teaspoons dried basil
1 teaspoon dried oregano
1 teaspoon salt
¼ teaspoon black pepper
5-6 potatoes, peeled and cubed
1 pound ditalini
Parmesan Cheese

In a large saucepan, heat the olive oil. Add the onions, celery, and garlic and cook over medium heat for about 7 minutes to soften. Add the tomatoes, tomato sauce, salt, pepper, fresh and dried basil, oregano and salt and pepper. Let simmer on low heat for about 30 to 35 minutes. In a small pot, parboil the cubed potatoes until they are almost done, drain; add to the tomatoes and let cook together for another 15 minutes. Set aside. Boil a large pot of salted water and cook the ditalini according to package directions. Drain the pasta over a pot retaining the boiling liquid. (You may need to add some of this water to the tomato mixture if too dry). Add the pasta to the tomato mix. Add the pasta water if necessary. Let stand 5 minutes. Top with grated parmesan cheese. Serves 4 to 6.

This is another of Nanny's wonderful pasta dishes. It's great with a loaf of crusty bread and a salad.

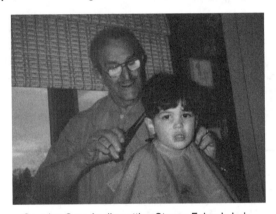

Grandpa Sam Avella cutting Steven Feiner's hair

SQUID CACCIATORE WITH LINGUINI
Josephine Mainella

2 pounds whole cleaned squid
¼ cup olive oil
1 cup finely chopped onion
1 clove garlic, finely chopped
½ teaspoon dried oregano
1 tablespoon fresh chopped basil

½ teaspoon salt, or more to taste
Freshly ground black pepper to taste
1½ cups canned plum tomatoes, partially drained and crushed
¼ cup dry red wine
½ pound (8 ounces) freshly cooked linguini or spaghetti

Cut squid into bite sized pieces. Rinse and dry with paper towels. Heat the oil in a large skillet, add the squid and cook over moderate heat for 3 to 4 minutes. The squid will give off some liquid. Add the onion, garlic, oregano, basil, salt and pepper, and cook for additional 3 to 4 minutes. Add tomatoes and wine bring to a boil, cover, lower the heat and simmer for 10 minutes. Do not overcook or the squid will be rubbery. Correct seasonings. Serve over well-drained linguini. Grind a little more black pepper over the top just before serving. Serve 4 as a first course.

"Nobody can do for little children what grandparents do. Grandparents sort of sprinkle stardust over the lives of little children."
-Alex Haley

PASTICHO
Peggy Spirakis

Meat Sauce Mix:

1 tablespoon butter
1 medium onion, peeled and grated
1 pound lean ground chuck
1 teaspoon salt
¼ teaspoon freshly ground black pepper
¼ teaspoon nutmeg

¼ teaspoon cinnamon
½ cup white wine
¼ cup tomato sauce
½ cup boiling water
¼ cup Parmesan or Romano cheese
1 cup plain breadcrumbs

In a large frying pan, sauté the onions in the butter for a few minutes, then add the chopped meat. Make sure you stir it while it is browning to separate the beef and avoid lumps; cook for about 10 minutes. Drain off any excess fat. Add the salt, pepper, nutmeg, cinnamon, and the white wine. Cover and simmer for about 8 minutes. Mix the tomato sauce with the boiling water; add to the meat mix. Cover and simmer for about 50 minutes. Stir in the breadcrumbs and cheese.

Macaroni:

½ pound elbow macaroni
3 quarts boiling, salted water
¼ cup butter

2 eggs, slightly beaten
½ cup Parmesan or Romano Cheese

Cook the elbows in boiling salted water according to package directions but decrease the cooking time by about 3 minutes. Drain well. In the same pot, add the butter and allow to melt. Add the elbows back into the pot. Add the eggs and cheese; mix well.

Cream Sauce:

¼ cup butter
4 tablespoon Wondra® flour
2 cups whole milk
2 cups heavy cream

¼ teaspoon nutmeg
1 teaspoon salt
3 whole eggs and three egg yolks
½ cup Parmesan or Romano cheese

To make the sauce, melt the butter in a large saucepan. Add the flour to about ½ cup of the milk and stir until smooth. Add to the butter mix; add the remaining milk, cream, nutmeg, and salt. Heat stirring constantly until the milk comes to a boil. Remove from the heat. Beat the eggs and yolks together. Add a little of the hot milk mixture to the eggs to temper them so they don't solidify. Then add the eggs to the milk/cream mixture. Mix well to keep smooth. Add the cheese and mix well.

Topping:

1 cup of grated cheese mixed with ½ cup plain dried breadcrumbs

1 bag of cheddar cheese, shredded (not part of topping mix)

Using a very large, deep casserole pan assemble in the following way: A layer of macaroni, ¼-cup topping mix, a layer of cream sauce, all the meat sauce ½ the cheddar cheese, ¼-cup topping mix, a layer of macaroni, remaining cream sauce, cheddar cheese and remaining topping mix. Bake at 375° for 45 minutes. Let stand until firm before serving. Freezes very well. May be done a day ahead. Serves 8.

A friend of Uncle Joe's of Greek descent who used to teach with him gave me several of these delicious Greek recipes.

"There is no love sincerer than the love of food."
-George Bernard Shaw

PASTA FAGIOLI A LA NANNY
Katherine Avella

1 large onion, peeled and chopped in small pieces
3 stalks of celery, diced in small pieces, use stems and leaves
4-5 tablespoons olive oil
4 cloves of garlic, peeled and crushed
1 (2 pound 3 ounce) can of plum tomatoes, (break up with your fingers if you like it chunky or put in blender if you like it smooth)
1 (15 ounce) can of Hunts Tomato sauce

1 (15 ½ ounces) can stewed tomatoes
6 fresh basil leaves, washed and cut fine
2 teaspoons dried basil
1 teaspoon dried oregano
1 teaspoon salt
¼ teaspoon black pepper
2 cans Cannellini beans, don't drain or rinse
1 pound ditalini
Parmesan Cheese

In a large saucepan, heat the olive oil. Add the onions, celery, and garlic and cook over medium heat for about 7 minutes to soften. Add the stewed and plum tomatoes, tomato sauce, salt, pepper, fresh and dried basil, oregano and salt and pepper. Let simmer on low heat for about 30-35 minutes. Add the 2 cans of beans with their liquid and let cook together for another 15 minutes. Set aside. Boil a large pot of salted water and cook the ditalini according to package directions. Drain the pasta over a pot retaining the boiling liquid. (You may need to add some of this water to the tomato mixture if too dry). Add the pasta to the tomato mix. Add the pasta water if necessary. Let stand 5 minutes. Top with grated parmesan cheese. Serves 4 to 6. You can also do this with dried beans - cook according to package directions; reserve the liquid you use to cook beans.

This was a staple food on Friday nights when I was growing up. If my mother wasn't making it, my Aunt Edith was. I always hated Friday's because it meant either fish or Pasta Fagioli, two of my least favorite things. Now, I love it. I made it just recently and spent the whole time cooking it laughing to myself thinking my Aunt Edith would never believe it, me making pasta fazoole as we called it! My son Steven loves this.

Steven Feiner's Graduation from The Trinity Pawling School - Class of 2000

NOODLE PUDDING
Edith Mainella

1 pound of noodles
4 eggs
½ stick of butter, melted
¾ cup milk
½ cup brown sugar

½ cup sugar
Raisins (optional)
1 large can of fruit cocktail, drained
Cinnamon

Cook noodles according to package directions in lightly salted boiling water. While the noodles are cooking, mix the butter, milk, sugars together. Drain the noodles. Mix with the butter/ sugar mixture. In a greased casserole, make a layer of noodles, a layer of fruit and raisins, and a layer of noodles. Sprinkle with cinnamon. Bake at 325 ° for 45 minutes to an hour.

I think this recipe came from Joan, a neighbor of my Aunt Edith's in East Hills. There are as many versions of Jewish kugel as there are of Italian pastas.

NONNY'S CANADIAN MACARONI
Fanny Christiano

1 pound ziti
2 pounds ground meat, (less if you want less)
2-3 tablespoons oil
Salt and pepper to taste

Basil or oregano (optional)
2 cans creamed corn
1 can tomato puree
1 pound of cheddar cheese (blocks, then shred it)

In a large frying pan, heat the oil; brown your ground meat. Fill a large pot with lightly salted water, and bring to a boil. Season the ground meat with salt and pepper or whatever spices your prefer. When the water comes to a boil, throw in the ziti. Don't let the macaroni boil for too long because they will cook a little more in the oven. Drain macaroni and pour them into a 13 x 9-inch baking dish that has been sprayed with PAM®. Then, add your ground meat to the dish, then your corn, tomato puree and finally top it all off with the cheddar (after you've shredded it). Bake in the oven at 350° for about an hour with some tin foil over it. Take it out a few minutes before its done and take off the tin foil. Place it bake in the oven to crisp and brown the top layer a little if desired. Wait until cool and serve! YAY!

This is one of my niece Nicole's favorite dishes from her other grandmother, Fannie Cristiano. Fannie worked in the cafeteria at the Masonic Home in Utica for years. Nicole says this is her favorite dish.

My very talented and beautiful niece Nicole Lynn Latini
Nicole is now an art teacher in Virginia...she did the drawings on the divider pages!

NANA'S KUGEL
Hannah Ostrow

1 pound broad egg noodles
6 eggs

¼ teaspoon freshly ground black pepper
½ tablespoon salt

Cook noodles according to package directions and drain. Add the six beaten eggs, salt and pepper and set aside.

Preheat oven to 475°. In a deep pan (9 x 13-inch) place 3 tablespoons of oil. Place pan in the oven and when the oil is hot, remove the pan. Spray the sides of the pan with PAM®. Add the noodle mixture to the pan. Reduce the heat to 350° and bake for 1 hour or until the top is brown and crisp. I sprinkle the top with a little seasoned salt before baking.

This is Barbara Schwartz's mother's noodle kugel. This can be used with meat. I love it because it is crunchy and slices firmly.

"Another appealing aspect to having grandparents is that they do help to give a sense of continuity—of his place in the world and in the generations. Not only do grandparents help him intellectually to comprehend that there are parents of parents, but they also aid him in understanding where he fits in the succession of things. Even a very young child can begin to feel a sense of rootedness and history."
- Lawrence Balter

NANNY NELLIE'S "THE BEST EVER" KUGEL
Nellie Reinisch

1 pound of Pennsylvania Dutch® Brand wide egg noodles
6 eggs beaten (add a dash of salt)
¾ cup sugar
2 Winesap apples (peeled and grated)
1 (8-ounce) can of crushed pineapple, drained (optional)
¾ cup white raisins (optional)
1 (16 ounce) container of sour cream

1 (8 ounce) package of Philadelphia® cream cheese
2 teaspoons vanilla extract
1 stick butter (melted)
1 (16-ounce) container of small curd cottage cheese or ricotta cheese
1-2 tablespoon orange juice
1 teaspoon cinnamon

Topping:
Graham cracker or cornflake crumbs, cinnamon sugar (I use the prepared one) or just make your own

Apricot jelly or jam (about ¼ cup melted down; heat over a very low flame or in the microwave for about 30 seconds)

In a large (9 x 13-inch) baking pan add half the stick of melted butter, and rock the pan to thoroughly coat the bottom and sides with the butter. In a large mixing bowl or Kitchen Aid mixer, mix the eggs, sugar, sour cream, cottage cheese or ricotta, cream cheese, vanilla, the rest of the butter, and orange juice, and cinnamon. Mix until well blended. Then add the grated apples, (pineapple and raisins, if desired). Mix just to blend. Cook the noodles in boiling salted water according to package directions, and drain thoroughly. Add to the prepared mix. Pour into the buttered pan. Brush with apricot jelly or jam sprinkle with the crumbs. Sprinkle on cinnamon sugar. Bake at 375° for 45 minutes to one hour or until nicely golden brown and set. Cut into squares to serve. Serves 8 to 10.

This is Nanny Nellie's recipe with a few very minor changes, but it is delicious. I switched to ricotta (the Italian in me?) because my family doesn't like the curds of the cottage cheese. I also added the apricot jam to the topping. This moist kugel is David's favorite holiday food. This is the kugel I always make and that people always want the recipe for. If you keep kosher, this is for a dairy meal.

SHIRLEY'S KUGEL
Shirley Flomenhoft

6 eggs, separated
½ pound dry cottage cheese
1 (8 ounce) container of sour cream
¼ pound (1 stick) butter

½ pound medium egg noodles
5 tablespoons sugar
2 teaspoons vanilla

Topping:
Graham cracker crumbs
¼ pound butter, melted

5 tablespoons sugar

Mix together the topping ingredients. Beat egg whites until stiff (set aside). Cook noodles and drain well, return to the pot. Add ¼-pound of butter to the noodles in the pot. Beat egg yolks. Add to the noodles. Add sugar, cottage cheese, sour cream, and vanilla. Mix well. Gently fold in egg whites. Pour into a greased glass 13 x 9 x 2-inch Pyrex® dish. Top with crumb mixture. Bake in a 350° oven for 45 minutes. Let cool then cut into squares. Serve with sour cream.

This is Aunt Shirley's favorite kugel recipe. She went through all of her recipes when we were in Florida and contributed several to this cookbook.

Aunt Shirley's Grandchildren, the
Weiner kids...
Clockwise from the top: Zach,
Hannah, Sarah and Rebecca

MOM MOM'S KUGEL
Betty Feiner

1 stick margarine, melted
1 pound egg noodles (cook in lightly salted water)
6 eggs separated (beat the whites until stiff)
¾ cup sugar
Raisins to taste
1-2 apples peeled and grated

1 small can crushed pineapple, drained
1 teaspoon vanilla
Zest of half of an orange
1 teaspoon cinnamon sugar
Graham-cracker-crumbs

Beat the egg yolks until light and fluffy. Add the sugar. Add as many raisins as you like, grate or cube (tiny) 1-2 peeled apples, and a small can of pineapple (crushed and drained). Add the cinnamon, vanilla, orange zest. Whip the egg whites in a separate bowl. In the meantime, boil the noodles. Drain the noodles; toss the noodles with the melted margarine and place into a buttered casserole. Add the egg yolk mixture; fold in the egg whites. Top with graham cracker crumbs and cinnamon sugar. Bake 350° for 45 minutes to an hour. Serves 8.

This is a traditional Jewish noodle kugel to be served with meat. It is delicious and different from the other kugel that we always make. Mom Mom gave me this recipe...she really can cook even though we tease her all the time!

APPLE NOODLE KUGEL
Pearl Borten

1 pound fine egg noodles, cooked according to package directions
¼ pound margarine, melted
6 eggs
1 cup sugar (scant)
Juice and rind of one lemon

1 cup white raisins
1 (23-ounce) jar Mott's® Chunky Applesauce
Cinnamon sugar
4 tablespoons margarine (for the top, cut in small squares)

Add melted margarine to the cooked egg noodles. Beat the eggs with the sugar and the juice of one lemon, and the zest of that lemon. Mix well. Add the raisins and applesauce to the noodles. Mix well again. Grease a 9 x 13-inch pan. Pour the noodle mix into the prepared pan. Dot with small cubes of margarine and sprinkle with cinnamon sugar. Bake for 1 hour, or if freezing for 45 minutes. Cool; cut into squares. If freezing, thaw and then cut into squares. Reheat at 350° for 15 minutes.

This is another great kugel recipe from Mom Mom's friend Pearl, one of her neighbors at Pine Ridge South, in Florida.

CUSTARD NOODLE PUDDING
Pearl Borten

8 ounces plus 1 cup of fine noodles
½ pound butter
½ (8 ounces) pint sour cream
2 cups milk
1 cup sugar

1 (8 ounce) package cream cheese, softened
6 eggs
2 envelopes Knox® gelatin
Cinnamon sugar (I use Dominos®)

Preheat oven to 350°. Cook noodles as per directions. Drain, and in a large bowl, cut up butter and put noodles over the butter. Mix until melted. Separate eggs. Beat whites until soft peaks form (not too stiff) and put aside. In a mixer, beat cream cheese, sugar, egg yolks and gelatin. Add sour cream and milk. Fold mixture into the noodles and mix well. Fold in the egg whites (mixture will be loose.) Pour into a greased 13 x 9 x 2-inch pan. Sprinkle with cinnamon sugar. Bake 1 hour. Cool and refrigerate. Cut into squares before reheating or freezing. Serves 6 .

This is a delicious noodle kugel recipe from Mom Mom's friend Pearl. She said it is a favorite with her grandchildren. It's great for the Jewish holidays.

CHEESY RICE CASSEROLE
Elise Feiner

4 cups cooked rice
1½ cups grated Monterey Jack Cheese
1½ cups grated cheddar cheese
1½ cups canned corn
⅓ cup milk
⅓ cup heavy cream
½ cup sour cream

½ cup thinly sliced scallion
1 (4-ounce) jar roasted red peppers, drained, patted dry and diced
1 can or jar sliced mushrooms, drained
Salt and cayenne pepper
1 can Durkee's fried onions
Paprika

Preheat oven to 350°. Combine all ingredients in a large bowl (**reserving 6 tablespoons of cheese and half the can of fried onions.**) Spoon into buttered soufflé dish. Sprinkle top with remaining fried onions. Top with reserved cheese and sprinkle lightly with paprika. Bake until top is golden, 25 to 30 minutes. Serves 8.

FRAN'S RICE CASSEROLE
Frances Zierler

4 bags Success® Rice, cooked
1 stick butter
4 large onions, peeled and thinly sliced
3 cans creams of mushroom soup
2 bags shredded cheddar cheese (white)

2 boxes frozen chopped broccoli, defrosted and drained (optional)
2 small cans Durkee® Fried onions
Garlic salt and black pepper to taste

Cook the Success Rice and drain. In a large frying pan, melt the butter. Sauté the onions until well browned and caramelized. Season with garlic salt and pepper to taste. In a large aluminum roasting pan which has been sprayed with PAM®, add the rice, sautéed onions, soup (don't dilute the soup with any liquid), cheese, and one can of the Durkee's onions. Add broccoli if desired. Bake at 350° for about 45 minutes. Top with remaining can of Durkee's onions and bake for another 15 minutes. Serves 8 to 10.

This is a wonderful side dish and tastes fabulous. My kids don't like the broccoli in it so I leave it out. You can make it in advance and freeze it if you want to. Just bring to room temperature before baking. I made this all the time for our summer barbeques on Thistle Court.

FRIED RICE
Elise Feiner

3 cups cooked white rice
3 tablespoons vegetable oil
2 eggs, beaten
2 cloves garlic, chopped
2 teaspoons fresh ginger, minced or grated
½ cup shredded carrots
1 small red bell pepper, diced

4 scallions, thinly sliced on an angle
½ cup frozen peas
⅓ cup Tamari (dark aged soy sauce) or regular dark soy sauce
1 cup leftover pork, chicken, or ham

If you don't have leftover rice, Make the rice from scratch using 1½ cups rice to 3 cups of water. Bring water to a boil. Add rice, reduce heat, cover and cook over medium low heat until tender, 15 to 18 minutes. Let the rice cool completely before stir frying it. Heat a large skillet or a wok. Add oil to the pan. Add egg to hot oil and scramble it as you cook it, breaking it into small pieces. When eggs are scrambled, add garlic and ginger to the pan. Add the leftover meat and stir fry 2 to 3 minutes. Add carrots, pepper, scallions to the pan and quick stir-fry the vegetables about 2 minutes. Add rice to the pan and combine with vegetables and meat. Fry rice with veggies 2 or 3 minutes. Add peas and soy sauce to the rice and stir fry 1 minute more, and then serve. Serves 4.

This is a great way to get rid of all those leftovers in your refrigerator.

"No one can make you feel inferior without your consent."
-Eleanor Roosevelt

ITALIAN RICE CASSEROLE
Elise Feiner

Leftover white rice
Eggs
Mozzarella
Heavy cream

Grating cheese
Parsley
Salt and pepper to taste

This is one of those recipes you can't give amounts for. It depends on how much rice you have leftover. Just add everything to taste. Mix well. Spray a casserole pan with PAM® or freeze in mini loaf pans for individual servings. Do not bake first if freezing. Bake at 375° for about an hour until thoroughly heated and mozzarella is melted.

Nanny use to make this whenever we had leftover rice. It freezes well. Just defrost before baking. It's a great side dish and is good for a buffet table or barbeque.

INDONESIAN RICE (NASI GORENG)
Caroline Wilson Kent and Mona Gilsenan

1 (3 pound) broiler chicken, cut in pieces
1 medium onion, peeled and quartered
1 bay leaf
A few celery tops, chopped
6 peppercorns
2 teaspoons salt
3 cups water
1½ cups uncooked long grain rice
2 tablespoons vegetable oil
1 large onion, chopped

1 clove garlic, peeled and thinly sliced
1 teaspoon coriander seeds
1 teaspoon ground cumin
½ teaspoon crushed red pepper
⅛ teaspoon mace
2 cups frozen deveined shelled raw shrimp, cooked and drained (from a one pound bag)
4 ounces sliced boiled ham, cut in strips
½ cup chopped salted peanuts
Soy sauce to drizzle

Combine chicken, quartered onion, bay leaf, celery tops, peppercorns, 1½ teaspoons of salt, and water in a large frying pan. Heat to boiling; cover. Simmer 50 minutes or until chicken is tender. Remove the chicken from the broth and cool until it is easy to handle.
    Then skim the chicken and take meat away from the bones; cut the meat into strips. Skim fat from the broth; strain broth into a medium size bowl. Sauté rice in vegetable oil, stirring constantly, until golden in the same frying pan you cooked the chicken. Stir in the chopped onion, garlic and remaining ½ teaspoon of salt. Stir in 3½-cups of the chicken broth (from when you cooked the chicken), coriander seeds, cumin, pepper and mace. Heat to boiling; cover. Cook following label directions for the rice or until most of the liquid is absorbed. Stir in chicken strips, shrimp, ham and peanuts; cover. Heat slowly, stirring several times, just until hot. Spoon into a large serving dish; sprinkle with more chopped peanuts, if you wish. Serve with soy sauce to drizzle over the top. Serves 8.

This is a recipe we used as a promotion for the Oberoi Resorts and Hotel group. It looked so good, so I saved it and reprinted it with Caroline and Mona's permission. This was the first spice promotion we did for the Oberoi group, and we dubbed ourselves the "Spice Girls"...we packaged so many spices that my house on Thistle Court smelled like a wonderful Indian restaurant.

L-R: Raina Goldbas, Lauren Feiner and Marta Godecki

PASTIERE
Katherine Avella

4 quarts of boiling salted water
1 cup Carolina® long grain rice
½ pound fine egg noodles
2 pounds ricotta
8 eggs
4 tablespoons parsley

1 teaspoon salt
¼ teaspoon black pepper
1 pint heavy cream
2 bags shredded mozzarella
2-3 cups grating cheese

Preheat oven to 375°. Add rice to the boiling water, bringing it back to a boil again quickly, while stirring with a fork. Boil for 12 minutes, then add the noodles to the boiling rice and then bring quickly to a boil again. Cook until noodles are just tender. Drain them in a colander. Beat eggs slightly in a large mixing bowl. Add all the remaining ingredients except the mozzarella cheese. When well mixed fold in the mozzarella. Add the pasta rice mix to the egg mix. Place into a greased baking dish. Bake for 1 hour or until golden brown and firm. Cut in squares to serve. If you want to, you can sprinkle cornflake crumbs or breadcrumbs and dot with a little butter before baking. Serves 6. My cousin John says you can bake this in a pie crust if you want to.

This is a recipe of my mothers that she used to make when I was a kid. My kids love this; it's even better leftover and reheated. It's a nice side dish for a holiday or a barbecue. It can fit in with any meal and it's a little different because it is rice and pasta together. What else could an Italian want????

PUMPKIN RISOTTO
Elise Feiner

⅓ cup chopped pancetta or proscuitto
2 to 2½ cups light chicken stock
2 large shallots, peeled and chopped
1 can or pumpkin puree, large
3 tablespoons olive oil
1 cup risotto rice, (Arborio)

1 cup dry white wine
½ cup heavy cream
4 tablespoons mascarpone or cream cheese
½ to 2 cups freshly grated Parmesan cheese
Salt
Freshly ground black pepper

Heat a dry non-stick frying pan and, when hot, fry the pancetta until browned and crisp. Drain and set aside. Heat the chicken stock to a gentle simmer in a saucepan. In a large pan, sauté the shallots in the oil for about 5 minutes. Stir in the rice and cook for a further 2 minutes. Add the wine and cook until reduced right down. Pour in ½ cup of the stock and stir well. Add the pumpkin puree. Cook gently until the liquid has been absorbed, then, stir in another ladle of stock. Continue cooking and stirring, gradually adding the stock, until the rice grains are just tender, and risotto creamy. Let it cook for about 15 to 20 minutes. Right before serving, stir in the heavy cream, pancetta, mascarpone, and half the Parmesan. Sprinkle with a little grating cheese before serving. Serves 4.

I tried to recreate this from a meal we had in a restaurant in Long Island where I met my friends from High School for an unofficial reunion.

RISOTTO ALLA BENEVENTO
Elise Feiner

½ stick butter
4 ounces minced shallots
12 ounces mushrooms, cleaned and sliced
2 yellow bell peppers, washed, seeded and cut into small dice
1¼ pounds Arborio rice

5 cups white chicken stock, heated
1½ cups grated Parmesan
4 ounces grated Fontina
1 cup heavy cream
Salt and pepper

Heat butter in a large pan set over medium heat. Add the shallots and sauté until translucent. Add mushrooms and sauté until cooked through. Add rice and stir until well coated. Add 2 cups of chicken stock and simmer until liquid is absorbed, stirring continuously. Add remaining stock one cup at a time, stirring continuously until liquid is absorbed before adding more. After about 10 minutes, add diced yellow bell pepper. Continue to cook. When the rice becomes creamy and the grains are still a little firm, add cheeses, and stir well. Add cream, salt and pepper to taste. Serves 10.

RISOTTO ALLA MILANESE
Virginia Casazza

4 cups Arborio rice, rinse and remove any stones
10 cups chicken broth; Bring the chicken broth to a boil in a large pot.
1 large onion, peeled and finely diced
1 stick sweet butter
4 tablespoons olive oil

1 cup dry white wine
1 pint heavy cream
1 cup grating cheese (more if you prefer)
Salt and pepper to taste
Pinch of saffron dissolved in a little hot water

In a large pan, melt the butter with the olive oil, and add the minced onions. Sauté to a light golden brown. Slowly add the rice. Keep cooking until most of the butter is absorbed by the rice. Slowly add the soup, 2 to 3 cups at a time cooking until the rice absorbs the soup before adding the next batch of soup. Stir frequently throughout the cooking process. Add the cup of white wine. Continue stirring. Add the saffron (to give it color); add the heavy cream and grating cheese last. Cook just until the cream is heated and starting to absorb. It should be a little loose so it stays creamy. Season with salt and pepper to taste if desired. If you want to add vegetables such as mushrooms (use about 3 ounces of sliced mushrooms) or asparagus, add them when you are sautéing the onions. If you are using asparagus, place it in boiling salted water for 2 minutes and then into an ice bath first. Cut into small pieces. I like to add both mushrooms and asparagus together. If you prefer a more yellow color you can add a drop of yellow food coloring. Serves 12. It's easy to divide for a smaller quantity. **NEVER** leave risotto unattended while cooking, it will burn quickly!

This recipe came from Cousin Virginia Casazza. This is a very basic risotto that you can use to add many things to, but it is delicious without anything extra added. I love it with some Pesto Sauce added to it.

Standing L-R: Virginia Casazza, Frank S. Mainella, M.D., Tee Tee Massimiano
Sitting L-R: Tina Massimiano, Angie Sanito, Frances Barone

L-R: Josephine Mainella and Angie Sanito

SPANISH RICE
Thirza Avella

½ pound bacon
1 large onion, chopped
2 cloves garlic, peeled and crushed
½ to 1 bell pepper
3 tablespoons olive oil
1 small can tomato paste

⅓ can water (tomato paste can)
2 tablespoons Lea & Perrins® Worcestershire Sauce
Bacon drippings
Salt to taste
2 cups cooked rice

Fry the bacon until crisp. Remove from pan, crumble; save the drippings. In another pot, sauté onions, garlic and bell pepper in the olive oil until browned. Add the tomato paste, water, Worcestershire sauce, crumbled bacon, bacon drippings, and salt to taste. Simmer slowly uncovered for about 2 hours. Stir occasionally. Add the cooked rice. Put in a double boiler and steam for 30 to 45 minutes. Serves 8.

THIRZA'S RICE
Thirza Avella

2 large bags Success® Rice, cooked as directed
1 bag mixed vegetables, frozen
3 tablespoons butter
3 chicken bouillon packets

Garlic salt
Salt and pepper to taste
1 cup grated cheese (more if you prefer)

Cook the vegetables in the microwave for about 5 minutes; turn. Add the butter and cook about another 5 minutes or follow package directions for cooking time. Place the vegetables in a large mixing bowl. Take about ¼ cup of water from the rice and add the chicken bouillon. Toss the rice, bouillon, and remaining ingredients together. Serves 6.

Thirza used to make this as a side dish with pork or chicken. It's fast and delicious!

L-R: Joseph Avella, Melissa Avella, Eva Castro, Douglas Avella

RICE BALLS (NEAPOLITAN)
John Grimaldi, Sr., Executive Chef

3 cups Carolina® Rice (raw)
6 cups water
3 tablespoons butter
Pinch of salt
¼ pound grated cheese
1½ pounds ricotta cheese
½ pound mozzarella cheese, grated
1 teaspoon salt
⅛ teaspoon pepper

1 tablespoon parsley
4 eggs, beaten
2 tablespoons milk (more if needed)
3 eggs (for dipping) beaten
Pinch of salt
Flavored bread crumbs
Oil for frying
1-2 large mozzarella, cut into small cubes, optional

Cook rice with salt and butter until water is almost all absorbed. Let cool. Add ricotta, 4 eggs, cheese, pepper, salt, parsley, grated mozzarella. Mix well. Shape into balls the size you prefer; refrigerate about 2 hours or more.

In a good size bowl, add the 3 beaten eggs, a pinch of salt and the milk. Whisk together until well blended. Roll the rice balls in beaten egg mix and then roll in flavored breadcrumbs. Deep fry. When shaping the rice balls you can place a small cube of mozzarella in the middle of each ball if you'd like. In Staten Island, they also add peas and ham to the rice balls. Makes about 40.

Cousin John is an Executive Chef and has done catering and worked in many Salumaria's on Staten Island for years. These are his famous rice balls. They are delicious!

"You will find as you look back upon your life that the moments when you have truly lived are the moments when you have done things in the spirit of love."
-Henry Drummond

WILD RICE WITH NUTS
Elise Feiner

1 (6.2 ounces) box Uncle Ben's® Long Grain and Wild Rice
Quick Cook Recipe
1 (13¾ or 14.2 ounce) can College Inn® Chicken Broth
2 tablespoons butter

¼ cup apple cider
½ cup chopped walnuts or pecans
Salt and pepper to taste

In a small saucepan, place the walnuts or pecans over low heat and toast for about 7 minutes; set aside. Cook the rice according to package directions substituting the chicken broth and apple cider for the water in the directions. Top with the toasted nuts, and season with salt and pepper to taste.

Aunt Fifi and "her boy" David Feiner

NANNY'S RICE CASSEROLE
Katherine Avella

Tomato Sauce (either Marinara or leftover Gravy, see
recipes under sauces)
Leftover white rice

Grating Cheese
Grated mozzarella
Ricotta

This is one of those recipes you can't give amounts for. It depends on how much you have leftover. Just add everything to taste. Mix well. Spray a casserole pan with PAM® or freeze in mini loaf pans for individual servings. Do not bake first if freezing. Bake at 375° for about an hour until thoroughly heated and mozzarella is melted.

Nanny use to make this whenever we had leftover rice. It freezes well. Just defrost before baking. It's a great side dish and is good for a buffet table or barbeque. This is similar to the Italian Rice Casserole but this one has tomato sauce in it.

L-R: Lucy Rumbutis, Marie George and Ronni Tichenor

Sue and Harold W. Baum, M.D....it's because of Harold, we came to Utica

Katie and her "boys": L-R: Joseph Avella, JoJo DiPierdomenico, and Katherine Avella Standing: Philip Avella

Top L-R: Frank S. Mainella, M.D. and Edith Mainella
Bottom L-R: Josephine Mainella and Katherine Mainella Avella

The Jenkins Girls L-R: Carly (7), Megan (12) and Taryn (9)
Their dad Rob, works with me and is responsible for the cover design of the book and the logos...

L-R: Trish and George Alsheimer
Trish and George and their children and extended family have been like our own family. Steven, David, and their son Mike have been friends for years.

Daniel and Helen Popeo –two very special friends...
Dan is responsible for a few of my favorite quotes found throughout the book

Side Dishes...

THE TIMOTHY J. TRAINOR FAMILY
L-R: Kyle, Katherine, Jonathan, Maria, Tim and Tessa

"Good friends are God's way of making up for some relatives."

– Dan Popeo

Stocking a Dream Kitchen!

Pots and Pans:

The more expensive brands you can afford the better off you are. In some cases, price doesn't matter, but in pots you get what you pay for...think All Clad®. If you are just starting out and can't afford them, you can always buy them in the future.

Saucepans (1-qt., 2-qt. and 3-qt.)
Stockpot (8-quart, 12 quart, 16 quart, and a real dream 20 quart or larger for making stocks, sauces etc.)
Skillets (8" and 10", 12 inches is a bonus, as is two sets, one set with a non stick finish)
Large Sautee Pan (deeper than a skillet, with a lid)
Dutch Oven

Utensils:

2 sets of Measuring Spoons (splurge on the heavy gauge stainless steel ones)
2 sets of Dry Measuring Cups
Glass Liquid Measuring Cups (1 cup, 2 cup and 4 cup are perfect)
2 Cutting Boards
Spatulas (hard rubber if you have nonstick cookware; you can never have too many)
Soup Ladle
Kitchen Tongs
Standing Grater (4-sided)
A set of Colanders or various sizes
Vegetable Peeler and brush
 Potato Ricer or Masher
A set of strainers (small ones)
Potato Peelers Long-Handled Fork
Wire Whisk in a few sizes (Hard Rubber Whisks are Available)
Garlic Press
Baster
Can Opener
Meat Thermometer
Oven Thermometer

Roasting Pan (three shallow, one deep)
Broiler Pan (usually comes with oven)
Double Boiler
Clay Pot Casserole
Egg Pan (Teflon) used only for eggs
Copper is great but is very expensive and requires a lot of work. If you do a lot of candy making or baking you may want to invest in some copper products.

Candy Thermometer
Timer
Corkscrew
Zesters
Slotted Spoons
Wooden Spoons
High-Heat Flexible Rubber Spatulas
Citrus Juicer
Strainers
Funnel
Nutcracker
Pepper Grinder
Coffee Pot and Tea Kettle
 Wooden Skewers
Ice Cream Scoop
Collapsible Vegetable Steamer
Meat Pounder (Hammer)
Mushroom Brush
Garlic Peeler
Corkscrew
Hand-Held Grater (great for parmesan cheese)
Mortar and pestle

ORZO WITH VEGETABLES
Elise Feiner

4 teaspoons olive oil
2 shallots minced
1 pound assorted fresh mushrooms (can include Crimini's, Portobello, etc), sliced thinly
½ pound of fresh snow peas, julienned

¾ cup toasted pine nuts
1 pound orzo, cooked according to box directions
4 tablespoon of butter
Salt and freshly ground black pepper
Grated parmesan or Locatelli Romano cheese

Heat 2 teaspoons olive oil in a sauté pan. Add shallots and sauté. Add mushrooms and sauté until brown. Add snow peas and cook for 1 minute. Add pine nuts. Add mixture to the orzo. Add butter. Season with salt and pepper, to taste. Add grated cheese before serving if desired. Serves 6.

PARSLEY POTATOES
Elise Feiner

5 pounds red potatoes
Salt and pepper to taste
½ cup chopped parsley
½ cup chopped scallions
¼ cup chopped basil
2 cloves of garlic, peeled and crushed

1½ teaspoons salt
½ teaspoon dry mustard
1 tablespoon sugar
1 tablespoon Worcestershire sauce
1 cup extra virgin olive oil
½ cup tarragon vinegar

Cook the potatoes in a pot of lightly salted water, about 40 minutes. Drain and cool. Cut into 1-inch cubes (you can peel them if you want, but you don't have too.) Place them in a mixing bowl. Put the parsley, basil and scallions over the potatoes. Mix the garlic, salt, mustard, sugar, Worcestershire sauce, olive oil and vinegar together. Mix well. Pour over the potatoes, and stir carefully. Let stand 4 to 6 hours. Serve at room temperature.

FRAN'S CABBAGE AND NOODLES
Frances Zierler

1 head cabbage, peeled and shredded
2 large Vidalia® onions or yellow onions, peeled and sliced
1 large Bermuda onion (red), peeled and sliced
Olive oil

⅛ teaspoon black pepper
1 teaspoon garlic salt
Caraway seeds (optional)
1 package of egg noodles

In a large sauté pan or deep pot, place enough oil to just cover the bottom. When oil is hot, add the onions and stir frequently until starting to brown. Season with garlic salt and pepper. Add the cabbage and sauté until soft. Add caraway seeds if desired. Serve as a side dish, or over egg noodles which have been prepared according to package directions. Serves 6.

This is another of Aunt Fran's tasty side dishes. I am not a cabbage lover but this is wonderful. The flavor of the onion and cabbage together is wonderful. If you serve them with noodles you just need meat and you have a meal. They are great reheated the next day for a light lunch.

L-R: Claire Van Waes and Fran Zierler

285

BAKED MACARONI
Katherine Avella

1 pound elbow macaroni
1 stick of butter
8 tablespoons flour (I use Wondra®)
Salt and pepper to taste
1 large box of Velveeta®, cut up into cubes
Dash of Worcestershire Sauce
1 bag of Monterey Jack Cheese (8 ounces) or shredded mozzarella

1 (8 ounce) bag of Cheddar Cheese
1½-2 quarts milk
1 tablespoon mustard
3 tablespoons butter
½ cup breadcrumbs or Panko crumbs
1 tablespoon grated cheese

Put up a pot of salted water and bring to a boil for the elbow macaroni. Start the sauce. Cook the elbows, but leave a little undercooked because they continue to cook in the oven; **DRAIN WELL.** Slowly melt the butter and stir in the flour. Slowly add the milk so it is smooth and doesn't get lumpy. Add salt and pepper to taste; add Worcestershire sauce and Velveeta cubes. Stir very frequently, and make sure you get the bottom of the pot so it doesn't burn. Cook until it starts to thicken. Add the remaining cheeses. Continue cooking until fairly thick. Add the elbows. Place into a large baking pan that has been sprayed with PAM®. Melt the 3 tablespoons of butter in a small frying pan, add the crumbs and toast lightly. Add the grated cheese. Sprinkle on top of the casserole before baking. Bake at 375° 45 to 60 minutes or until top is browned. If you are going to freeze this, don't bake it first. Let it defrost overnight in the refrigerator and then bake it. Serves 6 to 8.

This was one of my favorites growing up. I associate this with is Thanksgiving because we always had it instead of "Italian Macaroni" for the American Holiday

The Wedding:
Katherine and Sam Avella 6/11/39

The Honeymoon:
Katherine and Sam Avella in Canada
They say if you wait long enough, everything comes back in style…check out the necklace!

"Children are not casual guests in our home. They have been loaned to us temporarily for the purpose of loving them and instilling a foundation of values on which their future lives will be built."
-Dr. James. C. Dobson

ABBY AND JODY'S FETTUCCINE AND SPINACH
Barbara Feiner

2 packages frozen creamed spinach   **1 pound egg noodles or fettuccine noodles**

Cook the spinach according to the package directions. Cook the noodles or fettuccine in boiling salted water according to the directions. Drain the noodles. Quickly toss the noodles with the creamed spinach. Serves 4.

Aunt Barbara says that Abby and Jody love this side dish and it's so easy to make!

Jody, Lauren, Abby and Karen Feiner

Back Row L-R: Abby Feiner, Shelley Sussman
Front Row L-R: Jody, Barbara, and Kevin Feiner

L-R: Cousins Jody and Lauren Feiner

L-R: Jerry and Betty Feiner, Barbara Sussman Feiner,
Kevin Feiner, Ferne and Moe Sussman
Moe and Ferne owned Mo's Deli in Philadelphia for
years, and now Barbara's brother Mitchell owns it.

POTATO "SALAD"
Elise Feiner

6 cups of cooked potatoes, grated
6 hard boiled eggs, chopped
1 stalk of celery, chopped
1 cup Hellmann's® mayonnaise
¾ cup sugar

¼ cup heavy cream
2 tablespoons apple cider vinegar
2 teaspoons salt
2 teaspoons mustard

Mix the potatoes, eggs, and celery in a large bowl. Mix the mayo, sugar, heavy cream, vinegar salt, and mustard together with a whisk. Pour over the potato egg mixture. Stir until well blended. Refrigerate. Serves 8 to 10.

One day, I overcooked the potatoes and they fell apart. I mixed them anyway and they still tasted great. This is the result, but I caution you it has a very different texture than a regular potato salad.

287

ORIENTAL PASTA
Elise Feiner

6 cloves of garlic, peeled
¼ cup fresh ginger, peeled and cubed
¼ cup Wesson® oil
½ cup tahini
½ cup peanut butter
½ cup soy sauce
¼ cup cooking sherry
¼ cup rice wine vinegar

¼ cup honey
2 tablespoons dark sesame oil
½ teaspoon black pepper
¼ teaspoon cayenne pepper
1 pound linguine or spaghetti
1 red pepper, washed, seeded and cut into strips
1 yellow pepper, washed, seeded and cut into strips
3-4 scallions, thinly sliced

Put the ginger and garlic in a food processor, and chop. Add the oil, tahini, peanut butter, soy sauce, sherry, wine vinegar, honey, sesame oil, black pepper and cayenne pepper. Process until smooth. Cook the linguini in lightly salted water according to package directions. Drain and toss with the sauce. Serve warm or at room temperature.

This tastes as good any of the peanut noodles in the Chinese restaurants. It's a nice change of pace, great with a pork dish.

L-R: Hannah and Sarah Weiner Aunt Shirley's Grandchildren...

L-R: Rebecca and Zach Henry Weiner

Hal and Nicole's 4 children

NANNY'S POTATO CROQUETTES
Katherine Avella

5 pounds potatoes (about 9), boiled in their skin
1½ cups grated cheese
2-3 eggs
1 tablespoon dried or fresh parsley

Salt and pepper to taste
Plain breadcrumbs
Vegetable oil for frying

Boil the potatoes in their skins. When cooked (easily pierced with a fork). Remove from heat. Peel the skin. Place potatoes through a ricer. Add salt, pepper, grated cheese, and 2 eggs to start. Mix well. Mixture should be firm. Add the third egg if necessary. Wet your hands with a little water or oil, and shape the potatoes into logs or circles depending on your preference. Dip into plain breadcrumbs and fry until golden brown on all sides. You can also use leftover mashed potatoes, if they are not too loose.

I think my mother's potato croquettes are the best I've ever had.

POTATO PUDDING
Sheila Smith

5 pound Potatoes peeled and boiled
3 medium size onions chopped
¼ pound butter (can substitute olive oil for half the butter)

6 eggs (can substitute egg beaters for 4 eggs)
Salt and pepper

Sauté the onions until golden brown in the butter. In an electric mixer beat eggs until frothy. Add butter onion mixture. Add potatoes a few at a time while beating. Season to taste. Bake for 1 hour at 350°. This pudding can be frozen or refrigerated overnight before using. If baking the pudding cold add an additional 20 minutes to baking time.

This is Sheila Smith's grandmother's recipe, handed down in her family from generation to generation. Sheila's husband Bob was my husband Marc's partner until he retired. He is now enjoying retirement and his grandson Jamie.

LAUREN'S FAVORITE POTATO PIE
Barbara Schwartz

1 large box Hungary Jacks Instant Mashed potatoes
2-3 large onions, peeled and sliced
1 stick butter
1 teaspoon garlic salt

¼ teaspoon black pepper
Ingredients as per directions on box of potatoes (butter, milk or heavy cream if you like them rich, salt and water)
1 bag White cheddar cheese shredded (2-3 cups) (optional)

In a large frying pan, melt the butter and add the onions, black pepper and garlic salt (the above measurements are approximate, season to your own taste), until the onions are lightly browned and caramelized. Following the directions on the box for the whole box of potatoes, mix the butter,(**I usually a little less water than the box calls for**) milk, and salt. Heat until hot and the butter melts, but not until boiling. Add the onions to the liquid mixture. Spray a large baking pan with Pam. Pour the potato flakes in the pan. Add the milk and onion mix to the pan. Add the cheese if desired. Stir with a wooden spoon as the mixture is hard to stir sometimes. If the mixture is too thick, add a little more milk or heavy cream if you have it. Barbara says you can also spray muffin tins with PAM and make individual servings. Bake at 400° for about 45 minutes to one hour or until the top is golden brown. Let potatoes sit about 15 minutes before serving. The original recipe didn't call for cheese, so it's optional. If you make two, they freeze very well, but freeze unbaked, and then defrost before baking. Serves 6 to 8.

Aunt Barbara made this for dinner one night and it was delicious. When I asked her for the recipe, she laughed. "If I tell you what it is, you won't believe it", she said. They're instant mashed potatoes. I said, "you must be kidding". But, they were and it was so easy to make and it's delicious. Lauren loves this dish. Barbara always laughs that I have given this recipe to the entire world, including posting it on the internet. It's fast and easy. We make this all the time. I made it in Philadelphia to surprise Abby and Jody, they absolutely loved it. This is for you Abby and Jody...

Lauren and Abby Feiner...then

...and now

ROASTED POTATOES ITALIANO
Elise Feiner

2 cups plain bread crumbs or panko crumbs
½ cup olive oil
Salt and freshly ground pepper
1 teaspoon basil
1 teaspoon oregano

4 pounds russet potatoes, peeled and cut into large slices, lengthwise
2 cups shredded mozzarella or shredded cheddar
½ cup grated cheese

In a small bowl mix the bread crumbs, olive oil, basil, oregano and a pinch of salt and pepper together. Place the potatoes in a large well greased cookie sheet. Cover potatoes completely with bread crumbs. Bake potatoes for about 1 hour at 400° (cover with foil if getting too brown). Remove from the oven and top with mozzarella and grated cheese. Increase the temperature to 425° and bake until the cheese is melted. Serves 6

I made this accidentally one day by spilling breadcrumbs on my potatoes. Lauren suggested the mozzarella. They are a great side dish.

POTATO PIEROGI'S
Johanna Lewandrezwski

1 egg
2 heaping tablespoons sour cream
1 cup milk
4½ to 5 cups flour
4 tablespoons unsalted butter, melted
2 tablespoons cornmeal

5 pounds baking potatoes, peeled and quartered (about 10 medium potatoes)
¼ pound unsalted butter (1 stick), melted
2 ounces (about ½ cup) cheddar cheese, grated
4 ounces cream cheese
Coarse salt and freshly ground black pepper to taste

In a medium bowl, whisk the egg. Add the sour cream, and whisk until smooth. Add the milk and 1 cup of water, and whisk until combined. Slowly add about 3 cups of flour, and stir with a wooden spoon to combine. Turn dough out onto a well-floured surface and work in about 1 cup flour as you knead. Use a plastic scraper to lift the dough as it will stick to the counter before the flour is worked in. Continue kneading for about 8 to 10 minutes, working in ½ cup flour. The dough should be elastic in texture and no longer sticky. Be careful not to add too much flour as this will toughen the dough. Place dough in a lightly floured bowl and cover with plastic wrap and let rest while you prepare the filling.

Cook potatoes in salted boiling water until fork-tender. Drain and mash with a potato masher. Add melted butter and cheeses, and continue to mash until well-incorporated. Season with salt and pepper to taste. Place a large pot of salted water over high heat and bring to a boil. Lay a clean linen towel on your counter and evenly distribute cornmeal on it to prevent sticking. On a floured surface, roll out dough to about ⅛-inch thickness. Using a glass or cookie cutter measuring 2½ inches in diameter, cut out as many circles as you can. Gather dough scraps together, rolling out again, and continue cutting. Form filling into 1½ inch balls, and place a ball in the center of each dough circle. Holding a circle in your hand, fold dough over filling and pinch the edges, forming a well-sealed crescent. Transfer to linen towel. Continue this process until all dough circles are filled.

Place Pierogi's in the boiling water in batches. They will sink to the bottom of the pot and then rise to the top. Once they rise, let them cook for about a minute more. Meanwhile, drizzle the platter with melted butter. Remove Pierogi's from pot and transfer to platter to prevent sticking. Serve immediately.

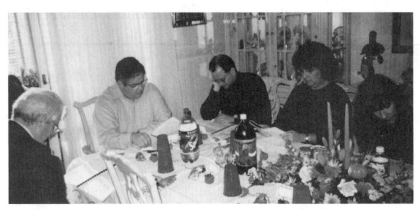

Reading the Thanksgiving "cookbook"/program that started it all…
L-R: Joseph Avella, Marc Feiner, Kevin Feiner, Barbara Feiner, Shelley Sussman

PARTY POTATOES
Edith Mainella

1 (32 ounce) bag frozen hash brown potatoes, thawed
1½ cups grated Cheddar cheese, divided
1 (10¾ ounce) can cream of chicken soup
1 (10¾ ounce) can cream of celery soup
½ cup sour cream

½ cup chopped onion
2 tablespoons melted butter
3 scallions chopped finely
Garlic salt and black pepper to taste
Paprika for garnish

Preheat oven to 350°. In a large bowl, combine the potatoes, 1 cup cheddar cheese, the soups, onions, sour cream and melted butter. Pour into a greased 9x13-inch baking pan. Bake one hour, or until bubbly. Remove from the oven and sprinkle with remaining ½-cup cheddar cheese and paprika, if desired. Bake 10 more minutes.

POTATO CROQUETTES WITH HAM
Rose Pacifico

3½ pounds baking potatoes, peeled and cut into chunks
4 eggs, separated
¼ pound proscuitto, or cooked or boiled ham, cut into
¼-inch dice
4 tablespoons butter
½ cup grated cheese

Dash of nutmeg
1 cup flour
1 cup fresh bread crumbs
2 cups extra-virgin olive oil, for frying

Bring 8 quarts of water to a boil. Cook the potatoes in the boiling water until easily pierced with a paring knife, about 15 minutes. Drain the potatoes and, while still hot, pass them through a food mill or ricer. Immediately add the egg yolks, proscuitto, butter, grated cheese, and nutmeg and mix well. Season with salt and pepper. With moist hands, divide the mixture into golf ball-sized portions and form circles of a 2-inch diameter or make into a pyramid shape. On three separate plates, place the flour, egg whites and bread crumbs. Dredge each croquette starting with the flour first, then the egg whites, then the bread crumbs. In a heavy-bottomed skillet, heat the oil until it's hot. Cook the croquettes in the oil, until they are deep golden brown. Drain on a plate lined with paper towels and serve. Serves 6.

Rose was our neighbor in Bayville, New York. She gave new meaning to cooking with love. There was always a feeling of love and warmth in her kitchen and in her house. I loved spending my days there. I learned so much about cooking from Rose and her mother, Grandma Festa.

POTATO CROQUETTES TARANTINO
Jenny Tarantino

6 Idaho baking potatoes
1 egg
2 eggs whites, beaten with 1 teaspoon of water
1 small fresh mozzarella, cut into pieces
½-inch thick and 2 inches long
¼ cup grating cheese

1 tablespoon fresh parsley, finely chopped
⅛ teaspoon fresh ground pepper
1 teaspoon salt
4 tablespoon melted butter
½ cup milk, heated
3 cups breadcrumbs

Peel potatoes. Cut into pieces and boil in lightly salted water, until a fork pierces through easily. Put potatoes through a masher or potato ricer. **DO NOT** use a food processor or mixer. Add the rest of the ingredients except the mozzarella and egg whites. Mix well. It should not be thin or it won't hold its shape. Use an ice cream scoop to measure each croquette. Place 1 piece of mozzarella down the center. Form into a rectangular log shape. Dip in egg whites then in bread crumbs. Place in refrigerator for 30-60 minutes to make firm. Fry in olive oil until golden brown. Drain on paper towels.

Ann said that Aunt Jenny would make these whenever she had leftover mashed potatoes. She didn't make them too often, as she couldn't stand to have her hands messed up, but she sure could cook! All of my father's sister's were great cooks and bakers!

"Sem and his sisters"…
Back Row L-R: Jenny Avella Tarantino, Flo Avella, Sam and Kay
Avella, Julia Avella Silvestri, and Mae Avella
Front Row L-R: Mary Avella Caccavale, Frances Avella Moreira

Jenny and Ralph Tarantino

BAKED POTATOES
Elise Feiner

6 large Idaho or Russet potatoes
Vegetable oil

Kosher salt or Seasoned Salt

Pierce the potatoes with a fork several times to allow the steam or escape. Roll the potatoes in vegetable oil. This will keep the skins crispy. Sprinkle with Kosher salt. Bake 400° about 45 to 60 minutes. Serves 6.

I love to eat the skin on my baked potatoes. These remind me of the potatoes at the Outback Restaurant; salty and crisp at the same time. Hint: use high starch potatoes (Russet, Idaho, baking potatoes) for baked, fried or oven roasted potatoes. Use low starch potatoes (red, new or all purpose potatoes for mashed.) You can even use Cooking with Love's Passion Spice Mix on the skins of the potatoes.

CORN CASSEROLE
Janet Saporito

1 can of kernel corn, do not drain
1 can of creamed corn
1 box of Jiffy® corn bread muffin mix
1 (8 ounce) container sour cream

1 egg
1 stick of butter or margarine, softened
½ cup of sugar or Splenda®

Mix all ingredients together. Pour mixture into a 9 x 12-inch pan. Bake at 350° for 1 hour.

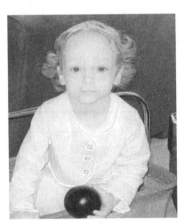

Two of Janet's Favorite's: Granddaughter Christina Molinari, age 18 months

and Shar-Pei "Dallas"

CRUSTY POTATO CASSEROLE
Elise Feiner

6-8 potatoes (Idaho or Russet)
Salt to taste
Freshly ground black pepper
Garlic salt to taste

1 stick of butter cut up into tiny cubes plus 2-3 tablespoons to grease casserole
2 scallions cut into very thin slices (optional)

Peel and cut the potatoes very thinly into rounds slightly wider than potato chips. Dry off the potatoes in a towel and place in a large mixing bowl. Sprinkle with salt and pepper and toss together to coat well. Arrange potatoes in a large (round if you have one) Pyrex® casserole that has been well greased with butter. Start in the middle and slightly overlap the potatoes in a circular pattern. When you finish the first layer, sprinkle with a bit of garlic salt, dot with butter, and sprinkle with scallions if using them. Add the next layer the same way, repeating the garlic salt, butter, scallions; continue until all the potatoes are used up. Bake uncovered in a 400° oven for 45 minutes to 1 hour. They should be very crisp. Loosen the edges of the pan with a wide spatula. If you used a round Pyrex®, try to invert it onto a serving plate; if not, just cut into wedges to serve. Serves 6.

This is a fast and easy side dish to prepare. It's great with a roast or chicken.

PERFECT FRENCH FRIES
Elise Feiner

4-6 large Idaho or Russet Potatoes, peeled, and cut into either thin rounds, or French fry shape Vegetable oil for frying	Salt, garlic or Seasoned Salt Pepper (optional) Ice Water

The key to the perfect French fry is to start with a great potato. Peel the potatoes, leaving them whole, and place in cold water. After a half hour, change the water. After another half hour change the water again. Now cut the potatoes in the shape you want. If you have a deep fryer, cut them in a traditional French fry shape. If you are going to use a frying pan, cut them in thin rounds. Place the potatoes in a bowl filled with ice water. Let them soak about fifteen minutes. Dry with a towel in small batches before frying. Let the remaining potatoes stay in the ice until ready to fry, them dry them off. Place the potatoes into a deep frying pan filled with **HOT** oil. Sprinkle with a little salt and pepper while they are cooking. Turn frequently until golden brown, drain on paper towels. Sprinkle with salt. These are good, but the next way **(if you have a deep fryer is the best).** Cook the French fries in hot oil (325°) until lightly browned, about 10 minutes. Drain on paper towels, paper plates, or paper bags. They will be a little soggy. Complete all the fries this way. Then turn up the fryer to 375°, and fry the potatoes for a second time, until golden brown and crisp, about 3 to 4 minutes. Drain on paper towels. Sprinkle with salt or a combination of salts. Serve immediately. Serves 6. Don't use a generic white potato, red new potatoes, or Yukon gold for French fries; the starch content isn't good for French fries.

Another twist on French fries is to peel and cut potatoes into ½-inch cubes. Place in a pot of lightly salted cold water, cover and bring to a boil. Boil for 10 minutes- no more than that. Drain carefully. Place on paper towels or a dishtowel to dry well. Fry. Sprinkle with Passion Spice or seasoned salt. These are crunchy on the outside, fluffy in the middle.

NOTE: Be very **CAREFUL** when dropping the potatoes into hot oil, if you **HAVEN'T DRIED THEM WELL**, they can splatter and cause burns...so dry them well with a clean dishtowel, and to be on the safe side, stand back a little when you place them in the oil!

When I lived in Brooklyn, one of my friend's mothers showed me this trick. It makes a great crispy French fry. If you have a French fry cutter or a mandolin, it makes the job much easier.

The Avella Grandchildren:
L-R: "Nanny" Katherine Avella, Jeffrey Feiner, Melissa Avella, Philip Avella, Jr., Lauren Feiner, Michael Avella, Douglas Avella, Steven Feiner, "Grandpa" Sam Avella
In front on the floor: David Feiner

ORANGE AND GOLD POTATO CASSEROLE
Katherine Avella

1 stick butter, divided 2½ pounds Yukon Gold Potatoes, rinsed and thinly sliced in rounds 1½ pounds Sweet Potatoes, peeled and thinly sliced in rounds 2 cups milk 2 cloves garlic, peeled and crushed	1 tablespoon Kosher salt 2 teaspoons fresh thyme leaves ½ teaspoon black pepper ⅛ teaspoon ground nutmeg 1 cup whipping cream 2 scallions thinly chopped

Preheat oven to 400°. Take a large baking pan and grease with 2 tablespoons butter. Place the potatoes and scallions in the pan, mixing together well. Mix the milk, salt, thyme, pepper and nutmeg together in a pot and bring to a boil. Pour over the potatoes. Cut 2 more tablespoons of butter into small cubes and scatter over the potatoes. Cover with foil and bake about 1 hour. Bring the cream to a boil in a small saucepan. Uncover the potatoes, pour the cream over the potatoes and cube (tiny) the remaining butter and scatter over the potatoes. Bake uncovered until golden brown about another 30 minutes.

OVEN ROASTED POTATOES
Elise Feiner

10-12 potatoes, Idaho or all purpose, not Yukon, peeled and sliced
2-3 large onions, peeled and sliced
½ cup olive oil
½ tablespoon garlic salt
¼ teaspoon black pepper

1 tablespoon dried basil
1 tablespoon dried oregano
1 tablespoon dried parsley
1 teaspoon paprika
¼ cup water

Preheat the oven to 450°. Peel the potatoes and cut into slices about ¾-inch thick. Peel the onions and cut into thin slices. Spray a large baking dish with Pam. Add the olive oil. Add the potatoes and onions and stir. Add the remaining ingredients and mix well. I like to use my hands for this. Bake the potatoes for about 45 minutes to an hour. Turn a few times while baking to ensure that all the potatoes become brown and crisp. As the potatoes start to bake, they will give off a lot of liquid. Drain liquid with a turkey baster periodically if the potatoes are too wet and discard the excess liquid. They will not get crisp if there is too much liquid in the baking dish. Bake for about 45 minutes to 1 hour or until very crisp any brown. Serves 6.

When I was little, every Sunday morning after church while my mother was cooking, my brothers and I would go with my father to visit his sisters. We would stop at each house and sample the goodies. At my Aunt Jenny's, she would often be making these potatoes. This is as close to her recipe as I have come. I think years ago, they used lard in the original recipes, but these taste almost the same. My cousin Ann just gave me my Aunt Jenny's recipe. This was close, but she didn't use all the spices I did. Her recipe is now listed separately.

Those were the days...L-R: Nicole Latini, Jeffrey, David, and Lauren Feiner, Mindy Rosenfeld, John-Michael Latini, Steven Feiner and Joshua Rosenfeld

CHEESEY POTATO CASSEROLE
Elise Feiner

6 large potatoes, peeled, boiled and put through a ricer
2 bags grated cheddar cheese or one bag of cheddar and another of mozzarella or Monterey jack

Salt and pepper to taste
Heavy cream

Butter a large casserole. Layer the ingredients in the following order: potatoes, grated cheese, salt and pepper. Repeat ending with a layer of cheese. Pour enough cream over the layers to almost reach the top of the casserole. Do not overfill or it will bubble over. Bake at 350° until the casserole is hot; reduce the oven to 250°, and continue baking for 3 hours.

This is great with barbequed ribs, steak, or chicken!

TWICE BAKED POTATOES DAVID
Elise Feiner

12 russet baking potatoes, peeled and left whole
2 teaspoon salt
1 to 2 cups heavy cream
1 (8 ounce) container of cream cheese with chives
1 cup ricotta
8 tablespoons butter
1 pound bacon, center cut, cooked crisp and crumbled
1 bag shredded sharp cheddar, grated
2 cups mozzarella, grated

1 bag Monterey Jack Cheese, shredded
½ cup grating cheese
1 cup sour cream
¼ cup chopped fresh chives
Freshly ground black pepper to taste
Garlic salt to taste (about 1-1½ teaspoons)
2 scallions, finely cut in circles (save some for top)
American cheese Slices (for the top) or grated cheddar

Place the potatoes in lightly salted water in a heavy 4-quart saucepan. Bring to a boil. Reduce the heat to a simmer and cook until the potatoes are fork tender, about 40 minutes. Drain in a colander and place through a ricer. Add the cream (start with one cup only add the second cup if mixture is very firm; this will depend on the type potato used), butter, cream cheese, ricotta, scallions, sour cream, salt, and black pepper. Don't make the mix too loose especially if you freeze it. Add the bacon (reserve 6 slices for the top), grated cheeses, and chopped chives and stir until thoroughly combined. Season with garlic salt, and pepper to taste. Place into a large greased casserole pan (I usually get two deep aluminum trays from this amount). Top with bacon, scallions, and break up the American cheese over the top. (May be frozen at this point). Bake 400° about 45 minutes. Cover with foil if it's getting too brown. Serve immediately. Serves 12 to16. You can divide this is half or freeze the second one for later use.

This is great to do for a Thanksgiving Casserole. It saves the time of baking the potatoes and stuffing then. This is one of David's favorites. If you want, do it ahead and defrost it and then bake it. Don't use instant mashed if you are freezing this.

"Mom Mom" Betty Feiner,
Jeffrey Feiner, "Nanny"
Katherine Avella
at Jeff's graduation from the
University of Pennsylvania

SCALLOPED POTATOES
Elise Feiner

4 cups very thinly sliced potatoes
1 onion, thinly sliced
2 tablespoons flour

Salt and pepper
4 tablespoons butter; divided in half
1½ cups hot milk

Put a layer of potato and onion in a 1½-quart buttered casserole. Sprinkle with the flour, salt, and pepper. Dot the potatoes with butter. Repeat; top with a layer of potato. Dot with butter again. Add enough hot milk to almost cover the potatoes. Bake covered with aluminum foil, in a preheated 375°oven for 45 minutes. Uncover and bake 15 minutes longer. Serves 4.

SAVORY CHEESE PUFF
Iryna Trociuk

1 regular size box (Red) of Stovetop® Stuffing
8 ounces sharp cheddar cheese cut in
½-inch cubes
3 tablespoons flour

3 tablespoons butter, melted
4 eggs at room temperature
3¼ cups milk

Preheat the oven to 350°. Place crumbs in a buttered 2-quart casserole. Add cheese, sprinkle flour over cheese. Drizzle butter over the cheese/flour mixture. Combine eggs, milk, seasoning packet from the stuffing mix, and mix well. Pour over the cheese. Bake at 350° uncovered for 1 hour. No peeking!

FAN POTATOES
Elise Feiner

6 large size Idaho or Russet Potatoes (try to make them about the same size)
1 teaspoons salt
1 teaspoon garlic salt
Black pepper to taste
1 stick butter, melted

5 tablespoons of chopped fresh herbs (thyme, basil, sage, chives, parsley, and oregano) whatever you prefer
5 teaspoons of the dried herbs of your choice
½ bag grated Cheddar or Monterey Jack cheese
4 tablespoons grated cheese

Peel the potatoes, and then score the potatoes into very thin slices but do not go completely through. They should look like a fan at this point. Put the potatoes in a baking dish and fan them slightly, being careful not to break them apart. Sprinkle with salt, garlic salt, pepper and drizzle with butter. Sprinkle with the herbs. Bake the potatoes 425° for about 1 hour. Remove from the oven. Sprinkle with the cheeses. Bake for another 15 minutes until lightly browned. The potatoes should be soft inside.

This is a takeoff of a potato I had in a restaurant in New Orleans in the late 70's. It's as close as I could come. Maria Trainor does something like this on the grill. She takes a potato and cuts it in thirds but not all the way through and sprinkles salt, pepper and places pats of butter between each section. She wraps them in foil which has been sprinkled with salt and pepper, places them on the grill on medium heat for about 30-40 minutes.

THREE POTATO CASSEROLE
Elise Feiner

2 tablespoons butter
2 whole heads garlic, halved
1 quart heavy cream
Salt to taste
Freshly ground black pepper
½ pound goat cheese, crumbled

1 pound russet potatoes peeled and sliced ¼-inch thick
1 pound sweet potatoes peeled and sliced ¼-inch thick
1 pound red or new potatoes, sliced ¼-inch thick
2 scallions cut in thin rings
½ cup grated cheese

Preheat the oven to 400° Grease a large soufflé or casserole dish with the butter. Cut the whole heads of garlic in half, removing any excess loose skins. In a sauce pot, bring the garlic and cream to a simmer. Season with salt and white pepper. Simmer for 15 minutes, or until the cream has reduced by a quarter and becomes slightly thickened. Whisk in the cheese. Season the potatoes with salt and white pepper. Layer the potatoes in the soufflé dish, alternating the white potatoes, sweet potatoes and red potatoes; sprinkle with the scallions and grated cheese as you layer. You should have a total of six layers. Remove the garlic from the cream and cheese mixture and pour over the potatoes. Cover the dish with aluminum foil and place in the oven. Bake for 30 to 35 minutes. Remove the foil and continue cooking for 10 minutes or until the top is golden brown. Cool the gratin for 10 minutes before serving. Serves 8.

This casserole recipe is very colorful, and as my Aunt Jean always said, you have to cook with color; this is for her.

L-R: Steven, Marc, Elise, David, and Jeffrey Feiner…
Club Med in Dominican Republic 1989
This is one of my favorite family photos.

WHITE POTATO PIE
Katherine Avella

10 pounds potatoes, peeled
5-6 eggs, lightly beaten
1-2 cups grating cheese
2 tablespoons parsley
Salt and pepper to taste
Dash or basil optional

1½ sticks butter, melted
1 onion, peeled and finely chopped
3 slices boiled ham, about ¼-inch thick cut into small cubes
1 pound ricotta cheese
2 (2 cup) packages grated mozzarella cheese
½ pint heavy cream

Boil the potatoes in lightly salted water until fork tender. Mashed or placed through a ricer. In a mixer, add riced potatoes with 1 stick of melted butter, heavy cream, salt and pepper to taste and mix well. Sauté the onion in the remaining ½ stick of butter, until lightly browned and soft. Add to the potatoes. Add the eggs, grating cheese, ricotta, mozzarella, and parsley and basil. The mix should not be too loose. Fold in the ham. Place in a greased casserole or deep aluminum pan that has been sprayed with PAM®. If freezing this don't bake first. (Allow to come to room temperature before baking). Score the top with a fork making lines both vertically and horizontally to resemble a basket weave. Bake 375° for about 1 hour until golden brown. Let set a few minutes before serving. Serves 16 as a holiday side dish.

We always make this at make this a Thanksgiving in place of mashed potatoes because it can be made in advance or do it the night before and refrigerate it and bake in the morning or, freeze it and let it defrost and bake it.

APPLESAUCE
Elise Feiner

6 medium Cortland or Macintosh apples, peeled, quartered, and cored
¼ cup cranberries
¼ cup dark-brown sugar

¼ cup granulated sugar, plus 4 tablespoons
1½ teaspoon ground cinnamon
⅛ teaspoon freshly grated nutmeg
¼ cup water

In a medium saucepan combine, apples, cranberries, dark-brown sugar, granulated sugar, cinnamon, nutmeg, and ¼ cup water. Cover, and cook over medium heat. Cook apples, stirring occasionally, until apples are soft and beginning to come apart, about 15 minutes. Process quickly in a food processor or a food mill. Use immediately, or cool before serving. Serves 6.

I think the cranberries add a nice pink color to the applesauce.

MASHED YAMS IN ORANGE CUPS
Elise Feiner

6 pounds large yams (red-skinned sweet potatoes)
¾ cup marshmallow Fluff®
9 tablespoons butter, at room temperature
3 tablespoons maple syrup
3 tablespoons honey
½ cup brown sugar
1 teaspoon cinnamon
Dash grated nutmeg

Salt and pepper to taste
3 tablespoons orange juice
3 tablespoons Grand Marnier
1 teaspoon vanilla
3 large eggs
9 large oranges
Additional marshmallow Fluff® or mini marshmallows
36 pecan halves

Pierce yams all over with a fork. Working in two batches, cook yams in microwave 15 minutes (or bake in oven 45 minutes at 400° until soft) Turn yams over; cook until tender, about 12 minutes longer. Cut yams in half; scoop pulp into a large bowl. Add ¾ cup marshmallow Fluff®, butter and syrup and honey; mash until smooth. Add salt, pepper, cinnamon, nutmeg, and vanilla. Add Grand Marnier, OJ, and brown sugar. Whisk in the eggs. Can be made a day ahead; cover and refrigerate) Preheat oven to 350°. Cut thin slice from the top and bottom or each orange to make flat surfaces. Cut the oranges in half. Scoop out pulp; reserve for another use. Place the orange cups on 2 baking sheets. Divide the yam mixture equally among cups. Top with a dollop of marshmallow cream or mini marshmallows and two pecan halves. Bake until beginning to brown, about 30 minutes. Serves 18.

I found this in a magazine and then jazzed it up a bit. They looked and tasted great.

AUNT MICHELE'S SWEET POTATO CASSEROLE
Michele Maida

3 cups sweet potatoes, mashed or a 40 ounce can
1 cup of sugar
1 egg lightly beaten
¼ cup milk

½ cup butter, melted
½ teaspoon vanilla (optional)
Dash of salt

If you are using fresh sweet potatoes, bake in a 400° oven for 45 minutes to one hour. Peel and mash. If using canned, mash well. Add remaining ingredients. Mix well and pour into a greased casserole dish.

Topping:
½ cup brown sugar
⅓ cup flour

1 cup of pecans or walnuts, chopped if desired

Preheat oven to 450°. Mix brown sugar, flour and nuts together. Spread over the potato mixture. Bake for about 20 minutes.

Aunt Michele says that she makes this at Thanksgiving. I love the topping! She said that you can also bake this in a ready made pie crust.

L-R: Cousins Michele and Maryann Maida

ROASTED POTATOES GRECIAN STYLE
Barbara Schwartz

Red New Potatoes or Idaho potatoes cut in small cubes
(amount will depend on number of people)

Vegetable oil
Cooking with Love's Passion Spice Mix

Place a little vegetable oil in a large roasting pan that has been sprayed with PAM®. Add the cubed potatoes and sprinkle liberally with Cooking with Love's Passion Spice Mix. Place in a 400° preheated oven about 45 to 60 minutes or until very crisp.

SPAGHETTI SQUASH SUPREME
Elise Feiner

1 large spaghetti squash
8 slices bacon, crisply fried and crumbled
4 tablespoon butter, melted
1 tablespoon Brownulated sugar

½ teaspoon salt
¼ teaspoon black pepper
¼ cup grated cheese
1 bag shredded Swiss cheese

Halve the squash carefully; removed seeds. Cover with plastic wrap and microwave about 10 minutes per half, turning once. Cook until soft and easily pierced with a fork. Let cool, rake with a fork until it resembles spaghetti. Preheat the oven to 350°. Fry the bacon and save the drippings. Mix the drippings with butter, sugar, salt, pepper, grated cheese and ¾ of the Swiss cheese. Mix well. Place in a baking dish that has been sprayed with PAM. Sprinkle with remaining cheese. Bake until thoroughly heated about 20 minutes. If cheese is getting too brown, cover with foil during the baking.

SWEET POTATO PIE
Julie Ann Juliano, M.D.

3 cups mashed sweet potatoes	2 eggs
¼ cup sugar	1 teaspoon vanilla
¼ cup butter	⅓ cup milk

Mix all of the above ingredients together and place in greased baking dish.

Topping:

¼ cup butter	½ cup flour
¼ cup brown sugar	1 cup chopped pecans

Mix together and sprinkle on top of potatoes. Bake at 350° for about 25 minutes, enjoy.

Julie Ann is my Aunt Julia's granddaughter. She is in Family Practice Medicine in New Jersey. Julie Ann sent this recipe; it is a family favorite in her house. Even with a busy medical practice, she finds time to cook, bake and sew, and teach her girls to do the same!

Julie Ann's Girls
Angela, Laura, and Maria

AUNT JENNY'S OVEN ROASTED POTATOES
Jenny Tarantino

Russet or Idaho Potatoes (amount depending on how many you are serving)	Olive oil
	Salt
Onions (Several, peeled and sliced)	Water

Peel and quarter the potatoes. In a large roasting pan, sprayed with PAM®, add the potatoes, onions, a generous amount of olive oil and salt. Add just a little water to the baking pan as well. Bake in a very hot oven 400° to 450° for 45 minutes to an hour or until very brown and crisp. Stir occasionally during the cooking process to evenly brown all the potatoes.

My Aunt Jennie was the best cook. I remember that the potatoes that she made were sliced, but Ann said they were quartered. They were always so crisp and delicious. Everyone used to fight to get to scrap the bottom of the pan, but when Aunt Jennie knew that her brother Sam (or Sem) as they called him (my father was the only brother with 6 sisters, talk about being spoiled...) she would put the pan away and save it for him. I think my Aunts, Jenny, Mary, and Frances, were probably the best cooks, my Julia was the great baker, and my Aunts, Mae and Flo went to work so they could spoil all the nieces and nephews rotten. I can still remember Sunday trips to the candy store in Ozone Park, and picking out everything I wanted. They never said no to any of us. The only problem was, they worked in a bathing suit factory and after too many trips to the candy store, who could ever fit into the suits?????

THERESA'S STUFFING
Theresa Feiner

2 stalks of celery, diced
1 medium onion, peeled and chopped
1 can of mushrooms drained
1 green pepper, seeded and diced

1 stick of butter
Salt and pepper to taste
Hot water
Pepperidge Farm® Seasoned Stuffing Mix

Sauté all the ingredients except the water and stuffing mix in the butter for about 30 minutes or until soft. Add salt and pepper to taste. Add the vegetables to the stuffing mix in a large bowl. Add enough hot water to soften the stuffing. Place in a greased casserole pan and bake at 350° for 45 minutes to an hour

Aunt Theresa makes this at Thanksgiving. It's a very good traditional stuffing mix . You can use chicken broth instead of water.

L-R Ivan, Karen and Theresa Feiner

SAVORY STUFFING
Elise Feiner

1 cup chopped broccoli or chopped mushrooms
½ cup chopped onions
½ cup chopped celery
6 green olives (optional), chopped
¼ cup butter
4 packages Ritz® Crackers, coarsely chopped

2 cups walnuts, pecans, or almonds, coarsely chopped
¼ cup fresh parsley
½ teaspoon ground black pepper
1 tablespoon poultry seasoning
1 can chicken broth (13 ounces)
2 eggs, beaten

In a frying pan or skillet, sauté the broccoli or mushrooms, onions, and celery in butter until tender. In a large bowl, mix the cracker crumbs, nuts, parsley, poultry seasonings, black pepper, olives and the sautéed vegetables together. Add the chicken broth and eggs, mixing until well combined. Place in a greased casserole (2 quart) and cover. Bake at 325° for 30 to 40 minutes or until thoroughly heated.

MATZOH STUFFING
Elise Feiner

1 (16 ounce box) Matzoh Farfel
1 stick unsalted butter or margarine
2 (13¾ or 14½ ounce cans) College Inn® Chicken Broth
3 stalks celery, finely chopped
1 bag Ore-Ida® Frozen onions

1 can or bottle Green Giant® mushroom slices
½ teaspoon black pepper
1-2 teaspoons garlic salt
¾ cup grating cheese (Parmesan or Pecorino Romano)

In a large frying pan, melt the butter; add the onions and celery and sauté until the onions are golden brown. Add the mushrooms, pepper, and garlic salt. In the meanwhile, in a large baking dish sprayed with PAM®, pour in the matzoh farfel and the cans of broth. Stir until well coated and soft. Add the vegetable mix. Stir in the grating cheese. Bake 375° 45 minutes to 1 hour. Serves 6.

Note: This cannot be served with meat if you keep a strict kosher kitchen unless you eliminate the grated cheese and use the margarine.

This is a great stuffing for Passover, but you can use it any time of the year. It makes a good traditional stuffing.

SWEET POTATO CASSEROLE
Katherine Avella

10 sweet potatoes, baked and mashed, or 4 large cans
sweet potatoes, drained and mashed
1 stick of butter, melted
1-1½ half pints of heavy cream
¼ cup orange juice
1 can pineapple chunks, drained or small can of mandarin
oranges, drained (optional)
1 teaspoon cinnamon
¼ cup corn syrup

¼ cup Mrs. Butterworth's® Syrup
⅓ cup brown sugar
3 tablespoons Grand Marnier
2 teaspoons vanilla
Dash of salt
1-2 apples, peeled and cut into very tiny cubes, or thin
slices
1 bag of mini marshmallows

Pierce the potatoes a few times with a fork and bake in a 400° oven about 45 minutes to one hour or until soft. When potatoes cool; peel. Place them potatoes in a large mixing bowl with the remaining ingredients except the apples and marshmallows. The amount of cream will be determined by the amount of potatoes. Don't make the mixture too loose. When well mixed, fold in about ¼ of the bag of marshmallows and the apple slices. Place in a large baking or casserole pan that has been well greased. Top with mini marshmallows. Cover with aluminum foil and bake at 375° for about 40 minutes. Uncover and bake about another 15 minutes until the marshmallows are golden brown. For a variation, you can cube the apples instead of slicing them. Take a stick of butter, ¼ -½ cup brown sugar, and 1 teaspoon of cinnamon and place in a frying pan (add the apples last. Fold half of the apples into the mix and place some of the remaining half in the middle of the casserole and the rest along the edges. Then top with marshmallows and bake as above.) Serves about 16 as a side dish.

We make this every year at Thanksgiving. It is always the same basic recipes but I always tweak it a little. This can be done in advance and frozen. Don't add the marshmallows until it defrosts. You can also serve this in oranges. Cut oranges in half and scoop out the insides. Fill with the sweet potatoes. Top with marshmallows and pecans halves and bake in the orange cups.

Jeanne Burkhardt and
her son Larry Joe

Jeane used to work
with Aunt Fifi and has
been a family friend for
over 55 years!

GRILLED POLENTA
Elise Feiner

8 cups water
1 teaspoon salt
2 cups polenta/yellow cornmeal
⅓ cup heavy cream

3 tablespoons butter, softened
1½ cup grated Parmesan
Fresh cracked black pepper, to taste
Olive oil

Bring water and salt to a boil in a large saucepan. Gradually whisk in the cornmeal in a slow steady stream. Lower heat and continue to whisk until the polenta is thick and smooth, about 20 minutes. Add the cream and butter and continue to stir until well blended.
Remove from heat, stir in Parmesan and black pepper. Pour the polenta into a buttered 9 x 13-inch shallow baking dish and spread evenly with a spatula. Cover and refrigerate a few hours. Cut the polenta into squares. Brush both sides with olive oil and transfer to a hot grill or a grill pan. Grill on both sides until golden brown.

I was in Italy for the first time in 1969; I became a fan of Polenta. I love it like this.

ELISE'S CORNBREAD- HERB STUFFING
Elise Feiner

1 package Pepperidge Farm® Herb Stuffing
1 package Pepperidge Farm® Cornbread Stuffing
2 sticks butter
2-3 large onions, peeled and diced
4-6 stalks celery, chopped
3 cloves garlic peeled and chopped
1 box mushrooms sliced
1 bag shredded carrots
Leftover mashed potatoes or make 4 potatoes and mash them with butter, milk, etc. (optional)
1 pint heavy cream

1 pint light cream
4-6 small cans chicken broth (14.5 ounces)
1 cup hot water
3 eggs, beaten
2 cups grating cheese
Salt and pepper to taste
Garlic and onion salt to taste
1 package Sazon Goya con cilantro y achiote seasoning
Fresh parsley, chopped about 2 tablespoons
Fresh sage, chopped about 2 tablespoons

In a large frying pan, melt the butter. Add the onions, celery and garlic and sauté until soft and slightly brown. Add mushrooms and carrots; cook until mushrooms are soft. Pour into a large bowl. Add stuffing mix and stir well. Fold in the mashed potatoes (they keep the stuffing moist) if desired. Add the creams, broth (add as much as you like to get the texture you like, but don't make it too loose), and water. Mix well. Add the beaten eggs, and grating cheese. Add remaining seasoning. Place into a well greased baking dish. (May be frozen at this point, bring to room temp before baking.) Bake at 375° for about 1 hour. Serves about 16.

You can add pecans, green olives, or hard boiled eggs. We make this every Thanksgiving in one form or another. Sazon Goya is in the Spanish food section. You can also use Cooking with Love's Passion Spice Mix or McCormick Season All Season Salt in place of Sazon.

Right: Standing: Joseph Avella
Sitting L-R: Rosemarie Moraglia Williams, and her mother
Frances Moraglia

Left: Rosemarie and Jerry Williams and their girls more recently!

Rosemarie taught with my mother at St. Fortunata's School in Brooklyn and my mother became her mentor. She in turn became a close family friend.

CRANBERRY-ORANGE RELISH
Elise Feiner

1 cup water
1 bag fresh cranberries (12 ounces)
¾ cup sugar

3 ounces freshly squeezed orange juice
Zest of 1 orange
1 can Mandarin orange segments (about 1 ounce)

In a medium saucepan, bring 1 cup water to a simmer. Add the cranberries, sugar, orange juice and zest. Stir until sugar is dissolved and the cranberries begin to pop, about 15 minutes. Remove from heat. Add orange segments to the cranberries. Stir to combine. Refrigerate and it will thicken.

We've been making this for Thanksgiving for years; I rarely buy prepared Cranberry sauce.

302

NANNY'S BAKED BEANS
Katherine Avella

4 (28 ounce) cans of B&M® Brick Oven Baked Beans
1 teaspoon dry mustard
½ teaspoon black pepper
1 cup ketchup

1 cup granulated light brown sugar
3 ounces molasses
½ pound bacon (optional)

Spray a pan with PAM®. Add all the beans and other ingredients except the bacon. Mix together. Top with slices of bacon and bake at 375° for 1 hour and 10 minutes.

These are Nanny's famous beans. They are great for a barbeque or buffet table.

L-R: Frances, Teddy and Eadie Barone

KASHA VARNISHKES
Barbara Schwartz

Kasha:
2 cups chicken broth or water
3 tablespoons butter
½ teaspoon salt

⅛ teaspoon pepper
1 cup of Kasha (whole grain)
1 egg

Heat the broth, butter, salt and pepper to boiling. Lightly beat the egg in a bowl. Add the kasha; stir to coat the kernels. In a medium frying pan or a saucepot, add the egg coated kasha. Cook over high heat for 2 to 3 minutes, stirring constantly until the egg has dried, and the kasha kernels are separate. Reduce heat to low. Quickly stir in the prepared boiling liquid. Cover. Simmer 8 to10 minutes until kasha is tender and liquid is absorbed.

Varnishkes:

3 large onions, peeled and sliced
1 pound fresh mushrooms, sliced
Oil

1 pound bow tie noodles
1 egg
Salt and pepper to taste

Before you start the kasha, put up a pot of lightly salted boiling water to cook the bowties. While waiting for the water to come to a boil, in a large frying pan, heat enough oil to cover the bottom of the pan. Sauté the onions and mushrooms until golden brown. Set aside. Drain the bowties when done. Mix the cooked kasha, bowties, and onion mix together, add egg, salt and pepper. Mix well. Can be served immediately, or kept in the refrigerator and reheated later in a 350° oven.

This is a very traditional Jewish family favorite. My brother Joe is always asking Barbara to make this and stuffed derma.

Stuart and Barbara Schwartz
and granddaughter Kayla Lipson

SWEET AND SOUR WALNUTS
DeAnn Jungkind

1 pound of walnuts halves
1 cup flour
1 cup of water
1½ teaspoons baking powder

¼ cup cornstarch
Salt and pepper to taste
Oil for deep frying

Mix all the ingredients into a batter. Add the walnuts, and deep fry. Try to keep the nuts separated. Use a large slotted spoon to scoop out the nuts from the oil. They can be done ahead to this point. Reheat for a few minutes on a cookie sheet. Otherwise just proceed with the sauce.

Sweet and Sour Sauce:
In a medium frying pan, coat the bottom of the pan with oil. Chop a few cloves of garlic in large pieces and add to the oil. Fry for a few minutes and remove the garlic.

Add:
½ cup sugar
½ cup white or rice wine vinegar

½ cup ketchup
½ cup pineapple juice

Mix 2 tablespoons cornstarch dissolved in ½ cup cold water. Pour in the above mix in a thin stream to thicken. Bring to a boil. Add the nuts and mix thoroughly. Serve immediately.

I got this recipe from DeAnn Jungkind. DeAnn and her husband Arnie used to cook Chinese meals in their home, and serve it in their dining room. You had to book it a year in advance. She only took reservations on January 1, and if you didn't call early enough, you didn't get in. She learned Chinese cooking from a Chinese woman neighbor of hers in exchange for English lessons. I have never had any Chinese food that compared to hers. We were all sorry when she stopped doing the dinners when Arnie retired. This was always one of my favorite courses and she shared the recipe with me.

L-R: Johann Gigliotti
and
Elise Feiner

CRANBERRY MOUSSE
Elise Feiner

1 (20 ounce) can Dole® crushed pineapple in juice
1 (6 ounce) package strawberry Jell-O®
1 cup water
1 (1 pound) can whole berry cranberry sauce
3 tablespoons fresh lemon juice

1 teaspoon fresh grated lemon peel
¼ teaspoon ground nutmeg
2 cups sour cream
½ cup chopped pecans

Drain the pineapple well, save the juice. Add juice to the Jell-O in a 2 quart saucepan. Stir in water. Heat to boiling, stirring to dissolve Jell-O; remove from heat. Blend in the cranberry sauce. Add lemon juice, lemon peel, and nutmeg. Chill until mixture thickens slightly. Blend sour cream into the mixture. Fold in pineapple and pecans. Pour into a two quart mold that has been sprayed with PAM®. Chill until firm. Unmold onto a serving plate. Serves 8 to 10.

CRANBERRY SALAD MOLD
Elise Feiner

2 envelopes Knox® Unflavored Gelatin
¾ cup sugar
1½ cups boiling water
1 cup ginger ale, chilled
1½ cups ground cranberries
3 envelopes Knox Unflavored Gelatin
⅓ cup sugar

1 cup boiling water
⅓ cup Hiram Walker® Cranberry Cordial
3 cups sour cream
2½ cups lemon or orange sherbet, softened
1½ cups walnuts, coarsely chopped

In a medium bowl, mix the 2 envelopes of unflavored gelatin with ¾ cup sugar; add the 1½ cups boiling water and stir until gelatin is dissolved. Stir in ginger ale and cranberries (you can substitute 1 can (16 ounces whole berry cranberry sauce and decrease the sugar to ½ cup). Turn into a 10-inch fluted tube pan or 12 cup mold sprayed with PAM®. Chill until almost set.

Creamy Layer:

In a large bowl, mix the 3 envelopes of gelatin with ⅓ cup sugar; add the 1 cup of boiling water and stir until gelatin is completely dissolved. With a wire whisk, blend in cranberry cordial, sour cream and sherbet. Let stand until mixture is slightly thickened, about 1 minute; fold in walnuts. Spoon onto almost set cranberry layer; chill until firm. Garnish with frosted cranberries. Serves 16.

This is a beautiful mold for Thanksgiving. I got it from a magazine about 25 years ago.

CINNAMON APPLESAUCE
Elise Feiner

8 McIntosh apples or other tart, red-skinned apples
⅔ cup freshly squeezed lemon juice
¼ cup sugar

2 tablespoon butter
2 teaspoon cinnamon (optional)

Quarter the apples, do not peel, and remove the seeds and cores. Place apples in a bowl, add the lemon juice, and toss thoroughly to coat. Place the apples, sugar, and 1 cup water in a heavy saucepan. Cover pot, and let simmer over low heat, about 30 minutes, or until the apples break down to a sauce like consistency. Remove pot from heat, uncover, and allow apples to cool slightly. Using a rubber scraper, gently push apples through a Foley food mill or wire sieve. Add butter and cinnamon. Throw out the skins. Refrigerate until ready for use.

A Chanukah favorite. Nanny Nellie always said, "Applesauce cuts the grease!"

How about these side dishes???
L-R: The Reinisch Girls…
Adele Reinisch Freedoff, Shirley Reinisch Flomenhoft, Betty Reinisch Feiner and
Nellie Reinisch

305

CHEWY CHEESES
Phyllis Jendzo

1 pound elbow macaroni
1 pound Jarlsberg cheese, shredded

2 (15 ounce) cans Delmonte® tomato sauce (heated to a boil)

Boil one pound of elbow macaroni in lightly slated water. Drain. Add the shredded Jarlsberg Swiss cheese, and two cans of Delmonte tomato sauce. Mix these three ingredients all together and enjoy.

My cousin Phyllis said that this recipe is for Uncle Joe...sounds easy enough for him to cook too!

Phyllis and Richard Jendzo

The Much Younger Jendzo Kids: Kimberly, Laura, Stephen holding Philip

Cousins Phyllis Jendzo and Elise Feiner
Although, we look more like sisters…

Adrianna Skonberg, Laura Jendzo Skonberg, and Kim Jendzo

306

Vegetables...

The Extended Avella-Mainella Clan

L–R Back Row: Douglas, Philip, Phyllis Avella, John-Michael Latini, Melissa Avella, David, Marc, Elise Feiner,
Thirza and Joseph Avella
L–R Front Row: Philip Avella, Jr., Steven Feiner, Katherine Avella, Nicole Latini, Lauren and Jeffrey Feiner, Michael Avella

**"I think people that have a brother or sister don't realize how lucky they are.
Sure, they fight a lot, but to know that there's always somebody there,
somebody that's family."**
-Trey Parker and Ma

Stocking a Dream Kitchen Continued:

Gravy Boats (2 - 3)
Glass Nesting Mixing Bowls (9 bowl set)
Microwave-Safe Casserole with Lid in different sizes
Rectangular Glass Baking Dishes, multiple sizes
Airtight containers for dry goods storage
Clear glass custard dishes
Ramekins or small stainless steel bowls come in handy for organizing

Cutlery – a good knife set is a must…I must tell you that if price is an issue, Chef Tony knives that you see on TV are great and reasonably priced! You can buy knives individually as well; you should consider the following in your start-up purchase:

Paring Knife
Chef's Knife
Carving Knife
Serrated Bread Knife
Serrated Tomato Knife

Heavy-Duty Blender
Toaster Oven
Kitchen Scale
Hand Mixer
Microwave Oven
Heavy Duty Mixer - Kitchen-Aid®
Food Processor - Cuisinart®
Crock-pot (a large oval 7 quart is the best and a smaller round one)
Coffee Maker
Ice Tea Maker

Sharpening Steel
Boning Knife
Cleaver
Kitchen Shears (great for trimming fat from meat)
Spice Rack
The Coffee Maker – who wouldn't love the built in Miele® coffeemaker – makes one cup at a time and grounds the beans, quite pricey but everyone can dream!
Showtime Rotisserie Oven (great for turkey breasts, chickens, etc.)…the best
Fajita Maker
Pizzelle Iron
Griddle

_____
_____
_____
_____
_____
_____
_____
_____
_____
_____
_____
_____
_____
_____

APPLE STUFFED SWEET POTATOES
Ann D'Amico

8 cooking apples
3 sweet potatoes, cooked in salted water
½ teaspoon orange peel
2 tablespoons orange juice
2 tablespoons butter, melted

2 tablespoons milk
1 egg, beaten
¼ teaspoon nutmeg
2 tablespoons lemon juice
½ cup corn syrup, light

Trim the skin from the tops of the apples and with the tines of a fork score in spirals all around the apples. Core the apples but don't go all the way through to the bottom. Brush with lemon juice after coring the apples. Peel and mash the sweet potatoes. Add remaining ingredients except for the 2 tablespoons of lemon juice and ½ cup corn syrup to the potatoes and mix well. Preheat oven to 325°. Fill a pastry bag with the potatoes mixture. Pipe the mixture into the apples. Mix 2 tablespoons of lemon juice with ½ cup corn syrup. Pour over each apple. Bake 45 minutes uncovered. Baste with corn syrup mixture several times during the baking. Serves 8.

This makes a great presentation for a holiday dinner.

GREEN BEAN CASSEROLE ALMONDINE
Edith Mainella

5 tablespoons butter
2 cups Kellogg® cornflake cereal, crushed to ½ cup
2 tablespoons Hidden Valley Ranch® Original Salad dressing mix, divided
3 tablespoons all purpose flour

1½ cups milk
1 cup shredded cheddar cheese
2 (10 ounce) packages frozen French cut green beans, cooked and drained
2 tablespoons slivered almonds, toasted

Melt 2 tablespoons of the butter. Combine with the cornflake crumbs, and 1 tablespoon of the Hidden Valley mix. Set aside for the topping. Melt the remaining 3 tablespoons butter. Stir in the remaining salad dressing and flour. Gradually add the milk, stirring until smooth. Microwave on high for 2 to 3 minutes until thick and buttery, stirring once during cooking. Add cheese, stir until melted. Place beans in a medium size casserole. Pour sauce over the beans. Microwave 5 to 6 minutes until heated thoroughly. Sprinkle with the reserved topping and almonds. Microwave 1 minute on high power. Let stand 5 minutes before serving. You can also bake it in the oven if you'd like at 350° for 20 minutes. Sprinkle on topping and bake an additional 10 minutes.

Another favorite that Aunt Edith used to make at the holidays. It's delicious!

BROCCOLI AND CAULIFLOWER AU GRATIN
Elise Feiner

1 large bunch of broccoli
1 head cauliflower
2 cups boiling water salted
3 tablespoons butter
3 tablespoons flour
2 cups milk

½ pound sharp cheddar cheese, grated
Salt and pepper, to taste
¼ cup flavored bread crumbs
⅓ cup parmesan cheese

Preheat oven to 350°. Cut up broccoli and cauliflower in floweret's and stalks. Remove any thick stalks. Place the vegetables in boiling water and cook until almost done about 7 to 10 minutes. Drain and place in a buttered baking dish. In a medium saucepan, melt the butter and while stirring, slowly add the flour. Add the milk and continue to stir until it thickens. Add salt and pepper to taste. Add the cheese and stir until it melts. Pour sauce over the vegetables in the casserole dish. Top with breadcrumbs and grated parmesan cheese. Bake about 30 minutes. Serves 6,

"Remember, we all stumble, every one of us. That's why it's a comfort to go hand in hand."
-Emily Kimbrough

ꞀIALLE

4 teaspoon capers
2-3 sprigs basil or parsley, finely chopped
1 teaspoon fresh oregano, finely chopped
1 clove garlic, finely chopped

⌐ and chopped
⌐ed and chopped

⌐gplants thinly and cut into 1-inch cubes. Sprinkle lightly with salt and leave in colander for 1 hour. Wipe dry. Heat oil ⌐t). Add eggplants and sauté over high heat for 15 minutes. Add tomatoes, olives, and capers. Lower heat and ⌐g for about 15 minutes or until eggplants is soft. Add the herbs (basil or parsley and oregano) and garlic. Taste for salt, ⌐rve either hot or cold. You can also put this on top of sliced toasted Italian bread and use as a Bruschetta.

A very young Josephine Mainella...our Aunt Fifi My Aunt Fifi never knew her father, he died before she was born, leaving my grandmother a 29 year old widow with 4 children to raise. She did a damn good job if I do say so myself.

"Aunt Fifi" Josephine Mainella enjoying some leftover Thanksgiving Turkey!

AVIVA'S RED PEPPERS
Aviva Philipson

12 red bell peppers, sliced in strips
Olive Oil (Just enough to cover a large frying pan's bottom)
8 cloves of garlic (4 cut in thick slices, 4 crushed)

About ½ cup balsamic vinegar
About 3 tablespoons brown sugar
1 teaspoon garlic salt

Heat the olive oil in a large frying pan. Fry peppers in the 4 cloves of garlic that have been sliced thickly. When the peppers are almost done, add the crushed garlic. Fry a few more minutes. Then add the balsamic vinegar, brown sugar and garlic salt. Stir and heat through.

Aviva and I were sitting together at Norm Siegel's birthday party and were exchanging recipes. She told me to try these and they were great!

BROCCOLI
Elise Feiner

2 package frozen broccoli spears, or fresh broccoli
2-3 tablespoons olive oil or vegetable oil

2-3 cloves of garlic, peeled and cut in half
Salt (or garlic salt) and pepper to taste

Cook broccoli according to package directions. Take one of the pieces of cut garlic and using the cut end, rub the garlic cut end down all over a serving platter (directly on the plate.) Then, place olive oil, remaining garlic cloves, salt ,(I usually add a little garlic salt as well) and pepper in the platter. When broccoli is done, drain and place on platter. Turn the broccoli spears in the oil mixture to coat well. Remove garlic cloves; I always count the number of pieces I've put in a recipe beforehand so I can remove them all later. Note: For a stronger flavor of garlic you can heat the olive oil and garlic in a small frying pan for a minute or two, but no longer.

This is a basic way to fix broccoli, no fuss, but delicious. This is one of Marc and Aunt Fifi's favorites.

ARTICHOKES (STUFFED)
Katherine Avella

6-8 large artichokes
2-3 large loaves of Italian bread remove crust and make into crumbs, not too fine
2-3 tablespoons dried parsley
6-8 cloves garlic, peeled and crushed
1-2 cups grated cheese
Salt and pepper to taste

Cut off a little piece from the stems of the artichokes and dice finely, don't use all the stems because you will need to add some to the pot you are using to cook.
Olive oil to dampen the crumbs but don't add too much
6-8 thinly sliced pieces of provolone or mozzarella cheese (optional)
8 cloves of garlic, peeled and left whole

Remove the crusts from the Italian bread and cut into small pieces. Put in a blender or food processor and pulse to make breadcrumbs, but **DO NOT** make them too fine, just on and off once or twice should do the trick. In a large mixing bowl, mix together the parsley, crushed garlic, grating cheese, salt and pepper, tiny cubes of the stems of the artichokes (see below), and olive oil; enough to lightly dampen the crumbs. Set aside

Wash and clean the artichokes. Take a scissors, and snip off **ALL** the pointed thorny parts of every leaf (Be **CAREFUL**, these are sharp.) Bang the artichokes on the counter or other hard surface top side down, to open the middles. With a scissor cut out as much stuff (thorns and fuzzy leaves) from the middle of the artichoke as you can. Create a wide pocket in the middle by using your hands. Season the middle pocket of the artichoke with salt and pepper to taste. Cut off the stems of the artichoke, peel them a little, and cut them into small cubes. Use some in the stuffing as directed above, and set the remainder of them aside to put into the pot. Stuff the middle of the artichoke with the breadcrumb mix, and carefully stuff the breadcrumb mixture between **ALL the outsides leaves** of the artichokes.

In a large cast iron, Dutch oven, or large pot (I do them in a crock-pot) carefully place the artichokes, stuffing side up, in a single layer. Add the rest of the cut up stems, add the whole cloves of garlic (1 per artichoke), add 1 tablespoon of oil per artichoke, salt and pepper to taste, and enough water to come up about ¼ ways up the artichokes. You can also add ½ cup of white wine if desired and top each artichoke with a thin slice of provolone or mozzarella cheese. Bring to a boil and then simmer on low heat for 1½ to 2½ hours or until you can pull out a leaf from an artichoke easily, and the leaf is tender. If doing them in a crock-pot put on automatic for about 6-8 hours. You can do them ahead, stuff them, place them in the crock-pot without all the liquid, and refrigerate. When you are ready to turn the crock-pot on, add the liquid (water and oil) as directed above, stem pieces, and garlic, and turn on early in the morning. They will be ready by dinnertime.

This is my mother's recipe. I think it was handed down to her from my grandmother. These are the best artichokes. At Daniele's they put proscuitto (cut into small pieces, and fried first) and a little mozzarella in their artichokes. You could probably add that to this mix as well. We always have these at Christmas. My kids love these.

L: Front to Back: Jerry, Kevin and Marc
R: Ivan and Betty Feiner
My father-in-law loved **my** mother's cooking

309

ARTICHOKES PARMIGIANA
Katherine Avella

2 tablespoons oil
1 medium onion, peeled and diced
1 (2 pound 3 ounce) can plum tomatoes
1 teaspoon basil
Salt and pepper to taste
Lemon juice
2 large mozzarella cheese, cut in slices
½ cup bread crumbs

4 tablespoons parmesan cheese
6 fresh artichokes
Flour
3 eggs, beaten
4 tablespoons parmesan cheese
Salt and pepper to taste
Oil for frying

Preheat oven to 375°. Make the sauce first. In a medium saucepan, heat the oil. Add the onions and sauté until translucent. Add the plum tomatoes and break them up gently with a fork or use your fingers. Add the salt, pepper and basil to taste. Bring to a boil and then lower to a simmer. Cook covered for about 15 to 20 minutes. Set aside. Slice the mozzarella and set aside. Mix the bread crumbs and parmesan cheese together and set aside. Take artichokes and trim down to the chokes, being careful when handling them. Be sure to remove all the sharp insides. Cut each choke into quarters and then into ⅓'s. Rub your hands and the artichokes with lemon juice to prevent discoloring. Dip the chokes in flour. Mix the beaten eggs with salt and pepper and grated parmesan cheese. Dip the floured chokes in the egg mixture; deep fry. Drain on paper towels. In a casserole dish, place a layer of tomato sauce. Then place a layer of chokes, mozzarella, sauce and alternate until everything is used up. Top with sauce and the crumb and cheese mixture you made earlier. Bake for 20 minutes. Serves 6 to 8.

This is a nice change from eggplant Parmigiana.

BALSAMIC ZUCCHINI
Elise Feiner

1 zucchini, peeled and sliced thinly on an angle
3-4 cloves of garlic, peeled and left whole
2-3 tablespoons olive oil

Garlic salt and black pepper to taste
Balsamic vinegar

In a large frying pan, heat the olive oil, add the garlic cloves. Fry the zucchini slices until done. Discard the garlic pieces. Sprinkle with a little garlic salt and pepper. Drizzle or sprinkle with a little balsamic vinegar to taste.

COUNTRY MUSHROOM SAUTÉ
Elise Feiner

6 slices of bacon, I prefer thick sliced for this dish
4 tablespoons butter
2 pounds sliced mushrooms, you can mix the types
1 medium onion peeled and finely chopped
2 cloves of garlic, peeled and crushed

4 tablespoons fresh breadcrumbs (made from day old bread) or fine dry unflavored breadcrumbs depending on the taste you prefer
¼ cup parmesan cheese
1 tablespoon finely chopped parsley
Freshly ground black pepper

Fry the bacon in a large frying pan until crisp. Remove from the frying pan, crumble, and set aside. Add the butter to the remaining bacon fat. Sauté the onions until slightly golden; add the garlic. Add the mushrooms, sauté for about 3-6 minutes. Add the breadcrumbs, salt, pepper, parsley; sauté another 3 minutes. Add the crumbled bacon and parmesan cheese. Serve hot. Serves 6.

I made this recipe up one day when Cousin Michele was visiting. She just loves mushroom, and loves this dish!

BROCCOLI WITH BUTTERED BREADCRUMBS
Elise Feiner

1 to 1½ pounds broccoli florets
Salt and freshly ground black pepper

4 slices firm white bread
6 tablespoons butter

Steam broccoli with whatever method you prefer or use a steamer. Remove to a platter and season with salt and pepper. In the meantime, process the bread in a food process or blender to make bread crumbs. In a small saucepan, heat butter on medium high until butter turns a nutty brown color. Add the bread crumbs and toss in the butter. Pour the buttered crumbs onto the broccoli and toss to coat.

BAKED STUFFED EGGPLANT
Katherine Avella

8 baby eggplants
1 pound ricotta cheese
1 bag shredded mozzarella cheese
Salt and pepper to taste
2 teaspoons dried parsley

2 eggs
½ cup grated cheese
1 pound of ground beef
Tomato sauce (see Eggplant Parmigiana recipe for sauce)

Brown ground beef in a frying pan with a little oil. Drain well and set aside. Mix all ingredients together except the eggplant and the beef. Add ground beef to the mix and mix well again. Peel the eggplants and boil in lightly salted water for about 10 to15 minutes. Let cool. Cut in half and remove seeds from center. Stuff the eggplants with the beef mixture. Place a layer of sauce in a baking dish. Put the stuffed eggplants on top of the sauce. Top with more sauce. Bake 350° about 30 to 45 minutes. You can also use this filling and fry the eggplant like the Parmigiana directions and roll them individually, if you'd like. Then, place a layer of sauce in a baking dish. Place the eggplant rollettes on the sauce; top with more sauce and grated cheese. Bake as above.

Standing L-R: Betty Arcara, Elise Feiner, Michele and Mary Ann Maida
Seated L-R: Nina Frank, Marie Caccavale, Phyllis Foster, Flo Avella,
Jean "Dolly" Caccavale

BALSAMIC MUSHROOMS
Elise Feiner

⅓ cup olive oil
3 cloves of garlic, peeled and crushed
1 pound of sliced mushrooms

2-3 tablespoons balsamic vinegar
3 tablespoons white vinegar
Salt and pepper to taste

Sauté the garlic in olive oil for 1 to 2 minutes. Do not brown the garlic. Add the mushrooms and cook for 2 minutes, stirring occasionally. Stir in the balsamic vinegar and wine, cook another 2 minutes. Season with salt and pepper to taste. Serve hot or cold.

ESCAROLE FEINER
Elise Feiner

5 heads escarole, washed, and cut small
5 tablespoons olive oil
8-10 cloves garlic, peeled and crushed
½ teaspoon black pepper

½ teaspoon salt
2½ cups grated cheese or more depending on your taste

Fill the sink with cold water. Cut the bottom off the escarole and then cut the leaves into two-inch pieces. Wash well and remove to strainer. Let the water out of the sink, wash out the sand. Fill with cold water again, wash it again, and remove to strainer. Repeat as many times as is necessary to wash the escarole, making sure there is no sand in it. Fill a large (16-quart) pot with salted water. Bring to a boil. Add the escarole. Boil for about 15 to 20 minutes until escarole turns bright green and is softened to your taste. Just before the escarole is cooked, take a large corning ware or heat proof bowl or large pot and add the olive oil. Heat the oil and then add the, garlic, salt and pepper. Heat until the garlic just starts to get hot and sizzle, (a few seconds at most). Take the escarole from the pot with a slotted strainer; drain well, but leave a little bit of water. Add it to the dish or pot with the oil. When the dish is half full, sprinkle half the cheese over it. Add the rest of the escarole. Add the rest of the cheese. Blend well. Cook for a few minutes just to fuse the flavors and melt the cheese.

This seems to be a favorite recipe of Lauren's. We all grew up eating escarole and nothing tastes better than escarole on a fresh Italian Bread sandwich. Sometimes in our house it seems that the escarole was just a side dish for the grating cheese! My grandmother has a saying in Italian," Chi mangia scarole mai muore."...he who eats escarole never dies! (Dialect) "It's delicious!" In Upstate New York where we now live, all the restaurants make "Greens" which are similar but with salami, cherry peppers, proscuitto, salami, and breadcrumbs. We like our greens plain sometimes, and this is that recipe.

BROCCOLI AU GRATIN
Elise Feiner

Fresh or frozen broccoli spears or floweret's, cooked as directed
2 tablespoons butter
2 tablespoons flour (I like Wondra®)
1 cup heavy cream

1 cup sharp cheddar cheese
Fresh bread crumbs (tossed with a little butter and lightly toasted)

Cook broccoli as directed; drain. In a medium saucepan, melt the butter; add flour and stir quickly to prevent lumps. Add the cream and continue to stir to prevent lumps. Cook over medium heat until sauce starts to thicken, stirring frequently. Add cheese and stir until melted and hot. Place broccoli in a casserole pan. Pour sauce over broccoli. Top with toasted breadcrumbs.

BROCCOLI CHEESE BAKE
Lucy Massimiano

2 packages frozen broccoli flowerets
1 pound cheddar cheese (You can also use Velveeta®), cut in ½-inch cubes

1 stick butter, melted
1½ stacks Ritz® Crackers, crumbled

Preheat oven to 325°. Cook the broccoli according to package directions until almost cooked. Place in a buttered casserole dish. Place the cut up cheese on the top of the broccoli. Melt the butter and add the Ritz crackers to the melted butter. Sprinkle the cracker mix over the cheese. Bake uncovered 20 minutes. Serves 6.

CORN ON THE COB
Elise Feiner

6-8 Fresh ears of corn, peeled and cleaned or Frozen Ears of Corn
4-6 teaspoons sugar

½ - 1 cup of milk
Cold water

Place the cold water, sugar and milk into a large pot. Place the corn into the cold water and bring up to a boil. Cover. Cook according to package directions for the frozen corn, or about 12 to 15 minutes for fresh corn. Drain. Serve. Add salt and pepper, Cooking with Love's Passion Spice Mix, chives, parmesan cheese, or melted butter if desired or whatever flavors you desire. Experiment with new tastes!

CREAMED SPINACH
Elise Feiner

2½ pounds fresh spinach, well washed (not dried) and tough stems removed
3 tablespoons unsalted butter
¼ cup all-purpose flour
1 cup milk or heavy cream

Coarse salt and freshly ground pepper
1 teaspoon sugar
Freshly grated nutmeg
Sour cream, for serving (optional)

Place spinach in a large pot over high heat. Cook, covered, with just the water clinging to leaves, stirring occasionally, until wilted, 2 to 4 minutes. Transfer to a colander, drain, squeezing out and saving excess liquid. Roughly chop spinach; set aside. In a medium skillet, melt butter over medium heat. Add flour, and cook, stirring, 1 to 2 minutes. Slowly whisk in milk; season with salt, pepper, and sugar. Thin with reserved spinach liquid. Stir in spinach. Sprinkle with nutmeg to taste and, if desired, top with a dollop of sour cream. Serve immediately. Serves 4.

CYNDI'S GREEN BEANS
Cyndi Koury

Large amount of flat green beans or string beans, cleaned and cut if desired
2-3 large onions, peeled and chopped

3-4 cloves or garlic, peeled and crushed
Enough oil to cover a large frying pan
Salt and pepper to taste

Place the oil in a large frying pan, **while the oil is still cold**; add the onions and garlic. Cook until the onions start to caramelize. Add the beans and continue cooking until the beans start to caramelize as well. Add a little water if necessary. Place the beans in a crock-pot. Add water to the frying pan to deglaze. Add the water to the crock-pot. Cook on high 1 to 1½ hours and reduce to low and let cook a few hours.

Cyndi Koury... Cyndi is an incredible Lebanese cook, learning from her mother-in-law.

EDAMAME
Elise Feiner

¼ cup coarse sea salt
½ teaspoon freshly cracked pepper
½ teaspoon garlic salt

½ teaspoon oregano
3-4 tablespoon melted butter
1 (1 pound) bag frozen edamame (soybeans in the pod)

Toast salt in a dry small heavy skillet over moderate heat until salt turns slightly tan, about 7 minutes. Add the pepper, garlic salt, and oregano; cook for about another minute. Cook the edamame in salted boiling water until tender about 4 minutes; transfer to a bowl of ice water to stop the cooking process. Pat dry. Toss the edamame with the melted butter and **a little of the salt mixture**. Place remaining salt mixture in a plastic container for future use. Serve hot or cold.

DEB'S GREENS
Deb Montero

4-5 heads of escarole
½ pound of proscuitto, cut into strips
1 stick of butter
½ - ¾ cup olive oil

2 cups of pecorino Romano cheese
2 cups fresh Italian breadcrumbs
Cherry peppers or sweet peppers
8-10 cloves of garlic, peeled and crushed

Carefully wash the greens and rinse in cold water several times to remove all the dirt. Cut the greens into medium size pieces. Blanch the greens in boiling water for a few minutes until slightly softened. Immediately drain into ice water to stop the cooking process. In a large sauté pan, melt the butter and olive oil together and add the proscuitto and cook until the edges curl. Add the garlic and cook for a few more minutes being careful not to burn the garlic. Add the greens, cheese, breadcrumbs and peppers. Heat thoroughly. These may be made in advance and reheated in the oven (350° for about 15 minutes). Serves 12.

This is Dr. Orlando's office manager Debs' recipe. She says that they are the best greens. She makes them up in large quantities at the holidays to share with her family. She was most generous in contributing them to our book.

FRAN'S DELICIOUS RED PEPPERS
Frances Zierler

6-8 large red peppers, washed and cut into 1-inch cubes
3-4 large onions (6-7 small onions or 2 bags frozen onions), peeled and diced
¼ - ½ cup olive oil

1 (15 ounce) can Del Monte® tomato sauce plus 1 (8 ounce) can if you use the large amount of peppers and onions
2-3 teaspoons onion salt or more depending on your taste

Heat the olive oil in a large frying pan. Fry the diced onions in olive oil for about 10 to 15 minutes on medium-hi heat, until soft but not too brown; stir frequently. Add the peppers and sauté for about another 20 minutes on medium-hi heat, stir frequently, add the tomato sauce and lots of onion salt and simmer for about another 15 to 20 minutes. Serves 6.

Fran always makes these and they taste just wonderful. I asked her for the recipe and she generously gave it to me. They are wonderful as a side dish, on sandwiches, or on cheese and crackers, great on just about anything.

FRAN'S VINEGARED PEPPERS
Frances Zierler

4-6 red peppers, seeded and cut into
1-inch strips
1 cup flavored breadcrumbs

½ cup Locatelli Romano or Parmigiana cheese
¼ cup oil
⅛ cup red wine vinegar

Wash, seed, and cut red peppers into wide strips. Place a little oil on a baking sheet. Place the peppers on the sheet. Mix the remaining ingredients together. Sprinkle on top of the peppers. Cook at 425° until the peppers are nice and soft, about 30 minutes. Cover with foil if the crumbs are getting too brown. You may need a little more oil and vinegar.

Aunt Fran always makes these delicious peppers at the holidays, but they are delicious anytime. They make a great side dish, and are even great on a sandwich.

"When you are a mother, you are never really alone in your thoughts. A mother always has to think twice, once for herself and once for her child."
-Sophia Loren

EGGPLANT CROQUETTES
Rose Pacifico

2 eggplants, peeled and cubed
1 cup shredded Sharp Cheddar Cheese
1 cup Italian breadcrumbs
2 eggs, beaten
2 tablespoons parsley
2 tablespoons chopped onion

3 cloves of garlic, peeled and minced
½ cup grating cheese
1 cup oil
1 teaspoon salt
½ teaspoon black pepper
Small cubes of mozzarella (optional)

Place the eggplant in a microwave and cook on medium-high for three minutes. Turn the eggplant and microwave another 2 minutes. The eggplant should be tender, cook another 2 minutes if not tender. Drain any liquid and mash. You can also bake the eggplants with the skin on in a 350° oven for about 45 minutes. Pierce the skin a few times with a fork before baking. Place on a baking sheet. When cool, peel and mash the eggplant and continue with the recipe. Combine the cheese, breadcrumbs, eggs, parsley, onion, garlic, salt and grating cheese with the mashed eggplant. Mix well. Shape the eggplant mixture into patties, either round or log shaped. Refrigerate for about an hour. Heat the oil in a large skillet. Fry the patties until golden brown on each side, about 5 minutes per side. You can also insert a tiny cube of mozzarella in the center of each croquette before frying.

I got this recipe from Rose Pacifico. She was our neighbor in Bayville. I have learned so many wonderful recipes from watching her cook as a teenager. I spent many hours in her kitchen and have many wonderful memories of holidays with her family. It wouldn't be uncommon to see Rose come home from a wedding and start to cook another meal for her husband John at 2:00 in the morning. She is a phenomenal cook.

My nephew, Michael Avella and Aunt Elise Feiner

EGGPLANT ZUCCHINI GRATINÉE
Ann D'Amico

2 narrow eggplants, don't peel
6 small zucchini, don't peel
6-8 tomatoes, vine ripened medium size
3 tablespoons Herbs de Provence
1 teaspoon salt

½ to 1 cup olive oil
⅓ cup grating cheese
Whole loaf of Italian Bread, remove crust, make fresh bread crumbs

Slice eggplant into ½-inch thick circles. Take a cookie sheet, smear with oil, and sprinkle the Herbs de Provence lightly. Take a slice of eggplant press into the cookie sheet and turn over. Roast at 400° for 15 minutes, until fork tender, slightly shriveled, but not mushy.
   While that's cooking cut the zucchini in ¼-inch slices lengthwise. Brush the top with oil. Sprinkle with salt, pepper and Herbs de Provence. Cut the tomatoes in circles and fix the same way. In a long gratin tin, smear with oil and start layering. Layer the eggplant across, then the zucchini, and then the tomatoes, so that the tops of each one are shown, not flat, sort of stand them up. In a bowl, put the breadcrumbs, cheese and one tablespoon olive oil; mix with your hands. You must see the tops of all the layers; the zucchini and tomatoes are raw at this point. Spread the crumb mixture over the top and drizzle with olive oil. Bake 350° 25 to 40 minutes until fork tender. Cover if the crumbs are starting to get too brown.

My cousin Ann D'Amico makes this all the time. It is a beautiful presentation, and easy to make.

315

EGGPLANT PARMIGIANA - AVELLA STYLE
Katherine Avella

1-2 large eggplants, peeled and sliced
6-8 eggs (more as needed)
⅛ teaspoon ground black pepper
½ teaspoon salt
1 tablespoon dried parsley
½ to 1 cup grated cheese

1-2 cups Wondra® flour, more if necessary
2-3 bags of shredded mozzarella or 2-3 large (1 pound)
mozzarellas, thinly sliced
Grated cheese to sprinkle between the layers
Marinara Sauce for eggplant (see index)
Vegetable oil for frying

Peel and slice the eggplant into ⅛-¼-inch slices lengthwise or in circles. I prefer lengthwise as it's faster to fry. Mix the eggs, salt, pepper, parsley, and grated cheese together with a whisk or fork. Dip each slice of eggplant in Wondra flour, and then into the egg mixture. Have a frying pan with about 1 cup of oil heating up. After you dip the slices in egg; fry them in the hot oil. Fry on both sides for a few minutes. Remove to a platter lined with paper towels. Layer paper towels between the eggplant slices. The oil may get foamy when you fry the eggplant, because of the high protein content in the egg. **If it gets too bad, change the oil or it will spill over onto the stove and cause a grease fire!** Don't forget **to heat the oil** before you start to refry. In a large baking dish, place a layer of marinara sauce (see recipe index for **Avella's Marinara Sauce for the Eggplant**) then a layer of eggplant, a layer of mozzarella, sprinkle a little grated cheese, a little more marinara sauce, and then start with eggplant, mozzarella, grated cheese, marinara, and keep repeating. End with a layer of eggplant, topped with marinara sauce and grated cheese. Do not put mozzarella on the top or it will burn. Cover with foil, and bake at 350° for about 45 to 1 hour or until it starts to bubble and is thoroughly heated through. Remove the foil and top with a very generous layer of mozzarella and a little more sauce, and return to the oven, bake uncovered for about 10 to 15 minutes until the cheese is melted. Let sit about 15 minutes before serving.

This recipe has been in our family forever. It is the most delicious eggplant. We make ours differently from most because many others use breadcrumbs. We like the taste of the egg flour mixture better. This is great when served hot and even better in sandwiches the next day. Personally, I like it cold for breakfast the next day. For a different twist take pizza dough and place it in a deep dish cake pan. Bake a few minutes until golden. Layer eggplant in crust and bake again for about 35 minutes.

FRAN'S CARROTS
Frances Zierler

2 bags baby carrots
1 stick butter

2 tablespoons mustard
½ cup brown sugar

Boil the carrots in lightly salted water until cooked to desired doneness. In a saucepan, melt the butter. Add the mustard and brown sugar. Cook stirring constantly until the sugar is dissolved. Drain the carrots. Add to the brown sugar mixture. Stir until coated. Serve immediately.

FRENCH'S® GREEN BEAN CASSEROLE
Elise Feiner

¾ cup milk
⅛ teaspoon black pepper
1 (10 ¾ ounce) can Campbell® Cream of Mushroom Soup

2 (9 ounce) packages frozen cut green beans, thawed
1⅓ cups French's® French Fried Onions

In a 1½-quart casserole, mix all the ingredients except ⅔ cup onions rings. Bake 30 minutes at 350° or until hot; stir. Top with ⅔ cup fried onion rings. Bake 5 more minutes or until golden. Serves 6.

This is everyone's favorite green bean casserole. It has been in every magazine from the beginning of the time. It is from the French's company.

"When a friend is in trouble, don't annoy him by asking if there is anything you can do. Think up something appropriate and do it."
-Edgar Watson Howe

VEGETABLES

FIVE VEGETABLE TORTE
Patty Cardinale

4-5 tablespoons olive oil
1 large Spanish onion peeled and sliced
¼-inch thick
3 medium yellow squash peeled and sliced ¼-inch thick
3 medium zucchini peeled and sliced
¼-inch thick
1 medium red pepper sliced ¼-inch thick
1 yellow pepper sliced ¼-inch thick
1 green pepper sliced ¼-inch thick
½ pound fresh mushrooms, including stems, sliced ¼-inch thick

6 large eggs
¼ cup whipping cream
2 cups stale bread cut in ½-inch cubes
8 ounces cream cheese, in small pieces
2 cups grated Swiss cheese
2 teaspoons salt
2 teaspoons pepper (this is a little spicy, so I use one teaspoon)
Rosemary to taste (optional)
Thyme to taste (optional)

In a large pot, heat the olive oil. Add onion, squash, zucchini, peppers and mushrooms. Cook over medium high heat about 15 minutes, until the vegetables are slightly cooked but still crisp, stirring constantly. Drain. (I needed two large pans to cook this volume of vegetables). In a large bowl, beat the eggs and cream. Add remaining ingredients. Stir vegetables into egg mixture. Mix well. Pour into a greased 9-inch spring form pan, packing the mixture tightly. Place on a baking sheet. Bake in a preheated 350° oven 1 to 1½ hours or until firm to touch, puffed and brown. If top browns too quickly during baking cover with aluminum foil. Serve torte hot, at room temperature, or cold. Torte may be reheated in a 350° oven for about 30 minutes. Serves 12 to 15.

This recipe came from Patty Cardinale during a recipe exchange we participated in. It was wonderful; I made it for Thanksgiving.

GRILLED VEGETABLES ON THE FOREMAN ® GRILL
Carmen Ferreiro

Cut an eggplant and/or zucchini lengthwise about ¼-inch thick. Brush both sides with olive oil, balsamic vinegar and seasonings to your taste. Place on the Foreman Grill and cook until tender and golden brown. You can also do this on the barbeque.

Carmen said these are so delicious and easy to make. She said they're also good the next day.

FRIED ASPARAGUS
Elise Feiner

1 bunch of asparagus (try to get very thin ones)
½ - ¾ cup all purpose flour or Wondra® (add more if necessary)
3-4 eggs
½ teaspoon salt

⅛ teaspoon pepper
1 teaspoon parsley
½-¾ cup grating cheese
½ cup plain breadcrumbs or more
Vegetable oil for frying

Bring a medium saucepan with lightly salted water to a boil. Prepare an ice bath (place several cubes with a cold water in a bowl). Place the asparagus into the boiling water for 2 to 4 minutes depending on the thickness of the stalks (they should just be pliable but not fully cooked). Remove immediately to the ice bath; remove to a dish and set aside. In a small dish (square if possible) beat the eggs, salt, pepper, parsley, and grating cheese together. On your counter or work surface, lay out two paper dishes or wax paper sheets and place the bowl with the egg mixture between them. Fill the first dish with flour and the second with breadcrumbs. Dip the cooled asparagus into the flour, then the egg mixture and finally into the plain breadcrumbs. Layer the breaded asparagus on a platter lined with waxed paper, and place waxed paper between the layers of asparagus. Heat a large frying pan with about 1-inch of oil in it. When the oil is hot, fry the asparagus until golden brown. Drain on paper towels. Place on a serving platter. Serve immediately.

My mother used to make these all the time for Sunday dinner. It is prepared on the order of a breaded cutlet and tastes delicious. My son David loves these and eats them like candy. They taste great leftover, even served cold!

FRIED SQUASH BLOSSOMS
Rose Pacifico

Squash blossoms
1 pound ricotta cheese
1 bag shredded mozzarella cheese
2 sliced of boiled ham (about ¼ " thick, cut in tiny cubes)
Salt and pepper, to taste
1 tablespoon dried parsley
½ cup grated cheese
1 egg for the cheese mixture

1 cup flour
1 egg for the batter mixture
Salt and pepper to taste
2 tablespoons sesame seeds
1 teaspoon baking powder
Water
Oil for frying

Gently wash squash blossoms in cold water and remove excess water. **These are very fragile**. In a large mixing bowl, mix ricotta, mozzarella, ham, salt and pepper, parsley, grated cheese, and one egg. Mix well. Mixture should not be too loose, but if you have to, you can add another egg. Make the batter: Mix the flour, 1 egg, salt and pepper, sesame seeds, baking powder and a little water. Mix well. Batter should be loose, but not watery. Add a little more water if necessary. Stuff the flower blossoms with the ricotta mixture. Dip in batter. In a large frying pan, heat about 1-inch of oil. Fry stuffed blossoms until golden brown.

I remember learning to cook in our neighbor Rose Pacifico's kitchen as a teenager, in Bayville, NY. I remember being so fascinated watching someone cooking flowers! In the Neapolitan dialect these are called sciuri 'e cuccozziello.

GREEN BEAN CASSEROLE
Elise Feiner

3 cans string beans, drained or 3 boxes frozen
Garlic salt to taste
1 (8 ounce) container sour cream
1 can cream of mushroom soup

8 ounces Velveeta®
24 crackers (Saltines®, Ritz® or your choice)
4 tablespoons butter, melted

Crush crackers and mix with melted butter. Preheat the oven to 375°. Place the string beans in the bottom of a 9x13-inch or 8x8-inch greased baking dish. Sprinkle with garlic salt. Mix the sour cream and the soup together; pour over the green beans. Slice the Velveeta and place on the top. Cover with buttered crumbs. Bake uncovered at 375° until hot, about 30 minutes. Serves 8.

ITALIAN CUCUMBER SALAD
Katherine Avella

2 cucumbers, peeled and sliced
Salt and pepper to taste
1 small onion cut in slices

½ teaspoon oregano
3 tablespoons olive oil
1 tablespoon red wine vinegar

Peel the cucumbers and then take a fork and score the outside vertically with the tines of the fork. Slice into rounds. Add the cucumbers and onions to a serving dish. Add salt and pepper to taste. Add oregano, oil and vinegar. Mix well. Adjust the flavor of oil and vinegar to your taste. Refrigerate overnight.

ITALIAN VEGETABLE SALAD
Katherine Avella

1 pound cooked vegetables of your choice (string beans, artichoke hearts, carrots, or asparagus)
1 small onion, peeled and thinly sliced
½ cup oil (vegetable or olive)
½ cup red wine vinegar
1 tablespoon fresh dill or 1 teaspoon dried dill

1 clove garlic, peeled and crushed
½ teaspoon dry mustard
½ teaspoon sugar
½ teaspoon salt
⅛ teaspoon black pepper

Mix everything together except the vegetables and onions. Shake well. Take vegetables and onions and mix with dressing. Let sit overnight in refrigerator to flavor.

AUNT LIZZIE'S STUFFED PEPPERS
Elizabeth Maida

4 large peppers
½ cup oil
1 cup toasted breadcrumbs
12 black olives (cut into pieces)
6 anchovy fillets (cut into very small pieces)
1 tablespoon chopped parsley

1 tablespoon chopped basil
1 tablespoon capers
½ teaspoon salt
½ teaspoon pepper
½ cup tomato sauce

Cut the top of the peppers, and remove all the seeds. Mix all the ingredients together, except for the peppers and tomato sauce. Make sure they are well blended. If the stuffing seems too dry add a little more oil. Stuff the peppers and place them standing up in a deep baking dish. Pour about 1 teaspoon of oil over the top of each pepper, and top each pepper with one tablespoon of the tomato sauce. Bake in a 350° oven for one hour.

My "Aunt" Lizzie is actually my mother's first cousin. All of the cousins cook in very similar fashion learning from their mothers, who were sisters. There was my grandmother, Clementina, "Aunt Lizzie's" mother Orsola, Philomena, grandmother of the Grimaldi, Sanito, DaBruzzo clan, Maddelena, and several brothers, John, Rocco, Francesco, and Barthlomeo.

Back Row L-R: Jean Mainella, Ursula Barone Marano, Kathy Barone Prato,
Maryann Maida, Elizabeth Barone Maida, Michele Maida
Front Row L-R: Orsola Barone, Rae Sessa Barone and Eadie Tucker Barone

JOPPY'S OVEN ROASTED TOMATOES
Joppy Basile

Roma Tomatoes sliced ¾-inch thick (about 15 to 20)
tomatoes to one pound of macaroni)
Olive oil
Garlic cloves, lots, peeled (about 6-8) cut into
about 4 pieces from each clove

Salt and pepper
Fresh basil
1-2 cups grating cheese
1 pound of pasta of your choice, cooked according to
package directions; drain

Preheat oven to 450°, about 50 minutes. Slice the tomatoes. Place a thin layer of olive oil on a cookie sheet. Line the tomatoes on the tray on a single layer. Sprinkle generously with salt and pepper. Place one piece of garlic on each piece of tomato. Sprinkle with basil. Sprinkle generously with olive oil. Top with grating cheese. Roast with 450° until soft and slightly charred. Mix with a spoon. Add a little extra olive oil if too dry. Toss pasta with the tomato mix.

Joppy taught Maria Trainor how to make this. She said it was just delicious and gave the recipe to me. Joppy is a great cook as is Maria so how can you go wrong!

GREENS DANIELE
Jeffery Daniels, Sr.

2-3 heads escarole, washed and cut in small pieces, boiled
Olive oil and a little chicken broth
¼ pound proscuitto, chopped
1 large onion, peeled and chopped in large cubes
Black pepper
Granulated garlic

Fresh bread crumbs made from Italian Bread
Parsley
Olive oil
Freshly ground black pepper
Grated cheese
Paprika

Cut ends off escarole. Cut in small pieces. Wash several times to remove sand. Fill a large (8 or 16-quart pot) with salted water. Bring to a boil. Add greens and cook for 15 to 20 minutes. Drain well. Place a little olive oil in a frying pan and quickly fry the greens with the olive oil for a few minutes. In another frying pan, add a little (very little) olive oil to the pan, fry the proscuitto until slightly brown. Remove proscuitto and add the onion and brown lightly. Add the greens, and then add back the proscuitto, black pepper, granulated garlic, a little chicken broth, breadcrumb mixture (mix fresh breadcrumbs with parsley, a little olive oil, black pepper, grating cheese, and paprika to taste) and a little more grating cheese. Heat thoroughly. Serves 6.

This is a Utica specialty; Jeff's are some of the best. He was nice enough to share his recipe with me. We have become big fans of these greens. They are much drier than the way we normally prepare them, and are absolutely delicious. I think the onions are the secret in this recipe. Don't forget to visit Daniele's when you're in the Utica area. They are open for lunch 6 days a week. Daniele's 1556 Mohawk Street, Utica, New York. The phone is 315 724-5821, or for dinner at Valley View Country Club 315 733-8358

A few of Jeff and Theresa Daniel's
Grandchildren:
Bottom to top:
Jeffery III, Alexandria, and Amanda
Daniels

ITALIAN VEGETABLE STEW

Elise Feiner

5 tablespoons olive oil
½ bag frozen onions (12 ounces bag)
3 large cloves garlic, peeled and crushed
2 yellow squash, peeled and cubed
1 green pepper cut in 1-inch pieces
6 small zucchini, peeled and cubed
2 small eggplants, peeled and cubed
4 stalks celery cut ½-inch thick
Garlic salt to taste

Freshly ground black pepper to taste
2 cans stewed tomatoes (large), more if you like more tomatoes
1½ cups grated cheese
1 teaspoon oregano (you can add more to taste)
1 tablespoon basil (you can add more to taste)
Shredded mozzarella cheese (optional)
Shredded Provolone cheese (optional)

In a large pot or Dutch oven, heat the oil; add the onions and cook until lightly browned. Add the garlic; stir for about a minute. Add the yellow squash, zucchini, eggplant, celery. Mix well. Add the tomatoes. Season with garlic salt, pepper, oregano and basil. Cover and simmer for about 1 hour until vegetables are soft. Add grated cheese and mozzarella and provolone if desired.

JEANE'S RED PEPPERS
Jeane Cassata

6-8 red pepper, seeded and cut in
1 to 1½-inch strips
Olive oil
Freshly ground black pepper

Garlic salt to taste
1-2 large onions, peeled and finely diced
Flavored breadcrumbs
Grating cheese

Cut red peppers in strips. Place a little olive oil in the bottom of the pan. Place strips on top of oil. Season with pepper, garlic salt, lots of onions, and flavored breadcrumbs. Drizzle more olive oil on top. Bake at 400° until they start to soften. Lower temperature to 350°, and sprinkle generously with grating cheese. Cook until soft. Mix well. Serve.

Nani Jeane recipe is a little different from Aunt Fran's recipe, but just as delicious.

L-R: Jean Greenspan, David and Fran Zierler, Rachel, Aviva, and Claire Akselrad and Jeane Cassata at Aviva's Bridal Shower

GREENS MORELLE
Brenda Johnson

2 pounds of escarole
½ pound of proscuitto
garlic to taste
½ - 1 cup seasoned fresh breadcrumbs
6 hot or sweet cherry peppers

1 (14 ounce) can chicken broth
½ cup olive oil
grated cheese to taste
1-2 potatoes, peeled, cut into small cubes and parboiled

Wash the escarole several times in cold water to remove all the sand; cut into 2 to 3 inch pieces. Boil escarole in lightly salted water until fairly soft; drain. Cut garlic into small pieces. Slice peppers and cut proscuitto into small pieces. Heat the oil in a frying pan. Sauté garlic, peppers and proscuitto in the olive oil. Remove from the pan and set aside. With the oil in the pan, add the escarole and chicken broth to moisten the escarole. Cook for awhile. Then add the pepper and proscuitto mix back in. Microwave the potatoes; cool. In a small bowl, place a little olive oil, a little garlic powder, salt, pepper and oregano to taste. Place the potatoes on a cookie sheet and broil until golden brown. Just before removing the escarole from the pan, add the breadcrumbs, potatoes, and grating cheese to taste. **NOTE:** to make seasoned breadcrumbs take a day old loaf of Italian bread, remove crust and put in a blender or food processor and pulse until the crumbs are fairly large. Don't make too fine. Season the breadcrumbs with a few cloves of crushed garlic, salt and pepper to taste, parsley, and grated cheese and a few drops of olive oil. Feel free to substitute sweet peppers for the cherry peppers if you don't like the greens hot.

Greens are an Upstate New York specialty and these are made at the Chesterfield Restaurant. Brenda got this recipe from a friend.

SPANAKOPITA (SPINACH PIE)
Peggy Spirakis

4 (10 ounce) packages of frozen spinach, thawed with only ¼ cup liquid drained off
9 eggs
1½ bunches of scallions (halfway up the stems) finely chopped
4 springs fresh dill, finely chopped
Salt and pepper

2 tablespoons (no more) chopped fresh parsley
1 pound feta cheese finely crumbled
1 tablespoon olive oil
1 pound phyllo dough
Combine 1 part olive oil, 3 parts butter, 2 parts safflower oil (or other tasteless oil), heated

Combine all the ingredients except for the phyllo dough and oil mixture. In a medium size baking dish, grease with a little of the oil mixture brushed on. Line with a sheet of phyllo dough; if it is too large it can overhang the size of the pan. Brush lightly with the oil mix. Place another 6 layers of dough brushing each layer with the oil mixture. Pour in the spinach mixture and spread evenly. Put seven more layers of phyllo dough in the pan brushing each layer with the oil mix. Brush the top completely with oil mix. With a sharp knife or a razor, trim the sides to the edge of the lip of the roasting pan. Cut through the top phyllo layers and spinach lengthwise in thirds or fourths depending on how big you want the pieces. Cook in preheated 350° oven for 45 minutes to an hour until the top is medium brown. Remove and **do not cover** or it will get soggy. It can be refrigerated covered and top recrisped by heating in the oven.

Ariana Cacoulidis, the cutest
"Greek-Polish Princess" I know

Ariana and Basia Stasik Cacoulidis
Look out world…this child will one day wow the world with her
talent and beauty and brains…what a combination!

MUSHROOMS WITH ONIONS
Elise Feiner

1 large onion, peeled and diced
3-4 cloves garlic, peeled and crushed
2-3 scallions, thinly sliced
2 tablespoons olive oil
3 tablespoons unsalted butter
2 boxes sliced mushrooms
⅛ teaspoon pepper

¼ teaspoon garlic salt
½ teaspoon dried oregano
½ teaspoon dried basil
½ teaspoon dried Parsley
1 cup fresh breadcrumbs (made with day old Italian bread) optional
¼ cup grating cheese optional

Heat the olive oil and butter in a large frying pan. Add the onions and sauté until soft. Add the scallions and garlic, sauté another minute. Add the mushrooms, and seasonings. Cook on medium heat until the mushrooms are soft. If necessary add a little water. At the end, just before serving add the grating cheese and breadcrumbs if desired. Heat thoroughly.

ONION RINGS
Edith Mainella

2 large Vidalia onions or Bermuda onions
2 eggs
4 tablespoons water
2 teaspoons baking powder

Salt and pepper to taste
Flour or bread crumbs
Oil to fry

Slice the onions about ¼-inch thick and separate into rings. Beat the eggs with the water and baking powder. Season with salt and pepper. Dip the rings into the egg mixture and then into flour or breadcrumbs. Deep fry.

ONIONS AND MUSHROOMS
Elise Feiner

2 large onions, peeled and sliced
2 boxes sliced mushrooms
1 stick butter

Garlic salt
Black pepper

In a large frying pan, melt butter; sauté the onions until soft and starting to brown. Add the mushrooms. Add garlic salt and pepper to taste. Continue sautéing until the mushrooms are cooked. Serve 4 to 6.

This is a great side dish. It works very well with steak.

NANNY'S FRIED PEPPERS AND TOMATOES
Katherine Avella

6-8 frying peppers (cubanelle, long thin skin, light green) do not use big bell peppers
Oil for frying (vegetable or olive oil is fine) about 6 tablespoons
3 large cloves garlic, peeled and halved
2 large onions, peeled and sliced

½ (2 pounds 3 ounces can plum tomatoes) (put in a blender)
1 teaspoon oregano
2 teaspoons basil
Salt and pepper to taste

Wash and dry the peppers. Remove the top, slice in half and remove the seeds. You can then either slice each half into strips or cubes, depending on your preference. Heat a large frying pan with enough oil to just cover the bottom (you don't want to deep fry the peppers). When the oil is hot, start frying the peppers in batches. Remove them to a platter but don't drain on paper towels, just let as much oil drip off as possible before removing from the pan. As you put the peppers in the platter, lightly salt each layer of peppers. When you finish frying the peppers, add the cloves of garlic to the oil and when golden brown, remove and discard. Add the onions to the oil and sauté until soft and golden brown. Add the tomatoes (if you like more tomatoes, you can use the whole can), salt, pepper, oregano, and basil to the tomatoes and cook for about 15 minutes. Pour the sauce over the fried peppers. If you prefer a chunkier sauce don't blend the tomatoes just break them up with a fork or your fingers.

This is great as a side dish or on sandwiches. The aroma when this is cooking is divine... another typical Italian peasant dish.

On Left:

L-R: Samantha Caplan Zierler and Lauren Feiner

On Right:

L-R: Rene, Camille and Andrew Sanabria
If there was a reality show to find the world's nicest family, they'd win, hands down!

JOPPY'S EGGPLANT PARMIGIANA
Joppy Basile

3 medium eggplants
6 or more eggs as needed
Salt and pepper to taste
1 cup of flour (or more if needed)

Good quality parmesan cheese
Tomato sauce (see index for sauce for eggplant)
Olive oil for frying

13 x 9-inch glass baking dish
Bake Time: 40 minutes
Temperature: 375°

Wash the three eggplants well, and cut into ⅛-inch slices, leaving the skin on (peeling is optional.) Beat the eggs with salt and pepper. Dip eggplant slices into the egg mix. Then dredge in the flour. Place on a tray lined with paper towels as you flour them and let them set. Heat the olive oil (about ½-inch deep) in a frying pan. Fry the eggplant slices until golden. Drain on paper towels. Layer in the following manner in the glass dish: Tomato sauce on the bottom, a layer of eggplant, a very generous sprinkling of parmesan cheese, tomato sauce, eggplant, parmesan cheese, make 4 layers, ending with the parmesan cheese. Preheat the oven to 375°Bake for 40 minutes, or until thoroughly heated.

Joppy Basile is the mother of our friend Frank. Her grandson Frank, Jr. and Lauren are also good friends. Maria Trainor says this is another one of the excellent peasant style cooking Joppy is famous for. Joppy and my mother have the same style of cooking. Maria said she made it for dinner and Tim, Frank, and the kids made the whole tray disappear. It is a little different from the traditional Eggplant Parmigiana because it has no mozzarella in it. This is a true Italian eggplant Parmigiana, it we Americans that added the mozzarella to what most of us refer to as Eggplant Parmigiana.

L-R: Frank Basile, Erica Basile and Joppy Basile at Erica's 1st Birthday

PEARL'S SPINACH SOUFFLÉ
Pearl Borten

2 boxes frozen Stouffer® Spinach Soufflé
2 boxes frozen creamed spinach

1 large can or 2 small cans Durkee® French Fried Onion Rings

Thaw all frozen items. Add ¾ of the onions to the spinach mixes. Mix together well. In a high soufflé dish which has been sprayed with PAM®, add the spinach mix and top with remaining onions. Bake 350° for 30 to 40 minutes. Serves 8.

Another easy recipe and delicious side dish from Pearl Borten.

"A good son-in-law is like the acquisition of a new son; a bad one is like the loss of your daughter."
-Old Jewish Proverb

PEAS
Elise Feiner

2 cans LeSueur® Baby Peas, partially drained	1 medium onion, peeled and diced
8 slices bacon	Salt and pepper to taste

In a large frying pan, fry the bacon until crisp; remove and crumble. In the same oil, sauté the onions until golden. Add the peas, and salt and pepper to taste. Heat thoroughly. Drain most of the liquid before serving; add the crumbled bacon to the peas just before serving.

PEAS AND EGGS
Katherine Avella

1 medium onion, peeled and diced	2 eggs
2 tablespoons oil	Salt and pepper to taste
1 can LeSueur® Baby Peas	½ teaspoon dried parsley
5 tablespoons tomato sauce (like Hunt's® or Del Monte®)	3 tablespoons grated cheese

In a medium saucepan, heat the oil. Add onions and brown until golden in color. Add the tomato sauce, and salt and pepper to taste. Let cook on a simmer for about 10 to 12 minutes. Add the can of peas but remove half the liquid first. Cook for a few minutes. In a separate dish, beat the eggs with salt and pepper to taste, parsley, tomato sauce and the grated cheese. Slowly drizzle the egg mix over the peas, and stir slowly. Cover the peas for 5 minutes. Remove from heat. Let sit a few minutes before serving.

My mother used to make this quite often when I was growing up. At the time I hated peas (and all vegetables) little did I know what I was missing. These are delicious.

PEAS WITH MUSHROOMS AND ONIONS
Elise Feiner

2 cans LeSueur® baby peas	2 tablespoons oil
1 jar or can of mushrooms, sliced	Garlic salt to taste
1 large onion, peeled and diced or about	⅛ teaspoon black pepper
¾ cup frozen diced onions	

In a medium saucepan, heat the oil. Add the onions and sauté until golden in color and translucent. Add the peas, mushrooms, garlic salt, and black pepper. Heat thoroughly and serve immediately.

PEPPERS IN VINEGAR
Edith Mainella

6-8 roasting peppers or bell peppers	3-4 tablespoons olive oil
Equal parts of white vinegar and water (about ¾ cup of each)	3-4 tablespoons white vinegar (more or less depending on your taste)
1-2 cans of anchovies, drained and cut into small pieces	2-3 cloves of garlic, peeled and crushed
3-4 tablespoons capers	1 tablespoon oregano
1 (2.25 ounce) can of black olives, pitted and sliced, drained	1 tablespoon parsley
Salt and pepper to taste	

Bring a large pot filled with the water and vinegar to a boil. Add peppers and cook until they turn a different color, and they softened a little. Let them cool. Cut in half; removes stems and seeds. Fill with anchovies, capers, olives. In a bowl, add oil, salt, pepper, white vinegar, garlic, oregano, parsley to taste. Pour over the peppers. Let it marinate.

This recipe was Aunt Edith's, but originally it came from Lena Sanito, Uncle Nick's sister. My mother-in-law ate these at Aunt Edith's, and loved them. She would always ask Aunt Edith to make them for her. They are a great appetizer.

SPINACH
Elise Feiner

2 packages frozen leaf spinach, or fresh spinach
2-3 tablespoons olive oil

2-3 cloves of garlic, peeled and cut in half or thirds
Salt and pepper to taste

Cook spinach according to package directions. Place olive oil, pieces of garlic, salt and pepper in a platter or bowl. When spinach is done, drain and place in bowl. Turn to coat well. Remove garlic pieces. **Note:** For a stronger flavor of garlic, heat the oil and garlic in a small pan for a minute or two but no longer.

A much younger Elise Feiner studying in medical school in the Philippines a la Abe Lincoln by candlelight during a brown-out.

A much younger Marc Feiner…

ROASTED PEPPERS
Elise Feiner

Red, Green, and Yellow Bell Peppers (any combination or one color is fine) about 10 pounds; washed, rinsed and left whole
Vegetable oil or olive oil
Salt and pepper to taste

Whole peeled cloves of garlic cut into 2 or three pieces each
Dried parsley
Brown paper bags (I use the size for school lunches)

Place the peppers under a broiler or on a barbeque grill and let their skin get blackened on all sides, turn frequently. Remove from broiler or grill and place in paper bags. Leave in the bags until fairly cool. Remove the blackened skins with the tip of a paring knife; slit open and scrape out the seeds, and remove the tops. Slice into strips about ¼ to ½-inches thick. Because it is so much work to make the peppers, I recommend making a large batch at a time. At this point, remove what you need for the day and then package the remaining peppers in zip lock sandwich size freezer bags and freeze. Leave a nice amount for your use and season as follows: Place the peppers in a bowl. Add black pepper and salt to taste (about ⅛ teaspoon of pepper and ¼ -½ teaspoon salt). Add parsley (about 1 to 1½ teaspoons), oil (about 1½ tablespoons depending on the amount of peppers you are making, you may need a little more) and garlic (about 2 to 3 cloves cut in ½). Mix well. Store the peppers in a Tupperware® type container. Refrigerate. Remove the garlic the next day and discard. These taste better if made a day or two in advance. They keep well in the refrigerator.

Do not season the ones you are going to freeze until you defrost them. Defrost and remove most of the water from the zip lock bag. Season as you did with the original batch. In a pinch, use Mancini® or Cora® roasted sweet peppers in a jar, pour off the liquid, and season the same way with salt, pepper, parsley, oil and garlic. I always keep some peppers in my freezer. I do them in the summer on the barbeque grill and they last through the whole year! Great alone or as a side dish.

I can remember my grandmother, mother and aunts all making these. It is a few hour production but well worth it. Do a lot in one day, and then freeze them. They are great with ham and mozzarella on Wheat Thins®, great on all sandwiches, cold cut subs, tuna fish, veal cutlets, etc. This summer my daughter Lauren asked me to teach her how to make them…another generation of mother-daughter bonding!

PICKLED ZUCCHINI - NANNY
Katherine Avella

3-4 zucchini, cut lengthwise into ¼-inch slices
3-4 tablespoons olive oil
2 tablespoons olive oil
2 cloves of garlic, quartered

½ teaspoon oregano
¼ teaspoon salt
1 bay leaf (optional)

Heat a skillet with about 3 tablespoons olive oil. Cook zucchini slowly until browned. Drain on paper towels. Cool. Mix remaining ingredients together. Pour mixture over zucchini and cover with wine vinegar. Store in the refrigerator. Serve cold. You can also add mushrooms to it.

SAUTÉED MUSHROOMS
Elise Feiner

1 pound small mushroom caps or slices
3 tablespoons olive oil
2 tablespoons unsalted butter
2 teaspoons fresh thyme, oregano, and basil, chopped

3 cloves garlic, peeled and crushed
Sea salt to taste
Freshly grated black pepper to taste

Heat the olive oil and butter until very hot. Add the mushrooms and toss quickly in the hot oil mix. Reduce heat and cover and cook 6 to 7 minutes. Remove the lid and continue cooking until most of the liquid evaporates. If serving immediately, sprinkle with herbs. Mix well, season with sea salt and black pepper. If not serving immediately, hold after liquid evaporates; then reheat and add the herbs, salt and pepper. Serves 6.

Marc and Elise Feiner now...
Still crazy (about each other) after all these years. He is my reason for living.

SPINACH KOURY
Cyndi Koury

2 boxes frozen chopped spinach
3 tablespoons oil
1 medium onion, peeled and diced
Salt and pepper to taste
Garlic salt to taste

2 teaspoons dried mint flakes
2 scallions chopped fine
Dash of lemon juice
¼ teaspoon cumin

Cook spinach according to package directions. In a medium frying pan, heat the oil. Sauté the onions until golden brown. Add the spinach to the onions and add remaining ingredients. Taste and adjust seasonings.

PEPPERS IN VINEGAR GRIMALDI
Anthony Grimaldi, Sr.

6-8 bell peppers
Salt
½ cup white vinegar mixed with ½ cup water

2 to 3 cloves of garlic PER jar
Oregano to taste
Olive oil

Wash, dry, and slice bell peppers in wide strips. In a Tupperware or plastic container, place peppers in layers, adding salt on top of each layer. Refrigerate 24 hours. Pour out any water that has formed. Add a mixture of white vinegar and water. Refrigerate 24 hours. In glass canning jars, place 2 to 3 cloves of garlic (in each Jar) peppers, and oregano. Before sealing the jars, add a little bit of oil on the top. The next day, eat and enjoy!

These are Uncle Tony's famous vinegar peppers. I guess all the Grimaldi's got into the cooking scene and did it very well.

Anthony Grimaldi Sr. at our house on Thistle Court
Uncle Tony was a kind and gentle man…He loved his Millie

SPINACH AND PEAS
Katherine Avella

2 medium shallots, or 1 small onion, peeled and thinly sliced
3 cloves of garlic, peeled and thinly sliced
2 tablespoon oil
2 tablespoon unsalted butter
1 (10 ounce) bag frozen peas or 2 cans LeSueur® Baby Peas

¼ cup water
1 bag spinach (triple washed)
1 teaspoon salt
¼ teaspoon pepper
½ teaspoon dried mint or dried oregano (optional)
Drop of olive oil (optional)

In a large sauté or frying pan over medium heat, melt the butter and the oil. Add the shallots and garlic and cook until soft, about 6 minutes. Stir in the peas and water; cover. Stir occasionally, cook about 5 minutes. Stir in spinach, salt and pepper, and mint. Stir until spinach is wilted. Place in serving bowl. Drizzle with a drop of olive oil if desired.

Peas go with anything, tomato and egg, mushrooms etc. Just another easy way my mother used to prepare them.

SPINACH BALLS
Elise Feiner

1 (10 ounce) package frozen chopped spinach, thawed and drained
2 cups dry bread stuffing mix
3 eggs, beaten

¼ cup grated Parmesan cheese
½ onion, chopped
2 tablespoons melted butter
¼ cup shredded Cheddar cheese

In a large bowl, mix together chopped spinach, dry bread stuffing mix, eggs, Parmesan cheese, onion, butter and cheddar cheese. Cover and chill in the refrigerator approximately 30 minutes. Drop the mixture by rounded spoonfuls onto a lightly greased large baking sheet. Place baking sheet in the freezer approximately 1 hour. When ready to bake, allow the balls to partially thaw, about 30 minutes. Preheat oven to 350°. Lightly grease a large baking sheet. Bake the balls 20 to 25 minutes, or until lightly browned. Makes about 16.

SAVORY SPINACH CUPS
Elise Feiner

1 tablespoon butter
½ cup finely chopped onion
1 (10 ounce) package frozen chopped spinach, thawed and drained
¾ cup mayonnaise

1 (8 ounce) package shredded mozzarella cheese
1½ teaspoons ground nutmeg
Salt and pepper to taste
1 (12 ounce) package refrigerated buttermilk biscuit dough

Preheat oven to 375°. Lightly grease a miniature muffin pan. Melt butter in medium saucepan over medium heat. Stir in the onion and cook until tender and lightly browned. In a medium bowl, mix together onion, spinach, mayonnaise, mozzarella cheese, nutmeg, salt and pepper. Unroll buttermilk biscuit dough. Separate each biscuit into two. Place biscuit dough halves into the prepared miniature muffin pan, forming small cups that extend slightly beyond the rim. Fill the biscuit dough cups with desired amounts of the onion and spinach mixture. Bake in the preheated oven 12 minutes or until biscuit dough and filling are lightly browned. Makes about 20.

SPINACH CASSEROLE
Elise Feiner

4 (10-ounce) boxes of frozen spinach, chopped
1 pounds ground beef
½ pound bulk sweet Italian sausage
5 stalks celery, chopped
1 medium onion, chopped
3 cloves fresh garlic, chopped
Fresh breadcrumbs made from one loaf of French or Italian bread

¼ cup chicken broth
½ teaspoon ground cinnamon
¼ teaspoon ground cloves
¼ teaspoon ground allspice
½ teaspoon nutmeg
Salt and pepper, to taste
¾ cup grating cheese of your choice
1 (2.25 ounce) can pitted, sliced black olives, drained

Preheat oven to 350°. Defrost spinach and squeeze out remaining liquid. In a large pan over medium heat, brown the ground beef and sausage, about 15 minutes. Add chopped celery, onion and garlic. Continue cooking until vegetables are translucent, about 5 minutes. Be sure to drain all grease. Add the fresh breadcrumbs. In a large mixing bowl, combine chopped spinach with cooked meat and mix thoroughly. Add ½-cup of broth. Season the mixture with cinnamon, cloves, allspice, nutmeg, salt, and pepper, and grating cheese. Add drained olives. Mix well. Spoon into 2½-quart casserole dish and cover with a lid. Bake for 1 hour and a half. Serves 6.

This recipe is a variation on our sausage stuffing that we make. It can be doubled for a holiday when you need a large amount. It's good anytime for a side dish.

SPINACH SOUFFLÉ
Theresa Feiner

4 eggs
1 cup sour cream
1 cup parmesan cheese
2 tablespoons flour
4 tablespoons butter, melted
1 tablespoon of butter

1 teaspoon salt
½ teaspoon black pepper
1 pound spinach (2 packages of frozen chopped spinach are fine too)
2 tablespoons onions sautéed in one tablespoon butter

Preheat oven to 350°. Thaw spinach. In a frying pan, place the one tablespoon butter. Sauté the spinach with two tablespoons of the onions. Drain the spinach and onions of any liquid. Beat the eggs with the remaining ingredients. Add in the spinach onion mix. Grease a large soufflé dish. Pour in the spinach mixture. Bake for 40 to 45 minutes.

Aunt Theresa made this recipe at one of the holidays when we were first married. It was absolutely delicious. You can make it a day in advance and just bake it when you are ready to serve it. Don't over bake it or it will separate. Aunt Theresa is from Alabama, and she is also of Lebanese descent. As you can see, we are a very ecumenical, ethnically diverse family. She is a great cook too!

SPINACH PIES
Cyndi Koury

Spinach Pie Dough:

4 cups flour
2 teaspoons salt
2 teaspoons sugar
1 teaspoon yeast

¼ cup oil
1⅓ cup (approx.) warm water

Add yeast, salt and sugar to a large bowl. Add half of the warm water, and let the yeast proof ("sponge") about 5 minutes. Add the rest of the water, oil and all of the flour mix well and knead in bowl. Let the dough rise in the bowl for 1 to 1½ hours.

After the dough has risen, knead it down in the bowl. Break off pieces of dough about the size of a small lemon. Ball dough up, and let rise on a floured cloth (covered with another cloth) about 45 minutes to 1 hour. Flatten dough balls with fingertips and let rise again (½ hour). Flatten balls and fill with heaping tablespoon of the filling mixture. Seal the edges into a triangle and bake on a greased baking sheet at 400° for 20 minutes.

Spinach Filling: (enough for 1 recipe of dough)

2 (10 ounce) packages fresh spinach, washed, dried, and coarsely cut up
Juice of 1 lemon
1½ cups finely chopped onion
½ cup oil

1 tablespoon salt
1 teaspoon pepper
½ teaspoon allspice
2 tablespoons finely crumbled dried mint

Mix all ingredients together in a large bowl.

Cyndi was one of the first people I met when we moved upstate. She was my next door neighbor and our kids were the same ages. Her husband Billy is Lebanese and she has become a fabulous Lebanese cook. She makes the best spinach pies in this town. She also makes great kibbee and tabbouli.

STIR FRIED GREEN BEANS
Elise Feiner

4 ounces fresh shiitake mushrooms
1 pound green beans
2 teaspoons cornstarch
1 tablespoon vegetable oil

2 teaspoons minced garlic
½ teaspoon salt
1 tablespoon oyster sauce or Hoisin sauce
½ cup chicken broth

Rinse the mushrooms in cold water and drain. Cut off and throw out the stems. Cut the mushroom caps into 1-inch strips. Rinse the green beans in cold water and drain. Snap off the ends. Mix the cornstarch and 2 teaspoons cold water in a small bowl.

Heat a wok or large non stick frying pan over high heat. Add the vegetable oil and rotate the wok to coat the sides. Add the garlic, green beans, and salt and stir-fry for 1 minute. Add the mushrooms and continue to stir-fry until mixed. Stir in the oyster or hoisin sauce. Stir in the chicken broth and heat to boiling. Stir in the cornstarch mixture; cook and stir until thickened, about 30 seconds. Place on a serving platter, removing carefully from the pan. Serves 4.

This is as close to the green beans in a Chinese restaurant as you can get.

"They say that blood is thicker than water. Maybe that's why we battle our own with

more energy and gusto than we would ever expend on strangers."

-David Assael

SQUASH FRITTERS
Katherine Avella

½ cup olive oil, plus ¾ cup, for frying
1 pound zucchini squash, peeled and quartered
1 large onion, chopped fine
6 tablespoons grated Kasseri Cheese or Mozzarella cheese
¼ cup grating cheese
2 tablespoons butter, melted
4 cups or bread crumbs
2 eggs

2 scallions, sliced thin
1 teaspoon finely chopped thyme
Salt and freshly ground black pepper
1 cup flour
2-3 eggs
Panko Crumbs or plain breadcrumbs
4 tablespoon butter, for frying

In a large sauté pan, heat ½ cup olive oil on medium-high heat. Cook the squash and the onion together until very soft. In a food processor, puree the squash onion mixture. Drain well to get out extra moisture. Put in a bowl with cheese, butter, grated cheese, bread crumbs, eggs, scallions, thyme, salt, and pepper. Mix well. Let it stand for 1 hour, refrigerated. Roll into about 2-inch balls. Lightly dredge in the flour, then the eggs, and finally the panko crumbs or plain breadcrumbs and fry in the remaining olive oil and butter until golden brown. You can also do this with eggplant. We are lucky to be able to buy Kasseri cheese at Symeon's. Serves 4.

STRING BEANS AND BACON
Elise Feiner

6 slices of thick sliced bacon cut in 1 inch pieces
1 (16 ounce bag) of frozen French cut string beans
⅛ teaspoon black pepper

¼ teaspoon garlic salt
1 medium onion, peeled and sliced
Sliced almonds (optional)

In a large saucepan, fry the bacon until crisp and remove, leaving the drippings. Add the onions to the drippings and sauté until soft and golden. Add the string beans, garlic salt and pepper. Cook covered over low-medium heat until string beans are cooked to your taste. Add a little water if dry. Serve with bacon and almonds sprinkled on the top.

STIR FRIED BROCCOLI
Elise Feiner

2- 3 bags of fresh broccoli floweret's
3-4 tablespoons oil

6 cloves of garlic, peeled and crushed

Liquid for Broccoli Mix:
9 tablespoons soy sauce
3 tablespoons sugar
3 tablespoons cooking sherry

1 tablespoon rice wine vinegar
2 packages chicken bouillon dissolved in
½ cup hot water

Mix above liquid ingredients for the sauce together. Set aside.

In a large frying pan or wok, heat the oil and the garlic. Quickly add the broccoli floweret's and stir fry until they turn bright green and begin to soften. Add the liquid mix and cook to desired doneness. If you want a thicker sauce, take about 2 tablespoons of cornstarch and dissolve in about 5 ounces cold water, mix until lump free. Pour into the broccoli, and heat until it thickens. Serves 6.

My kids are not great vegetable lovers but they love stir fried broccoli.

GEORGE'S VILLAGE GREENS
George Frattasio

Escarole
Proscuitto (cut in small pieces)
Fresh Breadcrumbs Oreganato

Grated Cheese
Cherry Peppers(cut in half) or Sweet peppers (cut in cubes)
Olive Oil

Wash the greens several times until all sand is removed. Drain well. Cut in small pieces. Fry the proscuitto in olive oil in a heated frying pan; remove. Fry the peppers in the oil; set aside. Mix fresh breadcrumbs with a little garlic, grated cheese and salt and pepper. Set crumbs aside. Fry the greens in the same pan. Add the peppers, proscuitto, and the breadcrumb mix. Add more grated cheese; serve.

My kids think that George's greens are the best, most delicious greens. Now, they live away, so they can make them!

STRING BEANS WITH MINT
Elise Feiner

2-3 tablespoons olive oil
1-2 onions, peeled and sliced
1 (16 ounce) bag frozen French cut string beans

⅛ teaspoon black pepper
¼-½ teaspoon garlic salt
1½ teaspoons dried mint

Heat the oil in a large saucepan. Add the onions and sauté until they are golden to medium brown. Add the string beans, garlic salt, pepper and mint. Cover and let sauté until cooked, stirring frequently. You may need to add a little water if too dry. Heat thoroughly. Serve.

This is a favorite of my niece Jennifer.

STUFFED CABBAGE (PROKEST)
Nellie Reinisch

1 head of cabbage
2 tablespoons oil
2 onions, sliced
3 cups canned tomatoes
3 teaspoons salt
½ teaspoon black pepper
Beef bones
1 pound chopped meat

3 tablespoons rice
4 tablespoons grated onion
1 egg
3 tablespoons cold water
3 tablespoons honey
¼ cup lemon juice
¼ cup raisins

Pour boiling water over the cabbage to cover and let soak 15 minutes (or freeze cabbage and let defrost overnight before using.) Take off about 12 to 18 leaves. Heat oil in a large saucepan; lightly brown the onions in it. Add tomatoes. Add half of the salt and pepper to the bones. Add the bones to the tomatoes. Cook bones over low heat for about 30 minutes to 1 hour; remove the bones. Mix the beef, rice, remaining salt and pepper, grated onion, egg and cold water together. Place meat mixture on each leaf of cabbage. Tuck sides in and roll. Add to the sauce. Cover and cook over low heat 1½ hours. Add honey, lemon juice and raisins. Cook another 30 minutes.

This is Nanny Nellie's stuffed cabbage recipe which we all thought was lost, but Aunt Shirley had a copy of it. So Terry, here it is for you.

"Nanny" Nellie Reinisch and great-granddaughter
Lauren Feiner

L-R: More of Nanny Nellie's great grandchildren
Top L-R: Jennifer and Jeffrey Feiner
Bottom L-R: Abby and Lauren Feiner

STUFFED CABBAGE OSTROW
Barbara Schwartz

1 onion, peeled and diced
1 can (10¾ ounces) tomato soup
1 can (8 ounces) tomato sauce
Juice of 2 lemons

½ teaspoon pepper
1 teaspoon salt
¼ cup sugar

Put the above ingredients in a large pot with 1 cup water and bring to a boil.

1 large Cabbage
2-3 pounds chopped meat
1 large onion, grated
1 tablespoon salt
Dash pepper

½ cup water
¼ cup raw rice (uncooked whole Carolina® Rice)
2 eggs
1 bag sauerkraut; set aside (for the pot)

To make it easier to make the cabbage rolls, place the head of cabbage in the freezer a few days ahead of time. The night before you want to make the rolls defrost the cabbage. Set aside the large outer leaves because you will need to place them over the top of the pot. Mix everything together except the meat and sauerkraut until well blended; mix in the meat. Put meat into each cabbage leaf and roll like an egg roll and place in bottom of prepared pot. When you have a complete layer on the bottom of the pot, sprinkle a layer of sauerkraut over the cabbage rolls and then make another layer of rolls. Continue this until you have made all the rolls you can. At the top, finish the sauerkraut with the juice and put on the top of the whole pot, the largest cabbage pieces which you had set aside (which makes it like a tent over the rolls.) Cook at a low heat for at least 2 hours. After about 1 hour, taste the juice to see if it needs any more seasoning.

This was Barbara's mother's recipe; now, she makes it for her family!

Stuart and Barbara Schwartz

Barbara and Stuart are an integral part of our lives here. Barbara is from Brooklyn and Stuart from the Bronx. Everyone up here says we "tawk" funny. I don't know, we all sound perfectly normal to me!

STRING BEANS WITH OREGANO
Katherine Avella

2 boxes frozen string beans (French or whole)
1 medium onion, peeled and diced
2 tablespoons oil
Garlic salt to taste

⅛ teaspoon black pepper
1 teaspoon dried oregano
A little water

In a medium sauce pan, heat the oil. Add the onions and sauté until golden. Add the green beans, black pepper, garlic salt, and oregano. Add a little water if too dry. Heat on a low simmer until green beans are as tender as you prefer.

"If someone cheats with you, they'll cheat on you!"
-Elise Feiner

SUGAR SNAP PEAS
Elise Feiner

1½ pounds snap peas, rinsed and drained   2 teaspoon sugar
4 teaspoons butter   ½ teaspoon (a couple of pinches) salt

Place snap peas in ½-inch boiling water with butter and a sprinkle of 1 teaspoon sugar. Reduce heat to simmer. Cover and steam snap peas 3 minutes. Remove cover and season snap peas with a little salt. Serves 4.

The Cousins…Mainella and Tretola Sisters…
Boy, could these woman cook!
Back Row L-R: Ida Tretola Grimaldi, Margie Tretola DaBruzzo,   Katherine
Mainella Avella, Josephine Mainella
Front Row L-R: Millie Tretola Grimaldi, Angie Tretola Sanito

STRING BEANS WITH TOMATOES
Katherine Avella

2 box frozen green beans, defrosted   2 teaspoons basil
3 tablespoons oil   Salt and pepper to taste
3 cloves garlic, peeled and crushed   ½ cup grated cheese
1 (15 ounce) can Hunts® Tomato Sauce

In a large saucepan, heat the oil. Quickly add the garlic, stirring for a few seconds. Add the green beans and cook a few minutes. Add the tomato sauce, salt and pepper, basil. Cook on a medium simmer until the beans are cooked to your taste. Stir in grated cheese and serve.

SUGAR SNAP PEAS WITH BACON
Elise Feiner

3 slices bacon, cut into ½-inch pieces   ½ cup water
1 small yellow skinned onion, peeled and chopped Salt and pepper
1 pound sugar snap peas

In a medium skillet over medium high heat, brown chopped bacon. Using a slotted spoon, remove bacon to a paper towel lined plate. Add onion to the pan. Sauté chopped onions 3 minutes or so, until they are just tender. Add peas and water to the pan. Cover and cook peas 5 minutes. Uncover and allow the liquid to cook almost out of the pan. Add bacon back to the skillet and remove pan from heat. Serves 4.

STUFFED CABBAGE ROLLS
Elise Feiner

Sauce:

2 tablespoons butter
1 tablespoon extra virgin olive oil
2 cup chopped yellow onions
3 cloves of garlic, peeled and crushed
5 (15 ounce) cans Hunts® Tomato Sauce

1 cup cream
1 tablespoon apple cider vinegar
3 tablespoons brown sugar
Salt and pepper to taste

Rolls:

1 head of cabbage (freeze and then let thaw to soften leaves)
4 teaspoons unsalted butter
1½ cup chopped yellow onions
6 clove of garlic, peeled and chopped
1 pound ground beef
1 pound ground pork
1½ cups cooked long-grain white rice

2 teaspoons McCormick® Season All seasoned salt
½ teaspoon garlic salt
¼ teaspoon ground black pepper
2 eggs
2 tablespoon tomato paste
Splash of red wine
A little olive oil

Preheat the oven to 350°. In a medium frying pan, melt the butter and olive oil over medium-high heat. Add the onions and cook, stirring, for 3 minutes. Add the garlic and cook, stirring, for 1 minute. Add the tomato sauce and cream and simmer, stirring occasionally, for 5 minutes. Add the vinegar and sugar and simmer, stirring occasionally, until the sauce thickens, about 5 minutes. Remove from the heat and adjust the seasoning to taste. Separate the cabbage leaves and remove the hard spine from each leaf if possible. Spread on paper towels and pat dry. Set aside. To make the stuffing, in a medium skillet melt the butter over medium-high heat. Add the onions and cook, stirring, until very wilted and starting to caramelize, about 5 minutes. Add the garlic, and cook, stirring, for 1 minute. Remove from the heat and let cool slightly. Lay the cabbage leaves, rib side down, on a flat work surface. Spread a thin layer of the sauce over the bottom of a baking dish. In a large bowl, combine the beef, rice, McCormicks' seasoned salt, garlic salt, pepper, eggs, tomato paste, red wine, and cooked onions. Mix well with a heavy wooden spoon or your hands. One at a time, spoon the filling into the center of the cabbage leaves, about ¼-cup in each, depending upon the size of the leaves. Line a baking dish with large cabbage leaves. Roll each into a neat egg-roll like shape and place in a layer on the sauce in the baking dish. Repeat with the remaining ingredients, stacking the cabbage rolls. Pour the remaining sauce over the rolls, drizzle the oil over the rolls, wrap the leaves up over the baking dish. Cover tightly with foil, bake until the meat is cooked through, rolls are tender, about 2 to 2½ hours.

This is another version of stuffed cabbage, baked in the oven. I tried to make it taste like Chanatry's (a local family owned grocery store) who make a great stuffed cabbage. The apple cider vinegar gives the sauce a little kick.

VEGETABLE MEDLEY
Elise Feiner

1 large onion, peeled and sliced in thin rings
6 scallions cut in 1 to 2-inch pieces
6 large zucchini, peeled and julienned
4 carrots cut in rounds
2 yellow squash, peeled and cut in rounds
1 can straw mushroom, drained
5 tablespoons olive oil
5 cloves garlic, peeled and crushed

2 packets chicken bouillon
Salt and pepper to taste
1-2 teaspoons garlic salt
1 teaspoon basil
1 teaspoon oregano
1 package Béarnaise sauce; prepared as directed
Grated cheese, optional

Place the olive oil in a large heated sauté pan. Add the onion and the garlic and sauté for a few minutes. Add the remaining vegetables and stir fry until soft but not soggy. Then add the bouillon that has been dissolved in about ¾-cup of hot water, salt, pepper, garlic salt, basil and oregano. Cook a few more minutes. Top with a little béarnaise sauce or serve it on the side. Sprinkle with grating cheese if desired.

I just made this up one night when I had a bunch of vegetables sitting in the refrigerator. The vegetables taste delicious when cooked together like this.

VEGETABLES

STUFFED FRYING PEPPERS
Katherine Avella

6-8 frying peppers (cubanelle, long thin skin, light green) do not use big bell peppers
Oil for frying (vegetable or olive is fine)
2 loaves day old Italian bread, crusts removed (save crusts)
3 cloves garlic, peeled and crushed
¼ teaspoon salt
⅛ teaspoon black pepper
2 cups grated cheese
2 teaspoons tiny capers
1 can sliced or chopped black olives (small) optional

5 tablespoons plum tomatoes liquid (open a large can you'll need it later)
2 tablespoons olive oil
3 tablespoons fresh parsley, finely chopped
2 large cloves garlic, peeled and halved
1 large onion peeled and sliced
¾ - 1 can plum tomatoes, (the rest of the open can from earlier); put in a blender or break with your fingers
1 teaspoon oregano
1 teaspoon basil
Salt and pepper to taste

Wash and dry the peppers. With a small paring knife, remove the top of the peppers, and carefully shake to remove the seeds; leave the peppers whole. In a blender or food processor, place the inside of the Italian bread (reserving the crusts for later) and process lightly to make bread crumbs, do not process too much, you do not want fine crumbs). Place the crumbs in a large bowl. Add all the remaining ingredients up to and including the parsley. You do not want a lot of salt because the capers and cheese are salty enough. You may need to add a little more oil or tomatoes so crumbs are moist, but not wet. Carefully stuff the peppers taking care not to break them (do not force the stuffing in). When you are finished stuffing them, take a piece from the reserved crust of the Italian bread and trim to a size that will fit the opening of the pepper. Gently insert the crust over the opening of the pepper to prevent the crumbs from falling out during frying. Heat a large frying pan with enough oil to just cover the bottom (you don't want to deep fry the peppers). When the oil is hot, start frying the peppers in batches; turn carefully to brown both sides. Remove them to a platter, **but don't drain on paper towels**, just let as much oil drip off as possible before removing from the pan.

When you finish frying the peppers, add the cloves of garlic that were cut in half into the oil and when golden brown, remove and discard. Add the onions to the oil and sauté until soft and golden brown. Add the remaining tomatoes, salt, pepper, oregano, and basil to the tomatoes and cook for about 15 minutes. Pour the sauce over the fried peppers. Note: We always do our peppers with breadcrumbs, however, if you prefer you can do them with rice and chopped meat. Take leftover cooked rice, brown some chopped meat (drain), add some grating cheese, some tomato sauce, a little salt and pepper, chopped black olives, some grating cheese, and stuff the peppers. Fry and make sauce as in above recipe.

My mother was close to 90, she was having difficulty remembering many things (don't wait to write down your family's collections). She was the most incredible cook. I was very fortunate to have sat with her several years ago, and we wrote down so many of her recipes. This is one of her better ones. This is truly the essence Neapolitan peasant cooking. When these are frying, you can smell it for miles; you are truly in the heart of an Italian home and kitchen!

Jeff and Janet Morse

Les and Abby Gross

SWEET POTATO BALLS
Elise Feiner

3 large (about 2½ pounds) sweet potatoes
2 tablespoons butter
⅛ teaspoon nutmeg
⅛ teaspoon allspice
¼ teaspoon cinnamon

1 teaspoon salt
1 cup chopped walnuts
Flour
Oil for frying

Cook potatoes in boiling salted water for about 40 to 50 minutes is until tender. Cool slightly; peel and mash. Add butter, nutmeg, allspice, and cinnamon, salt. Mix until blended. Stir in the nuts. Place about ½ cup of flour in a pie plate. Spoon about ⅓ of potato mixture into the flour. Shape into balls. Continue with remaining potatoes, adding flour as needed. Heat about 3-inches of oil to 375°. Cook until lightly browned on all sides.

Twins separated at birth?
L-R: Dr. Marc Feiner and Dr. Charles Antzelevitch

L-R: Marc and Jeffrey Feiner and Danny and Charlie Antzelevitch

VEGETABLES IN BEER BATTER
Katherine Avella

1¼ cups beer
1⅓ cups sifted all purpose flour or Wondra® flour
2 tablespoons grated cheese
1 tablespoon parsley
1 teaspoon salt
Dash of garlic powder

1 tablespoon olive oil
2 egg yolks, beaten
2 egg whites, beaten until stiff
Assorted vegetables of your choice (zucchini, mushrooms, peppers, artichoke hearts, etc.)

Let beer stand at room temperature for 45 minutes or until flat. In a mixing bowl, combine flour, grated cheese, parsley, salt, and garlic powder. Stir in the olive oil, the two egg yolks which have been beaten, and the flat beer. Beat until smooth. Beat the egg whites to stiff peaks and fold in to the batter. Dip the vegetables in batter and fry at 375° for 2 to 5 minutes depending on the vegetables used.

ZUCCHINI - PECAN SPLASH
Elise Feiner

4 tablespoons butter
2 cloves garlic, peeled and crushed
⅓ cup pecan, coarsely chopped
1 pound zucchini, peeled and sliced

3 tablespoons grated cheese
Dash of garlic salt
Black pepper to taste

In a large skillet, melt 1 tablespoon of butter over medium to low heat. Add the pecans and garlic; cook and stir until lightly browned, about 5 minutes. Remove the pecans and set aside. Add the remaining butter to the pan and melt; add the zucchini, dash of garlic salt, and black pepper. Sauté until soft. Sprinkle with grating cheese. Toss with the pecans and serve.

ZESTY BUTTER BEANS
Vicki Socolof

¾ cup brown sugar
2-3 teaspoons liquid smoke
½ cup catsup
1 medium onion, peeled and chopped

⅓ cup corn syrup
3 cans butter beans, drained
4-6 slices Beef Frye or Pastrami

Mix together well the first five ingredients. Pour over the three cans of beans. Turn into a 1½-quart casserole that has been sprayed with PAM®. Arrange 4 strips of beef frye or pastrami on top. Refrigerate. To serve, bring to room temperature, and then bake at 325° for one hour.

This recipe was given to me by Kal Socolof, our good friend and our Temple's Cantor. His wife Vicki makes it for all their family gatherings, and he was nice enough to share it with us. Use the Beef Frye, if you keep Kosher.

Vicki and Kalman Socolof

Rabbi Stanley and Aliza Gerstein

ZUCCHINI AND MUSHROOMS
Katherine Avella

1 large zucchini, peeled and sliced
Oil for frying
Salt and pepper to taste
1 large jar mushrooms, sliced or a container of fresh
mushroom slices

Dash of olive oil
½ teaspoon dried mint flakes
Dash or two of wine vinegar

Slice the zucchini in rounds. Heat just enough olive oil to cover the bottom of a frying pan. Fry the zucchini until soft; remove from the oil. Sauté the mushrooms until soft (if using fresh) or slightly heat the mushrooms from the jar or can in a small pan. Place mushrooms and zucchini in a serving dish. Season with salt and pepper, mint flakes, a dash of olive oil and wine vinegar.

Left:

Thirza and Joseph
Avella on their
wedding day...

Right:

Joseph Avella and his
daughter Melissa, my
beautiful niece...

SYMEON'S FRIED EGGPLANT
Symeon Tsoupelis, Jr.

1 eggplant, whole
All-purpose flour

Symeon's spices or Cooking with Love's Passion Spice Mix
Oil for frying

Cut off the top of the eggplant. Cut off a thin slice from both sides of the rounded edge of the eggplant. Leave the skin on. Slice the eggplant lengthwise into ½-inch slices. Soak the eggplant slices in lightly salted water for about an hour. Drain. Flour the eggplant slices and layer them on waxed paper. Refrigerate for awhile. Fry the eggplant but do not cook completely. Remove to paper towels. Right before serving, fry the slices again until crisp. Cut into smaller pieces (I usually cut them before I fry them.) Sprinkle liberally with Symeon's spices immediately. Serve with plain yogurt with has been mixed with Symeon's spices.

Symeon's is one of the best restaurants in this town, you never have a bad meal there. However, the food is not the only thing that makes it great, the Tsoupelis family is the best. Symeon Sr. and his late wife Ann set the tone for the restaurant and Symeon Jr. and Shelli are following in their footsteps. They are warm, caring and community oriented. Be sure to have a meal there when you are in upstate New York, you won't be sorry. Symeon's Greek Restaurant is located at 4941 Commercial Drive, Yorkville, NY. (315) 736-4074. Cooking with Love's Passion Spice Mix is available on our website www.cookingwithlove.com

ZUCCHINI IN VINEGAR
Vincent DeClementi

1-2 eggs
Salt and seasoned pepper

1-2 zucchini peeled and sliced
½ cup flour

Mix the eggs, salt and pepper. Dip the zucchini into egg mixture; then flour. Heat a little olive oil in a frying pan. Fry the zucchini, remove to paper towels. In a bowl, place a little olive oil, peel and slice a clove of garlic very thinly. Add the zucchini, salt and pepper to taste, a little chopped mint, and a little cider vinegar. Mix well. Refrigerate. Remove garlic before serving.

Uncle Jimmy is a genius with vegetables. This is simple side dish and is so delicious.

ZUCCHINI IN TOMATOES
Katherine Avella

4-5 tablespoons olive oil
3-4 zucchini peeled and cubed
1 large onion, minced
3 stalks celery, diced
2-3 carrots peeled and cut into thin slices but not paper thin
1 cup tomatoes, Italian plum tomatoes or stewed tomatoes

Salt and pepper to taste
Dash oregano
Lots of basil
Generous amount of grated cheese after you finish cooking it

Peel and cube the squash. Place the olive oil in a sauté or frying pan and heat; add the onions and sauté until they start to soften. Add the celery, carrots, zucchini, tomatoes and spices. Break the tomatoes apart with your fingers if using plum tomatoes, if stewed tomatoes are used, just add in. Cover and let simmer for about 1 hour and a half. Cook until tender, but not too soft. Add generous amount of grating cheese at the end. Serves 6.

This is one of Nanny's famous Italian vegetable side dishes. It smells wonderful when it cooks. You could also put this over pasta if you wanted to use it as a meal.

Our English Cousins L-R: Maddelena Stevens-Grassi, Katherine Avella, and Angela Grassi visiting the United States

ZUCCHINI MUSTARD TORTE
Elise Feiner

½ pound Challah bread, sliced
4 tablespoons Dijon mustard
4 tablespoons olive oil
2 cloves garlic, peeled and crushed
2 cups sliced mushrooms
2 cups yellow squash, peeled and shredded and squeezed dry
1 large onion, peeled and diced

Salt and pepper to taste
2 cups white cheddar cheese shredded or mozzarella cheese
1 cup parmesan cheese
4 eggs, lightly beaten
2 cups heavy cream or milk
1 cup marinara sauce; heated

Preheat the oven to 350°. Butter a large baking dish. Spread mustard on the slices of bread. Heat the oil in a skillet and sauté the onions and garlic until lightly brown. Add the mushrooms and zucchini and sauté for about another 10 to15 minutes until tender. Drain if the vegetables are too watery. Season with salt and pepper; let cool to room temperature. Place the bread mustard side up, mushroom mix, cheddar and parmesan cheese in alternating layers, ending with slices of bread, mustard side down. Mix the eggs with the cream and marinara sauce. Pour over the bread, poking some holes to allow mix to seep in. Let stand a half hour. Place the baking dish in a larger baking pan that has been filled with hot water. It should come halfway up the sides of the casserole. Bake 45 minutes or until set. Cool a few minutes before serving.

GREENS SAPORITO
Janet Saporito

2 large heads of fresh Escarole
2 bell peppers, (hot or sweet)
2 (⅛ -¼-inch) slices of Proscuitto from your butcher

⅓ cup grated Parmesan Cheese
2 tablespoons olive oil

Separate escarole leaves and rinse thoroughly in cool water. Place in a large pot with enough water to steam. Cover and steam escarole until tender, approximately 25 minutes. Drain well. Using a small bowl; press escarole in colander gently to remove the excess water. Clean and cut peppers into 1-inch wedges. Using the same pot, add oil and peppers and sauté until peppers are tender; approximately 10 minutes. Trim fat from Proscuitto and dice into ¼-inch pieces; add to peppers and sauté 5 minutes. Place drained escarole on a cutting board and cut into quarters. Add to pot with peppers and proscuitto. Gently mix thoroughly and sauté another 5 minutes until thoroughly heated. Add parmesan cheese toss before serving. Serve warm. Makes approximately 5 cups.

Janet says this may be served as an appetizer, side dish or main meal.

ZUCCHINI QUICHE
Elise Feiner

2 large onions, peeled and sliced
1 large or three small zucchini, peeled and sliced in rounds
4 tablespoons butter
½ teaspoon garlic salt
⅛ teaspoon black pepper
6 slices bacon

3 eggs
1 cup heavy cream
1 cup parmesan cheese
1 cup white cheddar cheese, grated
Salt and pepper
Chopped nuts of your choice, to taste

Heat the butter in a frying pan, and sauté the onions until golden brown and soft. Remove onions and set aside. Sauté the zucchini in the remaining butter, add more butter if necessary. Add the onions back into the pan and season with garlic salt and pepper.
Remove the zucchini and onions and place in a large greased 8x8-inch casserole pan. In a large bowl, beat the eggs with heavy cream, parmesan cheese, salt and pepper to taste, and cheddar cheese. Microwave the bacon until crisp. Crumble the bacon. Pour the egg mixture over the zucchini, sprinkle with bacon and chopped nuts. Bake 35 minutes at 400°.

"A real friend is someone who walks in when the rest of the world walks out."
-Anonymous

ZUCCHINI PIE
Estelle Zierler

3 small zucchini, peeled and sliced
1 onion, peeled and sliced
1 cup Bisquick® baking mix

4 eggs
5 tablespoons parmesan cheese
½ cup oil

Heat the oil in a large frying pan. Sauté the zucchini and onions. Mix the remaining ingredients together until well blended. Add the zucchini and onion mix. Pour into a well greased casserole pan. Bake 350° for 45 minutes.

Norm Zierler's mother, Nanny Estelle used to make this all the time. It's great for a luncheon or as an appetizer. Nanny's friend Jean Paragone also made this all the time.

A much younger Zierler-Feiner Crew at Shea Stadium…
Top: Darryl Strawberry
Middle L-R: David Zierler, Jeffrey Feiner
Bottom L- R: Jeremy Zierler, Steven and David Feiner

ZUCCHINI PIZZA
Elise Feiner

4 ounces mozzarella cheese, grated
4 ounces cheddar cheese, grated
4 cups zucchini, grated
2 eggs
2 tablespoons Bisquick® baking mix
¼ teaspoon salt
2 tablespoons oil
1 large onion, minced

1 clove garlic, minced
1 pound ground beef
1 cup tomato sauce
1 teaspoon oregano
Salt and pepper to taste
2 ounces mozzarella cheese, grated
2 ounces cheddar cheese, grated

Preheat the oven to 400°. Combine the 4 ounces of mozzarella and 4 ounces of cheddar cheese with the zucchini, eggs, Bisquick and salt. Press into a 10 x 15-inch greased jelly roll pan. Bake at 400° for 15 minutes.

Heat a frying pan with the oil. Sauté the onions, garlic and ground beef. Drain off any excess fat. Add the tomato sauce, salt and pepper to taste, and oregano to the beef mixture. Spoon beef mixture over the baked crust. Sprinkle the remaining mozzarella and cheddar cheese over the top. Bake for another 20 minutes at 400 °. Cover with foil if it's getting too brown.

The Marquino's Clockwise from top: Jennifer, Susan, Kenny, Kristen and Michael

The Werner's L-R: Hans, Ashley, Erich, Pat and Chelsea...P.E.A.C.H.

Jeffrey Feiner and Mindy Rosenfeld – best friends since kindergarten...way back when, then and (below) now...

Jay and Barbara Forgeron

Desserts...

Dessert Eating Experts Lauren and Steven Feiner
Same cake...same restaurant...same day...different cities...more twins separated at birth?

"Life is short, eat dessert first..."
- Unknown

Cheesecake Hints:

Preventing Cracks:

Make sure your pans are well greased. It is a good idea to chill the pan before you brush on the butter. This causes the butter to harden and it won't drip.

Place a pan of hot water (refill if necessary) on the bottom shelf of the oven or on the bottom of the oven itself to create steam or place the cake in a large pan filled with hot water that goes up the sides of the cake pan about 2 inches. Wrap the outside of your cake pan in aluminum foil before you pour the filling in the pan, and before you place it in the water bath.

Place the cake pan on the middle rack of the oven.

Do not over bake the cheesecake. A cheesecake will crack if the temperature is too high.

Don't open the door during the first half of the cooking time.

Checking for doneness with a cake tester or a bamboo skewer doesn't work with a cheesecake; it will always have batter on it – if it is dry, then it is way overcooked! It is almost set when 2-3 circles of batter still jiggle if shaken a little. Instead, check the surface of the cake, it will change from shiny to dull. The cake is done if the center doesn't jiggle when you tap it.

Make sure the crust doesn't burn. Cheesecakes are like meat; there internal temperature will rise for about 15 minutes after cooking.

Unless you are told not to in the directions, always turn off the oven and leave the cheesecake in with the door partially open for about an hour to cool the cake gently. Running a knife around the pan edges also helps to prevent cracks because it helps the cake to separate easily from the pan.

The worst scenario is a crack – don't fret, cover it with toppings, fresh fruit, confectioner's sugar, drizzled melted chocolate, etc.

Cutting a Cheesecake:

Use a knife dipped in hot water and wiped clean after **each** piece. Dip in hot water again before cutting the next piece; or use a piece of unflavored dental floss or monofilament (fishing tackle)...this works great on other cakes as well.

Freezing and Defrosting a Cheesecake:

Wrap the cheesecake in plastic wrap and then heavy duty aluminum foil. Label and date the cheesecake. To defrost, place the wrapped cheesecake in the refrigerator for 12 hours. Then unwrap the cake and return it to the refrigerator until completely defrosted. Remove from the refrigerator 30 minutes before serving.

APPLE CAKE SCHWARTZ
Barbara Schwartz

2 cups flour
2 cups sugar
3 teaspoons baking powder
4 eggs
1 cup vegetable oil
2½ teaspoons vanilla

½ cup orange juice, or the juice of one orange
3-4 Cortland apples, peeled, cored, and thinly sliced or
1 can sliced apples, drained
5 tablespoons sugar
1 teaspoon cinnamon

Preheat the oven to 350°. Mix the flour, sugar, baking powder, eggs, oil, vanilla, and orange juice in a bowl and mix very well until there are no lumps; set aside. Mix the apples, sugar and cinnamon together in a separate bowl. Grease and flour a large tube pan. Pour ½ the batter into the pan. Add the apples. Pour the remaining batter over the apples. Bake for 1 hour and 20 minutes. Cool about a half hour and then remove from the pan. This cake freezes beautifully; wrap in foil and place in a large zip lock freezer bag when cold.

Aunt Barbara always buys a bushel of apples at the beginning of the season and makes applesauce and several of these apple cakes. They freeze very well and are great to have in the freezer for unexpected company. This is one of the best apples cakes I've tasted, and simple to do.

L-R: Shelley, Kayla, and
Debbie Schwartz Lipson

Kayla Lipson Today

APPLE CAKE ROSENFELD
Rae Rosenfeld

2-3 apples, peeled, seeded, and sliced
2 eggs
1 cup sugar
¼ cup applesauce

2 cups flour
2 teaspoons baking powder
½ teaspoon cinnamon
¼ cup vegetable oil

Line the bottom of a greased, square glass or metal cake pan with sliced apples. In a medium bowl, mix together the eggs, sugar and applesauce. Set aside. Mix the flour, baking powder and cinnamon together; add this to the egg mixture, blend well. The batter will be heavy. Spread the mixture over the apples to the edge of the pan. Pour vegetable oil over the whole mix. Bake 350° for 35 to 40 minutes. It's done when it gets brown and stops bubbling. Serve with whipped cream.

Rae got this recipe from her neighbor Thelma. She said that it makes a wonderful dessert.

Stephen and Rae Rosenfeld...
Steve suffers from the Dick
Clark syndrome, he never ages!

CHOCOLATE CAKE (SOFT)
Shirley Flomenhoft

1 stick butter, softened
1 cup of sugar
4 eggs

1 cup sifted Swans® self rising flour
1 can Hershey® Chocolate Syrup
1 teaspoon vanilla

Put butter in a mixing bowl. Add sugar and blend well. Add eggs, one at a time. Add cake flour, Hershey's syrup and vanilla. Mix well. Grease and flour a 13 x 9-inch pan. Bake at 350° for 1 hour or 1 hour 15 minutes.

APPLE CAKE OSTER
Judy Oster

4 cups sliced Granny Smith apples
3 tablespoons cinnamon
5 tablespoons sugar
4 eggs
1 cup oil

¼ cup orange juice
1 tablespoon vanilla
3 cups flour
2 cups sugar
3 teaspoons baking powder

Preheat oven to 350°. Combine apples, cinnamon and sugar and set aside. Beat together eggs, oil, orange juice, and vanilla. Stir in dry ingredients. Pour ⅓ of the batter into a greased Bundt pan. Add half the apples, the ⅓ of the batter, then remaining apples and remaining batter. Bake for 1 hour to 1 hour and 15 minutes, or until a cake tester comes out dry. Cool for 10 minutes before removing from pan.

L-R: Marsha Silverman, Mel and Judy Oster

CHOCOLATE CAKE
Brenda Johnson

1 cup sugar
1 cup flour
½ cup cocoa
¼ cup oil
1 teaspoon baking soda

½ teaspoon baking powder
1 egg
1 teaspoon vanilla
Pinch of salt
1 cup hot water

Preheat the oven to 350°. Combine all the ingredients until well mixed. Pour into a greased 8 x 8-inch pan. Bake at 350° for 25 to -30 minutes.

AUNT LIZZIE'S POUND CAKE
Elizabeth Maida

1 pound of butter, softened	3 cups flour
1½ cups sugar	2 teaspoons vanilla
6 eggs	

Blend the butter and sugar together at high speed until well blended. Add the eggs, flour and vanilla. Grease and flour (or use Baker's Joy®) a large loaf pan. Pour mixture into the pan. Bake in a 300° oven for 90 minutes.

As a child, I spent so much of my time at my "Aunt Lizzie's." I have so many memories of vacations, holidays, and "school strikes" with Aunt Lizzie, Uncle Ernie, Mary Ann and Michele. We missed them so much, but we continue to spend all our happy occasions with Mary Ann and Michele, or "the girls", as we call them. David Edward (E for Elizabeth) is named in her honor.

There are some people who will always hold a piece of your heart forever, you are looking at two of them in this photo. The will live on in our memories forever.

Ernest and Elizabeth Barone Maida

ANN'S CRUMB CAKE
Ann D'Amico

2 tablespoons canola oil	2 teaspoons vanilla
4 cups flour	1 teaspoon lemon juice
½ cup sugar	1 teaspoon lemon zest
2½ teaspoons baking powder	1 cup lightly packed brown sugar
½ teaspoon salt	1½ teaspoons cinnamon
1 large egg	2 sticks unsalted butter, melted and cooled
½ cup milk	Confectioners' sugar

Preheat the oven to 325° Place the oven rack in the middle of the oven. Take a 9 x 12½-inch baking pan and put a little canola oil in it and grease the pan. Put a little flour in the pan and shake well to coat the entire pan. Shake out any excess flout. In a large bowl, sift together 1½ cups of flour, sugar, baking powder, and salt; set aside. In another bowl, beat the egg with the milk, canola oil, vanilla, lemon juice and lemon zest. Use a rubber spatula and fold the dry ingredients into the egg mixture.

Spread the batter evenly into the pan and set aside. In a medium bowl, mix the remaining 2½ cups of flour, brown sugar, and cinnamon. Add the melted butter and using a rubber spatula or your fingers, mix until large crumbs form. Sprinkle the crumbs over the batter. Place the pan in the oven and after 10 minutes, rotate the pan. Bake until a cake tester comes out clean about another 10 to 15 minutes more. Place the cake pan on a wire rack and let cool. Sprinkle with confectioners' sugar. Cut into squares to serve.

Ann says that this crumb cake is delicious. Just like we used to get in Brooklyn years ago.

BACARDI® RUM CAKE
Elise Feiner

Cake:
1 cup chopped pecans or walnuts
1 (18 ½) ounce package of yellow cake mix
1 (3¾) ounce package instant vanilla pudding
4 eggs

½ cup cold water
½ cup oil
½ cup Bacardi dark rum

Glaze:
¼ pound butter
¼ cup water

1 cup granulated sugar
½ cup Bacardi dark rum

Preheat oven to 350°. Grease and flour (or use Baker's Joy®), a 10-inch tube pan. Sprinkle nuts over the bottom of the pan. Mix all the cake ingredients together with a mixer. Pour batter over the nuts in the pan. Bake 1 hour. Set on a rack to cool. Invert on a serving plate. Prick the top of the cake with a long toothpick or bamboo skewer. Drizzle and brush the glaze evenly over the top and sides.

For glaze:

Melt the butter in a pan. Stir in water and sugar. Boil 5 minutes, stirring constantly. Stir in the rum. If you want to, you can decorate the borders of the sugar frosting with whipped cream. Serve with seedless grapes dusted with confectioner's sugar.

This recipe was in a woman's magazine years ago. I believe it was from the Bacardi Company

My wonderful in-laws
Betty and Jerry Feiner

CHOCOLATE CAKE ROSEN
Debby Rosen

1 package of Duncan Hines® Chocolate Cake Deluxe Mix
1 package of Instant Chocolate Pudding
1 cup oil
1 cup sour cream

4 eggs
½ cup warm water
1 teaspoon vanilla
1 (6 ounces) package mini chocolate chips

Mix the first seven ingredients until smooth. Fold in the chocolate chips into well mixed batter. Bake 350° 1 hour and 10 to15 minutes in a well greased tube or Bundt pan.

Debby is a great friend, classic beauty, an incredible role model, a woman to be admired. She is also a wonderful baker. She always makes trays of cakes and cookies and drops them off here. This was one of David's favorites so she sent along the recipe as well.

CASSATA CAKE COTRUPE
Brenda Johnson

Crust:

3 eggs
1 stick of margarine (softened)

1 cup sugar
flour

Beat the eggs together. Add the sugar. Add some flour (about ½ cup at a time) and work in the margarine. Add more flour, (as much as it takes to make a soft dough). Set aside.

Filling:

3 pounds fine ricotta
1 cup sugar
1 large Nestles® Chocolate Bar grated
10 eggs

1 teaspoon orange juice
1 tablespoon cinnamon
½ cup Maraschino cherries (cut into quarters)

Preheat the oven to 425° Mix together the ricotta, sugar, eggs, orange juice and cinnamon. Beat until well mixed. Fold in the grated chocolate and the cherries. Blend well. Roll out the dough for the crust into a large circle. Place the dough into a large 10-inch spring form pan that has been sprayed with PAM. Pour the filling into the crust. Bake at 425° for **10 minutes**. Lower the temperature to 300° and bake for an additional 30 minutes. Let cool. Sprinkle with confectioners' sugar. Keep refrigerated.

Brenda says that this recipe is her Aunt Sandy Cotrupe's recipe. Brenda makes it every Easter, and it's the best Cassata Cake. Her Aunt now says that Brenda's cake is better than hers!

Brenda's husband Robert Johnson and her Grandmother Nellie Plescia enjoying the holidays and Brenda's Cassata Cake.

Robert Johnson and son Mitchell

CHERRY NUT POUND CAKE
Katherine Avella

1 pound of butter
1 (16 ounce) package of confectioners' sugar
6 eggs
3 cups flour

1 teaspoon vanilla
1 cup whole nuts
1 cup whole cherries, pitted and cut in half

Dust cherries and nuts with some of the flour; set aside. Whip the butter and gradually add the sugar. Add eggs one at a time. Beat well; add 1 cup of flour at a time. Add remaining ingredients. Grease two loaf pans. Make at 350° one hour. Top will split. Dust with confectioner's sugar if desired.

BETTER THAN SEX CAKE
Ann D'Amico

1 box Devil's Food Cake Mix, bake as directed
3 (3 ⅛ ounce) size boxes My-T- Fine® Chocolate Pudding
Mix (don't use instant)
5¾ cups milk
¼ cup Kahlua

3 half pints heavy cream
¼ cup sugar
2 teaspoons vanilla
8 Skor® Bars, frozen and broken into small pieces

Bake the cake either the day before or very early in the day that you plan to use it, according to the directions on the box. Use either 2 (9-inch) cake pans or a loaf pan, depending on what you are going to serve the cake in. You can also use Angel Food if you prefer it to Devil's Food. Make the chocolate pudding by using 5¾ cups of milk instead of the 6 cups called for on the package directions, and substitute ¼ cup of Kahlua for the remaining milk. Chill the chocolate pudding. Remove the skin that forms on the top when you are ready to use it. Whip the heavy cream with the vanilla and sugar until it is thick. Be careful not to over whip or you'll have butter. When ready to assemble, take your trifle dish or a round glass salad bowl, or any deep bowl. Cut your layers in half so you end up with 4 rounds. If you are using a loaf pan slice into ½-inch slices and place a few on the bottom of your bowl. Add a layer of pudding, whipped cream, and top with Skor bars. Repeat the layers, cake, pudding, whipped cream, Skor bars. End with a layer of whipped cream topped with Skor Bars. Chill until ready to serve. Scoop out servings with a large serving spoon. Serves 12.

I was first given this recipe by my cousin Ann D'Amico. I don't know where it came from originally, however I've been told that the name came from the elderly in Florida. The kids love to make this, as well as eat it. We usually make it around Christmas time. It's great to bring to someone's house if you are asked to bring a dessert. Lauren just adores my cousin Ann!

Her Dad's favorite
picture of her…
Lauren Feiner age 8

Lauren and my cousin
Ann have a very
special relationship!

BLACK BOTTOM CAKE
Lucy Massimiano

Cake:
2 cups sugar
3 cups flour
½ cup cocoa
⅔ cup oil
2 cups water

1 teaspoon salt
2 teaspoons vanilla
2 teaspoons baking soda
2 teaspoons white vinegar

Middle Layer: Chopped walnuts and chocolate chips

Topping:
1 (8 ounce) package cream cheese
⅔ cup sugar
1 teaspoon vanilla

¼ teaspoon salt
2 eggs, beaten

Mix all ingredients for the cake layer together. Pour into an ungreased 9 x 13 x 3-inch pan. Top with chopped walnuts and chocolate chips. Mix all ingredients for the topping together until smooth. Top with topping mix. Bake 350° 45 to 50 minutes.

Our cousin Lucy used to bring this cake from Auburn to Brooklyn whenever she would come to visit.

CHOCOLATE CHIP CAKE
Marie Golden

1 cup chopped dates
1½ cups boiling water
2 teaspoons baking soda
2 cups sugar
½ cup shortening

2 eggs
2 cups flour
1 large package chocolate chips
1 cup chopped nuts

Mix dates, boiling water and 1 teaspoon of the baking soda together. Let stand while you prepare remaining ingredients. In a large bowl, cream 1 cup of sugar with shortening and eggs. In a small bowl, mix the flour and remaining teaspoon of baking soda. Add flour mixture, alternating with the date mixture to the egg mixture. Place into a greased and floured 9 x 13-inch pan. Top with chocolate chips, nuts, and the remaining cup of sugar. Bake at 350° for 30 to 35 minutes.

Marie said that it was her maternal aunt's recipe. It became one of her father's brother's favorites.

AUNT JULIA'S SPONGE CAKE
Julia Silvestri

4 eggs, separated
1 teaspoon vanilla
¼ teaspoon cream of tartar
1 teaspoon lemon juice
¼ cup water
1 cup sugar

1 cup sifted cake flour
¾ teaspoon baking powder
¼ teaspoon salt
½ cup rum (optional)
2 tablespoons Harvey's® Bristol Cream

Separate the eggs while still cold. Place the egg whites in a large mixing bowl. Let stand at room temperature for 1 hour. Preheat oven to 350°. Beat egg whites with the cream of tartar at medium speed until foamy. Gradually add in ½ cup of the sugar, 1 tablespoon at a time; continue beating until stiff glossy peaks form. Set aside. In a separate bowl, beat the egg yolks until thick and lemon colored; add the remaining ½ cup of sugar, 1 tablespoon at a time. Beat 2 minutes longer. In a small bowl or dish, combine the water, lemon juice, and vanilla. Sift the flour, salt, and baking powder onto a sheet of waxed paper. At low speed, combine the flour mixture ⅓ at a time into the egg yolk mixture, alternating with water mixture. Beat one minute until just combined. Fold in the egg white mixture, until no white shows. Pour into 2 ungreased 8-inch or 9-inch layer cake pans. Bake at 350° for 25 to 30 minutes. Invert pans on rims of two other pans; cool 1 hour. Loosen the edges with a spatula. Tap inverted pans on counter to remove. Cut each layer in half, filling each with fillings as listed below. Before filling you can brush each sponge layer with rum (mix ½ cup rum with 2 tablespoons Harvey's Bristol Cream) and brush on each layer. Frost with whipped cream or butter cream, and sprinkle with nuts or chocolate shavings.

Crème Pastissiere Filling Layer:
3 egg yolks
¾ cup sugar
3 tablespoons flour or 1 tablespoon cornstarch
¼ teaspoon salt

1½ cups milk
2 teaspoons orange extract
2 teaspoons vanilla extract

Beat egg yolks lightly. Combine the flour, sugar and salt. Add to the egg yolk mixture. Mix thoroughly; add the milk. Place mixture in a medium saucepan. Cook over moderate heat stirring constantly until it thickens and boils. Reduce heat; cook 2 more minutes. Remove from heat. Stir in flavorings. Cool. Divide in half and use half for the chocolate crème layer. Spread the remaining ½ of the mixture on the bottom layer of the sponge cake when completely cooled. (Note: this filling can also be used for cream puffs.)

CONTINUED ON THE NEXT PAGE

"It's much easier to turn a friendship into love, than love into friendship."
–Proverbs

AUNT JULIA'S SPONGE CAKE CONTINUED

Chocolate Crème Filling Layer:

4 squares of sweet Baker's® or semisweet chocolate

Melt 4 squares of sweet baker's or semisweet chocolate over a double boiler. Add to the ½ remaining crème Pastissiere filling. Use this as the filling for the third layer.

Cannoli Filling:

3 cups ricotta
1¼ cups of sugar
Zest of a small orange

2 teaspoons vanilla
Chocolate shavings or chocolate chips

Put the ricotta through a sieve to make it smooth. Combine well with remaining ingredients and beat until smooth. Chill until set (1½ hours.) Use for the middle layer.

Whipped Cream Frosting:

2 teaspoons unflavored gelatin
8 teaspoons cold water
2 cups heavy cream

½ cup confectioner's sugar, sifted
2 teaspoons vanilla

Combine gelatin and water in microwave proof cup. Let stand until thick. Heat briefly until dissolved. Cool slightly. Whip cream, until slightly thickened, add sugar, vanilla and beat. While beating, slowly add gelatin mixture. Whip at high speed until stiff peaks form. Don't over beat (it will turn to butter). You can also add melted chocolate or a little dissolved instant coffee.

My Aunt Julia was my father's oldest sister and he considered her to be a mother to him because his own mother died when he was very young. She was a fabulous baker. She always made this cake for any family celebration. I think my cousins Lucille and Julie Ann inherited her talents, in fact Lucille owned a bakery in Louisiana. Cousin Ann says she doubles the cake to make it higher instead of cutting the layers in half. She also stabilizes the whipped cream, and makes syrup of the rum so it doesn't make the sponge soggy. I've included this in the recipe.

L-R: Julia Silvestri, Ida Grimaldi, and Josephine Mainella

"Immature love says: 'I love you because I need you.' Mature love says '
I need you because I love you."

—Erich Fromm

BLUEBERRY CAKE
Pearl Borten

3 cups flour
3 teaspoons baking powder
1½-2 cups of sugar (depending on the sweetness of the berries)
1 cup oil
4 eggs
2 full teaspoons vanilla extract

¼ cup orange juice
1 pint fresh blueberries, washed, stemmed, and dried (or one half bag of frozen blueberries)
3 tablespoons sugar for top
½ to 1 teaspoon cinnamon for the top or you can use Domino's® Cinnamon Sugar

Mix the flour, baking powder, and sugar (use can use a little less than the 2 cups called for if desired), in a mixing bowl. I use a Kitchen Aid® mixer for this. Add in the oil, eggs, vanilla and orange juice. Mix well. **HINT:** After you wash the blueberries, dry on a paper towel and toss with about 2 teaspoons of flour. This will prevent the blueberries from sinking to the bottom of the batter. Fold in 1 pint of fresh or frozen blueberries. Spray a Bundt pan or Angel Food pan with PAM®. Spoon in the mixture. Mix the sugar and cinnamon together and sprinkle on the top. Bake at 350° for about 50 to 60 minutes (according to the oven) and turn out. Check for doneness with a cake tester or bamboo skewer. Use a rubber spatula to loosen if necessary. Pearl said that you can use the basic batter and add any fruit you want. She uses 4 to 5 Macintosh apples cut into cubes, sprinkle with sugar and cinnamon. Place half the batter in the pan, top with half the apples; pour the rest of the batter over apples, top with remaining apple mixture. This may need to bake a little longer, but check to make sure the apples don't burn. Cover with foil if necessary. I like to use peaches (just pit, slice and cube them; use about 5 to 6.)

This is from a friend of Mom Mom's in Florida. I've made this cake over and over since I got this recipe. There is always one of these cakes on the counter in my kitchen during blueberry season.

Marc and Elise Feiner 1977

CHOCOLATE CHIP ZUCCHINI CAKE
Elise Feiner

1 cup brown sugar
½ cup granulated sugar
½ cup butter, softened
½ cup oil
3 eggs
1 teaspoon vanilla
½ cup buttermilk
2½ cups flour

½ teaspoon allspice
½ teaspoon cinnamon
½ teaspoon salt
½ teaspoon baking soda
4 tablespoons cocoa
3 (about 6 inch long) zucchini peeled and grated; squeeze out excess liquid
1 cup chocolate chips (I like mini chips)

In a large bowl, cream the brown sugar, granulated sugar, butter and oil. Add in the eggs, vanilla and buttermilk and mix well. In a separate bowl mix the flour, allspice, cinnamon, salt, baking soda and cocoa. Sift into the egg mixture. Blend well. Add in the zucchini and stir until well blended. Pour into a greased and floured 9 x 13-inch baking pan. Sprinkle with chocolate chips. Bake at 325° for 45 minutes to1 hour or until done.

This is a great way to get rid of extra zucchini, healthy and delicious too.

CARROT CAKE TO DIE FOR
Elise Feiner

Cake Batter
2 cups flour
2 teaspoons baking soda
2 teaspoons cinnamon
½ teaspoons salt
3 eggs
¾ cup oil
¾ cup buttermilk

2 cups sugar
2 teaspoons vanilla
2 cups grated carrots
1 (8 ounce) can crushed pineapple, drained
4 ounces shredded coconut
1 cup chopped walnuts (optional)

Buttermilk Glaze:
1 cup sugar
½ teaspoon baking soda
½ cup buttermilk

1 stick butter
1 tablespoon corn syrup
1 teaspoon vanilla

Frosting:
1 stick unsweetened butter, at room temperature
1 package (8 ounces) cream cheese, at room temperature
1 teaspoon vanilla
2 cups powdered sugar

1 teaspoon orange juice
1 teaspoon orange peel
1 bag of shredded coconut

Preheat oven to 350°. Grease and flour two 9-inch cake pans. Sift the flour, baking soda, cinnamon and salt together; set aside. In a large bowl, beat the eggs. Add the oil, buttermilk, sugar and vanilla; mix well. Add the dry ingredients. Mix well. Add the carrots, pineapple, coconut and walnuts. Mix well. Pour into the prepared pans. Bake 55 minutes or until a toothpick inserted into the center comes out clean. While cake is in the oven, prepare the buttermilk glaze. Remove cake from the oven and slowly pour the buttermilk glaze **over the hot cake.** Cool in the pans until glaze is absorbed, about 20 minutes. Place one layer on a cake plate; frost with the cream cheese frosting. Sprinkle with a little coconut. Top with the second layer and completely frost with the cream cheese frosting. Press coconut into the sides and top of the cake. Refrigerate. Serve chilled. Serves 20.

Glaze:
In a small saucepan, combine sugar, baking soda, buttermilk, butter, and corn syrup. Bring to a boil. Cook 5 minutes, stirring occasionally. Remove from the heat and stir in vanilla.

Frosting:
Cream butter and cream cheese until fluffy; add vanilla, powdered sugar, orange juice and orange peel. Mix until smooth.

This is the best carrot cake I've ever tasted. I can't remember where the recipe came from; I believe I got in when I was in nursing school in the late 70's.

Julia Hutchins, Carol and Tom Zuchowski's Granddaughter

MIMI'S CHOCOLATE CHIP CAKE
Shirley Flomenhoft

1 box Baker's® semi sweet chocolate pieces (red boxes)
½ pound butter (2 sticks)
2 cups sugar
4 eggs, separated

1½ teaspoons vanilla
2¼ cups sifted Swan's-down® self rising cake flour
1 cup milk

Shave the Baker's chocolate with a peeler or knife, and refrigerate overnight. Cream the butter with the sugar. Add 4 egg yolks, and vanilla. Alternate Swan's-down flour with milk and blend in a medium bowl. Add to egg mixture. Add 1 cup shaved chocolate. Beat egg whites until stiff. Fold in egg whites. Grease and flour a large rectangular pan 14 x 10-inch. Bake 350° for 40 to 50 minutes. When cake is removed from the oven, immediately sprinkle with the rest of the chocolate shavings. Later, when cooled, sprinkle with confectioner's sugar.

Weiner kids then…
L-R Top: Terry and Leslie L-R: Bottom: Hal and Brad

Weiner kids now…
L-R: Brad Weiner, Terry Weiner Freedman, Leslie Weiner Solitrin and Hal Weiner

CHOCOLATE CHARLOTTE
Elise Feiner

2 packages unfilled ladyfinger cookies (12 in each)
¼ cup white crème de menthe or rum
2 packages semisweet chocolate squares (8 ounces each)
3 tablespoons instant coffee
½ cup boiling water

6 egg yolks
½ cup sugar
1 teaspoon vanilla
6 egg whites
1½ cups heavy cream, whipped

Split the ladyfingers, but do not separate into individual pieces. Brush the flat surface with the white crème de menthe or rum. Line the sides of a 9-inch spring form pan with the ladyfingers, rounded sides against the side of the pan, liqueur side facing in. Separate the remaining ladyfingers; line the bottom of the pan, overlapping to fit. Melt the chocolate in the top of a double boiler over hot water, stirring occasionally. Dissolve the coffee in boiling water. Beat the egg yolks in a small bowl until foamy. Beat in the sugar gradually; beating until thick. Reduce speed; add in vanilla, coffee, and melted chocolate. Wash the beaters. Beat the egg whites in a large bowl until stiff. Stir about 1 cup of the egg whites into the chocolate mixture to lighten it. Fold the chocolate mixture into the remaining egg whites. Fold in the whipped cream. Pour into the prepared pan. Freeze until firm. It will keep about a month frozen. Before serving garnish, with chocolate curls and pipe rosettes of whipped cream if desired. To serve, remove the sides of the pan, place on a cake plate. Serve semi thawed. This is very rich, so slice it thin. Serves 12 to 16

I have been making this favorite of Jeff's for Christmas and New Years for years.

L-R: David Zierler, Steven Feiner, Jeremy Zierler,
Jeffrey Feiner, David Feiner at Shea Stadium

Samantha Caplan
(soon to be Mrs.
Jeremy Zierler) and
Jeff "Noah Wyle- Dr.
Carter" Feiner

CHOCOLATE CHIP COFFEE CAKE
Edith Mainella

1 cup butter, softened
1 (8 ounce) package cream cheese, softened
1½ cups sugar, divided
2 eggs
1 teaspoon vanilla
2 cups flour
1 teaspoon baking powder

½ teaspoon baking soda
¼ teaspoon salt
¼ cup milk
1 (6 ounce) package chocolate chips
¼ cup chopped nuts (pecans or walnuts)
1 teaspoon cinnamon

In a large bowl, cream the butter, cream cheese, 1¼ cups of the sugar. Beat in the eggs and vanilla. Combine the flour, baking powder, baking soda, and salt. Add this to the creamed mixture. Add the milk. Stir in the chocolate chips. Pour into a greased spring form or angel food pan. Mix the remaining sugar, cinnamon, and nuts together; sprinkle over the batter. Bake 350° for 50 to 55 minutes or until a cake tester inserted in the middle comes out clean. Cool in the pan for about 15 minutes. Loosen the sides of the cake by running a knife blade along the edges. Cool before cutting.

This is another of Aunt Edith's wonderful coffee cakes.

CHOCOLATE MILKY WAY CAKE
Elise Feiner

8 large or 14 miniature Milky Way® bars
(I like the dark chocolate ones or mix them)
3 sticks butter, divided
2 cups sugar
4 eggs, well beaten
2½ cups all purpose flour

½ teaspoon baking soda
1¼ cups of buttermilk
1 teaspoon vanilla
1 cup chopped pecans
Confectioners' sugar

Combine the Milky Ways and 1 stick of the butter in a large saucepan. Melt and cool slightly. Cream the remaining 2 sticks butter and sugar together; add the eggs and cooled chocolate mixture. Sift the flour and baking soda together. Alternately add flour mix and buttermilk to the batter, blending well. Add the vanilla and nuts. Pour into a well greased Bundt or tube pan or three 8-inch layer pans that have been dusted with butter and confectionery sugar. Bake in a preheated 350°oven for 1 hour and 25 minutes for the tube pan, and 30 to 45 minutes for the layer cake pans.   Cool on a rack. You can sprinkle with confectionery sugar if desired or use frosting recipe below.

Icing:
2½ cups sugar
1 cup evaporated milk
1 stick of butter

1 cup of Marshmallow Fluff®
1 (6 ounce) package of chocolate chips
1 cup pecans, chopped

Combine sugar and evaporated milk. Cook to a soft ball stage (use a candy thermometer). Remove from heat and stir in butter, marshmallow cream, and chocolate chips, stirring until all have melted. Add pecans.

I got this recipe when we lived in Baltimore. There was a wonderful cake decorating store and one of the women gave it to me.

Steven's Graduation from Hofstra University...L-R: Betty Feiner, Sarah Burlingame, David Feiner,
Sharon, Melissa, and Joseph Avella, Elise, Steven, Kevin, Lauren, Jeffrey, and Barbara Feiner

COFFEE CAKE MAINELLA
Edith Mainella

½ pound butter (2 sticks)
1½ cups sugar
2 eggs
2 teaspoons vanilla
2 cups sour cream

4 cups flour
2 teaspoons baking powder
2 teaspoons baking soda
1 teaspoon salt

Filling:
1 cup chopped walnuts
⅔ cup sugar

2 teaspoons cinnamon

Mix the walnuts, cinnamon and sugar together. Cream the butter; add the sugar and mix well. In a separate bowl, beat eggs until light; add vanilla and sour cream. Beat until smooth. Add to the butter mixture; beat again. Mix the flour, baking powder, baking soda, and salt together; sift. Add flour mixture to the egg mixture; beat thoroughly. Pour half the batter into a greased and floured tube pan. Sprinkle half of the filling mixture over the batter. Add the rest of the batter; top with remaining filling mixture. Bake 350° for 1¼ hours.

HANNAH'S SPECIAL BIRTHDAY CAKE
Hannah Ostrow

1 cup sifted cake flour
¼ teaspoon salt
1 teaspoon baking powder
3 eggs

1 cup sugar
1 teaspoon vanilla
5 tablespoons water

Preheat oven to 350°. Sift together cake flour, salt, and baking powder, set aside. In a large mixing bowl, beat eggs until light and fluffy. Beat in sugar gradually. Beat in water and vanilla. Pour in flour mixture and beat until smooth. Pour at once into greased and floured pans 2 (9-inch rounds.) Bake for 20 minutes, the cake with be lightly browned (do not bake longer because if it gets too dark it will be too dry) and cool. Carefully split the 2 cold sponge cake layers in two, crosswise with a sharp knife to make four layers. Put the four layers together by spreading chocolate filling in between and on the sides and top. Chill overnight.

Chocolate filling:

3 sticks butter
1 cup confectioner's sugar
3 eggs, separated

4 (3 ounce) squares unsweetened chocolate, melted
1 teaspoon vanilla

Cream butter until fluffy. Add the sugar; gradually add egg yolks, one at a time. Beat well between additions. Beat in melted chocolate and vanilla. Beat egg whites until stiff, and then fold in to chocolate mixture until thoroughly blended.

This recipe is from Hannah Ostrow who is Barbara Schwartz's 91 year old mother. Barbara tells the history of this cake. Hannah only baked it once a year for her husband Harry and son Jesse's birthdays in August. She had been making this for the last 62 years, but only once a year. Aunt Barbara said that she used to make it for her birthday but when she got married, she lost out on the cake and gained Uncle Stuart!

L-R: Barbara Ostrow Schwartz, Elise Feiner, Linda and Jesse Ostrow

OLIVE OIL TEA CAKE
Mona Dunn

2½ cups unbleached all-purpose flour
2 teaspoons baking powder
Pinch of salt
1 cup sugar
2 eggs, lightly beaten

¾ cup milk
½ cup extra-virgin olive oil
½ cup golden raisins
Grated zest of 1 lemon
¼ cup pine nuts

Preheat oven to 350°. Butter and flour a 9 x 5-inch loaf pan. In a mixing bowl, stir together the flour, baking powder, and salt. Stir in the sugar. Add the eggs, milk, and olive oil, and beat well. Toss the raisins in a little flour to coat them lightly. Add the raisins and lemon zest to the batter and stir to distribute evenly. Spoon the batter into the pan and smooth the surface. Sprinkle the top with pine nuts. Bake for 55 minutes or until tester comes out clean. Let cool for a few minutes in the pan then unmold and cool on a rack.

Mona works with me at Trainor Associates. She said "this is a recipe my great-grandmother used to make for the children to enjoy, as well to have on hand in case of unexpected company. As it is not too sweet, it is perfect with a cup of tea or, as she used to serve it, with a strong espresso. It keeps very well wrapped in plastic wrap and foil."

COCA COLA ® CAKE
Elise Feiner

Cake:

2 cups flour	½ cup buttermilk
2 cups sugar	2 eggs, beaten
2 sticks butter	1 teaspoon baking soda
1 cup Coca Cola ®	1 teaspoon vanilla
3 tablespoons cocoa	2 cups mini marshmallows

Frosting:

1 stick butter	2 teaspoons vanilla
6 tablespoon Coca Cola ®	3 tablespoons Cocoa
1 box confectioner's sugar	1 cup toasted pecans, or almonds or both

Preheat the oven to 350°. Combine the flour and sugar and mix well. Heat the butter, Coca Cola, and cocoa, and bring to a boiling point. Pour this mix over the flour and sugar mix. Add the buttermilk, eggs, baking soda and vanilla. Mix well. Add the marshmallows and pour in a greased and floured 9x13-inch pan. Bake 30 to 35 minutes.

For the icing, cream the butter. Add the rest of the ingredients. Pour over the cake while it's still in the pan. Serve from the pan. This keeps well if you keep it in the pan you bake it in.

This recipe came from a friend in Baltimore years ago. It's rich and delicious.

Clockwise: Freda Feldman Feiner, Morris,
Jerome and Gene Feiner... Morris' Family,
the Bormels, lived in the Baltimore area –
they owned the Harvey House Restaurant on
Charles Street and made the best onion soup

L-R: Irwin Feldman, Ida Weinblatt Feldman,
Freda Feldman Feiner

"The higher you climb up the ladder, the more people get to take a shot at your ass!"
–Gene Feiner

TRIPLE CHOCOLATE DELIGHT
Elise Feiner

Cake Layers:
2½ unsweetened chocolate squares
3 eggs, separated
⅓ cup superfine granulated sugar

1 stick butter, softened
1 teaspoon vanilla
½ cup cake flour, sifted

Filling:
1 package semisweet chocolate squares (8 squares)
2 unsweetened baking chocolate squares

2 cups heavy cream
2 tablespoons Kahlua® or brandy

Glaze:
4 semisweet chocolate squares
½ cup heavy cream
3-4 teaspoons hot coffee or hot water

2 tablespoons butter, softened
3 tablespoons pistachio nuts, chopped fine

To make the cake, melt the chocolate over a double boiler; as soon as water starts to boil, remove from heat. Cool to lukewarm. Grease two 9-inch layer cake pans. Place waxed paper (cut to fit) on the bottom of the pans and grease well. Preheat oven to 350°. In a medium bowl, beat egg whites until foamy. Beat in 3 tablespoons of the sugar, 1 tablespoon at a time, until the meringue forms soft peaks. In a large bowl, beat the butter until creamy; beat in remaining sugar and the egg yolks until light and fluffy; beat in the chocolate and vanilla. Add the flour and stir until just blended. Fold the meringue mix into the chocolate mix ⅓ at a time until there are no streaks of white left. Divide the batter into the 2 prepared pans. Smooth the tops. Bake 350° for 15 minutes or until the center springs back when lightly presses with your fingertips. Cool in pans on a wire rack for 10 minutes; remove from pan; cool completely. Wrap and chill the layers.

Make the filling; chop the semisweet chocolate pieces coarsely. Place in a saucepan with the heavy cream. Cook stirring completely over medium heat until the chocolate melts and the mixture comes to boiling. Pour into a large deep bowl; stir in brandy or Kahlua. Cool stirring often, and then chill until mixture starts to thicken and set about 45 minutes. Beat the chocolate mixture with an electric mixture on high speed until it becomes light and fluffy about 3 to 5 minutes. Immediately spoon onto the chilled cake layer on a small cookie sheet. Spread quickly to a layer about 1¼ inches thick; top with second cake layer pressing lightly with hand; smooth side with spatula. Chill at least an hour until filling is firm.

Make glaze; Heat the remaining semisweet chocolate and cream in a small saucepan over low heat; stirring constantly until the chocolate is melted and mixture comes to a boil. Remove from heat; cool to lukewarm. Add a little hot water or coffee if too thick or mixture separates.

Place chilled cake over a pan to catch the excess glaze. Pour glaze on top of the cake. Spread with a long spatula, letting glaze run down the sides of cake to coat completely. Chill cake until glaze is set. Place on a serving plate. Beat 2 tablespoons of butter with about 4 tablespoons of the excess glaze until stiff enough to pipe onto the cake; chill briefly if necessary. Put into a pastry bag with a small star tip. Pipe small rosettes into a circle shape until about ¾ of the top of cake is covered with rosettes. Sprinkle pistachio nuts. Press nuts around the base about ¼- inch high from the bottom of the cake. Serves 10

PEARL'S COFFEE CAKE
Pearl Borten

¼ pound (1 stick) butter softened
¾ cup sugar
3 eggs
2 cups flour
1 teaspoon baking powder
1 teaspoon baking soda
1 (8 ounce) container of sour cream
3 tablespoon additional melted butter for topping

1 teaspoon of vanilla extract
¾ cup chopped walnuts
2 teaspoons cinnamon
1 cup (white/golden) raisins
¾ cup brown sugar
½ cup butter

Mix the ¼ pound of butter, sugar, and three eggs well. Add the flour, baking powder and baking soda; mix well again. Add the sour cream and vanilla and mix well again. Make the topping by mixing the walnuts, cinnamon, raisins, and brown sugar together. Cut in the ½ cup butter with 2 knives to make crumbs. Set aside. Grease a tube pan (Bundt or Angel Food). Put in half the batter, half the crumb topping, then add the remaining batter and remaining crumb topping. Pat down with a fork. Drizzle the remaining three tablespoons of melted butter on top of the topping. Bake 350° for 55 minutes.

DULCE DE LAS TRES LECHES (THREE MILK CAKE)
Carmen Ferreiro

Cake:
6 large eggs, separated
1 cup granulated sugar
1 cup flour

1 teaspoon baking powder
1 teaspoon vanilla extract

Cream topping:
1 (12-ounce) can evaporated milk
1 (14-ounce) can sweetened condensed milk

1 cup heavy cream

Icing:
3 tablespoons water
¾ cup granulated sugar

3 large egg whites

To make the cake: Preheat the oven to 350°. Lightly grease and flour a 9 x 11-inch baking dish and set aside. In the bowl of a mixer, beat the egg whites on low speed until soft peaks form. Add the sugar gradually with the mixer running and peak to stiff peaks. Add the egg yolks 1 at a time, beating well after the addition of each. Sift together the flour and baking powder and add to the egg mixture. (Do this quickly so the batter does not lose volume.) Add the vanilla. Bake until golden, 25 minutes.

To make the cream topping: In a blender, combine the evaporated milk, condensed milk, and heavy cream and blend on high speed. Remove the cake from the oven and while still warm, pour the cream mixture over it (with skewer make holes on top of cake so that the cake soaks the liquid). Let sit and cool to room temperature. Cover and refrigerate until well chilled, at least 4 hours or overnight.

To make the icing: Once the cake is completely chilled, in a saucepan combine the water and sugar. Bring to a boil. Reduce the heat and stir to dissolve the sugar. Cook until the mixture reaches the soft ball stage, 235° to 240°. Remove from the heat. In a medium bowl, beat the egg whites to soft peaks. While beating, add the hot syrup in a stream. Beat until all the syrup has been added, the mixture cools, and a glossy icing forms.

To assemble: Remove the cake from the refrigerator and spread the icing evenly across the top. Serves 10.

Carmen made this at one of her wonderful dinner parties, a perfect ending to a traditional Spanish Meal.

APPLE CAKE MONTICCIOLO
Fran Monticciolo

5-6 cups of apples sliced
1 cup chopped walnuts
¾ cup raisins
4 cups flour
4 cups sugar

1 teaspoon salt
4 beaten eggs
1⅓ cups oil
4 teaspoons vanilla

Glaze (Optional):
1 stick of butter, softened
1 egg yolk beaten

⅛ cup brandy
1 cup of confectioners' sugar

Using an electric mixer, mix flour, sugar, salt, eggs, oil, and vanilla in a large bowl. By hand, add the apples, raisins and nuts to the flour mixture because the flour mixture will be thick. Blend well. Place into a greased 9 x 13-inch pan. Bake for 1 hour at 350°. If not using the glaze sprinkle the top with ground nuts and raisins.

Glaze:
Beat the butter, egg yolk, brandy and confectioners' sugar together. When the cake is cool, spread the glaze over the top of the cake.

Fran Monticciolo was a very young, new teacher, when she was befriended by my mother, who became her mentor. She became a frequent visitor at our house, and a very good friend.

CRUMB CAKE
Elise Feiner

3 eggs
1 stick butter, melted
¾ cup sugar
3 cups sifted flour

4 teaspoons baking powder
Dash of salt
1 cup milk

Crumb mixture:

3 stick butter softened
1 cup sugar
3 cup flour

3 teaspoons cinnamon
1½ teaspoons white vinegar

Cream the eggs, melted butter and sugar. Sift the dry ingredients together. Add to egg mixture. Add the milk, blend well. Pour into a greased and floured 9 x 13-inch pan. Top with crumb mixture. Bake 350° for 35 minutes or until done. To make crumbs, mix together the softened butter, flour, cinnamon and vinegar and sugar. Using your fingers make into crumbs.

I must admit to having gotten very lazy and using Diane Longo's Recipe for crumb cake. It starts with a mix and is much faster. However, if you have the time, this is a great recipe too!

Betty Reinisch Feiner "prom" picture

Lauren Feiner – "look-alike"
the DNA doesn't lie…

RUTH'S POUND CAKE
Karen Selinsky

3 sticks butter or margarine
1 (8 ounce) package cream cheese
3 cups sugar
6 large eggs

2 teaspoons vanilla
3 cups flour
1 teaspoon baking powder

Grease and lightly flour a Bundt pan. Preheat oven to 325°. In a large mixing bowl cream butter or margarine and cream cheese. Add the sugar, eggs and vanilla; continue to cream the mixture together. Gradually mix in the flour and baking powder. Bake at 325° for 1 hour and 15 minutes or until light golden brown. You can sprinkle confectioners' sugar on the top or serve with fruit topping of your choice and/or cool whip.

Maria Trainor's sister Karen gave me this recipe. Karen says, "The pound cake recipe is from my sister-in-law Ruth who lives in Michigan. It has been in the family for years." My kids always called it "Aunt Ruth's pound cake." She said that it is the best pound cake ever!

MARY'S ULTIMATE CHOCOLATE CAKE
Mary Gaffney

The Cake:

6 tablespoons cocoa powder
3 tablespoons sugar
3 tablespoons water
⅔ cup milk
1 teaspoon vanilla
½ cup butter, softened

⅔ cup brown sugar
3 eggs yolks
1 cup flour
¼ cup cornstarch
1 teaspoon baking soda
¼ teaspoon salt
3 egg whites (beaten stiff)

Preheat the oven to 350°. Butter and flour 2 (10-inch) layer cakes pans. Combine the cocoa, sugar, and water in the top of a double boiler and cook over water until smooth and thick. Stir in the milk and vanilla, blend well, and set aside. In a large bowl, cream the butter and brown sugar. Beat in the egg yolks one at a time, then beat in the chocolate mixture. Sift the flour and cornstarch with the baking soda and salt three times. Blend into the chocolate mixture. Fold in the egg whites. Pour into prepared pans. Bake until firm to touch but no more than 25 minutes.

Mousse Filling:

11 ounces semisweet chocolate
¾ cup butter, cut into pieces
6 egg yolks
8 egg whites

4 teaspoons granulated sugar
2 tablespoons finely chopped walnuts
1 tablespoon hazelnut oil (may substitute)
2 ounces additional grated chocolate

Marinate the chopped nuts in the hazelnut oil; and have ready the 2 ounces of grated chocolate; set aside. Melt the 11 ounces of chocolate in top of double boiler over water; remove from heat. Add butter, stirring with a wooden spoon until smooth. Allow mixture to cool completely. Then add the egg yolks one at a time, beat well after each addition. Beat egg whites until stiff; halfway through add the sugar; fold chocolate mixture into egg whites with a wooden spatula or spoon. Add grated chocolate and drained walnut pieces. Set aside.

Topping:

12 ounces bittersweet chocolate
8 ounces heavy cream

1½ tablespoons butter
1 tablespoon sugar

Chop chocolate into small pieces. Place cream, butter, sugar on the stove; bring to a boil, remove. Stir in the chocolate. Allow to cool.

Assembly:

Allow cake to cool completely. Slice each layer in half to form four layers total. Place bottom layer into a 10-inch spring form pan, place some mousse on top, alternating with cake and mousse, ending with cake layer. Refrigerate several hours until firm or overnight. Remove cake from refrigerator and loosen spring form pan. Frost the cake with cooled chocolate icing. Finish with chocolate shavings.

Mary was pregnant with her first child and I was pregnant with Lauren and we had a baby shower given to us. Mary made this wonderful cake and shared the recipe with everyone. I think it originally came from the Washington Post.

"Love is a canvas furnished by nature and embroidered by imagination."
-Voltaire

COFFEE CAKE
Carmen Ferreiro

1 (18.5 ounce) package yellow cake mix
1 cup Colombo® plain yogurt or sour cream
⅓ cup water
2 eggs

1 cup chopped pecans or walnuts
2 teaspoons ground cinnamon
½ cup sugar

Prepare cake mix according to according to package directions, substituting sour cream or yogurt for the water. Pour ½ the batter into greased and floured 13 x 9 x 2-inch sheet cake pan, or an Angel Food or Bundt pan. Combine nuts, cinnamon, and sugar. Sprinkle half of mixture over the batter. Top with remaining batter. Sprinkle nut mixture over the top. Bake according to package directions. Cool in pan. While still warm glaze with 1 cup confectioners' sugar mixed with 4 teaspoons water. Serves 10.

This is Aunt Carmen's great coffee cake recipe. The first time I tasted it, was at Cristina's first birthday party...Cristina was 19 this year!

Hilda and Ed Ferreiro (Jorge's Parents)

Cristina Ferreiro – age 18

A very young Cristina Ferreiro- a vision of the beauty to come!

EGGNOG CHARLOTTE
Elise Feiner

12-14 ladyfingers, plain, unfilled
2 envelopes of Knox® unflavored gelatin
¾ cup sugar, divided
¼ teaspoon salt

4 eggs, separated
2¼ cups milk, divided
¼ cup rum or brandy
2 cups heavy cream

Split the ladyfingers; stand upright around the inside of a 9-inch spring form pan. Mix together the gelatin, ¼ cup sugar, and salt in a saucepan. Beat together the egg yolks, and 1 cup of milk; stir into the gelatin mixture. Place over low heat and cook stirring constantly until gelatin is dissolved and mixture thickens slightly 5 to 7 minutes. Remove from the heat; stir in the remaining 1¼ cups of milk, and rum. Chill the mixture, stirring occasionally until the mixture mounds slightly when dropped from a spoon. Beat egg whites until stiff but not dry. Gradually add the remaining ½ cup of sugar and beat until very stiff. Fold in the gelatin mixture. Whip the heavy cream until it holds its shape. Fold into the gelatin mixture. Turn into prepared pan. Chill until firm several hours or overnight. This can be done in advance and frozen. Let thaw in the refrigerator at least 24 hours. You can decorate the top with a mound of whipped cream in the middle and some cherries and chopped pistachio nuts. Serves 10.

I have been making this at the holidays for years. I found the recipe when I was a teenager. We usually have it at Christmas or New Years Eve. You can decorate it with whipped cream and cherries to give it a festive look.

GEORGE'S FLAKY COFFEE CAKE
George Koerner

1 package yeast	Pinch of salt
½ cup warm water	¾ cup sugar
1 tablespoon sugar	Cinnamon
2½ cups flour	Raisins
½ pound butter or margarine	1 cup chopped walnuts
4 eggs (separated)	

Mix the yeast, water and the tablespoon of sugar in a small bowl. Combine the flour, butter, egg yolks, and a pinch of salt. Add the yeast to the flour mixture and knead. Place the dough in the refrigerator overnight or for at least 1 hour. Remove from the refrigerator. Divide the dough in half and roll out with a rolling pin to a rectangle about 12x14-inches.

Beat the egg whites together with ¾ cup of sugar until it looks like whipped cream (meringue.) Spread half of the meringue over the first rectangle. Sprinkle cinnamon, raisins and chopped nuts over this, and roll up the dough. Shape into a horseshoe shape. Repeat with other half of dough. Let rise until double in bulk (about 1½ hours). Preheat oven to 350°. Place on a greased cookie sheet and bake for about 45 minutes until golden brown.

George says this recipe has been in his family for years. It was given to his mother by his grandmother.

George Koerner making his famous coffee cake

Zayda Koerner with George in the background

We had the most wonderful time visiting George, Zayda and the girls when we were in San Francisco…They made us feel so welcome and so at home.

"My friend, if I could give you one thing, I would wish for you the ability to see yourself as others see you. Then you would realize what a truly special person you are."

−B. A. Billingsly

ORANGE CHARLOTTE
Shirley Flomenhoft

2 packages of unfilled lady fingers
1 envelope of Knox® gelatin
½ cup sugar
⅛ teaspoon of salt
4 egg yolks (save the whites for later)
1 can (6 ounces) orange juice, thawed
3 tablespoons of lemon juice
3 tablespoons of water
½ teaspoon of orange peel

½ teaspoon of lemon peel
4 egg whites
⅓ cup sugar
1 cup heavy cream, whipped
2½ pints of heavy cream, whipped for topping with
¼ - ½ cup sugar and 2 teaspoons of vanilla.
1 large can of Mandarin orange slices, drained

Line a 9-inch spring form pan (bottom and sides) with lady fingers. Mix the Knox Gelatin, ½ cup sugar, and salt thoroughly in a heavy saucepan. Beat together the egg yolks and orange juice, and stir into the gelatin mixture. Add the lemon juice and water. Heat over low heat (**DO NOT BOIL**) until gelatin dissolves and mixture thickens slightly. Chill over ice water, stirring in the orange and lemon peel. Stir often until thick as egg whites. Set aside. Beat egg whites until foamy. Add ⅓ cup of sugar gradually and beat until soft peaks form. Whip 1 cup of cream and fold carefully into egg whites. Gentle fold gelatin mixture into egg whites and whipped cream mixture. Spoon the mixture into lined pan. Chill until set. Remove band from pan and spread top of cake with remaining 2½ pints of whipped cream that has been whipped with sugar and vanilla. Decorate with mandarin oranges. May be frozen but add whipped cream topping and oranges at the time of serving. Serves 12.

This is a great dessert from Aunt Shirley. It's perfect for a summertime dessert.

L-R: Brad Weiner, Leslie Weiner Solitrin, Shirley Flomenhoft, Terry Weiner Freedman, Hal Weiner

L-R: Shelley, Tara, and Scott Flomenhoft, Lori and Fred Wasa, Jill and Allison Roberts

MIMI'S COFFEE CAKE
Shirley Flomenhoft

4 eggs
½ pound butter, softened
2 cups sugar
1 pint sour cream

1 teaspoon vanilla
2 teaspoons baking soda
4 cups sifted all purpose flour
Pinch salt

Cream eggs, butter, sugar together. Mix sour cream with vanilla and baking soda. Alternate adding flour mix and sour cream mix to the egg mixture. Grease a 10-inch tube pan. Pour in ½ the batter. Mix 1 cup of chopped nuts of your choice with 1 cup of sugar and 2 teaspoons cinnamon. Spread ½ of nut mixture on batter. Top with remaining batter mixture. Top with remaining nut mixture. Bake at 350° for 1 hour.

This is Aunt Shirley's friend Mimi's recipe. It's another variation on a coffee cake.

CRUMB (LAUREN'S FAVORITE) BUNS DIANE
Diane Longo

1 box Duncan Hines® White Cake Mix

For Crumbs:

2 cups all-purpose flour
1 cup sugar
2 teaspoons cinnamon

1 teaspoon white vinegar
2 sticks butter, slightly softened

Mix the cake mix according to the package directions, and spread into a large buttered cookie sheet. I use disposable aluminum cookie sheets. Bake 15 to 20 minutes at 350° **(the cake will not be done.)** While this is in the oven, mix the ingredients for the crumb mixture together with your fingers. Mix well but leave crumbly, leaving some big crumb pieces. After the 20 minutes, place the crumb mixture on the top of the cake and bake another 15 to 20 minutes until done. Cool. Sprinkle with confectioners' sugar. Cut into squares.

Our next door neighbor, Diane Longo made this crumb cake when the kids were little. It's so delicious. Everyone always fights for the crumbs. This is a great dessert when you are having unexpected company. I always keep a box cake mix in the pantry. These rival the German Bakery crumb cakes of my youth in Brooklyn, and we always thought nothing could top those.

L-R: Rob, Michael, Diane, and Bob Longo

HARVEY WALLBANGER CAKE
Elise Feiner

1 package of any 2 layer Orange Cake mix
1 (3 ¾ ounce) package of instant vanilla pudding
4 eggs
½ cup oil

½ cup orange juice
½ cup Galliano®
2 tablespoons vanilla
2 tablespoons vodka

In a large mixing bowl, combine the cake mix and pudding mix; add the eggs, oil, orange juice, Galliano, vanilla and vodka. Beat on low speed 1 to 2 minutes, beat on medium speed 5 minutes; scraping the bowl frequently. Pour into a greased and floured Bundt cake pan or angel food pan. Bake at 350° for 45 minutes. Cool in the pan for 10 minutes. Remove to wire rack. Place on cake dish. Pour glaze over cake while still warm. Serves 10.

Glaze:

1 cup sifted confectioners' sugar
1 tablespoon orange juice

1 tablespoon Galliano
1 teaspoon vodka

Mix together; pour over warm cake.

ITALIAN SPONGE CAKE
Katherine Avella

½ cup butter flavored Crisco®
½ cup butter
2 cups sugar
1 teaspoon vanilla
5 eggs, separated
½ cup maraschino cherry juice

1 cup buttermilk
2 cups flour
1 teaspoon salt
1 teaspoon baking soda
2 cups coconut flakes

Preheat oven to 350°. Cream shortening and butter until they are evenly blended. Add sugar and vanilla, cream until well blended. Add egg yolks 1 at a time, creaming after each addition. In a separate bowl, mix the maraschino cherry juice and buttermilk. In a separate bowl, mix the flour, salt, and baking soda. Add half of the wet ingredients to the creamed mixture and then mix into the dry ingredients. Repeat with the other half of ingredients. Fold in coconut. Beat egg whites to stiff peaks and fold into the mixture. Divide mixture between 2 greased floured layer pans (I use Baker's Joy®) and bake for 45 minutes. Remove from oven and cool completely before icing. Serves 12 to 14.

Icing:
1 stick butter
4 cups confectioners' sugar
1 teaspoon vanilla

1 (8 ounce) package cream cheese
½ cups pecans or walnuts, broken and toasted

Beat first 4 ingredients until light and creamy. Spread icing between layers and over entire surface. Press toasted nuts around the border of the cake and sprinkle remaining nuts on the top.

L-R: Philip and Michael Avella

Melissa Avella

Michael and Sherry Avella

SOUR CREAM POUND CAKE
Elise Feiner

2¾ cups sugar
1 cup butter, softened
6 eggs
3 cups flour
½ teaspoon salt
¼ teaspoon baking soda
1 cup sour cream

½ teaspoon lemon extract
½ teaspoon orange extract
½ teaspoon vanilla extract
½ cup chopped nuts
½ cup chocolate chips
½ cup raisins (optional)

Cream butter and sugar together until light and fluffy. Add eggs one at a time, beating with each addition. Sift flour, baking soda and salt together, and add to creamed mixture alternating with the sour cream, beating well after each addition. Add the extracts, nuts, chips and raisins. Pour into a greased and floured 10-inch tube pan or loaf pan. Bake at 350° 1½ hours. Cool 15 minutes in the pan and then remove to a wire rack.

LEMON SOUR CREAM CAKE
Kitty Cully

Step 1:
1 Lemon Cake Mix (may have pudding in the mix)
1 cup (8 ounces) sour cream
⅓ cup oil

4 eggs
1 (2.9 ounce) package lemon pudding (NOT INSTANT)

Preheat oven to 350°. Mix all the ingredients together for 4 minutes on medium. Pour into a greased and floured 10-inch tube pan. Bake 55 minutes or until a toothpick inserted into the center comes out clean.

Step 2:
1 (4 ounce) small can frozen lemonade (thawed)

Remove cake from the oven. Let cool for 15 minutes. Poke holes all over the cake with a skewer. Pour thawed lemonade over the cake. Cake will still be warm. You may want to cut the amount of lemonade a little or it could be too tart.

Step 3:
Fresh strawberries
Confectioners' sugar

Fresh blueberries

Place strawberries in the center of the cake and around the sides of the plate. Sprinkle with confectioners' sugar. You can use blueberries or combine strawberries and blueberries.

This recipe came from Kitty Cully, Matt Cully's mother. Matt is a friend of Lauren and Jonathan Trainor. Maria Trainor said that Kitty baked this cake and sent to over to their house. She said it was so wonderful and asked her to add it to this cookbook.

Matt Cully relaxing in Old Forge

PINEAPPLE-CARROT CAKE
Janet Saporito

2 cups sifted flour
2 teaspoons baking soda
1 teaspoon baking powder
1 teaspoon salt
1 teaspoon cinnamon
1¾ cups sugar
1 cup oil

3 eggs
1 teaspoon vanilla
2 cups shredded carrots (shredded zucchini may be substituted)
1 cup coconut (optional)
1 cup chopped walnuts (optional)
1 can (8¼ ounces) crushed pineapple

Frosting:
1 (8 ounce) package of cream cheese
¼ stick of butter, softened
1 teaspoon vanilla

2 cups powdered sugar
3 tablespoons milk

Blend all the frosting ingredients well; set aside. Sift dry ingredients. Make a well; add sugar, oil, eggs and vanilla. Beat with a spoon until smooth. Add the carrots, pineapple, coconut and nuts; blend well. Pour into a greased and floured 9 x 12-inch baking pan. Bake at 350° for 45 minutes. Cool completely and frost.

CHOCOLATE COFFEE CAKE
Ruth Schwartz

1 package yellow cake mix
1 (4 serving size) package Jell-O ® Brand Chocolate Instant
Pudding and Pie Filling
4 eggs

½ cup oil
½ pint sour cream
1 (6 ounce) bag chocolate chips
¼ cup sugar plus 1 teaspoon cinnamon, combined

Preheat the oven to 350°. Grease and flour and Angel food cake pan. Blend cake mix, pudding mix, eggs, oil and sour cream in a large mixing bowl. Beat at medium speed of electric mixer for 10 minutes. Pour two thirds of the batter into the pan. Sprinkle half of the cinnamon sugar mix and half of the chocolate chips over the batter. Put the rest of the batter in the pan and top with remaining cinnamon sugar and chocolate chips. Bake 350° for about 1 hour.

Barbara Schwartz, Ruth's daughter-in-law gave me her whole collection of recipes. This was one of the many included in her cookbook, written in her own hand.

SOUR CREAM CAKE
Lucy Massimiano

1 cup sugar
2 sticks unsalted butter, softened
3 eggs
2½ cups flour

3 teaspoons baking powder
1 teaspoon vanilla
1 (8 ounce) container sour cream
½ teaspoon baking soda

Topping:

½ cup brown sugar
1 tablespoon butter
1 tablespoon flour

½ cup chopped nuts
6 ounces chocolate chips
1 teaspoon almond or vanilla extract

Mix all the topping ingredients together.

Cream the sugar and the butter together. Add and beat in one egg at a time. Add the flour, baking powder, and vanilla. In a separate bowl, mix together the sour cream and the baking soda. Set aside and let stand a few minutes. Add sour cream mixture to the flour mixture. Grease and flour (or use Baker's Joy®) an angel food tube pan. Pour in half the batter, and then a layer of the topping mix. Pour the remaining batter onto the topping mixture. Top with the rest of the topping mixture. Bake at 350° for one hour or until a cake tester comes out dry. Note: don't confuse the melted chocolate chips with the batter when testing the cake.

L-R: Sarah Burlingame, Mackenzie Raehm, Lauren and Abby Feiner

What a bevy of beauties!

MARBLE CAKE RECIPE
Hannah Ostrow

2 cups flour
2½ teaspoons baking powder
½ teaspoon salt
¼ pound butter
1¼ cups sugar

3 eggs separated
¾ cup milk
1 teaspoon vanilla
1 tablespoons cocoa
Walnut halves

Combine milk with vanilla. In a large bowl, cream butter, sugar and egg yolks together. Add dry ingredients alternately with milk and vanilla to the egg yolk mixture, until very smooth. In a separate bowl beat eggs whites until stiff. Add egg whites; fold in gently. Pour ⅔ of mixture into well greased and floured (9 x 13-inch) pan. Add cocoa to remaining ⅓ of mixture; blend well. Put blobs of cocoa mixture over white mixture and swirl a knife through to create a marble effect. Place walnut halves around the edge of the cake before baking. Bake moderately at 350° for about 1 hour. Watch until the center of cake is fully set. Debby(Hannah's granddaughter) said if you do this in a 9 x 13-inch pan you should double the recipe, otherwise use an 8 x 8-inch pan.

This is another of Hannah Ostrow's wonderful cake recipes. Her daughter Barbara Schwartz found this copy of her mother's recipe in her mother-in-law's cookbook and passed it on to me for this book. She said it is wonderful!

Harry Ostrow

Hannah Ostrow

COCONUT CAKE
Elise Feiner

1 package yellow cake mix
1 (4 serving size) package Jell-O ® Brand Vanilla Instant
Pudding and Pie Filling
1⅓ cups water

4 eggs
¼ cup oil
2 cups Flaked Coconut
1 cup chopped walnuts

Blend cake mix, pudding mix, water, eggs, oil and water in a large mixing bowl. Beat at medium speed of electric mixer for 4 minutes. Stir in coconut and walnuts. Pour into three greased and floured (I use Baker's Joy®) 9-inch layer pans. Bake 350° for 35 minutes. Cool in pans 15 minutes. Remove and cool on a rack. Fill and frost with coconut-cream cheese frosting. Serves 6.

Coconut-Cream Cheese Frosting:
4 tablespoon butter
2 cups Flaked Coconut
1 (8 ounce) package cream cheese

4 tablespoon milk
3½ cups confectioners' sugar
½ teaspoon vanilla

Melt 2 tablespoon butter in a skillet. Add coconut; stir constantly over low heat until golden brown. Spread coconut on absorbent paper to cool. Cream the remaining two tablespoons of butter with the cream cheese. Add milk and sugar alternately, beating well. Add vanilla; stir in 1¾ cups of the coconut. Spread on tops and sides of cake layers. Sprinkle with remaining coconut. Serves 6.

GERMAN CHOCOLATE CAKE
Elise Feiner

1 (4 ounce) package Baker's® German Sweet Chocolate	½ teaspoon salt
2⅓ cups sifted cake flour	⅔ cup butter, softened
1½ cups sugar	1 cup buttermilk
1 teaspoon baking soda	1 teaspoon vanilla
½ teaspoon baking powder	2 eggs

Melt chocolate over very low heat; cool. Sift flour with sugar, baking soda, baking powder and salt. Stir butter into a mixing bowl to soften. Add flour mixture, ¾ cup of the buttermilk and the vanilla. Mix to dampen the flour; beat two minutes at medium speed, scrapping the bowl occasionally. Add melted chocolate, remaining buttermilk, and eggs. Beat one minute longer. Pour batter into three greased and floured layer cake pans. Bake at 350° 30 to 35 minutes or until a cake tester inserted in the center comes out clean. Cool in pans for 5 minutes. Remove and cool on cake racks. Fill the layers and frost the sides with Coconut-Pecan Filling and Frosting. Serves 10.

Coconut-Pecan Filling and Frosting:

1 cup evaporated milk	1 teaspoon vanilla
1 cup sugar	1⅓ cups Baker's® Angel Food Coconut
3 egg yolks, slightly beaten	1 cup chopped pecans
½ cup butter	

Combine milk, sugar, egg yolks, butter and vanilla in a medium saucepan. Cook and stir over medium heat until the mixture thickens about 12 minutes. Remove from the heat. Add the coconut and pecans. Cool to spreading consistency, beating occasionally. Place between each layer and over the cake.

Our Boilermaker 2005 runners:

L-R: Jonathan Trainor, Lauren Feiner, Mindy Rosenfeld and Jake Stookey...
We are so proud of them!

"Adversity causes some men to break; others to break records."

—William A. Ward

LEMON CAKE
Maria Trainor

½ pound unsalted butter at room temperature
2½ cups sugar
4 jumbo eggs at room temperature
⅓ cup grated lemon zest (about 7 lemons)
3 cups flour
½ teaspoon baking powder

½ teaspoon baking soda
½ teaspoon kosher salt
¾ cup fresh lemon juice
¾ cup buttermilk at room temp
1 teaspoon vanilla extract

Glaze:
2 cups sifted confectioners' sugar

3½ tablespoons fresh squeezed lemon juice

Preheat oven 350°. Grease and flour 2 (8-inch) loaf pans. Line with parchment paper. Cream the butter with 2 cups of sugar with a mixer until light and fluffy about 5 minutes. Add the eggs one at a time and then add the lemon zest. Sift the flour, baking powder, baking soda, and salt together in a separate container. In another container, combine the buttermilk, vanilla and ¼ cup of lemon juice. Add the flour mixture and the buttermilk mixture alternating between the two to the egg/sugar mixture. Divide the batter between the two pans; tap the pans on the counter to smooth the mixture. Bake 45 minutes to 1 hour until a cake tester inserted comes out clean. Combine the remaining ½ cup sugar with the remaining ½ cup lemon juice in a small saucepan and cook over low heat until the sugar is completely dissolved. When the cakes are done, let cool 10 minutes and then invert them onto a rack. Spoon the lemon/sugar mixture over the cake. Let cool completely.

Glaze:

Mix the confectioners' sugar and the lemon juice in a bowl with a wire whisk. When smooth, pour over the cake and let the glaze run down the sides.

Maria says that this cake is one of her favorites; she says that people are always want the recipe from her so she graciously shared it with us!

BLUEBERRY BUCKLE
Brittany Butler

CAKE:
2 cups flour
¾ cup sugar
½ cup butter or margarine (softened)
2½ teaspoons baking powder

1 large egg
½ cup milk
2 cups blueberries (fresh or frozen)

TOPPING:
½ cup flour
½ cup sugar

½ teaspoon cinnamon
½ cup butter, softened

Make the cake batter. Beat the sugar and butter together; add the egg. Mix in the flour, baking powder and milk. Gently, fold in the blueberries. Grease a 9 x 9-inch glass baking dish. Place the batter in the prepared glass pan. In a separate bowl, mix all the ingredients for the topping until you have crumbs. You may want to use your fingers to make the crumbs. Sprinkle crumbly topping over the batter. Bake at 350° for 40 minutes.

Brittany is one of Lauren' closest friends since Junior High School. When Lauren left for Prep School, Brit gave Lauren her baby blanket to keep her company and safe! She still has it in her dorm room. Today, they attend Cornell together. She visited recently and wanted to give me a recipe for the book. This is her cousin's recipe and she says it's delicious!

L-R: Lauren Feiner and
Brittany Butler age 14

Lauren and Britt now!

L-R: Joanne, Sophia and Carl Fsadni

Sophia Fsadni

Anthony and Debbie Pedicini and Family
Anthony Jr, Thomas and Lisa

The Saracino Kids L-R: James, Cassie and Emily

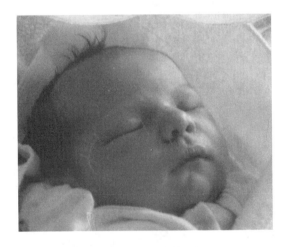

Adrianna Marie Skonberg

L-R: Nikki and Missy Appel

APPLE PIE
Ann D'Amico

Crust:
1-1¼ cups all-purpose flour
¼ teaspoon salt

⅓ cup shortening
4 to 5 tablespoons water

Filling:
¼ cup granulated sugar
2 tablespoons all-purpose flour
½ teaspoon ground cinnamon
⅛ teaspoon salt
6 cups thinly sliced, peeled tart cooking apples (about 2¼ pounds)

¾ cup packed brown sugar
½ cup all-purpose flour
½ teaspoon ground cinnamon
⅓ cup butter
1 cup chopped walnuts

In a medium mixing bowl stir together 1¼ cups flour and ¼ teaspoon salt. Using a pastry blender, cut in shortening until pieces are pea-size. Sprinkle 1 tablespoon of the water over part of the mixture; gently toss with a fork. Push moistened dough to the sides of the bowl. Repeat moistening dough, using 1 tablespoon of the water at a time, until all dough is moistened. Form into a ball. Roll dough into a 12-inch circle. Transfer to a 9-inch pie plate. Trim pastry to ½-inch beyond edge of pie plate. Fold under extra pastry. For a fluted edge, place your thumb against the inside of the pastry. Press dough around your thumb with the thumb and index finger of your other hand. Press the tines of a fork lightly into the center of each flute. Set aside. Preheat oven to 375°. In a large mixing bowl stir together sugar, 2 tablespoons flour, ½ teaspoon cinnamon, and ⅛ teaspoon salt. Add apple slices. Gently toss to combine. Transfer apple mixture to pastry-line pie plate. For the crumb topping, in a medium bowl stir together brown sugar, ½ cup flour, and ½ teaspoon cinnamon. Using a pastry blender, cut in butter until the mixture resembles coarse crumbs. Stir in 1 cup chopped nuts. Sprinkle crumb mixture over apple mixture. Gently pat mixture down over apples. Place pie on a baking sheet. Cover entire pie loosely with foil. Bake for 15 minutes. Remove foil. Bake for 35 to 40 minutes more or until top is dark golden brown and apples are tender. Cool on a wire rack. Makes 8 servings.

Make-Ahead Tip:

Prepare as above, except after sprinkling with crumb topping, wrap entire pie tightly in a double thickness of foil. Freeze up to 3 months. To bake frozen pie, remove foil wrapping and place frozen pie on a baking sheet. Cover entire pie loosely with foil. Bake in a 350° oven for 40 minutes. Remove foil. Bake 35 to 40 minutes more or until top is brown and apples are tender. Cool on wire rack.

CREAMY PUMPKIN PIE
Ann D'Amico

1¾ cups homemade or canned pumpkin puree
¾ cup firmly packed brown sugar
1½ (8 ounce) packages Philadelphia® cream cheese, at room temperature
3 eggs
1½ cups half and half
1 teaspoon vanilla extract

½ teaspoon ground ginger
½ teaspoon allspice plus more for garnish
¼ teaspoon ground cinnamon
⅛ teaspoon ground cloves
Pinch salt
1 unbaked 10-inch prepared or homemade pie crust shell,
Unsweetened chilled whipped cream for serving

Position a rack in the lower third of the oven and preheat to 425°. In a large bowl, whisk together the pumpkin puree, brown sugar and cream cheese until smooth. Whisk in the eggs one at a time. Add the half and half, vanilla, ginger, the ½ teaspoon allspice, the cinnamon, cloves and salt and stir to combine. Pour the filling into the pie shell. Place the pie in the oven and bake for 15 minutes. Reduce the oven temperature to 350° and continue to bake the filling until the filling is evenly but not firmly set, about 35 minutes more for a baking time of about 50 minutes total. Check the pie 10 minutes before it is ready; if it is browning too fast cover the crust with a collar of aluminum foil. Transfer to a wire rake and let cool to room temperature before serving. Cut the pie into wedges, top each wedge with whipped cream and lightly dust with Allspice. Serves 8.

Ann says, "This recipe came out of a Williams Sonoma Thanksgiving booklet. It is probably the best pumpkin pie I have ever made. It is so creamy and delicious." Check out their website www.williams-sonoma.com one of my favorite stores!

BLACK BOTTOM PIE
Elise Feiner

Crust:
1⅓ cups graham cracker crumbs
¼ cup sugar

⅓ cup butter, melted

Filling:
1 tablespoon unflavored gelatin
¼ cup cold water
1 cup sugar
½ teaspoon salt
¼ cup cornstarch
2 cups milk
4 eggs, separated

1 (6 ounce) package chocolate chips
¼ cup light rum
¼ teaspoon cream of tartar
½ cup heavy cream, whipped
Chocolate Shavings (Use a Hershey® Bar and potato peeler)

Preheat the oven to 350°. Make the crust: mix graham cracker crumbs, ¼ cup sugar and melted butter together. Press into the bottom and sides of a 9-inch pie plate. Bake 8 minutes. Cool. In a small bowl, sprinkle gelatin over water to soften. In a medium saucepan, combine ½ cup sugar, salt and cornstarch; gradually add the milk. Bring to boiling, stirring until thick. In a small bowl, beat the egg yolks slightly; gradually stir in half of the hot mixture to temper egg yolks. Pour back into saucepan. Return custard to heat; cook, stirring frequently another 2 minutes. Remove from heat. Measure 1½ cups of the custard into a large Pyrex® measuring cup or bowl. Add the chocolate chips and vanilla; stir until melted. Pour into prepared pie shell; refrigerate 45 minutes. Add the gelatin to the remaining custard, stirring until gelatin dissolves. Cool to lukewarm. Add rum. Refrigerate. Beat the egg whites with cream of tartar until soft peaks form. Add remaining ½ cup sugar, 2 tablespoons at a time until stiff peaks form. Fold whites into rum flavored custard; pour over chocolate mixture. Refrigerate at least 6 hours. Top with whipped cream piped from a star tipped pastry bag if you have one, and chocolate shavings.

L-R: Jennifer, Abby, Danielle and Lauren Feiner

PIE CRUST SILVESTRI
Julia Silvestri

2 sticks unsalted butter, chilled, cut into small cubes
2½ cups all-purpose flour
1 teaspoon salt
1½ teaspoons sugar

¼-½ cup ice water
A little extra butter and flour for buttering and rolling the dough

Place the flour, salt, and sugar in a food processor and pulse to blend. Add the chilled butter cubes and pulse for about 10 to 12 seconds or until it is crumbly and resembles small balls. Add about ¼ cup of ice water and pulse. The mixture should hold together but not form a ball in the processed. Add as much of the remaining ¼ of a cup as needed. When you squeeze the dough it should just holds its shape. Divide the dough into two equal circles wrap in saran wrap and refrigerate about 1 hour. Place some flour on a pastry board or clean work surface (wax paper works well and makes it easy to transfer). Place the circle of dough on the work surface and dust lightly with flour. I also dust my rolling pin with flour as well. Roll into a 10-inch circle about ⅛ to ¼-inch thickness. Grease your pie plate with the extra butter. Place crust into pie plate shaping with your fingers if necessary. Leave a one inch overhang. Fill with desired filling. Roll second crust for the top, or freeze for another use if a top crust is not needed. Crimp the crust in any style you desire. Makes 2 crusts.

This is another recipe from my Aunt Julia's collection. I modernized it by doing it in the food processor but it can be done by hand.

SWEET POTATO CHIFFON PIE
Elise Feiner

1 small box vanilla wafers	Pinch nutmeg
½ cup sugar	Pinch salt
½ cup finely chopped pecans	Pinch ginger
1 stick butter, melted	1 envelope unflavored gelatin
1½ cups eggnog	1 teaspoon pure vanilla extract
2 cups mashed sweet potatoes	3 egg whites
¾ cup light brown sugar	2 cups sweetened whipped cream
3 egg yolks	Confectioners' sugar
½ teaspoon cinnamon	8 sprigs fresh mint

Preheat the oven to 400 ° In a food processor, combine the vanilla wafers, ¼ cup sugar, and pecan pieces. Mix until the crust is smooth and resembles a coarse texture. With the machine running, add the butter and process until all of the butter is incorporated. Remove the crust from the processor and press into a deep-dish 10-inch pie pan. Place the pan in the oven and bake for 10 to 12 minutes or until the crust is set.

In a saucepan, combine the eggnog, sweet potatoes, brown sugar, egg yolks, cinnamon, nutmeg, salt, and ginger together. Mix well. Place the pan over medium heat and cook the mixture for 10 minutes, stirring constantly. Remove the pan from the heat and sprinkle the gelatin over the filling. Whisk the gelatin into the filling until the gelatin dissolves. Stir in the vanilla. Cover the filling and refrigerate until cool. Using an electric mixer, whip the egg whites until soft peaks form. Gradually add ¼ cup sugar and continue to beat until the peaks are stiff. Fold the egg whites into the sweet potato filling. Spread the filling evenly over the crust and refrigerate the pie for about 1 hour. Spread the whipped cream, evenly over the top of the pie. Serves 8.

CHOCOLATE CHIP PECAN PIE
Elise Feiner

Ready Made 9-inch Deep Dish Pie Crust	2 tablespoon melted butter
3 eggs, beaten slightly	1 teaspoon vanilla
1 cup corn syrup (light or dark)	1 cup coarsely chopped pecans
½ cup sugar	¾ cup chocolate chips

Preheat oven to 350°. In a bowl, combine eggs, corn syrup, sugar, butter and vanilla; blend well. Stir in pecans and chips. Pour into prepared crust and bake 1 hour until filling is firm around the outside and slightly firm in the middle. Serves 8.

PUMPKIN MASCARPONE PIE
Elise Feiner

1¼ cups all-purpose flour	½ teaspoon vanilla
¼ teaspoon salt	1 cup canned pumpkin
⅓ cup shortening	1 (5-ounce) can evaporated milk (⅔ cup)
4 to 5 tablespoons cold water	2 slightly beaten eggs
1 (8 ounce) package mascarpone or cream cheese, softened	⅓ cup packed brown sugar
1 slightly beaten egg yolk	1 teaspoon ground cinnamon
2 tablespoons honey	¼ teaspoon ground nutmeg

Preheat oven to 375°. In a medium mixing bowl stir together flour and salt. Using a pastry blender or two knives, cut in shortening until pieces are the size of small peas. Sprinkle 1 tablespoon of the water over part of the mixture; gently toss with a fork. Push moistened dough to the side of the bowl. Repeat moistening dough, using 1 tablespoon of the water at a time, until all dough is moistened. Form into a ball. Roll dough into a 12-inch circle. Transfer to a 9-inch pie plate. Trim and crimp edge high. In a bowl beat mascarpone or cream cheese, egg yolk, honey, and vanilla with an electric mixer on low to medium speed until smooth. Set aside. In another bowl stir together pumpkin, evaporated milk, the remaining 2 eggs, brown sugar, cinnamon, and nutmeg. Pour pumpkin mixture into pastry-lined pie plate. Drop the mascarpone mixture over pumpkin mixture. Pull a thin metal spatula or knife gently through the mascarpone mix to swirl fillings. Bake for 50 minutes or until top is puffed and a knife inserted near the center comes out clean. Cool for 1 hour on a wire rack. Cover and chill at least 2 hours before serving. In a hurry, use a prepared pie crust. Serves 8.

NUTTY PECAN PIE
Elise Feiner

½ package of pie crust mix
2 tablespoons chopped nuts
3 eggs
1 cup sugar
½ teaspoon salt
2 tablespoons butter, melted

½ cup dark corn syrup
½ cup whipped cream
1 teaspoon vanilla
¼ cup brandy or Kahlua®
1 cup shelled pecan halves

Preheat the oven to 375°. Prepare the pie crust according to package directions except add the chopped nuts before adding the water. Place crust into a 9-inch pie dish. In a small bowl, beat eggs, sugar, salt, butter, syrup and cream. Stir in vanilla, brandy and pecans. Pour into pastry crust. Bake 40 to 50 minutes or until filling is set and pastry is a golden color. Serves 10.

PEACHEESY PIE
Edith and Tina Terenzi

Crust:
2 cups flour
1 teaspoon salt
⅔ cup shortening (Crisco®)

6-7 tablespoons peach syrup (from the canned peaches)
2 tablespoons butter

Preheat oven to 425°. Combine the flour with the salt. Cut the shortening in until it is the size of peas. Sprinkle the peach syrup over the mixture while stirring with a fork until the dough holds together. Roll out half the dough on a floured surface to a circle 1½-inches larger than an inverted 9-inch pie pan. Turn the pan upright and place the pastry crust into the pan. Fill with the peach mixture and dot with butter. Flute the edges. Cover with the cheesecake topping. Roll out the remaining dough and cut into circles. Brush the circles with remaining peach syrup. Arrange the circles on top of the cheesecake layer. Bake at 425° for 10 minutes; cover the edges with foil, then reduce heat to 350° and bake for an additional 30 to 35 minutes or until the crust is golden brown.

Peach Cheesecake Filling:
1 (1 pound 13 ounce) can Cling Peach slices
½ cup plus ⅓ cup sugar
2 tablespoons cornstarch
2 tablespoons corn syrup
2 tablespoons pumpkin pie spice

2 tablespoons vanilla extract
2 eggs slightly beaten
1 tablespoons lemon juice
3 ounces cream cheese (softened)
½ cup sour cream

Peach mixture:
Drain the peaches and save the syrup. Combine the peaches, ½ cup sugar, corn starch, corn syrup, pumpkin pie spice and vanilla. Set aside.

Cheesecake topping:
Combine the eggs, ⅓ cup sugar, lemon juice and 2 tablespoons of the peach syrup in a small sauce pan. Cook stirring constantly until thick. Soften the cream cheese. Blend in the sour cream with the cream cheese. Add this mix to the hot mixture, beat until smooth.

This recipe is my friend Tina's mother Edith's recipe. Tina was my best friend from Roosevelt Hospital School of Nursing. Her mother passed away, but she was a terrific cook. She was a war bride from Germany and made the most wonderful dishes. I remember visiting their house in Franklin Square and sharing great times with Tina, her sisters, and her Dad. She now lives in Seattle but we still keep in touch.

PIE CRUST MAINELLA
Josephine Mainella

2 cups Wondra® flour
1 teaspoons salt
¾ cup butter

⅓ cup cold water

In a medium bowl, add flour, salt and butter; cut in and blend until coarse. Add the water and blend well but don't over mix. Divide in half and then roll into desired size circle. Refrigerate one half while working on the other. Use with any pie filling.

PEACH PIE
Elise Feiner

Filling:
4 cups of fresh peaches, sliced
¼ teaspoon nutmeg
⅛ teaspoon salt
¼ teaspoon cinnamon

1 (16 ounce) container sour cream
1½ cups sugar
5 tablespoons flour

Crust:
2 cups flour
1 teaspoon salt

¾ cup oil
¼ cup water

Mix flour and salt in a bowl. Add oil and water. Stir with a fork until well blended and dough hold together. Divide in half and roll into 2 circles to form a top and bottom crust for a 9-inch pie pan. Place crust into pie pan. Spread the peaches onto the pie crust. Combine the sugar (save 2 tablespoons), flour, salt, and sour cream. Spread over the peaches. Cover with top crust. Make several slits in the top crust with a knife and flute the edges of the crust. Combine the remaining sugar, cinnamon and nutmeg together, and sprinkle on the crust. Bake at 400° for 40 minutes. Refrigerate before serving if you like it firm, or serve warm and it will be a little runny.

I was about 15 when I started to make this pie. For some reason, it always reminds me of summers in Bayville, probably because that was peach season and I was always baking these pies for Joe, Warren, and Frankie.

PECAN PIE
Elise Feiner

1 cup white corn syrup
1 cup dark corn syrup
⅓ teaspoon salt
⅓ cup melted butter
1 teaspoon vanilla

3 whole eggs
1 heaping cup of shelled pecans, walnuts, or nut of your choice

Mix the syrup, sugar, salt, butter and vanilla. Add slightly beaten eggs. Pour into a 9-inch unbaked pie crust. Sprinkle the pecans over the filling. Bake at 350° for 45 minutes. You can serve it with whipped cream or ice cream. Serves 8.

I make this pie every Thanksgiving in one form or another.

PEANUT BUTTER PIE
Barbara Montelegro

½ cup creamy peanut butter
½ cup confectioner's sugar
1 (9-inch) Baked Pie Shell
¼ cup cornstarch
1 (12 ounce) can evaporated milk
4 eggs, separated

1 cup hot water
½ cup granulated sugar
1 teaspoon vanilla
¼ cup butter
½ teaspoon cream of tartar
4 tablespoons sugar

Bake a 9-inch pie crust until golden brown. Remove from oven and cool. Mix together the peanut butter and confectioners sugar. Mix until crumbled. Pour into the prepared pie crust. In a medium saucepan, mix together the cornstarch, evaporated milk, egg yolks, hot water, and ½ cup of sugar. Heat over medium high heat stirring constantly with a whisk until boiling. Boil for 2 minutes. Remove from the heat; add the vanilla, and butter. Whip until creamy. Pour into the pie shell on top of the peanut butter. Cover with plastic wrap and chill 2 hours. Beat the 4 egg whites, cream of tartar, and the 4 tablespoons of sugar until stiff peaks form. Place over the chilled pie going all the way to the edges with the meringue. Brown the top with a kitchen torch, or by placing it under the broiler for a minute or two. Serves 6.

The girl who used to do my hair years ago, Barbara gave me this recipe. She was from the Deep South, and this is a real southern peanut recipe. It is outstanding!

STRAWBERRY PIE
Sheila Bamberger

1 (9-inch) pie shell, baked	3 tablespoon cornstarch
1 quart fresh strawberries	1 cup water
1 cup sugar	6 drops red food coloring (optional – I don't use it)

Cut up 1 cup of strawberries into small pieces. Mix sugar, starch and water in 2-quart saucepan until smooth and clear. Add cut up berries. Cook and stir over medium heat until thick and clear. Stir in food coloring. Allow to cool completely. Cut remaining berries in halves and stir them into the sauce. Pour mixture into pie shell and chill for at least an hour. Garnish with whipped cream (or topping) and berries, if desired! Enjoy!!

This is a recipe from a friend, Sheila Bamberger. She made it for a barbeque we attended and it was wonderful. She was generous enough to share it with me.

FUDGY PECAN TART
Elise Feiner

1 prepared pie crust mix (mixed but not shaped)	1 cup sugar
3 squares unsweetened chocolate	1 cup light corn syrup
½ stick butter	2 cups pecan halves
4 eggs	Coffee whipped cream

Preheat oven to 400°. Take the prepared pie crust and place into a 9-inch tart pan with a loose bottom, form a stand-up fluted edge. Melt chocolate and butter in a small pan over low heat; cool. Beat eggs in a medium bowl; add sugar and corn syrup. Stir in chocolate mixture and 1⅓ cups of pecans. Pour into prepared crust. Arrange remaining pecans in a circular fashion into the pie filling. Bake in 400° oven for 5 minutes. Lower temperature to 350° and bake 35 minutes or until filling is set. Cool completely on a wire rack. Remove the side of pan. Spoon coffee whipped cream in the middle of the tart. To make coffee whipped cream, combine 1 cup heavy cream, 2 tablespoons confectioners' sugar, and 1 teaspoon instant coffee. Beat until stiff. Refrigerate until ready to use.

RICH AND CREAMY PUMPKIN PIE
Tina Dardano

1 can prepared pumpkin filling	3 eggs
1 (15 ounce) container fine ricotta	2 (9-inch) ready to bake pie crusts
1 (13 ounce) can evaporated milk	

Mix all ingredients until well blended. Pour into two pie crusts. Bake at 375° for one hour or until a knife inserted in the center comes out clean. Chill and serve with whipped cream.

My sister-in-law Phyllis' sister Tina gave me this recipe. She is a terrific cook and makes this at the holidays.

L-R: Orsola Barone, Elizabeth Barone Maida,
Clementina Mainella (my grandmother)
Orsola is my grandmother's sister and Lizzie is her daughter.

The Mainella Girls…
L-R: Katherine Mainella Avella and Josephine Mainella

CHOCOLATE AND COCONUT PECAN TART
Elise Feiner

Crust:
1½ cups all purpose flour
6 tablespoons unsweetened cocoa powder
¼ cup sugar
¼ teaspoon salt

½ cup (1 stick) chilled unsalted butter, cut into ½ inch pieces
2 large egg yolks

Filling:
1 cup light corn syrup
¾ cup (packed) golden brown sugar
¼ cup (½ stick) unsalted butter, melted
3 large eggs
2 teaspoons vanilla extract

¼ teaspoon salt
1 (6 ounce) bag miniature chocolate chips
¾ cup plus 3 tablespoons shredded, unsweetened coconut
1½ cups (about 7 ounces) pecan halves, toasted

For Crust: Preheat oven to 375°. Whisk flour, cocoa, sugar and salt in a large bowl to blend. Add butter; rub in with fingertips until mixture resembles coarse meal. Whisk yolks in a small bowl to blend; add to flour mixture. Stir until moist clumps form. Gather dough into a ball; press over the bottom and up sides of 11-inch diameter tart pan with removable bottom. Bake crust until set, about 15 minutes. Cool while preparing filling. Reduce oven temperature to 350°.

For Filling: Blend corn syrup, sugar and butter in a medium bowl. Whisk in eggs, vanilla, and salt. Stir in ½ cup chocolate chips, ¾ cup coconuts and the pecans. Pour into prepared crust. Bake tart until the filling is set and golden on the top, about 40 minutes. Place the tart on a rack. Sprinkle the remaining ½ chocolate chips evenly around the edges of the warm tart. Let stand just until chips soften, about 5 minutes. Using a small spatula spread the chocolate to form 1-inch border around the edge of the tart. Sprinkle the chocolate border with remaining 3 tablespoons coconut. Cool completely. This can be made a day ahead. Cover loosely with foil; let stand at room temperature. Serves 12.

This is one of my favorite pecan pie recipes. I usually make this one at Thanksgiving!

L-R: Marie Caccavale, Josephine Mainella,
Nina D'Amico (seated)

Aunt Flo Avella at her 90th Birthday Party!

CAROL MARDON'S FRUIT CRUMB PIE
Sheila Bamberger

Any fruit of your choice
1 cup flour
¾ cup sugar
½ teaspoon salt

1 teaspoon baking powder
1 egg
⅓ cup melted butter

Place fruit of your choice in 9x9-inch square pan or 10-inch pie pan. Make the topping; mix the flour, salt, baking powder, and egg together until crumbly. Sprinkle over fruit of your choice; pour ⅓ cup melted butter over topping Bake 35 to 40 minutes at 350 °.

Sheila Bamberger got this recipe from a friend, and said it's delicious!

Gina Mastrovito-Smith and Kris Smith

Maryann and Frank Mastrovito

L-R: Philip Jr., Gianna, and Jami Marissa
Di Pierdomenico

Richard and Julie Venezio

The Koerner Girls L-R: Renee, Sherylynn and Sandra our
neighbors and friends…they now live in California

L-R: Jonathan Sapio and his big
brother Julius "Joey".

CASSATA CAKE (ITALIAN CHEESECAKE)
Phyllis Latini

Crust:
7 eggs, beaten
¼ cup baking powder
¾ cup shortening

3 tablespoons of vanilla
¾ cup of sugar
5 cups of flour

In a bowl, mix the flour with the baking powder. In a separate bowl, beat the eggs and shortening together. Add the vanilla and the sugar. Mix in the flour mix and mix well together to form a pie crust. On a lightly floured surface, roll the crust out to make it about ⅛-inch thick round. Line a 10-inch deep cake pan with the crust, leaving some hanging over. Set aside.

Filling:
3 pounds of ricotta cheese
¾ cup confectioner's sugar
9 eggs
Juice from a half an orange

¼ cup of maraschino cherry juice
¼ pound Hershey® Bar (almonds optional), slivered
25 maraschino cherries, diced
1 (5.5 ounce) can of Hershey® chocolate syrup

Mix together the ricotta, sugar, eggs, orange juice, and cherry juice. Beat until smooth. You may also add 1 shot of liqueur when the filling is smooth, this is optional. Add the chopped Hershey bar and the diced cherries. Pour a layer of the filling on the bottom of the lined pan. Now, marbleize the filling with the chocolate sauce by pouring the sauce over the batter and taking a knife and running it through the batter to create a swirl effect. Bake 1½ hours in a 350° oven. Put a knife in the center to check for doneness, it should be dry when you remove it. Keep refrigerated when cool.

This is one of my niece Nicole's favorites. It's her grandmother's. When I asked who's name I should credit it to, this was her answer, "You can put Phyllis Latini for Shamm's recipes (I can't take credit for her marvelous cooking, no one would believe it, ha ha.)" Nicole is right...Phyllis is a great cook. When we first moved to Utica we shared many wonderful meals in her home!

L-R: Melissa, Sharon, Philly, Sherry, and Michael Avella, Nicole Latini

"A child's life is like a piece of paper on which every person leaves a mark."
-Proverbs

CHOCOLATE MARBLED CHEESECAKE
Elise Feiner

Crust:

1 cup of chocolate wafer crumbs (about
18-20 wafers)
½ cup finely chopped walnuts or pecans

2 tablespoons sugar
½ stick butter, melted

Mix the crumbs, nuts and 2 tablespoons of sugar in a small bowl. Add in melted butter. Press mixture over the bottom and sides of a well greased 8-inch spring form pan. Preheat oven to 350 ° Bake the crust for 10 minutes. Cool completely; chill.

Filling:

½ cup sugar
1 envelope Knox® unflavored gelatin
⅔ cup milk
2 egg yolks
2 (8 ounce) packages cream cheese, softened
1 tablespoon grated orange rind

½ cup sour cream
2 egg whites
3 tablespoons sugar
1 (6 ounce) package chocolate chips), melted and cooled
Mandarin orange segments (optional)

Combine the ½ cup of sugar and the gelatin in a small saucepan. Beat in the milk until well blended. Beat in the egg yolks until the mixture is smooth. Let stand 3 minutes. Cook over medium heat, stirring constantly, until gelatin is dissolved and mixture is slightly thickened, about 5 minutes. (Do not allow mixture to boil.) Remove from heat; cool completely. Beat cream cheese in a large bowl until smooth; beat in the orange rind and sour cream. Gradually add cooled gelatin mixture, beating on low speed until just blended. Chill over ice and water until the mixture mounds slightly when spooned. Beat the egg whites until foamy and double in volume. Gradually beat in the remaining 3 tablespoons of sugar until meringue forms soft peaks. Fold meringue into cheese mixture. Add about 2 cups of the cheese mixture to the cooled melted semisweet chocolate; stir until blended. Spoon plain and chocolate mixtures, alternately into the prepared pan. Swirl mixtures with a knife to create marble effect. Chill until firm, at least 4 hours or overnight. Remove from pan; garnish with orange segments, if you wish. Serves 12.

This cake makes a beautiful presentation and is easy to make especially in the summer because you only have to bake the crust.

CHEESECAKE MAINELLA
Frank Mainella, Jr.

2 (8 ounce) packages of cream cheese, at room temperature
1 (8 ounce) package sour cream
1 (16 ounce) package of cottage cheese with fruit, at room temperature (can use plain if desired)
3 tablespoons flour
3 tablespoons cornstarch

1 stick (¼ pound) butter or margarine, melted
1½ cups sugar
4 eggs
1½ tablespoons lemon juice
1 teaspoon vanilla

In a mixing bowl, cream the cream cheese until fluffy. Add cottage cheese. Gradually add sugar. Beat eggs, lemon juice and vanilla together and add to mixture. Add flour and cornstarch. Beat well. Add melted butter, and then add the sour cream. Pour into a 10 to 12-inch spring form pan that has been lined with foil and greased. Pour mixture into the prepared pan. Bake at 350° for 60 minutes. Shut off the oven. Leave in the oven for 2 more hours with the door closed. Cool in refrigerator and enjoy! Serves 12.

This was Aunt Edith's recipe. She always used to say that she was the best Italian cook of Irish/French descent. My cousin Frank gave me the recipe for the book.

L-R: Barbara Cacoulidis
holding Ariana, and
Lauren Feiner

ELISE'S BEST CHEESECAKE
Elise Feiner

Crust:
1 stick unsalted butter, melted
½ teaspoon ground cinnamon

1 teaspoon vanilla
2 cups graham cracker crumbs or chocolate wafer crumbs

Filling:
2 cups sugar
4 tablespoons flour
4 tablespoons cornstarch
5 (8 ounce) packages Philadelphia® Cream Cheese at room temperature
1 stick unsalted butter, melted

6 eggs
1 tablespoon vanilla
1 tablespoon lemon juice
Zest of half a lemon, finely grated
1 pint heavy cream
1 (8 ounce) container sour cream

Topping (Optional):
2 tablespoons butter
2 pints blueberries, washed and dried
¾ cup granulated sugar

1 teaspoon cornstarch
Juice of 1 lemon

To prepare crumb crust: In a mixing bowl, combine the crust ingredients together with a fork until evenly moistened. Lightly coat the bottom and sides of a 10-inch spring form pan (3-inch deep if possible) with non-stick cooking spray, or chill the pan and then brush the pan with melted butter. Firmly press the mixture over the bottom and 1-inch up the sides on the pan, use your fingers or the smooth bottom of a glass. **Cover the outside of the pan with aluminum foil** to protect it later in the water bath. Refrigerate the crust while preparing the filling.

To prepare filling: In a medium mixing bowl, combine the sugar, flour and cornstarch and sift. In a large bowl, beat the cream cheese on low speed for 1 minute just until smooth and free of any lumps. Gradually add the sugar mixture and beat until creamy, 1 to 2 minutes. Periodically scrape down the sides of the bowl and the beaters. Add the melted butter, and then add the eggs, 1 at a time, and continue to slowly beat until combined. Stir in the vanilla, lemon juice and lemon zest. Add the heavy cream. Blend in the sour cream. The batter should be well mixed but not over beaten. Over beating incorporates too much air and will cause the cake to puff when baking, then fall and crack when cooling. Pour filling into the crust-lined pan and smooth the top with a spatula.

To prepare water bath: Set the pan on a large piece of aluminum foil and fold up the sides. This will prevent water from seeping into the seams of the spring form pan. Carefully set the cake pan in a larger roasting pan. Pour hot water into the roasting pan until the water is about halfway up the sides of the cheesecake pan; if you can't do this, place a large roasting pan filled with water on the lowest shelf and bake cheesecake on the middle shelf. **DO NOT** open the door while the cake is cooking, at least not for the first half hour. The cheesecake will be done when it is set on the edges but still jiggles a little bit in the middle.

Bake in a preheated 325° oven for 60 to 90 minutes. The cheesecake should still jiggle; it will firm up after chilling. Be careful not to overcook! Turn the oven off and let cake sit for another hour. Do not do a toothpick test in the cake's center, this will make a crack.
   Loosen the cheesecake from the sides of the pan by running a thin metal spatula around the inside rim. Let cool in the pan for 30 minutes. Chill in the refrigerator, loosely covered, for at least 4 hours to set. Unmold and transfer to a cake plate. Slice the cheesecake with a thin, nonserrated knife that has been dipped in hot water and wiped dry after each cut, or with unflavored dental floss. Serves 12.

Topping (Optional):
   Wash and remove stems from the blueberries. Dry the blueberries on a paper towel. Combine all ingredients in a 2-quart saucepan over medium-high heat. Bring up to a slow boil and stir gently until the berries breakdown and release their natural juice. The consistency should remain a bit chunky. Cool to room temperature and serve on top of cheesecake, by drizzling a little over each piece, or serve in a bowl and let people add it themselves.

You can put strawberries or any other topping you desire or just leave it plain. This recipe evolved from several other recipes that I put together. It is wonderful. Wrapping the spring form pan in aluminum foil, and cooking it in a water bath prevents the top from cracking. This dessert is always Marc and David's favorite, but they like it plain, or with the toppings on the side. You can also do these in small spring form pans and put different toppings on them. Check baking time, it may only take 30 to 45 minutes at 325°, leave in oven 30 minutes with door open. This mixture is quite large and you may not fit it all into a 10-inch spring form. You can bake the leftovers in smaller pans, but don't bake at the same time because if you open the oven door to take out the smaller cake you could jeopardize the larger one. Bake the smaller one's later or bake in two 8- inch pans. You can also cheat for the topping and buy fresh strawberries and blueberries and put them in Marie's Glaze (sold in the produce section...works for me!) I actually am quite fond of the Marie's Glaze(it comes in strawberry and blueberry) and use it quite often.

CHOCOLATE CARAMEL CHEESECAKE
Elise Feiner

2 cups vanilla wafer crumbs
2 tablespoon unsalted butter, melted
1 (14 ounce package) individually wrapped caramels
1 (5 ounce) can evaporated milk
1 cup chopped pecans

2 (8 ounce) packages cream cheese, softened
½ cup sugar
1 teaspoon vanilla
2 eggs
½ cup semisweet chocolate pieces

Preheat oven to 350°. In a large bowl, mix together the cookie crumbs and melted butter. Press into the bottom of a 9-inch spring form pan. In a heavy saucepan over low heat, melt the caramels with the evaporated milk. Heat and stir frequently until smooth. Pour caramel sauce into crust, and top with pecans. In a large bowl, combine cream cheese, sugar and vanilla; beat well until smooth. Add eggs one at a time, mixing well after each addition. Melt the chocolate, and blend into cream cheese mixture. Pour chocolate batter over pecans. Bake in preheated oven for 40 to 50 minutes or until filling is set. Loosen cake from the edges of pan, but do not remove rim until cooled to prevent the top from cracking. Chill in refrigerator for 4 hours, or overnight.

S'MORES CHEESECAKE
Elise Feiner

Crust:
½ cup butter, melted
2¼ cups graham cracker crumbs

⅓ cup sugar

Filling:
2 (8 ounce) packages cream cheese, softened
1 can sweetened condensed milk (Eagle Brand, 300ml)
2 teaspoons vanilla

3 eggs
1 cup miniature chocolate chips
1 cup miniature marshmallows

Topping:
1 cup miniature marshmallows
½ cup chocolate chips

1 tablespoon butter

Combine butter, graham cracker crumbs, and sugar. Press into the bottom of a 10-inch spring form pan. In a large bowl, beat the cream cheese, condensed milk, and vanilla until smooth. Add the eggs and beat until well combined. Stir in the chocolate chips and marshmallows. Pour into crust. Bake at 325° for 40-45 minutes, or until the center is almost set. Remove cheesecake from oven and sprinkle marshmallows over top. Return to the oven and bake another 4 to 6 minutes, until the marshmallows are puffed and golden brown. Melt chocolate chips and butter together. Drizzle over the marshmallows. Let cool to room temperature and then refrigerate overnight.

I love anything that looks like a s'mores, tastes like a s'mores, and I am always on the look out for new recipes with s'mores. I can't remember where this came from, but I've had it a long time.

L-R: Michele Maida, Elise
Feiner, and Toni Mollico

L-R: Michele Maida,
Toni Mollico, and
Elise Feiner today!

DOUBLE CHOCOLATE CHEESECAKE SQUARES
Ann D'Amico

1¾ cups chocolate wafer crumbs
⅓ cup butter, melted
PAM® Spray
4 (6 ounce) white chocolate flavored baking bars, divided
(white chocolate may be substituted)
2 (8 ounce) packages cream cheese, at room temperature

½ cup sour cream
4 large eggs
2 teaspoons vanilla extract
¼ cup heavy cream
2 tablespoons Frangelico® or any other hazelnut liqueur

Preheat oven to 300°. Mix the chocolate crumbs and melted butter together and set aside 2 tablespoons of the mixture. Press the remaining crumbs onto the bottom of a 13 x 9 x 2-inch pan lined with aluminum foil and sprayed with PAM. Place 16 ounces of white chocolate baking bars in a heavy saucepan over low heat until the chocolate melts. Let cool slightly. Beat the cream cheese and sour cream with an electric mixture at medium speed until fluffy. Add eggs, one at a time, beating after each addition. Stir in vanilla and melted chocolate. Pour into prepared pan, and bake at 300° for 30 minutes; turn oven off, and leave in the oven an additional 30 minutes. Cool on a wire rack. Place remaining 8 ounces white chocolate in a heavy saucepan; cook over low heat until chocolate melts. Remove from heat; stir in heavy cream and Frangelico. Pour over cheesecake, and sprinkle with reserved 2 tablespoons crumb mixture. Cover and chill at least 8 hours. Lift cheesecake from pan, and remove foil. Cut cake into squares; place in individual paper baking cups to serve. Makes 24.

I think Ann got this recipe from one of our recipe exchanges. She made them and said that they were wonderful.

L-R: Nina D'Amico, Ann D'Amico, Tina Massimiano, Frances Barone, Virginia Casazza

RASPBERRY CHOCOLATE TRUFFLE CHEESECAKE
Elise Feiner

1 (9 ounce) package chocolate wafer cookies
3 tablespoons butter, melted
1 (12 ounce package) semisweet chocolate chips
1 cup heavy cream
¾ cup Raspberry jam

2 (8 ounce) packages cream cheese, softened
¾ cup sugar
4 Eggs
2 teaspoons vanilla extract

Grind cookies to a fine crumbs, mix with the butter and press into the bottom and up the sides about an inch of a 9-inch spring form pan. Refrigerate while making the filling. Combine the chips and cream in a microwave safe bowl and heat on high for 3 to 4 minutes or until mix is smooth; stirring every minute. Mix in the jam, stirring until dissolved; let cool 10 minutes Mix the cream cheese and sugar until smooth. Add the eggs, one at a time, mixing well after each addition. Add the vanilla and the chocolate raspberry mixture. Mix well. Bake 1¼ to 1½ hours at 325° or until cake is set around the edges but still jiggles slightly in the center. Cool and refrigerate at least 6 hours.

CHOCOLATE CHEESECAKE ROSENFELD
Rae Rosenfeld

Crust:
1¼ cup graham cracker crumbs
2 tablespoons sugar

¼ cup melted butter

Mix together and pack into a 8 or 9-inch greased spring form pan.

Filling:
1 (6 ounce) semi-sweet chocolate chips
½ cup sugar
2 (8 ounce) packages cream cheese
¾ cup sugar

½ cup sour cream
1 teaspoon vanilla (or ½ teaspoon vanilla and
½ teaspoon almond extract)
4 eggs

Take the semi-sweet chocolate and ½ cup sugar and put them in the top of a double boiler. Heat over hot but not boiling water until melted and smooth stirring constantly. In a mixing bowl, beat the cream cheese until light gradually adding ¾ cup sugar, sour cream and vanilla. Beat eggs one at a time until mixed. Divide batter in half and add melted chocolate to one part blending completely. Pour chocolate mixture in pan and top with plain mixture. Swirl with a knife to marbleize. After baking at 350° for 50 minutes, turn off the oven. Keep the oven door open slightly and keep cake in the oven another 30 minutes. Either refrigerate or freeze. Serves 12.

Joshua and Mindy Rosenfeld

Joe Avella and Eli Lipetz
(Rae's Father)

COOKIE DOUGH CHEESECAKE
Elise Feiner

2 tablespoons butter, melted
2 ½ cups chocolate cookie crumbs
4 (8 ounce) packages
Cream cheese at room temperature
1 cup sugar
4 eggs

1 teaspoon all-purpose flour
1 teaspoon vanilla
1 cup sour cream
1 pound packaged refrigerated chocolate chip cookie dough
2 ounces chocolate chips

Topping:
1 pint Heavy cream, whipped
Chocolate chips

Chopped walnuts

Preheat oven to 325.° Grease the bottom and sides of a 10-inch spring form pan. Mix the butter with the chocolate cookie crumbs. Press onto the bottom and sides of the pan. Using an electric mixer on high speed, combine cream cheese, sugar, eggs and flour and mix until smooth. Add vanilla and sour cream and mix just until blended. Pour ½ of the batter into prepared crust. Cut cookie dough into small sized chunks and drop into batter. Sprinkle in chocolate chips. Top with remaining batter. Bake for 1 hour. Turn off the oven; open the door slightly. Keep in the oven 30 more minutes. Refrigerate until ready to serve. Top with fresh whipped cream. Sprinkle with chocolate chips and walnuts.

CHOCOLATE CHEESECAKE FEINER
Elise Feiner

Crust:

1¼ cups chocolate wafer crumbs
¼ cup melted butter

2 tablespoons granulated sugar
¼ teaspoon each of nutmeg and cinnamon

Mix all the ingredients together and press in a greased 9-inch spring form pan.

Filling:

⅓ cup sifted flour
Pinch of baking soda
¼ teaspoon salt
2 (4 ounces) packages German or sweet chocolate
3 large eggs
¾ cup sugar

3 (3 ounce) packages cream cheese, softened
2 cups heavy cream
1 teaspoon vanilla
1 tablespoon sifted confectioners' sugar
½ jigger crème de cocoa

Sift together the flour, baking soda, and salt. Set aside. In the top of a double boiler; melt the chocolate, stirring occasionally. Remove from the heat to cool slightly. In a small bowl, beat the eggs until thickened and lemon colored. Beat in the sugar 1 tablespoon at a time. Mixture will be thick. Without washing the beaters, in a large bowl, beat the cream cheese until soft and fluffy. Add 1¼ cups of heavy cream and vanilla; beat until smooth and of a whipped cream consistency. Add slightly cooled melted chocolate and beat gently to blend. With a rubber spatula, fold in egg mixture; sift in flour as you do so. Place into prepared pan. Bake at 325° 1 hour and 15 minutes. Cool. Top may crack. Remove pan. Before serving beat the remaining ¾ cup heavy cream with the confectioners' sugar and cream de cocoa. Top each slice with whipped cream. Serves 8.

To try to prevent cracking place a pan of water on a lower shelf of the oven to create steam. See index page on cheesecake tips.

L-R: Lauren, David, Jeffrey, Marc, and Elise Feiner, Brenda and Charlie Antzelevitch

"One of life's greatest mysteries is how the boy who wasn't good enough to marry your daughter can be the father of the smartest grandchild in the world."
-Old Jewish Proverb

CHOCOLATE-SWIRLED CHEESECAKE
Katherine Avella

For The Crust:
1 cup chocolate graham cracker crumbs
3 tablespoons butter or margarine, melted

2 tablespoons granulated sugar
Non-stick cooking spray

For The Filling:
1 (6-ounce) package semisweet chocolate morsels
2 (8-ounce) packages cream cheese (regular or nonfat) softened
1¼ cups sour cream (regular or nonfat)

1 egg
2 teaspoons vanilla extract
1 cup granulated sugar
6 tablespoons all-purpose flour

Preheat oven to 300°. To make the crust, combine graham crackers, melted butter and sugar in a medium bowl. Mix well with a fork to combine. Press the mixture into the bottom of a 9-inch spring form pan that has been coated with non-stick spray. Set aside. To make the filling, melt chocolate in a double boiler or medium bowl over simmering water. Set aside to cool slightly. In a large mixing bowl, combine cream cheese, sour cream, egg, and vanilla. Mix on low speed until smooth and creamy. Fold in sugar and flour. Pour filling into prepared pan. Drizzle melted chocolate over surface of cheesecake. Using a toothpick, swirl the chocolate into the filling, just until decorative swirls form (don't over-swirl or you'll lose the effect). Bake 1 hour, or until center is set. Turn off oven, prop open the oven door (not all the way, just slightly), and allow the cake to cool 15 minutes. Transfer pan to a wire rack and cool completely. Cover with plastic wrap and refrigerate until ready to serve. Serves 12.

David's Graduation from Phillips Exeter Academy...
Back Row L-R: David, Elise, Marc, Lauren, Jeffrey and Steven Feiner
Front Row L-R: Katherine Avella and Josephine Mainella

The previous generation of
Feiner Boys:
L-R: Philip (Pinky), Morris,
Gene and Jerome

ITALIAN CHEESECAKE
Elise Feiner

1 (2 pound) container of ricotta
¾ to 1 cup sugar
6 large eggs, slightly beaten
1 tablespoon vanilla extract

1 tablespoon flour
¼ teaspoon cinnamon
⅛ teaspoon nutmeg
1 cup heavy cream, lightly whipped but not too stiff

When ready to fill the crust, mix all ingredients for the filling together except the cream. When well blended fold in the cream. Pour into prepared crust. Preheat the oven to 350°.

Crust:
3 cups flour
¾ cup sugar
2 teaspoons baking powder
Pinch of salt
⅛ teaspoon cinnamon

4-5 teaspoons of lemon peel or orange peel or combination of both
1 stick of cold, unsalted butter, cut into small cubes
4 large eggs, lightly beaten

Make the pastry in a food processor by combining the flour, sugar, baking powder, salt, cinnamon. Process for about 35 seconds. Add the lemon/orange peel, and butter and process until it resembles coarse crumbs. Keep the processor on; add the eggs one at a time and process until the mixture forms a ball. Wrap in saran wrap and chill for about 30 minutes. Take two thirds of the dough and roll into a circle about ⅛ to ¼-inch thick. Spray a 10-inch spring form pan with PAM®. Place the crust into the spring form pan. Place in refrigerator until you are ready to fill it. Roll the remaining pastry into a circle and cut into strips about 1-inch wide. Use a pastry cutter with fluted edges if you have one. Place on waxed paper and refrigerate until ready to use. Fill the crust with the filling mix. Lay the strips of cut pastry across the top by putting one strip vertically, and then one horizontally; then continue in this fashion placing the strips about 1-inch apart to form a lattice like pattern. Take on egg yolk and mix with a teaspoon of water. Brush the lattice and crust with the egg wash. Bake 1 hour or until set, check with cake tester. Let cool 30 minutes, and chill at least 4 hours before serving. Serves 12.

This is a traditional Italian cheesecake made with ricotta and not cream cheese This is traditional around the Easter holidays. I can't remember where this came from but I believe it was one of our neighbors in Bayville, perhaps Rose Pacifico.

OREO® CHEESECAKE
Elise Feiner

1½ cup Oreo® Cookie Crumbs (about 23 Oreo cookies finely chopped)
2 tablespoons melted butter
3 (8 ounce) packages cream cheese
1 cup sugar
5 large eggs

¼ teaspoon salt
2 teaspoon vanilla
¼ cup flour
8 ounces sour cream
5 Oreo® Cookies (coarsely chopped for the batter)
10 coarsely chopped Oreo® Cookies for the top of cake

Make the crust by mixing the 2 tablespoons of melted butter with Oreo crumbs and press into a 9-inch spring pan (butter the bottoms and sides) cover the bottom and 1½-inches up the sides with crumbs, set aside. All ingredients need to be at room temperature before beginning. Beat cream cheese until light and fluffy. Keep mixer on a low setting during the mixing and beating process. Add sugar gradually and continue beating cream cheese until mixed through. Add eggs one at a time and continue to beat until blended. Measure the vanilla, salt and flour, pour into cream cheese and egg mixture and beat until smooth. Add the sour cream and beat well. Turn off the mixer and stir in the coarsely chopped Oreo cookies with a spoon. Pour cream cheese into the spring pan and place the nine coarsely chopped Oreo Cookies on to of the cream mixture. Place pan on the top rack and in the middle of a preheated oven at 325° and bake for one hour and 15 minutes. When time is up prop the oven door open and let the cheese cake stay in the oven for one hour. Remove from oven and let cool enough to place in the refrigerator for 24 hours. Serves 12.

L-R: Lauren Feiner and Kristin Furino

A "Bit of Cheesecake" L-R: Lauren Feiner and Kristin Furino. Check out Page 395 to see them now

ZEBRA CHEESECAKE
Ann D'Amico

1½ cups chocolate wafer cookie crumbs, about 30
3 tablespoons butter, melted
½ (6 ounce) package semisweet chocolate pieces (½ cup)
4 (8 ounce) packages cream cheese at room temperature
1¼ cups sugar
3 tablespoons cornstarch
¼ teaspoon salt

5 large eggs
1 (8 ounce) container sour cream
2 teaspoons vanilla extract
1½ cups heavy cream
1½ (8 ounce) packages semisweet chocolate squares = 12
(1 ounce) squares
8 ounces white chocolate

Early in the day or a day ahead:

Preheat oven to 350°. Grease 9 x 3-inch spring form pan. In a bowl mix chocolate crumbs and butter. Firmly press on to the bottom of spring form pan for crust. Bake crust 12 to 15 minutes. Remove crust from oven; sprinkle with ½ cup chocolate pieces. Let stand several minutes until chocolate pieces soften, then spread evenly over the crust. Refrigerate while preparing filling. In a large bowl, with a mixer at medium speed, beat cream cheese until light and fluffy. In a small bowl, mix sugar, cornstarch and salt; gradually beat into cream cheese mixture until blended. With mixer at low speed, gradually beat in eggs, sour cream, vanilla and 1 cup of heavy cream until blended and smooth. Divide batter evenly into two 4 to 8-cup measuring cups or other containers with a pouring spout. In a small saucepan over low heat, melt the 8 squares of semisweet chocolate over very low heat with ¼ cup remaining heavy cream. Do the same thing with the white chocolate. Stir melted semisweet chocolate into batter in one measuring cup and stir melted white chocolate into the batter in the second measuring cup.

To create zebra design, pour half of the dark batter into spring form pan. Holding the white batter about 2 feet above the pan, pour about half of the batter directly into the center of the dark batter (pouring from this height will cause the batter in the center of the cake to be pushed toward the edge of the pan, forming a zebra or bull's eye design). Repeat the procedure 3 times, alternating dark and light chocolate, decreasing the amounts of batter each time and pouring from high above pan only into the center, ending with white batter. (Top of cake should look like concentric circles.) Bake cheesecake 30 minutes at 350°. Lower oven to 225° and bake 1 hour and 45 minutes longer or until center is set. Turn off oven and let cheesecake sit in the oven for 1 hour more. Remove cheesecake from the oven. Run a thin blade spatula or knife around edge of the cheesecake to loosen from the side of the pan. Cool cake on a wire rack. Refrigerate at least 6 hours or until well chilled. Serves 12.

My cousin Ann said this is scrumptious, easy, and makes a great presentation.

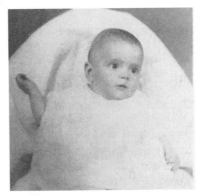
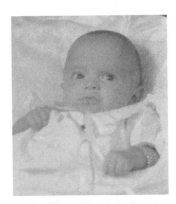

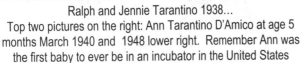
Ralph and Jennie Tarantino 1938...
Top two pictures on the right: Ann Tarantino D'Amico at age 5
months March 1940 and 1948 lower right. Remember Ann was
the first baby to ever be in an incubator in the United States

AMBROSIA
Theresa Feiner

3 (30 ounce) cans of fruit cocktail, drained
1 (15.4 ounce) can fruit cocktail
1 (16 ounce) container sour cream
1 (8 ounce) container sour cream
1 cup chopped pecans

1 bag mini marshmallows
2 (15 ounce) cans Mandarin Oranges, drained
1 small bag coconut
5 cups (half pints) heavy cream, whipped with a little vanilla
(about 2 teaspoons) and sugar (about ¼ - ½) cup

Combine everything together except the whipped cream. When well blended, fold in the whipped cream. I usually do this a day ahead and freeze it. Remove to the refrigerator about 3-4 hours before serving or you can just refrigerate until time to serve it.

Aunt Theresa made this for several parties' years ago. It is great in the summer...fast and easy to make. You can even freeze this and take it out a few hours before serving and it will be well chilled.

BAKED APPLES
Katherine Avella

6 apples, Rome preferred
¼ cup brown sugar
¼ cup granulated sugar
2 teaspoon cinnamon

1 teaspoon vanilla
¼ finely chopped pecans (optional)
3 tablespoons butter, cut into small cubes
Dash of lemon juice

Mix the sugars, cinnamon, vanilla and pecans in a bowl. Slice off about ¼-inch of the top of each apple. Scoop out the seeds and core of the apple with a melon-baller to make a pocket, being careful not to go all the way to the bottom of the apple. Peel off about a ½-inch band of the apple's skin along the upper half of the apple with a vegetable peeler. Brush the peeled part and the interior of the apple with lemon juice. Fill the center of each apple with the sugar mixture, leaving a little room for the butter. Add a few butter cubes to each apple. Place the apples in a baking pan, and put about 1 to 1½-inches of water into the pan. Bake in a 400° oven for 45 to 50 minutes. Serve with heavy cream or whipped cream. Maybe served warm or chilled. Makes 6.

I remember coming from school as a child and smelling these when I walked through the door. The aroma of these baking is just wonderful!

BANANAS FOSTER
Elise Feiner

½ stick of butter
6 heaping tablespoons of brown sugar
4 bananas, peeled and sliced in quarters
Pinch of cinnamon

1 tablespoon banana liqueur, overflow a bit
1 tablespoon light rum
2 tablespoons brandy
Vanilla Ice Cream

Mix the butter and brown sugar in a skillet. Cook over medium heat until sugar is melted. Slice the bananas in quarters, and add to the butter mixture cooking until tender. Add liqueur and stir. Sprinkle rum and brandy over the top. Ignite. Spoon gently a few times. Serve over vanilla ice cream. Serves 6.

I got this recipe from the wife of my Cousin Warren's friend when he lived in New Orleans. I spent several weeks there at Mardi Gras time when I was in nursing school. It was the first time I ever tasted this dish. It was a Louisiana favorite but it is now well known everywhere.

"Living well is the best revenge."
-Dan Popeo

FRIED CHOCOLATE AND BANANAS
Elise Feiner

2 milk chocolate Hershey® bars
16 wonton skins
2 bananas, sliced

Vanilla or chocolate ice cream
½ cup cinnamon sugar
Vegetable oil for frying

Break each bar into 8 equal pieces. Break again to make a small square of the chocolate. Place the wonton skins out on a surface and 1 at a time; brush the edges with water. In the center of the wonton skin, place a square of chocolate and a banana slice on top of the chocolate. Fold the wonton skin corner to corner to make a triangle and press together well to seal completely. Cover with plastic wrap and store chilled until ready to fry and serve, up to 10 hours ahead. Heat the oil in a deep pot to 350°. Drop the wontons into the oil, a few at a time (you may have to work in batches) and fry, turning often, until golden brown. Meanwhile, place the cinnamon sugar in a bowl. Remove the wontons with a slotted spoon and immediately dredge them in the cinnamon sugar to coat heavily. Serve with ice cream. Serves 4

This is a great fast and easy dessert. Wontons are really versatile. They can be stuffed with anything and baked or fried. Years ago there was a great cookie recipe in Bon Appetit using dates and peanut butter in a wonton wrapper; I wish I could find it again. If anyone has a copy please e-mail it to elise@cookingwithlove.com

FRUIT AND CHIPS
Elise Feiner

2 kiwis, peeled and diced
2 apples, peeled, cored, and diced
1 (8 ounce) package raspberries, thawed and drained
1 pound strawberries cut into slices
2 tablespoons granulated sugar
1 tablespoon brown sugar

3 tablespoons strawberry preserves, or flavor of your choice
10 (10-inch) flour tortillas or very thin pita bread
Melted butter or Butter Flavored PAM®
2 cups cinnamon sugar
Cool Whip®

In a large bowl, thoroughly mix kiwis, apples, raspberries, strawberries, white sugar, brown sugar and fruit preserves. Cover and chill in the refrigerator at least 15 minutes. Preheat oven to 350°. Coat one side of each flour tortilla with butter flavored cooking spray or melted butter. Cut into quarters to form triangular wedges and arrange in a single layer on a large baking sheet. Sprinkle wedges with cinnamon sugar to taste. Spray again with cooking spray. Bake in the preheated oven 8 to 10 minutes. Repeat with any remaining tortilla wedges. Allow to cool approximately 15 minutes. Serve with chilled fruit, top with Cool Whip and sprinkle with cinnamon sugar.

This can be made low fat by using Fat Free Cool Whip and I Can't Believe It's Not Butter™ Spray. Lauren loves kiwi and tortilla chips...this dessert combines the two.

FRUIT BOWL
Elise Feiner

2 cups water
1½ cups sugar
3 tablespoons lemon juice
2 tablespoons anise seed
½ teaspoon salt
1 medium pineapple
1 small honeydew melon

1 small cantaloupe
2 oranges
2 large nectarines
2 large purple plums
½ pound seedless grapes
2 kiwi fruit, peeled and sliced

Do this a day ahead: In a large saucepan over medium heat, cook the water, lemon juice, sugar, anise seeds, and salt 15 minutes or until the mixture becomes a light syrup. Refrigerate until the syrup is cool. Remove the skin from the pineapple, cantaloupe, and honeydew and cut into chunks. Peel and section the oranges. Slice the nectarines and plums into wedges, but do not peel. Slice the grapes in half. In a large bowl, combine the cut up fruit. Pour the chilled syrup over the fruit. Cover and refrigerate; stir occasionally.

You can add other fruits too. This looks great served in a clear trifle like bowl.

ORANGE BAKED ALASKA
Elise Feiner

3 large oranges
1 pint of orange sherbet, lemon sherbet, or orange
sherbet/vanilla ice cream mix

3-4 egg whites
¼ teaspoon cream of tartar
¼ cup plus 2 tablespoons of sugar

Scoop the ice cream or sherbet in to 6 large scoops. Wrap in wax paper and freeze until firm; at least 5 hours. Cut the oranges in half cross-wise; cut a very thin slice from the bottom of each half so the orange will lay flat on a plate being careful not to cut into the orange or you won't be able to refill the shell. Cut around the inside edges and the membranes; remove the orange segments and remaining membranes. Separate the orange slices and cut into smaller segments. Refrigerate the pieces in a container, and wrap the orange rinds in saran wrap and refrigerate. When ready to serve, heat the oven to 500°. (If you have a small kitchen blow torch like the kind used for crème brulee you can eliminate this step). Make the meringue mixture by beating the egg whites and cream of tarter until foamy; beat in the sugar one tablespoon at a time and continue beating until stiff and glossy. **DO NOT OVERBEAT!** Place the orange shells on an ungreased baking sheet. Place a few of the orange sections at the bottom of each orange half. Remove the ice cream balls from the freezer, unwrap, and place on top of the orange segments. Cover with meringue mixture. Seal to the edges of each shell. Bake 2 to 3 minutes until the meringue is golden and serve immediately. You can also do this under the broiler for a minute or use the kitchen blow torch to just brown the meringue. Serves 6.

This is a great, elegant looking dessert that can be prepared ahead of time. It's a perfect dessert for a hot summer day.

MARIA'S APPLE DIP
Maria Trainor

1 (8 ounce) package Philadelphia® Cream Cheese
4-5 apples, sliced
Half a bag Heath® Bar Bits

1 (20 ounce container) T. Marzetti's® Caramel Apple Dip or
Peanut-Caramel Apple Dip

Spread the cream cheese in a thin layer in a serving plate. Spread ½ the container of caramel dip on top of the cream cheese. Sprinkle with the half bag of Heath Bits. Place the apples around the dip. To serve, dip the apples in the mixture. During preparation you may want to put the apples slices in a bowl with a little lemon juice to prevent them from turning brown.

Maria said one of the hockey mothers made this for a dinner and the kids loved it. It's a fast, easy, and delicious dessert.

PEACH MOLD
Elise Feiner

1 (16 ounce) can sliced peaches, drained and diced
2 tablespoons apricot brandy
2 (3 ounce) packages Jell-O® orange flavor

2 cups boiling water
1½ cups cold water
1 (4 ounce) container Cool Whip® thawed

Sprinkle the peaches with the brandy and set aside. Dissolve the orange Jell-O in boiling water. Stir in the cold water and chill until thickened. Fold peaches into half the Jell-O mix and place into a 6 cup mold that has been lightly sprayed with PAM®. Chill until set but not firm about 10 minutes. Beat the Cool Whip into the remaining Jell-O and spread over the clear layer in the mold. Chill until firm about 4 hours. Serves 10.

COFFEE FLAVORED FRUIT DIP
Elise Feiner

1 (8 ounce) package cream cheese, softened
1 (8 ounce) container sour cream
½ cup brown sugar

⅓ cup coffee-flavored liqueur (Kahlua®)
1 (8 ounce) container frozen whipped topping, thawed
Assorted fresh fruit

Place cream cheese, sour cream, brown sugar and coffee-flavored liqueur in a medium bowl. Blend together with an electric mixer until smooth. Fold in thawed frozen whipped topping. Chill in the refrigerator until serving. Serve with assorted cut up fresh fruit.

CARMEN'S FRUIT DIP
Carmen Ferreiro

1 cup of sour cream
¼ cup brown sugar (I use Dominos® Brownulated, it's
easier to pour)

Dash of lemon juice (about teaspoon)
¼ teaspoon cinnamon
Dash nutmeg

Mix everything together and refrigerate. Serve with a mixture of sliced fruit, strawberries, bananas, peaches, kiwi etc. Make sure if you are using apples or bananas you dip them in ice water to which you have added a little lemon juice to stop them from turning brown.

This is a great to serve with a bowl of cut up fruit. Make in advance so the flavors blend (the night before is perfect).

FRUIT DIP
Elise Feiner

1 (8 ounce) package cream cheese, softened
½ cup sour cream, for topping
1 cup whipped cream
¼ cup brown sugar

¼ cup white sugar
1 tablespoon maple syrup
1 teaspoon vanilla extract

In a mixing bowl, combine the cream cheese, sour cream, whipped cream, brown sugar, sugar, maple syrup and vanilla extract. Mix until smooth. Serve immediately or chill for later.

BERRIES AND CREAM
Elise Feiner

Fresh strawberries, blueberries, raspberries, or
blackberries

Heavy Cream
Sugar (about ¼ cup)

Wash the fruit, remove stems. If using strawberries, cut into slices. Place heavy cream and sugar to taste in a large bowl and add the fruit. Chill until ready to serve. The amount of cream and sugar will depend on the amount of fruit. Note: do not whip the cream.

My kids love berries and cream for dessert in the summertime.

KAHLUA® FRUIT DIP WITH NUTS
Elise Feiner

1 (8 ounce) package of cream cheese
1 (8 ounce) carton of heavy cream, whipped
¾ cup light brown sugar

⅓ cup Kahlua®
1 cup sour cream
1 (3 ounce) package of unsalted peanuts, finely chopped

Blend together cream cheese, whipped cream. Add brown sugar and Kahlua. Mix well. Add sour cream and peanuts. Refrigerate 1 to 2 days before serving. Serve with fresh fruit.

Brenda Plescia Johnson and
soon-to-be Alexander Johnson

L-R: Gabrielle Johnson, Abby,
Jody and Lauren Feiner

CHOCOLATE COVERED STRAWBERRIES
Maria Trainor

48 large strawberries with leaves still attached   2 teaspoons vegetable oil
2 bags (12 ounces) Hershey® or Nestle® chocolate chips

Wipe the strawberries off with a paper towel, but do not wash them. Keep the stems and leaves attached. Fill the bottom of a double boiler with hot water. Place the chocolate and vegetable oil in the top of a double boiler, and melt the chocolate pieces and the vegetable oil together, (making sure that the water does not boil but just gets hot and simmers.) When the chocolate is completely melted, dip each strawberry into the chocolate and place into a Reynolds™ mini size foil baking cup (mini cupcake holder) and place on a cookie sheet. Place in the refrigerator until the chocolate hardens and strawberries are chilled. This can be done a day in advance.

These make a great dessert for a special occasion or for no reason at all. My friend Maria makes them the best and drops a tray off every now and then. Maria prefers the Hershey Chips. My kids love them and they are so fast and easy to do.

L-R: Jonathan Trainor, Lauren and Abby Feiner, Kristin Furino

L-R: Melissa Avella and Kate Trainor
Brains and Beauty…Melissa will be teaching Spanish on the University level and Kate has a
BS from Boston College and is studying for a Masters Degree from Columbia University's
School of Journalism…This girl can write and will surely go places.

L-R: Sherry and Daniella Avella and David Feiner

L-R: Lindsey Ulrich and Josh Rosenfeld

Daniella Faith Avella – our newest addition
and our great-niece!

L-R: Aviva and David Zierler, Antoinette Valenti, M.D.
and Jeffrey Feiner, M.D.

Maria and Tessa Trainor

Our favorite "General" Vincent and Dorothy DeClementi

CARMEN'S FLAN
Carmen Ferreiro

1 (14 ounce) can sweetened condensed milk
1 (12 ounce) can evaporated milk
4 eggs (slightly beaten)
1 tablespoon vanilla

Cinnamon sticks
½ cup milk plus as much as needed in below directions
Pinch of salt
½ cup sugar (for the caramel)

Using a container such as a cake pan, spring form pan, or flan pan, pour ½ cup sugar in it and slowly melt the sugar on medium heat, making sure it does not burn. With the caramel hot, coat the bottom and sides of the pan **(BE VERY CAREFUL NOT TO SPILL ANY ON YOUR HANDS AND ARMS)**. After that is done, set it aside and let cool. It will crack a little. In a saucepan, boil ½ cup of milk with the cinnamon sticks until it flavors the milk. Set aside. In a mixing bowl, empty contents of condensed milk. Using the condensed milk can as a measuring device, measure a total of two cans using the evaporated milk and the cinnamon milk (strained and cinnamon sticks removed), and then add the balance in regular whole milk. Pour those two cans into the bowl with the condensed milk and add the 4 eggs that have been slightly beaten. Add the vanilla and a pinch of salt. Mix well and pour into the caramelized pan. Bake at 350° in a Bain Marie (water bath) for 60 to 70 minutes. A Bain Marie is a larger pan filled with hot water into which you place another pan with the ingredients to prevent burning. The water should come up about 1" around the sides of the pan. Remove from the oven. Let it cool and refrigerate. When you are ready to serve it, loosen the sides, put the serving dish on top and turn it over. Serves 6.

This is the best we have ever tasted. Carmen would make them and send them over at the holidays. My mother, the dessert-o-holic loved this.

RICE PUDDING MAINELLA
Edith Mainella

1 cup water
Pinch of salt
½ cup uncooked rice
½ cup sugar
¼ cup butter
1 quart milk

3 eggs
1½ teaspoons vanilla
½ cup raisins (optional)
Cinnamon to sprinkle on the top
Whipped cream (store bought or homemade)

In a saucepan combine the water, salt and uncooked rice. Cook for 7 minutes. Then, add the milk and butter. Cover and simmer 1 hour. Remove from heat. Beat the eggs, vanilla and sugar. Add a couple of tablespoons of the hot rice mix to the egg mixture stirring quickly to temper it. Then add the egg mix to the cooked rice mix. Stir frequently. Remove from heat. Add raisins if desired. Mixture will thicken as it stands. Spoon into individual dishes and chill before serving. Top with cinnamon and whipped cream. (see index for whipped cream recipe).

FLAN LIZA
Bettina Arcara Liza

4 eggs
1 cup sugar
1 (14 ounce) can Eagle Brand™ sweetened condensed milk

1 (13 ounce) can Carnation evaporated milk
1 ounce vanilla extract, or to taste

Break eggs into a bowl, add condensed milk, evaporated milk and vanilla extract. Stir until well mixed. Put sugar into sauce pan and melt over low heat, stirring constantly to avoid burning. Pour sugar into a flan dish (about 9-inch diameter) and tilt the dish to coat the bottom and the sides evenly; work fast because the sugar solidifies quickly. Pour in custard. Preheat oven to 350 degrees. Set flan pan in oven in a larger pan that contains about 1/4 inch of water in the bottom; bake for about an hour. To check if it's cooked insert knife in the center of the flan. If it comes out clean the flan is done. After removing the flan from the oven, invert it onto a serving dish. Do this carefully to avoid breaking the custard and not to spill sugar on you. Serve warm or cold.

My cousin Bettina sent this in, she is now living in Texas and we miss her...

RICE PUDDING FERRIERO
Carmen Ferreiro

1½ cups medium grain rice
1 (14 ounce) can sweetened condensed milk
1 (12 ounce) can evaporated milk Cinnamon sticks (2-3)

1 tablespoon vanilla extract
Ground cinnamon

In a large saucepan, boil the rice in about 6 to 7 cups of water with the cinnamon sticks until the rice is tender (make sure the rice doesn't stick to the pot). At this point, all the water will be gone. Pour the evaporated milk and condensed milk into the rice and continue to cook, stirring constantly so that the mixture does not burn. Cook for about 5 more minutes. Remove from the heat. Take out the cinnamon sticks. Stir in the vanilla and pour into individual bowls. Sprinkle with ground cinnamon and refrigerate.

Carmen says, "You can also use risotto rice, but you have to add more water - If you like the taste of lemon rinds, add them when you are boiling the rice." For a low fat version, use regular milk and sugar instead of condensed and evaporated milk.

CREAMETTE®PUDDING
Shirley Flomenhoft

1 (7 ounce) box of Creamettes® (elbows or shells)
¾ stick of butter
¼ (8 ounce) package of cream cheese (or a few spoons more if you like
⅓ cup sugar

Pinch of salt
2 eggs
½ pint of sugar
½ cup milk
A few extra tablespoons butter for top, cut into small cubes

Preheat oven 350° to 375°. Grease a round Pyrex® bowl. Cook Creamettes according to package directions. In another small pan, melt butter and cream cheese together (break cheese in quarter size pieces, cheese does not have to melt.) Put into a bowl with the Creamettes. Mix well. Add sugar and salt; mix well. Add 2 eggs; mix well. Add sour cream; mix well. Add milk; mix well. Scatter a few pieces of butter (cubed) over the top. Bake 45 minutes to 1 hour. The sides of the Pyrex will start to brown, the top will not; a custard will form. Cool. It's delicious!

This came from a friend of Aunt Shirley's. She said it's wonderful.

BANANA MERINGUE PUDDING
Elise Feiner

3 tablespoons flour
1 cup sugar
Dash of salt
6 tablespoons water
3 egg yolks
3 cups of milk

1 stick of butter
1 teaspoon vanilla
6 large bananas
1 (16 ounce) package of Vanilla Wafers
3 egg whites
6 tablespoons sugar

Mix the flour, sugar, and salt in a double boiler; add water and make a smooth paste. Mix the milk and egg yolks together well, and then add to flour mixture. Place over simmering water until mixture thickens and comes to a boil. Remove from the heat and add butter and vanilla. Butter a 2-quart Pyrex®, and layer the bananas and vanilla wafers in it. Pour the custard over the banana/vanilla wafer mix. Beat the egg whites into soft peaks. Gradually add the sugar and beat to stiff peaks. Spread over the pudding. Bake meringue at 350° a few minutes until golden. Serves 10 to 12.

RICE PUDDING BAKED
Josephine Mainella

1 cup rice (cook 1 cup rice in 3 cups lightly salted water
2 tablespoons butter
3 eggs

1 teaspoon vanilla
4 cups milk
¾ cup sugar

Cook the rice in the salted water. Drain; add butter. Beat 3 eggs, add sugar and mix well. Add to rice. Mix well. Add vanilla and 4 cups of milk. Bake a greased pan. Place pan in a larger pan to which you have added hot water (Bain Marie). Preheat the oven to 350°. Bake 1 hour at 350°. When done, sprinkle with cinnamon before serving.

This is a friend of Aunt Fifi's recipe.

RICE PUDDING SANITO
Angie Sanito

½ cup rice
½ cup sugar
1 quart milk
2 eggs

1½ teaspoons vanilla
Cinnamon to sprinkle on top
Whipped cream, homemade or store bought is fine

Cook the rice in milk with ¼ cup sugar, until the rice is cooked. Beat the eggs, vanilla, and remaining ¼ cup sugar. Add a couple of tablespoons of the hot rice mixture to the egg mixture stirring quickly to temper it. Then add the egg mixture to the cooked rice mixture. Cook for a few minutes until it reaches desired thickness. Stir frequently so it doesn't scorch. Spoon into individual dishes; chill before serving. Top with cinnamon and whipped cream. Serves 6.

To make homemade whip cream, take a ½ pint of heavy cream, about 1 to 2 tablespoons of sugar and a teaspoon of vanilla, and whip together at high speed until firm.

I like this rice pudding recipe because you don't have to bake it; it's all done on top of the stove. This recipe is my mother's cousin Angie Sanito's recipe; she used to make this for Uncle Nick, Mario, Joe, and Nicky. It's so easy to make delicious.

L-R: Pam, Joseph and Rose Sanito
Aunt Angie is now living with Rose and Joe
in Florida

L-R: Cousins Ronald DaBruzzo, Philip Avella, Joseph and Nicholas Sanito

GREEK RICE PUDDING IN A CROCK POT
Sandra Cotrupe

3 quarts of milk
1 pint heavy cream
1⅓ cups short grain rice only
½ stick butter

1 cup sugar
¾ cup raisins
3 eggs beaten
Cinnamon

Place all ingredients into a crock-pot. Place on low and leave uncovered. Cook for 3-4 hours stirring occasionally. This can also be done on top of the stove by following the following directions. In a large pot, bring the 3 quarts of milk to a boil reserving ¼ cup for later on. Add the heavy cream. When it starts to bubble, add the rice, butter, sugar and raisins. Stir constantly. Simmer 1 hour. Stir occasionally. Blend and temper the eggs with the milk rice mixture and the remaining ¼ cup milk. Add slowly to rice mixture until thick and blended. You can serve this hot or cold. Cover with Saran Wrap. Top with cinnamon.

This recipe came from Brenda Johnson who said it is her Aunt Sandy's recipe. She said it is the best rice pudding. It is so much easier to make in the crock-pot rather than have to stir it constantly on top of the stove.

MY FAVORITE GREEK RICE PUDDING
Elise Feiner

2½ quarts of milk
¾ teaspoon salt
2 cups long grain Carolina® rice, rinsed and drained
1 cup raisins (optional)
1 cup evaporated milk
2½ cups sugar

5 eggs, slightly beaten
3 teaspoons vanilla
2 cups heavy cream
Nutmeg
Cinnamon

In a heavy saucepan, cook the milk and salt until slightly heated; stir in the rice. When the mixture starts to boil, lower and simmer for thirty minutes, stirring occasionally. Add the raisins and simmer another 5 minutes; if omitting the raisins, add the five minutes to the cooking time of the rice. Check to see if rice is cooked. Add an extra minute or two if necessary. Add ¼ cup of the evaporated milk. Cool a few minutes. In a mixing bowl, combine the eggs, sugar, vanilla, remaining evaporated milk. Stir some of the rice mixture into the egg mixture to temper it. Add egg mixture into rice mixture, stirring frequently so it doesn't cook the egg. Return to heat and cook slowly (until it just **STARTS** to thicken) for a few minutes, stirring constantly so the bottom doesn't burn. Add cream. Stir pudding often as it cools. Top with nutmeg, cinnamon and whipped cream if desired. This is a very loose rice pudding, but it thickens as it cools. Serves 12.

This is the best and richest rice pudding made on top of the stove. It was Grandpa Sam's favorite dessert. I got this recipe from a friend's mother in Staten Island.

L-R: Phil Avella, Jeannie DaBruzzo, Michael Avella and
Ronald DaBruzzo

Dawn and Philip DiPierdomenico

BREAD PUDDING
Elise Feiner

1 large Challah bread
¾ stick butter, melted
1 pound white chocolate; cut in chunks
2 cups milk
2 cups heavy cream

⅔ cup sugar
1 vanilla bean, split in half
8 large eggs

Preheat the oven to 325°. Cut the bread in 1-inch cubes. Grease a 2-quart baking dish. I use an aluminum pan. Drizzle the cubes with the melted butter. Add in the chucks of chocolate (you can use milk chocolate if you prefer). Mix the milk, cream, sugar and vanilla bean together and bring to a boil over medium heat. Stir until the sugar is dissolved. Beat the eggs. Add the hot cream mix to the eggs, very slowly, stirring constantly with a whisk but do not allow custard to form too much foam. Remove excess foam. Slowly pour the custard over the bread. Let it stand at least 10 to 15 minutes so the custard soaks into the bread. Place the baking dish in a larger baking pan and add enough hot water to come up 1-inch on the sides of the baking dish forming a Bain Marie. Bake for 50 minutes to 1 hour until the custard sets and pudding is golden. Serves 12 to 14.

You can use any sweet bread if you can't find Challah. I got this recipe from a friend of Uncle Warren's years ago in New Orleans. New Orleans must be the home to 100's of different bread puddings...every restaurant has its own variation.

APPLE CRISP
Pearl Borten

1 cup flour
1 cup sugar
1 teaspoon baking powder
1 egg

6 apples (Granny Smith) peeled, seeded, and cut in chunks
2 tablespoons cinnamon sugar (Dominos®)
Juice of 1 lemon
¾ stick unsalted butter or margarine

Preheat oven to 350°. In a small bowl, mix the flour sugar and baking powder well. Add egg and cut in with 2 knives to make crumbs. Mix the apples, juice of lemon and cinnamon sugar; stir well. Using a square 8-inch pan or Pyrex® 8-inch pan, that has been sprayed with PAM®; layer the apples, crumbs, apples, crumbs, etc. ending with crumbs. Drizzle the melted butter over the top. Bake about 1 hour until brown on top. Cover with foil if it's getting too brown. Serve with ice cream or cool whip.

This is a favorite dessert at Mom Mom's condo group in Florida. Everyone raves about Pearl's baking. This is delicious.

BLUEBERRY PEACH CRISP
Pearl Borten

1 cup flour
¾ cup sugar
1 teaspoon baking powder
1 egg
2 cups fresh blueberries

3 cups peeled sliced peaches
2 tablespoons sugar
½ teaspoon cinnamon
¼ cup butter, melted

Preheat oven to 375°. Combine the flour, ¾ cup sugar, and baking powder in a bowl. Add the egg and using 2 knives, cut into crumbs. Place the blueberries and peaches in a 2-quart lightly buttered baking dish (you can use an 8 x 8-inch Pyrex® square). Mix together the 2 tablespoons of sugar and ½ teaspoon of cinnamon. Sprinkle the cinnamon sugar mix on the fruit. Sprinkle with the crumb topping. Drizzle melted butter over the topping. Bake at 375° for 35 to 40 minutes or until top is well browned. Serves 6 to 8.

This would be great topped with vanilla ice cream. Pearl is an excellent baker!

TIRAMISU - THE VERY BEST
Elise Feiner

7 egg yolks
1 cup sugar for the yolks
3 cups mascarpone cheese or (1) 750 gram container
4½ tablespoons water
1½ tablespoons Knox unflavored gelatin
3 egg whites
¼ cup sugar for the whites

1 cup heavy cream; whipped
2½ cups espresso coffee; cooled
½ cup Kahlua
20 to 24 ladyfingers, plain unfilled
1 cup chocolate shavings
2 teaspoons cocoa powder

In a mixer with the whip attachment, whip yolks and sugar until thick and pale in color. Add mascarpone and whip until well mixed. Pour water into a small bowl then pour powdered gelatin over it. Do not stir. Allow gelatin to absorb the entire amount of water (about 15 minutes) then place the bowl on top of a small saucepan containing simmering water (creating a double boiler). Immediately turn off the heat and allow the gelatin to dissolve completely. In a separate bowl, whip egg whites to a soft peak, gradually add sugar, and then slowly pour in dissolved gelatin. Whip to a stiff, glossy peak. Fold whites into mascarpone and yolk mixture then fold in whipped cream (mousse mixture.) In a separate bowl, combine espresso and Kahlua. Dip 1 ladyfinger at a time in the espresso mixture; don't leave it in the mixture too long or it will begin to fall apart. In an 8 x 10-inch pan, arrange soaked ladyfingers close together in neat rows until the bottom of the pan is completely covered. Pour ½ of the mousse over the ladyfingers and smooth with a rubber spatula. Sprinkle ½ of the chocolate shavings over mousse. Create another layer and chill until set. Smooth the surface and dust liberally with cocoa powder and chocolate shavings. Serves 12. To really make this spectacular, serve in large individual chocolate cups or bowls or wine goblets...just get creative!

This is one of Jeffrey's favorite desserts; it is very easy to make and very delicious!

L-R: Jeffrey Feiner and
Uncle Kevin Feiner

MUDDY BUDDIES
Johann Gigliotti

2 teaspoon vanilla
2 pounds powdered sugar
1 cup peanut butter

2 (12 ounce) package semisweet chocolate chips
2 sticks margarine or butter*
2 boxes (18 cups) Chex® cereal (any variety)

Measure cereal into large bowl; set aside. Microwave chocolate chips, peanut butter and margarine in 1-quart microwavable bowl, uncovered on High 1 minute; stir. Microwave 30 seconds longer or until mixture can be stirred smooth. Stir in vanilla. Pour chocolate mixture over cereal in bowl, I use a very large plastic storage container, stirring until evenly coated. Pour into large plastic bag; I use a large kitchen size (13 gallon) garbage bag; add powdered sugar. Close the bag tightly; shake until well coated. Spread on waxed paper to cool. Store in airtight container in refrigerator. 18 cups snack. *Do not use spread or tub products. Important: Because microwaves cook differently, time is approximate.

Range Top Directions: Measure cereal into large bowl; set aside. Heat chocolate chips, peanut butter and margarine in 1-quart saucepan over low heat, stirring frequently, until melted. Remove from heat; stir in vanilla. Continue as directed above.

These are Lauren's favorite. Johann Gigliotti made them and said the recipe came from the Chex ®Cereal boxes. Chex® Cereal is a registered trademark of General Mills.

Johann and Bernie Gigliotti

They don't come any nicer
than Bernie and Johann.
They give new meaning to
the term open house.

PUMPKIN ROLL
Angela Pohleven

3 eggs
1 cup sugar
⅔ cup pumpkin
1 teaspoon lemon juice
¾ cup all purpose flour

1 teaspoon baking powder
2 teaspoons cinnamon
1 teaspoon ginger
½ teaspoon nutmeg
½ teaspoon salt

Filling:
1 (8 ounce) packaged cream cheese
4 tablespoons butter

1 cup powdered sugar
½ teaspoon vanilla

In a large bowl, combine eggs, and sugar, beating them well. Add pumpkin and lemon juice, mixing until blended. In a separate bowl, combine flour, baking powder, spices, and salt. Add to egg mixture, mixing well. Spread batter into a greased and waxed paper lined 10 x 15-inch jelly roll pan. Bake at 350° for 15 minutes. Remove from the oven. Cool for 15 minutes. Place cake on a clean tea towel. Cool 10 minutes longer. From the 10 inch side, roll cake up in a towel. Set aside.

Meanwhile prepare filling. Beat together cream cheese and butter. Stir in sugar and vanilla, blend until smooth. Unroll cake. Evenly spread filling over the cake. Roll up cake. Remove towel. Cover and chill at least one hour. Slice before serving. Keep any leftovers refrigerated. Serves 10.

This recipe is from one of the girls I met in my real estate class. She said this is her mother- in- law's recipe. It's great for the holidays.

LEMON OR LIME MOUSSE
Eleanor Sulzman

2 (3¾ ounce size) packages Lemon or Lime Jell-O®
2 cups boiling water
2 cups 7 UP® (well chilled)

Juice of 1 lemon
1 (8 ounce) container Cool Whip®

Add the Jell-O to the boiling water and mix well. Add 2 cups of **COLD 7 UP** and the lemon juice. Whip with a mixer for 5 minutes. Refrigerate until thickened. Add container of Cool Whip. Beat for an additional 10 minutes. Refrigerate until firm.

This recipe is from another friend of Mom Mom's. This is a great summertime dessert...cool and refreshing.

LEMON MOUSSE PIE
Elise Feiner

6 (3-inch graham cracker squares) or 9 mini individual prepared graham cracker pie crusts
1 (1.5 ounce) box sugar free, fat free vanilla pudding mix, dry

½ plastic package Crystal Light® Lemonade mix, yellow
2 cups skim milk
1 (8 ounce) container Fat-Free Cool Whip®, thawed
A few drops of yellow food coloring

Line the bottom of an 8 x 8-inch square pan with the graham crackers, if using crackers. In a large mixing bowl, stir in the pudding mix and lemonade mix. Add the milk and beat with a wire whisk or hand mixer for about two minutes until well blended and starting to thicken. Add ¾ of the container of Cool Whip. Add a few drops of yellow food coloring; mix well. Pour over the graham crackers or fill the mini shells. When it sets or before serving, top with remaining Cool Whip. Serves 9.

This came out of a Shape Magazine recipe. I changed it a little by added the food coloring and put into individual graham cracker crusts. It's great when dieting, quick to prepare and tastes great. It has less than 1 gram of fat and is about 208 calories a serving.

JEAN'S BROWNIES
Jean Glorius

1 pound unsalted butter
1 pound plus 3 cups semisweet chocolate chips, divided
6 ounces unsweetened chocolate
6 jumbo eggs
3 tablespoons instant coffee or espresso
2 tablespoons vanilla extract

2¼ cups sugar
1¼ cups flour, divided
1 tablespoon baking powder
1 teaspoon kosher salt
3 cups chopped walnut pieces (optional)

Preheat oven to 350°. Spray a 13 x 18 x 1½-inch sheet pan with Bakers Joy® or grease and flour the pan. Melt the butter, 1 pound chocolate chips, and unsweetened chocolate on top of a double boiler or very carefully (minute by minute in a microwave). Cool slightly. Mix together the eggs, instant coffee, vanilla and sugar. Stir in the warm chocolate mixture and let cool to room temperature. In a medium bowl mix together the flour, baking powder and salt. Add to cooled chocolate mixture. Mix the chopped walnuts and 3 cups chocolate chips with a little flour to coat them, this prevents from sinking to the bottom of the batter. Add to the chocolate batter. Pour into floured pan. Bake for about 30 minutes, or until tester just comes out clean. After 15 minutes, tap the pan against the oven rack. This will allow air to escape from between the pan and the brownie dough. Don't over bake. Cool, refrigerate and cut into squares.

This came from a neighbor in Staten Island years ago.

CHOCOLATE MOUSSE D'AMICO
Ann D'Amico

2 cups semi sweet chocolate pieces
12 eggs, separated

4 teaspoons vanilla

Melt the semi sweet chocolate over hot water. Remove from heat. With a spoon, beat in yolks, then vanilla. Beat whites until stiff. Fold in chocolate mixture. Serve with flavored whipped cream. Add nuts or sprinkles. Serves 16.

Ann sent this recipe as part of a recipe club we had. It is a fast easy dessert.

FUNNEL CAKES
Elise Feiner

2 beaten eggs
1½ cups milk
2 cups sifted flour

1 teaspoon baking powder
½ teaspoon salt
2 cups cooking oil

In a mixing bowl, combine the eggs and milk. Sift together the flour, baking powder and salt. Add to the egg mixture; beat until smooth. Test to see if the mixture will flow easily through a funnel or pastry bag with wide tip. If too thick add a little more milk, if too thin add a little more flour. Pour oil into a large skillet (8-inch) and heat to 350°. Pour a generous half cup of batter into a funnel keeping your finger on the opening. Hold near the surface of the oil and remove your finger and release batter in a spiral shape. Fry until golden about 3 minutes. Turn and cook another minute. Drain on paper towels; sprinkle with confectioner's sugar.

Just like at all the street fairs and state fairs!

JO ANN'S CARAMEL BROWNIES
Jo Ann Tehan

1 box of Betty Crocker® Chocolate Cake Mix with Pudding
1 (14 ounce) bag of caramels, unwrapped
⅔ cup evaporated milk

½ cup (1 stick) of margarine, softened.
1½ cups walnuts, chopped
1 cup chocolate chips (mini)

Unwrap the caramels and place in a microwave safe bowl with ⅓ cup of the evaporated milk. Microwave one minute at a time until they are melted. Combine the cake mix **(DO NOT FOLLOW PACKAGE DIRECTIONS)** with the remaining ⅓ cup of evaporated mix and the stick of margarine. Stir until well blended, with a spoon. Mixture will be thick. Press half of the mixture into a well greased 13 x 9-inch pan. Bake for 6 minutes at 350°. Remove from oven and sprinkle 1 cup of walnuts, and chocolate chips over the hot crust. Top with the melted caramel mix. Then drop the remaining batter by teaspoonfuls (or just use your hands) over the caramel mixture. Top with remaining ½ cup of walnuts. Continue baking about another 28 minutes. Refrigerate before cutting.

Maria Trainor got this recipe from her friend JoAnn. It's a great brownie recipe!

FRUIT AND PASTA SALAD
Kathy Schabert

1 pound orzo or Rosa Marina Pasta
2 (20 ounce) cans pineapple chunks
2 (15 ounce) cans Mandarin oranges
¾ cup sugar

2 eggs well beaten
2 tablespoons flour
1 (16 ounce) container of Cool Whip®, thawed

Cook pasta in salt water, according to package directions; drain. Drain the pineapples and the oranges, save the juice. Put the reserves juice in a saucepan. Stir in the sugar until dissolved. Add the eggs and flour. Heat and cook, stirring until slightly thickened. Pour over pasta in a large bowl. Mix well. Refrigerate. The next day, mix the fruit and cool whip together. Add to the pasta.

Kathy got this recipe from Cheryl Martin's grandmother. She made it for a party at Fran's house and it was delicious. It's great for a buffet table, or a summer barbeque.

The Schabert's:
L-R: Dan, Gretchen,
Meredith and Kathy

ENGLISH TRIFLE
Ann D'Amico

2 (3 ¾ ounce) packages vanilla flavored instant pudding
and pie filling
2¼ cups milk
2 cups heavy cream
¼ cup Grand Marnier
1 (10 ounce) package frozen raspberries thawed and
drained, reserve syrup
¼ cup raspberry preserves

⅓ cup sweet sherry
3 (3 ounces each) packages ladyfinger cookies 36 double
ladyfingers
2 tablespoons confectioners' sugar
2 teaspoons vanilla extract
½ cup whole unblanched almonds

Prepare the instant pudding with the milk, 1½ cups of the heavy cream, and the Grand Marnier (totaling 4 cups of liquid) following the package directions. Combine 3 tablespoons of the reserved raspberry liquid, the raspberry preserves, and the sherry in a small bowl; mix well. Separate the ladyfingers. Brush the mixture over the flat side of half of the ladyfingers; arrange against the flat side of a 2-quart glass bowl or trifle bowl; rounded sides out, lining bowl completely. Spoon in half the pudding and top with remaining ladyfingers. Top with drained raspberries and remaining pudding. Cover and refrigerate several hours or overnight until completely chilled. Just before serving, beat the remaining ½ cup heavy cream with the 2 teaspoons of vanilla extract and confectioner's sugar. Spoon cream into a pastry bag with a star tip. Pipe the cream into a lattice pattern on top of custard. Garnish with the almonds. Serves 12.

CHRISTMAS BOMBE
Ann D'Amico

1 quart vanilla ice cream
1 quart pistachio ice cream
1 pint raspberry sherbet

½ cup shelled, unsalted pistachio nuts, crushed
Raspberry Sauce (see index)

Put a 3 quart bombe mold or metal mixing bowl in the freezer for at least half an hour. Put vanilla ice cream in refrigerator until soft but not melted. Using a spatula, line the sides and bottom of the frozen mold or bowl evenly with a layer of vanilla ice cream, working quickly. Immediately return mold to the freezer. Put pistachio ice cream in refrigerator until soft but not melted. Using a spatula, evenly line the firm vanilla ice cream with a layer of pistachio ice cream, working quickly. Immediately return mold to the freezer. Put raspberry sherbet in refrigerator until soft but not melted. When mold is firm, fill the center of the mold with the raspberry sherbet and return to the freezer for at least 3 hours. To unmold, dip bowl into hot water for a few seconds to loosen. Quickly turn onto a frozen serving platter. Sprinkle with pistachios and immediately return to the freezer until ready to serve. To serve, heat a knife in hot water, dry and slice. Repeat between slices. Drizzle with raspberry sauce. Garnish with mint leaves and raspberries if desired.

CRÈME BRULEE
Elise Feiner

9 egg yolks
¾ cup superfine white sugar plus 6 tablespoons

1 quart of heavy cream
1 vanilla bean

Preheat your oven to 250°. In a large bowl, beat together the egg yolks and the sugar with a whisk until pale yellow and thick. Split the vanilla bean down the middle and scrape out the seeds and place them into a medium saucepan; add the cream and heat the cream by bringing it to a simmer, but **DO NOT** boil it. Remove from the heat. Add a few tablespoons of the hot cream mixture to the egg mixture to temper it. Whisk constantly. Very slowly, add the remaining cream to the egg mixture, whisking it so the eggs won't cook. Place into individual custard dishes or ramekins (6 ounce size). Place the ramekins into a baking pan and fill the pan with water so that the level of the water reaches halfway up the sides of the pan. Bake about 40 minutes or until set around the edges. You may to cover loosely with foil if they are getting too brown. Remove from oven and let cool to room temperature. Chill in the refrigerator for at least two hours. When ready to serve, sprinkle the top with a table spoon of sugar and caramelize by using a kitchen torch, or placing them under the broiler to caramelize the sugar. If you prefer chocolate crème brulee, add 3 ounces of shaved dark chocolate to the custard mix before you put it in the ramekins.

One of my favorite desserts; I like chocolate crème brulee, but both are delicious!

"You can never be too rich, too thin or eat too much chocolate!
-Author Unknown

ÉCLAIRS
Elise Feiner

Pastry:
¾ cup water
⅓ cup butter
⅛ teaspoon salt

¾ cup flour
3 large eggs

Preheat oven to 400°. In a medium saucepan, bring water, butter, and salt to boiling. Remove from the heat. Quickly add the flour all at once. With a wooden spoon, beat constantly over low heat until the mixture forms a ball and leaves the sides of the pan. Remove from heat. Place the flour mixture into a mixing bowl. Using the mixer beat in the eggs one at a time, beating well after each addition. Continue beating vigorously until shiny and satiny, and breaks away in strands. Dough will be stiff. Drop dough or pipe out the dough with a pastry bag with a large opening, to strips about 4-inches long by 1½-inches wide, onto an ungreased cookie sheet. Use a knife to round the edges and indent the sides slightly. Bake 35 to 45 minutes until puffed and golden. Let cool.

Filling:
1½ cups milk
¼ cup sugar
1½ tablespoons cornstarch

2 egg yolks, beaten
1 teaspoon vanilla extract
½ cup heavy cream, whipped

In a small heavy saucepan, heat the milk until bubbling around the edges. In a separate dish, mix the sugar and cornstarch together. Add to the hot milk mixture stirring all at once. Cook over medium heat, stirring frequently until bubbling. Reduce heat, simmer one minute. Beat a little of the hot mix into the yolks to temper it. Then, add the yolks to the hot mixture, stirring over medium heat until thick. Add the vanilla extract. Remove from heat. When cool, refrigerate. When the mixture is cold, fold in the whipped cream. Fill the éclairs by cutting them in half and spooning some of the filling into each one. Place the tops back on the éclairs. Frost the top with chocolate glaze. Place on a serving tray. If not using right away, keep refrigerated.

Chocolate Glaze:
1 (6 ounce) cup semisweet chocolate pieces
2 tablespoons butter

2 tablespoons corn syrup
3 tablespoons milk

In the top of a double boiler over hot water, melt the chocolate and butter. Blend in the corn syrup and milk. Heat for 5 minutes. Spread over the top of each éclair.

In my youth (of course, I can't remember that far back), when I had time, I used to make these for dessert if we were having company. Delicious, but time consuming

ALFREDO'S DESSERT
Flo DeSimone

1 cup flour
½ cup butter
1½ cups chopped nuts (save a few for the top)
1 cup confectioners' sugar
1 cup Cool Whip®
1 teaspoon vanilla

1 (8 ounce) package cream cheese
1 package instant vanilla pudding
1 package instant chocolate pudding
2½ cups milk
German Chocolate bar, shaved
Cool Whip® for the top

Preheat oven to 350°. Mix the flour, butter and chopped nuts together and press into a 9 x 13-inch pan; bake at 350° for 25 to 30 minutes. Let cool. Mix the confectioners sugar, cool whip, vanilla and cream cheese together and spread over cooled crust. Mix the vanilla and chocolate puddings together with the milk; let thicken. Spread over the cool whip layer. Finally top with extra Cool Whip, sprinkle with leftover chopped nuts and shaved chocolate. Refrigerate. Cut in squares to serve.

This is the dessert served at Alfredo's Ristorante in New Hartford. All of our Bar and Bat Mitzvah's were there, and they did a wonderful job with the catering. When the restaurant was open, this was their signature dessert!

CREAM PUFFS
Katherine Avella

1 stick butter, unsalted	4 eggs
½ teaspoons salt	1 cup water
1½ teaspoons sugar	1 cup sifted flour

Combine butter, water, salt and sugar in a saucepan and stir over moderate heat until the butter melts and it reaches a rolling boil. Remove from heat; add flour all at once, and stir vigorously, return to heat for about 1 to 2 minutes or until the mixture forms a ball and leaves the side of the pan. Remove from heat. Stir in the eggs, one at a time beating thoroughly with a wooden spoon or electric mixer. Continue mixing until spoonfuls of the mixture break away sharply from the rest of the mixture. Drop by heaping teaspoonful on an ungreased cookie sheet. Bake 425° 35 to 40 minutes. Cool on wire rack. Cut and fill.

Filling:

2 cups milk	1 cup flour, sifted
6 egg yolks	1 cup sugar
2 teaspoons finely grated lemon zest	

Place the milk on the top a double boiler; heat until warm. Add the egg yolks to the warm milk. Blend; add lemon zest. Add flour. Add sugar, cut for about 10 minutes until thick. Remove from heat. Cool. Fill cream puffs. Refrigerate.

You can also fill with instant pudding, or chocolate whipped cream and bananas or strawberries, etc. To make chocolate whipped cream, whip heavy cream, add a little vanilla and sugar and semisweet chocolate shavings.

Jean and Pat Mainella my Aunt and Uncle... My Uncle Pat is my mother's brother. I lived with them for most of my senior year of high school because my parents moved to Staten Island and I didn't want to transfer there.

CHOCOLATE MOUSSE
Elise Feiner

1¾ cups whipping cream	1 tablespoon dark rum
1 (12 ounce) package quality semi-sweet chocolate chips	4 tablespoons unsalted butter
3 ounces espresso or strong coffee	1 teaspoon Knox® unflavored gelatin

Chill 1½ cups whipping cream in refrigerator. Chill metal mixing bowl and mixer beaters in freezer for about 15 minutes. In top of a double boiler, combine chocolate chips, coffee, rum and butter. Melt over barely simmering water, stirring constantly. Remove from heat while a couple of chunks are still visible. Cool, stirring occasionally to just above body temperature. Pour remaining ¼ cup whipping cream into a metal measuring cup and sprinkle in the gelatin. Allow gelatin to "bloom" for 10 minutes. Then carefully heat by swirling the measuring cup over a low gas flame or candle. Do not boil or gelatin will be damaged. Stir mixture into the cooled chocolate and set aside. In the chilled mixing bowl, beat cream to medium peaks. Stir ¼ of the whipped cream into the chocolate mixture to lighten it. Fold in the remaining whipped cream in two batches. There may be streaks of whipped cream in the chocolate and that is fine. Do not over work the mousse. Spoon into bowls or martini glasses and chill for at least 1 hour. Garnish with fruit. If mousse is to be refrigerated overnight, chill for one hour first, and then cover each with plastic wrap. Serves 6.

To die for!!!!!!

CHOCOLATE FONDUE
Christina Terenzi

½ cup light cream or half and half
1 pound milk chocolate pieces
2 tablespoons light corn syrup
1 teaspoon vanilla

24 ladyfingers, plain split in half
Finely chopped walnuts or pecans (in a separate bowl)
Flaked coconut (in a separate bowl)
Colored sprinkles (in a separate bowl)

In a fondue pot, combine the cream and corn syrup. Heat; stirring until blended. Add the chocolate pieces and heat, stirring until melted. Add the vanilla. Place the ladyfingers on fondue forks, twirl in the chocolate. Dip in nuts, coconut, or sprinkles. Serves 8.

This is my friend Tina's recipe. Fondue was big in the 70's when we were in nursing school, and it's making a comeback so I thought I'd include it in this book.

BROWNIES
Elise Feiner

½ pound (2 sticks) unsalted butter
2½ cups light brown sugar (I use Brownulated)
6 ounces unsweetened chocolate
4 large eggs

2 teaspoons vanilla extract (for a different taste, use Kahlua®)
2 cups flour
½ teaspoon salt

Preheat oven to 325°. Butter a 9 x 13-inch glass baking pan; cut a piece of waxed paper to fit the bottom. Place over the butter. Lightly butter the waxed paper. In a microwave safe bowl, combine the butter, brown sugar, and the chocolate. Microwave on high for 1 minute. Stir. Continue to microwave at 10 second intervals until the chocolate is very soft but not completely melted. Beat the eggs and vanilla into the chocolate with a wooden spoon. Beat in the flour and salt. Pour into the pan, smooth and bake. Bake for 35 to 40 minutes or until a toothpick inserted into the center comes out clean. Let cool. Run a knife around the edges of the pan. Turn onto a baking sheet, and turn over onto a work space. You can cut the brownies into squares or cut them out with a cookie cutter into any shape you want. Roll the extra pieces of brownies into rounds and roll in confectioners' sugar, cocoa, or decorative sugars.

I love this recipe. It's easy, delicious, and great for holidays. I use bunny cutters, hearts, etc. My cousin Ann told me about this recipe. I made these for Lauren when she was at Exeter for every occasion. These are my kid's favorite brownies!

CHOCOLATE CHERRY SNACK MIX
Elise Feiner

2 cups Wheat Chex® cereal
1 cup dry-roasted peanuts
¼ cup margarine or butter
1 (6 ounce) package semisweet chocolate chips (1 cup)
1 cup natural-flavor malted milk powder

2 cups miniature marshmallows
1½ cups coarsely chopped malted milk balls
½ cup dried cherries, chopped
2 cups Corn Chex® cereal
2 cups Rice Chex® cereal

Measure cereals and peanuts into large bowl; set aside. Melt butter and chocolate chips in 1-quart saucepan over low heat, stirring occasionally. Pour over cereal mixture in bowl, stirring until evenly coated. Gradually stir in malted milk powder until evenly coated. Stir in remaining ingredients. Store in airtight container. 12½ cups snack. Tip: Coarsely chop malted milk balls in a food processor.

CANNOLI
Elise Feiner

3 boxes of Cannoli Shells
1 pound ricotta
2 ounces mascarpone cheese
1 cup powdered sugar
½ cup chopped pistachios
½ pint heavy cream

2 teaspoon vanilla
1 teaspoon cinnamon
Glacee fruit chopped (optional) about 4 tablespoons
Orange zest (optional) about 2 tablespoons
1 (12 ounce) package mini chocolate chips, divided in half (save ½ to dip ends in)

Mix everything together except for the shells and half the chocolate chips. Refrigerate until fairly firm about three hours. Fill a pastry bag with a wide tip, with chilled filling. Fill the shells. Dip the ends into the mini chips. You can also add espresso or Kahlua or Amaretto to the mix if desired. You can also melt chocolate and dip the Cannoli shells into melted chocolate before filling if desired.

BISCUIT TORTONI
Ann D'Amico

¼ cup Amaretto® liqueur
1 teaspoon unflavored gelatin
4 egg yolks
¼ cup water

½ cup sugar
1 cup whipping or heavy cream
½ cup chopped toasted almonds
¼ cup crushed almond macaroons

Place the gelatin and liqueur in a heat resistant cup and mix until gelatin is softened. Place cup in simmering hot water and heat until completely dissolved (can use a double boiler) 2 to 3 minutes. Beat yolks with a mixer until lemon colored. Combine sugar with water in a medium saucepan on medium heat until it boils and sugar is dissolved. Keep stirring. Lower the heat and stir until a candy thermometer says syrup is 230° (about 5 minutes.) With a mixer on low speed, beat syrup in a steady but slow stream, into egg mixture until well blended, about 6 minutes more or until thick. Cool. Beat heavy cream until thick peaks form. Fold cream, almonds, and macaroons into cooled mixture. Spoon into 12 foil cups or custard cups and chill or freeze. Serve with whipped cream, a cherry or sliced toasted almond on the top. Serves 12.

Ann says she usually makes this for dessert after a holiday dinner or for company after a heavy Italian meal. Can be frozen, covered for up to three weeks

BAKLAVA SPIRAKIS
Peggy Spirakis

1 pound shelled walnuts, toasted
½ pound blanched almonds, toasted
½ pound shelled pistachios, toasted
⅔ cup brown sugar

1 tablespoon ground cinnamon
½ teaspoon ground cloves
½ pound unsalted butter, melted
1 pound phyllo pastry sheets

Preheat oven to 350°. Finely chop the nuts in a food processor or coffee grinder. Transfer nuts to a bowl and mix in brown sugar, ground cinnamon, and cloves. Brush a 13 x 9-inch baking pan with melted butter and set aside. Cut a piece of cardboard into a 13x9-inch rectangle. Unroll the phyllo dough and lay the sheets flat on a work surface. Set the cardboard template on the stack of phyllo and trim the excess so they fit the pan. Keep the pastry covered with a damp, not wet, towel as you work to prevent drying out. To build the baklava, you will alternate 3 layers of dough with 2 layers of nuts. Start with a stable base of 8 sheets on the bottom, brushing each with melted butter. Spread ½ the nut mixture evenly over the stacked sheets. Cover with 4 sheets of phyllo, painting each with melted butter, then sprinkle again with remaining nut mixture. Top the last layer of nuts with 8 layers of phyllo as you did for the bottom. Drizzle any remaining butter over top. If you have time, cover and refrigerate for 30 minutes so the butter will set and make the baklava easier to cut. Using a sharp knife, make 5 cuts across lengthwise, then cut diagonally to form diamonds. Baklava is more difficult to cut after it is cooked because the pastry becomes so flaky. Bake for about 40 minutes until golden and flaky. If the top browns too quickly during baking, tent with foil.

Syrup:
2 cups sugar
2 cups water
½ cup orange blossom honey
1 teaspoon vanilla extract

½ lemon, juiced
2 large strips orange peel
1 cinnamon stick
3 whole cloves

To make the syrup: combine the ingredients in a saucepan and bring to a boil. Reduce the heat and let simmer for 10 minutes until thickened. Remove the orange peel, cinnamon stick, and whole clove; set aside to cool. Remove an end piece of the baklava and tilt the pan to allow the butter to collect in the corner. Spoon out the excess and discard. With the pan flat, pour the syrup evenly over the hot baklava. Allow to stand for several hours before serving.

Back Row L-R: Rae Barone,
Millie Grimaldi, Frances Barone,
Katherine Avella
Front Row L-R: Elizabeth Maida,
and Edith Mainella...Mother's
Day 1943

BAKLAVA AVRAMIDIS
Athena Avramidis

1 pound of walnuts mixed with ½ cup sugar
1 tablespoon cinnamon

1½ packages phyllo dough
2 sticks sweet butter, melted

For the syrup:
2 cups sugar
2 cups water

1 cup honey
Orange or lemon rind

Butter the pan and start layering the phyllo dough, buttering as you go until you have about 10 to15 sheets of phyllo dough at the bottom of the pan. Then, start layering and scattering the nut mixture on the top sheet and then place a single sheet of buttered phyllo, and continue to after each buttered single phyllo (phyllo) addition. After all the nuts are gone then layer another 10 to 15 phyllo sheets on the top buttering between each sheet. Score into diamond shapes. Bake in a 350° oven for about 45 minutes or until light brown on top. Cool. In a large pot, bring the sugar, water, honey, and rind to a boil for 10 minutes. Pour hot over **COOL** Baklava.

Athena makes this at Christmas, and it's one of the better recipes and fairly easy to make. This can be made in advance.

L-R: Katherine Avella, Marcia Archibald and Athena Avramidis at our Holiday Cookie Exchange

PUMPKIN CRÈME BRULEE
Elise Feiner

2 cups heavy cream
¼ cup light brown sugar
¼ cup plus 4 teaspoon sugar
8 large egg yolks

½ teaspoon vanilla
¼ teaspoon cinnamon
⅛ teaspoon nutmeg
1 cup cooked mashed pumpkin

Preheat the oven to 325°. Place 8 (½ cup) ramekins or custard cups in a big baking pan. In a medium pot, heat the heavy cream. Add the brown sugar, and ¼ cup sugar. Bring to a low simmer over medium heat, stir until sugar is dissolved. Remove from heat. Beat the egg yolks until frothy and lemon colored. Slowly, add a little of the hot mix to the egg yolks, whisking continuously. Add the egg mix to remaining hot cream; whisk. Add vanilla, cinnamon, nutmeg and pumpkin; whisk until smooth. Strain through a strainer into bowl. Fill custard cups. Place hot water around the cups in the pan (coming up halfway up the sides). Bake 45 to 55 minute until set but not stiff. Remove from oven; cool and refrigerate at least 4 hours or overnight. Before serving sprinkle each cup with ½ teaspoon of remaining sugar. Using a kitchen torch, caramelize the sugar or place under the broiler for a few minutes, 1-2 minutes, **watch carefully!**

RAINBOW JELL-O®
Ann D'Amico

1 (6 ounce) package
Orange Jell-O®
1 (6 ounce) package
Lemon Jell-O®
1 (6 ounce) package

Lime Jell-O®
1 (6 ounce) package
Cherry Jell-O®
4 cups (2 pints) sour cream

Dissolve the orange Jell-O in 2 cups boiling water. To ½ cup of the liquefied Jell-O add 1-cup sour cream and stir well. Pour sour cream/Jell-O mixture into a 9 x 13-inch glass baking dish and reserve 1½ cups orange Jell-O. Put the baking dish on a level shelf in your refrigerator and chill until set. When firm, pour reserved orange Jell-O over the creamy layer; chill until firm. Repeat with remaining colors of Jell-O each with a creamy layer and clear layer.

The person who gave this to Ann said that it is a gorgeous dessert and so festive looking. It's great for a holiday dinner.

POPSICLE MOLD
Pearl Borten

6 (3 ounce) boxes small green Jell-O®
6 cups boiling water

4 cups cold water
1 box chocolate covered vanilla Popsicles (12)

Add the Jell-O, and hot water to dissolve it. Immediately add the cold water. Mix well; refrigerate to jell slightly. Whip with a mixer until chiffon consistency. Break up the Popsicles with your fingers and fold in. Spray a mold or baking pan with PAM®. Add Jell-O mix. Refrigerate until firm. Pearl says this is a large amount and you can easily cut it in half. Serves 12.

This is another recipe from Mom Mom's friend Pearl. She gave me several of her dessert recipes. Everyone in Florida raves about this one.

L-R: Great grandmother Ida and Great Grandfather Dave Feldman, Morris and Freda Feldman Feiner, Betty Reinisch Feiner, Nellie and Judah Reinisch, Shirley Reinisch Flomenhoft In front: Philip (Pinky) Feiner and Adele Reinisch Freedoff
Picture taken by Gene Feiner

Freda and Morris Feiner

APPLE CRÈME BRULEE
Elise Feiner

3 Granny Smith apples
1 tablespoon cinnamon
2 tablespoons butter
¼ cup sugar, plus 6 tablespoons

¼ cup water
6 egg yolks
1 teaspoon vanilla
1½ cups heavy whipping cream

Peel and core apples. Cut into bite sized chunks. Cook the apples in the cinnamon, ¼ cup sugar, butter, and water for 7 to 8 minutes until tender, but not mushy. Set aside to cool. Preheat oven to 325°. Whisk egg yolks and 6 tablespoons sugar. Whisk until light yellow in color. Add vanilla; while whisking, gradually add in whipping cream. Divide apple mix evenly into 6 ramekins. Pour cream mixture evenly over the apples. Place ramekins in a baking dish. Make a Bain Marie by pouring hot water halfway up to the sides of the ramekins. Bake the custard until set, approximately 40 minutes. Keep the ramekins in the water bath and let them cool for about 30 minutes. Remove from water and chill overnight in the refrigerator. Sprinkle sugar on top of crème and then torch or under a broiler until golden brown. Serves 6. You can do this with peaches as well. Peel them first, then, cube them. Don't cook as long as the apples (about 3 to 4 minutes.)

Standing L-R: Michael Alsheimer, Andrew Massoud, Rich Kiersnowski, Steven Feiner, Anthony Alsheimer, Adam Morton
Kneeling L-R: Brittany Butler, Lauren Feiner

Clockwise from the left: Lauren Feiner, Kristin Gigliotti, Kristin Furino, Alison Houck, and Britt Butler

L-R: Cousins Karen, Abby, and Lauren Feiner

L-R: Steven Feiner, Jeremy Zierler, and Joshua Rosenfeld

On Left:
Joseph , Edith
and Warren
Mainella

On Right:
A young Jeremy
Zierler

Cookies and Candy...

The Extended Feiner Family

Standing L-R: Jerome Feiner, Alvin Freedoff, Harvey Flomenhoft, David Freedoff, Leslie and Howard Sheldon, Kevin Feiner, Brad Weiner, Elise and Marc Feiner, Marc and Terry Freedman, Kathy Freedoff, Hal Weiner, Theresa and Ivan Feiner
Sitting L–R: Shirley Flomenhoft, Betty Feiner, Clara Karasch, Nellie and Juda Reinisch, Adele Freedoff, Barbara Forgeron

"If God wanted us to be thin, he wouldn't have made fattening foods taste so good."
-Unknown

Shipping Cookies:

When we had the gift basket business we shipped lots of cookies. Here are some hints to ship your cookies. Use a sturdy box or can or plastic container. Put container in a large box and pack with shipping material, i.e. bubble wrap or packing peanuts. Make sure you label the box well; place your return address as well as the recipients address in a large bold print done with a permanent marker. Tape over the address with clear packing tape to protect address.

Certain cookies tend to ship better than others do. Try not mail cookies with custard or custard-like fillings or toppings, including Cheesecake Bars. The cheese could spoil, making a very unwelcome gift. For that matter, any cookie that requires refrigeration is not a good cookie to mail. Another type of cookie that doesn't hold up well for mailing is one with a delicate, cake-like texture such as Madeleine's. The best cookies to mail are those that have a crunchy or hard texture or a chewy texture such as Biscotti, Chocolate Chip, Oatmeal, Shortbreads make excellent choices for mail delivery. They tend to be fairly sturdy, so you don't have to worry too much about breakage. Cookies that are chewy tend to dry out if they are in the mail for more than a week, so if their destination is a long way off, you might want to ship them by express to ensure that they arrive just as tasty as when they left. Dense bar cookies such as Fudge Brownies, or Peanut Butter Bars are delicious; just be sure to individually wrap each one with plastic wrap to keep that moist, dense texture from drying out.

Macaroons, Italian Pignoli (pine nuts) or marzipan based cookies mail beautifully. Their chewy, moist textures get better after they've aged a few days. Who wouldn't want to receive a single, chocolate-dipped coconut macaroon as a special snack? Be careful of shipping chocolate covered cookies in a warm climate or in warm weather. Use dry ice or ice packs and express ship. Label them "Do Not Leave Outside", Unpack immediately…

Baked and cool your cookies before packing them. There are a few guidelines you should follow when it comes to preparing cookies to be mailed. Follow these and your packages should arrive fresh, in one piece, and great tasting. Don't pack crisp and soft cookies together. The moisture from the soft cookies will seep into the crisp cookies, making them lose their delightful crunch.

Don't overstuff your container. Your cookies may be damaged. Likewise, don't under-pack your container. The cookies should fit snugly. If you have too much space, crumple up a bit of tissue paper to fill the holes. Pack cookies in a sturdy tin or airtight container. On the bottom of the container place a piece of bubble wrap, then line the container with parchment paper or cellophane, leaving enough to tuck over the top once the container is fully packed. Place one layer of cookies in the container. Cover with parchment paper. Arrange another layer of cookies, followed with more parchment paper, and continue this layering until the container is full. Tuck the cellophane or parchment paper over the top, then place another piece of bubble wrap on top, and seal your container.
Never pack soap or perfumed products with food, they will absorb the smell! The same goes for strong smelling cheeses like parmesan…don't pack with the cookies.

Wait for rave reviews, requests for recipes and lots of thank you notes!

ALMOND JOY COOKIES
Elise Feiner

4 egg whites
1 cup confectioners' sugar
1 teaspoon vanilla extract
1½ cups coconut

1½ cups flour
1 cup semisweet chocolate chips (I like mini chips)
1 cup toasted almonds, chopped

Beat the egg whites until stiff. Add the sugar and vanilla gradually. Add in the coconut and flour; mix well. Stir in the chocolate chips and almonds. Drop by teaspoonfuls onto lightly greased cookie sheet. Bake at 350° for 15 minutes. Remove and cool. Makes 48 cookies.

These taste like Almond Joy Bars; you often find them on my Christmas Cookie Tray.

L-R: Marc Feiner, Ivan Feiner,
Grandparents Juda and Nellie Reinisch, and mother Betty Feiner

CORN FLAKE COOKIES
Toni Mollico

1 (12 ounce) bag mini chocolate chips
2 tablespoon peanut butter

6 cups corn flakes

In a large microwave safe bowl or a double boiler, melt the chocolate chips with the peanut butter. If you are doing it in a microwave, microwave for 1 minute and stir, continue to microwave at 10 second intervals until the chocolate is melted. Add the corn flakes and mix well. Spoon onto a cookie sheet lined with waxed paper. Freeze or refrigerate for a few minutes until hardened. Store in a glass jar or airtight container in the refrigerator.

Toni gave me this recipe years ago. They take 5 minutes to make. Lauren loves these cookies. They're one of her favorites.

L-R: Steven Feiner and Brian Mollico – circa 1982

CHOCOLATE NUT KISSES
Elise Feiner

1 (12 ounce) package chocolate chips   1 package of whole filberts

Melt the chocolate chips in the top of a double boiler. Dip whole filberts into melted chocolate. Spoon coated filberts onto a cookie sheet and peak the top with a fork to look like a kiss. Chill until firm.

ANGINETTE'S ARCIERI
Joan Arcieri

6 eggs   4 cups of flour (enough to form soft dough)
Pinch of salt   6 teaspoons baking powder
½ cup sugar   ½ cup oil
2 teaspoons vanilla

Preheat the oven to 350°. Beat the eggs lightly. Add oil, salt, sugar vanilla, baking powder and enough flour to make soft dough. Knead well. Allow the dough to rest about ½ hour. Divide and wrap in Saran Wrap®. Shape by taking piece of dough and rolling into thin pencil shapes about 5 to 6 inches long. Wrap the roll of dough around your finger and then push it off. Place on a lightly greased and floured cookie sheet. Bake at 350° for about 10 to 15 minutes. When cool ice the cookies. See below. Yield about 60.

Confectioners' Sugar Icing:
1 box of Confectioners' Sugar   ¼ cup strained fresh lemon juice
3-6 tablespoons ice water

Combine the above ingredients in a deep bowl and stir until smooth. If icing is too stiff, beat in up to 3 tablespoons more of water (1 teaspoon at a time). Store in a tin box or freeze them.

This is my Cousin Joan's version of the Anginette's.

Joan Arcieri
Aunt Toni Mollico's mother. Joan was so beautiful and full
of life, tragically we lost her at a very young age.

ANISETTE TOAST
Janet Saporito

1 tablespoon baking powder   1½ cups sugar
1 teaspoon baking soda   1 cup butter or margarine, melted and cooled
Dash salt   1 teaspoon vanilla extract
5 to 5¾ cups flour   1 teaspoon lemon extract
6 large eggs   1 tablespoons anise extract

Sift dry ingredients in medium bowl. In a large bowl, beat in eggs for 3 minutes until foamy. Add sugar ½ cup at a time, beating well. Slowly pour in butter and extracts. At slow speed, mix in 5 cups of flour ⅓ at a time. If too soft add, remaining flour. Form dough into a circle and cut into 6 portions. Shape each into a cylinder 15 x 1-inch. Place on ungreased cookie sheet 4-inches apart. Bake in oven preheated to 350° for 25 to 30 minutes. Remove. Cut 1-inch slices on sharp diagonal. Replace on baking sheet, standing up, 1-inch apart. Bake 10 to 15 minutes until golden brown. Cool. Coat with powdered sugar and store in airtight container to develop flavor.

ANGINETTE'S MAINELLA
Josephine Mainella

1 cup of eggs (about 6-8) at room temperature
4 ounces of vegetable oil
¼ teaspoon salt
1 cup sugar
Juice of one fresh orange (about ½ cup)

2 teaspoons lemon juice
2 teaspoons vanilla
4-6 cups of flour (enough to form soft dough)
2 tablespoons baking powder

Preheat the oven to 350°. Beat the eggs lightly. Add oil, salt, sugar, juices, flavorings, baking powder and enough flour to make soft dough. Knead well. Allow the dough to rest about ½ hour. Divide and wrap in Saran Wrap. Shape by taking piece of dough and rolling into thin pencil shapes about 5 to 6-inches long. Wrap the roll of dough around your finger, starting at the base and working up to the tip, and then push it off. Place on a lightly greased and floured cookie sheet. Bake at 350° for about 10 to 15 minutes. When cool ice the cookies. See below. Yield about 60.

Confectioners' Sugar Icing:

1 box of Confectioners' sugar, sifted
3-6 tablespoons ice water
¼ cup strained fresh lemon juice

Few grains of salt
Zest of half an orange (optional)

Combine the above ingredients in a deep bowl and stir until smooth. If icing is too stiff, beat in **UP** to 3 tablespoons more of water (1 teaspoon at a time). Store in a tin box or freeze them.

All the woman in our family have some version of this cookie. I've included three here; Aunts Fifi and Julia's and Cousin Joan's. These are one of Lauren's favorite cookies; she is always begging Aunt Fifi to make them. Hopefully, someday she'll use this book to make her own memories. These cookies appeared at every family occasion that I can remember.

Jennifer and Jeffrey Feiner...then
Today they are Dr. Jennifer Feiner and Dr. Jeffrey Feiner;
Jeff is a Plastic Surgeon and Jen is a Veterinarian

BUTTER COOKIES
Elise Feiner

5 cups sifted flour
1 pound of unsweetened butter, softened
1 cup sugar

2 eggs, beaten
1 teaspoon vanilla

Cream the butter and sugar together. Add the egg and vanilla. Gradually add the flour. Use a cookie press to shape the cookies. You can use food coloring to tint the dough if desired. Sprinkle with sugar before baking. Bake 300° for about 10 minutes. Do not over bake.

This is a generic butter cookie recipe. Great for cookie presses!

CHOCOLATE CHUNK CHIP COOKIES
Elise Feiner

1 cup flour
½ teaspoon baking powder
½ teaspoon salt
1 stick of butter, softened
½ cup sugar
¼ cup brown sugar, firmly packed

1 teaspoon vanilla
1 egg
1 (8 ounce) package Bakers® Semi-Sweet chocolate, cut into chunks, or package chocolate chunks
¾ cup chopped walnuts (optional)

Mix the flour, baking powder and salt and set aside. Beat the butter, sugars, vanilla and egg until fluffy. Blend into flour mixture; stir in chocolate chunks and nuts. Chill dough 1 hour before baking. Drop 2-inches apart by heaping tablespoons onto an ungreased baking sheet. Bake at 350° for 12 to 15 minutes or until lightly browned. Cool 2 minutes. Place on wire racks. To make chocolate chunks, melt 1 square of the chocolate; cool and add to the butter sugar mixture. Another variation, melt and cool 1 package of Bakers German Chocolate. Partially dip the cookies into the chocolate. Place on waxed paper. Let stand until firm.

L-R: David, Marc, Uncle Frank Mainella, Elise, Jeffrey and Lauren Feiner

Uncle Frank Mainella -1923…When Uncle Frank was 6 he told my grandmother he was blind. She took him to the Doctor, who asked "Frankie, why are you lying to your mother, I know you can see?" My Uncle said, "Because I want to wear glasses like you and be a Doctor when I grow up " and so he did…Dr Frank S. Mainella, Graduate of Hahnemann Hospital School of Medicine in Philadelphia, Pa.

ALMOND COOKIES
Frances Zierler

1 can or tube of Almond Paste
2 egg whites

1¼ cups sugar

Preheat oven to 325°. Line cookie sheets with parchment paper. Break almond paste into small pieces and place in a medium mixing bowl or food processor. Add sugar and process until smooth. Add egg whites and mix well. Drop by rounded teaspoonfuls on to baking sheets 1-inch apart. Bake 18 to 20 minutes or until golden brown. Cool completely. Store in an airtight container.

This recipe was given to Fran by a close friend, Kathy Schabert. It has become a Zierler family favorite and it's a fast easy cookie to make. Fran made them at our Christmas Cookie Exchange.

"All our dreams can come true, if we have the courage to pursue them."
-Walt Disney

ANISETTE COOKIES
Josephine Mainella

6-8 cups of flour
1 teaspoon salt
½ cups oil
2 cups sugar

8 teaspoons baking powder
½ bottle anisette extract
6 eggs

Beat eggs in bowl; add anisette, oil, and sugar. Add salt, flour and baking powder. Knead well. Pull off pieces of the dough. Roll out into a long roll. Cut into 2½ to 3-inch pieces; twist the dough to form the cookie. Repeat with remaining dough. Bake at 300° on an ungreased pan until lightly brown about 11 minutes.

These are the very traditional examples of Italian cookies that we grew up with for every holiday.

ANN'S LINZER TARTS
Ann D'Amico

3 cups all-purpose flour
1 teaspoon salt
1 large egg
1½ teaspoons vanilla or almond extract

1 cup butter softened or use ½ cup butter and ½ cup margarine
1½ cups sugar
Raspberry Jam
Confectioner's sugar

Sift together flour, salt, and set aside. With mixer, cream butter, margarine and sugar until light and creamy. Add egg and flavor extract, beat again. Add sifted flour mixture; blend first with mixer, then with your hands to form smooth dough. Wrap in waxed paper, chill for two hours. Preheat oven to 375°. Roll out half the dough onto a well floured board to ⅛-inch thickness. Cut with 2 or 3-inch round cookie cutter. Repeat with remaining dough, this time cut a circle (or heart, tree, leaf, etc) in the center of each cookie (apple corer is fine). Place on cookie sheet. Bake 375° oven, 6 to 8 minutes or until the edge is golden. Cool. Fill with raspberry jam. Dust top of cut out cookie with confectionery sugar. Place on top of the jam half. At Christmas or Valentines Day use seasonal cut outs.

Ann uses all butter instead of margarine mix. She makes these for all of her friend's important occasions. There isn't a bridal or baby shower in East Setauket, where these don't appear.

TRAY COOKIES FOR PARTIES
Nellie Plescia

8 cups Maple Leaf Flour
2 cups spry (or Crisco)
2½ cups sugar
2½ teaspoons baking powder
2 teaspoons honey

½ cup milk
4 eggs
2 teaspoons vanilla, brandy, rum or any flavor you have or mix them

Mix all the ingredients together to form a dough. Make them into little round balls and flatten a little. Beat and egg yolk with a little water and brush on the top of each cookie. Sprinkle with sugar. Bake at 375°to 400° for about 15 minutes. You can also divide the dough and add a few drops of food coloring to each batch to have different color cookies.

Brenda gave me this recipe of her grandmothers. Brenda said that her grandmother called these her cookie tray cookies and they were made for every family occasion and holiday. Her grandmother used to make each batch in a different color to make the trays of cookies look festive. This recipe was given to me written in her grandmothers own handwriting, She wrote, " will keep in fridge couple of days or more cover with plastic wrap and mapeen." This really brought back memories for me because many of the women in my own family used the term "Mapeen" which for those of you who don't know is a dishtowel!

"In every marriage more than a week old, there are grounds for divorce. The trick is to find, and continue to find, grounds for marriage."
-Robert Anderson

ANGINETTE'S SILVESTRI
Julia Silvestri

9 eggs
About 2 pounds of flour (8 cups)
9 teaspoons baking powder
1½ cups sugar
½ pound sweet butter

2 teaspoons of orange extract
2 teaspoons of lemon extract
1 teaspoon vanilla extract
⅛ teaspoon salt
The juice and zest of one lemon and one orange

Mix together to make a soft dough. If you need more flour, you can add it. If too hard add more eggs. Make the dough nice and soft. Let the dough rest covered 1 to 1½ hours. Make into ropes about ½-inch thick and about 6-inches long. Twist around your fingers 3 times and tuck ends in. Place on a lightly greased and flour cookie sheet. Bake 350° about 10 to 12 minutes or until golden brown on the bottom. When cool, dip the cookies into the icing. Store in a tin or cover tightly. Makes 80 cookies.

Icing:

1 box of confectionery sugar
1 teaspoon orange extract

1 teaspoon lemon extract
A few tablespoon of milk (add one at a time)

Beat the icing ingredient together, adding enough milk to hold it together and make a smooth glaze. Divide icing and tint in pastel colors (pink, yellow, blue, green), leaving some white. Put cookies on a wire rack to dry icing. Store in tins for up to one week. Place in small decorator cups when serving.

This recipe was given to me by my cousin, Ann D'Amico. It was my father's sister Julia's recipe. She was a wonderful baker. She was his oldest sister and more like a mother to him because he was the next to youngest. She would always do the desserts for all our family parties. She would always make these and Rice Krispies treats. She also made wonderful sponge cakes and fillings. This has been passed on in our family. Ann remembers sitting by her side and helping make these cookies as a little girl. Ann said they appeared at every wedding; a beautiful tray of pastel cookies, to celebrate the day. I remember my Aunt Julia baking in her tiny kitchen on Livonia Avenue, turning out trays of delicious treats from this tiny space. I am just like her; she loved to bake at night!

BISCOTTI A L'ANISE
Julia Silvestri

Dough:

6 eggs, beaten well
¼ pound butter, softened
1 cup sugar
4 teaspoons baking powder
4½-5 cups flour
4 ounces heavy cream or milk
2 teaspoons anise seeds
Pinch of salt

1 teaspoon vanilla
1 teaspoon lemon extract
1 teaspoon anise extract
Toasted nuts (½ pounds of mixed nuts (blanched almonds, walnuts, pecans, filberts etc) coarsely chopped) roasted on a cookie sheet in a 375° oven for about 5 to 7 minutes; cool

Preheat the open to 250°. Mix all ingredients except the flour together. Slowly add the flour, until you get a soft dough. Knead for a few minutes. Dip hands into flour and shape the dough into loaf shape. Flatten the loaves. Place on a greased cookie sheet. Dent with a knife to the width of the slices you desire (about ½-inch wide). Bake for 15 minutes then remove from the oven and using the indentations that you make before slice the cookies through. Place back on a baking sheet and return to oven to brown on both sides, about 10 to 15 more minutes. This is like making biscotti.

This was my Aunt Julia's recipe and one of my father's favorite cookies. He was always asking her to make these for him. He said his sister Julia "baked with love!"

MAPLE COOKIES
Nellie Plescia

2 cups brown sugar
1 cup shortening (butter)
1 teaspoon salt
2 eggs
1 cup buttermilk

1 teaspoon baking soda dissolved in 1½ teaspoons maple flavoring
1 teaspoon baking powder
4 cups flour
Chopped nuts (optional)

Mix the brown sugar, shortening, salt and eggs together. Add in the remaining ingredients. Beat thoroughly; drop by teaspoonfuls onto a greased cookie sheet. Bake at 425° until golden brown depending on the size you make them. Nellie's notes say that she uses a tablespoon to drop the cookies and bakes them on the second rack and them moves them to the third rack for a few minutes. You can frost them of you want by mixing confectioners' sugar with maple flavoring and a little milk

Brenda Johnson gave me this recipe and she said that her grandmother Nellie is most famous for her Maple Cookies. She always makes them for special occasions and holidays. Her family loves them. She said her Grandmother always made them very large, and that they had a cake-like consistency.

.

Nellie Plescia then…

Nellie Plescia now…

L-R: Gabrielle Johnson and Brenda Plescia Johnson…Nellie's great-granddaughter and granddaughter…you can see where they inherited their beauty!

BUTTER TOFFEE COOKIES
Elise Feiner

2½ cups all-purpose flour
1 teaspoon baking soda
½ cup salted butter
1½ cup granulated sugar

1 tablespoon vanilla extract
2 eggs
2 cups toffee pieces (home-made butter toffee or store-bought bits)

Preheat oven to 350°. Sift together flour and baking soda and set aside. Cream together, butter, sugar, and vanilla; add eggs one at a time. Add toffee pieces to mixture. Mix creamed mixture and dry mixture together. Use rounded tablespoon to measure dough. Place dough at least 2-inches apart on baking sheet. Bake for 10 to 12 minutes. Makes 40.

L-R: Elizabeth Barone Maida, Orsola Barone, Dr. Michael C. Barone, Rae Sessa Barone, and Frances Barone…Mother's Day 1943

419

BOCA RATON HOTEL PECAN BARS
Elise Feiner

¾ cup unsalted butter, softened
¾ cup sugar
2 eggs

Topping:
¾ cup unsalted butter
¾ cup light brown sugar
½ cup honey

1 teaspoon grated lemon zest
2¼ cups all purpose flour
½ teaspoon baking powder

3 cups pecans, toasted
½ cup heavy cream

In a mixing bowl, cream the butter and the sugar together until light and fluffy. Add eggs and lemon zest, beat well. Combine flour and baking powder. Stir into the creamed mixture until well mixed. Press dough into a 9 x 13-inch baking pan. Refrigerate about 30 minutes. Preheat oven to 375°. Make the topping (see next paragraph.) Prick the dough with a fork. Bake 10 minutes. Remove from oven. Reduce temperature to 350°.

Topping: Meanwhile in a deep heavy saucepan, combine butter, sugar and honey. Bring to a boil, stirring constantly. Cook 5 minutes. Remove from heat; cool slightly. Stir in pecans and cream. Spread evenly over partially baked dough. Bake for another 30 minutes. Cool in the pan on wire racks before cutting into 2 x 1-inch bars. Makes 4½ dozen cookies, about 150 calories each.

BROWNIE BISCOTTI
Elise Feiner

⅓ cup butter
⅔ cup white sugar
2 eggs
1 teaspoon vanilla extract
⅓ cup unsweetened cocoa powder
1¾ cups flour

½ cup mini chocolate chips
¼ cup chopped walnuts
1 egg yolk, beaten
1 tablespoon water
2 teaspoons baking powder

Beat butter until soft and add sugar and baking powder. Beat in eggs and vanilla, add cocoa and as much flour as you can by mixer add rest by hand. Stir in chocolate chips and nuts. Divide dough into two equal parts. Shape into 9 x 2 x 1-inch loaves. Place on sheet 4-inches apart. Brush with mixture of water and yolk. Bake at 375° for 25 minutes. Cool on sheet for 30 minutes. Cut loaves into thick slices diagonally. Lay cut side down and bake at 325° for 15 minutes. Turn over and bake other side for 10 to 15 minutes until dry. Cool. Store in air tight container. Makes 30.

BUTTERFLYS
Josephine Mainella

1 cup flour
1 cup milk
½ teaspoon salt
5 teaspoons sugar

1 egg, unbeaten
3 teaspoons vanilla
3 teaspoons brandy
Oil for frying

Mix all the ingredients together until smooth. This is the batter that is used to mold the cookies that are available on a long handle. Dip the molds into the batter and then into a deep saucepan filled with hot oil, or a deep fryer. Sprinkle with confectioner's sugar when done. The sell these molds in Bed, Bath and Beyond; I think they are called rosette molds.

This is a quick, easy and fun cookie to make. These molds have been around for years.

On Left: Aunt Fifi
Mainella age 88

On Right: L-R: Aunts
Jean and Fifi Mainella
1940

CANDY CANE COOKIES
Elise Feiner

½ cup butter, softened
1 cup confectioners' sugar
1 egg
1 teaspoon vanilla

½ teaspoon almond extract
2½ cups Wondra® Quick-mixing flour
1 teaspoon salt
Red food coloring

Combine the butter, confectioners' sugar, egg, vanilla, and almond extract. Mix well. Blend in the flour and the salt. Mix together to form a medium dough. Divide the dough in half and add red food coloring to one half. Chill a half hour to 1 hour. Using about 1 teaspoon of each color, roll into 4 inch strips and twist them together. Bend into a candy cane shape. Place on a lightly greased cookie sheet. Bake at 350° for about 9 minutes or until light brown. If desired, combine ½ cup sugar and ½ cup crushed peppermint candy and sprinkle over the cookies. Remove cookies from the sheet immediately and cool on a rack.

L-R: Steven, Lauren and David Feiner

LISA'S PINE NUT COOKIES
Lisa Frank

1 stick (½ cup) unsalted butter, at room temperature
½ cup plus 2 tablespoons sugar
1 teaspoon vanilla extract
1 teaspoon ground fennel seed

¼ teaspoon salt
1 large egg
1¼ cup flour
¼ cup pine nuts

Using an electric mixer, beat the butter, sugar, vanilla, fennel seed, and salt in a large mixing bowl until light and fluffy. Beat in the egg. Add the flour and mix until just blended. Transfer the dough to a sheet of plastic wrap. Shape the dough into an 8-inch log. Wrap the log in plastic wrap and refrigerate two hours. Preheat the oven to 350°. Line heavy baking sheets with a silpat or parchment paper. Cut the log crosswise into ⅛ to ¼-inch slices. Transfer the cookies to the prepared cookie sheets, spacing evenly apart. Press the pine nuts decoratively atop the cookies. Bake until the cookies are golden around the edges, about 15 minutes.

L-R: Bettina Arcara Liza, Lisa
Frank and Cookie Frank

421

BROWNIE PEANUT BUTTER BITES
Cathy LaRosa

1 (15 ounce) package Brownie mix
¼ cup oil
⅓ cup hot water
1 egg

48 miniature chocolate covered peanut butter cups;
unwrapped
Mini muffin tins

Preheat oven to 350°. Combine water, brownie mix, oil and egg. Beat well with a spoon. Fill paper lined mini muffin cups about half full. Press one peanut butter cup into batter in each cup. Bake 15 to 20 minutes or until brownie is set. Cool completely. Yield 40 to 48 pieces.

A LaRosa family favorite; Bryan, Andrew, Alison and Jenna can't wait for these to come out of the oven. My David loves them. Cathy shared her recipe at our Christmas Cookie exchange.

CARAMEL FILLED CHOCOLATE COOKIES
Cathy LaRosa

1 cup butter, softened
1 cup white sugar
1 cup packed brown sugar
2 eggs
2 teaspoons vanilla extract
2¼ cups all-purpose flour

1 teaspoon baking soda
¾ cup unsweetened cocoa powder
1 cup chopped walnuts
1 tablespoon white sugar
48 chocolate covered caramel candies (Rolos®),
unwrapped

Beat butter or margarine until creamy. Gradually add sugars, beat well. Add eggs and vanilla, beat well. Combine flour, baking soda and cocoa. Gradually add to butter mixture, beating well. Stir in ½ cup nuts (optional). Cover and chill at least 2 hours. Preheat oven to 375°. Combine remaining ½ cup nuts with the 1 tablespoon sugar. Divide the dough into 4 parts. Work with one part at a time leaving the rest in the refrigerator. Divide each part into 12 pieces. Quickly press each piece of dough around a chocolate covered caramel (Rolo). Roll into ball. Dip one side into sugar. Place sugar side up 2 inches apart on baking sheets. Bake for 8 minutes. Let cool one minute. Remove to wire rack and cool completely.

The LaRosa's L-R: Andrew, Alison, Jenna and Bryan

CAVATOONAS -FRUTTA DI CECI
Mary DeSalvatore

Filling:

1 can chick peas, pureed and drained (you can use chestnuts if you want)
1 package (¼ pound) sweet cooking chocolate, grated
¼ cup espresso coffee
Dash salt
¼ teaspoon cinnamon

2 tablespoon citron, or currants, or lemon rind
½ teaspoon vanilla
½ cup finely chopped toasted almond or nuts or your choice
½ cup honey

Dough:

4 cups sifted flour
2 eggs
⅓ cup oil

Dash salt
½ cup plus 2 tablespoons water

Coating:

1 cup honey
½ cup water

Finely chopped nuts, powdered sugar

Drain the chick peas. Puree the chick peas. Add chocolate, espresso, salt, cinnamon, currants, vanilla, ½ cup nuts and honey. Mix well. Cook over boiling water in a double boiler, stirring occasionally, for 10 minutes or until mixture becomes sticky. Remove from heat and cool. Place flour in Kitchen Aid® with a dough hook. Add eggs, oil, salt, and ½ cup of water. Process to make a soft dough. Add more water if needed, but dough should not be sticky. Divide dough into three equal parts. Roll each part out thin and cut into 2-inch circles. Place 1 heaping tablespoon of the filling in center of each circle. Moisten edges of pastry with water, fold over and seal with the tines of a fork. Fry in 2½-inches of hot oil at 400° for about 30 seconds or until pastries are golden brown. Drain and cool. Makes about 30.

Coating:

Heat honey and the ½ cup water to a rolling boil in a small saucepan. Drop pastries in a few at a time into the honey mixture and coat thoroughly about 20 seconds. Drain on a cake rack. Sprinkle pastries with chopped nuts. Cool and dust lightly with powdered sugar. Store pastries in loosely covered container. They will keep at least five weeks. If they soften in storage, heat them in a slow oven 250° for a few minutes.

This recipe is Rosemary Grimaldi's mother's recipe. It is almost exactly the same as Maria Di Pier's recipe. Maria used espresso in hers so I added it to Mary's recipe. Basically, they're the same, Maria just used powered sugar and not honey on top. In her dough she used one tablespoon of oil and sugar for each egg. She used 12 eggs, for 2 cans of chick peas.

CHOCOLATE CHIP COFFEE COOKIES
Elise Feiner

2¼ cups flour
1 teaspoon salt
1 teaspoon baking soda
¼ teaspoon fresh ground nutmeg
1 teaspoon cinnamon
½ pound butter
1 cup light brown sugar
½ cup sugar

2 tablespoons Hershey® chocolate syrup
1½ teaspoons vanilla
2 eggs
1½ teaspoons mocha or instant coffee mixed with 2 tablespoons hot water
1 (12 ounce) package chocolate chips
1 (6 ounce) package chocolate chips
1½ cups chopped walnuts

Preheat the oven to 350°. Mix flour, salt, baking soda, nutmeg and cinnamon and put aside. In mixer, beat butter, sugars, chocolate syrup, and vanilla until smooth. Add eggs one at a time; beat until smooth, approximately 5 minutes. Add dry ingredients, coffee mixture, chocolate chips, and nuts and mix by hand with wooden spoon until mixed. Drop on baking sheet by rounded teaspoons, about 2-inches apart, and bake for 12 to 14 minutes. Makes 36 cookies.

CHOCO-NUT DAINTIES
Maria Trainor

2¼ cups flour, sifted
½ teaspoon salt
1½ sticks margarine, softened
¾ cup sugar
1 egg

1½ teaspoons vanilla
1 (6 ounce) package mini chocolate chips
2 cups finely chopped walnuts
¼ cup margarine
1 (12 ounce) package chocolate chips for melting

Preheat oven to 350°. Sift flour and salt onto waxed paper. Beat together margarine, sugar, egg and vanilla in a large bowl until well mixed. Blend in flour mixture. Stir in chocolate pieces (6 ounce package.) Shape dough on lightly floured surface into logs (2 x ½-inch) Place on an ungreased cookie sheet. Bake at 350° for 12 to 15 minutes, or until cookies are set. Cool on wire racks. Dips ends of cookies into chocolate coating; roll ends in chopped nuts. Place on waxed paper until set. Makes about 4½ dozen cookies.

Chocolate coating: Melt together the 12 ounce package of chocolate chips and ¼ cup margarine in the top of a double boiler over hot water, stir until blended and smooth. If the mixture is too thick, add more margarine, one tablespoon at a time until it is a good consistency.

Maria brought these cookies to our Christmas cookie exchange. What a wonderful aroma fills the house when these are in the oven...Maria's house is a houseful of kids and a houseful of love.

Jonathan Trainor and Lauren Feiner

CHOCOLATE BUTTER CRUNCH SQUARES
Ann D'Amico

40-50 (unsalted tops) Saltine Crackers
2 sticks butter
1 cup light brown sugar

1½ teaspoons vanilla
2 cups mini chocolate chips
1 cup finely chopped pecans

Grease a 12 x 17-inch cookie sheet with PAM®. Place Saltines face up on the cookie sheet, making them fit snuggly without overlapping (you may have to break some in half.) Preheat oven to 375°. In a saucepan combine butter and brown sugar. Once melted, simmer three minutes, stirring occasionally. Remove from heat, stir in vanilla and pour over the Saltines, spreading evenly. Bake 5 minutes. Be very careful and watch them to make sure they don't burn. Bake on top rack of oven. Remove from oven, fix crackers (they will have shifted a bit) and press them down slightly. Pour chips over the top and once they are melted, spread chocolate evenly and sprinkle with nuts. Shake cookie sheet back and forth to evenly distribute nuts. Then with a sharp knife, score surface into saltine sized squares. Refrigerate for 20 minutes. Once cooled, cut into squares. Makes 40 to 50.

This recipe came from my cousin Ann, who could put Martha Stewart to shame, and she's much nicer too! All joking aside, she is one of the best cooks, and does a ton of gourmet parties in Long Island. Ann should be a professional caterer. Her touches are just beautiful and her presentations wonderful.

CHOCOLATE COOKIES
Elise Feiner

2½ flour
1 teaspoon baking powder
½ teaspoon baking soda
¾ teaspoon salt
1 teaspoon cinnamon
½ teaspoon ground cloves
10 tablespoons unsalted butter, softened
½ cup sugar
½ cup dark brown sugar

1 egg
1 egg yolk
¼ cup molasses
1 teaspoon vanilla
1 (4 ounce) bar bittersweet or semisweet chocolate bar chopped into large chunks or store bought chocolate chunks
Confectioners' sugar

Preheat oven to 350°. Place parchment paper on two cookie sheets. Sift the flour baking powder, baking soda, salt, cinnamon and cloves together, and set aside. With a mixer, beat the butter, ¼ cup sugar, and brown sugar together until light and fluffy (about 6 minutes). Add the egg and the egg yolk; mix. Add the molasses and vanilla and mix again. Put the mixer on low and add the dry ingredients in small amounts until combined. Fold in chocolate. Shape in balls. Roll in sugar. Place on baking sheets and press with a fork to flatten. Bake until light brown about 14 minutes. Place on a wire rack to cool. Repeat with the remaining dough.

Jody Feiner then…

Jody Feiner now…

CHOCOLATE CHIP COOKIES ESPRESSO
Elise Feiner

½ cup unsalted butter, softened
1 cup brown sugar
3 tablespoons granulated sugar
1 egg
½ teaspoons vanilla extract
½ teaspoon baking soda

½ teaspoon baking powder
½ teaspoon salt
1¾ cups flour
1½ teaspoons instant espresso coffee granules, crushed fine
1 (6 ounce) package semisweet chocolate chips

Cream the butter with the sugars until fluffy. Beat in the egg, and vanilla extract. Combine the dry ingredients and beat into the butter mixture. Stir in the chocolate chips. Drop by large spoonfuls onto a greased cookie sheet. Bake 375° for 8 to 10 minutes or for a crisp cookie 10 to 12 minutes.

PIGNOLI DE BISCOTTI
Elise Feiner

1½ cups sugar
1 tablespoon prepared almond paste
4 eggs
⅛ teaspoon salt
2 cups all-purpose flour

½ teaspoon baking powder
2 teaspoons almond extract
½ cup pine nuts
¼ cup confectioners' sugar

Preheat the oven 350°. Butter and flour two cookie sheets; set aside. Put enough water in the bottom of a double boiler so there is just enough water on the bottom of the pot, but not high enough so that the top pot is touching the water. Add the sugar, almond paste, eggs and salt to the top pan. Barely bring the water to simmer and with a hand mixer beat the mixture until frothy and feels lukewarm; make sure the water only heats to lukewarm or the eggs will curdle when they are beaten.

Remove the top pan from the double boiler and continue to beat for another o until the mixture is cool. Transfer the mixture to a bowl. Sift the flour and baking powder together and add to the egg mixture along with the almond extract. Mix the batter well; it will look like cake batter. Drop by teaspoonfuls of batter onto the cookie sheets, spacing 1-inch apart as the batter spreads. Sprinkle each cookie with a few pine nuts dust each cookie with a little confectioners' sugar. Let stand about 5 minutes before baking. Bake the cookies on the middle rack for about 10 minutes or until the edges begin to turn golden brown. The cookies **should** be a pale color. **Don't be in a hurry to take the cookies off the cookie sheet or they will crack.** Let cool for at least 5 to 10 minutes before removing to a wire rack. Makes about 48 cookies.

Top L-R: Elise and Marc Feiner
Bottom L-R: Steven Feiner and Christina Malecki

Marc A Feiner, M.D. Then (above)
Now (below)

Marc and Elise Feiner - 1979

CHOCOLATE CHIP COOKIES
Elise Feiner

⅔ cup Butter Flavored Crisco®
⅔ cup butter, softened
1 cup granulated sugar
1 cup brown sugar
2 eggs
2 teaspoons vanilla

3 cups flour
1 teaspoon baking soda
1 teaspoon salt
1 cup chopped nuts (optional)
1 (12 ounce) bag chocolate chips

Preheat oven to 375°. Thoroughly blend the shortening, butter, sugars, eggs and vanilla. Blend in remaining ingredients. Drop by rounded teaspoonfuls or use a cookie scoop, onto an ungreased cookie sheet. Bake 8 to 10 minutes until light brown. Cool slightly before removing from baking sheet. Makes about 7 dozen.

This is a basic chocolate chip cookie recipe. I used to make these all the time until I found the recipe for what is now called The Feiner Kids Favorite Oatmeal Chocolate Chip Cookie (See Index).

Clockwise from Top: Betty, Jerry, Marc, and Ivan Feiner

Philip Feiner - Uncle "Pinky"

CHOCOLATE FIG COOKIES
Sadie Koury

¼ cup butter (half a stick)
¼ cup cocoa
½ box confectioners' sugar
½ teaspoon vanilla

¼ cup milk
2 packages of Fig Newtons®
Coarsely chopped nuts (whatever kind you like)

Melt butter, add cocoa. Add sugar, vanilla, and milk and beat until smooth. Cut the Fig Newton's in half lengthwise, and dip each cookie in the chocolate mixture. Then, roll in coarsely chopped nuts. Place on wax paper on a cookie sheet and refrigerate overnight. Makes approximately 1½ to 2 packages of Fig Newton's. If chocolate gets to thick while using, keep thinning it with a little milk.

Billy Koury's Aunt Sadie gave me this recipe. We were at the Koury's for a family party and she had brought them over. I didn't even like Fig Newton's, but these were so good. She was nice enough to share this recipe. These are great Christmas cookies, or for a party cookie tray.

OATMEAL CHOCOLATE CHIP COOKIES - THE FEINER KIDS FAVORITE
Elise Feiner

1½ cups all-purpose flour (Gold Medal®)
1 teaspoon baking soda
1 teaspoon salt
1 cup vegetable shortening (I use 1 stick of butter flavored Crisco®)
¾ cup light brown sugar, packed (I use Brownulated)

¾ cup granulated sugar
2 eggs
1 teaspoon hot water
1 teaspoon vanilla
2 cups Quaker® Instant Rolled Oats
1 (12 ounce) package Nestles® mini chocolate chips

Preheat oven to 375°. Butter 2 baking sheets unless you are using non stick cookie sheets. Mix flour, salt and baking soda in a bowl and set aside. In a bowl with mixer at medium speed beat shortening until smooth, 1 minute. Beat in sugars, ½ cup at a time, until fluffy. Reduce speed to low. Beat in eggs one at a time, until just combined. Beat in hot water, and then add the flour mixture, until just combined. Add vanilla. Beat in chips and oatmeal until combined. Drop by rounded teaspoonfuls about 2-inches apart onto baking sheets. Bake in batches 8 to 10 minutes, or until lightly browned around the edges. Do not overcook, Lauren, because you like everything burned! Cool on pans on rack 1 minute. Remove from sheets, and cool on racks. Makes 6 dozen. I use a large cookie scoop to make the cookies uniform size and bake them 14 minutes, 7 on the top rack, 7 minutes on the bottom rack.

I found this recipe in a women's magazine. It was sent in by a reader telling of a story of a cookie jar that had been in her family for generations. It was her Aunt Mary's and it was always filled with these cookies. She inherited the jar and always filled it with her aunt's cookies. One day her cousin came over and saw his mother's jar and became very emotional. She gave the jar and the recipe back to her cousin and shared it with all of us. I just love this story, it is so full of warmth and love and family unity. This has now has become our family's favorite as well.

L-R: David, Steven, and Jeffrey Feiner
In front: Lauren Feiner

COCONUT HEAPS (MACAROONS)
Elise Feiner

2 eggs at room temperature
½ cup sugar
3 tablespoons butter, melted and cooled

3⅓ cups coconut, grated or flaked
3 (1 ounce) squares semisweet chocolate, melted

Preheat oven to 375°. Grease and flour 2 cookie sheets or use Bakers Joy if you are not using Teflon cookie sheets. In a large mixing bowl (use Kitchen Aid if you have one) beat eggs until light. Gradually add sugar, beating until mixture is thick and sugar is dissolved. Beat in melted butter (you can melt the butter in a glass dish in the microwave by placing it in the microwave for a few seconds). With a rubber spatula, fold in the grated coconut. Let stand 10 minutes. Drop by teaspoonfuls onto the cookie sheets. Bake 15 to 20 minutes until the tops are golden brown. Cool on wire racks. Drizzle the tops with the melted chocolate (melt in the top of a double boiler or in a glass dish in the microwave - do it one minute at a time stirring after every additional minute) by using a tablespoon. Makes 4 dozen cookies, about 50 calories each.

I found this recipe when I was in elementary school. I have been making them for about 40 years. They are fast and easy to make and I always try to make some for my Christmas cookie tray. This was a favorite of my father's and I always think of him when I make them.

CHOCOLATE PEPPER COOKIES
Lucy Massimiano

4 cups flour
1 cup sugar
½ cup cocoa
1 teaspoon baking powder
¼ - ½ teaspoon black pepper
½ teaspoon baking soda

½ teaspoon cinnamon
½ teaspoon ground cloves
½ teaspoon salt
½ cup butter, melted
1 cup milk
2-4 (2 ounce shot glass) shots of whiskey

Mix the dry ingredients together for 2 minutes. Add the butter, milk, and whiskey. Knead well. Chill for about 1 hour. Roll into small balls the size of a walnut. Bake at 375° on a greased cookie sheet for 12 to 15 minutes. Roll the balls in the frosting while warm, but not hot.

Frosting:
1 box confectioners' sugar
1 tablespoon oil

4 tablespoons cocoa

This is another cookie recipe of Cousin Lucy Massimiano from Auburn.

CHOCOLATE CRANBERRY COOKIES
Elise Feiner

1 cup hazelnuts or pecans, chopped
1 package extra large semisweet chocolate morsels,
½ cup sun-dried cranberries
1 cup sugar
1 cup unsalted butter softened
1 (3 ounce) package cream cheese softened
1 egg
2 tablespoons milk

2 ounces unsweetened chocolate, melted
1½ teaspoons vanilla
2 cups plus 2 tablespoons flour
½ teaspoon baking powder
½ teaspoon salt
¼ cup Dutch processed cocoa
1 cup marshmallow Fluff®

Preheat oven to 325°. Spread nuts on an ungreased cookie sheet and roast for 7 to 12 minutes, or until they are lightly browned and some skins have loosened. Set aside to cool. Grease 2 cookie sheets. In a large bowl, combine the chocolate chips, cranberries, and cooled nuts, set aside. In another large bowl, beat together the butter, sugar, cream cheese, and eggs until very smooth and creamy. Beat in the milk, melted chocolate, and vanilla. Sift together the flour, salt, baking powder and cocoa, then add to butter mixture. Blend in the Marshmallow cream, stirring thoroughly until well combined. Add the chips, cranberries, and nuts. Stir until well mixed. Batter will be thick. Using a ¼ cup measure or a 4 tablespoon ice cream scoop, measure out batter and place 2-inches apart on cookie sheets, putting no more than 6 cookies per sheet. Bake 13 to 17 minutes, until puffed and cooked through. Cool one minute on sheets; transfer to wire racks to cool completely. Makes 24.

MADELEINES
Elise Feiner

4 eggs, at room temperature
1½ cups sugar
1 heaping teaspoon finely grated lemon zest
1 teaspoon vanilla

2 cups flour, sifted
1½ cups clarified sweet butter
Confectioners' sugar to sprinkle

Melt four sticks of butter over low heat and continue until foam disappears from the top and light brown sediment is in the bottom of the pan. Pour off the clear butter and measure 1½ cups of clarified butter. Let cool; store any leftover butter in the refrigerator. Mix eggs, sugar and lemon zest in the top of a double boiler. Place over 1 to 2 inches of hot water. When the mixture starts to feel warm remove and start beating at high speed until they are light and fluffy and tripled in bulk. It will look like whipped cream. Add vanilla. Carefully, fold in the flour followed by the melted cooled butter. Fill well buttered Madeleine mold ⅔ full. Bake 10 minutes at 425° or until golden. Rebutter pan before refilling.

CHOCOLATE LOGS
Cyndi Koury

Dough:
2 sticks soft margarine or butter
1 (8 ounce) package of cream cheese, at room temperature

3 cups flour

Cream together the margarine and cream cheese. Mix in the flour and chill.

Filling:
1 (12 ounce) package chocolate chips
1 can sweetened condensed milk

1 cup chopped walnuts

Cook chips and condensed milk until melted, add chopped walnuts and remove from heat and cool. Divide dough in half and roll into large rectangle (approximately 10 x 14-inch). Spread half of filling and roll lengthwise into a jellyroll. Repeat. Place on a baking sheet. Bake 350° for 20 minutes. Cool and slice.

This recipe is one of the famous cookies from the Cyndi Koury "Cookie Tray" collection. It the one most requested by the Feiner kids who have had the pleasure of sampling such wonderful delights from her kitchen...

BLACK BOTTOM COOKIES
Lucy Massimiano

3 cups flour
2 cups sugar
½ cup cocoa
2 teaspoons baking soda
1 teaspoon salt
2 cups water
2 tablespoons white vinegar
1 package (8 ounces) cream cheese, softened

1 cup vegetable oil
2 teaspoons vanilla
1 egg
⅓ cup sugar
½ teaspoon salt
1 (6 ounce) bag mini-chocolate chips

Preheat oven to 350°. Mix the flour with the 2 cups sugar, cocoa, baking soda, and 1 teaspoon of salt. Add in the water, vinegar, oil, and vanilla. Mix well. Set aside. In a separate bowl, mix the cream cheese, egg, ⅓ cup sugar, and ½ teaspoon of salt together. Beat until creamy. Fold in the mini chips. Using the batter from the first bowl, fill a lined cupcake tin (I like mini muffin lined tins) half full. Add 1 teaspoon of the filling to each tin. Bake 15 to 18 minutes. If you are using mini tins; you may have to adjust your cooking time.

VIENNA COOKIES
Hilda Lanier

½ cup butter
2 tablespoons sugar
1 teaspoon vanilla

1 cup finely chopped nuts
1 cup cake flour
Confectioners' Sugar

Preheat oven to 350°. Cream together the butter, vanilla, and the sugar. Add the finely chopped nuts and flour a little at a time until well mixed. Grease a cookie sheet or spray with PAM®. Take rounded teaspoonfuls of cookie mixtures and roll into little round cookies in the palm of your hand. Put on cookie sheets. Bake at 350° for 20 minutes. While hot, roll in confectioners' sugar. When cool, roll in confectioners' sugar again. Hilda usually doubles this recipe.

This is Uncle Jorge Ferreiro's sister Hilda's recipe. Carmen says they are delicious!

"The weak can never forgive. Forgiveness is the attribute of the strong."
-Mohandas Ghandi

PORTUGUESE SIGH COOKIES
Elise Feiner

1 cup ground almonds
½ cup confectioners' sugar
⅛ teaspoon salt

2 egg whites
1 teaspoon vanilla extract
¼ teaspoon almond extract

Preheat the oven to 325°. Line 2 cookie sheets with parchment paper or foil. In a small bowl, mix the ground almonds, sugar, together. Add salt to the egg white and beat until stiff. Combine with the sugar mixture. Fold in the extracts. Drop from a teaspoon 1-inch apart onto a well greased cookie sheet, or pipe from ¾-inch plain pastry tube 1½-inches apart. Bake at 325° for 15 minutes or until lightly browned. Transfer on the parchment paper to a wire rack to cool. Makes 24.

I made these for a school project in the fourth grade; studying foods of the world.

L-R: Kevin. Marc and Ivan Feiner
Speak no evil, See no evil, Hear no evil!
Like fathers ....

Hear no evil the next generation…
L-R: Jody, Lauren and Abby Feiner
.............Like daughters

CHOCOLATE PISTACHIO COOKIES
Elise Feiner

1 cup butter
⅔ cup packed brown sugar
1 teaspoon vanilla
1 egg, beaten
2¼ cups all purpose flour

¼ cup unsweetened cocoa
¾ cup finely chopped pistachio nuts
¼ cup semisweet chocolate pieces
1 tablespoon shortening
½ cup finely ground pistachio nuts

In a heavy saucepan combine the butter and the brown sugar. Cook over low heat, stirring frequently until the butter is melted. Remove from the heat, stir in vanilla. Cool 15 minutes. Stir in egg, flour and cocoa until just combined. Stir in the ¾ cup finely chopped pistachios. Divide the dough in half. Cover and chill in the refrigerator about 30 minutes or until dough is easy to handle. On a lightly floured board, roll half of the dough at a time into ¼-inch thickness. Using a 2-inch heart shaped or round cookie cutter, cut out cookies. Reroll trimmings as necessary to make about 48 cookies. Place the cookies 1 inch apart on an ungreased cookie sheet. Bake at 350° about 9 minutes, or until edges are firm. Transfer to a wire rack to cool. In a heavy saucepan, heat and stir the chocolate pieces and shortening over low heat until melted. Remove from heat. Dip half of each cookie into chocolate mixture; roll edges of the cookie in ground pistachio nuts.

I always do this at Christmas because it has my two favorite things, chocolate and pistachio nuts. Yummy! I remember sending David on a wild goose chase all over Buffalo for shelled pistachios!

"Save the apple for the bite."
-Elizabeth Maida

EASY ROLLED COOKIE DOUGH
Elise Feiner

1½ cups sugar
1 pound of butter
5½ cups flour

3 teaspoons vanilla
1 teaspoon baking powder
3 large eggs

Cream the butter and sugar together. Beat in the eggs and vanilla. Sift the flour and baking powder together; gradually add to the creamed mixture. If the texture is too soft, batter can be refrigerated. Roll out on a lightly floured board to desired thickness. Use cookie cutters to cut your cookies. Place on an ungreased cookie sheet and bake at 400°10 to 12 minutes or until delicately browned. Decorate as desired when cooled.

This makes a large batch so you can cut it in half.

ANN'S PIGNOLI COOKIES
Ann D'Amico

3 cups (about 20 ounces) blanched slivered almonds (don't pack down)
1½ cups sugar

⅓ cup plus 1 tablespoon egg whites (about 3-4 eggs)
1 teaspoon almond extract

For Top of Cookies:

2-3 egg whites

3 cups pine nuts (about 10 ounces)

Preheat the oven to 325°. Put your oven racks on the top two spaces. Line your cookies sheets with parchment paper. **Do not use ungreased pans or greased pans**. You must use parchment paper for these cookies. Place the almonds in a food processor and process (use metal chopping blade) for about 1 minute. Add the sugar ; process for another 15 seconds or so. Add the egg whites and almond extract; process until the paste sticks around the blade. Scrape down the sides and corners of the food processor. Process again until a stiff dough forms (like a marzipan consistency) something you can shape, about 5 seconds. If the mixture is crumbly, add a drop of two or water until the consistency desired is reached. Use about 2 tablespoons of paste for each cookie; roll into a ball. Place the cookies about 1½-inches apart. Beat the remaining 2-3 egg whites lightly. Roll each cookie into the egg whites and them into the pine nuts. Press them lightly with your fingers to flatten them a little so they are about 1-inch wide. Bake until golden brown about 20 to 25 minutes, rotating them halfway through the cooking time. **Don't over bake!** Let them cool completely before removing them from the parchment paper. Makes about 2 dozen 2-inch cookies.

Ann's made a ton of Pignoli cookies for Aunt Flo's 90th birthday party.

Aunt Flo then…

L-R: Flo Avella and great-niece Joan Calabrese at her 90th Birthday Party. My cousin Joan is a very talented writer and wrote a beautiful tribute to our Aunt Flo on her birthday.

432

CHOW MEIN-NOODLE HAYSTACKS
Elise Feiner

2 ounces spaghetti or 5 ounces packaged fried chow mien noodles
1 tablespoon vegetable oil, plus oil for frying

5 ounces semisweet or bittersweet chocolate
¼ cup unsweetened coconut flakes, toasted
½ cup unsalted roasted peanuts, coarsely chopped

In a large pot of boiling water, cook the spaghetti until tender. Drain well, and then toss with 1 teaspoon of vegetable oil to prevent sticking. In a skillet or electric fryer, heat 1-inch of oil to 365°. Working in batches of 3 or 4 tangled strands; fry the spaghetti until golden brown. Let the spaghetti intertwine to form interesting shapes. Drain on paper towels. Break the spaghetti or chow mien noodles into pieces no larger than 1-inch long. In a completely dry bowl or in the top of a double boiler set over barely simmering water, melt the chocolate. Mix in the noodles, coconut, and peanuts. Drop walnut size haystacks of the mixture on a cookie sheet and refrigerate for 30 minutes to set. Served chilled.

Rocky Road Chow Mien-Noodle Haystacks:
1 recipe chow mien-noodle haystacks, stir in 1 cup-2 cups mini marshmallows

White-Chocolate Chow Mien-Noodle Haystacks:
Substitute white chocolate for the semisweet chocolate and chopped pecans for the peanuts in the original chow mien-noodle haystacks recipe.

These cookies have been around for years, everyone has their own version.

The Freedoff's...
L-R: David, Kathy, Aunt Adele, Barbara, and Uncle Alvin

CHRISTMAS KISSES
Elise Feiner

¾ cup Crisco®
½ cup granulated sugar
¼ cup brown sugar
1 egg
2 teaspoon vanilla
½ teaspoon almond extract

1¾ cups flour
½ teaspoon baking powder
¼ teaspoon salt
½ cups very finely chopped or ground blanched almonds or pecans
4 dozen Hershey® Kisses, unwrapped

Preheat oven to 350°. Using an electric mixer, cream Crisco, and sugars, until fluffy. Add the egg, vanilla and almond extracts; beat well. Add the flour, baking powder, salt and nuts; mix until well blended. Roll the dough into 1-inch balls. Press a kiss into each ball making sure it is completely covered by the dough. Bake 12 minutes on an ungreased cookie sheet. Cool on wire racks. Makes 3½ to 4 dozen cookies. You can decorate by drawing bows and flowers on the top with the icing in the tubes and then putting on some nonpareils.

I started to make these Christmas favorites when Mike and Philly were babies, and now they have babies of their own..

CHOCOLATE FUDGE COOKIES
Ann D'Amico

2 cups all-purpose flour
2 teaspoons baking powder
5 ounces unsweetened baking chocolate
1 stick unsalted butter
4 large eggs
Pinch of salt

1 cup dark brown sugar, firmly packed
1 cup granulated sugar
1 tablespoon dark rum
Confectioners' sugar
Several cookie sheets lines with parchment paper or foil

Mix the flour and baking powder together and set aside. In the top of a double boiler, combine the chocolate and the butter, stirring occasionally until melted. In a large bowl, whisk eggs with salt. Then whisk in the both sugars. Add chocolate mixture, then the rum. Stir in the flour mix to form a soft dough. Scrape the dough onto a piece of plastic wrap and wrap tightly. Chill for 2 hours. Preheat oven to 350° and set the racks on the upper and lower thirds of the oven. Flour your hands and roll the chilled dough into 2 teaspoon balls. Roll each ball in confectioner's sugar and place 2 to 3 inches apart on the prepared cookie sheets. Bake about 12 minutes. Cool pans on a rack before removing cookies from the pan. Store cookies between sheets of waxed paper in a tin or other air tight container. Makes 60.

CREAM CHEESE LOGS
Clementina Mainella

½ cup butter, softened
4 ounce package cream cheese, softened
1 teaspoon vanilla extract
1¾ cups flour

1 tablespoon sugar
Dash salt
1 cup pecans, finely chopped
Confectioners' sugar

In a large mixing bowl, cream the butter and cream cheese. Beat in the vanilla. In a separate bowl, combine the flour, sugar and salt; gradually add to the cream cheese mixture. Stir in the pecans. The dough will be the consistency of crumbs. Shape into 2 inch logs. Place 2 inches apart on ungreased cookie sheets. Bake 375° for 12 to 14 minutes. While the cookies are still warm, roll them in confectioners' sugar. Cool on wire racks. Makes 1½ to 2 dozen.

This was a recipe of my grandmother's.

FENNEL SEED HOLIDAY COOKIES
Josephine Mainella

1 cup butter, softened
1½ cups sugar
1½-2 teaspoons fennel seeds
1 teaspoon grated lemon zest
2 tablespoons anisette

2 cups flour
1 teaspoon baking powder
½ teaspoon salt
½ cup chopped pistachios

In a large mixing bowl, cream butter and sugar until light and fluffy. Add fennel seeds, lemon zest, and anisette; mix well. In a small bowl, combine flour, baking powder and salt. Gradually add the flour mixture and nuts to the creamed mixture to make a stiff dough. Refrigerate at least 30 minutes. Preheat oven to 350°. Roll dough into ¾-inch balls. Place on an ungreased cookie sheet. Bake 10 to 12 minutes, until lightly browned. Cool 5 minutes on cookie sheet. Transfer to wire rack to cool completely. Makes 7 dozen.

My grandmother
Clementina Mainella
A woman way ahead of
her time...
She set the standards for
all the women in the
Mainella gene pool!

GEORGE WASHINGTON COOKIES
Elise Feiner

1½ cups flour
½ cup unsweetened cocoa
½ cup butter
1 cup sugar
¼ teaspoon baking soda
¼ teaspoon baking powder

¼ teaspoon salt
1 egg
1½ teaspoons vanilla
48 undrained maraschino cherries
1 cup semisweet chocolate pieces
½ cup sweetened condensed milk

Combine the flour and cocoa powder; set aside. In a medium mixing bowl, beat the butter until softened. Add the sugar, baking soda, baking powder, and salt. Beat until combined. Beat in the egg and vanilla. Gradually beat in the flour mix. Shape into 1-inch balls.
    Place 2-inches apart on ungreased cookie sheet. Press down the center of each cookie with your thumb. Drain the cherries, saving the liquid. Place a cherry in the center of each cookie. In a heavy saucepan combine the chocolate pieces and milk over low heat until the chocolate is melted; stir in 4 teaspoons of the saved cherry juice. Spoon 1 teaspoon of frosting over each cherry. Thin with additional cherry juice if necessary. Bake in a 350° oven about 10 minutes or until edges are firm. Cool on cookie sheet for about 1 minute, and then transfer to a wire rack. Makes about 48.

These are delicious, like eating a box of chocolate covered cherries!

GOLDEN MACAROONS
Elise Feiner

2½ cups (about 7 ounces) flaked sweetened coconut
2 cups unsweetened coconut (health food store) finely shredded
1 cup sugar
3 tablespoons flour

¼ teaspoon salt
4 egg whites
1 tablespoon honey
1 teaspoon vanilla

In a large bowl, combine flaked and shredded coconut until evenly mixed. (Flaked coconut should be broken into separate flakes with only a few small clumps present.) In a medium mixing bowl combine sugar, flour, and salt. Add egg whites, honey and vanilla. Whisk rapidly until smooth. Pour sugar and egg white mixture over the coconut mixture. Stir with a wooden spoon, and then use hands to continue to blend until evenly mixed. Cover with plastic wrap; chill for 30 minutes. Preheat oven to 300°. Line a large cookie sheet with baking parchment. Drop rounded tablespoons of macaroon batter onto cookie sheets about 2-inches apart. Gently pinch mounds into triangle shape. Bake 17 to 19 minutes or until golden brown. Remove from oven. Transfer macaroons immediately to a cooling rack. Makes 24.

Chocolate Lovers Macaroons:

Using above mixture, pack a tablespoon with macaroon dough. Transfer to parchment sheet and press gently to form flattened mounds. Bake at 300° for 20 to 22 minutes. Cool. In a small saucepan, heat ¾ cup heavy cream to near boiling; remove from heat.
    Add 6 ounces chopped semisweet chocolate. Let stand 5 minutes, then whisk until smooth. Cool completely. Make a sandwich by spooning a mound of chocolate onto the bottom of one macaroon. Top with a second macaroon, pressing sandwich together gently, similar to a sandwich cookie.

Right Side: Lauren Feiner and
her Poppy Jerry Feiner

Lauren loves this picture of her
and her Poppy

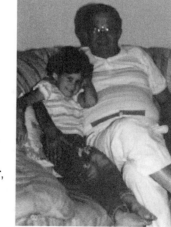

Roosevelt Hospital Nursing School
Graduation -1973
L-R: Katherine Avella, Elise Avella Feiner,
Samuel Avella

HELLO DOLLY'S
Marcia Archibald

⅓ cup sweet butter, melted
1 cup of graham cracker crumbs
1 (12 ounce) bag chocolate chips
1 cup chopped nuts

1 (12 ounce) bag butterscotch morsels
1 bag of shredded coconut
1 (15 ounce) can condensed milk

Preheat oven to 350°. Melt the butter and place it into a 9 x 13-inch pan. Sprinkle the graham cracker crumbs evenly over the melted butter. Next sprinkle the following layers in order: chocolate chips, nuts, butterscotch pieces, coconut. Pour one can of condensed milk over the top. Bake 30 minutes until the coconut is lightly browned on the top. Cool and then cut into squares.

These cookies are known by many names. Marcia made them for our Christmas Cookie Exchange, and shared the recipe. Grandpa Sam used to love a cookie that was very similar to these because he loved the flavor of butterscotch.

Marcia Archibald and Gordon Archibald M.D. Marcia is an attorney and realtor and Gordon is a radiologist in town. He is also a gourmet cook.

One of our Cookie Exchanges… Left side in rear Joanna Basile Right side back to front: Maria Trainor, Cathy Sleeper holding Peter, and Eileen Furino

KOURABIETHES
Athena Avramidis

1 pound sweet butter (4 sticks)
1 egg yolk
½ cup confectioners' sugar, plus additional for the coating
½ cup brandy

½ cup corn oil
¾ cup almonds ROASTED (it makes a difference), chopped
4 cups flour, more if needed
1 teaspoon vanilla

Preheat the oven to 350°. Cream the butter until light and fluffy. Add the rest of the ingredients, except the nuts. Knead lightly, add the almonds, and add more flour until it is not sticking to the fingers. Shaped into flattened balls or cut with a cookie cutter into shapes.
Place on a greased cookie sheet. Bake 15 to 20 minutes or until light brown. As they are baking, sift some confectionery sugar on to a platter. As the cookies come out of the oven place them on top of the sugar, then sprinkle the top of the cookies very generously with the remaining powdered sugar. They should be fully coated.

This is a traditional Christmas cookie in Greece. I think Athena's are the best of all. She generously shared her family's recipe with me.

MANDELBROT
Barbara Schwartz

1 cup oil
1 cup sugar
2 eggs
1 teaspoon baking powder

2 teaspoon vanilla extract
¾ cup chopped walnuts
1 (6 ounce) bag chocolate chips
3 cups flour

Mix everything together but the flour. Then add the flour and mix into a dough. Shape the dough into three oval shaped loafs and bake on a greased cookie sheet at 350° for 30 minutes. Take out of the oven and slice on an angle when warm and let cool.

Barbara is a wealth of knowledge for Jewish recipes. This is a very traditional Jewish cookie.

GRANDMA RUTH'S COOKIES
Ruth Schwartz

1½ sticks margarine
2½ cups flour
1 cup sugar
1 teaspoon vanilla

1 teaspoon baking powder
3 eggs
Pinch of salt

Preheat oven to 350°. Beat all the ingredient together and drop on to cookie sheets. Bake for 20 minutes. You can also add chopped nuts or chocolate chips for variety. These can also be made for diabetics by substituting 16 packets of sweet 'n low for the sugar.

This is the recipe for Grandma Ruth's cookies (Uncle Stuart's mother). She always made them for her family. Everybody loved them. When she passed away, Aunt Barbara found her cookbook and these were listed as "My Cookies."

MACADAMIA MACAROONS
Betty Saracino

2½ cup shredded coconut
1 cup unsalted macadamia nuts, finely chopped
1 (14 ounce) can condensed milk
1 teaspoon vanilla

20 saltine crackers, finely crushed
2 egg whites
1 (6 ounce) package chocolate chips, chopped and melted
PAM® cooking spray

Preheat oven to 350°. Place coconut and macadamia nuts on a 15 x 9½ x ½-inch cookie sheet. Bake until lightly roasted, about 10 minutes, stirring frequently. Let cool. In a large bowl, combine milk and vanilla. Stir in coconut mix and crushed crackers. Blend well. Beat egg whites until still and gently fold into the coconut mixture. Grease a baking sheet lightly with PAM. Drop by rounded teaspoonfuls onto the sheet. Bake 12 to 14 minutes or until golden. Cool completely. When cool, dip in melted chocolate. Place on waxed paper. Refrigerate until set. Make 36 cookies.

This recipe is my cousin Betty's. She made a ton of these for my Aunt Flo's 90th birthday party. She inherited her mother Julia's talents.

TONI'S POTATO CHIP COOKIES
Toni Mollico

½ cup crushed potato chips
½ cup finely ground pecans
1½ cups flour
½ cup sugar

1 cup butter, at room temperature
1 large egg yolk
1 teaspoon vanilla
Confectioners' sugar

Preheat oven to 350°. In a medium bowl, combine chips, pecans and flour. In a large bowl, cream sugar and butter until fluffy, then beat in dry ingredients until well mixed. With damp hands, form dough into 1 inch balls and place 1½-inches apart on ungreased cookie sheets. Bake until cookies just start to color, 15 to 18 minutes. Cool slightly and roll in powdered sugar.

HORSESHOE COOKIES
Ronni Tichenor

1 package dry yeast
½ cup milk
1 egg yolk

Walnut filling:

1 pound of walnuts
1 cup sugar

1 cup butter
3 cups flour

½ cup water

In a small bowl mix the yeast and milk together. Add the egg yolk. In a separate bowl, cut the butter into the flour as if you were making a pie crust to make a crumbly mixture. Add yeast/milk/yolk mixture to dough. Separate dough into small pieces, forming balls. Roll out each ball. Place 1 tablespoon of nut filling (see below). Fold and seal edges, and shape into a crescent. Bake at 350 for 12 to 15 minutes.

Filling: Grind one pound of walnuts (semi-fine) in a food processor. Add in the sugar and water. Simmer for 15 minutes, or until thick. Cool before using.

Jim Tichenor, my husband's partner told me that this recipe needed to be in the book. He couldn't remember the name but Ronni said they were called "Horseshoe Cookies", which his mother has always made, though Jim wisely tells Ronni that hers are better!

James Tichenor Jr., M.D.,
Veronica Tichenor,
and their daughter
Michael
Jim is a wonderful OB/GYN
and Ronnie is a Sociology
Professor at SUNY IT. She
recently published her first
book.

MERINGUE KISSES
David Feiner

4 egg whites, room temperature
¼ teaspoon salt
1 teaspoon vanilla

¾ cup sugar
1 (12 ounce) package mini chocolate chips
1 cup pecans, finely chopped

Preheat oven to 250°. Make these at night, because they need to sit in the oven overnight. In a mixer on medium-low speed, beat the egg whites until frothy, about 2 minutes. Increase the mixer speed to high, add salt and whip to stiff, but not dry peaks. Reduce the speed to medium. Add the vanilla and then the sugar, a few tablespoons at a time. Whip to glossy peaks, about 2 minutes. Gently fold in the chocolate chips and the pecans. Drop by the tablespoon onto cookie sheets lined with parchment. Bake 45 minutes. Turn oven off and leave in oven overnight without opening the oven door. You can eliminate the nuts and just use the chips if you have someone who doesn't like nuts. Makes 36 cookies

David watches his fat content so these cookies work well since they have no butter or shortening. With the nuts they are 74 calories and have 3.9 grams of fat, and without the nuts they are 63 calories and have 2.8 grams of fat.

HOLIDAY TRIANGLES
Elise Feiner

2 cups flour
3 tablespoons sugar
¾ cup unsalted butter at room temperature
1 egg, beaten
½ teaspoon vanilla
½ cup orange marmalade
5 egg whites
1 ½ cups sugar

3 tablespoons flour
1 tablespoon light corn syrup
1 teaspoon cinnamon
2⅔ cups broken pieces pecans
½ teaspoon orange extract
¼ teaspoon baking powder
1 recipe Double Chocolate Dip (see below)

Line a 15 x 10 x 1-inch pan with aluminum foil. Butter the foil well (Better yet use a disposable aluminum cookie sheet!). Set aside.

In a Cuisinart: Place steel blade in work bowl. Add the 2 cups of flour and 3 tablespoons sugar; process 5 seconds to mix. Cut the butter into chunks. Add butter to the work bowl process until crumbly. Add the beaten egg and vanilla. Process until dough forms a ball. Press dough onto prepared pan. Chill 1 hour. Spread the marmalade over the dough. In a 1½ quart saucepan, combine the egg whites, 1½ cups sugar, 3 tablespoons flour, corn syrup, and cinnamon. Bring to a boil over medium-high heat. Reduce heat to medium. Stir constantly until mixture reaches 200°. Mix will be brown and may appear overcooked. Stir in pecans, orange extract and baking powder. Spread hot mixture over marmalade. Bake 350° 30 minutes or until golden. Cool in pan on wire rack. Lift foil to remove baked mixture from the pan. Cut into 24 squares. Diagonally cut each square to form 48 triangles. Dip edges of each triangle in warm double chocolate dip. Let dry on a rack. To store place cookies between layers of waxed paper in airtight container. Store in a cool place.

Double Chocolate Dip:
3 squares semisweet chocolate
1 square unsweetened chocolate

2 tablespoons shortening

In top of double boiler combine all ingredients. Place over, but not touching, hot water. Stir to melt. Remove from heat. Dip cookies on one edge.

MICHAEL AVELLA'S COCONUT KISS COOKIES
Elise Feiner

2 packages Pillsbury® Sugar Cookies
1 bag Bakers® Angel Flake coconut

1 large bag Hershey's® Kisses unwrapped

Preheat oven to 350°. Cut the package into 10 slices and each slice each circle into 4. You will have a total of 40 cookies from each package. Roll each cookie in the coconut and place on a cookie sheet and bake according to package directions (7 to 11 minutes) or until golden brown. As soon as you remove the cookies from the oven, immediately place a chocolate kiss in the middle of each cookie by pressing with a slight twisting motion. Always have the kisses peeled before the cookies come out of the oven.

I found this recipe in a magazine when my nephews Michael and Philly were very little. They always wanted to help make Christmas Cookies and these were very easy to make with kids. It became a Christmas tradition and so I always call them Michael's Coconut Kisses. I guess things never change because it was the year 2000, and Mike and Phil are now married, but, they were here for Christmas and still wanted these cookies. We ended up making them three times that year and even sent home a care package with Mike and Sherry for the long ride home.

Michael and Sherry Avella

MOCHA CHOCOLATE CHIP COOKIES
Elise Feiner

(2 cups) all-purpose flour
½ teaspoon baking powder
¾ teaspoon ground cinnamon
¼ teaspoon salt
2½ sticks unsalted butter, softened at room temperature
(make it very soft)

3 tablespoons instant espresso powder (or 4 tables instant
coffee granules, crushed)
1 cup confectioners' sugar
½ cup packed light brown sugar
1½ cups semisweet chocolate chips
About ¼ cup granulated sugar for dipping

Heat the oven to 350°. Line a cooling rack with paper towels. In a medium bowl, combine the flour, baking powder, cinnamon, and salt. In a larger bowl, beat the butter and coffee until well combined. Add the confectionery sugar and brown sugar and beat until combined. Stir in the flour mixture about ½-cup at a time, mixing well after each addition. Stir in the chocolate chips. Pour the granulated sugar in a small bowl or paper plate. Scoop out about 1 tablespoon of dough and flatten it slightly into a disk. Dip one side in granulated sugar and then, set the cookie, sugar side up, on an ungreased baking sheet. Repeat with remaining dough, spacing disks about 2-inches apart. Bake until the edges start to darken, 12 to 14 minutes. Begin checking after 12 minutes, but don't be tempted to remove them too soon. Let the cookies cool for 1 to 2 minutes on the baking sheets. Transfer them to paper towel lined racks to cool completely. Bake the rest of the dough the same way. Once the cookies are cooled, wrap them in plastic to keep them crisp. They also freeze well.

L-R: Jeffrey, Steven, David and Lauren Feiner

Steven Feiner learning how to "Razzle Dazzle"…
He's now in law school !

OATMEAL COOKIES
Elise Feiner

1¼ cups unsifted flour
1 teaspoon baking soda
1 cup butter, softened
¼ cup granulated sugar
¾ cup light brown sugar
1 teaspoon vanilla

1 (4 ounce) package Jell-O® Instant Vanilla
Pudding and Pie Filling
2 eggs
3½ cups quick cooking rolled oats
1 cup raisins
1 (6 ounce) package chocolate chips (optional)

Mix the flour with the baking soda. Combine the butter, sugars, and pudding mix in a large mixing bowl. Beat until smooth and creamy. Beat in eggs and vanilla. Gradually add the flour mix, and then stir in the oatmeal, raisins and chocolate chips. Batter will be stiff.
Drop by rounded teaspoonfuls onto ungreased cookie sheets or use cookie dropper, about 2 inches apart. Bake at 375° for 10 to 12 minutes. Makes about 5 dozen cookies.

This is a recipe that was in a magazine years ago. I tweaked it a little. I used to make these quite often when my father was alive because oatmeal cookies were his favorite.

OLD FASHIONED OATMEAL RAISIN COOKIES
Elise Feiner

1 cup raisins
1 cup water
¾ cup shortening
1½ cups sugar
2 eggs
1 teaspoon vanilla
2½ cups Gold Medal® flour

1 teaspoon baking soda
1 teaspoon salt
1 teaspoon cinnamon
½ teaspoon baking powder
½ teaspoon cloves
2 cups oats, rolled (raw)
½ cup chopped nuts, optional

Heat the raisins and water over medium heat until the raisins rehydrate, about 15 minutes. Drain raisins, saving the liquid. Add enough water to the liquid to make ½-cup of water.

Preheat oven to 400°. Mix the shortening, sugar, eggs and vanilla until well blended. Add in the ½ cup of raisin water. Add the remaining ingredients. Drop by rounded teaspoonfuls 2-inches apart onto an ungreased cookie sheets. Bake 8 to 10 minutes or until golden brown.

PEANUT BUTTER COOKIES
Elise Feiner

1 (14 ounce) can sweetened condensed milk
¾ cup peanut butter
2 cups Bisquick

1 teaspoon vanilla extract
Granulated sugar

Preheat oven to 375°. In a large mixing bowl, beat the milk and peanut butter until smooth. Add in the Bisquick and vanilla; mix well. Shape into 1-inch balls. Roll in sugar. Place 2-inches apart on ungreased cookie sheet. Flatten with a fork (first vertically and then horizontally to make a weave effect.) Bake 6 to 8 minutes or until lightly browned; do not over bake. Cool. For a different variation, do not flatten with a fork. Bake as above, and press a candy kiss in the center of each ball immediately after baking. **Make sure you unwrap the kisses in advance.**

I always made these cookies when my children were little. They prefer the kiss in the middle.

Back L-R: Marc, Betty, Ivan and Kevin Feiner
In front: Kevin Feiner

L-R: Lauren, Steven and David Feiner

"Youth is the gift of nature, but age is a work of art."
-Stanislaw Lec

PEANUT BUTTER KISSES
Sam Sternick

1 cup butter
1 cup peanut butter, creamy
1 cup brown sugar, firmly packed
1 cup granulated sugar
2 eggs
¼ cup milk

2 teaspoons vanilla
3¼ cups all-purpose flour
1 teaspoon salt
2 teaspoons baking soda
Sugar for rolling
72-90 Chocolate kisses, unwrapped

Preheat oven to 375°. Combine the butter, peanut butter, brown sugar and granulated sugar in a large bowl. Beat at medium speed with an electric mixer until well blended. Beat in eggs, milk and vanilla. Combine flour, baking soda and salt. Mix into the creamed mixture at low speed until just blended. Dough will be stiff. Form into 1-inch balls. Roll in granulated sugar. Place 2-inches apart on ungreased cookie sheet. Bake 8 minutes. Press chocolate kiss into the center of each cookie. Return to the oven and bake 3 more minutes. Cool 2 minutes in cookie sheet, remove to a cooling rack. Makes 6 to 7½ dozen cookies.

Sam Sternick says that she is not a cookie baker but you would never say that if you tasted these. She made them for the Christmas Cookie exchange.

PECAN OR ALMOND MANDELBREAD
Pearl Borten

1 stick margarine
1¼ cups sugar
4 eggs
2 teaspoons vanilla extract

2 cups flour
½ teaspoon baking powder, heaping
3 cups pecan halves or whole almonds or
2 cups chopped walnuts and 1 cup mini chocolate chips

Preheat oven to 350°. Cream the margarine and sugar together. Add the eggs, one at a time, blend well. Add the vanilla. Add the flour and baking powder and mix well. Fold in the nuts. Put into 2 well greased loaf pans and bake at 350° for 30 minutes. Cool upside down. Remove and wrap in foil and freeze. Take out 10 minutes before slicing and then toast in a 350° oven for a few minutes.

CHOCOLATE SAMBUCA® COOKIES
Elise Feiner

12 semisweet chocolate squares (1 ounce each)
4 tablespoons butter
3 large eggs
⅓ cup Sambuca® (anise-flavored liqueur)
1 cup sugar

1 cup blanched almonds, finely ground
⅔ cup all-purpose flour
¾ teaspoon baking soda
⅓ cup confectioners' sugar

In the top of a double boiler or a 2-quart saucepan, melt chocolate with butter over low heat stirring frequently. Remove the saucepan from heat; cool chocolate mixture slightly. In a medium bowl, with wire whisk, mix eggs, Sambuca, and ½ cup sugar; blend in chocolate mixture. With a spoon, stir in ground almonds, flour, and baking soda into the chocolate mixture until combined (dough will be very soft). Cover bowl with Saran Wrap and refrigerate at least 4 hours or overnight. Preheat oven to 350°. In a small bowl, combine confectioners' sugar with remaining ½ cup sugar. With lightly floured hands, roll dough by rounded tablespoonfuls into balls. Roll balls in sugar mixture to coat. Place balls about 2-inches apart on an ungreased cookie sheet. Bake 10 to 12 minutes until cookies are just set and look puffed and cracked. Keep on cookie sheet for about 1 minute. With a spatula, remove to a wire rack. Repeat with remaining dough. Yield: 48

This cookie was done at a cookie exchange and the recipe given out there.

"Grow old with me! The best is yet to be."
-Robert Browning

PECAN TASSIES
Hilda Lanier

Tart Crust:
1 (8 ounce) package cream cheese at room temperature
½ pound unsalted butter

2 cups all purpose flour
Mini cupcake tins

Cream butter and cream cheese together. Gradually add the flour until the mixture is soft. Roll into small balls the size of walnuts, and place one in each mini muffin tin. Chill for about 30 minutes, or until firm. Remove from refrigerator, and pat each ball to line the mini muffin tins.

Filling:
3 eggs slightly beaten
3 tablespoons melted butter
2 teaspoons vanilla

1½ cups light brown sugar
1 cup of pecans (you can use walnuts)
Confectioners' sugar to sift over the top

Mix all ingredients together except the nuts. Then add one cup of chopped walnuts or pecans. Fill cups and bake at 350° for 20 minutes. The sides of the cups will get slightly brown. Let cool and flip them onto wire racks. When cool sprinkle with powdered sugar.

This recipe was given to Carmen by Jorge's sister Hilda, and is the most requested cookie in the Ferreiro house at the holidays, when all the family is up from Florida. A true family effort...

Hilda Ferreiro Lanier (Uncle Jorge's sister)

RAINBOW COOKIES
Ann D'Amico

4 eggs, separated
8 ounces almond paste
3 sticks unsalted butter
1 cup sugar
1 teaspoon almond extract
2 cups flour

8 drops red food coloring
10 drops green food coloring
¼ teaspoon salt
1 (12 ounce) jar raspberry or apricot preserves
6 ounces semisweet chocolate

Preheat oven to 350°. Grease three 9 x 13-inch pans or 12¼ x 8¼-inch tin foil tin pans lined with parchment paper. Grease again. Beat egg whites until stiff. Place in another bowl and set aside. In the mixing bowl, break up the almond paste with a fork. Add butter, egg yolks, extract, and sugar and beat until light and fluffy. Add the flour and salt. Mix well. Fold in the egg whites. Remove 1¼ cups of the batter and spread evenly into the first pan. Remove another 1½ cups of batter and add the red food color. Spread into the second pan. Remove the last 1½ cups of batter and add the green food color and spread into the three pan. Bake 15 minutes or until the edges are golden. Remove from pans. Peel off paper. Cool on racks. Melt preserves and strain. Place green layer on plate. Spread with preserves. Add yellow layer. Add rest of preserves. Place red layer on top and weight down. Refrigerate overnight. Melt chocolate in microwave or top of a double boiler. Spread on top of cookies. Cool. Spread on bottom too. Trim and cut into squares.

PIZZELLE - MARIA DI PIER
Maria DiPierdomenico

6 eggs
4-5 teaspoons oil
⅔ cup sugar

Lemon zest of one whole lemon
1-2 teaspoons baking powder
Enough flour to be able to roll the dough

Roll out dough to about 2½-inch strips. Make sure iron is hot before starting. Turn iron over after each use. Flame should be high. Cook one minute. Today, you can use the pizzelle iron. Heat pizzelle iron; spray with PAM®. Place tablespoon of batter in the middle of iron. Close the iron. Cook until golden.

Filling:
Grate 1 square of semisweet chocolate, ¼ cup grated walnuts, ½ cup grape or strawberry jelly. Mix together and put a little of the filling on the pizzelle and top with another pizzelle.

You can tell how old this recipe is because Maria was still using a pizzelle maker that was done over a flame. She was our next door neighbor on Alabama Avenue in Brooklyn, and one of my mother's dearest friends. I can remember watching her make these as a very little girl. She was the only one I knew who filled the pizzelle. I can still picture her in her kitchen with her hearty laugh, making pizzelles, and her homemade soap. She had retired to Pescara, Italy. She passed away recently at the age of 100. Our families have become more than friends through the years and sometimes we forget that we are not related by blood, but by love!

Maria and Philip DiPierdomenico

PIZZELLE - RO DI PIER
Rosemarie DiPierdomenico

½ cup butter
⅔ cup sugar
3 eggs
1¾ to 2 cups flour

1 teaspoon baking powder
1 teaspoon vanilla
1 bottle anise extract
Pinch of salt

Beat shortening until smooth. Gradually add sugar and beat well. Add eggs, vanilla, and beat. Sift flour, baking powder, and salt into egg mixture. For best results, make soft sticky batter. Finely chopped nuts may be added. Heat pizzelle iron; spray with PAM®. Place tablespoon of batter in the middle of iron. Close the iron. Cook until golden. Pizzelle can be made in advance, and keep forever. May be frozen if desired. Makes about 3½ dozen.

PEANUT BUTTER BALLS
Karen Selinsky

2 cups crunchy peanut butter (I use Skippy® Super Chunk)
2 cups Rice Krispies®
1 stick butter or margarine (melted)

1 pound confectioner's sugar
Chocolate coating (1 bag semisweet chocolate chips and 1 tablespoon Crisco® or vegetable oil, melted over hot water)

Mix peanut butter and butter. Add powdered sugar. Mix in cereal. Form mixture into 1-inch balls and swirl the top half of the ball into the slightly cooled chocolate coating. Chill at least 1 hour before serving to set chocolate or can be stored in fridge until ready to serve.

Karen makes these for the Christmas holiday and other important family occasions. Karen says, "The peanut butter balls can be made larger and formed around lollipop sticks - it is time-consuming to do but well worth the effort. If you make them into lollipops, you need more chocolate chips and oil and melt as needed."

Karen Selinsky and her mother Connie DiMare

Jonathan Trainor and his grandmother
Connie DiMare

POTATO CHIP COOKIES
Elise Feiner

1 cup butter
½ cup sugar
1 cup light brown sugar
2 eggs
1 teaspoon vanilla

2 cups flour
1 teaspoon salt
1 teaspoon baking soda
2 cups crushed potato chips
1 cup chopped nuts (optional)

Cream together the butter and sugars. Add the egg and vanilla; mix well. Add flour, salt and baking soda; blend. Stir in potato chips and nuts. Drop by teaspoonfuls on a lightly greased cookie. Bake 325° for 10 to 15 minutes.

SCHNECKEN
Nellie Reinisch

4 cups flour, sifted
¾ cup butter
3 eggs, separated

1 (8 ounce) container sour cream
2 teaspoons of vanilla
3 tablespoons confectioner's sugar

Cut in butter into flour with 2 knives to make a very fine crumb-like mix. Add the 3 egg yolks, sour cream and 1 teaspoon of vanilla. Knead with fingers. Put in refrigerator at least 1 hour. Beat 3 egg whites with confectioners' Sugar until stiff. Add 1 teaspoon of vanilla.
Take the dough and divide into 8 to10 parts. Sprinkle a board with confectioner's sugar, and a rolling pin with confectioner's sugar. Roll each piece into a round shape and paint on the egg white mixture. Sprinkle with cinnamon sugar (Dominos). Take a knife and divide into 8 to 10 wedges. Take each wedge and roll from wide end to the point (very loosely). Put on a greased cookie sheet. Dab on egg white mixture and cinnamon sugar. Bake in a 400° oven until golden brown about 15 minutes. Immediately remove from cookie sheets.

This recipe came from Aunt Shirley. It was Nanny's recipe, written in her own hand.

PIZZELLE COOKIES PICANO
Lynn Picano

6 eggs
3½ cups flour
1½ cups sugar
2 tablespoons vanilla or anise extract

1 cup butter, melted and cooled
4 teaspoons baking powder
½ cup anisette (optional)

Sift flour and baking powder. Beat eggs in a large mixing bowl. Gradually add the sugar mixing until smooth. Add butter and vanilla (anisette if desired). Add flour mixture. Beat until smooth. Dough will be sticky enough to drop with a spoon. Spray pizzelle iron with Pam or grease with a little oil. Heat pizzelle iron over medium heat. Place 1 tablespoon of batter in the center. Close the iron, squeezing the handles together. When the mixture stops sizzling, turn the iron over and continue cookies until both sides of the cookie are golden, checking frequently and turning as necessary. Place on a wire rack. Makes about 60 cookies.

For chocolate pizzelle: Sift ½ cup unsweetened cocoa, ½ cup sugar and additional ½ teaspoon baking powder to the flour mixture. Then add to egg mixture, blending well.

Lynn made these for our cookie exchange. They have been in her family for years.

L-R: Lynn Picano and Iryna Trociuk

The Picano Kids
L-R: Cara, John and Danny

RANGER COOKIES
Catherine Sleeper

1 cup chocolate chips
1½ cups all purpose flour
½ teaspoon baking powder
½ teaspoon baking soda
¼ teaspoon salt
1 egg

1 teaspoon vanilla
1¾ ounces flaked coconut (optional)
½ pound butter
½ cup granulated sugar
½ packed brown sugar
2 cups Rice Krispies® Cereal

Mix dry ingredients together in a bowl. Beat butter, add sugar and brown sugar, and beat until fluffy. Add egg and vanilla. Add to dry ingredients. Add chocolate chips, coconut, and cereal. Drop by teaspoonfuls onto a cookie sheet 2-inches apart. Bake at 350° for 8 to 10 minutes.

Cathy made these for our Christmas cookie exchange. They are a favorite of the Sleeper kids; Lauren, David, Peter and Amy.

Catherine and Richard Sleeper, M.D.

The Sleeper Kids:
Top L-R: Lauren and David
Bottom L-R: Amy and Peter

One of our Holiday Cookie
Exchanges...
L-R: Ronni Tichenor, Barbara
Schwartz and Joanna Basile

RICOTTA-CHEESE COOKIES
Edith Mainella

2 cups sugar
2 sticks butter, softened
1 (15 ounce) container ricotta cheese
2 teaspoons vanilla extract
2 large eggs
4 cups all-purpose flour

2 tablespoons baking powder
1 teaspoon salt
1½ cups confectioners' sugar
3 tablespoons milk
Red and green sugar crystals

Preheat oven to 350°. In a large bowl, with a mixer at low speed, beat sugar and butter until blended. Increase speed to high; beat until light and fluffy; about 5 minutes. At medium speed, beat in ricotta, vanilla, and eggs until well combined. Reduce speed to low. Add flour, baking powder, and salt; beat until a dough forms. Drop by level tablespoonfuls, about 2 inches apart, onto an ungreased cookie sheet. Bake about 15 minutes or until cookies are lightly golden (they will be soft). With a spatula, remove cookies to a wire rack to cool. Repeat with remaining dough. When cookies are cool, prepare icing: In a small bowl, stir in confectioners' sugar and milk until smooth. With a small knife spread frosting on the cookies; sprinkle with crystals (you can also use nonpareils). Set cookies aside to allow the icing to dry completely, about 1 hour. These freeze very well. Makes about 6 dozen cookies.

Anyone who tells you it's not about the money lies! It's all about the Benjamin's!
-Elise Feiner

RICOTTA COOKIES
Cindy Circelli and Johann Gigliotti

1 pound ricotta
4 eggs
1 cup sugar
1 cup oil

2 teaspoon flavoring (vanilla, orange, or lemon)
8 teaspoons baking powder
5 cups flour

Cream together the ricotta, eggs, and sugar in a large mixing bow until well blended. (You can use an electric mixer.) Add the oil, flavorings, baking powder, and flour. Spray cookie sheets with PAM® (only after the first batch.) Roll the dough into small balls.
   Cindy said that when she makes them she does some with each of the extracts. She also said that if you like them in chocolate you can add about 3 tablespoons of cocoa to the mix and increase the sugar by about ¼ cup. Bake 350° for 10 to 15 minutes until brown on the bottom.

Frosting:
Combine confectionery sugar and milk to make a glaze (about 1 cup of sugar to 3-4 tablespoons of milk). Place sprinkles of the top if you want.

Johann gave me her sister-in-law Cindy's recipe for these cookies. She said that these are Bernie's favorite cookies, and she always makes them at Christmas.

SNOW BALLS
Rosemarie DiPierdomenico

2 sticks of softened butter
1½ to 2 cups flour
4 tablespoons sugar

1 teaspoon vanilla
Dash of salt
½ cup chopped nuts

Cream together the butter, flour and sugar. Then add the vanilla, salt, and chopped nuts. Roll into little balls. Place on a lightly greased cookie sheet. Bake at 300° 10 to 15 minutes. Don't brown the tops. When cool, roll in powdered sugar

Rosemarie and Joe DiPierdomenico on their Wedding day…
and enjoying many years of marital bliss!

RUGELACH KAPLAN
Sylvia Kaplan

Dough:
½ pound unsweetened butter, melted
½ pound cream cheese
2 cups of flour

Pinch of salt
1 tablespoon sugar
¼ teaspoon baking powder

Filling:
1 cup sugar
1 tablespoon cinnamon
1 cup raisins

1 cup of chopped pecans or walnuts or mixed
Mini chocolate chips

Mix all ingredients well by hand and chill. May be refrigerated overnight. Divide the dough in four equal parts. Roll into a circle. Place filling on the top of each circle. Cut each circle into 6 to 8 pieces and roll up from the wide end. Brush with an egg wash. Bake at 350° until done, about 15 to 20 minutes.

Aunt Barb Feiner's' Aunt Sylvia gave me this recipe years at Barb's Bridal Shower.

WALNUT CRESCENTS
Iryna Trociuk

2 cups ground walnuts
½ cup sugar
2 cups flour, sifted
1 cup butter

1 teaspoon vanilla
1 egg white, unbeaten
Confectioners' sugar, to roll cookies in

Cream butter and sugar together. Add the egg white and vanilla; beat. Add the flour; mix well. Add the walnuts; blend. Shape dough into half moons, crescents, balls, or circles. Place on a greased cookie sheet. Bake at 375° for 15 minutes. Immediately roll each cookie into confectionery sugar until evenly coated.

These cookies are a Ukrainian favorite of the Trociuk kids. Iryna made them for our Christmas Cookie Exchange. They are delicious.

The Trociuk Family
L-R: Roman. Larissa, Iryna, Dr. Michael, Natalie and Daniel
Mike is an anesthesiologist, and Iryna a gourmet cook.

RUGELACH
Edith Mainella

2 sticks butter, softened
4 cups flour
1 teaspoon salt
¼ cup sugar

1 cake of yeast
1 cup heavy cream
3 egg yolks

Filling:
¾ cup sugar
3 teaspoons cinnamon

½ cup chopped pecans
¼ raisins

Mix the butter with the flour until it is the consistency of crumbs. In a separate bowl, using your fingers, crumble the yeast into the cream, and add the egg yolks. Add the wet ingredients to the dry ingredients and make a dough. Chill 3 to 4 hours or overnight. Roll ⅓ of the dough into a circle.

Preheat oven to 375°. Mix the filling ingredients together; sprinkle ⅓ onto the dough. Cut into triangles and roll from the wide end up. Place on a greased cookie sheet point side down. Repeat with the remaining dough. Let rise 30 minutes at room temperature. Bake for 15 to 10 minutes until golden brown in color.

Aunt Edith got this from one of her neighbors when they lived on Flamingo Road in East Hills, New York.

Standing L-R: Joe, Thirza, and Katherine Avella, Harvey Flomenhoft, Josephine Mainella
Seated L-R: Jean, Frank, Edith Mainella, Shirley Flomenhoft, Betty Feiner

ZURICH NUT COOKIES
Elise Feiner

¾ cup butter
2¼ cups sugar
5 eggs
½ cup milk
7 cups cake flour

½ cup almond paste
¼ cup apricot preserves
1 tablespoon Kirsch®
8 (1 ounce) squares semisweet chocolate
1½ teaspoons salad oil

Preheat the oven to 400°. Grease 2 cookie sheets. In a mixing bowl, cream the butter and the sugar together until light and fluffy. Slowly add the eggs and milk. Add flour one cup at a time, mixing until combined. Spoon batter into a pastry bag fitted with a star tube. Pipe small teardrop shapes onto cookie sheet. Bake 10 minutes. Cool on a wire rack. Meanwhile, in a small bowl, beat together almond paste, preserves, and kirsch. Spread a very thin layer of the filling on the bottom half of the cookies. Top each with a second cookie. In the top of a double boiler melt the chocolate and oil together. Dip the narrow end of each cookie ½ inch into the melted chocolate. Place on waxed paper to harden. Makes 7 dozen

SARAH BERNHARDT COOKIES
Ronni Tichenor

Almond Macaroons:

1½ cups slivered almonds
1½ cups powdered sugar

3 egg whites (reserve yolks)

Process almonds until finely ground. Sift sugar and add to almonds, stir until lump free. Beat egg whites until stiff moist peaks form. Gently fold into the almond mixture, a third at a time. Drop teaspoon size mounds on parchment lined cookie sheets, two inches apart. Bake 350° for 15 to 18 minutes. Let cool 5 minutes, and then remove with spatula.

Chocolate Buttercream:

In a small pan, stir together 7 tablespoons each of sugar and water. Bring to a boil over high heat, until syrup reaches 230° to 234°. Beat four egg yolks until blended. Beating constantly, slowly add syrup in thin, steady stream. Beat until mixture is thick and has returned to room temperature. Beat in ⅔ cup softened butter, one tablespoon at a time, just until blended. Stir in 4 teaspoons unsweetened cocoa. **Spread the flat side of the cookie with the buttercream.** Refrigerate cookies for at least 15 minutes.

Coating:

Melt 5 ounces of semisweet chocolate and 1 tablespoon plus two teaspoons solid vegetable shortening in a double boiler. Dip cookies, buttercream side down in the chocolate. Refrigerate. These cookies will keep in the fridge or may be frozen. If buttercream becomes dark and runny, refrigerate it for 45 minutes, and then beat again until fluffy. Makes 30 cookies.

Ronni Tichenor gave me this recipe. She made these for dessert when we went for dinner. Ronni said, "They are wonderful cookies. They take a little effort to get them right and it might take one or two tries but it's worth it."

L-R: Jim Tichenor, M.D., Ronni and Michael Tichenor

TOFFEE BARS
Ronni Tichenor

2 cups butter
2 cups packed brown sugar
2 egg yolks
2 teaspoons vanilla

4 cups flour
1 (12 ounce) package chocolate chips
2 cups chopped pecans

Beat butter for 30 seconds. Add brown sugar and beat until fluffy. Add egg yolks and vanilla; beat well. Gradually add flour, beating constantly. Stir in chocolate chips and chopped pecans. Press into jelly roll pan and bake at 350° for 20 to 25 minutes. Cut into bars while warm.

Ronni's mother makes batches of these cookies every year at Christmas time. Ronni made these for our Christmas cookie exchange and they were great.

SPRITZ COOKIES
Eileen Furino

1 margarine or butter, softened	½ teaspoon salt
1 teaspoon almond or vanilla extract	2¼ cups all purpose flour
½ cup sugar	1 egg

Heat oven to 400°. Mix margarine and sugar. Stir in remaining ingredients. Fill cookie press with dough. Form desired shapes on an ungreased cookie sheet. Bake until set but not brown, 6 to 9 minutes. Makes about 5 dozen cookies.

Chocolate Spritz: Stir 2 ounces of melted unsweetened chocolate (cooled) into margarine mixture.

Butter-Rum Spritz: Substitute rum flavor for almond extract. Tint parts of dough with different food colors. After baking glaze cookies with butter rum glaze. Glaze: heat ¼ cup butter over low heat until melted; remove from heat. Stir in 1 cup of powdered sugar and 1 teaspoon of rum flavoring. Beat 1 to 2 tablespoons of hot water in, until it is the desired consistency.

Christmas Spritz: Before baking, top cookies with currants, raisins, candies, nuts or candied fruits. Or after baking, decorate with colored sugar, nonpareils, red cinnamon candies, or finely chopped nuts; use corn syrup to hold decorations on cookies.

Holly wreaths: Use star press to form wreaths by moving in circular motion. Gently push ends together to form a wreath. Use bits of red and green candied cherries to form holly berries and leaves.

These are a favorite cookie in the Furino house. Uncle Anthony does the cookie press, Felicia and Kristin do the decorating and Aunt Eileen says she is in charge of the cleanup.

L-R: John Burt, Eileen Burt Furino,
Dorothy Burt, Anthony Furino, D.D.S.
Bottom: Kristin Furino
All of our friends have voted Anthony
and Eileen the perfect couple...if they
ever got divorced, we would all lose faith
in this world.

WORLD'S BEST COOKIES
Elise Feiner

1 stick butter	1 teaspoon salt
1 stick margarine	1 teaspoon baking soda
1 cup granulated sugar	1 teaspoon cream of tartar
1 cup light brown sugar	1 cup finely chopped nuts
2 teaspoons vanilla	1 cup Old-fashioned Quaker® Oats
¾ cup Crisco® oil	1 cup shredded coconut
1 egg	1 cup Rice Krispies®
3½ cups all-purpose flour	

Preheat oven to 325°. In mixing bowl, cream butter and margarine; add sugars, vanilla, and oil. Beat until smooth. Add egg and beat again until smooth. Add flour, salt, baking soda, and cream of tartar. Add nuts, oats, coconut and Rice Krispies. Fold in until well blended. Cover bowl with waxed paper and refrigerate for an hour. Dough will be stiff enough to handle. Spray cookie sheets lightly. Pinch off small piece about the size of a marble. Flatten with your fingers. (Regular size cookie sheet will hold 24) Bake for 8 to 10 minutes. After taking them out of the oven, leave on the cookie sheets for a few minutes. Cool on racks. Makes about 150 cookies

THE BEST RUGELACH
Ann D'Amico

3 cups flour
1 package yeast
1 cup butter (melted)
3 egg yolks

1 (8 ounce) carton sour cream
1 jar of strawberry preserves or apricot preserves melted (optional)

Filling:
1¼ cup chopped walnuts, finely chopped
1½-2 cups sugar
Raisins

3 to 4 tablespoons cinnamon
Mini chocolate chips

Mix nuts, sugar and cinnamon separately in a bowl and put to the side. (I sometimes leave the nuts separately and do some with nuts, some without. Sprinkle yeast on flour, add melted butter and blend with fork in bowl. Stir yolks into sour cream in another bowl then add to flour mixture. Mix until a dough is formed. Pack and round into large ball and refrigerate overnight or place in freezer for ½ hour.

The next day, preheat oven to 350º. Cut and divide ball into quarters. Sprinkle ¼ cinnamon/sugar (nuts) mixture onto bread board or wax paper. Place dough on top of the mix. Roll out (one quarter at a time) with rolling pin into a circle. Brush with raspberry preserves before filling if desired. Sprinkle desired fillings on the circle. Cut each circle into 8 triangles and roll up from the wider end. Bend into a crescent shape; pinch the ends. Repeat with all remaining dough. Bake at 350º for 15 to 18 minutes until golden brown. Cool on rack.

Rugelach is a staple dessert in Jewish families and ours is no exception. My kids like the chocolate chips and raisins, Marc and I like chocolate chips, nuts and raisins. This is by far the best rugelach recipe there is! These are the ones we always make.

RUGELACH FILLINGS:
Rugelach are so versatile because you can really fill them with anything. Here are just a few that you may want to try:

Raspberry-Chocolate

¼ cup raspberry preserves, ¼ cup mini chocolate chips. Mix well. You can add coconut or chopped nuts to this as well.

Apricot or Prune Coconut Mixture:

In a food processor, pulse ¾ cup of dried apricots or prunes with 1 tablespoon of freshly squeezed orange juice, and 2 teaspoons of orange zest until finely chopped. Stir in ¼ cup flaked coconut. You can also add some mini chocolate chips in the above mix.

Peanut Butter – Chocolate Chip:

Mix ¼ cup of mini chocolate chips and ¼ cup chunky peanut butter together and blend until thoroughly mixed.

Orange Cranberry:

In a small container, mix ¼ cup orange marmalade, ¼ cup chopped cranberries (fresh or frozen) or craisins, and 1 tablespoon of orange zest together. Stir until well blended.

Poppy Seeds:

In a food processor take ½ cup raisins, ¼ cup poppy seeds. 1 tablespoon sugar, 1 teaspoon lemon juice, and dash of cinnamon. Process until well chopped and blended. You can also add ¼ cup finely chopped walnuts.

Cannoli Filling:

Mix ½ cup ricotta, ¼ cup chopped raisins or maraschino cherries, 2 tablespoons sugar, 1 egg yolk, 1 teaspoon of lemon zest, ¾ teaspoon vanilla, and ground cinnamon and nutmeg to taste. You can also add mini chocolate chips to this as well.

Caramel Filling:

2 cups caramels peeled and cut into small pieces, 1 cup chopped pecans, ½ cup brown sugar. Mix well.

TOFFEE SQUARES
Elise Feiner

1 cup butter, softened
1 cup brown sugar, packed
1 egg yolk
1 teaspoon vanilla

2 cups flour
¼ teaspoon salt
5 (⅞ ounces) bars Hershey® Milk Chocolate Bars
½ cup chopped nuts

Preheat the oven to 350°. Mix the butter, sugar, egg yolk, and vanilla. Measure flour by the dipping method, or sifting. Stir in flour and salt until dough is well blended. Spread dough in a rectangle about 13 x 10-inch on a greased baking sheet leaving about 1-inch all around the edge of the baking pan. Bake 20 to 25 minutes, or until nicely browned. Crust will be quite soft. Remove from the oven. Immediately place separated squares of chocolate on the top. Let stand until they melt, then spread evenly over the surface of the crust. Sprinkle with the nuts. Cut in small squares while warm. Makes 6 to 7 dozen.

Believe it or not this was given to me by a friend from Weight Watchers named Elizabeth. She does catering locally and generously shared this recipe with me. I wish I knew her last name to give her credit for the recipe.

Uncle Gene Feiner and David Feiner

The Original Feiner Boys L-R:
Philip "Pinky", Gene and Jerome

NUT HORNS
Ruth Schwartz

2¼ cups sugar
1 cup butter
2 eggs
4 cups flour
½ teaspoon salt

1 teaspoon baking powder
1 cup sour cream
¼ teaspoon cinnamon
2 cups ground walnuts
1 lemon rind, grated

Beat ¼ cup sugar, butter and eggs until light and fluffy. Add the dry ingredients (flour, baking powder and salt), alternating with sour cream and blend well. Form into 4 balls. Roll each ball into a circle ⅛-inch thickness. Combine remaining ingredients with reserved sugar and spread filling on each circle. Cut into 12 wedges. Roll loosely from the outside edge towards the center. Bake on a greased cookie sheet at 350° for 30 to 35 minutes.

SNICKERDOODLES
Ruth Schwartz

1 cup shortening
1½ cups sugar
2 eggs
2¾ cups flour

2 teaspoons cream of tartar
1 teaspoon baking soda
½ teaspoon salt
Cinnamon sugar

Cream shortening, sugar, and eggs together. Add the dry ingredients. Roll dough into 1-inch balls. Roll balls in cinnamon sugar. Bake on an ungreased cookie sheet at 400° until golden brown.

WINE COOKIES
Joanna Basile

Dough:
1 cup Chablis, (I use Inglenook®) or Chardonnay
1¼ cups sugar
2 large eggs at room temperature

4 teaspoons baking powder
1 cup canola oil
4-5 cups flour (as much as it takes)

Buttercream Frosting:
4-6 tablespoons butter, softened
2⅔ cups confectioners' sugar
4 tablespoons milk

1 teaspoon vanilla

Bake Temperature: 350°
Cooking time: 20 to 25 minutes (in my oven I need 28 minutes) until very light brown

Mix in a large bowl **in the following order**, whisking **AFTER** each addition: (Chablis, sugar, eggs, baking powder, oil, and flour.) Mix together with a large spoon. Knead on a counter or lightly floured work surface until a soft dough forms (the consistency of a pizza dough). You made need to work in a little more flour (about ½ cup) Dough will be soft and a little sticky.   Shape into three logs, 12-inches long by 2½-inches wide. Place two of the logs on an ungreased cookie sheet, and the third log on its own cookie sheet. Bake the two first, and when they are done, bake the third one by itself. The cookies will barely be brown when they are done; start checking them after18 minutes. **Do not over bake to get them brown or they will be too dry.** Frost the logs while still warm but not hot.   Slice the logs in to 1 to 1½-inch cookies after they are frosted. Joanna says that you can also roll them into balls about 1 to 1½-inches in diameter and bake for about 10 minutes.

To make the frosting, mix the softened butter with the milk and vanilla. Add in the confectioners' sugar. You can mix by hand or with a mixer. Consistency should be on the thicker side. Spread the frosting over the cookies when they are warm.

Maria Trainor made these cookies for me when I was recovering from surgery. They are absolutely delicious. Maria got the recipe from Joanna. Joanna said this is her mother's recipe. Maria said that she makes these at least once a week. They are fast and easy to make. Sarah and Sachi love these.

L-R: Shirley Eadline, Joanna Basile, Maria Trainor, and Katie Cominsky

SESAME COOKIES
Josephine Mainella

3 eggs
½ pound of butter or 1 cup of oil
Pinch of salt
4 teaspoons baking powder
1 cup sugar
2 teaspoons vanilla

3 teaspoons anisette
1 teaspoon orange zest (optional)
Approximately 6 cups of flour
For rolling: 3 tablespoons milk and 3 tablespoons anisette
Sesame seeds

Preheat oven to 350°. Combine all ingredients except the flour. Then add the flour, starting with 3 cups. The dough should be a medium consistency. Add flour until you reach this consistency. Knead the dough on a floured board until it is well blended. When you put two fingers in the dough the dough should spring back. Cut dough in pieces and roll into 2 inch thick, long pencil like logs, slit the top of the log with a knife but don't go all the way through. Then cut each log into 2 to 3-inch cookies. Make a mixture of 3 tablespoons milk and 3 tablespoons anisette. Roll the cookies in the milk mixture, and then roll them in sesame seeds until they are completely covered. Place on a lightly greased (PAM®) cookie sheet, slit side up. Bake 15 to 20 minutes. Makes about 100 cookies.

Aunt Fifi made these cookies at the holidays. I love the smell of the anisette!

OREO® COOKIE DESSERT
Tessa Trainor

1 bag (1pound 2 ounces) Oreo Cookies
1 stick butter, melted
1 (8 ounce) package (Philadelphia® Cream Cheese at room temperature

1 cup confectioners' sugar
2 (3¾ ounce) boxes Chocolate pudding mix (not instant)
4 cups milk
2 (8 ounce) containers Extra Creamy Cool Whip®

Cook the chocolate pudding according to package directions. Let cool. You can also use instant chocolate pudding if desired. Place the Oreo cookies in a food processor or blender and pulse them into crumbs. Reserve about 1 to 1½ cups for the top of the cake. Add the remaining crumbs to the butter and place into the bottom of a 9 x 13 inch cake pan.

Mix the cream cheese, confectioners sugar and 1 container of Cool Whip together. I used the food processor. Place on top of the Oreo layer. Place the chocolate pudding on top of the cream cheese layer. Spread the remaining container of Cool Whip over the chocolate pudding. Top with remaining Oreo crumbs and or chocolate curls if desired. Chill until serving. Cut in squares to serve.

L-R: Kyle, Tessa and Jonathan Trainor...Tessa is quite the beauty!
Jonathan is debating between law school and medical school and Kyle will one
day be on the red carpet with an Oscar for Best Producer or Director in his
hands.

ROLLED DELIGHTS
Pearl Borten

3½ cups flour
½ pound butter
¼ cup sugar
4 eggs
1 teaspoon baking powder
Cinnamon sugar mix (I use Dominos®)

Apricot or seedless raspberry jelly
Chopped nuts of your choice
Raisins
Mini chocolate chips (optional)
A few tablespoons of milk
Powdered sugar

Preheat oven to 350°. Mix together the flour, sugar and baking powder. Add butter and eggs. Mix and knead (by hand) for a few minutes. Divide in three parts. Wrap in saran wrap. Refrigerate for ½ hour. Roll out dough as thin as possible into a 10 x12-inch rectangle. Spread generously with seedless raspberry or apricot jelly. Sprinkle with cinnamon sugar mixture, nuts and raisins. Roll as a jelly roll. Start at the 12-inch side (do not start too close to the edge) and place on a cookie sheet (ungreased.) Brush with milk. Repeat with remaining 2 sections of dough. Bake until brown about 50 minutes. Slice into ½-inch rounds while warm. Sprinkle with powdered sugar when cool. May be frozen.

This is another of Mom Mom's friends Pearl's cookies. She said that these are a favorite of her family. She was generous enough to share the recipe with me.

TAYLOR'S CHOCOLATE CHIP TOFFEE COOKIES
Taylor Cocalis

1 cup (2 sticks) unsalted butter, softened
½ cup granulated sugar
¾ cup light brown sugar, packed
1½ teaspoons vanilla extract
1 large egg
2¼ cups all purpose flour

1 teaspoon baking soda
1 teaspoon cornstarch
½ teaspoon salt
2 cups (12 ounce) semi-sweet chocolate chips
1 bag (8 ounces) Heath or Skor Bites, smashed

Preheat oven to 375°. Combine flour, baking soda, cornstarch and salt in small bowl. Cream the butter with the two sugars (this can be done by hand or with a mixer). Add vanilla. Add egg and beat until combined. Gradually stir in the dry ingredients. Stir in the chocolate chips and toffee. Place clumps of dough on ungreased baking sheet. Bake until golden brown. Bake time will vary according to size of cookie. The average times are as follows: Small 7 to 8 minutes, Medium 11 to 12 minutes, and Large 14 to 16 minutes. Cool cookies on baking sheet for a couple of minutes; remove to wire racks to cool completely. Recipe will yield 4 dozen small, 3 dozen medium, or 2 dozen large cookies.

Taylor is a friend of Lauren's from the School of Hotel Administration at Cornell University. Lauren says, "Taylor makes the best cookies ever!" Lauren gave me this recipe after Taylor made them for their class. She wanted to surprise her by including it in our cookbook. Lauren said she prefers chocolate chunks to chocolate chips.

Taylor Cocalis…expect great things from Taylor in the food industry!

ITALIAN BUTTER COOKIES
Elise Feiner

½ cup butter, softened
1¼ sugar
4 eggs
1 teaspoon vanilla
1½ teaspoons almond extract

4 cups all purpose flour
1 teaspoon salt
4 teaspoons baking powder
Crushed Almonds

Cream the butter and sugar together; beat in the eggs, one at a time. Add in the extracts. Sift together the dry ingredients (except almonds) and then add to the egg mix. Chill. Roll into balls and dip into crushed almonds. Bake on an ungreased cookie sheet at 350°for about 17 minutes.

Clockwise from top left: Susan Alexander Marquino, Pat Tromba Werner, David DiJohn, M.D., Linda Gebhart Smart, and Angela Sarcia Murphy

Can't have the Alsheimer boys and not Megan... Megan Alsheimer

On Left: More Cousins... The Vennen's L-R: Brian, Robert, Lucille, Tom, Kristine, and David

On Right: Betty Silvestri Saracino and Julia Silvestri, Lucille's mother and grandmother

The Sullivan's: Top L-R: Katie, Eileen, Colleen and Jimmy Bottom L-R: Jim and Kathy

L-R Top: Flo Avella, Betty Silvestri Saracino, and Mae Avella Bottom: Marie Caccavale

JOANNA'S ALMOND BRITTLE
Joanna Basile

¼ cup butter (½ stick)
1 cup granulated sugar

2 cups whole blanched Almonds or 1½ cups sunflower
seeds (roasted unsalted)

Combine all of the above ingredients in a large Teflon skillet. Cook over **MEDIUM** heat stirring (using a wooden spoon sprayed with PAM) until the sugar melts and the mixture is a golden brown (cooking time can be up to 40-50 minutes.)The mix will first look like light brown beach sand, then it will start to clump together and then get like loose caramel Pour mixture quickly into buttered 15 x 10 x 2-inch pan (pizza pan, I use a disposable aluminum cookie sheet. It may not fill the whole pan.) When cool, break into pieces. **Don't ever double the recipe, make two separate batches if you need more.** Store in a plastic container with wax paper between the layers.

Note: Sugar must meet the mixture (it will be a loose, but thick consistency). Please be careful when stirring the mixture, it gets **very hot** and sometimes will splatter. **I wear long sleeves when I make this.** If you can find blanched almonds, I have used the whole almond with the brown skin on them and it works just fine.

This recipe has been passed down from Frank's grandmother and mother. It is a Basile family Christmas favorite. Joanna was gracious enough to share it with me. She made it at our Christmas Cookie Exchange.

ESPRESSO TRUFFLES
Ronni Tichenor

¾ cup heavy cream
1 tablespoon instant espresso powder
¼ cup granulated sugar
1 ounces semisweet chocolate, chopped into ¼ inch pieces

4 ounces of unsweetened chocolate, chopped into
¼ inch pieces
30 individual chocolate covered espresso beans

Heat the heavy cream, instant espresso powder, sugar, and butter in a 1½ quart saucepan over medium high heat. When hot, stir to dissolve the sugar. Bring to a boil. Place the semisweet and unsweetened chocolate in a 4 quart bowl. Pour the boiling cream mixture over the chocolate and allow to stand for 5 minutes. Stir until smooth and presto, espresso ganache. Place foil candy cups in mini muffin tins on a baking sheet. Spoon 2 level tablespoons of ganache into each foil cup. Use your index finger to push out the ganache if necessary. Top each cup with a chocolate espresso bean. Refrigerate until firm, about 1 hour. Serve immediately or store in a tightly sealed plastic container in the refrigerator.

Ronni makes these every Christmas. They are fabulous and keep very well in the refrigerator. These make a great holiday gift.

EBONY AND IVORY CHOCOLATE TRUFFLES
Ronni Tichenor

7½ ounces white chocolate, chopped into ¼ inch pieces
¾ cup heavy cream
8 ounces semisweet chocolate, chopped into ¼ inch pieces

¾ cup heavy cream
5 tablespoons unsweetened cocoa

Place the white and dark chocolates into separate stainless steel bowls. Heat the cream in a 1½ quart saucepan over medium heat. Bring to a boil. Pour ¼ cup of boiling cream over the white chocolate and the remaining ½ cup over the dark chocolate and allow to stand for 4 to 5 minutes. Stir each with a separate whisk until smooth, and allow to cool for 1 hour at room temperature. Refrigerate the two ganaches for 15 minutes, stirring every 5 minutes. Line a baking sheet with parchment paper. Portion 36 heaping teaspoons of dark chocolate into separate mounds onto the parchment paper. Top each teaspoon of dark chocolate with a level teaspoon of white chocolate. To fashion the truffles, roll each portion of chocolate in your palms in a gentle circular motion, using just enough pressure to form smooth rounds. Roll the rounds of chocolate in cocoa until completely covered. This recipe can easily be doubled. You can make them all dark chocolate, add 1 teaspoon orange extract, and roll in chopped pecans. Makes 36.

These are the truffles that Ronni always makes for the holidays. They are wonderful, especially with the orange flavoring.

ROCKY ROAD CANDY
Ann D'Amico

1 (12 ounce) package of chocolate chips
1 (14 ounce) can Eagle Brand Sweetened Condensed milk
2 tablespoons butter

2 cups dry roasted peanuts (or walnuts)
1 (10 ½ ounce) package of miniature marshmallows (use colored ones)

In a heavy saucepan, over low heat, melt morsels with condensed milk and butter. In a large bowl combine marshmallows and nuts. Stir in chocolate mixture. Spread in greased 9 x 13-inch pan. Chill 2 hours or until firm. Cut into squares. Store loosely covered at room temperature.

MACADAMIA BRITTLE
Elise Feiner

3 tablespoons unsalted butter, at room temperature
1 cup chopped macadamia nut, leave them coarse
1½ cups sugar
½ cup light corn syrup

½ cup water
½ cup finely chopped semisweet chocolate (I like Ghirardelli)
Butter for baking sheets

Brush a disposable aluminum cookie sheet 9 x 13-inch with butter. Place on a regular cookie sheet for stability. Sprinkle the macadamia nuts over the cookie sheet. Combine the sugar, corn syrup, water and butter in a medium saucepan. Cook over medium heat, stirring frequently until the sugar dissolves. Use a pastry brush dipped in water to brush down the sides of the pan if any crystals appear. After the sugar has dissolved, stop stirring the mix, and continue to cook until it reaches 300°, or the hard crack stage on a candy thermometer. Remove the pan from the heat and stir in the chocolate; stir constantly. Pour the chocolate mix over the nuts. Spread over the nuts using a spatula that has been sprayed with PAM® or oiled. Let cool, and then break into pieces. Store in an airtight container.

I like to make this at the holidays. You can substitute different nuts if you like, but I love Macadamia nuts.

L-R: Jody and Abby Feiner

L-R: Jody, Abby and Lauren Feiner roasting their grandmother Mom Mom at her 80th birthday

L-R: Abby and Lauren Feiner at Famous 4th Street Deli in Philadelphia

CHOCOLATE TRUFFLES
Elise Feiner

¾ cup hazelnuts, walnuts, or pecans
6 (1 ounce) squares semisweet chocolate
⅓ cup heavy cream
1⅓ cups confectioners" sugar

1 egg white
2 tablespoons Grand Marnier, Cointreau or Rum
Chocolate Sprinkles

Grind the nuts in a food processor until fine, **but do not over process** or they'll turn to a butter. Line the bottom of a 9 x 5 x 3-inch loaf pan with waxed paper. In a small saucepan, combine chocolate with cream. Heat over very low heat until chocolate is just melted. Remove from heat. In a medium bowl combine nuts, sugar, and egg whites. Stir with a wooden spoon until just combined. Stir in chocolate mixture and liqueur. Combine well. Turn into prepared pan. Refrigerate until firm. Shape into round balls using ½ teaspoon for each. Roll the balls into chocolate sprinkles. Place in mini cupcake holders. Freeze if desired, and thaw before serving, or keep refrigerated.

I've been making these at the holidays for years; they're fabulous and easy to make.

L-R: Betty and Jerry Feiner, Elmer and Shirley Snyder

L-R: Shirley Snyder and Betty Feiner today!

Shirley and Elmer Snyder today

L-R: Betty and Kevin Feiner with Louise Altman, they have been best friends since they were young girls. Today they were celebrating Betty's 80th Birthday!

461

DEATH BY CHOCOLATE ALMOND CRUNCH
Elise Feiner

4 cups sliced almonds
6 ounces unsalted butter
1½ cups granulated sugar
½ cup water
¼ cup Myers's Dark Rum

¼ cup honey
8 ounces semisweet chocolate, chopped into ¼ inch pieces
4 ounces unsweetened chocolate, chopped into
¼ inch pieces

Preheat the oven to 325°. Toast **2 cups** of almonds on a baking sheet in the preheated oven until golden brown, about 12 to 14 minutes. Remove the almonds from the oven and allow to cool to room temperature. Transfer the almonds to a large dish or other suitable container and set aside until needed. Melt the butter in a 2½ quart saucepan over low heat, stirring constantly as it melts so it does not simmer or boil. As soon as the butter is completely melted, add the sugar, water, rum, and honey. Increase the heat to medium high. Heat the mixture to a temperature of 220°, as measured on a candy thermometer, stirring constantly. Add the untoasted almonds and continue to heat and stir until the mixture reaches a temperature of 225°. Evenly divide the honey-almond mixture between two baking sheets. Place the baking sheets on the top and middle shelves of the preheated oven and bake until the mixture is evenly caramelized, about 24 to 26 minutes. Rotate the baking sheets from top to bottom about halfway through the baking time. Remove from the oven and allow to cool for 5 minutes. Combine the semisweet and unsweetened chocolate pieces and evenly divide and sprinkle over the surface of the caramelized honey-almond mixture. Allow to stand for 5 minutes. Use a spatula sprayed with PAM® to spread the chocolate throughout the mixture. Evenly divide and sprinkle the toasted almonds over the chocolate. Place both baking sheets in the freezer for 20 minutes. Remove the Chocolate Almond Crunch from the freezer and break into irregular pieces. Store in a sealed plastic container in the freezer or refrigerator.

The Venezio Family
L-R: Jennifer, Brittany, Rich and Julie

MIXED NUT BRITTLE
Elise Feiner

1½ cups sugar
½ cup light corn syrup
¾ cup cold water
Pinch of salt

2½ cups of mixed nuts (don't use salted from a can)
1 teaspoon vanilla
1 teaspoon baking soda
1 cup shredded coconut

Brush a disposable aluminum cookie sheet well with unsalted butter at room temperature. Place on a regular heavy cookie sheet for stability. In a large saucepan, combine the sugar, corn syrup, water and salt. Bring to a boil over medium heat; stir until sugar is dissolved. Brush down the sides of the pan with a pastry brush dipped in water to prevent any crystallization. Cook, stirring occasionally, until the mixture reaches 238° (soft ball stage). Stir in the nuts and coconut, stir frequently so the nuts don't burn, until light amber in color. Stir in the vanilla and baking soda. The mixture will foam up. Pour onto the cookie sheet, and spread with a spatula sprayed with PAM® or vegetable oil. When cool, break into pieces.

I love to do the candies at the holidays. They make great gifts as well. I like to use, pecans, almonds, pistachios and pumpkin seeds.

WHITE TRASH
Candie Mitchell

6 cups Crispix® Cereal
1 pound M & Ms® plain chocolate candies
3 cups Cheerios®

2 cups small pretzels
1 cup salted peanuts, no skin
1½ pounds white chocolate wafers

Mix all above together except white chocolate wafers. Melt white chocolate in a bowl in the microwave 1 minute at a time and stir after each minute. Once melted, pour over cereal mixture. Mix together and lay out on wax paper to dry. After about 1 hour, break into pieces. Store in Tupperware bowl.

My friend Candie Mitchell made this as a favor for a graduation party and wrapped it in pretty bags. This is a great snack for kids, fast and easy to make and taste great...

COFFEE-WALNUT TOFFEE
Elise Feiner

1¼ cups unsalted butter (2½ sticks)
1 cup sugar
⅓ cup packed light brown sugar
⅓ cup water
1 tablespoon dark molasses
2 teaspoons instant espresso powder

½ teaspoon cinnamon
¼ teaspoon salt
2 cups coarsely chopped walnuts
4½ ounces imported bittersweet chocolate (not unsweetened), finely chopped
4½ ounces Lindt white chocolate, finely chopped

Butter a small cookie sheet (I use a disposable aluminum one). Melt butter in a heavy 2½ quart saucepan over low heat. Add sugars, water, molasses, and espresso powder, cinnamon and salt; stir until the sugar dissolves. Attach a clip on candy thermometer to the pan. Increase heat to medium; cook until temperature registers 290°; stirring slowly but constantly and scraping bottom of the pan with a wooden spatula, about 20 minutes. (Hint: do not leave unattended and spray the wooden spatula with PAM). Remove from the heat. Mix in 1½ cups of the chopped nuts. Immediately pour mixture into prepared buttered pan. Tilt the pan (use potholders) so that the toffee spreads to ¼ inch thickness. Sprinkle the chocolates on the top of the hot toffee as follows; alternating white and dark to form a checkerboard pattern about 4 squares across and about 7 squares lengthwise. Let the chocolate sit on top of the hot toffee about 1 minute. With the back of 2 spoons (one for the white, one for the dark chocolate) swirl the chocolate to help it melt. Shake the sheet to form an even layer. Then, using a tip of a knife, swirl the chocolates together to make a marble pattern. Sprinkle with remaining ½ cup chopped nuts. Refrigerate until toffee is firm. Break toffee into pieces. You can make these 2 weeks ahead and chill in an airtight container. You can serve it cold or at room temperature.

I found this recipe in a magazine years ago and always make it at the holidays. It is one of my favorites and Nanny's favorite too! My mother could never finish a meal, but always had room for dessert!

Back Row L-R: Jerry, Kevin holding Jody, Barbara and Betty Feiner Front Row L-R: Abby and Lauren Feiner at Famous' Deli in Philadelphia – a Feiner Family tradition for Sunday Brunch! After years under the same ownership Famous' was sold to Ilene and Russ Cowan, who have done a great job remodeling and improving the menu. The Cowans come from a long line of Brooklyn Deli owners (Radins, etc). If you haven't been there recently or you are in the Philadelphia area, stop in, you won't be sorry. Famous Fourth Street Deli is located at 700 South 4th Street, Philadelphia, PA. 215 922-3274

MINTED MARBLE BARK
Nancy Blaker

1 cup sugar
⅓ cup light corn syrup
⅓ cup water

1¼ teaspoons peppermint oil (not extract)
¾ pound white chocolate, finely chopped
½ bittersweet chocolate, finely chopped

Note:You can substitute one scant cup of crushed hard peppermint candy for the homemade peppermint candy in this recipe. Proceed as directed in Step three. If you make the mint candy, the leftover sugar can be reserved for stirring into coffee, tea, or hot chocolate. Be sure to use peppermint oil, and not extract. Use more white chocolate than dark chocolate. Makes about 1¾ pounds

Line a baking sheet with parchment paper or foil. In a medium saucepan, stir the sugar with the corn syrup and ⅓ cup water. Wash down the sides of the pan with a wet pastry brush and bring to a boil over high heat. Set a candy thermometer in the pan and boil, **WITHOUT STIRRING**, until the temperature reaches 290°, about 7 minutes. **IMMEDIATELY REMOVE** from the heat. As soon as the mixture stops boiling, stir in 1 teaspoon of the peppermint oil, cover the pan and let sit for **10 SECONDS**. Stir once and pour the sugar mixture onto the prepared baking sheet, tilting the baking sheet to spread the mixture evenly over the bottom. Let cool completely. **IMMEDIATELY PUT THE POT IN THE SINK WITH WARM SOAPY WATER.** When the candy has cooled break candy into 1½ to 2 inch pieces. (The candy can be done up to 1 day ahead and stored in an airtight container.) Place the candy in a food processor and pulse until the largest pieces are no larger than ¼-inch. Place the crushed candy in a coarse strainer set over a bowl to sift out the finely ground sugar; reserve the sugar for another use.

Line a baking sheet with parchment paper or foil. Put the white chocolate and bittersweet chocolate in separate medium bowls and set each over a saucepan of gently simmering water (or use a double boiler). Stir the chocolate until half melted, about 4 minutes for the white and 6 minutes for the bittersweet. Remove from the heat and stir until completely melted. Stir the remaining ¼ teaspoon of peppermint oil into the white chocolate, and then add a generous ½ cup of the chopped peppermint candy. Stir the remaining peppermint candy into the bittersweet chocolate. Pour the white chocolate onto the prepared baking sheet in 3 long strips about 2 inches wide and 2 inches apart. Pour the bittersweet chocolate in three strips next to the white chocolate. Draw the tip of a small knife crosswise through the chocolate to create a swirling marble effect. Holding the parchment paper down with your thumbs, gently shake the pan to level the chocolate. Give it 3 to 4 quick taps on the counter to remove any air bubbles; then refrigerate until hardened, about 1 hour. Break into 2 inch pieces before serving. Store in an airtight container in the refrigerator.

Maria Trainor gave me a copy of this recipe that Nancy Blaker made as Christmas gifts one year. I made it for Thanksgiving and it was great. Be careful not to over melt the white chocolate, and be careful to only cover the candy for 10 seconds or it will start to harden.

L-R: Jeffrey, David, Nanny
Nellie Reinisch, Lauren, and
Steven Feiner
Visiting together in Florida

BAILEY'S IRISH CREAM TRUFFLES
Katherine Avella

1 (12 ounce) bag semisweet chocolate morsels
¼ cup heavy cream
1 tablespoon sweet butter

2 egg yolks
¼ cup Baileys Irish Cream

Melt chocolate, Baileys and heavy cream together over very low heat. Whisk in yolks, one at a time. The mixture will begin to thicken. Whisk in butter. Refrigerate overnight, or until firm. Roll into small balls. You can then roll the truffles in powdered sugar, cocoa, chopped nuts, colored sugar or sprinkles.

NOT QUITE CHOCOLATE COVERED PRETZELS
Elise Feiner

24 waffle shaped pretzel square   1 bag of M & M's
24 Hershey Kisses or Rolos

Line a cookie sheet with parchment paper. Place the pretzels in a single layer and top each with a kiss. Preheat the oven to 350°. Put into the oven for 1-2 minutes just until the kisses start to melt. Remove from the oven and place an M & M onto each kiss. Refrigerate to harden. Store in a plastic container.

My family loves chocolate covered pretzels but this is a little twist on that theme. These are great for parties as you can coordinate the M&M's to your theme colors. They are very easy to make.

ROCKY ROAD FUDGE
Elise Feiner

⅓ cup unsalted butter, cut into chunks   12 ounces semisweet chocolate, chopped
1 cup evaporated milk   ½ cup slivered almonds, toasted
1½ cups sugar   1 cup mini marshmallows
¼ teaspoon salt

Combine butter, evaporated milk, sugar, and salt in a medium saucepan. Bring to a hard boil for 5 to 7 minutes, stirring constantly. Remove from heat. Stir in the chocolate until melted and smooth. Fold in the almonds and marshmallows. Pour into an 8 x 8-inch square baking pan. Chill until firm, about 2 to 4 hours. Cut into 12 squares.

MARGARITA CHEX® FIESTA MIX
Elise Feiner

½ cup butter   3 cups Rice Chex®
2 tablespoons Tequila or lime juice   2 cups Wheat Chex®
2 teaspoons seasoned salt   1 cup mixed nuts
¼ teaspoon cayenne pepper   1 cup small pretzel twists
2 envelopes (3.3 ounce) instant Margarita Mix dry 1 cup dried cranberries
4 cups Corn Chex®

Preheat the oven to 250°. Melt the butter in a large roasting pan. Stir in the Tequila, seasoned salt, cayenne pepper and Margarita mix. Stir in the cereals, nuts, and pretzels until evenly coated. Bake 1 hour stirring every 15 minutes. Stir in dried cranberries. Spread on paper towels to cool.

This recipe was generously reprinted with the permission of the General Mills Company. Chex® is a registered trademark of General Mills. This would be great in the summer with a tall pitcher of Margaritas. Maria Trainor makes a great Margarita!

Clockwise from the top:
Katherine, Jonathan, Tessa
Trainor, Connie DiMare, and
Kyle Trainor

Equal time for mothers and sons... could it get any better than this?

L-R: Betty Feiner and her boys...
Marc, Betty, Ivan and Kevin

Betty Feiner and her men...
L-R: Ivan, Betty, Marc and Kevin

L-R: Elise and her boys...David,
Elise, Jeffrey and Steven Feiner

Elise and Jeffrey Feiner

Maria Trainor and Jonathan

Donna Feiner and Noah Gabriel

Marinades, Sauces, and Dressings

The Gene Feiner Family

L-R: Brett, and Hallie Feiner, Sharon, Julia and Mulford Fisher, AnnDee, Adam, Larry and Marti Feiner
Sitting L-R: Ann, Gene, and Greg Feiner

"Once the game is over, the king and the pawn go back in the same box."

-Italian Proverb

Stocking a Dream Kitchen continued...

George Foreman® Grill
Pannini Grill
Pizzelle Maker
Fajita Maker
Sandwich Press
Electric Griddle
Cookie Cutters
Biscuit Cutters (different shapes, round, hearts, etc.)
Food Processor
Standing Mixer
Electric Juicer
Ice Cream Maker
Waffle Iron
Coffee Grinder
Chafing Dishes (Metal with covers) 2 or 3 are ideal; BJ's carries some that work quite well and are around $25.00 These are great if you do a lot of brunches or Sunday breakfasts)
Pasta Maker
Bread Machine Baking
Dehydrator
Spice Grinder
Disposable Aluminum Cookies sheets, muffin tins, loaf pans, square pans etc, so much easier!
Serving Trays
Bed Tray
Utensil Caddies
Glass Trays
Doilies

Corn on the Cob holders and dishes
Candles
Sterno's
Paper Dishes
Bagel Cutter
Deep Fryer
Immersion Blender
Ice Cream Maker
Vegetable Steamer
Griddle
Ice Cube Trays
Electric Slicing Machine
Wok
Paella Pan
Flavor Injector
Pasta Drying Rack
Egg Slicer
Tuna Can Strainer
Cherry or olive pitter
Wooden Spoons
Crumb Sweeper
Apple Cutter
Funnels
Metal Skewers
Trivets
Potholders
Paper Towel Holder
Magnetic Spice Racks
A disposable rubber glove – great when you can't open a jar
Jar Opener
Laser Thermometer

_____

_____

_____

_____

_____

_____

AUNT THIRZA'S TURKEY MARINADE AND TURKEY
Thirza Avella

2 lemons, cut in half and squeezed of their juice, keep the lemon shell halves as is
1-2 medium onions, peeled and cut in slices
1 packet of Sazon Goya® seasoning mix (con culantro y achiote)
Wesson® oil about 1½ cups
Garlic flavored wine vinegar (about ½ cup)
Garlic salt (about 1-2 tablespoons)
Onion powder or salt (about 2 teaspoons)
Oregano (about 4 tablespoons)

Parsley (about 4 tablespoons)
Basil (about 4 tablespoons)
Black pepper to taste (about ¾ teaspoon)
Paprika (about ½ tablespoon)
McCormick® Season All Seasoned Salt (about 2 teaspoons)
Cooking with Love's Passion Spice Mix (about 2 teaspoons)
Water (enough to make it a little looser) about ½ cup
For the cheesecloth: Melt 3 sticks of butter and a bottle of white Zinfandel (This is an optional step)

In a large disposable roasting pan, mix lemon juice, oil, vinegar, and all the seasonings. Don't add the water, onions and the lemon halves (do not grate, leave as is) yet. Mix well. Add in the onions and lemon rinds and mix again. Add a little water now if mixture is too thick. Rinse and wash turkey. Remove the gizzard packages if possible. If the turkey is too frozen at this point, be sure to remove them later, before baking. Marinade the turkey in this mix at least overnight or up to two days (make sure you rub the marinade all over the turkey, top and bottom and place some mix into the bird's cavities. . Preheat the oven to 500°. Spray a large roasting pan and rack with PAM®. When ready to bake the turkey, stick the lemon halves in the bird's cavities. Keep as much of the onion and about 1 cup of the liquid and discard the rest. Put the remaining cup of marinade and the onions in the prepared roasting pan.

At this point, you have a few options. You can do nothing and leave with the marinade all over it, or you can soften some butter and rub over the top of the bird and sprinkle with a little paprika, or you can sprinkle a little garlic salt and paprika on the turkey, or you can melt 3 sticks of butter with a bottle of white wine and dip a four layer cheesecloth in the butter mixture and place it over the bird's breast, and keep adding butter/wine mixture to keep cloth moist. (Remove the cheesecloth during the last half hour of cooking. Check the package for directions for cooking time. Check with a meat thermometer and cook until about 10° lower than the thermometer says for poultry. The turkey will go up 10° after it is removed from the oven, and then it won't dry out. When you remove the bird, place the cheesecloth back over the top to keep it moist until sliced.) Place the bird on the rack in the pan. Start the bird in the 500° oven **FOR 30 minutes**, breast side down, then **DECREASE** temperature to 350°, turn the bird over and continue to bake breast side up depending on the weight. **If you are afraid to turn the turkey when it is hot, just start it off breast side up and don't worry about it, it won't make much of a difference.** The marinade is so delicious that no matter what you do you can't hurt this turkey! Baste frequently. When **10° less** than the right temperature for poultry is reached, remove the turkey from the oven. Let cool a few minutes. **Remove the lemon carefully from the cavities** (they will be hot.) Let the turkey rest on a cutting board at least 20 minutes before carving. See Brown Gravy Recipe Gravy and use the cooked marinade drippings to make a delicious brown gravy!.

Aunt Thirza always used to marinade her turkeys like this. They are the best tasting turkeys in the world. Of course, she got the recipe from her mother, Eva Castro. Both were excellent cooks. She also used this to marinade a loin of pork, just leave out the lemons. I can still hear her infectious laughter in my ears whenever I make this recipe. We all miss her terribly.

Ann and Phil D'Amico's Wedding:
Back Row L-R: Phil Avella, Marie Caccavale, Rudy, Phil and Ann D'Amico, Mario Simat, Lisa Dambrosio, Joe Avella
Front L-R: Elise Avella Feiner, Giannina Schwendemann, Marlene Simat and Lucille Saracino Vennen

MAPLE SYRUP RIB MARINADE
Elise Feiner

3 pounds pork or beef spareribs, parboiled in pot with 2 peeled whole onions
1 cup water
2 teaspoons salt
2½ tablespoons chili sauce
2 tablespoons onions, peeled and finely chopped
¼ teaspoon chili powder
1½ cups maple syrup

⅛ teaspoon pepper
2 teaspoons Cooking with Love's Passion Spice Mix
Zest of half a lemon
1 tablespoon Worcestershire sauce
2 teaspoons salt
½ teaspoon dry mustard

In a medium bowl, combine the cup of water and 2 teaspoons salt to make a salt water mixture. In a medium bowl combine remaining ingredients except the spareribs; mix well. Spray grill with PAM® about 5 to 7 inches above the coals on low temp, for about 45 minutes, spraying with the salt water mixture. Then, start basting with the maple marinade sauce, brushing frequently for the next 15 to 20 minutes

L-R: John Grimaldi, Jr., Philly Avella,
John Grimaldi, Sr.

Ellie and Norm Neslin, M.D.

SPARERIB MARINADE
Elise Feiner

1½ cup ketchup
3 tablespoons cider vinegar
2 tablespoons corn syrup
2 teaspoons salt

1 teaspoon paprika
¾ teaspoon chili powder
4 tablespoons maple syrup
1 onion, peeled and left whole

Mix all ingredients together. Parboil your spareribs in lightly salted water in which you have placed a whole onion for about 15 to 20 minutes. Drain; cool and place into marinade. Let marinade overnight.

STEVEN'S MARINADE
Steven Feiner

Salt and Pepper to Taste
Garlic Salt
A1 Steak Sauce
Jack Daniels No. 7 Mustard

McCormick Spicy Season All Seasoned Salt
Chili Powder
Oregano
Parsley

Mix all the ingredients to taste and marinate your steaks overnight or for a few hours at least.

As you can see Steven likes his food spicy. He made this marinade up to put on his Omaha Steaks, and called me with the recipe. Adjust the amounts based on how much you are marinating.

UNCLE PHIL'S CHICKEN MARINADE
Elise Feiner

2-3 lemons
2 medium to large onions, peeled and sliced
3 sprigs fresh mint leaves or dried if fresh not available
Extra virgin olive oil
Red wine vinegar to taste
1 tablespoon oregano
1 tablespoon dried parsley

4-5 cloves garlic, peeled and crushed
Paprika
½ cup grated cheese
Salt and pepper to taste
20-30 chicken pieces of your choice (legs, breasts, thighs. etc.)

In a large plastic bowl, cut the lemons in half, taking care to remove the seeds, squeeze the juice into the bowl, and then add the halves of the lemons back into the bowl as well. Add the onions, mint, vinegar, salt, pepper, and oregano. You can add a little water if it's thick. Add the chicken and let refrigerate overnight. Cook the chicken on a grill in aluminum trays with the marinade. At the end, remove from pan and place directly on grill to brown. Brush with the marinade mix frequently while the chicken is cooking. You can also use boneless breasts, slice in strips after cooking, and put them on skewers and serve with peanut dipping sauce (satay sauce – see index)   (or slice in strips before and barbeque on skewers as an appetizer and use satay sauce..

Making the chicken marinade was always Uncle Phil's job when we lived in Brooklyn. We had barbecues every weekend in the summer. The smell of this chicken cooking is outstanding. We used to have a small vegetable garden in the backyard and Uncle Phil grew the mint for the marinade and for his iced tea there.

The Avella Boys L-R: Joseph and Philip

Phyllis and Philip Avella

SYMEON'S MARINADE
Symeon and Ann Tsoupelis

Symeon's Spices or Cooking with Love's Passion Spice Mix
Red Wine

Vegetable or olive oil

Mix the ingredients to taste. Marinate the meat of your choice for a few hours or overnight.

This is a fast, easy marinade made with wonderful Symeon's spices.

"It's surprising how many persons go through life without ever recognizing that their feelings toward other people are largely determined by their feelings toward themselves, and if you're not comfortable within yourself, you can't be comfortable with others."
- Sydney J. Harris

THIRZA'S DUCK SAUCE MARINADE
Thirza Avella

1 large bottle duck sauce
1 teaspoon lemon juice

2 teaspoons each garlic powder, onion powder, paprika, oregano, salt, pepper, parsley and basil

In a large bowl, mix duck sauce, lemon juice, garlic powder, onion powder, paprika, oregano, salt, pepper, parsley, and basil. Mix together and add meat; marinate one to two hours or longer. This is great for pork chops or spare ribs. To use for chicken, add fresh onion, peeled and sliced, and more onion powder.

Aunt Thirza made the most delicious meats. This is one of the marinades that she used. You can probably use it on anything. However, nothing beats her turkey marinade, it's the greatest!

Thirza Castro Avella in Old Forge, New York
My beautiful sister-in-law Thirza with the most infectious laugh, smart, talented, and beautiful. She was taken way too young, and we miss her dearly…she is always in our hearts.

L-R: Melissa Avella, Eva Castro, and Douglas Avella

AUNT CAMY'S MARINADE
Camille Sanabria

½ cup oil
1 cup soy sauce
2 tablespoons brown sugar

2 tablespoons sherry or Jim Beam ®
Grated Ginger to taste

Mix all ingredients together. Add your favorite meat or chicken. Refrigerate one hour or overnight. Bake or grill as desired.

Aunt Camille says this is one of her favorite marinade mixes.

Back L-R: Claire Akselrad, Aviva Akselrad Zierler, Rene Sanabria, Jeane Cassata, Samantha Caplan, Jonathan Zierler, Norm Zierler, Fran Zierler, David Zierler, Andrew Sanabria, Camille Sanabria
Front L-R: Zach Zierler, Jeremy Zierler

BEER MARINADE
Elise Feiner

½ cup olive oil
1 cup dark beer
¼ cup lemon juice
4 cloves garlic, peeled and crushed
1½ teaspoons kosher salt
1 teaspoon freshly ground black pepper

2 bay leaves
1½ teaspoon dry mustard
1½ teaspoon basil
1½ teaspoon oregano
1½ teaspoon thyme

To prepare the marinade, whisk together the oil, beer, and lemon juice. Add garlic, salt, pepper, bay leaves, mustard, basil, oregano, and thyme. Mix well.

JOJO'S STEAK MARINADE
Joseph Mainella, Jr.

1-2 tablespoons McCormick® Montreal Steak Seasoning
About ½ to ¾ cup Lea and Perrins® Worcestershire Sauce
½ to ¾ bottle of Zesty Italian Salad Dressing

Garlic powder
1-2 tablespoons balsamic vinegar

Mix all together and add steak of your choice to the mix. This is great for London Broil. Insert the fork several times into the meat on both sides to allow marinade to penetrate. Turn frequently and pierce both sides with the fork frequently. Marinate for about 2 hours or more. Grill steak starting on high for a few minutes and reduce to low. Cook to desired doneness.

JoJo made this marinade when we were in Florida. It was one of the best steaks I have ever eaten. JoJo was a cook at the Outback for years.

ORIENTAL MARINADE
Elise Feiner

¾ cup soy sauce
¼ cup rice wine vinegar
⅓ cup olive oil
⅓ cup orange juice
1 tablespoon lemon juice

1 tablespoon grated ginger
6 cloves of garlic, peeled and crushed
2 tablespoon Coleman's Dry Mustard
2 tablespoons brown sugar
2 teaspoons garlic salt

Mix all the ingredients together in a large plastic container. This is good for beef and chicken. Place the meat in the container so that it is submerged. Refrigerate at least 8 hours or overnight. If you are marinating beef, prick the meat several times with a fork on both sides.

COFFEE MARINADE
Elise Feiner

2 cups strong coffee or espresso
1 cup brown sugar
2 tablespoons dried mustard
2 tablespoons Worcestershire sauce
¼ cup lemon juice
1 teaspoon cayenne pepper

4 cloves garlic, peeled and crushed
4 tablespoon Kahlua
1 tablespoon Cooking with Love's Heavenly
Greek Spice Mix
1 teaspoon cornstarch
¼ cup water

Mix everything together except the Kahlua, Cooking with Love's Passion Spice Mix, cornstarch and water together in a pot. Bring to a boil. Mix the cornstarch and water together until there are no lumps. Add to the coffee mix and stir well to prevent lumps. Bring to a boil again, cook for about 5 minutes; cool. When cool add the Kahlua and Cooking with Love's Passion Spice Mix. Use this for beef.

COOKING WITH LOVE'S BASIC SPICE MARINADE MIX
Elise Feiner

2 tablespoon garlic salt
1 tablespoon Cooking with Love's Heavenly
Greek Spice Mix
1 tablespoon dried parsley
4 tablespoons dried oregano
4 tablespoons dried basil
4 tablespoons dried parsley

½ teaspoon black pepper
½ tablespoon paprika
2 teaspoons onion salt
2 teaspoons McCormick® Seasoned Salt
1 packet of Sazon Goya® seasoning mix (con culantro y achiote) available in the Spanish Food section of your grocery store

Mix the dry ingredients together. Depending on what you are marinating, add the following according to your taste:

1 medium to large onion, peeled and sliced (good with everything)
½ cup vegetable oil (good with everything)
½ cup water (good with everything)
½ cup red wine vinegar (good with everything)
4 tablespoons Kahlua (good with beef)
1 to 2 lemons, cut in half and squeezed, add lemon halves too (good for poultry)
1 tablespoon rosemary (good with lamb)

My son Steven is always taking home this marinade blend to cook his meat with. You can alter it to your own taste, this is just a suggestion.

Back Row:
Jeffrey Feiner
Middle Row L-R:
Jennifer, Betty, Karen,
Danielle, David,
Steven and Lauren
Feiner
Front Row L - R:
Abby and Jody Feiner

L-R: Danielle, Abby,
Barbara, Elise, Betty,
Jody, Karen and
Lauren Feiner

OLIVE OIL BREAD DIPPING SAUCE
Elise Feiner

1 tablespoon fresh chopped basil
1 tablespoon fresh chopped parsley
1 tablespoon fresh minced garlic
1 teaspoon thyme
1 teaspoon oregano
¼ teaspoon black pepper

½ teaspoon minced fresh rosemary
½ teaspoon kosher salt
¼ teaspoon garlic salt
¼ teaspoon crushed red pepper flakes (optional)
½ cup extra virgin olive oil
⅛ teaspoon fresh lemon juice

Mix everything together except the olive oil and lemon juice in a small food processor. Pulse briefly until everything is about the same size. In a separate container mix the olive oil and lemon juice. To serve, combine about 1½ teaspoons of the chopped herb mix with 3 to 4 tablespoons of the olive oil mix on a small dish. Dip sliced bread in mixture.

ROASTED GARLIC DIPPING OIL
Elise Feiner

To roast the garlic:
2 heads garlic tops removed
2 teaspoons extra virgin olive oil

Salt
Ground black pepper

For the dipping sauce:
Freshly ground black pepper to taste
Salt to taste
Roasted garlic cloves left whole after roasting

Grating cheese of your choice
1-2 cups extra virgin olive oil

Preheat the oven to 350° Cut off the top end of the whole garlic bulb, but don't go too deep. Place a drop of olive oil, salt and pepper on a piece of aluminum foil. Place the garlic bulb on top of oil and then, rub 1 teaspoon of oil into the top of each head. Sprinkle lightly with salt and pepper. Wrap each head separately in the aluminum foil. Bake until the cloves are soft and golden, about 1 hour. Remove from the oven and let sit until cool enough to handle. Carefully remove the cloves if using in oil, or squeeze each head of garlic to expel the cloves into a bowl if using for a paste. Place the bulbs of garlic into olive oil; set aside until needed. When ready to serve, spoon the olive oil and garlic mixture onto a dish, Season with salt and pepper to taste. Sprinkle with grating cheese. Dip bread and enjoy.

LAMB MARINADE
Elise Feiner

1 tablespoon black peppercorns, plus ground pepper
¼ cup Dijon mustard
¼ cup soy sauce
½ cup red wine or burgundy (Livingston)
2 teaspoons dried thyme or 2 sprigs fresh thyme
10–12 cloves of garlic, peeled and crushed
½ cup olive oil
2 teaspoons garlic salt

1 teaspoon sea salt
2 teaspoons seasoned salt
1 large onion peeled and chopped
2 teaspoons Cooking with Love's Passion Spice Mix
4 teaspoons dried rosemary
Juice of one lemon plus the zest on one lemon or orange
Lamb chops or rack of lamb, or leg of lamb; amount depends on how many you are serving.

This marinade is enough to do about 15 loin chops or 2 to 3 small racks of lamb. In a small skillet, heat the peppercorns over medium heat, about 4 to 6 minutes. Add to a large bowl. Add remaining ingredients. Add lamb chops or rack of lamb and marinate in the refrigerator overnight. Turn occasionally. Season with salt and pepper. Grill or broil the chops or racks turning once until crisp about 12 to 15 minutes or bake leg of lamb in a preheated 350° oven until meat thermometer reaches desired temperature.
Note: I usually cut the racks into individual chops to marinade them and then put on the grill or use a grill pan.

These lamb chops are delicious on the grill. This marinade is wonderful! Serve with Gorgonzola Sauce (see index)

"The three hardest tasks in the world are neither physical feats nor intellectual achievements, but moral acts: to return love for hate, to include the excluded, and to say, "I was wrong."
-Sydney J. Harris

More Mothers and sons, grandmothers and grandsons, godmothers and godsons…

Fran Zierler and her sons…
L-R: David, Jonathan, Fran, Zachary, and Jeremy Zierler
Fran an Norm have done a great job with their boys, or should I say
men. Where did all those little boys go?

Elise Feiner and her sons…
Clockwise from the top: David Steven, Jeffrey
and Elise Feiner

Elise Feiner and Godson Philip Avella, Jr.
Philly will be graduating from the Police
Academy in New Jersey soon

Betty Feiner and her grandsons…
L-R: Jeffrey, David, Mom Mom and Steven Feiner

GEORGIO'S VODKA SAUCE
George Frattasio and Judy Gorea

1 stick of butter
4 ounces proscuitto, chopped fine
2 cups red onion, chopped fine
2 shots vodka

2 pints of 40 percent heavy cream
8 cups marinara sauce
Grating cheese
1 pound cooked pasta

Cook butter, proscuitto and onion until onion is translucent. Add vodka and cook until it burns off. Mix in heavy cream and let the cream reduce, and then add marinara sauce. Cook together and add a large handful of grated Pecorino Romano cheese. Add vodka sauce to cooked pasta in a large bowl. Serves 4.

George Frattasio from Georgios Restaurant in New Hartford gave us permission to print this recipe. Georgios is a wonderful Restaurant owned by George and his cousin Judy, and if you are in the Upstate New York area be sure to dine there. Their number in New Hartford is (315) 792-1111. They are located on 60 Genesee Street in the Village of New Hartford. Georgio's is one of the best Italian Restaurants in the city.

George Frattasio at his restaurant. He co-owns it with his cousin Judy Gorea. What a
great restaurant, what a great chef and incredible person...the same goes for Judy!

GRIMALDI'S FAMOUS TOMATO SAUCE
John Grimaldi, Sr., Executive Chef

½ large onion, peeled and diced
6-8 cloves of garlic, peeled and crushed
6 cans of Montini Plum Tomatoes, or brand of your choice
(Place into a blender to just puree and place back in each
can. Do this before you start the sauce)
1 (18 ounce) can tomato paste

18 ounces of water
Parsley
4 slices of Proscuitto
Salt and Pepper to taste
1-2 tablespoons basil
4-5 tablespoons vegetable oil

Heat the vegetable oil in a large (8-quart) pot. Add the onions and garlic, until lightly golden. Add the proscuitto. Add the tomato puree and 18 ounces of water. Cook 15 minutes. Add the first can of tomatoes. Cook another 15 minutes. Add salt, pepper, and basil. Add the remaining 5 cans of tomatoes, and 1 can of water (use the empty tomato can to measure it.) Bring to a boil, and lower to a simmer. Let simmer for 2 hours.

This is Cousin John Grimaldi's recipe. He is a caterer on Staten Island and has generously shared his recipe.

AVELLA'S MARINARA SAUCE
Katherine Avella

4 (1 pound 12 ounce or 2 pound 3 ounce) cans of Italian plum tomatoes or crushed tomatoes or you can mix them
2 (8 ounce) cans Tomato sauce (use either Hunts, Del Monte, Contadina or Cora)
7-9 cloves garlic, peeled and crushed
¼ cup olive oil or vegetable oil

½ teaspoon black pepper
1½ tablespoons salt
1½ - 2 tablespoons dried basil
1-2 (2.25 ounce) cans of black olives, drained (optional) don't use if making sauce for Parmigiana

Before starting the sauce, peel and crush the garlic and put in a little dish. Open all the tomatoes and put each can of plum tomatoes (omit this step if using crushed tomatoes) into a blender turn on and off quickly to liquefy the tomatoes, and place each back in its own can. Place the oil in a large pot. Heat the oil and add the garlic stirring rapidly. As soon as it starts to sizzle quickly add the rest of the tomatoes so the garlic won't burn. Add about ½ can of water to the 8 ounce can of tomato sauce and pour from can to can to get all remaining tomato that is stuck to the cans from all 6 cans. Add that water to the sauce. Add the rest of the seasonings to the sauce. Bring to a boil stirring frequently. Then lower to a simmer for about 35 minutes to an hour. Sauce will change color from orange to red as it cooks. You can cook uncovered for about 35 minutes and then you may want to cover it so it does not get too thick. You can also add a can of sliced and pitted drained black olives or mushrooms, if you'd like.

This is your basic marinara sauce. It can be used to make Veal or Chicken Parmigiana, or served by itself with pasta. It's especially good with long macaroni (spaghetti, angel hair, linguini) It has been handed down from generation to generation. This is not the sauce used with Eggplant Parmigiana. That sauce is made with onions. This is a good sauce if you need to make a quick dinner or if you get unexpected company and you have to feed a lot of people. (When making pasta, figure 4 people to a pound). Freeze the leftovers.

Cousins…L-R: Anthony Grimaldi, Jr., Philip Avella, Ronald DaBruzzo, and Joseph Avella

AVELLA'S PIZZA SAUCE
Katherine Avella

4 (1pound 12 ounce or 2 pound 3 ounce) cans crushed tomatoes
8 cloves garlic, peeled and crushed
¾ tablespoon salt
¼ teaspoon black pepper

1 tablespoon dried oregano
Olive oil (about 4 tablespoons)
Store bought or homemade pizza dough (see Index)
Mozzarella
Grating Cheese

Peel and crush the garlic and put it in a little dish. Place enough olive oil to cover the bottom of a large saucepan. Heat the oil, and quickly add the garlic. As it starts to sizzle, quickly add the tomatoes. Add the salt, pepper, and oregano. Bring to a boil, and then lower to a simmer for about 40 to 45 minutes. Taste to adjust seasonings. If you want to you can pre bake your crust for a few minutes to prevent it from becoming soggy. Top pizza dough with sauce. Top with mozzarella and grating cheese. Top with a little more sauce. Bake pizza in a hot oven 500° about 15 to 20 minutes or until crust is brown. Don't use too much sauce or your crust will be soggy. This will make enough sauce to make about 8 large square pizzas. Use what you need and freeze the rest in 4 cup containers so you can use the rest later. It freezes beautifully, so I also keep some in the freezer for last minute dinners. You can easily cut this recipe in half.

I remember as a kid, Fridays in my house were always filled with the smell of homemade pizza. In those days, you couldn't eat meat on Friday so we always had pizza or macaroni with ricotta. I can remember my mother making the dough in a large pot and putting it in a dark place to rise. I loved the smell of the yeast as it was rising. Today, you can buy the dough already made, but I have put in the recipe to make the dough as well.

AVELLA - MAINELLA FAMILY'S "FAMOUS" GRAVY
Katherine Avella

Please read the entire recipe before starting to make the gravy.

Vegetable or olive oil
2 (2 pounds 3 ounce) cans Italian plum tomatoes
4 (2 pounds 3 ounce) cans Italian Crushed tomatoes
2 (8 ounce) cans Hunts® or Del Monte® Tomato Sauce
Garlic cloves, peeled and crushed about
10-12 large cloves
1½ tablespoons salt (you may want to add more to taste)
½ teaspoon black pepper

2 - 2½ tablespoons basil dried
2 medium to large onions, peeled and left whole
1 package sweet Italian sausage links
1-2 packages boneless country style pork ribs
Meatballs (see recipe index)
Pasta of your choice (1 pound will feed 4 people as a guide)
Grating cheese (to fix the pasta)

Note before starting the sauce: The flavor in the sauce is dependent upon the meats that you choose to add. You can use whatever meat you want to, but we usually use a package of sweet Italian sausage links, 1 to 2 packages of boneless country pork spareribs, meatballs, and beef Braciole if you can get it. However, the sausage, ribs, and meatballs are enough to make very flavorful gravy. You can add any other meat you want (you can use pork skin, Braciole (see recipe index for these recipes), stuffed breast of lamb or veal, eye round etc.), but you really don't need to add anything else. This is all a matter of personal preference. If you are using other meats as well as the sausage and boneless pork ribs, just brown them all at the same time.

Before you start to make the gravy, do a little prep work: Peel and squeeze the garlic through a garlic press; about 2 cloves of garlic for every large can of tomatoes (Don't count the little cans of Hunt's tomatoes in this amount). Place this is a small glass dish or a paper plate so that you can add it to the hot oil quickly. If you squeeze the cloves in one at a time, they will burn. It's much easier to have the garlic cloves all ready to go at one time. Open all the tomatoes (any brand of whole plum tomatoes is fine, Cora, De Cicco, Tuttorosso etc.) As you open each can of plum tomatoes put it into a blender and turn the blender on and off fairly quickly. You just want to puree the tomatoes but not beat them to death.) Place each batch of tomatoes back in their can so you can add them to the oil quickly when you eventually start to heat the garlic. When directed later on in the recipe, you will pour the crushed tomatoes and small cans of Hunts or Del Monte tomato sauce directly into the sauce **WITHOUT** putting them in the blender.

After you have added the tomatoes to the pot, keep all the empty cans. Set aside one large can of empty tomatoes. Use this empty can and fill it about ⅔ of the way with water. Swish the water around that can and then pour the water from that can into the next empty can to rinse it. Discard the cans as they are rinsed and continue to place water in all the remaining cans until they have all been rinsed. You will eventually add this water/tomato mix to the sauce as directed below.

To start the sauce, get a very large pot (8 or 12-quart), and place just enough oil (Wesson or olive oil is fine here) to cover the bottom of the pot. Place the onions, which have **been peeled, but left whole in the oil.** Brown the sausage and the boneless pork spareribs until well browned. (The meat **WILL NOT** be thoroughly cooked at this point, so don't eat it. It will continue cooking in the sauce later). As the meat browns, place it on a platter, and continue browning the meats until **ALL** the meats have been browned. If you are adding any other meats like breast of veal, brown them at this point as well. Leave the onion in the pot, and add the garlic to the remaining oil and stir quickly so it doesn't burn. As soon as the garlic begins to sizzle, begin adding the can of tomatoes right away, so the garlic doesn't burn. Add the Hunt's tomato sauce now too. Then, add the water/tomato mix that's in the empty can. Season with black pepper (about ½ teaspoon), salt (a small handful for 6 to 8 cans), better to use less and add more later if necessary, and about 2 to 2½ tablespoonful of dried basil. You can add some of the oil (about ¼ to ½ of what's left in the frying pan,) that you fried the meatballs in now. Bring to a boil, then lower to a low-medium simmer for about half hour, then add **ALL** of the browned meats, including the meatballs back into the tomatoes, add any drippings that remained on the platter where the meat was as well. Cover and cook on a low-medium simmer for about 2½ to 3½ hours, until the meat is well cooked. Check again for seasonings and add salt, pepper and more basil to taste **IF** necessary. Stir frequently, making sure you go all the way to the bottom of the pot. If you like a thicker sauce, you can add a small can of tomato puree, but we don't, so we don't add it. When you put the leftovers in the refrigerator you can skim off any grease that forms on the top. You can also freeze the leftover gravy, as this will make a large amount. Cook the pasta of your choice according to the package directions; drain. Place a few ladles of gravy in the bottom of a large serving bowl. Add the drained pasta. Mix well. Add more gravy and a handful of grated cheese. Mix well again. Top with the gravy and grating cheese. Enjoy.

CONTINUED ON NEXT PAGE

AVELLA - MAINELLA FAMILY'S "FAMOUS" GRAVY

NOTE: If you want to increase or decrease the sauce always keep this ratio: 1 can of plum tomatoes: 2 cans crushed tomatoes: 1 can of Hunts tomato sauce

I always double this recipe because you can divide this and freeze it for several meals. If you double the recipe, you really don't need to double the meat, just the tomatoes. There is enough meat to flavor a lot of tomatoes. If you prefer a thinner sauce, you can use all whole plum tomatoes, or if you prefer a thicker sauce you can use all crushed tomatoes. I prefer a combination of both as listed in the recipe; it seems to be the perfect mix. The choice is yours.

This is our family's wonderful tomato sauce or as we call it "gravy". It has been handed down through the generations. I can remember my grandmother making it on Sunday mornings and then my own mother doing the same thing. There was nothing more wonderful than waking up to the smell of meatballs frying on Sunday morning. Of course, we all wanted to eat the meatballs before they ever made it to the gravy. Today, it is the next generation asking how to make it, Mike, Philly, Jeff, Melissa, Steve, Dave and Lauren. These directions therefore are very user friendly. It's up to them to keep the traditions going...and the aromas filling the air.

BEEF BRACIOLE FOR "AVELLA - MAINELLA GRAVY"
Katherine Avella

1-2 pieces of beef Braciole
2-3 cloves of garlic, peeled and crushed
1 cup fresh breadcrumbs
½ teaspoon salt

⅛ teaspoon black pepper
2-3 tablespoons grating cheese
2 teaspoons dried parsley

Mix the fresh breadcrumbs (use day old Italian Bread and putting them in a blender process until crumbs, but not too fine), salt, pepper, grating cheese and parsley together. Rub the garlic over the surface of the Braciole. Place some of the stuffing mix onto the Braciole leaving a little border all around. Roll the Braciole jelly roll fashion, tie with kitchen twine. Brown the Braciole with the remaining gravy meats (sausage, spareribs, etc). Remove when browned. Add back into the tomato sauce and let cook with the rest of the gravy meat. To serve, slice into round slices about ½-inch thick.

Philip and Sharon Avella...My nephew Philly is the reason that
I wrote this book. He wanted me to make a video showing him
how to make our family "Gravy."

PORK SKIN (FOR "AVELLA-MAINELLA GRAVY")
Katherine Avella

1-2 pieces of pork skin (ask butcher or go to an Italian
specialty shop)
2-3 cloves of garlic, peeled and crushed
1 cup fresh breadcrumbs

½ teaspoon salt
⅛ teaspoon black pepper
2-3 tablespoons grating cheese
2 teaspoons dried parsley

Mix the fresh breadcrumbs (use day old Italian Bread), salt, pepper, grating cheese and parsley together. Rub the garlic over the surface of the pork skin. Place some of the stuffing mix onto the pork skin leaving a little border all around. Roll the pork skin jelly roll fashion, tie with kitchen twine. Brown the pork skin with the remaining gravy meats (sausage, spareribs, etc). Remove when browned. Add back into the tomato sauce and let cook with the rest of the gravy meat. (See Avella-Mainella Sauce recipe). To serve, slice and place on platter with sausages, meatballs, etc.

MEATBALLS FOR "AVELLA - MAINELLA GRAVY"
Katherine Avella

2 pounds of chopped meat (ground round or chopped
chuck will do)
4 eggs
Pinch salt (about ¼ teaspoon) because the cheese is salty
Ground black pepper (a little less than a ½ teaspoon)
Grating cheese (Parmesan or Locatelli Romano) about 1-1½
cups or 2 good handfuls

Dried parsley about 1½ - 2 ½ tablespoons
6 large garlic cloves, peeled and put through a press
Plain breadcrumbs (don't use seasoned) about ½-¾ of a
cup
Water about ¼ -½ of a cup
Vegetable oil for frying

Mix everything together but the meat. When well mixed, add the meat; blend until the egg mix and meat are very thoroughly blended. Shape into balls about 2½ inches in diameter. Put about ½ inch of oil in a large frying pan, and heat. When oil is hot, fry (use Wesson or another vegetable oil **but not olive oil**) until well browned on both sides; try to turn them only once if possible. Put the meatballs on a platter with paper towels as they are done and don't eat all of them before you put them in the gravy ☺ You will add meatballs to the gravy after it has simmered for about 25 to 35 minutes. Do not throw out the oil you have fried the meatballs in; you will add some of it to the tomato sauce later on. See previous page 477 as to when to add the oil. You don't have to add **ALL** the oil from frying the meatballs, but add a good amount. This is what will flavor the sauce. I usually double this recipe because they eat half of the meatballs before they ever get put into the gravy.

There is nothing that tastes or smells as good as these do when they are cooking! This is the smell of Sunday mornings in an Italian house...it was always a competition as to who's mother made the best meatballs...of course, it was mine. When I was a kid in Brooklyn, we lived next door to the Gellis family, the maker of Isaac Gellis Kosher Hotdogs, etc. Their son Sammy would always hang out in the backyard on Sunday whenever the meatballs were frying. My mother would always sneak him a few meatballs. They were a wonderful family. I adored Mr. Gellis, what a wonderful man. Mrs. Gellis and Lynda would be tanning in the backyard with a reflector. They had three children, Henry, Sam, and Lynda. Henry and Sammy have since passed away, but Lynda lives in Beverly Hills and is married to Peter Guber (Sony Pictures, Mandalay Entertainment, etc.)

L-R: Abby and Lauren Feiner

L-R; Alison Steates, Toby Usenheimer, Eileen Furino, Lauren Feiner,
Athena Avramidis, and Johann Gigliotti

"There is one art of which man should be master, the art of reflection."
--Samuel Taylor Coleridge

JOPPY BASILE'S MARINARA SAUCE
Joppy Basile

Olive oil
1 medium onion, peeled and diced
3-4 cloves of garlic, sliced thin
4-5 (28 ounce) cans Cora® whole plum tomatoes leave
whole

Salt and pepper to taste
1½ teaspoons sugar, level
Generous handful of fresh basil, chopped
A little fresh parsley, optional
Crushed red pepper, optional

Place enough olive oil in a pot to cover the bottom. Peel and dice a medium onion, slice cloves of garlic thinly. Heat the oil and sauté the garlic and onions. Add the whole tomatoes (left whole), and basil; season to taste with salt, pepper and sugar. Bring to a boil and then lower heat. Mash the tomatoes with a potato masher, not to fine, leave some chunks, and then a hand blender to medium consistency. Do not over blend. Lower to a simmer and cook uncovered 40 minutes. Add the end, add the parsley and crushed red pepper if desired. Serve over pasta; add grating cheese and fresh basil.

Maria Trainor gave me this recipe from Joppy. This is real "peasant" sauce, nice and chunky.

AVELLA'S MARINARA SAUCE FOR EGGPLANT PARMIGIANA
Katherine Avella

3 (1 pound 12 ounce) cans Italian Plum tomatoes or
crushed tomatoes
1 (8 ounce) can Hunts® Tomato Sauce
1 large onion, peeled and chopped

4 tablespoons olive oil
1-2 teaspoons salt
¼ teaspoon black pepper
1-1½ tablespoons basil

If you are using plum tomatoes, put through the blender quickly to puree. Place the olive oil in a large saucepan. Add the onions and sauté until soft and transparent. Add tomatoes, salt, pepper, and basil. Bring to a boil stirring frequently. Lower to a simmer and let simmer for about 45 minutes. Taste to adjust the seasonings. You don't want this too salty because the cheese will make the eggplant salty. This makes enough sauce for 2 large eggplants.
Note: **I prefer crushed tomatoes** because you want a little thicker sauce when making the eggplant, so when the mozzarella melt and gives off a little water the sauce will still coat the eggplant.

This is the sauce for the Eggplant Parmigiana. See the Eggplant Parmigiana recipe in the vegetable section for the rest of the directions.

SAMI JO'S HEALTHY ALFREDO SAUCE
Samantha Caplan

4 cups well cooked Cannellini beans or white beans
4 cups plain soy milk
1 teaspoon garlic powder

¾ teaspoon salt
½ cup Pecorino Romano Cheese, grated

Puree the beans with the milk, garlic powder and salt in a blender until creamy. Place the mixture into a pot and bring to a boil, stirring occasionally. Lower the mixture to a simmer. After five minutes, remove from the heat and stir in the Pecorino cheese.

This is Jeremy Zierler's fiancée Sam's recipe for a healthy alternative. Jeremy prefers a vegetarian diet so Sam shared this with us. Who said there are no healthy recipes in this book!

"If you find it in your heart to care for somebody else, you will have succeeded."
-Maya Angelou

CARBONARA SAUCE
Frank S. Mainella, M.D.

3 tablespoons olive oil
4 cloves garlic, peeled and crushed
¼ pound pancetta (Italian ham) sliced thin and then cut into thin strips

1 cup heavy cream
3 large egg yolks
½ cup parmesan cheese
Fresh ground pepper

Pasta of your choice (this sauce lends itself to a long pasta, linguini, fettuccine, spaghetti) Before making your sauce, put up a pot of salted water to cook the pasta. The sauce is done quickly, so when you throw the pasta in, you can then start the sauce. In a large frying pan, heat the olive oil. Add the garlic and sauté for about 30 seconds. Add the pancetta, cooking until its crisp about 2 to 3 minutes. Beat the egg yolks and cream together in a separate bowl. Drain the pasta, and add it to the bacon mixture. Remove from the heat, add the cream mixture and toss well. Add the parmesan cheese; mix well. Add fresh ground black pepper. If you can't find pancetta you can use bacon or proscuitto, but the taste is not quite the same.

My Uncle Frank who was 90 years old when he sent this recipe, along with a note to my mother that said, "Elise got in touch and told us she would like us to help with getting some good recipes for Jeffrey. I will enjoy giving all the help I can to Jeffrey. God bless him. He's such a fine boy. And Elise! I can't praise her enough and Marc too." This lovely and gushy note from my uncle, who used to promise to hang us up by our ears in the dining room if we misbehaved. He used to have a giant safety pin to tease us with. As I was the only girl on my mother's side, he used to tell all the boys they would have holes in their ears like me if they didn't listen. He pierced my ears and Lauren's ears at age three months. They don't come any better than him, or any gentler. He was a surgeon in Brooklyn for years and beloved by all his patients and family alike. My Uncle would have been so proud of Jeffrey, graduating number 1 in his medical school, and scoring on of the highest Board Scores in the nation.

Frank S. Mainella, M.D.

"One in a million"

BROWN GRAVY (FOR BEEF, TURKEY OR PORK)
Elise Feiner

Pan drippings
Wondra® Quick-mixing flour
Cold water

Salt and pepper to taste
Gravy Master®

To make a brown gravy take a few tablespoons of Wondra flour and dissolve in about 1½ cups cold water. (Try to remove as much of the grease from the drippings as possible if you are health oriented...if you are flavor oriented, you can leave some of the grease.) Add to the drippings in the pan. Pour that mix into a medium sauce pan. Season with black pepper and garlic salt to taste. Add Gravy Master for color. Stir constantly and bring to a boil. Lower the heat and let it simmer for a few minutes. The gravy will only thicken after it comes to a boil. If too thick add more water, if too thin add a little more Wondra (mix with a little cold water first.)

You can make this brown gravy with the drippings from any meat, turkey, beef or pork. It's great over the meat and mashed potatoes too. The secret to making any lump free gravy is to dissolve your thickening agent (flour, cornstarch, or potato starch) in cold water first, before adding it to the hot drippings.

COCKTAIL SAUCE
Elise Feiner

¾ cup chili sauce or ketchup
2 tablespoons horseradish (drain any liquid)
1 tablespoon lemon juice
½ teaspoon salt

⅛ teaspoon pepper
½ teaspoon Worcestershire sauce
Dash of Cayenne pepper
Tabasco sauce (optional)

Mix all the ingredients together except the Tabasco sauce. Add the Tabasco sauce to taste if you like your cocktail sauce hotter. Chill until ready to serve with shrimp.

I usually use ketchup when making the cocktail sauce. They tend to like it very spicy in our house so you may want to use a little less horseradish if you don't like it as hot.

MUSHROOM GRAVY IN A PINCH
Katherine Avella

1 tablespoon butter
¼ cup very thinly sliced onion
1 tablespoon finely chopped green pepper
2 tablespoons pimento strips

1 can Campbell's® Cream of Mushroom Soup (don't dilute)
⅓ cup chicken stock
salt and pepper to taste (optional)

Melt the butter in a small saucepan. Add the onions and the pepper and sauté for about 5 minutes. Take the pan off the heat. Add the remaining ingredients; mix well. Return to the heat and simmer for about 5 minutes, until thoroughly heated; stirring periodically. You can add salt and pepper to taste if desired.

SPINACH PESTO SAUCE
Katherine Avella

4 cups lightly packed baby spinach leaves
¼ cup toasted Pignoli (pine nuts) or walnuts
Zest of one lemon
4 tablespoon lemon juice
⅔ cup olive oil

⅔ – 1 cup grated cheese
½ teaspoon salt
½ teaspoon freshly ground black pepper
2 - 4 ounces heavy cream (optional)

Preheat your oven to 400° Place the Pignoli on a cookie sheet and place in the oven for about 5 to 7 minutes. Do not over brown or they will become bitter. Place the spinach, toasted Pignoli, lemon zest, and lemon juice into the bowl of a food processor. Turn the food processor on and keep it running, gradually add the oil, processing until the mix is a creamy consistency. Place the pesto in a bowl. Add the grated cheese, and salt and pepper to taste. You can use this as a dip or over pasta. If you are using it with pasta, I usually add a little heavy cream to the sauce.

BROWN BUTTER AND SAGE SAUCE
Katherine Avella

1 stick of unsalted butter
6 fresh sage leaves
½ teaspoon salt

¼ teaspoon black pepper
Dash of nutmeg
½ cup grated cheese

In a large frying pan, melt the butter over medium-high heat until golden brown in color. Add the sage leaves and cook until they begin to crisp. Add in the salt, pepper, and nutmeg. Adjust seasonings to taste. Add the grated cheese. Serve with gnocchi, or any stuffed pasta (tortellini, ravioli). You can also use this over broccoli or other vegetables.

If you are serving this with the pasta, you may want to incorporate some of the water that the pasta was cooked in to may it go further. You can substitute basil or any other herb of your choice.

MADEIRA SAUCE
Elise Feiner

2 tablespoons butter
¼ cup carrots, minced
¼ cup celery, minced
¼ cup onions, minced
2 tablespoons flour
2 cups brown beef broth

½ cup fresh or canned tomatoes, diced
1 bay leaf
Pinch of thyme
3 tablespoons Madeira wine
Salt and pepper to taste
1 tablespoon butter

Heat 2 tablespoons butter in a heavy saucepan. Add the carrots, celery, and onions and cook stirring once or twice until they begin to brown. Add the flour and continue to cook, stirring frequently until browned. Bring the broth to a boil and add to the vegetables. Add the tomatoes, bay leaf, and time and simmer for about 30 to 45 minutes or until reduced to about 1½ cups. Strain, pressing the vegetables to squeeze all the liquids into the sauce. Add the Madeira, salt and pepper, and return to a simmer. Remove from the heat and add in the last tablespoon of butter. Serve immediately.

This is a wonderful sauce that I serve with Beef Wellington! I have been making this for special occasions for years.

Phil Avella and our Mother Katherine Avella

GARLIC MAYONNAISE DIPPING SAUCE
Carmen Ferreiro

6-8 cloves of garlic, peeled and crushed

1 cup of mayonnaise

Mix the garlic with the mayonnaise. Let flavor for a little while. Serve with baked pork loin. You can use with French Fries too.

Carmen serves this with her pork loin. It is wonderful, except you need a bottle of mouth wash afterwards. Caution: Do not serve at a Valentine's Day dinner...Not a meal on a hot date night!

TARTAR SAUCE
Elise Feiner

¾ cup mayonnaise
4 tablespoons sour cream
1 tablespoon Dijon mustard
2 teaspoons lemon juice
1 tablespoon parsley, finely chopped
1 tablespoon capers, finely chopped
1 hard boiled egg, mashed finely

2 tablespoons scallions, finely chopped
1 clove garlic, peeled and crushed
2 tablespoons pickle relish
1 teaspoon dill
⅛ teaspoon cayenne pepper
Salt and pepper to taste
Dash of paprika

In a medium bowl, mix the mayonnaise, sour cream, mustard, and lemon juice until well blended. Add remaining ingredients, stirring until well blended. Refrigerate until ready to serve. This is best when used within 24 hours.

CHICKEN DIPPING SAUCE
Elise Feiner

1 cup ketchup
½ teaspoon dried mustard
1 tablespoon brown sugar

2 tablespoon white vinegar
¼ cup vegetable oil

Blend together in a small saucepan and cook for about 5 minutes until sugar is melted. Serve with chicken nuggets.

This is an excellent sauce for the sesame chicken nuggets. When I was a nurse in Doctor's Hospital in Staten Island, these were always requested whenever there was a party.

L-R: Jeffrey, Steven, David and Lauren Feiner at her graduation from Phillips Exeter Academy

RASPBERRY SAUCE
Ann D'Amico

2 (14 ounce) bags unsweetened raspberries, thawed
¼ cup sugar

⅓ cup Framboise® or Kirsch®

In a saucepan, simmer all the ingredients over low heat for 3 minutes. Place in a food processor and process until smooth. Push through a fine sieve. Yields 2½ cups.

SMOKIN' BARBEQUE SAUCE
Elise Feiner

10 pound ripe tomatoes
8 medium onions, peeled
2 red hot peppers
1 cup sugar

1 cup white vinegar
1 teaspoon cinnamon
4 teaspoons salt
¼ cup honey

Quarter the tomatoes. Peel and quarter the onions. Seed and core the peppers (**wear gloves and don't touch your eyes**) and cut into pieces. Put the vegetables in a pot and cook until soft. Put in a food mill to puree. Return to the pot and add the rest of the ingredients. Cook until it thickens. Reduce heat and simmer 45 minutes, stirring frequently. Use with chicken or ribs as a marinating or basting sauce.

ONION BARBEQUE SAUCE
Elise Feiner

1 chopped onion
¼ cup oil
1 cup water
½ cup ketchup
1 tablespoon sugar

1 teaspoon garlic salt
2 tablespoons vinegar
2 tablespoons Worcestershire sauce
1 beef bouillon package or cube

Mix all ingredients together. Use to marinade or brush on your meat as you barbeque.

PESTO SAUCE A LA TRAINOR
Maria Trainor

2-3 cups of fresh basil wash and pat dry
½ cup fresh parsley
Salt and pepper to taste
3-4 cloves of garlic
¼ cup Pignoli (pine nuts) toasted

¾ - 1½ cups olive oil
1 cup Locatelli Romano or Parmesan cheese, more to sprinkle at the end
½ pint heavy cream

Mix basil, parsley, pine nuts, garlic, salt and pepper in a food processor until a fine paste forms. Drizzle in olive oil. The amount of oil will depend on the amount of basil. (It's hard to get an exact measurement with fresh basil leaves.) Process until well mixed (basically, just on and off.) You could do this in advance and refrigerate until ready to serve. Right before serving, add ½ pint of heavy cream and the grating cheese to the pesto sauce. Place the pesto in the bottom of your serving dish. Cook 1½ pounds of ziti or other macaroni, according to the package directions. Drain the pasta reserving about 2 ladles of the pasta water to add at the end if the sauce seems too thick. Toss pasta with the pesto. Add extra Locatelli Romano or parmesan cheese.

Maria Trainor gave me this recipe for the pesto sauce. It is delicious and very easy to make. It's great as a luncheon, main course, or a side dish. Her family loves it and I can see why...It's the best pesto sauce you'll ever taste! This freezes very well so when basil is in season, make plenty of pesto sauce. If you plan to freeze it , DON'T ADD THE CREAM OR GRATING CHEESE until you are ready to use the sauce.

L-R: Connie DiMare and her grandson
Jonathan Trainor

Maria Trainor enjoying a rare free moment... relaxing at
their camp in Old Forge.

SWEET AND SOUR SAUCE
Elise Feiner

1 cup sugar
½ cup white vinegar
½ cup plus 1 tablespoon water
1 tablespoon chopped green pepper
1 tablespoon chopped pimentos

½ teaspoon kosher salt
2 teaspoons cornstarch
1 teaspoon paprika
2 tablespoons ketchup

In a medium saucepan mix the sugar, vinegar, ½ cup of water, pepper, pimento, salt and ketchup; simmer for about 5 minutes. Mix the cornstarch and the remaining tablespoon of water (cold) together. Add this to the sugar mixture. Remove the pan from the heat and stir until thickened. Add the paprika to taste. Cool completely. Use with fried shrimp, chicken, or pork cubes or fried walnuts.

BEARNAISE SAUCE
Elise Feiner

1 teaspoon chopped shallots
½ teaspoon chopped chervil
½ teaspoon chopped tarragon
12 peppercorns, crushed
2 tablespoons dry white wine

1 tablespoon vinegar
1½ cups butter
5 egg yolks
2 tablespoons heavy cream
Salt and cayenne pepper to taste

Mix the shallots, chervil, tarragon, peppercorns, white wine, and vinegar. Simmer until you have reduced the mixture by half. Melt the butter and pour off the clear portion (save; this is the clarified butter) Beat the egg yolks with the cream. Beat the vinegar into the egg yolks and put in the top of double boiler. Cook over boiling water until creamy. While the sauce is cooking, whisk constantly to prevent curdling. Add in the clarified butter. Season with salt and cayenne pepper to taste.

L-R: Maureen Finnegan, Rae Barone and Frances Barone

GORGONZOLA OR BLUE CHEESE DIPPING SAUCE
Jeffery Daniels, Sr.

4-6 ounces of crumbled gorgonzola cheese

½ pint heavy cream

Place the cheese and cream in a small saucepan and heat on a low flame until the cheese is melted and begins to thicken. You can serve this with lamb, filet, or pork, or place it over cooked spinach.

This is Jeff's recipe for the Gorgonzola sauce. He serves it at Café Daniele. He is a marvelous chef and this is one of his signature sauces. He was very generous in sharing this recipe with me. I use this sauce with baby lamb chops that been grilled, they are to die for!

PESTO DIPPING SAUCE
Jeffery Daniels, Sr.

1-2 tablespoons of prepared pesto sauce
¼ cup mayonnaise

Balsamic vinegar to taste

Mix all ingredients well. Serve with grilled chicken breast topped with roasted peppers and melted provolone cheese.

MUSTARD SAUCE (FOR HAM)
Elise Feiner

2 tablespoons sugar
1 tablespoon Coleman® dry mustard
Salt and pepper

2 tablespoons white vinegar
½ cup cream
1 egg yolk

In a small saucepan, off heat, combine sugar, mustard, salt and pepper. Whisk in vinegar until it forms a paste. Add cream whisking, and beat in yolk. Heat over low heat, whisking constantly, until sauce thickens slightly, do not boil or sauce will curdle. Serve the sauce warm with slices of baked ham.

This is a wonderful tangy sauce to serve with a spiral or any type of ham. My kids love this sauce!

WHITE SAUCE
Elise Feiner

5 tablespoons butter, divided
3 tablespoons flour
2 cup chicken stock
Salt to taste

Freshly ground black pepper to taste
½ cup heavy cream
1 teaspoon Worcestershire sauce

In a saucepan, over medium heat, melt 3 tablespoons of butter. Stir in the flour and cook for 2 minutes. Whisk in the stock, ½ cup at a time. Whisk until smooth. Season with salt and pepper. Bring the liquid to a boil and reduce the heat to low and cook for 15 minutes. Whisk in the cream and continue to cook for 2 minutes. Add the Worcestershire sauce. Season with salt and pepper. Remove from the heat and whisk in the remaining butter. This is the sauce to use with chicken or turkey croquettes.

PEANUT DIPPING SAUCE (SATAY SAUCE)
Elise Feiner

1 tablespoon olive oil
1 tablespoon dark sesame oil
4 tablespoons butter
1 small red onion, peeled and diced
3 cloves garlic, peeled and crushed
1 teaspoon freshly grated ginger
2 tablespoon red wine vinegar with garlic
¼ cup Brownulated light brown sugar
2 tablespoons soy sauce

1 tablespoon Worcestershire sauce
1 tablespoon tamari (dark soy sauce
½ cup smooth peanut butter
2 tablespoons chunky peanut butter
¼ cup ketchup
3 tablespoons sherry
1½ teaspoons fresh lime juice
1 scallion, very finely chopped

Sauté the onions, garlic, ginger and scallions in the olive oil, butter, and sesame oil until the onion is soft and transparent (about 12 to 16 minutes.) Gently stir or whisk in vinegar, brown sugar, soy sauce, Worcestershire sauce, tamari, smooth peanut butter, ketchup, lime juice and sherry; cook for another 2 minutes. Add the chunky peanut butter. Cool. You can use this with Uncle Phil's Chicken or over noodles.

L-R: Joseph Avella, Steven Feiner, Philip Avella, Michael Avella, Nicole Latini, Phyllis Avella, Melissa Avella, David Feiner, John Michael Latini, Douglas Avella, Katherine Avella, Elise Feiner, Marc Feiner, Josephine Mainella, Flo Avella, Jean Mainella
Sitting: Sharon and Philip Avella, Jr.

More mothers and sons…snips and snails and puppy dog tails…

Rae Rosenfeld and son Joshua

Ann Silvestri with son Joseph

Ann Mainella with sons (L) Michael and (R)
Joseph Jr.

Julia Silvestri with son Philly

L-R: Elise and David Feiner at his "White
Coat Ceremony" at UB's Medical School

CREAMY LEMON VINAIGRETTE
Elise Feiner

8 cups assorted baby greens, such as Bibb, Radicchio, and Endive
1 shallot, minced
1 tablespoon Dijon mustard
2 tablespoons white wine vinegar
1 lemon, zested and juiced

Pinch cayenne pepper
⅓ cup extra-virgin olive oil
½ cup sour cream
Salt and pepper

Combine the baby greens in a salad bowl. In a mini food processor, pulse together the shallot, mustard, vinegar, lemon juice, zest and cayenne. Add the olive oil and pulse again to combine. Add the sour cream and blend for 30 seconds until creamy. Season with salt and pepper to taste. Drizzle over the greens and toss to coat and serve.

CREAMY VINAIGRETTE DRESSING
Elise Feiner

½ cup olive oil
1 small red onion, peeled and finely diced
1 small shallot, peeled and finely diced
2 cloves garlic, peeled and crushed
¼ teaspoon dried basil
¼ teaspoon salt
1 tablespoon honey
2 tablespoons Dijon mustard

¼ cup Balsamic vinegar
1 cup sour cream
1 cup mayonnaise
1 cup grated cheese
¼ teaspoon black pepper
½ cup Balsamic dressing (You will make this from above ingredients...see directions)
Blue cheese, crumbled

Heat the olive oil in a frying pan, and add the onions and shallots, sauté for about 4 minutes. Add the garlic. Sauté about another 30 seconds. Add the basil, and salt. Whisk in the honey, Dijon mustard and vinegar. Set aside and let cool. When cool take ½ cup of the dressing and add to the remaining ingredients except blue cheese. Refrigerate any remaining vinaigrette. Refrigerate the creamy dressing and serve with the layered antipasto salad. Place blue cheese in a bowl next to dressing.

LEMON BALSAMIC SALAD DRESSING
Ann D'Amico

2 tablespoons Dijon Mustard
1 teaspoon salt
¼ teaspoon pepper
¼ cup vinegar

¼ cup lemon juice
1 cup oil
1 tablespoon sugar (for diabetics decrease to ¼ teaspoon)

Mix together and serve over salad.

Ann made this dressing for dinner when we were there one evening. It was delicious and very light and I'm not a lemon lover but this was great. Very subtle!

LEMON VINAIGRETTE
Josephine Mainella

¼ cup olive oil
2 tablespoons lemon juice
1 teaspoon oregano

½ teaspoon salt
⅛ teaspoon pepper
1 clove of garlic, finely chopped

In a small bowl, combine all ingredients. With a wire whisk, beat until blended.

ITALIAN VINAIGRETTE
Josephine Mainella

1 cup olive oil
¼ cup red wine vinegar
1 teaspoon garlic powder
1 teaspoon onion powder
1 teaspoon parsley

½ teaspoon oregano
½ teaspoon basil
1 teaspoon salt
¼ teaspoon pepper

In a jar with a tight fitting lid, combine all ingredients. Shake until well blended. Drizzle desired amount immediately. Refrigerate remaining vinaigrette.

Standing L-R: Josephine Mainella, Angie Sanito
Sitting L-R: Katherine Avella, Joseph Avella

GREEN GODDESS MAYONNAISE
Elise Feiner

¾ cup mayonnaise
2 scallions, thinly sliced
3 tablespoons parsley, chopped

2 tablespoons freshly chopped tarragon
2 teaspoons chives, chopped
2 anchovy fillets, minced, optional

Combine all ingredients in a bowl. Cover. Refrigerate before serving at least 1 to 2 hours. Use with fish, chicken, or meats.

ROQUEFORT DRESSING
Elise Feiner

1-quart mayonnaise
6 ounces Roquefort cheese, crumbled
1 (16 ounce) container sour cream
½ large onion, chopped
1 dash Worcestershire sauce

Salt and pepper, to taste
1½ lemons, juiced
½ handful fresh parsley, finely chopped
Dash of garlic salt

Mix the mayonnaise and the Roquefort cheese together and refrigerate overnight. The next day, in a blender mix all remaining ingredients with the mayonnaise mixture. May be halved or doubled. You might want to add some extra crumbled cheese after it is blended if you like chunks in your dressing.

SYMEON'S GREEK SALAD DRESSING
Symeon and Ann Tsoupelis

1 cup of oil
¼ cup red vinegar

3 heaping tablespoons Symeon's Spices or
Cooking with Love's Passion Spice Mix

Mix all ingredients well. Use as a dressing over a mixed salad. Add feta cheese, Greek olives, and sliced onions. You can also use this as a marinade for meats. You can order the spice mix from our website **www.cookingwithlove.com**

This is the salad dressing served at Symeon's Restaurant. This is the most wonderful Greek restaurant, and you should definitely give it a try if you are in the central New York area. The address is 4941 Commercial Drive, Yorkville, New York. The phone number is (315) 736-4074. The restaurant started by Symeon and Ann Tsoupelis was quite small when we first moved to New Hartford. It has grown through the years, and is now run by Symeon Jr. and his wife Shelli. Sadly, Ann passed away a few years ago, but she has left a tremendous legacy behind. Don't miss an opportunity to dine here! Try the fried calamari and fried eggplant appetizers...they are the best!

THOUSAND ISLAND DRESSING
Elise Feiner

1 egg
1 lemon, juiced
¼ cup green bell pepper, chopped
¼ cup sweet pickles, chopped
¼ green olives, chopped
1 tablespoon pimientos, chopped
1 hard boiled egg, finely chopped
3 tablespoons ketchup
1 tablespoon freshly chopped chives
1 tablespoon chili sauce

Salt to taste
Freshly ground black pepper to taste
1 cup oil
1 egg
1 lemon, juiced
¼ cup chopped onions
¼ cup chopped green bell peppers
¼ cup chopped sweet pickles
¼ cup chopped green olives
1 tablespoon chopped pimientos

Combine all the ingredients (except the salt and pepper, and oil) in a food processor with a metal blade and process until smooth. Season with salt and pepper. While the machine is running, slowly add the oil, a little at a time, until thick. Taste for seasonings.

BLUE CHEESE DRESSING WITH SOUR CREAM
Edith Mainella

1½ teaspoons minced garlic
½ teaspoon dry mustard (Coleman's)
¾ teaspoon black pepper
⅛ teaspoon white pepper
¼ cup red wine vinegar
1 teaspoon Worcestershire sauce

¼ teaspoon hot pepper sauce
1 cup sour cream
3 cups mayonnaise
½ cup buttermilk
½ pound Maytag blue cheese, crumbled

In bowl whisk together garlic, mustard, black pepper, onion salt, and white pepper and whisk in the vinegar, Worcestershire sauce, and hot pepper sauce. Add the sour cream, mayonnaise, buttermilk and whisk the dressing until it is combined well. Fold in the blue cheese and chill the dressing, covered, overnight. It will keep for a week.

As you can see, we're a blue cheese family! We all have our own version.

"Holding on to anger is like grasping a hot coal with the intent of throwing it at someone else; you are the one who gets burned."
- Buddha

BLUE CHEESE DRESSING
Elise Feiner

1 cup Hellmann Mayonnaise
2 to 4 ounces blue cheese, crumbled
2 tablespoons milk
2 tablespoons white vinegar
2 teaspoon sugar

¼ teaspoon onion salt
¼ teaspoon dry mustard
⅛ teaspoon garlic powder
4 tablespoons of sour cream

Stir together all ingredients. Add 2-4 ounces of blue cheese to make as crumbly as you prefer. May be halved easily. Cover; chill.

This is my favorite blue cheese recipe.

BLUE CHEESE DRESSING WITH CHIVES
Elise Feiner

½ pound crumbled blue cheese, plus ¼ pound for garnish
¾ cup sour cream
½ lemon, juiced

2 tablespoons red wine vinegar
Pinch cayenne pepper
1 tablespoon minced chives

To prepare the creamy blue cheese dressing: Whisk together ½ pound blue cheese with sour cream, lemon, vinegar and cayenne until smooth. Fold in chives, cover, and chill until ready to serve. Stir in the remaining ¼ pound of crumbled blue cheese for garnish.

CREAMY BLUE CHEESE DRESSING
Katherine Avella

6 ounces (about ⅓ pound) double cream blue veined
cheese, softened to room temperature
½ cup heavy cream
2 pinches ground cayenne pepper

½ cup sour cream
Salt and pepper

Mash softened cheese with fork in a bowl. Whisk in the cream and sour cream into cheese, the consistency should be smooth with an occasional small bit of blue. Season with salt, pepper, and cayenne pepper.

FRENCH DRESSING
Katherine Avella

½ cup fresh lemon juice or vinegar
1½ cups of olive oil or vegetable oil
2 teaspoons salt

¼ teaspoon pepper
1 teaspoon powdered mustard
Dash of cayenne

Mix all ingredients in a container you can shake; shake until well blended. Cover tightly. Store in the refrigerator. Makes 2 cups.

L-R: Frances, Johnny and John Anselmo 1938

Aunt Frances is one of my father's six sisters

L-R: Isabelle and Joseph Silvestri

Their children Debbie and John look just like their parents!

FRENCH DRESSING SUPREME
Katherine Avella

½ cup fresh lemon juice or vinegar
1½ cups of olive oil or vegetable oil
2 teaspoons salt
¼ teaspoon pepper
1 teaspoon powdered mustard
Dash of cayenne

3-4 cloves of garlic, peeled and crushed
⅓ cup chili sauce
1 tablespoon horseradish
1 teaspoon paprika

Mix all ingredients in a container you can shake; shake until well blended. Cover tightly. Store in the refrigerator. Makes 2 cups.

CREAMY SWEET AND SOUR DRESSING
John Brown

1 cup mayonnaise
⅓ cup evaporated milk
3 tablespoons red wine vinegar

⅛ cup of sugar (or more to taste)

Mix all ingredients together and blend well. Let sit in refrigerator at least 20 minutes.

John is my favorite realtor and one of my favorite people. He and Veronica have become our close friends. He used to own the Whiffletree Inn in Ilion years ago. He said that this dressing is great for spinach salad, veggie dip and chicken wings too! He said that it's perfect on the following; 1 bag cleaned washed chopped spinach, 4 hard boiled eggs, sliced, 4 strips of bacon, crumbled into bits, chopped and diced red onions. Toss well with dressing.

JOHN'S EASY BALSAMIC VINAIGRETTE
John Brown

1 tablespoon Nance's® sharp and creamy mustard
Pinch of ground oregano
Several grinds of a peppermill

6 tablespoons balsamic vinegar
Extra virgin olive oil (to taste)

Mix the mustard, oregano, pepper, and vinegar and blend well. Slowly add the extra virgin olive oil, blending to taste.

"The John Brown Team" L-R: Laurie Zdyb, Veronica Bunce,
John "Bunny" Brown, and Lori Scalise

493

And yet more mothers and sons…That's what little boys are made of!

Maryann Mastrovito and son Frank, Jr.

Camille Sanabria and son Andrew

Thirza Avella and son Douglas

Julie Ann Sapio and son Julius (Joey)

Holiday Cooking...

The Rene Sanabria Family
L-R: Andrew, Camille, and Rene

"Tomatoes and oregano make it Italian; wine and tarragon make it French. Sour cream makes it Russian; lemon and cinnamon make it Greek. Soy sauce makes it Chinese; garlic makes it good."
– Alice May Brock

Stocking a Dream Kitchen continued...

Round Cake Pans (at least two 8-inch and 2 9-inch)
Spring form Pans in various sizes
2 Rectangular Baking Pan (13 x 9-inch)
2 Square Baking Pan (9 x 9-inch)and (8 x 8-inch)
Loaf Pans (at least two)
Mini Loaf Pans
4 Flat Baking Sheets
Baking Sheet with Rim
Glass Pie Plate (8, 9, and 10-inch)
Muffin Tins, mini muffins tins, popover pans
Flour Sifter
Rolling Pin
Cooling Racks

Pastry Brush
Pastry Bag with Decorating Tips
Tart Pans (fluted edges, removable bottoms)
Jelly-Roll Pan
Angel Food Cake Pan
Bundt Pan
Palette Knife for Cake Decorating
Pastry Blender
Pie Weights
The ultimate kitchen goodies – a faucet above the oven so you don't have to carry heavy pots...
A vacuum opening at the base of one kitchen cabinets, so you can sweep the crumbs right into it (part of a central vacuum setup)

Dinnerware - one everyday set, one good china set
Glassware - one everyday set, one good stemware set
Flatware - one everyday set, one good set of Sterling
Serving Dishes of all Shapes and Sizes
Baskets

Live in help!!!! A live in Chef...a true fantasy.......

Add your own dreams to this list:

_____
_____
_____
_____
_____
_____
_____
_____
_____
_____
_____
_____
_____

THE MAINELLA-AVELLA-FEINER FAMILY'S FAMOUS NEW YEARS EGGNOG
Elise Feiner and Edith Mainella

12 eggs separated
1½ cups sugar
1½ quarts heavy cream
1 quart milk
Candy canes
2 pints heavy cream whipped with ¼ cup sugar and 3 teaspoons vanilla

1 (half gallon) container of eggnog or French vanilla ice cream, softened
1 bottle each of red and green maraschino cherries, drained
Freshly ground nutmeg
1 pint whiskey or cognac (optional)

Beat the egg whites until stiff but not dry, gradually add the 1½ cups of sugar until stiff peaks form. In a separate bowl, beat the egg yolks until thick and lemon colored, fold into the egg whites. Gradually add the 1½ quarts of heavy cream, milk, and whiskey and rum if desired. Stir until well mixed. Whip the remaining heavy cream with the ¼ cup sugar and vanilla until it becomes a thick whipped cream, being careful not to over beat (or you'll have butter.). Add to the eggnog mix by large spoonfuls. Soften the ice cream slightly and add by large spoonfuls to the eggnog mix. Add the red and green cherries. Grate fresh nutmeg on the top. Decorate the punch bowl with candy canes, and place one in each cup to serve. This is so thick you probably need to use a spoon to eat it. It probably has 1000 calories a cup, not for the squeamish! **Buy the eggs the day before so they will be super fresh.** Some people are skeptical about raw eggs but I have made this for years with no problem. Serves 18 to 24.

My best memories of Christmas and New Years as a kid was going to Aunt Edith and Uncle Frank's house in Bayville, N.Y. We would go from house to house on Valley Road and share the holiday spirit with all our friends, family, and neighbors. Basically, we always hung out at the Pacifico's. We were like one family connected by a driveway. This will always be my happiest childhood memory...Bayville... Christmas and New Year's and Family. Not putting up a Christmas tree was truly one of the hardest sacrifices I made when I converted to Judaism. I always tease my kids that when I die, no flowers at my funeral, just one last tree and a Christmas ornament from everyone! It was always my job to fix the eggnog. Aunt Edith bought the canned or store bought kind, and I was supposed to jazz it up. One year I found this basic recipe and then jazzed it up, adding the whipped cream and ice cream. My kids love this and beg to have it more than once a year but then it wouldn't be special. Not a year goes by that I make it that I don't think of Aunt Edith, and all those good times we had as kids. Steven is now in charge of the eggnog making. He even made it for his Fraternity brothers at Hofstra. He will never allow me to miss a year and always goes down to get the punchbowl ready. I'm sure when I'm long gone, he will continue this tradition. Because the kids were small we never added any alcohol, and we prefer the non-alcoholic version.

AUNT EDITH'S IRISH SODA BREAD
Edith Mainella

3 cups of flour
4 teaspoons baking powder
½ teaspoon baking soda
⅓ teaspoon salt
¼ cup sugar

4 tablespoons shortening (oil)
2 tablespoons caraway seeds
½ cup buttermilk
1 egg
1 cup raisins

Mix all dry ingredients together. Make a hole in the center of the mix and add the liquids. Mix well. Add the raisins and caraway seeds. Grease a round loaf pan. Bake at 350° for 15 minutes. Make a cross on the top of the loaf with a knife. Bake another 45 minutes or until done.

Aunt Edith was of Irish-French descent and St. Patrick's Day was her favorite holiday. She always made this bread on St. Patrick's Day every year for as long as I can remember.

"Make sure your words are always sweet; someday you may have to eat them!"
-Claire Akselrad

CORNED BEEF AND CABBAGE
Edith Mainella

1 large corned beef brisket
5-6 new potatoes, peeled and cut in half
1 bag of carrots, peeled and cut in half
1 large head of cabbage, cut into wedges
2 onions, peeled and left whole

3 whole cloves
2 ribs of celery
2 sprigs parsley
3 scallions
Pepper to taste

Place the corned beef into a large pot and cover the corned beef with water. Bring to a boil, lower to a simmer, and let simmer 1 hour. Discard all the water in the pot, and start over with fresh water. Bring the water to a boil again, and then reduce to a little more than a simmer. The corned beef will need to cook another 3 to 4 hours. During the last hour and a half, add the potatoes, carrots, celery, scallions, cloves, parsley and onions. During the last 45 minutes add the cabbage. Slice the corned beef against the grain and serve with fresh rye bread and mustard. I like to parboil the potatoes in lightly salted water for about 10 to15 minutes before adding them to the corned beef.

It wouldn't be St. Patrick's Day if my Irish-French Aunt Edith didn't make corned beef and cabbage. As a child, I remembered thinking what a smell! As an adult, I just thought what a great taste. I will always think of my Aunt Edith, but on Saint Patrick's Day, she comes back to us and fills our hearts! I have a St. Patrick's Day Tree with ornaments that I always put up in her memory. She's is always in my heart!

UNCLE ERNIE'S HOLIDAY SODA BREAD
Ernest Maida

½ cup white raisins
9 cups flour
3 teaspoons baking soda
3 teaspoons baking powder
3 teaspoons salt

¾ cup sugar
6 eggs
1 quart buttermilk
1 stick plus 1 tablespoon butter or margarine, melted

Heat the oven to 350 °. Wash the raisins; remove any bad ones and set the rest aside; leave them slightly moist. Sift the dry ingredients together in a large mixing bowl. Mix well. Add the eggs, stirring with a wooden spoon. Slowly stir in the buttermilk, and add the melted butter. Stir in the raisins. Because this dough is rather soft, it bakes well in a greased pan. Uncle Ernie used an angel food pan (pan with a removable tube in the center.) Bake 1 hour and 10 minutes or until a cake tester or toothpick inserted in the center of the bread comes out clean and dry.

After Aunt Lizzie passed away, Uncle Ernie took over some of the cooking. This was his special bread. My Aunt Edith would have been proud of him as well, as she loved her Irish Soda Bread on St. Patrick's Day! My "Uncle Ernie" was a real gem. When I was a kid, my father could never close his barbershop to go on vacation, so my beloved "Uncle Ernie" volunteered to drag me along with his family through Florida, Canada, and everywhere else...just him and a carload of women. When I was growing up, he, my Uncle Frank, and my Uncle Pat were three of the most important men in my life besides my father!

L-R: Maryann, Ernest and Michele Maida

Ernest Maida

ITALIAN EASTER BREAD
Phyllis Jendzo

1 cup scalded milk (just to boil)	10 cups of flour
½ pound sweet butter	2 teaspoons salt
1 cup sugar	6 eggs
1 cup warm water	1 teaspoon of each vanilla, lemon, and orange, extract
3 packages of yeast	1 orange rind
1 tablespoons sugar to put in with the yeast	1 lemon rind

1st bowl (Small pot)
Scald (heat the milk on medium to low heat until it foams but do not bring to a boil) 1 cup of milk, add ½ pound of butter, let melt, add 1 cup sugar stir to dissolve

2nd bowl (Medium size)
Dissolve 1 cup of warm water, 3 packages of yeast and 1 tablespoon of sugar. Let this bowl stand for about 15 minutes and bubble up. Place it in a warm spot.

3rd bowl (Large size)
Sift together 8 cups of flour and 2 teaspoons salt

4th bowl (Medium size)
Beat together 6 eggs with all the extracts, add the lemon rind and the orange rind. Mix well

Combine all bowls and pots into one very large bowl. Gradually, knead in 2 more cups of flour on a floured wooden board. Work with the dough (15 to 20 minutes or so) until it does not stick to your fingers. If you need to add more flour, do so. Place this dough into a large greased pot. Cover with a towel and place in a warm place. (On top of a warm oven is good) Let this rise for one hour. Punch it down to get all the air out. Cover it again and let it rise for ½ hour more or until it doubles in size. Divide this dough into 4 balls and form braids with each of these balls. Place in greased loaf pans or round cake pans. Let them rise again covered and in a warm place until at least doubled in size. Brush with beaten eggs and garnish with multi colored sprinkles. You can tuck into the braid one or two previously colored, hard boiled eggs if desired. Bake at 350° for 30 to 40 minutes or until golden brown. Slice and enjoy!

This recipe came from my cousin Phyllis Jendzo. It was her grandmother's (my father's sister Julia's) recipe. Phyllis and I have been cooking together since we were kids. We spent an entire summer with her friend Nancy making more chocolate chips cookies than Mrs. Fields

Stephen, Richard, Laura Jendzo Skonberg holding Adrianna Skonberg,
Kim Jendzo, Cookie Frank, Philip and Phyllis Jendzo

SWEET CONGO
Josephine Mainella

1 cup milk	2 teaspoons salt
1 cup vegetable oil	2 cups sugar
1 pound butter, melted	1 cup warm water
12 eggs, at room temperature, beaten well	4 teaspoons sugar
4 teaspoons vanilla	4 packages yeast
2 teaspoons lemon extract	About 4 pounds of flour
2 teaspoons orange extract	

Scald the 1 cup of milk, and let cool. When cool, add 1 cup of oil (vegetable) and butter (total shortening should always equal 24 ounces). Set aside. Mix the eggs, vanilla, lemon and orange extracts, salt and two cups of sugar well in a large bowl and set aside.

Dissolve the yeast in the warm water and 4 teaspoons sugar in a large bowl, and set aside. When thoroughly dissolved, add the beaten egg mixture to this bowl. Then add the milk mixture. Add approximately 4 pounds of flour (about 16 cups) and knead together to form a soft dough. Place in a large pot and cover with a towel and let rise until double in bulk about 1½ hours. Punch down and shape in bread. This dough will yield 5 loaves, 2 shaped in tube pans, 2 shaped in loaf pans, 1 shaped in a small loaf pan. To shape divide the dough and then **make each division into three long ropes of dough** and form into braids. Place the braided loaves into their respective pans that have been well greased and floured. Before baking, beat an egg with a little milk or 1 egg yolk with 1 tablespoon of water. Brush the tops of the loaves with the egg wash mixture. Place tiny colored nonpareil sprinkles on the top of each loaf. Bake at 350°, after 15 minutes; cover with foil and reduce heat to 300°. Bake 35 minutes for the small loaf, and 1 hour for the large pans.

This is our family's traditional Easter sweet bread. The recipe was my grandmothers' but has been refined over the years by Aunt Fifi. This is really her version. It is delicious lathered with butter and dipped in a good cup of coffee. It is very similar to the Easter Bread with the hard boiled eggs in it, and in fact you could boil and color some eggs and use in this recipe if desired.

L-R: Sachi Ide
and
Lauren Feiner

CONGO - UNSWEETENED
Josephine Mainella

5 packages yeast	8 ounces oil
1 teaspoon sugar	3½ tablespoons of salt
1 cup warm water	3 tablespoons coarsely ground pepper
2 dozen eggs	Approximately 5 pounds of flour
¾ pound butter, melted	

Dissolve the yeast in the cup of warm water and 1 teaspoon of sugar. Beat the eggs with the melted butter, oil, salt and pepper. Add the yeast mixture. Then add enough flour to make a soft dough. Turn on dough onto a floured board and knead well. The dough is well kneaded when you lightly press two fingers into the dough and it bounces back. Place a little oil in a large pot and add the dough, covering the dough with a little oil so it won't stick to the pot. Cover with a towel, and let rise until double in bulk. Punch dough down. Place your fingers in the dough if the indentation remains the dough is ready to be shaped. Shape the dough by dividing it in half. Then divide each piece into three long ropes and braid, place in a well greased tube pan. Let rise again (about one hour) in the tube pans. Preheat oven to 400°. Bake for 15 to 20 minutes and then lower the heat to 350° for another hour.

This traditional Easter bread is not a sweet bread it's dry. It is delicious served right out of the oven with butter and a cup of coffee...one of Aunt Fifi's specialties.

EASTER RICE PIE (PIZZA DI RISO)
Clementina Mainella

1 pound rice
4 quarts milk
6 eggs
2 cups sugar

Rind of one lemon, grated
3 tablespoons citron
1 teaspoon vanilla extract
Crust for the Easter Rice Pie (Pizza di Riso)

Cook the rice in the 3 quarts of milk. Add the 4th quart slowly, and cook until the rice is done. While the rice is cooking, beat the eggs with the sugar. Add the lemon rind, citron and vanilla (you can also add orange rind if you want.) Cool the rice slightly and add some of the cooled rice to egg mixture to temper it. Add remaining rice mixture. Pour into a prepared baking pan (approximately 9 x 13-inch) which has been lined with pie crust (see below). Allow some of the crust to overhang so you can crimp it up at the end for a decorative look. Reserve some pie crust to roll out and cut in thin strips to lay across the top of the pie in a lattice fashion. (Lay one strip horizontally, and the next vertically, and repeat to make a weave effect.) Serves 8.

There are traditional Easter pies made in all Italian households. This is ours.

CRUST FOR EASTER RICE PIE AND WHEAT PIE (PIZZA DI RISO AND PIZZA GRANA)
Clementina Mainella

5 eggs
½ pound sweet butter, melted
8 tablespoons sugar

1 teaspoon baking soda
2 teaspoons baking powder
6 cups flour (you will need to use your judgment here)

With a mixer with a dough hook attachment or a food processor with dough hook attachment, mix the eggs, butter and sugar. Mix the baking soda, and baking powder with two cups of the flour. Add to the egg mixture. Add two more cups of flour. Add the last two cups as you watch the consistency of the dough. If should be the consistency of a pie crust and easy to roll out. Let stand one hour. Spray a baking pan with PAM®. Divide the dough into two unequal pieces. Use the larger piece to roll into a rectangle and line the baking sheet. Pour in the filling. Roll the remaining piece in a rectangle and cut into strips with a pizza cutter or macaroni cutter wheel. Arrange in a lattice pattern. Fold up any overhanging crust to encase the lattice and crimp like you would for and apple pie, using your thumb to push in to make a **V** shape all around the pie. Bake at 350° for 1 hour, on the middle rack. Lower the temperature to 300° and bake an additional 45 minutes or until firm. Check frequently to be sure the crust does not get too brown and cover with aluminum foil if necessary.

EASTER WHEAT PIE (PIZZA GRANA)
Clementina Mainella

3 pounds ricotta cheese
1 pound of wheat grain (soak overnight and cook 1 hour according to directions or cook in a pressure cooker with 3 cups of water)
2 cups sugar
18 eggs
1 tablespoon citron

1 tablespoon orange juice
1 tablespoon lemon juice
1 tablespoon vanilla
1 tablespoon orange rind
1 tablespoon lemon rind
2 ounces whiskey

Preheat the oven to 300°. Whisk the eggs and sugar together. Add the ricotta cheese. Add the remaining ingredients except for the grain, mix until well blended. Fold in the grain. Pour into a prepared baking pan (9x13-inch) which has been lined with pie crust (recipe preceding). Allow some of the crust to overhang so you can crimp it up at the end for a decorative look. Reserve some pie crust to roll out and cut in thin strips to lay across the top of the pie in a lattice fashion. (Lay one strip horizontally, and the next vertically, and repeat to make a weave effect.)

"Trust your hunches. They're usually based on facts filed away just below the conscious level."
-- Dr. Joyce Brothers

AUNT LIZZIE'S NO CRUST RICOTTA PIE
Elizabeth Maida

3 pounds of ricotta
14 eggs
¾ - 1 cup of sugar
3 tablespoons orange juice

1 tablespoon lemon juice
1 tablespoon vanilla
1 cup boiled milk
½ cup flour, sift before mixing

Boil the milk, stirring so the bottom won't burn. Watch this carefully so it doesn't boil all over the stove. Combine milk with remaining ingredients in a large bowl. Pour into a large well greased casserole or round Pyrex®. Bake at 325° for 1 hour.

This is a family favorite at Easter time. Michele gave me Aunt Lizzie's recipe to share. She was an excellent cook, and is greatly missed.

Elizabeth Maida and daughter Michele Maida

MIGLIACCIO
Clementina Mainella

3-quarts of milk
1 pound very fine semolina
Pinch of salt
3 teaspoons vanilla
1 dozen eggs, slightly beaten

½ pound sweet butter
1¾ cups sugar
2 tablespoons orange zest or peel
Citron

Cook the milk and sugar together in a large saucepan. Bring to a boil. Then add the salt and vanilla. Add the orange peel. Add the semolina a little at a time, stirring constantly; keep at this point for about another 10 to 15 minutes **NO LONGER**! Remove from the heat and stir in the butter. Let cool for a few minutes. Add the eggs to the mixture a little at a time stirring constantly. Add citron if desired. For a richer consistency, add 1 to 1½ pounds of ricotta to the mixture (prepare as follows before adding.) Add additional 1 cup of sugar to the ricotta beat to a fine consistency. Add 2 additional eggs beating the whole mixture together. Then add to the above mixture, whipping until smooth. Butter a large baking dish. Pour mixture into prepared dish. Bake at 350° 45 minutes to 1 hour or until golden brown and firm.

This is a traditional dish served at Easter and was one of my grandmother's recipes. I can remember my Mother and Aunt Fifi making it at the holidays when I was a little girl. There were always so many wonderful baked goods around at the time of the Easter holiday.

EASTER HAM
Elise Feiner

6-8 pound boneless ham, fully cooked
2½ cups chopped onion
1 stick of butter
1½ cup packaged cornbread stuffing
¾ chopped parsley

2½ cups chopped pecans or nuts of your choice
3 teaspoons mustard (I like Dijon)
3 eggs, lightly beaten
¾ cup honey
3 tablespoons frozen orange concentrate, thawed

Remove any fat and skin from the ham. Make a pocket about 2-inches round in the middle of the ham using a sharp knife, going from the front of the ham to the back. Set aside. In a large frying pan, melt the butter and sauté the onions until golden brown and soft. Place the onions in a bowl and add the stuffing mix, parsley, pecans, mustard, and eggs. Mix gently. Place about ⅔'s of the stuffing into the pocket you created in the middle of the ham. You can make a diamond pattern on the top with a knife if you'd like. Score it about ¼-inch deep. You can do this up to 2 days ahead. Refrigerate the ham and the remaining stuffing. Preheat the oven to 325°. Bring the ham to room temperature before baking. Spray a roasting pan with PAM®. Bake for 60 to 90 minutes.

Mix the honey and orange juice together. After the ham has cooked for 90 minutes, pour the honey mix over the ham; and bake another 20 minutes. Then, take the ham out of the oven and spread the remaining stuffing mixture over the top of the ham. Baste with any juices that are in the pan. Cook another 20 to 30 minutes until the top is a nice brown color and it is crusty.

This is a great holiday ham that I have made several times. You can use any stuffing and do it the same way, but I like pecans.

L-R: Steven Feiner, Sarah Burlingame, David Feiner, Jeffrey Feiner, Alana Kivi

MINESTRA MARITATA
Clementina Mainella

20 pounds dandelion greens (this amount is not a mistake!)
5 pounds escarole
3-5 pounds Savoy cabbage
1 proscuitto bone (scrape of most of the pepper and rinse the bone)
2-3 slices of proscuitto skin
½ pound dried sweet sausage

½ pound dried hot sausage
1 pork hock
3 pounds spare ribs
2 sweet pepperoni sticks
2 hot pepperoni sticks
1 Hormel® salami
Grated Cheese

Place all the bones and meat (except the spareribs) (don't worry if you can't find proscuitto bone and skins, there are enough other meats to flavor the stock) into an 8-quart stockpot and fill with water. Leave the pepperonis, etc whole, don't slice them. Bring to a boil and then lower to a high simmer and cook for about 4 to 5 hours, so that meats are tender and stock is thick. You may need to add water from time to time because you will need 4 quarts of stock later on. Add the spareribs and cook another 1½ to 2 hours. Remove the meat and strain the stock. Clean and wash greens separately. Boil the greens in lightly salted water, drain, cool and set aside. After you have strained the stock, add the cooked greens to the stock. Slice all salami's and meat and add to the greens. Heat the greens thoroughly before serving. Top with a generous amount of grated cheese.

This was only served at Easter and is a very traditional dish in many Italian Families at the Easter Holiday. I can still remember my grandmother making this. We would all go outside and gather up all the dandelions in the neighborhood, walking around with our brown bags. It's hard to image that all those strange ingredients when combined could taste so delicious. It wouldn't have been Easter in our house without this dish.

PIZZA CHIENA OR PIZZA RUSTICA
Clementina, Josephine Mainella, and Katherine Avella

Crust Recipe:
2 packages of Fleischmann's yeast
4-6 cups flour
6 eggs
1 teaspoon of salt

¼ teaspoon black pepper
½ stick sweet butter, melted
½ cup warm water

Dissolve the yeast in the warm water. Add all the remaining ingredients and knead into medium soft dough, or use a food processor with a dough hook attachment. Place in a warm dry place and let rise for 1 hour. Punch down and let rise a second time. This will make two pie crusts, one for the top and one for the bottom.

Filling:
1 pound of proscuitto, sliced thinly
½ pound Genoa salami
1 dried sausage (optional)
½ pound soppressata (sweet)
½ pound pepperoni
1-2 large mozzarellas (grated) or 1½ pounds sliced mozzarella or 2 bags shredded mozzarella
½ pound sliced provolone
3 pounds of ricotta

2 pounds of formaggio fresca or coarse ricotta or basket cheese
10-12 eggs
1 - 1½ cups Parmigiana or Pecorino Romano grating cheese
½ teaspoon salt
¼ teaspoon black pepper
2 tablespoon dried parsley

Egg Wash:
1 egg

1 tablespoon of water

Mix egg and water well with a fork.

Preheat oven to 350°. Cut the meats into small pieces (I use a scissor and cut them into strips and then into small squares.) Mix the ricotta, formaggio fresca, eggs, salt, and pepper, grating cheese, and shredded mozzarella together. Mix the meats with the cheese mixture. If you prefer using the sliced mozzarella and sliced provolone cheese, just put it to the side at this point. Take ½ of the dough and roll into a large rectangle. Spray a large rectangular deep baking pan (9x13-inch is fine) with PAM®. Place the dough in the pan so that you have an overhang of dough around the pan. Start by layering the ricotta mixture, top with a layer of the mozzarella and/or provolone cheese, then another ricotta layer, cheese layer, etc. End with ricotta layer. Roll the other half of the dough to make the top crust. Place the top crust on the pie and roll together with the overhang piece from the top layer to make an edge like you would for an apple pie. Make a few slits in the top to allow the steam to vent. Brush the top of the crust with an egg wash. Bake at 350° for about one hour. Lower the heat to 300° and bake another hour. Check while baking and if the crust is becoming too brown cover with aluminum foil to prevent browning. You have to use your judgment to see if it is done. When cool, remove from the pan, if you are able to. If not you can refrigerate it at this point until it is firm and you are able to cut it in smaller pieces. Years ago my mother always wrapped a dish towel around this so the bottom crust did not become soggy and then wrapped it in foil. Keep refrigerated. Slice in thin pieces to serve. Serves 12.

Note: You can use the mozzarella of your choice (sliced or shredded). If you use shredded, add it directly to the ricotta mix. If you prefer it sliced, layer it with the provolone.

My grandmother and then my mother and Aunt Fifi always made this at Easter. The aroma while it is cooking cannot be described. I made it using pizza dough for the crust but Nanny and Aunt Fifi said it wasn't the same. I have to agree, the right crust is much better. The crust is easy to make though. This tastes better as it stays in the refrigerator. This is traditionally made at Easter.

"In the garden of life, you plant the seeds of love around your kitchen table..."
-Elise Feiner

RICOTTA DOLCE (EASTER SWEET PIE) VANILLA AND CHOCOLATE
Clementina Mainella

Crust:
3 eggs
½ cup sugar
2 ounces oil

1-2 teaspoons of vanilla
3 teaspoons baking powder

Mix the eggs and sugar together with a whisk attachment. Add the oil, then the vanilla and the baking powder. Add enough flour (about 4 cups) to make dough of a medium consistency. It needs to be thick enough to roll into a crust. You can use a dough hook attachment of a food processor or mixer to do this. Spray two (10-inch) Pyrex® pie plates with PAM®. Divide the dough in thirds. Roll two of the pieces into circles to make the bottom crust for the two Pyrex dishes. Allow some of the crust to overhang so you can crimp it up at the end for a decorative look. Reserve the last third of dough to roll out and cut in thin strips to lay across the tops of the pies in a lattice fashion. (Lay one strip horizontally, and the next vertically, and repeat to make a weave effect.) You can choose either of the two fillings given below. Serves 10.

Choose filling 1 or 2:

Filling 1:
3 pounds of ricotta
1½ cups of sugar
12 eggs

2 teaspoons vanilla
3 tablespoons of cocoa

Preheat the oven to 350°. Whisk the eggs and sugar together in a mixing bowl. Add the vanilla. Add ricotta and mix well. Divide the mix in half. Add the cocoa to one half. Taste to see if that half needs any additional sugar. Divide the two halves (vanilla and chocolate) to place in the two Pyrex pie plates. You can pour the vanilla in first and then swirl the chocolate in, or if you are really skillful, place the vanilla on one side of the pan and chocolate on the other. Top with strips of the pie crust arranged in a lattice fashion. Bake at 350° for one hour. Check to make sure the crust doesn't get to brown and if necessary cover with aluminum foil.

Filling 2:
3 pounds ricotta
2½ cups sugar
18-20 eggs

2 tablespoons vanilla
¾ cup dried fruits (citron)

Mix everything together. Follow above directions (pour into crust, etc.) Bake 350° 1 hour.

This is another variation of the Easter pies. It was always my favorite because I wasn't a fan of the rice or grain pies. This is more like a cheesecake. You can also use the wheat pie crust if desired.

L-R: Bettina Arcara Liza, John Arcara, and Marie "Cookie" Frank

Lauren Feiner and John-Michael Latini

PASSOVER BROWNIES
Elise Feiner

½ cup margarine
2 cups sugar
4 eggs
1 cup matzoh cake flour
½ cup cocoa
⅓ cup potato starch

¼ teaspoon salt
½ cup water
1 teaspoon vanilla
1 cup chopped walnuts (optional)
1 cup mini chocolate chips (Hershey®)
Confectioners' sugar for top

Blend butter with an electric mixer until creamy. Gradually add the sugar; beat well. Add the eggs, one at a time, beating well after each addition. Add remaining ingredients. Mix well. Grease a 13 x 9-inch baking dish. Preheat oven to 350°. Place mix in prepared pan. Bake 30 to 35 minutes or until a cake tester comes out clean. Cool and cut into squares. Dust with confectioner's sugar.

You can never have too many Passover dessert recipes.

PASSOVER CHEESECAKE
Elise Feiner

1 cup crushed Mandelbrot
1 cup pecans, finely crushed
¼ cup sugar
⅓ cup margarine, melted
2 (8 ounce) packages cream cheese
3 eggs
1 teaspoon of vanilla

1 (14 ounce) can condensed milk
½ pint heavy cream
1 (8 ounce) container sour cream for the batter
¼ cup sugar
2 teaspoons lemon zest
¼ cup freshly squeezed lemon juice
1 (8 ounce) container sour cream for the topping

Preheat oven to 300°. Put the Mandelbrot into a blender to make into crumbs. Mix the Mandelbrot, pecans, ¼ cup of sugar and margarine together. Press into the bottom and 2-inches up the sides of a greased spring form pan. Beat the cream cheese for a few minutes until light and fluffy. Add the eggs, one at a time, beating well after each addition. Add the vanilla. Add the milk, heavy cream, sour cream, sugar, zest, lemon juice, and beat until well mixed. Pour into crust. Place a pan of water on the bottom shelf of the oven to prevent cracking. Bake for 1 hour or until almost set (middle will jiggle a little). Turn the oven off, and let cake stand in oven for 30 minutes. Remove to a wire rack. Spread sour cream over the top, and let cool completely. Cover and chill 8 hours. Decorate with lemon zest or lemon slices if desired. Serves 10.

PASSOVER PANCAKES
Elise Feiner

3 large eggs
⅓ cup matzoh meal
2 tablespoons matzoh cake meal
¼ cup sour cream
2-3 teaspoons vegetable oil

¼ cup ricotta cheese
Pinch of salt
1 ripe banana, cut in small pieces

In a large bowl, whisk the eggs. Whisk in the matzoh meal and matzoh cake meal. Add in sour cream, ricotta, and salt. Fold in bananas. Heat a griddle or frying pan. Add the oil and heat the oil. Pour the batter to make 3-inch pancakes. Cook until the pancake starts to bubble. Turn over and cook other side. Serve with butter and syrup.

Counterclockwise from bottom:
Lauren, Steven, Jeffrey and
David Feiner

PASSOVER CHOCOLATE CHIP KAMISH BREAD
Pearl Borten

6 eggs
1½ cups sugar
1½ cups matzo cake meal
1 cup oil

1 tablespoon orange juice
1 teaspoon vanilla extract
1 bag (12 ounces) mini-chocolate chips
1 cup chopped walnuts

Preheat oven to 350°. Beat eggs in a mixer for 5 minutes. Add all the ingredients in order except for the chocolate chips and the nuts. Beat for another 5 minutes. Fold in chips and nuts. Pour into a well greased rectangular pan. Bake at 350° for 40 minutes only. Slice when hot as follows: Slice the pan in half lengthwise, and then cut across the narrow length of the pan in 1 to 1½-inch slices. Remove to a cookie sheet and toast in a 350° oven until brown as desired.

A great Passover dessert!

PASSOVER LASAGNA
Brenda Antzelevitch

1 Box of Passover Matzoh (depending on the size of your pan)
2 boxes frozen chopped spinach (thaw and squeeze out excess water)
1 pound ricotta cheese

½ cup grating cheese
½ teaspoon oregano
1 bag mozzarella
Marinara sauce

In a large 8 x 8-inch baking dish sprayed with PAM®, place a layer of tomato sauce on the bottom of a large baking dish. Place a layer of matzoh on top of the sauce. Place a little more sauce on top of the matzoh. Mix the ricotta, spinach, grating cheese; oregano and mozzarella (reserve some for the top) together. Spread on top of the matzoh. Top with sauce. Continue layering with matzoh, spinach mixture, and sauce. End with a layer of matzoh, cover with tomato sauce and sprinkle with grating cheese. Cover with foil and bake at 350° for 15 minutes. Uncover and sprinkle the top with mozzarella. Place back in the oven until the mozzarella melts, about 3 to 5 minutes. Serves 4.

This is a favorite of the Antzelevitch family, in fact, they like it so much that Brenda makes it all year long.

PASSOVER PECAN CANDY
Pearl Borten

1½ sticks of butter (must be butter, not margarine)
1 cup lite brown sugar

1 cup chopped pecans
3 sheets Passover matzoh (more if need)

Melt the butter and add the brown sugar. Heat and mix; add in the pecans. Spray PAM® all over a cookie sheet and place three sheets of the matzoh and add pieces to fill in and cover the sheet. Spread pecan mix on the matzoh. Bake at 350° for 7 to 8 minutes to brown. Cool and break into pieces.

I bet this would be good if you also melted some mini chocolate chips over the top!

CHAROSET
Elise Feiner

3 apples, peeled and finely chopped
½ cup shelled walnuts, coarsely chopped
½ teaspoon cinnamon

5 tablespoon sweet wine (I use Manischewitz® Concord Grape)
3 tablespoons of honey

Placed the apples and walnuts in a small bowl. Add the remaining ingredients and mix until smooth. I usually double this amount.

This is my favorite food on the Passover Seder plate and Passover Dinner. It's even better left over the next day.

MATZOH-APPLE KUGEL
Nellie Reinisch

2 tablespoons plus 2 teaspoons unsalted butter
4 apples, peeled, cored, and cut into
¼-inch thick slices
¼ cup raisins
½ cup sliced blanched almonds
10 square plain unsalted matzo

4 eggs, beaten
2 cups sour cream
½ cups whipped cream cheese
¾ cup sugar
1 teaspoon cinnamon
½ teaspoon salt

Melt 2 tablespoons of the butter in a large skillet and sauté apple slices on high heat, stirring occasionally, until soft and lightly browned. Remove to a large bowl with a slotted spoon. Add 2 teaspoons butter to the skillet, lower heat to medium, and quickly sauté raisins and almonds, stirring constantly. Be careful not to burn them. Add to the apples, and set aside. Preheat oven to 350°. Place matzo squares in another large bowl, and run cool water over them to soften. Crumble the matzo, and drain in a colander. Return drained matzo to bowl. Combine eggs with matzo and stir well. In another bowl, mix sour cream and cream cheese thoroughly. Then add it to the matzo mixture, along with sugar, cinnamon, salt, and fruit-nut mixture. Mix all ingredients thoroughly. Grease a 10-inch square Pyrex® baking pan liberally with butter, pour mixture into pan, and bake for 50 minutes or until top is a light golden brown. Let cool on counter. Loosen sides with a knife, place a large platter over the baking pan, and carefully turn the kugel out onto the platter. If any pieces stick in the pan, just put them in place. Right before serving, sprinkle top with confectioners' sugar. You can serve this kugel warm, at room temperature or chilled. Serves 6.

BANANA YOGURT KUGEL
Elise Feiner

6 matzoh, soaked in water and squeezed dry
4 eggs
⅔ cup sugar, divided
1 container of pineapple or pina colada yogurt
3 mashed bananas
1 (8 ounce) container of sour cream
½ cup crushed pineapple in its juice

1 teaspoon vanilla extract
1½ teaspoons cinnamon, divided
¼ cup chopped walnuts, finely chopped (optional)
1 tablespoon sugar
Butter
Pineapple or apricot preserves to glaze, melted

In a large bowl, combine the matzoh, eggs, sugar (reserve 1 tablespoon for later use), yogurt, sour cream, pineapple, bananas, vanilla, ½ teaspoon cinnamon, and walnuts. Turn onto a greased 8-inch square baking dish. Combine the remaining sugar and cinnamon and sprinkle over the kugel. Dot the kugel sparingly with butter. Bake at 350° for 45 minutes or until center is firm. Brush with melted preserves. Serve hot or at room temperature. This can be made ahead and frozen. Freeze after it has been baked. To serve remove from the freezer and put in the refrigerator the day before serving. Heat in a 325° oven for 20 minutes to reheat. Serves 6.

I found this recipe years ago and played with it to get this version. It makes a great kugel for Passover when you need a little variety. It can be used as a side dish or dessert.

THANKSGIVING MOLD
Katherine Avella

2 small boxes of lemon Jell-O® dissolved in 2 cups hot water
1 package frozen raspberries (10 ounces)

1 small can crushed pineapple, drained
1 mashed banana
½ cup chopped walnuts

Mix all ingredients together. Spray a gelatin mold with PAM®. Add ingredients to the mold. Refrigerate until solid. Remove from mold and serve on a serving platter. Serves 10.

Nanny always made this at Thanksgiving. I think it tastes even better a day later.

THANKSGIVING CORNUCOPIA
Elise Feiner

3 cups warm water
3 packages active dry yeast
3 tablespoons sugar
1½ tablespoons salt

⅓ cup oil
9 cups flour, more if needed
1 egg mixed with 1 teaspoon water

Place the yeast and water in a large bowl. Stir until dissolved. Add sugar, salt and oil. Add about three cups of flour and stir vigorously until smooth. I do this with a Kitchen Aid® with a dough hook attachment). Stir in additional flour until the dough pulls away from the bowl. Place on a floured board and knead until smooth and elastic. Place the dough into a greased bowl, turning over once to grease top of dough. Cover and let rise in a warm place until double in bulk about 45 minutes. Punch down and remove to a floured board. Make a cornucopia out of aluminum foil that is thirty inches long and twelve inches wide at the mouth. Curl into a cornucopia shape. Place on a cookie sheet. Spray the cookie sheet with PAM®. Cut dough into 24 pieces; roll each into a rope about one inch thick. Lay rope of dough over the cornucopia form, using a double thickness at the mouth. Tuck ends under. Brush with beaten egg yolk to which 1 teaspoon of water has been added. Bake at 400° for 35 to 40 minutes. Allow to cool. Set on a wide serving platter. Remove as much foil as you can from the mouth of the bread. Place cranberries or grapes and other fruits to look as though they are coming out of the cornucopia. Surround with other fruit. It makes a beautiful and elegant centerpiece for the table.

Thanksgiving - 1974

SAUSAGE - MEAT STUFFING (AVELLAS)
Katherine Avella

1 pound chopped meat
1 pound Italian sweet sausage
Fresh breadcrumbs (made from day old Italian bread about
1 loaf)
1-2 sticks butter
2 large onions peeled and chopped

5 stalks celery, finely chopped
Salt, pepper, parsley, oregano to taste
6 chestnuts boiled and chopped
1 jar sliced mushrooms
Grating cheese about 2 cups

Take the day old bread and put it into a blender or food processor to make the crumbs. Don't make the crumbs too fine; just pulse on and off. Brown the chopped meat in a frying pan sprayed with PAM®. Drain off liquid. Remove and set aside. In the same pan, brown the sausage, taking a little longer to brown than the chopped meat. Drain and set aside. In a large frying pan, melt the butter and add the onions and celery. Cook until translucent, add the mushrooms. Remove from the heat and add to the meat. Add the seasonings, the bread, chestnuts, and the grating cheese. Mix well. If too dry add a little chicken broth or water. Place in a large baking dish that has been sprayed with PAM®. The stuffing can be frozen at this point. Bake at 375° for about 30 minutes. For another variation you can cut up some Genoa Salami and mozzarella and add to the above.

This is our families traditional Thanksgiving stuffing. We have always had it. It was my father's favorite and Uncle Joe and Uncle Phil's favorite too. It's delicious leftover too. I can remember helping my mother make this when I was a little girl.

SOUP A LA SANDELLA (THANKSGIVING SOUP)
Katherine Avella

This soup can be done two ways...you can make the chicken soup from scratch which is what I do, but for years, we did it the easy way which is to use College Inn Chicken Broth. If you want to use the College Inn, just heat 6 to 8 **LARGE** cans of College Inn Chicken Broth in a large stockpot. Make the meatballs according to the recipe (see index for Meatballs for the Soup a la Sandella). Add the meatballs to the broth. Make the omelets according to the recipe directions (see index for Egg Omelet's for Soup a la Sandella). Add to the broth and meatballs. Heat the soup before serving. This can be done in advance and frozen. You can also do all the parts separately, and freeze and then combine them the day you are using them. If you decide to go with the Chicken Soup made from scratch, see index for Elise's Best Chicken Soup) but **don't add the chicken to the soup.** (Use the chicken for chicken salad instead). This soup is just basically eggs and meatballs.

I have always loved the smell of this soup cooking on Thanksgiving morning. Uncle Phil, Steven and Lauren need about a pound of cheese each when they eat this soup. Usually, they eat so much soup that they never eat much of the food.

EGG OMELET'S FOR SOUP A LA SANDELLA (THANKSGIVING SOUP)
Katherine Avella

12 eggs
½ teaspoon salt
½ teaspoon black pepper

1½ cups grating cheese
1½ tablespoon dried parsley

Please note that the amounts of salt, pepper, and parsley are approximate, you can alter these to your taste. Whisk all ingredients in a large bowl until all ingredients are well blended. In a very small, (4 to 6-inch in diameter) non stick frying pan (or your egg pan if you have one) place about 1 teaspoon of oil, and rub it around with paper towel. This will make the omelet's flow easily, but not make them greasy. Take a small gravy ladle, the size used for a gravy boat, fill with the egg mix, and then put it into the pan. Rotate the eggs quickly around the pan, to make a thin layer of egg. Flip to cook on both sides. This will take only a minute or two. **CAREFULLY** remove from the pan being careful to keep the round shape. Continue doing this until you have used up all the egg mixture. Place onto cloth kitchen towels, (not paper towels, they will stick) for a few minutes until they cool. When they are cool, you can stack them in groups of about six...you don't need to stack them on hundreds of towels, they can be stacked quickly (after you have completed about five the first few are cool enough to be stacked. They don't have to be ice cold, just not hot. With a sharp, long, wide knife, slice the circles into strips about ½-inch wide. When finished, rotate the circles and do the same thing in the opposite direction, so that this time when you make the strips, you will create cubes about ¼ to ½ -inches. Add to the chicken stock. If you like, you can make the omelet's ahead, and freeze them in a large Tupperware at this point, before adding them to the soup. Take them out of the freezer the day before and let them defrost. You can then add them to the soup that morning. You can also assemble the soup and freeze it already assembled. The choice is really up to you. See Soup a la Sandella recipe.

I remember as a kid getting to slice up the eggs for the soup. It was my favorite job. You always got to cheat a little and eat as you were slicing. I love this soup, because it reminds me of family, home, comfort, and love. My children love this soup so much that sometimes when she knows that they are coming home from school, Nanny will make it even if it isn't Thanksgiving.

A Typical Thanksgiving...
L-R: Abby, Lauren and Jody Feiner

MEATBALLS FOR THE SOUP A LA SANDELLA
Katherine Avella

3 pounds of chopped meat (ground round or chopped chuck will do)
6 eggs (2 eggs per pound of meat)
Pinch salt (about ¼ to ½ teaspoon) because the cheese is salty
Ground black pepper (about ½ teaspoon)

Grating cheese (Parmesan or Locatelli Romano) about 1½ to 2 cups or 2 to 3 good handfuls
Parsley (dried) about 1-2 tablespoons
Plain breadcrumbs (don't use seasoned) about ¾ of a cup
Water about ¼-½ of a cup

Mix everything together but the meat. When well mixed, add the meat and mix well. Before shaping the meatballs have cookie sheets lined with waxed paper or aluminum foil ready to place the meatballs on. Do not stack the meatballs on top of one another; use more cookie sheets if necessary. Shape into balls about ¼-inch in diameter. **These meatballs are very tiny**. Take a tiny bit of meat with the tip of your fingers and shape into tiny balls. Put up a large pot of water with about 1 tablespoon of salt added to it. Bring to a boil, and throw in the meatballs. Boil for about 5 to 6 minutes until cooked. Use a large slotted spoon to add the meatballs to chicken soup. Do not add the remaining water or pieces of meat in the water that might be floating around. If you need more broth, then strain the water that you cooked the meatballs in and then add it, but I don't usually like to do this because this is really chicken soup, not beef soup. If you want to make this soup at another time in a smaller amount follow the meatballs for beef soup recipe which is cut down to one pound of meat.

My favorite story in making this soup is one that occurred years later when Mom Mom was helping Nanny make the meatballs, Nanny was rolling microscopic meatballs, and well the best way to tell the story is to repeat what Dad said, "Mom, do you see the size of the meatballs my mother-in-law is making?...You're making golf balls!" With that, we all started to roll on the floor with laughter. Anyway, you put these into chicken soup that also has tiny omelets added to it. My mother has done it with only College Inn Chicken Broth, but I usually make it from scratch.

L-R: Elise Feiner, Lauren Feiner and "daughter" Sachi Ide

CHRISTMAS BOWS FURINO
Theresa Furino

5 cups of flour
¾ cup sugar
2½ teaspoons vanilla
6 eggs

2½ teaspoons baking powder
½ stick of unsalted butter, softened
2½ ounces of Amaretto
Oil for frying

Mix all ingredients together and knead like pizza dough. Roll out the dough until it's very thin and cut into strips with a pastry cutter. Shape into bows. Deep fry or cook in very hot oil. Drain on paper towels. Dust with confectioners' sugar if desired.

This is a favorite in the Furino house and Uncle Anthony and Aunt Eileen make them at the holidays. This is Uncle Anthony's mother's recipe.

"Thanksgiving dinners take eighteen hours to prepare. They are consumed in twelve minutes. Half-times take twelve minutes. This is not coincidence."
-Erma Bombeck

FAVETTI -FEINER
Elise Feiner

9 egg yolks plus 2 eggs
1 teaspoon salt
½ stick butter, melted
2 teaspoons vanilla
4 tablespoons Grand Marnier®
1 cup sugar

1 (8 ounce) package cream cheese, at room temperature
1 (8 ounce) container of sour cream
2 ounces oil
Orange and lemon zest
1-2 pounds of flour (8 cups)

In a Kitchen Aid® or food processor, cream the sour cream and cream cheese together. Add the remaining ingredients and mix well in the machine until a dough forms. Shape the dough into a log shape and cover. Keep dough covered while you shape the favetti. Roll into long pencil like sticks. Cut each stick into ½-inch pieces. Deep fry for a few minutes until golden brown. Drain on paper towels. Coat with honey glaze.

Honey Glaze:
2 cup honey
1 cup sugar
Juice of one orange

2 tablespoon Grand Marnier®
Grated orange peel if desired
1 large bag of slivered almonds (optional)

Heat honey and sugar until sugar is melted, and started to boil. Lower flame and cook until smooth, and mixture is close to a clear yellow. Add the orange juice and Grand Marnier. Mix in Favetti. Add the almonds. Place on platters. Sprinkle with confetti. Cover the favetti with plastic wrap.

These are a tradition in every Italian house at Christmas. Aunt Edith always made them at Christmas. They keep well covered with saran wrap. You can also add slivered almonds into the honey when coating the favetti.

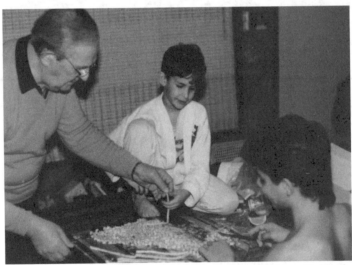

Grandpa Sam practicing what he preached…Cooking with Love!
L-R: "Grandpa" Sam Avella, Jeffrey Feiner, and Michael Avella making Favetti

CHRISTMAS BOWS MAINELLA
Josephine Mainella

5 cups of flour
1 teaspoon baking powder
1 tablespoon sugar
1 (8 ounce) package cream cheese

6 eggs
1 tablespoons vanilla
Enough flour to make a soft dough
1 quart Wesson® oil to fry

Beat eggs in a large bowl. Mix cream cheese, sugar, and vanilla well. Add the baking powder to one cup of flour. Add that to the egg mixture. Then, pour as much flour as the egg mixture will take to make a soft dough. Knead on a floured board. Roll very thin. Cut into 2-inch strips and shape to form bows. Put oil in a frying pan, and fry bows until golden brown. Drain on paper towels. Sprinkle with powdered sugar or dip into honey. (Heat 1 cup of honey and 1 tablespoon of sugar in a very large pot until sugar is dissolved.) Pour over the bows or dip the bows in honey. Sprinkle with nonpareil confetti sprinkles.

FAVETTI - MAINELLA
Josephine Mainella

4 eggs plus 1 yolk
4 tablespoons brandy, rum, or whiskey
Pinch of salt
2 ounces of oil

¾ cup sugar
1 teaspoon vanilla
Approximately 4 cups of flour (1 pound)

Mix well in the machine (Kitchen Aid® or food processor), or mix all ingredients together by hand. If mixing by hand knead the dough until soft to medium. Keep dough covered while you are working. Roll into long pencil like sticks. Cut into ½-inch pieces. Deep fry for a few minutes. Drain on paper towels. Glaze with honey. This is best done with 2 people.

Honey Glaze:
½ cup sugar
¾ cup honey
Juice of one orange, about ½ cup

2 tablespoon Grand Marnier®
¾ cup Grated orange zest if desired

In a large pot, heat honey and sugar until sugar is melted, and started to boil. Lower flame and cook until smooth, and mixture is close to a clear yellow. Add the orange juice and Grand Marnier. Mix in Favetti. Place on platters. Sprinkle with confetti or slivered almonds. Cover the favetti with plastic wrap.

This is Aunt Fifi's recipe. I use one that has cream cheese in it. These are the little honey balls you always see at Italian houses during Christmas and Easter. These are much easier to make if you have two people doing it. Otherwise, it's hard to keep up with the cutting and the frying.

The Sussman-Feiner Clan...
Back Row
L-R: Ferne Sussman, Barbara
Sussman Feiner
Front Row
L-R: Moe Sussman, Jody, Kevin and
Abby Feiner
The Sussman-Feiner clan
has shared many a holiday with us!

CHRISTMAS BOWS CATAPANO
Neva Catapano

3½ cups flour
½ teaspoons baking powder
1 teaspoon dry yeast

6 teaspoons extra fine sugar for honey dipped bows OR 12 tablespoons sugar for plain bows
1 (8 ounce) sour cream
12 egg yolks

Mix flour, baking powder, yeast, sugar, and sour cream together. Add egg yolks and mix. Run the dough through a macaroni machine on the **#5** setting. Cut in strips about 1 to 1½ -inches; shape into bows, and deep fry. They can be eaten plain but if you want to coat them in honey do the following: Fill the bottom of a very large pot with 1 small jar of honey, and add 1 tablespoon sugar. Heat until sugar is dissolved. Turn heat on low, put several bows in the pan and cover with honey. Drain and place on a platter. **NOTE:** Be careful when working with honey, when it boils it grows tremendously in volume. This is why you need a very large pot for a small amount of honey.

This recipe is from one of our neighbors in Brooklyn, Neva Catapano. She was an excellent cook, and would be serving meals at all hours of the day and night at her house on Arlington Avenue. Her husband Jack was a physician who had office hours in his house, and when he finished at 9 or 10 at night she would first start to cook dinner.

CHRISTMAS BOWS - DIPIERDOMENICO
Rosemarie DiPierdomenico

½ cup sugar
3 eggs
3 tablespoons brandy
1 teaspoon vanilla
3 ounces of oil

Pinch of salt
3 teaspoons baking powder
3-4 cups of flour
Oil to fry

Mix all the ingredients together but the flour. Start to add the flour slowly. Dough should be soft. Roll out the dough in pieces. Use a pastry wheel to cut the strips. Shape into a bow. Deep fry until golden brown. Top with confectioners' sugar or honey icing.

Honey Icing:
¼ cup honey
¼ cup sugar

Juice of fresh orange

Bring to a boil, and cook for about 5 minutes. Dip the bows in the mix, or pour over the bows.

Ro Di Pier serving up her wonderful specialties.

Ro was a beauty and she and Joe made one of the most beautiful couples.
As a little kid, one of the things I remember about Ro was, after Johnny was born, she said she couldn't curse, so she would say, "Son of a Pup"…I thought that was the greatest thing! I was about 7 and would go around repeating that.

FISH SALAD (CHRISTMAS)
Josephine Mainella

2 pounds of baccala, cleaned (dry cod)
2 pounds of calamari
1½ pounds medium shrimp
2 pounds scungilli
½ cup olive oil
Juice of 1½ lemons
3 small cloves of garlic, peeled and cut up

1½ ribs of celery, chopped
1 can pitted black olives
12 vinegared peppers
Salt and pepper to taste
Lemon or Italian Vinaigrette dressings if desired (add as much or as little as you prefer) (recipes in index))

Boil the baccala in water for about 10 minutes; remove from the pot. Boil the rest of the fish for about the same time in another pot; then remove from pot. In a large bowl, mix the fish, lemon juice, garlic, celery, olives and vinegar peppers. (If thin peppers are used leave them whole if not cut them in half.) Add salt and pepper to taste and mix well. Add lemon or Italian vinaigrette if desired (see recipe index). Refrigerate for at least one hour before serving.   Note: You must soak the cod in water for a few days before making the salad, changing the water frequently. Clean and remove any membranes from the cod.

This is a traditional dish in Italian families on Christmas Eve.

Abby Feiner and Melissa Avella enjoying the holidays! The best of both of my worlds sharing and caring together…

CHRISTMAS TRUFFLES
Elise Feiner

8 ounces of a high quality premium bittersweet chocolate broken into 2-inch pieces
¼ cup heavy cream
2 tablespoons butter

3½ tablespoons Kahlua®
1½ tablespoons Smirnoff® Vodka
1 cup finely chopped roasted nuts (walnuts or pecans)

Chop the chocolate in a food processor until finely chopped. In a small pot, place the butter and cream over medium heat until the butter melts and the cream just begins to boil. Turn the food processor back on and add the hot cream mixture through the feed tube, into the chocolate. Add the Kahlua and vodka and process until blended. Put the chocolate into a bowl, cover and refrigerate until firm (overnight.) The next day, roll into 1-inch balls; roll in the nuts. Store in the refrigerator in a plastic container. Serve at room temperature. Makes about 30.

CANDY CANE KISSES
Elise Feiner

4 large egg whites
⅛ teaspoon salt
1 teaspoon cram of tartar

1 cup sugar
½ teaspoon peppermint extract

Beat the egg whites at medium speed until they become frothy. Add the salt and cream of tartar. Beat for about 3 more minutes until soft peaks form. Add the sugar slowly, and beat until stiff peaks form. Beat in the extract until well blended. Take a parchment pastry bag and put a star tip in it. Use a paintbrush and paint 4 vertically spaced stripes up the bag with red food coloring paste. Space the stripes evenly. (I learned how to do the stripes when I took the Wilton® cake decorating course in the 70's.) Carefully put the mix into the bag, and pipe kiss shaped cookies on parchment lined cookie sheet. Bake at 225° for 1 to 1½ hours. Turn oven off and leave in the oven overnight.

MICROWAVE PEANUT BRITTLE
Elise Feiner

1 cup sugar
½ cup light corn syrup
⅛ teaspoon salt
1 cup shelled raw peanuts

2 tablespoons butter
1 teaspoon baking soda
2 teaspoons vanilla

Combine the sugar, corn syrup, and salt in a large microwave bowl. Microwave on high 5 minutes. Add the peanuts; and microwave on high 2 minutes. Stir in the butter, baking soda and vanilla. Pour into a greased 15 x 10-inch cookie sheet, and spread with a wooden spoon that has been sprayed with PAM®. Let stand until hardened. Break into pieces.

L-R: Mackenzie Raehm, Sarah Burlingame, David Feiner,
Jonathan Trainor, Katherine Trainor and Lauren Feiner

POTATO LATKES
Shirley Collins

6 large white potatoes
2 large onions
2 3 eggs
2 egg whites
⅔ cup of matzoh meal or flour

1 teaspoon baking powder
½ teaspoon garlic salt
1 teaspoon salt
½ teaspoon white pepper
Oil for frying

Peel potatoes and onions. (If not using immediately, place in cold water.) Grate the potatoes and onions with a shredding blade of a food processor. Put grated potatoes and onions in a fine strainer and press out as much liquid as you can. Transfer to a large mixing bowl. Beat eggs and egg whites until thick. Add to potatoes and onions. Add flour or matzoh meal (I like Matzoh meal), baking powder and seasonings. Mix well. Heat oil in a frying pan (about 1-1½-inches of oil). When ready drop by large soup spoonfuls or shape with your hands to form oval shapes. Fry over moderate to high heat until brown on one side, turn to brown the other side. Remove from frying pan and drain on paper towels. Serve with sour cream or applesauce.

This is my friend Cathy's grandmother's recipe for Latkes. I can remember the smell of onions frying in the hallway of her apartment near Atlantic Avenue in Brooklyn. These are wonderful! David and Abby, my latke critics loved these. This is my favorite recipe for latkes.

POTATO LATKES - NANNY NELLIE
Nellie Reinisch

6-8 Potatoes, peeled and grated
Salt and pepper to taste
1 teaspoon baking powder
2 onions, peeled and grated

2-3 eggs
Flour if needed
Vegetable oil, to fry

Mix in a large bowl all ingredients with a wooden spoon. Add small amounts of flour if needed to bind ingredients together. Heat a generous amount of vegetable oil in a pan. Make patties of potato mixture and fry until golden brown. Don't drain all the liquid from the potatoes in this recipe, it should be wet. Serves 6.

This is Nanny Nellie's recipe. I made these for Chanukah when we were trying different versions of latkes. These were crisp and very good.

L-R: Abby, Jennifer and Jody Feiner

*"If you're photographing them in color, you are showing the color of their clothes...
if you use black and white you are showing the color of their soul."*
-Author unknown

HANUKKAH POTATO LATKES
Freda Feiner

2½ pounds baking potatoes, peeled and quartered
2 large onions, quartered (about 1 1/2 cups grated)
3 large eggs, lightly beaten
1 teaspoon baking powder
1¼ cups vegetable oil

1 cup all-purpose flour
2½ teaspoons kosher salt
¼ teaspoons freshly ground black pepper
2 cups matzo meal

In a food processor, finely grate potatoes; leave some texture. Drain to eliminate excess liquid. Transfer to a large bowl. Finely grate onions, and mix 1½ cups into potatoes. Add eggs, baking powder, ¾ cup corn or vegetable oil, flour, salt, and pepper. Stir to combine. Fold in matzo meal, blending well.

Heat remaining half cup vegetable oil in a deep skillet over low heat. With a large kitchen spoon, drop batter into pan, make the pancakes about 3 to 3½ inches in diameter. Don't crowd them. Fry until underside is a deep golden brown, 3 to 4 minutes. Turn and fry for 1 to 2 minutes more. Repeat with remaining batter. Drain latkes on a paper towel-lined baking sheet. Serve with applesauce and/or sour cream.

Freda's Boys...

Gene and
Pinky Feiner

Betty Feiner with Philip "Pinky" Feiner

Uncle Gene is truly one of the most
philanthropic men I know, and a great
family historian.

L-R: Gene, Betty and Pinky Feiner
Uncle Pinky is our family fashion plate and used to work for Ralph Lauren.

"You go to sleep with dogs, you wake up covered with fleas!"
- Freda Feiner

Freda's Boys, Betty's Boys and Elise's Boys…
Back Row L-R: Kevin, Pinky, Gene, Steven, and Ivan Feiner
Front Row L-R: Jeffrey, David and Marc Feiner

The Feiner Girls: L-R: Back Row: Jennifer,
Barbara, Elise Betty and Danielle Feiner
Front L-R: Theresa, Lauren, Abby, Jody and
Karen Feiner

The Venezio Family: Rich, Julie, Brittany, and
Nick and Jennifer Venezio Garcea

The Avella Girls: Back Row L-R: Phyllis Avella, Nicole Latini, Flo Avella,
Lauren Feiner, Elise Avella Feiner
Front Row: Melissa and Katherine Avella, Josephine Mainella, Thirza Avella

L-R: Basia, Ariana and George Cacoulidis

Julie Ann Saracino Juliano, Laura, Angela, Maria and John Juliano

516

A Bit of This...A Dash of Love!

"The King of My Heart"...Marc Feiner
Thanks for making it all possible!

Clockwise from Left: Danielle, Marc, Betty, Lauren, Abby and Jennifer Feiner

Safety Stuff...

This was sent to me over the internet, and since we've nourished your heart and soul, here are some things to keep you safe!

This was sent out in an attorney's office and has some great tips:

Next time you order your check have only your initials (instead of first name) and last name put on them. If someone steals your checkbook, they won't know if you sign with your initials or whole name, but the bank will know how you sign your checks.

When writing your checks to pay credit card accounts **DO NOT** put the complete account number on the "For" line. Instead, just put the last four numbers of your account. The credit card companies know the rest of the numbers; this way, no one handling your check as it passes through check processing will have access to your account number.

Put your work phone number on your checks instead of your home phone. If you have a PO Box use that instead of your home address. If you don't have a PO Box, use your work address.

Never print your Social Security number on your checks...you can add it if necessary but if you print it, anyone can get hold of it.

Photocopy the contents of your wallet, do both sides of your license, and each credit card. You'll know exactly what was in your wallet if it's stolen, all the account numbers and phone numbers to call to cancel. Keep the photocopy in a safe place. If you travel abroad, also photocopy your passport.

If someone does steal your wallet or identity, limit the damage by doing the following:

Cancel your credit cards immediately. The key is having the toll free numbers to call and the account numbers. Keep them where you can find them.

File a police report in the jurisdiction where it was stolen; this proves to credit providers you were diligent, and is the first step towards an investigation if there is on.

Notify your banks, Department of Motor Vehicles, Passport Office or whatever is appropriate.

MOST IMPORTANT:

Call the three national credit reporting agencies and immediately place a fraud alert on your name and social security number. The numbers are:

Equifax: 1 800 525-6285
Experian (formally TRW) 1 888 397-3742
Trans Union 1 800 680-7289

Social Security Administration Fraud Line – 1 800 269-0271   10-4 EST Monday – Friday

These numbers were all correct at the time of printing.

BUTTER CREAM FROSTING
Elise Feiner

2 cups butter or shortening   2 teaspoons vanilla
3½ cups confectioners' sugar

Cream shortening and sugar together until smooth. Add vanilla and blend well. You may have to make some adjustments, especially in the summer. If the mixture is too soft, add more sugar. Do not over mix, just mix until smooth.

Butter Cream Version 2:

⅓ cup butter, cold and firm   ½ teaspoon vanilla
2 cups confectioners' sugar   1-2 tablespoons milk or heavy cream

Place the butter in a bowl and with an electric beater beat several minutes until creamy. Add sugar, about ½ cup at a time, and beat well after each addition. Add vanilla, then milk or cream. Beat well. Store in an airtight container in refrigerator. Whip again before using. For snow white icing, use white vegetable shortening (Crisco®) and butter flavoring.

CHOCOLATE BUTTER CREAM FROSTING
Elise Feiner

1 cup sugar   1 teaspoon vanilla
⅛ teaspoon cream of tartar   2 (2 ounce) squares unsweetened chocolate
Dash of salt   ⅔ cup butter, softened
¼ cup water
2 egg whites

Combine the sugar, cream of tartar, salt, and water in a small saucepan. Stir over low heat until the sugar dissolves. Bring mixture to a boil. Without stirring, cook to 234° to 238°. Remove from heat. Beat egg whites until stiff peaks are formed. Slowly pour the warm sugar syrup into the beaten egg whites in a steady stream beating constantly. Fold in vanilla. Cool. Melt chocolate over a double boiler. Cool. Cream the butter until light and fluffy. Beat in the egg white mixture 3 tablespoons at a time. Add the chocolate. Beat well. Refrigerate at least 5 minutes before using. Yield 2 cups.

This makes a delicious frosting but it is not very good to decorate or pipe with.

MOCK BUTTERCREAM FROSTING
Elise Feiner

⅓ cup cornstarch or flour   ½ cup butter
1 cup milk   ½ cup Crisco®
1 cup sugar   1 teaspoon vanilla

Cook the cornstarch and milk together in a small pot, stirring constantly until thick. Set aside and let cool. Blend the butter and the Crisco together until fluffy. Add the sugar slowly and beat until fluffy. Add cooked milk mixture and vanilla. Beat until fluffy again.

I got this recipe from a cake decorating course I took in New Jersey years ago. It makes a great filling for a cake. This is good if the weather is too hot for real buttercream.

CHOCOLATE SOUR CREAM FROSTING TWO
Elise Feiner

1 box of confectioners' sugar   1 egg
¾ stick of butter, melted   ½ cup sour cream
2 teaspoons vanilla   3 envelopes Nestle Choco Bake chocolate

Beat everything together until fluffy.

CHOCOLATE DOUBLE SOUR CREAM FROSTING
Ann D'Amico

1¼ pounds fine quality milk chocolate, finely chopped
10 ounces fine quality semisweet chocolate, finely chopped

3 cups sour cream
2 teaspoons vanilla

Melt chocolates in a double boiler or a large metal bowl set over a saucepan of simmering water, stirring occasionally. Remove bowl from heat, then whisk in sour cream and vanilla. Cool to room temperature, stirring occasionally (frosting will become thick enough to spread). You must work quickly and spread the frosting before it becomes too thick. (If icing does become thick, reheat over simmering water, then cool and try again.)

STRAWBERRY MOUSSE FILLING
Elise Feiner

1 (3 ounce) package of strawberry Jell-O®
¼ cup sugar
1 cup boiling water
¾ cup cold water

1 envelope of Dream Whip®
¼ cup cold milk
½ teaspoon vanilla

Dissolve the Jell-O and sugar in boiling water. Add the cold water. Chill until slightly thickened. Prepare the Dream Whip with the milk and vanilla as directed on the package. Stir Jell-O and blend in prepared Dream whip. Refrigerate for about three hours. Stir well before filling the cake. Recipe can be doubled for a larger amount.

They make great fillings for a cake!

CHOCOLATE MOUSSE FILLING
Elise Feiner

1 (6 ounce) package of Jell-O® pudding mix
2¼ cups of milk
1 envelope of Dream Whip®

½ cup cold milk
½ teaspoon vanilla

Combine Jell-O and 2¼ cups milk and cook as directed on the package. Remove from heat. Cover surface with waxed paper and chill in refrigerator at least two hours. Prepare Dream Whip with ½ cup milk and vanilla as directed on package. Stir the pudding until smooth. Blend in the Dream Whip. Cover and refrigerate until ready to use inside the cake. Best if prepared ahead.

PINEAPPLE FILLING
Elise Feiner

1 (8 ounce) container frozen Cool Whip®, thawed
1 (14 ounce) can sweetened condensed milk
1 cup shredded coconut

1 (8 ounce) can crushed pineapple including the juice
1 cup chopped pecans
¼ cup lemon juice

Gently spoon whipped topping into a large bowl and set aside. Combine remaining ingredients. Fold into the topping. Blend well. Chill at least 1 hour. Use as a filling for cakes (yellow).

"Life is an adventure in forgiveness."
-Norman Cousins

ICING FOR FIGURE PIPING
Elise Feiner

4 tablespoons meringue powder
⅔ cup lukewarm water
1¼ cups confectioners' sugar, sifted

3 cups granulated sugar
⅔ cup water
¼ teaspoon cream of tartar

Beat the meringue powder with the lukewarm water into peaks. Slowly add the confectioner's sugar and beat at medium speed until blended. Combine the granulated sugar with ⅔ cup water and cream of tartar; and in a saucepan heat to 234°. Pour cooked mixture into meringue mixture and continue beating at medium speed until peaks form. Use a heavy duty mixer to do this or you'll **BURN OUT** a hand mixture.

When Jeff was a baby, Cousin Michele and I took a cake decorating course at Sears in New Jersey. We became quite proficient at decorating, and I used to love to do piped figures on a cake. This is a great icing to accomplish this. You can use food coloring paste to tint it to whatever color you want. This is a very stiff icing, not used to frost a cake but for decorating.

BOILED ICING - MERINGUE
Elise Feiner

4 level tablespoons meringue powder
1 cup warm water
2 cups granulated sugar

¼ teaspoon cream of tarter
3½ cups confectioners' sugar, sifted

Boil the granulated sugar, ½ cup water, cream of tarter to 240°. Brush the sides of the pan with warm water to prevent crystals. Meanwhile, mix the meringue powder with ½ cup water and beat 7 minutes at high speed. Turn down to low speed, add the confectioner's sugar, and beat 4 minutes at high speed. Slowly add the boiled sugar mixtures, beat 5 minutes at high speed. This will keep for a week refrigerator covered with a damp cloth. Beat again before using icing.

Clockwise from left: Elise Feiner, Joe Avella, Phil Avella and Lauren Feiner

STRAWBERRY BUTTER
Ann D'Amico

1 cup sliced fresh strawberries, pureed
2 sticks sweet butter at room temperature

2 tablespoons confectioners' sugar

Use a food processor to beat the strawberry puree into the butter. When mixture is pretty smooth (don't worry about a lump here and there) add the sugar. Pack into a mold or crock and chill until ready to serve.

ORANGE BUTTER
Ann D'Amico

2 tablespoons orange rind, freshly grated
2 sticks sweet butter, at room temperature

2 tablespoons confectioners' sugar

Beat the orange rind with the butter and when well mixed add the sugar. Pack in a small crock or bowl and chill until serving. This is great on muffins, waffles, pancakes, French toast. It will last several days in the refrigerator.

ORANGE CREAM CHEESE SPREAD
Elise Feiner

1 (8 ounce) package of Philadelphia® cream cheese, softened
3 tablespoons sugar

2 teaspoons vanilla extract
1 teaspoon grated orange peel

In a bowl beat all ingredients until smooth. Store in the refrigerator. This is great on bagels or muffins.

We love to find new and different cream cheese spreads for our bagels.

What every smart girl needs... a good plastic surgeon and a good orthodontist!
L-R: Richard Sleeper, M.D., Lauren Feiner, and Anthony Furino, D.D.S.

ORANGE MARMALADE BUTTER
Elise Feiner

1 stick unsalted butter at room temperature
¼ cup sweet orange marmalade

2 teaspoons honey

In a bowl, cream the ingredients together. Place in a small bowl or crock until serving time.

VANILLA SUGAR
Elise Feiner

2 pounds superfine sugar

4 vanilla beans

You need a food processor for this one. Put your vanilla beans in the mixer, process, scrape the sides and process again. Add all the sugar and process for about 2 minutes. Sieve the mixture into a bowl, return any lumps to the food processor and process again. (You may want to repeat this process if you want it really fine). Sprinkle on fruit or use in whipped cream.

WHIPPED CREAM
Elise Feiner

2½ pints heavy or whipping cream   ¼ cup granulated sugar or sifted confectioners' sugar
2 teaspoons vanilla

In an ice cold bowl, place ingredients. With a whipping attachment on high, whip until cream holds its shape. Do not over beat or you'll get butter. Taste to adjust sugar to your liking.

This whipped cream can be used for any dessert topping. I use this in my eggnog.

Top L-R:
Betty Reinisch Feiner,
Shirley Reinisch Flomenhoft,
Adele Reinisch Freedoff
Seated: Nellie and Judah
Reinisch

QUICK PIZZA SAUCE/ENGLISH MUFFIN PIZZA
Elise Feiner

1 (15 ounce) can of Hunt's Tomato sauce   ⅛-teaspoon black pepper
1-2 small cloves of garlic peeled and crushed   ½ teaspoon salt
1-2 tablespoon olive oil   ½-¾ teaspoon oregano
Jumbo English Muffins   Grating Cheese
Shredded mozzarella or fresh if you can get it (sliced)

In a small saucepan heat the oil, add the garlic and cook for about one minute. Add the tomato sauce, salt, pepper and oregano. Bring to a boil and then simmer for about 15 minutes. This is a quick sauce to use on an English muffin pizza, or a pita pizza. It won't make enough for a regular size pie. Place about a teaspoon of the sauce on a **TOASTED** (muffin should be fairly brown so sauce doesn't make it soggy) English muffin, place mozzarella and a little grated cheese on top and add another drop of sauce. Place under a broiler or toaster oven until cheese is melted.

This is for you David so you can make a fast midnight snack!

David Feiner Then…

Future "Doc" David Feiner
State University of New York at Buffalo
School of Biomedical Sciences Class of 2009

ARMENIAN STRING CHEESE
Shemoney Koury

15 pounds of salt free mozzarella cheese curd   Black caraway seeds (not the kind for rye bread)
Kosher Salt or canning salt

Slice the cheese curd thinly. Rinse the curd in water. Add cold water to an 8 quart pot and put about 26 ounces of salt in the pot - there should be enough salt to float an egg the size of a half dollar. Measure 6 ounces of curd at a time, and microwave 60 to 75 seconds. Knead the melted curd with some of the caraway seeds. Stretch the cheese several times (be careful as it's hot). Braid it, and put it into the cold water rinse. Let stay in the water about 2 hours. Wrap and freeze. Shred before serving.

We had the most fun making this cheese with Cyndi Koury and her mother-in-law. We were all novices, except for Shummy, and pulling and braiding the cheese and making a mess, but we made delicious cheese. It takes a while to get the hang of cheese making, but what fun it is.

MOZZARELLA CHEESE
John Grimaldi, Sr., Executive Chef

Salt   1 pound Fresh Mozzarella Curd
2 gallons water

In a large pot, add the water. Add enough salt to the water until it tastes like saltwater. Bring the temperature of the water up to about 120° to 130°, until the touch of the water is like hot bath water. Place a colander in the water. Crumble the cheese curd into the water. Using a wooden spoon, stir the mixture until the curd starts to pull. Using your hands or a spoon, pull the cheese until it begins to hold shape. It's like pulling taffy. Do not over pull the cheese because the end product will be rubbery. If the cheese hardens to soon, dip the cheese back in the water and repeat the pulling process. After the desired size is achieved dip the cheese in an ice bath. Store in salted water or in plastic wrap.

No one makes mozzarella the way they do in Staten Island, N. Y….John's is the best!

Back Row L-R: Tom and Toni Mollico, John, John Jr., Rosemary Grimaldi, Marc Feiner
Front L-R: David Feiner, Brian Mollico, Jeffrey, Steven Feiner, Christopher Grimaldi, Lauren Feiner

ROASTED PUMPKIN SEEDS
Elise Feiner

Separate the seeds from the fibers after cleaning out the pumpkin interior. Discard the fibers. Rinse the seeds off. Spread the seeds out on a cookie sheet. Toast in a 250° oven for about an hour. Turn up the oven to 350°. Mix the seeds with a scant tablespoon vegetable oil for each cup of seeds, spread again on a cookie sheet. Salt lightly if desired with kosher salt, and return to oven for 14 minutes. When cool, store in a covered plastic container.

This is for you Steven, I know you love to make and eat these!

"MOCK" CLUB MED® MARINATED OLIVES
Elise Feiner

4 cups assorted olives, such as Kalamata, Picholine, Sicilian green, and Nicoise
½ cup extra virgin olive oil
½ cup lemon juice, or ¼ cup lemon juice and ¼ cup fresh squeezed orange juice
3 cloves minced garlic
2 tablespoons minced fresh rosemary or 2 teaspoons dried rosemary
2 teaspoons fresh oregano, chopped or ½ teaspoon dried oregano

½ teaspoon dried basil
⅛ Teaspoon ginger
Zest of ½ lemon and zest of ½ orange
1-2 mini limes cut into very thin slices
1 teaspoon dried hot pepper flakes (optional)
½ teaspoon fennel seeds
1 teaspoon garlic salt
1 teaspoon black pepper
Extra virgin olive oil

Place everything in the food processor except the olives, lime slices, and olive oil. Pulse until you have a paste. Add the olives to the paste and mix well. Add the mini lime slices. Cover with olive oil and refrigerate in a glass jar. They will keep for about a month. In a large bowl, combine all the ingredients and stir well to mix. Marinate the olive mixture, covered and chilled, stirring occasionally, for at least 1 day before serving. Let come to room temperature before serving. To store indefinitely, transfer the olives to a 1-quart glass jar with tight-fitting lid and keep chilled.

We had these olives on a vacation to a Club Med in the Dominican Republic when the kids were really small. I tried to duplicate the recipe. It may be hard to find the mini limes in New York.

LEBANESE OLIVES
Shemoney Koury

Buy large green uncured Sevillano olives if possible. Crack the olives on their sides open with a hammer (hit once, don't remove the pit.) Put olives in a large kettle or kettles and cover with water for at least 10 days. Change the water at least twice a day. When olives are ready to bottle, rinse well and put in 1 quart canning jars (to the neck of the jar if glass topped, and almost to the neck if brass dome lidded). To each quart jar add the following:

1 jigger white vinegar
1 jigger lemon juice (use fresh lemons)
1 jigger olive oil

1 tablespoon canning salt
1 tablespoon oregano (optional)

***The jigger glass that we used measures 2 tablespoons

After adding the ingredients, place half of the juiced lemon, cut side down over the olives. Fill the jar with water, and press down to remove any air. Add additional water if necessary. Seal the jar. Turn each jar over to check for leaks. Let the jars side upside down for two days to make sure the ingredients are distributed, and then **store right side up in a cool dark place. Let season for at least three months before opening.**

Marc, Billy, Cyndi and I experimented with some of the jars. We did a total of twelve jars. Six we did the regular way. Two, we added the oregano too, and the other four we got adventurous with, and added the following to the basic mix:

(In each jar)
3 cloves of garlic
Zest of lime or orange about 1 tablespoon per jar
1 tablespoon dried mint
1 small bunch of fresh tarragon (just break off a small piece)

1 small bunch fresh oregano   (just break off a small piece)
1 spring of fresh thyme
4-5 basil leaves fresh
Or other herbs of your choice

This recipe came from Cyndi Koury's mother-in-law Shummy. I went to visit the Koury's one evening and they were talking about making these olives. Cyndi asked me if I wanted to do some, and I said sure. I don't know what was more fun, watching Dad hitting the olives with a hammer, changing that darn water everyday (it weighs a ton) or having the Koury's over to help jar the olives. What a great time sharing with old friends.

SUGARED PECANS AND WALNUTS
Elise Feiner

1 pound pecans or walnut pieces or a mix of both	⅛ teaspoon ground cloves
½ cup unsalted butter, melted	1½ teaspoons cinnamon
½ cup confectioner's sugar	¼ teaspoon ginger
¼ teaspoon ground allspice	

In a small bowl, mix the allspice, cloves, cinnamon, and ginger together and set aside. Preheat a crock-pot on high for about 15 minutes. Add the butter and nuts and stir well until evenly mixed. Add the confectioner's sugar and stir well to coat. Cover and slow cook on high for 15 minutes. Reduce the heat to low, and remove the cover. Continue cooking uncovered, stirring occasionally until the nuts are coated with a crisp glaze (this takes about 2 hours). Put into a bowl and sift the spices over the nuts. Let cool before serving.

These are great at the holidays and they practically cook themselves. They make great holiday gifts too!

TRADITIONAL CHEX MIX
Elise Feiner

½ stick butter	2⅔ cups Rice Chex®
1¼ teaspoons seasoned salt	1 cup salted mixed nuts
4½ teaspoons Worcestershire sauce	Pretzel sticks
2⅔ cups Corn Chex® mix	1 cup Cheerios®
2⅔ cups Wheat Chex®	½ stick butter

Preheat oven to 250°. Heat butter in a shallow roasting pan (about 15 x 10 x 2-inches) in oven until melted. Remove. Stir in the seasoned salt and Worcestershire sauce. Add the Chex cereal, nuts, pretzels, Cheerios. Mix well until all the pieces are coated. Heat in the oven for 1 hour, stirring every 15 minutes. Spread on absorbent paper to cool.

This is from the cereal boxes and everyone has probably made it at one time or another. It is so much better than the packaged kind. I included it in the book because at least three people called to ask if I had the recipe. This way, it is right at your fingertips. Reprinted with permission of General Mills. Chex® is a registered trademark of General Mills.

SPICY PECANS
Elise Feiner

3 teaspoons of butter	Salt or garlic salt to taste
⅓ cup Worcestershire sauce	2 cups of large pecan halves
2 dashes Tabasco	

Melt butter, add the other ingredients. Remove from heat and add the pecans. Stir and mix, 5 minutes or more so that each nut is coated and the sauce is absorbed. Line a cookie sheet with parchment paper, pour nuts out onto the cookie sheet and bake at 300° for 15 minutes.

MARIA'S NUTS (CHINESE FRIED WALNUTS)
Ann D'Amico

6 cups water	A little salt
4 cups walnuts	Salad oil for frying
½ cup sugar	

Boil water, add the nuts and bring to a boil and cook 1 minute. Rinse with hot water. Drain. Add to a bowl with ½ cup sugar and let stand five minutes. Clean pot and put in oil and heat to 350°. Fry walnuts about 5 minutes until golden brown. Take out with a slotted spoon and put in a colander to drain. Add just a little bit of salt and mix well (keep moving them) Put on paper towels to absorb the shortening and keep moving them as they tend to stick to the paper towels, or use brown paper grocery bags. Put in a container and cover tightly.

This recipe is from Ann's friend Maria; a great munchie, appetizer or dessert.

CANDIED SUGAR NUTS
Katherine Avella

6 cups sugar
3½ tablespoons cinnamon
2 teaspoons ginger powder
1 teaspoon nutmeg

2 teaspoons salt
6 cups whole pecans or walnuts
Vegetable oil, for frying

Mix the sugar, cinnamon, ginger, nutmeg, and salt, together in a large bowl.

Boil a small pot of water and put the nuts in for 1 minute. Drain the nuts and let them dry them off in a kitchen towel. Lightly toss them into the sugar mixture until coated. Remove nuts. Put the sugar spice mixture away for the time being. Bring the oil in a deep fryer or a heavy-bottomed pan to 330° to 350°. (Do not let the oil burn). Like frying anything, test the oil test by placing a little bread or a nut in it and if starts to sizzle, it's hot enough. Add the nuts, about 1 cup at a time. Fry approximately 1 minute, the nuts will turn golden in color, and float. Remove from the oil and add directly to the remaining sugar mixture and toss again. Remove nuts and shake off excess sugar, let cool and serve. These are great as dessert, or tossed in a salad.

Elise Feiner and Lauren Feiner in an "after picture"…be careful of all these delicious recipes… Eat in moderation and enjoy!

PLAY DOUGH
Don Orilio

1 cup flour
1 cup water
½ cup salt

2 tablespoons oil
1 teaspoon cream of tartar

Cook in a saucepan over medium heat until dough sticks together. Add food color to make it different colors. Store in zip lock bags.

This is great to make with little kids. It's actually better than play dough, it doesn't seem to dry out as much. Don Orilio was a teacher up at E.R. Hughes School in New Hartford.

L-R: Katherine Avella, Eva Castro, Josephine Mainella

EDIBLE CONFECTIONERS' GLUE
Elise Feiner

Method 1:

¾ cup water
2 tablespoons corn syrup
1 teaspoon vinegar

½ cup cornstarch
¾ cup cold water

Mix the water, syrup and vinegar in a small saucepan. Bring to a rolling boil. In a small bowl, mix the cornstarch and the cold water. Add this mixture slowly to the first mixture. Stir constantly. Let stand.

Method 2:

4 teaspoons Meringue Powder
¼ cup water

3 cups confectioners' sugar

Whisk gently the meringue powder and the water together until completely dissolved. Beat in the 3 cups confectioners' sugar until thick and smooth.

This is useful for certain craft projects, such as candy topiary trees.

BUBBLES FOR WAND
Elise Feiner

2 cups Joy® dishwashing liquid
6 cups water

¾ cup white Karo® corn syrup

Combine, shake and let settle 4 hours. Store covered in refrigerator to extend shelf life. Allow to warm before using. This is non toxic, but not for human consumption. Use with large bubble wand. If you can't find a large wand, shape one out of a wire hanger in a heart or circle shape.

This is great for kids to make jumbo bubbles.

L-R: Cathy D'Andrea and Godmother Katherine Avella
My mother and Cathy had a very special relationship, especially after her own mother
passed away

HOT PEPPER JELLY
Nancy Herr

1 cup ground bell peppers
½ cup ground hot peppers (you decide how hot you want them, I use California)
6½ cups sugar

1½ cup cider vinegar
1 bottle pectin (or pouch)
7-8 drops green food color

Be careful handling peppers. You might want to wear gloves. They sting the skin and eyes. Grind peppers in Food Processor. Mix peppers, sugar and vinegar together in a large pot. Boil about 2 minutes (if boiling over add a touch of margarine). Strain through a jelly sack or sieve several hours or overnight. (I use a sieve). Later or next day bring to a hard boil, and then add pectin and coloring. Bring to a boil again, hard for 1 minute. Pour immediately into prepared jelly jars; I boil the jars and lids in advance after washing them with soap and water first. Seal with lids or paraffin. I use lids and the hot bath method. I believe it keeps the jelly from spoiling or growing bacteria.

This recipe is from Lauren's friend Dan's mother Nancy Herr. She sent us a jar for Thanksgiving and it was wonderful. I asked her for the recipe and she sent it along. Nancy says, "Nice served with roast meats or on crackers with cream cheese."

THE BEST GRILLED CHEESE SANDWICH
Maria Trainor

String Cheese (Lebanese or Armenian type with the black seeds) shredded
Pita Bread (small size about 6-inch diameter)

Melted Butter
Ham (Optional)

Take the string cheese, and carefully shred by pulling it apart with your fingers and set it aside. Very carefully, using the tip of a knife, score the pita bread carefully to cut it in two. In a frying pan, melt some butter and place the inside of the pita bread facing down into the butter. Top with cheese and a slice of ham if desired. Place the other half of the bread with the crust side down. Lift to turn and add a little more butter to the pan; turn sandwich over. Continue to cook until crisp and the cheese is melted.

Maria said this is the way Johann Gigliotti's mother makes the grill cheese. Now, my kids won't eat it any other way

BAKED GRILLED CHEESE
Elise Feiner

8 slices of white bread, crust removed
¼ pound cheese of your choice, provolone, mozzarella, cheddar
2 ounces ham (I like Black Forest, Sahlen's smoked ham or Boar's Head Baby Ham)

3 eggs
2 cups milk
1 tablespoon grated cheese (optional)
Salt and pepper to taste

Grease an 8 x 8-inch square baking dish. Place four slices of the bread on the bottom of the dish. Top each slice with cheese and ham. Place the remaining 4 slices over the top. Whisk the eggs together with salt and pepper to taste and grated cheese. Whisk in the milk. Blend well; pour over the bread. Refrigerate, covered for at least 1 hour. Preheat the oven to 350°degrees. Bake the sandwiches for about 45 minutes until lightly brown. Slice and serve.

These makes a great light supper on a Sunday night especially if there is a football game on, add a bowl of soup and you've got it all!

"Death is God's way of saying you're fired."
-Author Unknown

HAM AND CHEESE PITA ROLL-UPS
Mary Ann and Segean Karam

Lebanese String cheese, shredded	**Butter**
Deli Ham, thinly sliced	

Take the string cheese, and shred by pulling it apart with your fingers; set it aside. Very carefully, using the tip of a knife, score the pita bread carefully to cut it in two. In a frying pan, melt some butter and place the **INSIDE** of the pita bread facing down into the butter.

Top with cheese and a slice of ham if desired; leave as open face sandwich, and when the cheese is melted and the outside is crisp, roll it like a tortilla; cut in half to serve. Repeat with the other half.

We get our pita bread and string cheese from Karam's Middle East Bakery and Restaurant. I was telling Mary Ann how much my kids love the grilled cheese made with their bread and string cheese. She told me to try this. She said it was the way her father always made it. Karam's is a little restaurant with wonderful Middle Eastern food. My husband and my son Jeff love the Falafel. Isn't it wonderful how here in America, the Jews and the Arabs can live together in such harmony. You never go into Karam's without finding half of the Jewish physicians in this town having lunch there. Karam's will ship the bread and the cheese to you. Call (315) 736-1728 or FAX them at (315) 736-1720. They are located at 137 Campbell Avenue, Yorkville, N.Y. 13495. Another great Upstate N. Y. Restaurant. Stop in for lunch!

Mary Ann and Segean Karam

BAKED GRILLED CHEESE TOO
Elise Feiner

1 package of Pillsbury Crescent Rolls	1 egg, beaten
4 cups shredded cheese (1 cup of each) Muenster,	Salt and pepper to taste
Monterey Jack, Swiss and Cheddar	1 tablespoon butter, melted
1 (8 ounce) package of Philadelphia Cream Cheese, sliced	1 tablespoon sesame seeds

Unroll the crescent dough and divide in half. Seal the perforations. Spray a 8 x 8-inch pan with PAM. Line the bottom of the pan with half of the dough. Layer the cheeses, and the cream cheese. Beat the egg with the salt and pepper. Pour the egg over the cheese. Top with the remaining dough. Brush with the butter, sprinkle with sesame seeds. Bake, uncovered at 350° for 30-35 minutes until golden brown.

This is another version of a baked grilled cheese sandwich. My family loves grilled cheese in any form. You can also add ham to this. I've made this twice, but it is very, very, rich. I think the next time, I would cut the quantity of cheese in half.

528

TABBULI SALAD
Theresa Feiner

¾ cup Bulgur #1 (cracked Wheat)
2 large bunches of parsley, (washed and drained well; spin it) finely chopped
¼ cup fresh mint or ⅛ cup dried mint, if available
4 Green onions with green ends, finely chopped
2 large tomatoes, finely chopped

1 small onion, finely chopped
2-3 teaspoons salt
Pepper to taste
½ to ⅔ cup fresh lemon juice
½ cup olive oil

Rinse Bulgur (cracked wheat) by pouring enough water to over it; rinse and drain, and then squeeze excess water out. Place in large mixing bowl. First, finely chop tomatoes. Using a food processor, chop parsley, mint, onion and green onions together. Place vegetable on top of bulgur; tomatoes first, then parsley mix. Add seasoning and mix well; add lemon juice and toss. Just before serving, add oil and toss thoroughly. This is eaten by hand by using very tender grape leaves, Romaine or Iceberg lettuce leaves to pick up tabbuli in bite-size servings. **Note:** Tabbuli may be prepared 1-2 hours ahead of time by omitting tomatoes and oil; cover with plastic wrap and refrigerate. Add tomatoes and oil just before serving. You can also add ½ cup whole black olives, ½ cup feta cheese and 1 small cucumber, peeled and diced if desired

My sister-in-law Tre is Lebanese. She converted to Judaism when she married Ivan!

Theresa Feiner and her mother Barbara Boohaker who was a fabulous cook!

L-R: Jennifer and Theresa Feiner

Jennifer Feiner today

CRANBERRY LAYERS
Elise Feiner

1 (8 ounce package) of Philadelphia Cream Cheese, at room temperature
2 tablespoons sour cream
1 tablespoon brown sugar

¼ cup chopped pecans
1 (16 ounce can of jelled Cranberry Sauce (whole) chilled
¼ teaspoon cinnamon
Dried blueberries and cranberries, Chopped

Mix the cream cheese with the sour cream until creamy. Add in the brown sugar and cinnamon and mix again. Blend in the pecans and chopped blueberries and cranberries. Mix well. Slice the cranberries into ¼-inch rounds. Place about 1 tablespoon of the mix on the cranberry slice. Top with another cranberry slice. Repeat until everything is used up. You can cut these is half or quarters to serve. Refrigerate uncut until ready to serve.

I saw Paula Deen do this on the Cooking Channel and decided I liked the idea but not the mayonnaise called for in her recipe. I changes the mayonnaise to sour cream, added the brown sugar and cinnamon. I was in B.J.'s at the time and saw the dried blueberries and cranberries and added that as well. It was delicious and a great hit at Thanksgiving. I hope Paula Deen doesn't mind me borrowing her idea!

MIKE'S HOMEMADE CHEESE CANVAS
Michael Miller

2 quarts whole milk
1 cup heavy cream
2 cups fresh buttermilk
2 tablespoon fresh lemon juice
Salt and Pepper to taste

3 cloves garlic peeled and crushed
6 leaves fresh basil, finely chopped
3 tablespoons fresh parsley, finely chopped
1 teaspoon olive oil

In a large heavy pot, mix the milk and cream. In a separated bowl, mix the buttermilk with the lemon juice; stir to blend and add to milk mix. Place a candy thermometer in the pot. Cook over **low** heat stirring **once** with a flat spatula using **ONLY TWO STROKES** when the **temperature reaches 125°F** and then one **more time at 150° F** the same way. **Do not over stir or you will destroy the mix by breaking up the curds.** You will see the mix begin to crystallize and the curds form. Check the temperature often, but it takes quite awhile when the temperature is low to reach 175°. **When temperatures reaches 175° remove** from heat immediately **and let sit 10 minutes undisturbed.** Place two layers of cheesecloth over a strainer or colander and **gently ladle** the mix into the cheesecloth. Let as much liquid drain off as possible. You may squeeze **very gently** to help get rid of the water. Let the cheese sit overnight in the cheesecloth in the refrigerator to allow any remaining liquid to evaporate. In the morning, remove the cheesecloth and mix in the salt, pepper, herbs, garlic and olive oil. Serve with crackers. It will keep for a week plain and for about a month with oil and herbs added to it (refrigerate.) **This cheese is quite temperamental so follow directions to the letter!**

Mike is my niece Jen's boyfriend, soon to be veterinarian and gourmet cook. He used to work in his family's restaurant in New Jersey. Mike says this cheese is like a blank canvas, you can add anything you like to it. We tried grated cheese and roasted peppers in the mix and it was delicious. You can add scallions, capers, olives, or whatever you like. This is great on bagels, crackers or French bread toasted with a little olive oil and garlic. You can also do a sweet version with honey, fruit, raisins, mini chocolate chips, vanilla, and cinnamon or whatever else you like in it.

My niece Jennifer Feiner and her boyfriend Mike Miller. They are both veterinary students
at the University of Pennsylvania Mike is also a gourmet cook!

AJ'S FAMOUS CINNAMON SNAILS
Abby and Jody Feiner

6 slices of white bread
Philadelphia Cream Cheese (at room temperature)

Domino's Cinnamon Sugar or make your own
½ to 1 stick of melted butter

Place the cinnamon sugar in a bowl. Place the melted butter in another bowl. Remove the crust from the bread, and with a rolling pin, roll the bread until it is flat. Spread the cream cheese on a slice of bread and then roll the bread, jelly roll style. Cut in half. Dip into the butter and then into the cinnamon sugar. Heat a medium frying pan that has had some melted butter placed into it; be careful not to burn the butter. Fry the cinnamon snails until golden brown.

Abby says that she and Jody make these at Southampton Summer Day Camp, where they are counselors.

"Winners never quit and quitters never win."
-Vince Lombardi

AND FINALLY, EVERY WOMAN'S FAVORITE RECIPE…

RESERVATIONS
Betty Feiner

1 yellow page local phone book   1 calendar
1 telephone

Check calendar for available date and time. Look up restaurant section of the yellow pages. Pick a restaurant. Lift phone off cradle. Dial the number. **CALL FOR RESERVATIONS!** Enjoy your dinner…

Nanny Nellie used to joke that although she was a great cook she never taught Mom Mom, Aunt Adele and Aunt Shirley how to cook so they needed to learn to make reservations. We always tease Mom Mom about that. Even though I love to cook, this is truly my favorite recipe!

Nellie Reinisch

L-R: Adele Reinisch Freedoff, Nellie Reinisch, Shirley Reinisch Flomenhoft, and Betty Reinisch Feiner

"When one door closes, another opens. But we often look so long and regretfully upon the closed door that we do not see the one that has opened for us."
-Helen Keller

Teriann Mainella Abbott with daughters
Brittany Abel and Jennifer Abbott

Robert (Apgar 10) Smith, M.D.
and Marc Feiner, M.D.
Partners and friends…at Bob's retirement

Pnina and Paul Feiner

The Socik's Clockwise from top: Bob, Mary Ann, Michele, and Eve

Clockwise from top: Debbie, Emily, Guy,
James, and Cassie Saracino

The Sleepers…Standing L-R: Amy, Lauren, Cathy, David
Sitting L-R: Dick and Peter and their beloved pets!

Boilermaker Race - Utica 2005
Our Heroes...

Jonathan Trainor giving his brother Kyle
a high 5 as he races by!

L-R: Mindy Rosenfeld and her
"little Sis" Lauren Feiner at the post
race party

Mindy Rosenfeld and Jake Stookey after the race...
Jon and Jake had great running times, Mindy and Lauren were
right behind them!

Lauren Feiner and Jonathan Trainor

The Ferreiro Family
L_R: Cristina, Carmen, Eric, Jorge, Marc and Alex

Ariana Cacoulidis...
Growing more beautiful every day

The La Rosa Family
Clockwise from top: Andrew, Bryan, Allyson and Jenna

The Sapio Boys...
Jonathan, Santa Claus, and Joey

L-R: Mackenzie and Ian Emery

Kathy and Jim Sullivan's newest additions...
Their three new grandchildren
L-R: Kaitlyn Sullivan Zezza, Seamus Michael Sullivan
and Jonathan James Sullivan Roost

Every time I thought I was finished putting this book together, someone else would say, "I have this great recipe you just have to put in"…finally I said, "that's it, we're done. But I just couldn't leave these last few recipes out because they came from such very special people…

WAFFLE OR PANCAKE BATTER
Marc A. Feiner, M.D.

4½ cups flour
¼ cup sugar plus 2 tablespoons
½ teaspoon salt
1 package of dry yeast

4 cups milk
½ cup butter
6 eggs, lightly beaten
½ teaspoon vanilla

Mix the flour, sugar, salt and yeast together in a large mixing bowl. Heat the milk and butter in a medium saucepan until warm. Together with the eggs, add the milk and butter mixture to the flour mixture. Add in the vanilla. Beat until smooth (you can use an electric mixer or Kitchenaid. Cover and refrigerate. Mix may be refrigerate for four days, but no more. On the second day, add in 2 extra tablespoons of sugar. If you are making pancakes, heat the griddle (spray with PAM or grease with a little oil or butter)) pour about ¼ cup of batter onto the hot griddle for each pancake. Cook for about 3-4 minutes and them turn and cook an additional 1-3 minutes. You can add chocolate chips, or pieces of fruit if desired. For waffles, pour into a **HOT** waffle iron and cook until the streaming is complete about 5-8 minutes.

As Marc gets closer to retirement, I keep telling him he either has to get a hobby or a girlfriend. Luckily, he chose a hobby. We bought a professional waffle iron and he is mastering waffle making 101. He wants to be an expert before his grandchildren start to arrive! This recipe is great because you can make it in advance. We have measured out exactly how much our waffle iron takes and we fill plastic cups with the individual amounts so as the kids wake up we just pour and watch them devour the waffles. For late night snacks, what's better than Waffles and Ice Cream. Marc says it reminds him of the time he spent growing up in Atlantic City, New Jersey, spending his summers at his grandparents and going to Lambert's, a local ice cream parlor…great memories!

FRIED CANDY BARS
Cyndi Koury

1 cup of self rising flour
1 cup club soda
Miniature candy bars of your choice Mounds, Mars Bars,
Milky Ways, Three Musketeers, about 8

Confectioners' sugar
Oil for Frying

Heat the oil in a deep-fat fryer to maximum heat. Measure the flour into a bowl, and whisk in ¾ cup of the soda water to make the batter, adding the rest of the water if the consistency is still too thick: you want this just thick enough to adhere easily. The best way to check is to turn a Mounds bar in it, if the batter sticks well enough, it's fine. Deep fry until golden. Sprinkle with confectioners' sugar.

This is much **easier** to do if you put **lollypop sticks, or bamboo skewers** in the candy bars and **then freeze them** before dipping them into the batter

Cyndi, Barbara Schwartz and I were having lunch just before the book went to print and of course all we talked about was food and recipes and she told me this recipe. This originated in Scotland, and now is very popular at state fairs all around the country. There is even a restaurant in New York City called A Salt and Battery where these are a specialty of the house.

UNCLE JIMMY'S MARINARA SAUCE
Vincent DeClementi

1 teaspoon salt
1 teaspoon sugar
5-7 cloves of garlic, peeled and left whole

1 can plum tomatoes
Fresh basil (a few leaves torn up in pieces)
Extra Virgin Olive oil

In a medium sauce pan, heat the olive oil and add the whole cloves of garlic. Add the tomatoes (you can mash by hand or put in a blender or a quick turn on and off to make smooth), salt, sugar and fresh basil. Bring to a boil and then let simmer for about 60 minutes to one hour. Mash the garlic cloves and add back into the sauce. Serve over your favorite pasta. You can easily double or triple this.

Uncle Jimmy, who is now is his 90's and affectionately known to all of us as "The General," had a heart attack recently. We all went down to visit him and he was so down in the dumps until he saw the final draft of the cookbook and he perked up and said we had to include these other recipes of his as well as all the others in the book, so here they are!

UNCLE JIMMY'S GREEN BEAN SALAD
Vincent DeClementi

Extra virgin olive oil to taste
Apple cider vinegar to taste
Oregano

Salt and Pepper to taste
Fresh Green Beans about 1 pound
Fresh basil (about 4-5 leaves) torn into pieces

Wash and snap off the ends of the green beans, and leave whole. In a pot of lightly salted boiling water, cook the green beans until cooked but still firm. Drain and place in an ice bath to stop the cooking. Place into a container and add a little olive oil and vinegar, salt and pepper, oregano and fresh basil to taste. Refrigerate until ready to serve.

Uncle Jimmy says that the secret to keeping all your vegetables green when cooking them is to wet the tip of your finger in water, dip your finger into baking soda and then dip your finger into the water that you will be cooking your vegetables in. He says it never fails to keep your vegetables green!

UNCLE JIMMY'S MEAT SAUCE
Vincent DeClementi

Extra Virgin Olive Oil
½ pound hot sausage (about 4 links)
½ pound sweet sausage (about 4 links)
1 pound chopped meat (ground round, chopped chuck or sirloin your choice)
1 onion, peeled and chopped

1 green pepper, diced into small pieces
2 cans plum tomatoes
10-12 cloves of garlic, peeled and left whole
½ teaspoon ground (powdered) fennel
Fresh Basil (about 6 leaves), torn into small pieces

Heat the olive oil in a large frying pan, add the onions and peppers; sauté for a few minutes until starting to soften. Remove the sausages from their casing and add to the pan; add the chopped meat and brown well. Drain off all the fat and set aside. Heat a little more olive oil in a deep saucepan (a few tablespoons or enough to cover the bottom of the pot). Add the 2 cans of plum tomatoes (break apart with your fingers or put into a blender, add browned meat, garlic cloves, salt and pepper to taste and the ground fennel. Add the fresh basil and let simmer for about 1 hours. When the garlic is soft, remove and mash and add back into the sauce. Serve over the cooked pasta of your choice.

Uncle Jimmy says that this is one of his most requested recipes from all his friends and neighbors. He says that the secret is in the ground fennel and recommends putting it in any dish that has sausage in it.

Beauty fades, character never does.
-Unknown

UNCLE JIMMY'S PIZZA RUSTICA
Vincent DeClementi

CRUST: (This makes ONE crust (top and bottom) You will need to make this recipe THREE times to make the 3 pies)

2 cups flour
pinch of salt
1 tablespoon sugar

1½ sticks COLD butter (12 tablespoons)
5-6 tablespoons COLD water

In a large mixing bowl, mix the flour, salt and sugar. Cut the butter into thin pats and then using two knives or a pastry cutter, cut the butter into the flour mix until it resembles small peas. Add about 3 tablespoons of cold water until the dough begins to hold together. Add the remaining two tablespoons of water, one at a time, if necessary. The dough should be on the dry side but yet, it shouldn't be too dry or you won't be able to roll it out. Shape the dough into a ball. Wrap in waxed paper and refrigerate at least 1 hour. **Repeat the recipe two more times** until you have three balls of dough in the refrigerator. When you are ready to make the pies, do the following: Preheat the oven to 400°. Divide each ball of dough in half to form a top and bottom crust. Roll each half out on a pastry sheet or a lightly flour piece of waxed paper to form a 10-inch circle. Lightly grease a 9-inch glass pie plate. Place the bottom crust into the pie plate, and with a fork, prick the bottom of the crust. Place enough filling (see recipe below) to fill the pie crust until it is just about level with the top of the pie pan. Roll out the top crust and place on top of the pie pan. Crimp the crust together with your fingers. Using a fork, prick the top crust with a fork. Brush with an egg wash (take 1 egg and mix with 1 tablespoon of water). Repeat with two remaining crusts. When all the pies are ready to go, bake in the 400°oven for 15 minutes, **THEN, lower the heat to 325°,** bake another 40-50 minutes. Insert a toothpick or bamboo skewer carefully into the crust to test for doneness (it should be dry when removed from the middle of the pie.)

FILLING: This will make enough filling for ALL three pies)

A total of 32 ounces of cold cuts (Uncle Jimmy uses the following ¼-½ pound of proscuitto, ½ pound Genoa Salami, ½ pound sweet Soppressata, and ½ pound of pepperoni) cut into small pieces
1 pound of Polly-O Whole Milk Mozzarella (cut into tiny cubes
3 pounds whole milk ricotta

¼ cup sugar
9 eggs
3 tablespoons fresh parsley, finely chopped
⅓ cup grated cheese (Reggiano Parmigiana or Locatelli-Romano)

Make the filling by cutting the cold cuts into small pieces, and cubing the mozzarella into small cubes. Put the ricotta in a large bowl, and add the eggs; blend well. Add the sugar, parsley and grated cheese and mix well again. Fold in the cold cuts and mozzarella and mix well. Divide the filling into the three pie pans as described in the crust recipe above. Follow baking instructions above.

UNCLE JIMMY'S CAULIFLOWER AND MACARONI
Vincent DeClementi

1 head of cauliflower (cut into flowerets, saving some of the tender green leaves as well)
½ cup extra virgin olive oil
2-3 cloves of garlic, peeled and thinly sliced

salt and pepper to taste
grating cheese to taste
1 pound of the pasta of your choice

Place the cauliflower flowerets and green leaves in a large frying pan or medium saucepan of slightly salted water. Cook for a few minutes until finger tender but not soft. Drain; and place in an ice bath to stop the cooking. Drain and set aside. In the meantime, place a large pot of lightly salted water on the stove and bring to a boil for the pasta. While the pasta is cooking do the following: In a large frying pan, place the olive oil; and heat. Add the garlic and let it brown but **DO NOT LET THE GARLIC BURN.** Add the prepared cauliflower and sauté until fairly soft but not mushy. Season with salt and pepper to taste. Drain the pasta reserving some of the hot water in case the pasta is too dry. Toss the pasta with the cauliflower and top with grating cheese. Add a little of the pasta water if it's too dry.

Uncle Jimmy says to always cut a few of the tender leaves of the cauliflower when you are making this dish as it adds a little color to the final presentation. Uncle Jimmy was so excited about this book and he really wanted to include all of these recipes as his legacy.

COCONUT CHICKEN GRAN MARNIER
John Grimaldi, Sr., Executive Chef

Main Dish Ingredients:

1½ pound boneless chicken breasts, cut into strips (like for stir fry)
1½ pounds of size 16-20 (size of shrimp is based on the number of shrimp to a pound) shrimp (cooked, peeled, deveined, and cut in half LENGTHWISE
About ½ cup flour
Salt and pepper to taste to season flour
Garlic powder to taste to season flour
Oil for frying
1 (12 ounce) bag of coconut (toasted if desired)

Salt and pepper to taste
4 cloves of garlic, peeled and finely chopped
Fresh parsley, chopped, about 1-2 tablespoons
½ cantaloupe melon, peeled, seeded and diced into small cubes
½ honeydew melon, peeled, seeded and diced into small cubes
1 (12 ounce) frozen baby peas, defrosted
1 cup chopped walnuts
A little oil to fry walnuts

Gran Marnier Sauce:

1 (16 ounce can) Coco Casa Cream of Coconut
½ can Gran Marnier (use the can from the Cream of Coconut to measure)

1 jar of Heinz Chicken Gravy (or 16 ounces of homemade chicken gravy)
Salt and pepper to taste

In a small bowl, take the flour, add a little salt and pepper to taste, and a little garlic powder to the flour. Flour the strips of chicken. Fry the chicken strips in a deep fryer if you have one, or in a frying pan with about 2 inches of oil in it. After frying the pieces, drain on paper towels and set aside. After the chicken in fried, place in a large bowl. Add the shrimp and half the bag of coconut. (**You may toast the coconut if you prefer it that way. To toast the coconut, place in a shallow cookie sheet. Preheat the oven to 325°. Place pan in the oven and stir frequently for about 15 minutes or until golden brown)**, add the defrosted peas. Add salt and pepper to taste; add the garlic. Add the fresh parsley to taste. Spray a baking pan (lasagna pan size) with PAM. Place the chicken mixture into the pan. In a small frying pan, heat a little oil and quickly stir fry the walnuts just to heat them. Sprinkle over the chicken. Make the Gran Marnier sauce (see below). Ladle the sauce over the chicken, **reserving 1 cup of the sauce**. Sprinkle with the coconut. Bake 350° for about 30-40 minutes, but do not let the sauce get too brown. When you remove the chicken from the oven, ladle reserve sauce over the chicken. Arrange the cubed honeydew and cantaloupe around the chicken in the tray or serving dish, alternating the two melons..

Sauce:

Mix the Coconut Cream, ½ of the can of Gran Marnier, and the chicken gravy together in a medium saucepan. Bring to a light boil. Season with salt and pepper to taste, set aside.

SPINACH RICE BALLS
John Grimaldi, Sr., Executive Chef

1 recipe for Rice Balls (Neapolitan) on page 282

1-2 bags Fresh Baby Spinach, stems removed, cut into large pieces (2-3 pieces per leaf)

Follow the recipe for the rice balls on page 282, and when you are adding the ricotta, eggs, etc., add the spinach into the mix and proceed with the rest of the directions as given.

SHRIMP RICE BALLS
John Grimaldi, Sr., Executive Chef

1 recipe for Rice Balls (Neapolitan) on page 282

1 Pound of size 16-20 shrimp, cooked, peeled and deveined, and coarsely chopped)

Follow the recipe for the rice balls on page 282, and when you are adding the ricotta, eggs, etc., add the shrimp into the mix and proceed with the rest of the directions as given.

THREE MUSKETEERS
John Grimaldi, Sr., Executive Chef

2 pounds boneless chicken breasts (cutlets) , cut in half
2 eggplants, peeled and cut in ½-inch slices lengthwise and then cut each long slice in half
2 pounds of beef eye round cut into ¼ -inch slices (the butcher can do this for you) to make beef cutlets
2 pounds of slicing mozzarella, sliced
4-5 tomatoes, sliced about ¼ -inch thick
Flour for breading (I use Wondra flour)
12 eggs or more as needed to use to bread the chicken, beef, and eggplant)

salt and pepper to taste for egg
½ -¾ cup grated cheese for egg
Flavored breadcrumbs
6 whole mushrooms
½ cup white wine
salt and pepper to taste for mushrooms
1 tablespoon fresh parsley, chopped
Oil for frying

ROUX:

8 tablespoons flour
8 tablespoons butter

½ cup oil

MARSALA SAUCE;

2 cans (14 ounces) College Inn Beef Broth
2 cups good quality Marsala
Roux

Salt and Pepper to taste
Garlic powder to taste
2-3 cloves of garlic, peeled and crushed

Make the Roux. In a small frying pan, melt the butter; add the oil. Stir in the flour and cook over low - medium heat until it turn a light grayish brown, stirring constantly until the flour is all absorbed and the roux in lump free. Remove from the heat and set aside. You will use the roux to thicken the Marsala sauce. You can freeze any leftover roux for another use.

In a large bowl, mix the eggs with salt and pepper to taste and the grated cheese. Beat until well blended. Place the flour in a paper dish and the flavored breadcrumbs in another paper dish. Prepare several sheets of waxed paper cut to the size of three platters or disposable paper platters. Dip the chicken into the flour, then into the egg, and finally into the breadcrumbs. Place on a platter separating the layers with waxed paper. Set the chicken aside. Next, dip the beef cutlets into the flour, egg mixture and breadcrumbs the same way you did the chicken; layer on waxed paper; set aside. Do the same with the slices of eggplant (flour, egg, and then breadcrumbs) Make more egg mix if necessary; add more flour and breadcrumbs as needed. Heat a large frying pan with about an 1-inch to 1½ -inches of oil. Fry the chicken cutlets in the oil, browning on both sides until golden; set aside. Fry the beef cutlets in the oil the same way; set aside. Change the oil whenever necessary, remembering to preheat the oil again before you start to fry. Fry the eggplant slices and set aside. The pieces of chicken, beef, and eggplant should be about the same size (about 3-inches by 3-inches). When everything if fried, get a large baking dish (you may need 2) and spray with PAM.

Layer as follows to make individual "bundles" : place the pieces of chicken across the pan, top with a slice of tomato and a slice of mozzarella. Next, place the beef cutlet on top of the mozzarella, top with another slice of tomato and another slice of mozzarella. Finally, top each bundle with a piece of fried eggplant. After if is assembled, bake in a preheated 350°oven about 25 minutes. **While this is in the oven make the Marsala sauce**. Cut the very end of the mushrooms off and then slice into about 5 slices lengthwise per mushroom. In a medium frying pan, sauté the mushrooms slices in the white wine; add a little salt and pepper to taste; add fresh parsley.. Cook for about 5-7 minutes; set aside. In a medium sauce pan, mix the beef broth with the Marsala wine, salt, pepper, crushed garlic, and garlic powder to taste, and blend in the roux one tablespoon at a time until the sauce is thickened to the consistency of a brown gravy. Add the mushroom mix and bring to a light boil. In a hurry and don't have time to make a roux, use 2 jars of Heinz Chicken Gravy and add 2 cups of Marsala to it; season as in the other Marsala sauce with salt, pepper, mushrooms, etc. bring to a light boil.) When the chicken has been cooking for 25 minutes, remove it from the oven and place an additional slice of mozzarella over each bundle. Place back in the oven for a few minutes to melt the mozzarella to mold over each bundle. Remove from the oven once this is done. To serve, ladle a small gravy ladle of sauce over each bundle.

When we were growing up, cousin John was our family's favorite pest... He was always getting us in trouble, one way or another. In high school, he was a year ahead of me. I used to ask him if he ever went to class because he was always helping out in the math department, and was never in classes. He always said school was not his thing, but it sure didn't get in his way, because he sure can cook!. He started to work in a deli in Woodhaven when he was very young. Now, he is a certified Executive Chef, at Seven Brothers Gourmet Food Market. It's located at 2914 Long Beach Road, Oceanside, New York 11572. The phone number is 516 678-5999. Be sure to stop in if you need catering, John is the best and most inventive chef. I think the males are getting to be better cooks than the females in this family, my son Steven is getting really talented in the kitchen, John's nephew Dean Grimaldi, just graduated from the Culinary Institute of America! We'll be eating well in the next generation, that's a given...

RAVIOLETTI BRUSCHETTA SALAD
John Grimaldi, Sr., Executive Chef

2 pounds of cheese ravioletti (the tiny squares used for soup, usually in the refrigerated section of the grocery store)
8 plum tomatoes; diced fine
2 small onions, peeled and diced
About 15 leaves of fresh basil, cut into a chiffonade,
1 fresh mozzarella cut into ¼ -inch slices and then cut into small cubes
Salt and Pepper to taste

4 cloves of garlic peeled and cut into 2-3 pieces (count the number of pieces so you can remove them before serving)
¼ teaspoon dried oregano
4 tablespoons (brown) balsamic vinegar
¼ cup extra virgin olive oil
1 teaspoon garlic powder
¼ teaspoon salt
¼ teaspoon black pepper
Fresh mint and fresh basil cut in small pieces for the top

Heat a large pot of lightly salted water, and add about ¼ cup of oil to it and bring to a boil. Cook the ravioletti's until al dente; drain. While the ravioletti's are cooking, place all the remaining ingredients (except the mint and basil for the topping) into a large serving bowl. When the pasta is done, carefully stir into the remaining ingredients. Taste for seasonings. **Remember to remove the garlic cloves.** Sprinkle with a little fresh mint and fresh basil before serving

John says this makes a great salad especially in the summertime, it's a twist on the original bruschetta served on bread slices.

EGGPLANT SALAD
John Grimaldi, Sr., Executive Chef

2 eggplants, peeled and sliced lengthwise into about ¼-inch to ½-inch slices (about 10 slices per eggplant)
Flour for breading eggplant slices (I use Wondra)
8-12 eggs
Salt and pepper to taste
About ¾ cup grating cheese
Flavored breadcrumbs
Oil for frying
1 red bell pepper (Cut EACH pepper the following way, cut into about 12 slices per pepper and then each slice into 4-5 cubes
1 green bell pepper (cut as above)

1 yellow bell pepper (cut as above)
1 orange bell pepper (cut as above)
2 small red onions, peeled and cut into thin slices
5 cloves of garlic, peeled and crushed
garlic powder and onion powder to taste
5 teaspoons sugar (add one at a time, you may not need all five)
1 cup white balsamic vinegar
½ cup extra virgin olive oil
Fresh parsley, finely chopped about 2 tablespoons
6 plum tomatoes, diced into small cubes (this is used for the garnish)

Place the flour and the breadcrumbs in two paper plate. Place the egg into a large bowl, add the salt and pepper and grating cheese. Mix well. Dip the eggplant slices in the flour, then into the egg mixture and finally into the breadcrumbs. Place on a sheet of waxed paper and continue until all the eggplant is breaded. Keep waxed paper between the layers. Place about 1-inch of oil in a large frying pan, Heat the oil and then fry the eggplant until golden brown on both sides. Remove to paper towels to drain. When cool, cut the eggplant into cubes. In a large mixing bowl, add remaining ingredients,). **EXCEPT FOR THE PLUM TOMATOES. (being careful to add the sugar one teaspoon at a time, tasting after each addition.)** To serve place the mixture on a platter and garnish the border of the platter with the diced tomatoes.

SHRIMP SCAMPI
Elise Feiner

½ cup flour
¼ teaspoon salt
½ teaspoon black pepper
¼ teaspoon cayenne pepper
1½ pounds fresh shrimp, shelled and deveined without tails
½ cup olive oil

5 cloves garlic, peeled and crushed
1 shallot, peeled and chopped finely
4 tablespoons fresh parsley, chopped
½ teaspoon oregano
3 tablespoons white wine
3 tablespoons brandy

Mix the flour, salt, pepper, and cayenne pepper in a bowl. Dredge the shrimp in the mix. In a large frying pan, heat the oil; sauté the shrimp over high heat for about 5 minutes. Stir frequently to prevent burning. Remove shrimp to a platter; keep the oil. In the oil, sauté the garlic, shallot, parsley and oregano over low-medium heat for about 3 minutes, stirring frequently. Spoon the mix over the shrimp. In the same pan, mix the wine and brandy and **ignite carefully** with a match **(stand back when doing this.)** When flames are gone, stir well. Pour over shrimp. Place in an over proof pan and place under the broiler for about 2-3 minutes. Serve with rice pilaf. This is for Lauren, she loves Scampi.

FRIED EGGPLANT BALLS
John Grimaldi, Sr., Executive Chef

2 eggplants (about 6 inches in length) peeled and cubed
1 small white onion, peeled and chopped or 4 small
shallots, peeled and chopped
Oil for frying
1 pound of Italian sweet sausage, (no fennel) removed from
the casing or use bulk sausage
2 cups of Carolina long grain rice
4 cups of water
4 tablespoons butter
1 cup of grated cheese

salt and pepper to taste
¾ - 1 pound of mozzarella, coarsely grated
fresh parsley to taste, finely chopped (about 2 tablespoons)
2 eggs, slightly beaten for the mixture
Flour for dredging
4-5 eggs
salt and pepper to taste for the eggs
½ cup grated cheese for the eggs
Flavored breadcrumbs

Place just enough olive oil to cover the bottom of a large frying pan. When the oil is hot add the onions or shallots, and the eggplant and sauté until softened but still firm. (The eggplant will continue to cook when you fry it.) Remove from the frying pan and set aside. Brown the sausage in the same pan, when cooked, drain off the grease and set aside. Cook the two cups of rice in 4 cups of boiling water and 4 tablespoons of butter, according to the package directions. Set aside. In a large bowl, mix the eggplant, sausage, and the rice together. Add the cup of grated cheese, salt and pepper to taste, shredded mozzarella, parsley, and the 2 eggs. Blend well. Place the flour and the flavored breadcrumbs on paper plates or dishes. In a large bowl, mix the 4-5 eggs, salt and pepper to taste, and the ½ cup grated cheese, beating well. Roll the eggplant mixture into balls. Dredge in flour, then in the egg mix and then in the breadcrumbs, place back in the egg mix and then back in the breadcrumbs again. Deep fry the balls until golden brown.

GIANNINA'S FRIED CHRISTMAS BOWS
Giannina Schwendemann

1 cup flour
1 large egg
pinch salt
1 level teaspoon baking powder

Vegetable Oil for frying
Confectioners' sugar
Honey

The proportions above are for 1 cup of flour. Giannina says when she makes the recipe, she usually uses 4 cups of flour (4 eggs, 4 pinches of salt, and 4 teaspoons of baking powder.) Just remember if you want to increase the amount, to always keep those proportions. After you measure the flour, shake it through a sifter or strainer. Add the salt and baking powder to the flour. Place the flour on a wooden board or whatever work surface you have available (you can use sheets of waxed paper if you want. Make a hole in the middle of the flour to create a well. Break the eggs into the middle of the flour. Start working the dough from the outside of the well into the middle until the eggs are well blended with the flour and you have created a dough that is slightly sticky. Roll the dough into a ball and cover the dough with a large mixing bowl; leave covered for 45 minutes to 1½ hours. Pinch off a small piece of dough at a time and roll the dough out until it is thin, but not paper thin. Using a fluted pastry cutter, pizza cutter or a knife, cut the dough into small strips. Tie each strip into a knot or make a small slit in one end of the dough and feed the other end through the slit to make a "bow".

In a deep fryer or a frying pan filled with a few inches of oil **(make sure the oil is hot first...a reminder for Lauren and Melissa)** deep fry the bows a few at a time (they will expand in the oil) until they float to the surface and are golden brown. Drain on brown paper bags if you have some (I use brown lunch bags) or several layers of paper towels (change frequently.) Sprinkle with confectioners' sugar or heat some honey in a saucepan over low heat until it becomes the consistency of water **(use a large pot because honey expands very rapidly when heated)**, and then drizzle over the bows. These keep very well in plastic containers.

When we went to visit Uncle Jimmy after he had his heart attack and I surprised him by showing him the draft of the cookbook, he had several recipes he wanted to add. At the time, his grandson Michael was there taking care of him, and they both said at the same time, you have to put "Giannina's bows" ("my mother's bows") in the book, they're the best. After a few phone calls back and forth, I managed to track down Giannina (who is Uncle Jimmy and Aunt Dottie's daughter) and get her recipe. She said that this recipe was her Aunt Rose's (Uncle Jimmy's sister) recipe. When she asked her Aunt Rose for the recipe, she told her, "I can't give it to you, I don't measure, you'll have to watch me." Giannina did just that and was finally able to get this recipe. She said they are easy and delicious, and her whole family obviously agrees with her!

...

In Loving Memory of

Christopher Donalty

The Christopher Donalty CURE Benefit honors the memory of Christopher Donalty, who died on February 21, 2002 of Sudden Unexplained Death from Epilepsy (SUDEP). Chris, the son of Barry and Jeanne Donalty, was born and raised in Utica, New York; graduated tenth in his class from Proctor High School in 1998, and was a star baseball player for both the Proctor Raiders and Utica Post's American Legion Team. He was 21 years old and a candidate for a degree in business administration from Stetson University at the time of his death.

Chris' family and friends have joined together to help pay tribute to Chris through education and public awareness about the potential devastation of epilepsy. Contributions will help fund critical research which offers the hope of finding a cure to those afflicted with this terrible and debilitating disease. We ask that if you have no preference to where your donation from this cookbook goes that you consider CURE, or perhaps you would consider an additional donation on your own. Please visit their website at **www.CUREepilepsy.org**

Chris' mom Jeanne has become a good friend and is doing incredible things so that this will never happen to your children and grandchildren...please help!

Once again, we want to thank all of our wonderful family and friends who graciously allowed us to share their recipes, histories, pictures and their heritage. Without all of you, this book could never have turned out as wonderful as it has. We hope as you turn the pages, you too will have wonderful memories of the times we spent together. Each of you has a special place in our hearts. You have all touched our lives in a very special way. There are no words to describe how blessed we are to have all of you in our lives… To the friends we haven't met yet, those who will come to know us through this book, we suggest that you make a book like this for your own family and friends. I won't say that it wasn't time consuming, but the rewards are incredible…touching base with people you haven't seen in a while, remembering things you haven' thought about in years, and most importantly in this day and age of change and moving, giving your family firm roots to look back on. Remember to take the time to thank all those people in your life who always cooked with love, and by doing so, gave their gift of love to you. Check our website to nominate them to the **Cooking with Love's Cooking Hall of Fame**… www.cookingwithlove.com

With Love
and
Our Sincere Thanks,

Elise and Marc

Remember...
Always
Cook
With
Love!

COOKING WITH LOVE

Index

Happy Recipe Hunting...

547

549

CHILI

CHOCOLATE (ALSO SEE DESSERTS, CANDY, COOKIES)

555

557

559

560

Cooking with Love

Presents

Chefs with Heart...Whisking Up a Better World!™

Please select ONE charity from the list below, circle it on the enclosed letter and we will make a $5.00 donation to the charity of your choice.

Visit our website **www.cookingwithlove.com**

Or e-mail us for information at **elise@cookingwithlove.com**

Our List of Charities, Foundations, and Schools: (Check our website for updates)

By appearing in the list below, these charities DO NOT endorse this cookbook or are in NO WAY AFFILIATED with We Are Cooking with Love. They are charities WE have chosen to receive your donation.

American Diabetes Association
American Heart Association
American Kennel Club Canine
Health Foundation (AKCCHF)
American Lung Association
American Society for the Prevention of
Cruelty to Animals (ASPCA)
Arnold Palmer Hospital
Autism Society of America
Baylie For Brains
Business and Professional Women of
New York State Career Development
Opportunities, Inc
Central Association for the Blind and
Visually Impaired

Children's Miracle Network at Faxton-
St. Luke's Healthcare
Christopher Reeve Foundation &
American Paralysis Association
Cinderella Project of Central NY (giving
prom gowns to underprivileged girls)
Corporate Angels Network
CURE (Citizens United for
Research in Epilepsy)
Cystic Fibrosis Foundation
Elizabeth Glaser Pediatric
AIDS Foundation
Fisher Center for Alzheimer's Research
Foundation

FOR MORE LISTINGS TURN PAGE

Gilda's Club New York City (for Ovarian Cancer)
Guiding Eyes for the Blind
Klaas Kids Foundation
Little Flower Children and Family Services of NY
MADD (Mother's Against Drunk Drivers)
Make-A-Wish Foundation® of Central of New York
March of Dimes
Masonic Medical Laboratory Research Intern Scholarship Fund
Muscular Dystrophy Association
National Colorectal Cancer Research Alliance
NIAF (National Italian American Foundation) Scholarship Fund
Operation Smile
Papanicolaou Corps for Cancer Research
Phillips Exeter Academy Annual Giving Fund
Ronald Mc Donald's House Charities
Shriners Hospitals
St. Jude Children's Research Hospital
The Amyotrophic Lateral Sclerosis Association (ALSA)
The Arc Advocacy and Services for People with Disabilities Oneida-Lewis Chapter NYSARC
The Boomer Esiason Foundation for Cystic Fibrosis
The Caring Community Foundation, Inc.
The Carol M. Baldwin Breast Cancer Research Fund, Inc.

The Hole in the Wall Gang Camp(for children with cancer and other life-threatening illnesses and conditions).
The Hospice & Palliative Care, Inc.
The Joe Torre Safe at Home Foundation
The Leukemia and Lymphoma Society
The Lower Eastside Girls Club (providing girls with the vision to plan - and the tools to build - their future).
The National Multiple Sclerosis Society
The Starlight Starbright Children's Foundation
The Women's Fund of Herkimer-Oneida Counties
Trinity-Pawling School (Carol and Theodore Kneeland Scholarship Fund)
World Wildlife Foundation (WWF)